The
Change Handbook

The Change Handbook

THE DEFINITIVE RESOURCE ON TODAY'S BEST METHODS FOR ENGAGING WHOLE SYSTEMS

Peggy Holman, Tom Devane,
Steven Cady, and Associates

BERRETT-KOEHLER PUBLISHERS, INC.
San Francisco

Berrett-Koehler Publishers, Inc.
235 Montgomery Street, Suite 650
San Francisco, CA 94104-2916
Tel: (415) 288-0260 Fax: (415) 362-2512 www.bkconnection.com

ORDERING INFORMATION

Quantity sales. Special discounts are available on quantity purchases by corporations, associations, and others. For details, contact the "Special Sales Department" at the Berrett-Koehler address above.

Individual sales. Berrett-Koehler publications are available through most bookstores. They can also be ordered directly from Berrett-Koehler. Tel: (800) 929-2929; Fax: (802) 864-7626; www .bkconnection.com

Orders for college textbook/course adoption use. Please contact Berrett-Koehler. Tel: (800) 929-2929; Fax: (802) 864-7626.

Orders by U.S. trade bookstores and wholesalers. Please contact Publishers Group West, 1700 Fourth Street, Berkeley, CA 94710. Tel: (510) 528-1444; Fax: (510) 528-3444.

Printed in the United States of America

Berrett-Koehler books are printed on long-lasting acid-free paper. When it is available, we choose paper that has been manufactured by environmentally responsible processes. These may include using trees grown in sustainable forests, incorporating recycled paper, minimizing chlorine in bleaching, or recycling the energy produced at the paper mill.

Library of Congress Cataloging-in-Publication Data

The change handbook: the definitive resource on today's best methods for engaging whole systems/edited by Peggy Holman, Tom Devane, and Steven Cady.—2nd ed.
p.cm.
Includes bibliographical references (p.) and index.
ISBN-10: 1-57675-379-8; ISBN-13: 978-1-57675-379-8
1. Organizational change.   I. Holman, Peggy, 1955–   II. Devane, Tom, 1954–   III. Cady, Steven, 1964–
HD58.8.C4537 2006
658.4'06—dc22   2006042909

Second Edition

12 11 10 09 08 07   10 9 8 7 6 5 4 3 2 1

Copyedited by Frances Lyon. Production services and composition by Westchester Book Group. Proofread by Katherine Deyell. Indexed by WordCo Indexing Services.

Contents

Preface

Change is disturbing when it is done to us, exhilarating when it is done by us.
—Rosabeth Moss Kanter

Why We Wrote the Second Edition

In 1999, *The Change Handbook* provided a snapshot of a nascent field that broke barriers by engaging a "whole system" of people from organizations and communities in creating their own future. In the last seven years, the field has exploded. Robust, international communities of practice grew around many approaches. The pioneers influenced each other's practices. Inspired by the potential, seasoned practitioners invented a wide variety of creative processes, and people from other fields more fully embraced these ideas and integrated them into their practices. Also, we uncovered practices of systemic engagement emerging through completely different disciplines from strategic planning and process improvement to street theatre and urban development.

Clearly, it was time to capture what was happening.

This second edition of *The Change Handbook* is a meeting of theory and best practices from a variety of disciplines. Over the past seven years, we have noticed growing influences among several of them:

People who use human methods such as World Café and Dialogue who are seeking a "harder," results-oriented edge that will contribute to success;	*and*	people who use "harder" methods such as Six Sigma and Rapid Results who want to tap into human energy to fuel success.
People in organizations who wish to bring some of the democratic practices of community engagement, such as Nonviolent Communication and Charrettes into the workplace;	*and*	people in communities who wish to bring the action-oriented successes of processes that inspire employees, such as Appreciative Inquiry and Scenario Planning, into civic engagement.

Our research for this edition showed that organizations using methods typically thought of as "hard" or "soft" were most successful when they incorporated aspects of what their method was not. For example, when done well, Six Sigma is an engagement exercise as well as an application of powerful statistical tools that can vault an organization to dramatically higher levels of performance. Dialogue, when done well, spurs people to deploy new strategies, technical tools, and processes to achieve performance levels previously not imagined.

A remarkable convergence is under way as people who developed methods for public participation meet people working in organizational settings. They have discovered their common commitment to broad engagement—of citizens and employees. They are just beginning to learn what they have to offer each other.

Whether your situation, calls for "hard" or "soft" practices, organizational or community applications, we believe you'll find something that serves your needs.

The core purpose of the book has remained constant:

Supporting people committed to changing whole systems—organizations and communities—in making wise choices for their work and for their lives.

We also remain committed to providing a practical resource. Given that aim, we began by connecting with our diverse audience—the managers, internal and external consultants, academics, community activists, and students who use the book. They told us:

- Interest in whole system change continues to grow

- Keep the current format

- Address four requests:

  - Include more methods—bring the rigor of *The Change Handbook*'s standard format to other processes

  - Include more information on outcomes and measurable results

  - Include more contemporary stories and examples

  - Tell us about mixing and matching methods

What's Different?

The new edition contains:

- *More than Sixty Methods*

  Up from 18 in the first edition, this book contains 61 processes. Nineteen are highlighted with "in-depth" chapters and 42 others have "thumbnails" to whet your appetite. Some practices are well established; others are quite new. All are approaches that we believe further the theory and/or practice of whole system change.

  Most of the in-depth chapters were chosen because they are well-established practices with sizable, international communities of practice: Appreciative Inquiry, Dialogue and Deliberation, Open Space Technology, Technology of Participation, World Café, Future Search, Scenario Thinking, Rapid Results, and Six Sigma. We believe that no book on high-participation, systemwide change would be complete without the pioneering work of Whole-Scale Change and foundational methods based in Open Systems Theory: Search Conference and the Participative Design Workshop. While most of these approaches have their roots in organization development, we widened our reach to include methods of engaging people from other disciplines. Charrettes originated in the world of architecture and urban planning and Playback Theatre has its roots in the performing arts. We've also included in-depth chapters on two of the most frequently used supporting practices for change: Online Environments and Visual Recording and Graphic Facilitation. Finally, we've added a bit of spice by offering three "young" methods that we believe are exciting contributions to the field: Collaborative Loops, a design-it-yourself practice; Community Weaving, a highly original approach to change that started life in communities; and Integrated Clarity, an exciting application that integrates Nonviolent Communication into work with organizations and communities.

The thumbnail chapters are brief overviews that showcase the range of applications available. Some of the processes are longtime practices; others are new, just finding their "legs," but bringing something original. A few are innovative hybrids of well-established methods that we believe contribute something original. There are creative adaptations of "foundational" practices. For example, Scenario Planning inspired Large Group Scenario Planning. Appreciative Inquiry is the root of SOAR and the Appreciative Inquiry Summit. Our intent is that the thumbnails provide enough information for you to see what might fit your situation, and visit online to learn more.

- *A Guide to Selection*

  With more than 60 methods, we would be remiss not to provide a road map! Our contributing authors have helped us create a "Summary Matrix" of some useful characteristics to help you find your way among the choices.

- *A New Chapter on Preparing to Mix and Match Methods*

  We spoke with a number of seasoned practitioners about how they approach their work. Combined with our own knowledge, we offer you some insights into this emerging discipline.

- *A New Chapter on Outcomes, Sustainability and Measurement*

  We've woven thoughts from our contributing authors with our own experiences to reflect on this important but challenging and elusive subject.

- *Completely Revised Chapters Speculating about the Future*

  As practitioners gain experience and influence each other, how do the practices evolve? These processes introduce increasingly democratic practices into organizations. They provide new highly interactive models of community engagement influencing what it means to be a citizen. How are they changing the way humans organize themselves? We offer three views on the future of the field and what this field means to our future.

We were stunned as we realized how much this field of whole system change has matured in the last seven years! We believe the breadth and depth of the new material is a testimony to the inherent potential in engaging collectives in cocreating their future.

What Is the Book About?

This book is about effective change. It describes methods for changing "whole systems," that is, change based on two powerful foundation assumptions: high involvement and a systemic approach to improvement. High involvement means engaging the people in changing their own system. It is systemic because there is a conscious choice to include the people, functions, and ideas that can affect or be affected by the work. Whole system change methods help you initiate *high-leverage*, sustainable improvements in organizations or communities. "High-leverage" is empha-sized because in any improvement effort, we want the highest possible value for the effort invested. We believe that involving people in a systematic way is a key to high leverage and that the methods in this book can provide this leverage for you. You'll need to determine the one(s) best suited to moving your organization or community to the culture you want. We wrote this book to support your efforts.

The book is intended to answer questions such as:

- What methods are available that have proven successful in addressing today's needs for organizational or community change?

- What are the key distinctions among these methods?

- How do I know if a method would be a good fit for my organization or community?

- How do I get started after I select one or more methods?

To make a good choice, you'll need some basic information. Rather than provide details of how to do each method, we give you an overview of what's available and some tools to help focus your exploration. If you'd like more in-depth information, we've provided convenient references and a Web site—www.thechangehandbook.com—for learning more.

Intended Audience

This book is for anyone who needs a change that involves people. In particular, we intend it for lifelong students of effective, sustainable change. It is a guide that is useful to readers irrespective of their current functional discipline, community or organizational position, age, country of origin, or educational background. The principles and approaches covered have wide applicability around the world in organizational and community settings for a variety of human conditions. If you are interested in change that involves people, you'll likely find some of the methods and principles in this book extremely useful. For example, these practices are for anyone who wants people in organizations or communities to:

- Commit to a shared vision of the future
- Operate from the "big picture"
- Make change happen
- Seek responsibility and take initiative
- Use their creative powers to their fullest potential.

This book is written for people in organizations and communities who are seeking dramatic, sustainable change. It supports people focused on achieving better results, higher quality of life, improved relationships, and increased capacity for succeeding in turbulent times. It is

Among the audience are . . .	Who are . . .
Middle managers and project managers	Searching for proven methods to accomplish the daunting task of successful, sustainable change
Community leaders and activists	Seeking effective approaches to sustainable development and citizen involvement
Senior managers	Meeting an overall responsibility for significant organizational performance
Internal organization development consultants	Seeking proven methods for systemic, large-scale change
Internal Total Quality consultants	Searching for meaningful, reliable ways to involve the organization in continuous improvement
Internal business reengineering groups	Enhancing process redesign efforts with "the people side of change" to increase individual motivation, commitment, and performance
Project leaders of large information systems projects	Seeking ways to make the new technology more effective and the people more productive by engaging them in the change process
Process owners for reengineered processes	Seeking methods to enhance process performance
External consultants	Assisting clients with high-leverage methods that dramatically improve organizational performance and community development efforts
Students of change	Learning the range of possibilities for making a difference in organizations and communities

Table 1. Examples of the Intended Audience

intended for leaders who want to create workplaces and communities that foster high commitment through participation.

We know that interest in high-participation change is growing, with a diverse audience, as shown in table 1.

Finding and Including Today's Best Methods

We sent out a call for proposals, attracting over 100 methods for our review. We used ten criteria for inclusion. The first eight came from our review of successful, sustained change efforts. Each selected method:

- Involves people in a meaningful way, improving individual and collective awareness and connectedness,

- Enables people to discover and create shared assumptions about their work processes and ways of working together; fostering the emergence of collective thought and action,

- Has been practiced for at least five years to establish a track record,

- Is a systemic approach to change,

- Achieves dramatic and lasting results with a moderate amount of people's time and other resources,

- Provides support from multiple sources (e.g., books, articles, Web sites, practitioner networks, user conferences, user groups/communities, training programs and materials, etc.),

- Has been applied in a variety of environments, cultures, and industries, and

- Is grounded in solid theory, and makes strong theoretical and practical contributions to the field of change.

In addition, when considered in totality, the collection of methods:

- Approaches change from a variety of disciplines (e.g., systems thinking/dynamics, quality improvement, organization development, creativity), and

- Reflects international and gender diversity.

While many methods are rooted in organization development, others bring rich traditions from community development, total quality, social science, system dynamics, public participation, the wisdom of indigenous cultures and studies of intelligence, creativity, and the arts. Practitioners from these different disciplines independently embodied the eight criteria in their approaches. The implications for changing organizations and communities are profound, as these practices from different fields have influenced each other and contributed to a rich and growing practice field.

Numerous methods met our criteria. To make the hard choices among them, two factors played a major role: Was there a vibrant community of practice growing around the approach? Was there an underlying generosity of spirit, a willingness to share?

We felt that a multifaceted support base—books, Web sites, formal or informal practitioner associations, training as well as consulting practices—indicated generous access to critical knowledge and support. In a few cases, though proprietary, if we felt the work contributed something important to the theory and practice of the field and there were at least some tools for self-study, we included it. We also included a handful of processes with less than five years of history because of their promise. There were many hard calls! We hope these selections serve you well.

How to Use This Book

This book is designed for quick and easy access to information. It is a tool—a hands-on reference guide that answers questions about high-leverage change. We encourage you to skip around in the book—orient yourself to whole system change through reading the opening chapters, look at the quick summaries (one page for each method), browse through the references that follow each chapter, or simply read about the methods that interest you most. The book is organized into five parts.

PART I: NAVIGATING THROUGH THE METHODS

This section provides a framework for selecting and working with change methods. The first chapter is a "big picture," offering a taxonomy for thinking about the methods. It contains a "Summary Matrix" that is an overview of some characteristics helpful in making choices among the methods. Chapter 2 guides you through what to consider when choosing among processes and selecting a consultant. Chapter 3 contains insights into preparing to mix and match methods. The fourth chapter reflects on outcomes, sustainability, and measurement.

PART II: THE METHODS

The methods are arranged into five subsections by their basic purpose—adaptable, planning, structuring, improving, and supportive. Within their section, the processes are organized alphabetically in two groups—in-depth descriptions and thumbnails. We offer some questions to consider when determining how each method might work for your organization or community.

Every chapter contains:

A Story of Its Use

- Could we envision this scenario unfolding in our environment?

- What would make it happen?

The Basics: Answers to Frequently Asked Questions

- Would the outcomes described be useful to us?

- How would using this method benefit us? Can we articulate a clear case?

Table of Uses

- How would we describe our situation?

- What can we learn from the situations described here—even ones that are different from our own?

About the Author(s)

- How do we think the authors' backgrounds might have influenced their work?

- What does that tell us that might be useful for our situation?

Where to Go for More Information

- How might these resources (books, organizations, Web sites, etc.) help us?

- How can we learn more about this process—by ourselves or with others?

The in-depth chapters also contain information on:

Getting Started

- How can we apply the author's advice for starting in our environment?

- Do the guiding principles make sense for what we are trying to accomplish?

Roles, Responsibilities, and Relationships

- Are the sponsors ready to assume their responsibilities?

- Do we have skilled facilitators available? Where might we find them, and how much would they cost?

- How effective are outside facilitators in our culture?

Conditions for Success

- Are the conditions for success present in our environment?

- If not, how might they be created? Is it worth the effort?

Theory Base

- How does the theory fit our culture?

- Could we explain whatever is needed to proceed?

Sustaining the Results

- How successful is our culture in sustaining change? What would improve the odds?

- What sort of leadership and associated leadership development are required to sustain the results?

Burning Questions

- What are *our* burning questions?

- What do our burning questions tell us about ourselves?

- What questions can we ask that will make an even bigger difference?

Some Closing Reflections

- Let's step back and think about what we've read. What's our reaction to it?

- If several methods seem like they fit, what criteria would help us choose?

While the contributors may use different words to describe these sections, you'll know where you are by looking at their accompanying icons (above).

PART III: THOUGHTS ABOUT THE FUTURE FROM THE LEAD AUTHORS

We've gained a lot of insight over the last seven years from our own work and from spending time with the pioneers. We offer you some speculations about the future.

PART IV: QUICK SUMMARIES

We designed a reference tool that provides a snapshot of each method, answering frequently asked questions including: an image of the process, purpose, outcomes, a brief example, when to use, when not to use, number and types of participants, typical duration, and historical context of the work. We've also provided a link to more information. There's a page for each method, in alphabetical order.

PART V: REFERENCES SUGGESTED BY MULTIPLE CONTRIBUTING AUTHORS

Although each method chapter has a section on where to go for more information, we thought you would be interested in knowing which references were identified as valuable by multiple contributors. They are gathered together in this section. In addition, check out www.thechangehandbook.com to learn more about methods, selection, and to join a community of practice for all who do whole system change work.

WWW.THECHANGEHANDBOOK.COM

It is inevitable in a nascent and growing field that the moment a selection is made, something with significant potential emerges. As this book entered its final stages of editing, a powerful process with a growing community of practice came to our awareness: the "U" Theory, developed by Otto Scharmer. While it was too late to add a chapter, it became a perfect case for establishing the means for continuing to highlight the best work emerging in the field. We invite you to visit www.thechangehandbook.com to see a chapter on the "U" Theory. We expect as time passes that other promising practices will also make their way onto the site.

About the Contributors

The 95 contributing authors have helped businesses, governments, nonprofits, communities, and associations around the world achieve their goals. They have joined us in creating a rich collection of writings on whole system change. Their biographies appear in their respective chapters.

Peggy Holman, Tom Devane, and Steven Cady are practitioners of several of these change methods. They bring in-the-trenches experience and consulting advice to some of America's best-known companies and communities. Peggy conceived the book's design and kept the practitioner in mind throughout its development. Tom contributed a strong theory base and senior management perspective from his years in industry and consulting. Steve Cady, new to this edition, brought his scholar practitioner perspective to the mix.

Our hope is that the pages of this book will be dog-eared because it is so easy to use and answers your most important questions on change! We hope it speeds you on your way to creating the organizations and communities in which you really want to work and live.

Peggy Holman,
Tom Devane,
and Steven Cady
January 2007

Acknowledgements

We are immensely grateful to all the contributing authors. We thank them for their contributions, their numerous insights on change, their flexibility, and their thoughtful revisions that helped make this book an easy-to-read reference guide.

We are indebted to Christine Valenza for the wonderful images she created for many chapters. An incredible graphic facilitator and coauthor of the Values Into Action chapter, she generously gave her time to contributing authors to bring their processes visually to life. The book is far more attractive because of her work. We are also grateful to Nancy Margulies, coauthor of the chapter on Visual Recording and Graphic Facilitation, for providing additional graphic images.

We thank Jackie Stravos. If she hadn't asked, "What do you think about doing a new edition?" this project never would have begun.

Our thanks to Michael M. Pannwitz, who opened the door to the creative change work happening in the German-speaking world.

We thank the graduate students who interviewed seasoned practitioners on our behalf: Patti Coutin, Michael Hotchkiss, Amanie Kariyawasam, Amber M. Linn, Judy Marriott, Sue Ellen McComas, Kelly L. Niksa, Andrew Sauber, and Seneca Vaught. We thank the practitioners who gave their thoughts to us: Michael Arena, Tom Atlee, Lisa Beutler, Lyn Carson, Chris Corrigan, Susan Dupre, Rick Lent, and Christine Whitney Sanchez.

We owe a big thanks to the reviewers for their excellent suggestions that greatly improved the manuscript: Ela Aktay Booty, Larry Dressler, Jeff Kulick, and Leigh Wilkinson.

We thank Steve Piersanti for his conviction that this book contributes to people in communities and organizations who want to make their world a better place. To Jeevan Sivasubramanian, who made our lives better with his remarkable ability to always be there with just the answer we needed when we needed it, we are immensely grateful. We are deeply indebted to all of the people "behind the scenes" at Berrett-Koehler who edited, designed, and produced this book.

The entire field of whole system change is greatly indebted to the early work of Fred Emery, Kurt Lewin, Larry Lippitt, and Eric Trist. Most of the truly high-leverage principles in this book's methods gain their power from the action research of their early observations, experiments, and theory building. We are fortunate to have original contributions in this book from Merrelyn Emery, who has made additional valuable contributions to the field after working with Fred Emery for so many years.

We wish to acknowledge Kathie Dannemiller, whose passing leaves this field of change without one of its most original and courageous pioneers. Without her gumption to give it a go, who would have guessed anything useful could happen with hundreds of people in a room?

We also want to acknowledge Billie Alban and Barbara Bunker for their groundbreaking work, which first made this work—in which the people of the system participate in creating their future—visible.

Coediting a book is a lot like marriage—if everything is always smooth, one of you is redundant. We want to acknowledge each other—we believe the different perspectives we brought to the book coupled with our commitment to making it work by sorting out our differences have provided a better offering.

From Steven Cady

I would like to acknowledge five groups that are very important to this book. First and foremost are my Bowling Green State University colleagues and my clients. Students, faculty, and staff have played an important role in my work in this area and particularly with the concepts in this book. I'd like to thank Kelly Ashbacher for her help in the beginning phase of preparing the manuscript. As for all the students, there are too many to name here. I have learned so much from wrestling with and exploring ideas with them. In addition, many of the ideas for this book have come from my field experience and research with such organizations as DaimlerChrysler, the Toledo Diocese, and more.

Second, my close mentors have encouraged me and provided me with the foundation necessary to do this work. I can't say enough about people like Jimmie Ferrell, Kathie Dannemiller, Marguerite Foxon, Patricia Fandt, and Rasesh Thakkar.

Third, my family always asks how things are with the book, and when I am too busy to call . . . they call me: the Bellomys, Bonds, Browns, Cadys, MacDonells, Odins, Thakkars, and Smiths.

Fourth, my best friends in Orlando have been my advocates and cheerleaders, and that too goes for my friends and brothers in Ohio.

Finally, thank you Peggy and Tom . . . I am so glad you invited me to join you on the journey.

From Tom Devane

I am indebted to the many people in my professional and personal networks who enabled me to make some valuable contributions to this book as an author and coeditor. I thank Helena Dolny of the Land Bank of South Africa for inviting me to help in the postapartheid transformation of the part-government, part-financial institution that she headed. This project had a profound impact on my consulting practice and it helped shape, and reshape, many ideas I had about successful large-scale, sustainable change.

I'm fortunate enough to have some great business colleagues who are also personal friends, and I thank Robert Rehm, Nancy Cebula, Gary Frank, Dennis Mayhew, and Tony Singarayar for long hours of collegial work and nonwork time spent observing organizational behavior and building successful theories and approaches for improving organizations and communities.

I also thank Merrelyn Emery for her extensive research and collaboration with me on this and other publications. I thank Larry Kinney of AT&T for his advice and inviting me in to help with AT&T's postdivestiture conversion from a monopolistic to entrepreneurial mind-set.

My special thanks go out to my wife, Susan Conway Devane, and my kids, Krista and Kiernan, who exhibited extreme patience and support during the long writing and editing hours spent on weekends and holidays.

From Peggy Holman

There are so many thanks at so many levels! To Anne Stadler and Harrison Owen for being great companions in this journey through the amazing world of change. To Mark Jones, my fellow traveler and frequent partner in crime. To Kenoli Oleari for his complex and challenging suggestions on the Mix and Match chapter. To Tree Fitzpatrick for her friendship, insight, writing suggestions, and support. To Tom Atlee, for his many direct and indirect contributions to my thinking and writing.

And to my husband, Neil Holman, who not only provided invaluable advice, but who wholeheartedly dove into the production of an unbelievably complex manuscript to help us out as the deadline loomed. On top of that, he managed to live with me during the process—he has my love and enduring thanks.

Introduction and Essential Fundamentals

What we do not understand we do not possess.
—Goethe

Effective, sustainable change can be elusive, particularly if its core principles are not grasped and actively applied. Change efforts are often like the little girl in the nursery rhyme, who, "when she was good, she was very, very good, and when she was bad, she was horrid." There's often no middle ground when it comes to describing the success of a change effort. Consider the following two cases:

Case 1: A Major Pharmaceutical Manufacturer

The CEO of a major pharmaceutical manufacturer in New Jersey sat quietly in his office, wondering what had gone wrong. After eight months of intensive efforts to improve product quality and reduce production cycle time, the company had spent more than $1.6 million on external consultants and allocated five full-time internal people who had developed detailed process maps, used tools to diagnose problems, and conducted training in the improvement concepts of Lean and Six Sigma. The returns to date had unfortunately not even covered one-tenth of the effort's cost. He thought he'd done all the right things, having one-on-one conversations with his VPs, publishing progress in the company newsletter, and putting posters around the plant that extolled the virtues of doing things "right the first time." He'd even conducted several all-employee Town Hall meetings and explained the program to people, taking adequate time for questions and answers afterward. He thought he'd even addressed that pesky "people part" of change that organizations so often forget, and still his effort had fallen flat. The people didn't own the change. They exhibited behavior that maximized personal power in functional silos instead of taking an enterprise-wide view. Regarding the few improvements that were made, the people at middle management and frontline workers rapidly slid back as soon as the high-priced consultants finished their project stint.

Case 2: A Sleepy Mountain Town

Seventeen hundred miles away in a Rocky Mountain state, the residents of a sleepy mountain town rose to trudge down the hill to another day of meetings at the municipal center. The controversy: Many residents opposed changing local zoning laws to permit gambling in their town. They were very concerned about what would happen to their quality of life and their children's future. On the other side, the real estate developers thought they had indeed been very generous to townspeople in future profit sharing and putting money back into the town's infrastructure. The primary means each side had to voice their concerns and influence outcomes were personal pressure on local politicians and rowdy behavior in new zoning meetings. Unfortunately, these usually started out as polite exchanges and quickly deteriorated into shouting matches. The result: a stalemate for both sides, as the debate had already dragged on for more than a year.

What Really Happened?

As the organizers of these efforts sat back and debriefed the results that didn't match their intended objectives, they pondered four questions:

- Why was there no energy for change beyond the change proposers?
- Why didn't people "get it" that this change was ultimately for the good of everyone?
- Is conflict a natural state of being when people with different needs and views get together? If so, is there a way to harness it and move forward in a productive fashion?
- What could be done to create ownership of the problems and the solutions among all people involved?

One powerful high-leverage strategy that could address the four questions above was noticeably absent from the two scenarios—a concerted effort to engage groups of people in productively working together toward identifying common ground and expanding it together. That is, people were not involved in group settings where they could collectively explore possibilities, surface and test assumptions, and develop plans to address areas that they agreed would benefit all involved.

One might argue that there was group involvement in both cases. In each, there was certainly one-on-one communication, and there were meetings where information was broadcast from the change leaders to the general population. There were even gatherings where people could express their opinions and debate. However, merely getting people together in a room does not ensure they'll be productive. What's needed for effective, sustainable change are sessions in which people collectively explore each other's assumptions, seek and expand common ground, shape a desired future, and jointly take ownership of the solutions to the issues at hand. Methods that contain these objectives are precisely what this book provides. We'll explore some high-leverage strategies for addressing these issues, and also dispel some common misconceptions about change. Specifically, this chapter covers:

- Global patterns and trends that bring the methods into the spotlight
- What drives people to use change methods
- How change methods affect people and desired outcomes
- Misconceptions about change methods
- Financial considerations
- Common elements of change that engage the people of the system.

Global Patterns and Trends

When talking about the need for changing the way we change, it makes sense to round up the usual suspects: increasing global competition, escalating customer demands, and rapid pace of change in both public and private sectors. These all exert influences that lead people to the methods described in this book. However, we believe some trends go beyond that usual laundry list and we've honed in on some particular patterns/trends that exert tremendous forces screaming for changes in the way we work together and make the need for organized group events an imperative for any leader—at any level—seeking improvements in his or her organization or community. Table 1 shows such items and associated impacts that favor the use of methods.

After looking at the data, it makes sense that change methods present logical options for addressing some of the unfolding global issues affecting organizations and communities. However, just realizing that change methods can capitalize on favorable trends and thwart unfavorable ones does not necessarily mean that all who could benefit will readily embrace them. There are

DILBERT: © Scott Adams/Dist. by United Feature Syndicate, Inc.

Figure 1. Increased Immunity to Change

Pattern/Trend	Impact	How Change Methods Help
Rapid advancements in, and global dissemination of communications technology	More people can get information about policies, events, and situations that shape their lives. An informed populace can, and quite often does, crank up a strong desire to participate in decisions that affect them. They deeply grasp the issues previously unknown (consider Tiananmen Square) and start to care. Communities of practice around particular topics are on the rise, and in a peer-to-peer fashion, people freely contribute to these to advance the body of knowledge.	Channel the energy of information to people. Provide a structure in which they can quickly and productively seize ownership and responsibility for improving their lot in life, whether it is in an enterprise-wide computer implementation that promises dissemination of decision making or local political issues surrounding a zoning decision for urban planning. The information is there, and the change methods described here can help people get productive around it.
Spread of increased participation and democratic principles around the world	Whether it is the collapse of the Soviet Union, demonstrations in Indonesia, elections in the Middle East, or demands for empowerment in organizations, more people are wanting to take an active role in determining policies, decisions, and actions that affect them. Many exhort that command and control is dead, but their overt actions demonstrate just the opposite.	The methods in this book are proven practices that can systematically increase participation and energy, while simultaneously addressing concerns of organizations or communities wildly spinning out of control.
Increased education levels around the world	Generally speaking, the more people learn, the less likely it is they will enjoy being told what to do and how to do it.	Methods provide a systematic means to capitalize on internal desires to participate and develop quality results.
Increased global mobility	In organizations and communities throughout the world, there are increasingly diverse populations, and within those diverse populations there are numerous chances for conflict and gridlock.	Methods provide the means for people from different backgrounds to productively explore common ground that benefits them individually and as an organization or community.

Pattern/Trend	Impact	How Change Methods Help
Increased conflicting demands of multiple stakeholders	Organizations and communities must balance the sometimes conflicting needs of many different customer segments, workers, and other stakeholders. Increased mobility has made neighborhoods around the world far less homogenous. Multiple conflicting interests must be adequately addressed for the common good of all involved.	Methods often include multiple stakeholders and establish conditions in which they cocreatively meet their individual and collective needs.
Tight time and work/life balance	In today's post-reengineering and lean world, many organizations have not just trimmed fat, but have also cut muscle and scraped bone. Scarce time resources make it difficult to balance technical work, improvement work, and outside work interests.	Methods save time by productively using people's time to pursue opportunities and fix problems. Common understanding and commitment reduce the need to revisit issues multiple times, thus conserving scarce resources.
Declining participation in community, family, and social life	In his landmark book, *Bowling Alone*, Harvard sociologist Robert Putnam notes, based on 500,000 interviews in 25 years, how declining connections have begun to impoverish American lives and communities (data was collected only for the United States, but similar conditions exist worldwide).	Methods provide a cost-effective way to satisfy the human need to connect with other people, and can be done efficiently at work or in community interactions.
Increased immunity to change	Many companies have been exposed to numerous change initiatives over the past 15 years. After being Total Quality Managed, reengineered, and downsized, workers have adopted attitudes of extreme skepticism to downright sabotage of new change attempts to a "this too shall pass" attitude. Traditional forms of public participation, with little interaction or cooperative solution seeking, has decreased trust in government and created greater challenges for making change in communities.	As shown in figure 1, modern-day business commentator Dilbert observes that introducing change can be ill received in a workplace. Methods provide people with an immediate opportunity to have their voices heard, and in many cases, immediately acted upon, thus gradually building people's positive attitudes toward change and avoiding the all-too-common change-averse attitudes. Similarly, these methods are rekindling civic engagement in cities and countries around the world.

Table 1. Global Patterns and Trends That Favor the Use of Methods

forces and factors that tend to drive people toward using these methods, and some misconceptions that drive people away from them.

What Drives People to Use a Change Method?

The change methods described in this book have experienced an increasing popularity over the past 15 years as an element of programs where effective change was essential. While the global, big-picture patterns and trends listed in the previous sections may be the motivators, we offer eight reasons to use one of the methods described in this book.

Reason 1. They accelerate action. Since considerable time in most methods is devoted to articulating personal assumptions, imagining desirable futures, seeking common ground, finding innovative answers, and codeveloping action plans, there is a high level of commitment to quickly implementing what was developed, and lots of ownership that helps fuel rapid action.

Reason 2. They increase shared understanding and dissemination of shared strategy/direction. When strategic direction is merely passed down from the top of the organization or from government officials, often there is minimal understanding of the strategic details and related assumptions because only select people were present during strategy development. With the use of whole system change methods, typically more people are involved in setting the strategy and therefore understand the nuances and reasons for selected options. Sometimes an entire organization is involved in strategy formulation; more often there is substantial involvement in *strategy dissemination*. The result is that there are more points of contact throughout the organization or community who understand nuances and reasons, and more widespread motivation to succeed because of personal ownership.

Reason 3. They take some of the continual pressure off the top. Organization and community leaders have their hands full: staying in touch with customers and citizens, prioritizing tactical issues, and keeping their strategic antennae up looking for emerging trends and patterns. Also, effective leaders devote time at the start of the change effort to demonstrate that elusive, often watched-for element of "leadership commitment." However, in organizations and communities that use methods, ongoing demands for positional leadership commitment can taper off a bit *if* they intelligently use change methods to create leader-full environments, disseminating ownership and energy for change throughout an organization. In communities, these methods can be a remarkable force for reengaging a disinterested public.

Reason 4. They create emotional attachment to outcomes. Great leaders know that people need to be emotionally attached to improving their own condition, or there won't be any traction. Since the change methods can create emotional attachment through meaningful involvement, cocreating the future, seeking common ground, collective goal setting, and joint implementation planning, great leaders channel their own emotional commitment through large group methods to jump-start change and move it along.

Reason 5. They promote a seeing-is-believing effect. People who have witnessed one of these large-group events and the power that is unleashed become the greatest advocates for using them. One California semiconductor executive stated, "I was in such awe of the energy created by our first group planning meeting that I had a difficult time expressing its power to other executives I talked with about our change effort."

Reason 6. They increase sustainable results. Sustainability is a key watchword in organizations and communities today (in fact, this book has devoted an entire chapter to it). The methods highlighted here foster sustainability through meaningful participation, co-discovery, and coplanning, often among groups with very different interests and experiences.

Reason 7. They enhance management effectiveness. Though many organizations espouse the death of command-and-control styles, unfortunately many ingrained practices die hard. These methods provide a way for top managers to begin to distribute responsibility while simultaneously establishing critical controls to ensure that boundaries exist to avoid often-feared "the organization will be spinning out of control" situations.

Reason 8. They convey a visible "hey-this-could-be-different" message. The widespread implementation of numerous change initiatives has inured many people to any new change effort. In some cases, they overtly oppose or covertly sabotage it. When these change methods demonstrate how quickly people can have a voice and an impact, it fuels their further enthusiastic participation.

How Change Methods Affect People and Desired Outcomes

The change methods in this book are practical applications of social systems theory that engage the complexities of human behavior. In our experience, there are three "soft" value propositions that capture business leaders' attention for their "hard" effect on measurable results. These methods generate:

Group energy. What drives a group to move forward no matter the odds? What creates a sense of collective accountability and the strong belief that "we are all in this together"? More than the sum of the parts, bringing together people with different knowledge and experiences often leads to breakthrough solutions and effective action. Because group energy is contagious, it can be highly effective in replicating its benefits, through creative and collaborative peer-to-peer interactions that capitalize on the momentum created by the peer support and coaching provided. The capacity to generate authentic human connections across siloed organizations, among diverse demographics, and between highly conflicted factions in a community, is a central strength of effective large group change. Such group energy is instrumental in bringing about high-quality decisions and results.

Intrinsic motivation. What keeps an individual going when things look dim? What causes a person to act from the heart, not the pocketbook? While group work may produce the breakthroughs, dedicated individual action is its companion for success. Through these methods, people connect with what is important to them as individuals, fueling a motivation that comes from within. For example, Participative Design Workshop accomplishes this by supporting people in structuring into their environment local work autonomy, variety in daily tasks, local goal setting, feedback, learning, opportunity for achievement, and recognition. This intrinsic motivation (coupled with appropriate doses of extrinsic motivation, like bonuses) gets people up every morning, genuinely asking from within, "What can I do to support the desired outcomes?" It is through intrinsic motivation that people take the initiative—not waiting to be told what to do—to reach the desired results.

Emotional engagement. What causes someone to express how much he or she truly cares about a specific outcome beyond all logic? What helps to foster strong feelings about something that matters? Rarely are people swayed through white papers or fact-filled lectures. Rather, it is by putting a human face on an issue, making it personal, that people commit 100 percent. For example, a pharmaceutical company sought to improve the stock-out situation on a life-saving drug. They kicked off the effort with a film of testimonials from people whose lives had been saved by the drug. They also showed the adverse effects when the drug was unavailable. That helped fuel a very rapid improvement effort. Within two months, the stock-out situation was eliminated and 100 percent of the patients received their medication on time. Without some sort of emotional connection to critical behaviors, people can end up simply going through the motions of executing work plan tasks. This usually results in lackluster outcomes, or projects that die a slow death. With emotional engagement, people go out of their way to seek the assistance of others, to find time in their busy schedules to do the necessary work (even though it may not have been budgeted), and to innovate ways to circumvent obstacles to implementing the desired outcome.

These characteristics do not exist in isolation. Rather, as group work inspires individual motivation and engenders emotional commitments to the work and to colleagues, these qualities reinforce each other. It is a tribute to the underlying theory that such powerful practices are available to benefit our organizations and communities.

RESPONSIBILITY OF THE CHANGE LEADER

As with any powerful tool, using change methods appropriately is incumbent on change leaders. Being clear about their true intentions and acting with integrity in carrying out those intentions is not only ethical but also fundamental to success. These change methods ask people to open their hearts and get involved. No less can be expected of the change leader. If this seems a lot to ask, consider the stakes of the intended change and make a clear choice about what it is worth to challenge an organization or community to be its best.

Having seen the power of these change methods, it raises an important question: Why are they not in even more widespread use? To understand this, we turn now to clearing the air on some misperceptions that have hindered their growth.

Misconceptions

Some of these methods have been around for several decades. As pioneers have brought them into organizations and communities, we have learned a great deal about what makes them effective. Along the way, some perceptions have arisen that cause leaders to avoid using them. Table 2 contains some of those misconceptions, as well as realities and mitigating strategies.

Misconception	Reality and Mitigating Strategy
Methods are just touchy-feely, feel-good events with minimal practical impact.	It's certainly true that there is more time spent than in an average meeting devoted to what might be dubbed "people issues" such as establishing conditions for effective interpersonal communication and joint exploration of issues. However, when done well, these are set up in the context of addressing an important opportunity or problem, and actually address it more productively by reducing the number of future required iterations of understanding and buy-in.
Most people will change based on pure logic, so methods that seek to engage people are unnecessary.	People need an emotional, gut-level connection to a challenge to inspire engaging with it. Large group methods can help provide that by generating intrinsic motivation through direct involvement.
It's expensive to get lots of people in a room to decide something, and it's just not worth it!	There is no "law" of methods that states that everyone has to be called into a room for every decision. Typically, careful attention is paid in discerning who gets invited to ensure that the optimal mix to address a challenge is present. Effective preplanning ensures the right people are gathered at the right time to address challenges in a systemic way, instead of just "fixing errors."
Methods should bear the brunt of the large-scale change work for successful change.	Large group methods are not the only way of accomplishing successful large-scale change, though they are among the most rapid. Other approaches include one-on-one conversations, training, coaching, role modeling of new behaviors, day-to-day management practices, and changes to the reward system.
Top managers and government officials should not give up control to middle managers and front-line workers or to ordinary citizens.	The issue of control has some elements of emotion to it, and some elements of well-founded logic. Historically, many managers and civic leaders have been burned by pushing decisions lower in the organization or out to community members, but when large group methods are used well, appropriate boundaries, alignment, internal controls, and monitoring mechanisms are present. In fact, when selected decisions are distributed to groups, the groups may actually provide more control because more people are watching for positive overall outcomes. Futurist Karl Albrecht speaks about empowerment as "responsible freedom."

Table 2. Misconceptions and Associated Realities About the Methods

Misconception	Reality and Mitigating Strategy
A large group method is just like any other meeting, just with more people.	Large group methods are quite different. It's an entirely different type of meeting because people are in conversations with each other that they truly care about. While starting and finishing on time are great to apply to any meeting, including large group methods, beyond that, traditional facilitation rules may not all apply.
Conflict is bad and will naturally emerge in a method when members having different interests show up in one place, resulting in discomfort and catastrophe.	There are places in every city where people are together and there is no conflict. These places are called cemeteries. The reality is that whenever you have more than one living person in a room, you'll have more than one set of interests, and that's not a bad thing. Most methods are designed to surface conflict and deal with it productively.

Table 2. Continued

Once people have gotten over some commonly held misconceptions about the methods, they are ready to move along in the decision process to use one or combine several methods. Once they start thinking about committing to using a method, it's completely natural to start thinking, "What will this cost and what will it get me?"

Financial Considerations

As people enter the method selection process, they typically develop a healthy interest in the following:

- Costs
- Benefits
- Other Resource Considerations

Costs

Once people decide to use large group methods to meet their organization or community challenges, an early question that arises is, "Hey, what's this thing going to cost?" Well, it would be great if we could give you a standard cost for each method, or even a formula to figure it out. We can't.

The two big variable costs for a method are facility costs and facilitator costs. Both can vary widely. For example, the strategic planning vice president of a Fortune 100 company booked an island resort for a three-day Search Conference. The total cost of the session was $55,000. Five weeks later, a Colorado mountain community held a Search Conference—the same exact agenda—at a free local community center using pro bono facilitators, where total out-of-pocket costs were $68.73 for donuts and coffee. Value of each event: priceless. Costs: highly variable. The bottom line is that costs are more determined by the organization or community culture and event structuring than they are by specific method type. For sample budgeting templates, visit www.thechangehandbook.com.

BENEFITS

A challenging question for many methods is, "What benefits were realized?" Some methods, such as Six Sigma, are wired from the start to identify potential benefits, tactically pursue them, and then audit the results. For other methods, such as Dialogue (that helps surface important unstated assumptions) or Participative Design Workshop (that converts organizations into structures of high-performing teams), it is a bit more difficult to find a direct tie to the bottom line. A majority of the contributing authors in the first edition stated that while there was definitely a benefit to doing the method, the connection between the method conduct and the financial results was too loose to definitively provide a specific return on investment figure.

Authors suggested several alternatives. Benefits are best defined in the context of the desired outcomes. Clarity about the purpose of the work provides the basis for determining its effectiveness. Whether this is best measured financially or through other means, it is an opportunity for a rich and useful conversation as the initiative is defined.

Another approach suggested by contributing authors was to qualitatively consider the cost of not doing the method, and then assessing if it would make sense to do it. For example, such questions might include: "What is the cost of not having a strategic plan that all the vice presidents helped create and are motivated to implement?" "What are the implications of not having a major community segment present in zoning discussions?" and "What are the costs of hidden and overt resistance if frontline workers are not involved in decisions that affect their local working conditions?"

Finally, it's important to consider that not all benefits arrive with a monetary price tag. Some benefits, such as quality of work life, vibrancy in communities, and increased collaboration are extremely worthy objectives and can make an immediate difference in people's lives as well as a long-term difference that has positive economic implications.

RESOURCES

An often-missed consideration is one of resources. Typical resource requirements for large group methods include flip charts, easels, markers, LCD projectors, a laptop computer, and a large room, preferably with a window. Everything you may need for a session may not require a financial outlay, or it may be a minimal expense for something that can make or break the session. For example, if you require an LCD projector and you're conducting the session in a remote location, make sure you order it early, and that they have backup bulbs for the projector. If you're up at a rustic mountain lodge, make sure the conference room they've put you in has electrical outlets. If your method requires a big circle of chairs and no tables, make sure the hotel staff can remove the tables from the room so it won't look like a table warehouse during your session. And if you will be generating many flip charts full of information, be sure it is okay to use tape on the walls. You get the picture.

Now that you know why people might use methods that engage others in changing their systems, what might turn them off, and what it might cost, you may want to know *what it is about the methods that makes them effective.*

Common Elements Across the Methods

By looking across the many methods in this book, we uncovered some common elements that we believe are keys to their success. We offer seven shared characteristics:

Contributing to a meaningful purpose *compels people into action.* When people see the possibility of contributing to something larger than themselves, they operate differently. The emphasis shifts from focusing on "Why can't something be done?" to "How can we make this happen?" There is a tangible difference in the atmosphere of organizations and communities that have made this shift—they feel alive with possibility and excitement.

The power of individual contribution *is unleashed.* When people understand the whole system, when they see the possibility of meaningful intentions, and when they feel their voice matters, they commit. While it doesn't happen every time, the potential for extraordinary accomplishment exists within each of these approaches.

The whole person, *head, heart, and spirit, is engaged.* Over the years, words such as "hands" or "heads" have become a way to count numbers of people in organizations. They reflect a focus on what is considered important—hands to do the manual work; heads to do the thinking work. These methods reengage the whole person: hands for doing, heads for thinking, hearts for caring, and spirits for achieving inspired results.

Knowledge *and* wisdom *exist in the people in the organization or community.* This belief that the people in the system know best is a profound shift from the days of bringing in the outside "efficiency" expert with the answer. While several of these approaches rely on new ideas, not one of them presumes to have the answer. Instead, they engage people in the organization or community in making choices about what's best for them.

Information *is cocreated by members of the organization or community.* What keeps the system whole over time is a commitment to collaborative meaning making, a profound shift from information provided on a "need-to-know" basis. When people share stories of what is important to them and to the system, they are more connected to each other and make more informed decisions about their individual and collective actions.

The method creates a whole system *view among members of the organization or community.* Each method enables people to understand their system at a deeper level. They begin to see interconnections among departments, neighborhoods, processes, and relationships. When this occurs, system members know better how to contribute and therefore make commitments that were previously unlikely. Because more people understand the whole system, they can make intelligent, informed contributions to substantive decisions.

Change is a process, *not an event.* While most of the authors describe a half-day to three-day event, they are all quick to say that the sum total of a transformational effort is *not* just one change event. While events help focus people's attention, they are only one part of the change equation. Leaders—at all levels—of organizations and communities also need to focus on actively supporting the plans and improvements achieved during the event. Without such ongoing support, conditions may return to what they were before the event occurred.

These elements form a pattern, linking the individual with the collective, and the inner being with the outer "doing" or work, integrated through communication that connects, and bounded by two key assumptions: a commitment to a systems view and change as an ongoing process (figure 2).

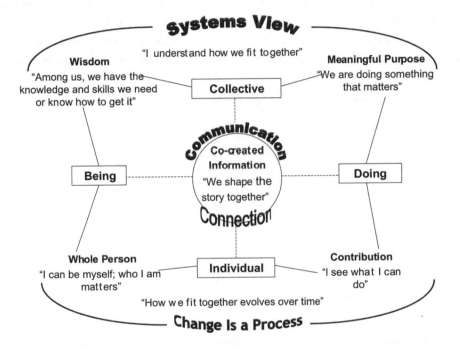

Figure 2. Common Elements Among the Methods

In summary, the methods in this book provide a way to address the complex emerging global trends and patterns that provide huge challenges to the very survival of organizations and communities today. Indeed, the collaborative and common ground–seeking methods may provide one of the only solutions to such complex problems. Once people recognize that the methods can have such a profound impact, they need to decide if, when, and how they will use them. The forces that drive people to use the methods in this book—such as the need for speed, the need for intrinsic motivation, and previous exposure to the dramatic success of the methods— are currently being experienced by a growing number of progressive leaders who seek positive, sustainable change. Unfortunately, misconceptions about the use of methods abound, and, in many cases, are keeping people from using them. By taking a critical look at historical use of the methods—both good and bad—and correctly applying their underlying principles, leaders can advance the positive development of their organizations and communities in a sustainable way.

A Word on Terminology

We have encountered a variety of terms that are nearly synonymous: large group methods, whole system change, enterprise-wide change, large group interventions, change methods, change processes, and the process arts are among the most common. Many of these are used throughout the book, depending on the author's background and audiences with whom he or she typically works. We have found that a term one person really resonates with can often set off alarm bells and near anaphylactic reactions in another. For now, our advice is to *use the term that you think best for your environment*. Think about how you'll want to explain what you're trying to accomplish to key decision makers, your fellow change agents, and the population that will be most affected by the change, and select a good match.

Part I: Navigating Through the Methods

Every journey of substance benefits from a road map. Particularly when entering unknown territory, any reference points from those who have gone before can make the trip a little easier. When there are many choices, a little orientation goes a long way! The chapters in this section prepare you for traveling through the vast and rapidly expanding discipline of highly participative change in human systems.

Chapter 1: "The Big Picture: Making Sense of More than Sixty Methods" is like a travel guide, providing a set of characteristics to help you begin orienting yourself to the 61 change methods in the book. It gives you a glimpse into these methods through the purpose of the process—whether it is for use in an organization, community, or both—with regard to the size of events it is intended to support, its typical duration, what it takes to prepare new practitioners, its cycle of use, and any special resource needs.

Chapter 2: "Selecting Methods: The Art of Mastery" provides a framework for thinking about mastering the work of change. It offers a pathway to follow for making a choice among methods and takes you through a story of making a choice. It also offers some counsel on selecting a consultant to work with your community or organization and some guidance in getting started.

Chapter 3: "Preparing to Mix and Match Methods" travels deeper into the territory for those who are considering how different approaches might blend with each other. It shares some stories from the field as well as some practices to guide you in this work.

Chapter 4: "Sustainability of Results" prepares you for starting with the end in mind, so that the time, money, and effort you invest leave a lasting legacy.

This opening section grounds you in the basics of change, preparing you to take your first steps into the new and liberating terrain of cocreating a future that serves the people, communities, and organizations in which we live and work.

1

The Big Picture
Making Sense of More Than Sixty Methods

Make everything as simple as possible, but not simpler.
—Albert Einstein

Whole system change methods continue to increase in recognition, variety, and use. The first edition of this book included 18 methods and just a few short years later, there are more than 60 methods in this second edition. This creative explosion provides great opportunities for reaching further into organizations and communities to engage people in making a positive and productive difference.

So, let's say you need to make a change, you have looked at a variety of methods, and you come across this compendium of more than 60 methods. Where do you start? What's the difference between one method and another . . . how do you make sense of them all? How do you speak intelligently about them . . . helping clients, coworkers, employees, community members, stakeholders, leaders . . . understand the distinctions? WHAT DO YOU DO? This chapter defines seven characteristics to help you see the whole of the methods available to support your work. These seven characteristics are gathered in a "Summary Matrix" that provides you with a quick, "at-a-glance" way to compare and contrast the methods.

Understanding Options: Seven Characteristics to Consider

Categorizing anything is tricky. On one hand, we strive to simplify our world with models, categories, and taxonomies. On the other hand, simplification limits and potentially undermines the essential concepts we strive to better understand. Classification does not stand alone; it is a starting point for consideration. With elaboration and context, a fuller picture emerges. The framework that follows is one lens into that picture. Coupled with the information in the rest of the book, we believe you will have what you need to make sound choices regarding which method(s) can best help you. The method chapters, quick summaries, and end-of-chapter references offer the means to further investigate the possibilities.

Purpose

In *Alice's Adventures in Wonderland* by Lewis Carroll, the cat said, "If you don't know where you are going, any road will get you there." Purpose ensures we go somewhere intentional. It answers the questions: What is the focus and aim of our work? What methods are designed to do this? We identified five overarching dimensions of purpose. Planning, structuring, and improving describe processes designed to accomplish a specific purpose. Adaptable methods span these purposes. Supportive processes enhance the work, whatever its purpose (see figure 1).

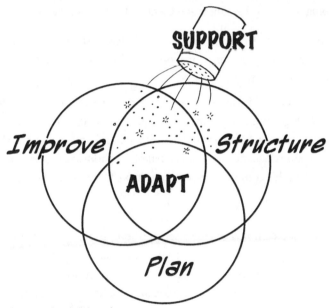

Illustration by Christine Valenza

Figure 1. The Five Dimensions of Purpose

- *Adaptable* methods are used for a variety of purposes in organizations or communities, including planning, structuring, and improving. This group uses principles and practices that adjust to varying needs.

- *Planning* methods help people in communities and organizations shape their future together. These methods set strategic direction and core identity through activities such as self-analysis, exploration, visioning, value clarification, goal setting, and action development.

- *Structuring* methods organize the system to create the desired future. They rely on an effective plan and result in redefined relationships among people and redesigned work practices.

- *Improving* methods increase effectiveness and create operational efficiencies in such areas as cycle time, waste, productivity, and relationships. Basic assumptions of how the organization works often stay the same, while breakthroughs are achieved in processes, relationships, individual behaviors, knowledge, and distributive leadership.

- *Supportive* refers to practices that enhance the efficacy of other change methods, making them more robust and suitable to the circumstances and participants. They are like spices in a meal, enriching methods to satisfy the unique tastes of the client. They weave into and often become permanent elements of other methods.

TYPE OF SYSTEM

Who do these methods help? What kinds of people are coming together? How might we think of the system undergoing the change? A simple and useful distinction is organizations and communities.

- *Organizations* have discernable boundaries and clearly structured relationships that help determine which employees, functions, organizational levels, customers, and suppliers to include in a proposed change.

- *Communities* are more diffuse, often involving a range of possible participants—citizens, different levels of government, associations, agencies, media, and more. These systems are often emerging entities that exist around a common bond, sometimes based in purpose, sometimes in relationships. Alliances, cities, associations, cohousing groups, and activist rallies are examples of geographic communities, communities of interest, and communities of practice.

EVENT SIZE

Most of the methods employ one or a series of events along the change journey. Though they all focus on whole systems, some engage large numbers of participants at one time, while others involve smaller numbers over time. Still others use technology to bring people together across time and space. What best serves your situation? Size has many implications, both strategic and practical. Do we involve the whole system or a meaningful subset? What facilities do we need? How many people do we include? What are the potential costs per person and how much can we afford? It's a tough balance to include as much of the system as you can while dealing with the constraints of space, time, and cost.

DURATION

When determining what process to use, time is always a factor. What is the sense of urgency? What sort of pace can the organization or community assimilate? What is possible in terms of how frequently people gather? Whatever the nature of the process, it requires time for preparation, for event(s), and for follow-up. This is often tough to characterize because it is highly dependent on the complexity of the initiative. The contributing authors have given us a range based on how their process is typically used.

CYCLE

Some methods have a natural beginning and ending. Others are suited for a periodic planning cycle, and some become "the way things are done around here." We have identified the following cycles:

- *As Needed.* Done to accomplish an intended purpose, these methods are not typically scheduled to be repeated. Sometimes they are used only once; however, they may be used again if a new purpose arises.

- *Periodic.* Repeated over time, these methods are commonly used for planning processes. For example, repetition may be scheduled every few years.

- *Continuous.* For some methods, the objective is for the event to cease being an event. The full benefit is realized when the application becomes everyday practice.

PRACTITIONER PREPARATION

People often ask, "How quickly can I get started with using this method on my own?" Some methods are deceptively simple to "just do," yet there is art and nuance to mastering them over time. Mastery of virtually any process is a lifetime's work. The more complex the change effort, the more advisable it is to get skilled support. Still, knowing what's involved to prepare new practitioners provides insight into how quickly and broadly change can spread. Here are the distinctions we offer for getting started as a new practitioner:

- *Self-Directed Study.* Given a background in group work, with the aid of a book, a video, support from a community of practice (perhaps via the internet), or some in-person coaching, a new practitioner can take his or her first steps independently. Because these practices look so simple, this caution is especially important: Start with straightforward applications!

- *General Training.* Before attempting this work on your own, attend a workshop or work with someone skilled in the process. In some cases, training workshops offer follow-up field experiences that provide opportunities to work as part of a support team.

- *In-depth Training.* These methods require a significant investment in training and practice before working on your own. Often, there is formal training, certification from a governing body, and mentoring.

SPECIAL RESOURCE NEEDS

Almost every process involves at least one face-to-face or online event. We've asked the contributing authors to make visible any unusual needs for people (e.g., many volunteer facilitators), exceptional technology requirements (e.g., proprietary software or hundreds of linked computers in a room), or other out-of-the-ordinary items or resource-intensive requirements.

All processes require a knowledgeable facilitator or facilitation team. Most face-to-face events require adequate space, breakout rooms, comfortable seating, clean air, good lighting, appropriate acoustics, and supplies (e.g., flip charts, markers, tape). Many online processes require a computer and Internet access. Very large events often require audiovisual support. Beyond these basics, is something special required?

An Interlude: A Tale of Multiple Intelligences

We invite you into a behind-the-scenes story with a cliff-hanger ending:

As we searched for how to communicate the qualitative distinctions among the methods in the book, educator Howard Gardner's multiple intelligences offered an exciting possibility.[1] Drawing from neurophysiology, Gardner identified the site location in the brain that correlates with each of the intelligences.[2] Just as people have natural gifts in different areas—art, math, music, etc.—we thought, "Why not approach these processes by considering their different emphases among the intelligences?" Characterizing the methods this way could open the door to rich conversations about the relationships among the processes and their fit with the purpose of an initiative or the culture of the organization or community. We could also see the intelligences as useful to practitioners in discerning what methods resonated with their skills and talents.

Excited by the idea, we asked the contributing authors to identify the three most dominant intelligences (in order of dominance) for their method. One or two told us they liked the idea and others told us that they didn't. Most just responded with an answer. A few identified four or more intelligences and were a bit frustrated that we asked them to limit their choice to the dominant three. Then, as our due date for delivering the manuscript neared, three elders of the field weighed in, flatly refusing to play. Merrelyn Emery put it this way, "I object to it [multiple intelligences] being applied to Open Systems Theory methods because whether you like it or not, it is the human implications that will be drawn from the entry and these methods have been designed to be as nondiscriminating as possible."

In a separate conversation, Sandra Janoff and Marv Weisbord said, "There is equal opportunity to access all the intelligences in Future Search. Future Search is like an empty bottle. People pour in their experiences, history, aspirations, then seek common ground and act based upon it. What is key is to get the right diversity into the room, that's what gives the event its rich character. Not the method, nor the facilitator."

It was the eleventh hour and we faced a dilemma: Include the intelligences or drop them from the book? After our initial consternation, we realized that we were in a situation that brings many people to whole system change methods: a complex subject, deeply held beliefs, and the need to find an answer—fast! We faced a consultant's worst nightmare: the need to practice our own teachings! Taking a deep breath, we embraced the controversy, knowing that disturbances are a doorway to learning and an opportunity for something innovative to emerge. We then did what we advise our clients to do and revisited our purpose: to support readers in discerning enough about the processes to make useful choices.

We discussed the value of the intelligences in meeting this purpose, and specifically how this lens of the intelligences had already benefited our own work. For example, we realized that the book did not have a single process with rhythmic intelligence among the three most dominant. Steven Cady went searching and found two gems: JazzLab and Drum Café.

Peggy Holman talked about how awareness of the intelligences had immediately affected a gathering she did with Juanita Brown, using both The World Café and Open Space. Together, they consciously brought all seven intelligences into play, creating a powerful, rich experience that continues to ripple in its effect on participants. Did bringing music and movement—intelligences that might not have otherwise been incorporated—matter? It is difficult to say; it is clear that the conference accessed parts of participants that might not have been otherwise present.

As we reflected, Tom Devane pointed out that our use of the intelligences had morphed. We didn't use them to classify; rather, they served a higher purpose, consciously inviting more of ourselves and our participants into the work. Steven Cady added that inventing and incorporating activities that tap the intelligences was a way to evolve the methods.

Yes, we concluded, the intelligences had something valuable to add, but perhaps not in the way we had originally envisioned, and not without more in-depth exploration among the contributing authors. That, we felt would be a disservice to them, to the field, and to our readers. But how could we bring the value, give it the time needed to "simmer," and meet our publication deadline?

As often happens when we embrace rather than resist disturbances, we found an innovative answer that we believe accomplishes far more than we originally envisioned. We are convening a conversation at www.thechangehandbook.com among the contributing authors. Our eleventh-hour monkey wrench became an opportunity to meet another desire we had: to create an online space to grow a vibrant community of practice across the many process disciplines. What better way to start than with a meaty, substantive issue? We invite you to visit, see how the story is unfolding, and join in the continuing conversation.

The Summary Matrix

The following tables provide an overview of all the processes in the book. Because purpose is paramount to starting a change initiative, we use it as the primary organizing dimension, with a separate table for each purpose. Within purpose, the in-depth methods are grouped alphabetically followed by the thumbnails, also in alphabetical order. Please note that "Org/Com" abbreviates "Organization/Community." We hope these tables guide you to the methods that can best serve your needs.

Summary Matrix

ADAPTABLE METHODS

Adaptable methods are used for a variety of purposes, including planning, structuring, and improving.

Page	Process Name	Org	Com	Event Size	Prep	Events	Follow-up	Cycle	Practitioner Prep	Special Resource Needs
In-depth										
73	Appreciative Inquiry	x	x	20–2,000	1 day–many mos	1 day–many mos	3 mos–1 year	As needed–Continuous	Self-study	
89	Collaborative Loops	x		10–200	4–6 wks	2–3 days	3–12 mos	As needed	General	
102	Dialogue & Deliberation	x	x	5–5,000	1–6 mos	90 min–many years	1–3 mos	As needed–Periodic	Self-study	
118	Integrated Clarity	x	x	1–500	2 wks–2 mos	1 day–many mos	Ongoing, as needed	As needed–Periodic–Continuous	General	Integrated Clarity Feelings & Needs lists
135	Open Space Technology	x	x	5–2,000	1 day–6 mos	1–3 days	As appropriate to purpose	As needed–Continuous	Self-study	
149	Technology of Participation	x	x	5–1,000	1–3 days	1–3 days	Immediately to quarterly and annually	As needed	General	ToP Sticky Wall
162	Whole Scale Change	x	x	10–10,000	2–4 days per event	Several 2- to 3-day events	1 month to 1 year	As needed	General	1 logistics assistant per 5 tables
179	The World Café	x	x	12–1,000+	<1 day to several mos	2 hrs–several days	As appropriate to purpose	As needed–Periodic–Continuous	Self-study	Hospitable space (e.g., flowers, tablecloths)
Thumbnails										
195	Ancient Wisdom Council	x	x	1–500	2–5 days	2–5 days	1–3 mos	Continuous	In-depth	
201	Appreciative Inquiry Summit	x	x	30–3,000	2–6 mos	3–5 days	2 mos–1 yr	As needed–Periodic	General	
207	Conference Model	x		40–700	1–3 mos	Three 2-day events	6–12 mos	As needed	General	
212	Consensus	x	x	2–1,000+	Varies	<1 hr–several days	Determined by agreements	Continuous	General	
218	Conversation Café	x	x	3–1,000+	None	60–90 mins	None	As needed–Periodic	Self-study	
223	Dynamic Facilitation	x	x	2–40	Not required	1–4 mtgs	Written conclusion	As needed–Continuous	General	

Page	Process Name	Org	Com	Event Size	Prep	Events	Follow-up	Cycle	Practitioner Prep	Special Resource Needs
227	The Genuine Contact Program	x		12–500	1–3 mos	Four 2–3-day events	6–12 mos	Continuous	General	At times: OpenSpace-Online SW, computers on site, HeartMath's Freeze Framer
234	Human Systems Dynamics	x	x	10–200	4–12 hrs	2 hrs– 3 days	1 wk–1 mo	Continuous	General	
239	Leadership Dojo	x	x	8–1,000	2–3 days	Two 4-day conferences	Coaching	Periodic	In-depth	
244	Open System Theory Evolutions	x	x	4–100+	2 wks– 6 mos	1 hr– 3 days	Ongoing	As needed	In-depth	
250	OpenSpace-Online	x	x	5–125	1 hr– Ongoing	2–8 hours	1 hr– Ongoing	As needed– Continuous– Periodic	Self-study	OpenSpace-Online Software
256	Organization Workshop	x		24–50	2–3 hrs	1–3 days	Varies	As needed	General	
261	PeerSpirit Circling	x	x	5–20	3–4 hrs	1–2 hrs/ 1–2 days	As requested	As needed– Periodic	General	
267	Power of Imagination Studio	x	x	12–120	1–6 mos	1–5 days	1–3 mos	As needed	General	
273	Real Time Strategic Change	x	x	1– 10,000+	1–3 mos	1–10+ events	Immediately– 18 mos	Continuous	General	
278	SimuReal	x	x	35–125	3 days	1 day	Immediately	Periodic	General	
283	Study Circles		x	100– 1,000+	2–4 mos	4–6 wks	Ongoing	As needed– Continuous	General	2 facilitators per study circle
288	Think Like a Genius	x		12– 1,200+	3 hrs– 1 day	3 hrs– 1 day	Within 1 wk	As needed	General	Building materials
294	Web Lab's Small Group Dialogues	x	x	200– 10,000+	1–3 mos	2–4 wks	2 wks–1 mo	As needed	In-depth	Small Group Dialogue Software

Summary Matrix

PLANNING METHODS

Planning methods help people shape their future together.

Page	Process Name	Org	Com	Event Size	Prep	Events	Follow-up	Cycle	Practitioner Prep	Special Resource Needs
In-depth										
300	Dynamic Planning Charrettes		x	10–100+	6 wks–4 mos	4–7 days	4–18 mos	Periodic	In-depth	
316	Future Search	x	x	40–100+	3–6 mos	2.5 days	As appropriate to purpose	Periodic	General	
331	Scenario Thinking	x	x	15–500	1–2 mos	Two 1–2-day events over 3–6 mos	Varies	Periodic	General	
347	Search Conference	x	x	20–35	1–18 mos	2 days, 2 nights	Self-sustaining	Periodic	In-depth	
Thumbnails										
365	Community Summits		x	64–2,048	3–4 mos	2–3 days	6 mos	Periodic	General	
370	Large Group Scenario Planning	x	x	32–512	1–4 mos	2–3 days	6 mos	Periodic	General	
375	SOAR	x	x	10–400	0.5–1.5 days	1.5–3 days	Immediately and continuously	Periodic	General	
381	Strategic Forum	x	x	2–50	1–6 mos	1–2 days	6 mos	As needed	In-depth	
386	Strategic Visioning	x	x	5–75	6 wks	1–2 days	3–6 mos	Periodic	In-depth	Futures research, Graphic Templates
393	21st Century Town Meeting		x	100–5,000	6–12 mos	1 day	3–12 mos	As needed	In-depth	Polling keypad system, wireless laptop groupware system, 1 networked laptop & 1 facilitator/table

STRUCTURING METHODS

Structuring methods redefine relationships and/or redesign work practices.

Page	Process Name	Org	Com	Event Size	Prep	Events	Follow-up	Cycle	Practitioner Prep	Special Resource Needs
In-depth										
400	Community Weaving	x	x	10–2,500	1 day–6 wks	1–5 days	Ongoing	Continuous	General	Community Readiness Assessment
419	Participative Design Workshop	x	x	15–200	2 wks–many mos	1–3 days	Active Adaptation via Redesign	As needed	In-depth	
Thumbnails										
436	Collaborative Work System Design	x		5–30	2–6 wks	1–5 days	Several mos–yrs	As needed	In-depth	
441	Whole-Systems Approach	x		6–1,500	3–12 mos	6–30 mos	12–24 mos	Continuous	In-depth	

Summary Matrix

IMPROVING METHODS

Improving methods increase effectiveness in processes, relationships, individual behaviors, knowledge and/or distributive leadership.

Page	Process Name	Org	Com	Event Size	Prep	Events	Follow-up	Cycle	Practitioner Prep	Special Resource Needs
In-depth										
450	Rapid Results	x	x	12–100	2 wks	1 day	30–100 days	As needed	General	
465	Six Sigma	x		4–6 per project team	2 days–1 mo	<4–6 mos per project	Financial audit at 6 mos, cyclic control plan audits	Continuous	In-depth	Substantial data collection and statistical software
Thumbnails										
479	Action Learning	x	x	3–30	4–16 hrs	2–8 hrs	Monthly up to 12 mos	Continuous	General	
484	Action Review Cycle/ AAR	x		5–15	30 min	15 min–3 hrs	Continuous	Continuous	General	
490	Balanced Scorecard	x		Up to 20 initially, then entire org	2–6 wks	1–3 days	2–4 mos	Continuous	General	
496	Civic Engagement		x	15–200	1 wk	2 wks	1 wk–6 mos	Continuous	Self-study	
501	The Cycle of Resolution	x	x	2–100	Interview key players	1–3 days	4–6 wks	As needed	General	
507	Employee Engagement	x		Up to 100 per group	1–3 mos	3–4 hrs	1–3 mos	Periodic	General	Survey
513	Gemeinsinn-Werkstatt (Community Spirit)		x	27–	6 wks–6 mos	3 mos–2 yrs	6 wks–6 mos	Periodic	General	
519	Idealized Design	x	x	3–50	2 days	0.5–5 days	2 days	As needed	General	
524	The Practice of Empowerment	x	x	15–40	1–3 mos	3 days	12 mos	Continuous	In-depth	
530	Values Into Action		x	30–1,000+	3 mos	1–3 days	Optional tracking	Periodic	General	
535	WorkOut	x	x	20–100	2–4 wks	1–3 days	3–4 mos	As needed	General	

SUPPORTIVE METHODS

Supportive refers to practices that enhance the efficacy of other change methods.

Page	Process Name	Org	Com	Event Size	Prep	Events	Follow-up	Cycle	Practitioner Prep	Special Resource Needs
In-depth										
542	Online Environments	x	x	2–10,000+	Integrated w/ change process	1 hr–weeks–ongoing	Integrated w/ change process	As needed–Continuous	In-depth	Technology
561	Playback Theatre	x	x	10–150+	0.5–2 days	1–2 hrs	0.5 day min	As needed	In-depth	Props (chairs, boxes, +)
573	Visual Recording & Graphic Facilitation	x	x	Any size	Short design meeting	Integrated w/process	Graphic reports in 2–3 days	As needed	General	Large wall for murals and/or 2–4 flip charts
Thumbnails										
588	Drum Café	x	x	10–22,000	1 day	1 hr–1 day	Minimal	As needed	In-depth	Percussion instruments
593	JazzLab	x	x	20–2,000	1 day	1 hr–1 day	Minimal	As needed	In-depth	Instruments
598	Learning Maps	x	x	Any size	3 wks–6 mos	1 day–1 yr	None–yrs	As needed	In-depth	
603	Visual Explorer	x	x	2–100+	20 min	1–4 hrs	Weaves flexibly into other methods	As needed	General	Set of images available from Center for Creative Leadership

1. Gardner's original seven intelligences are: Linguistic, Logical, Rhythmic, Kinesthetic, Spatial, Interpersonal, and Intrapersonal. For more on their application to whole system change processes, see www.thechangehandbook.com.

2. LdPride (2006). Multiple Intelligence Explained. www.ldpride.net/learningstyles.MI.htm#Learning%20Styles%20Explained; Infed (2006). Howard Gardner, Multiple Intelligences and Education. www.infed.org/thinkers/gardner.htm; Howard Gardner, "Intelligence Reframed," in *Multiple Intelligences for the 21st Century* (New York: Basic Books, 1999).

Selecting Methods
The Art of Mastery

The intuitive mind is a sacred gift and the rational mind is a faithful servant.
We have created a society that honors the servant and has forgotten the gift.
—Albert Einstein

If you watch footage of the 70+-year-old founder of Aikido, Morihei Ueshiba (1883–1969), practicing his martial art, you will see men more than half his age are rushing at him; with little effort, the master flings one person this way and another that way.[1] It's hard to actually believe this elderly man of slight build could be seriously doing this . . . and he was. Master Ueshiba began his journey to the invention of Aikido through blending other combat methods. He would bring aspects of the various methods together in an instant to meet the moment. In mastering each of these methods and then blending them, he discovered that they shared common principles. He combined their essence into a new form called Aikido. He considered Aikido to be advancement beyond the originating methods. Aikido is an art in which each training session is a step in the quest for perfection, where the apprentice learns through practice to be patient, relaxed, and focused while acting intuitively.[2]

Whether you want to become a master or simply select a method for a particular situation, the principles and advice espoused here can help you achieve greater success with any change initiative. This chapter begins with an overview of mastery, and follows with a description of the first step to mastery—method selection. The chapter ends with a discussion on selecting a consultant and advice for those embarking on the journey to mastery.

What Is Mastery?

Mastery refers to having the consummate skill, commanding knowledge, and intuitive sensibility that can be successfully applied to a particular situation or activity. At the heart of mastery is the dilemma in which one must conduct rational analyses while drawing on intuition. Gary Klein, one of the foremost researchers and consultants on the power of intuition, states, "In order to take that path, we have to reject the dilemma. We shouldn't simply follow our intuitions, as they can be unreliable and need to be monitored. Yet we shouldn't suppress our intuitions either, because they are essential to our decision making and can't be replaced by analyses and procedures. Thus, our only real option is to strengthen our intuitions so that they become more accurate and provide us with better insights."[3] This is the key to mastery.

Mastering Whole System Change

In reviewing the paths of inventors, developers, and leading voices of established methods, I uncovered a subtle yet essential shared journey called the Cycle of Mastery (see figure 1). These masters flow through this cycle in three phases: Method, Blend, and Invention. A person begins a phase as an apprentice, develops mastery, and then begins the next phase as an apprentice, and so forth. The apprentice versus master delineation is intended to give a sense of where the journey begins and ends for each phase in the cycle. There is no shame in being a novice. Contrarily, it is an exciting time to be learning and, yes, it can be scary. Actually, a healthy dose of fear, doubt, and self-reflection is required for the journey to mastery. It is necessary to give up old ways of doing things that are familiar in order to step into new ways of being. The experience can be likened to the transformation of a caterpillar into a butterfly. A caterpillar crawls while the butterfly flies—they are the same being, yet their mode of operation is fundamentally changed. Anyone who chooses to learn something is daring to be great! Bravely putting themselves out in the world, choosing to claim what they know, admitting what they don't know, and then trying something new . . . these are the characteristics of the leading voices for methods in this book.

While it is often said that these methods take a lifetime to master, there is an arriving that people express when working with a method. This arriving is often described with a sense of wonder, excitement, and confidence. It also signifies that the person is moving to the next phase of mastery, a new journey is beginning.

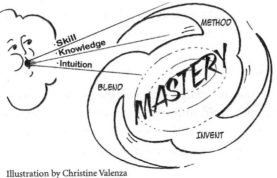

Illustration by Christine Valenza

Figure 1. The Cycle of Mastery

METHOD MASTERY

Method Masters focus on one particular approach to whole system change. The practitioner takes a "deep dive" into the history, theory, research, values, language, tools, techniques, and applications of the method. These masters require little documentation when in the midst of the change process; they have embodied the method . . . they know it by heart, and they can sense when the method requires adjustment in order to adapt it to a particular situation. The apprentice, on the other hand, is more inclined to strictly follow the method guidelines with little deviation from what is written in the documentation or taught in courses and workshops.

BLEND MASTERY

Blend Masters build on method mastery. They have mastered multiple methods and continue to add more to their repertoire. While they may not articulate it in the moment, blend masters intuitively know what to use when, where, and why. There is an effortless mixing and matching, recognizing which aspects of the methods are best integrated for a particular situation. On the other hand, the apprentice may not see the distinctions and the blending may appear more disjointed or choppy. Here, the apprentice might be at a loss as to which method or methods to use, and might make a less-than-optimal match.

INVENTION MASTERY

Invention Masters focus on the natural evolution of method mastery and blend mastery. Alban and Scherer stated, "We are standing on the shoulders of giants. It is now up to us, their descendents, to do what they did so many years ago; discover new principles and methods of assisting leaders and their organizations to be as effective as they can be."[4] In the process of perfecting their knowledge of methods and increasing their ability to blend them, invention masters push outside conventional boundaries to innovate. When faced with a situation that cannot be addressed with a method or set of methods, these masters draw upon their expertise to create new connections and patterns that lead to advances and inspired approaches. On the other hand, the apprentice draws from the pool of what is available and blends methods effortlessly, yet does not see nor seize the opportunity to craft a new way.

Selecting Methods

Mastery begins with selection. If you choose to master a particular method, combine methods, or develop a new one, you must begin with selection; and there is so much that goes into this decision. Consider, for example, the Catholic Schools Initiative in the Toledo Diocese of northwest Ohio. This example will be used throughout this section of the chapter to bring to life the process for method selection.

There were 95 schools located throughout northwest Ohio. The schools operated somewhat autonomously and often found they were competing for the same students. Enrollments were declin-

ing and some schools had to close. A question often raised was, "How can we sustain ourselves, collaborate, and serve our calling?" In one planning meeting, they described how their purpose was to go from being a network of individual schools to a truly interdependent school system. As they looked ahead, they determined that they had to craft a unified vision of their future, find a better structure, and improve the way they collaborated.[5]

Which method or methods would you recommend using? What about all the factors at play here and all the additional questions you would like to ask? How can the Summary Matrix (see chapter 1) and all the information in this book help you consider options and design a change road map? Making sense of all these methods and then choosing is not a straightforward process. While designing a change initiative, Ron Lippitt, one of the founders and thought leaders for the field of organization development, intuitively asked three simple questions (see figure 2). Years and many methods later, these questions are still relevant. The three questions can be thought of as a sequence of steps to consider when selecting a method.

Illustration by Christine Valenza

Figure 2. Lippitt's Three Questions for Planning a Change

WHAT IS THE PURPOSE?

The primary organizing theme for this book is purpose. Purpose is about meaning. In the context of change, it captures the essence of how the people in the system aspire to be different because they have come together, in person or virtually, in order to collectively create their future. Getting to purpose is hard work. Bold questions about what is desired become a powerful source for clarifying the intentions and aspirations for change. Uncovering purpose can lead to lengthy debates, crumpled-up paper, and starting over. Ironically, conflicts, problems, and issues are something to be welcomed rather than resisted or feared because they provide clues to what is best and needs to emerge. Inviting people to shape the specifics ensures the investment is worthwhile.

Purpose is the collective answer to the question, "What do we want to accomplish on this change journey, what aspirations do we hold?" The answer differs from one change to the next. One way to develop purpose is to clarify a set of outcomes using an appreciative approach in which participants in the planning of the change share stories of an amazing or successful experience with a change. Another approach is to ask people to speak one by one of their most deeply held aspirations for the change. As they share and listen to each other, common themes emerge that coalesce into the desired outcomes for the impending change. In developing the outcomes, consider the following general guidance:

- *Keep the end in mind.* Too often, facilitators and participants jump right into action . . . determining the tasks to be accomplished, timing, locations, and even specific agenda items. Then, someone involved in the process asks, "Why do we want to do that?" When this question is raised, the process can unfurl—a pregnant pause, looks to the ceiling, and even frustrated glances suggesting that to ask such a question is heresy. It is natural to start with action and often comes from the desire to be tangible and concrete. Clarifying the "why" provides an opportunity for taking the conversation deeper in a way that brings out the meaningfulness of the change. A powerful question to ask of any activity is, "In order to what?" The answer will uncover the real desires—the compelling inspirations and aspirations.

- *Focus on the intentions for the change.* It's seductive for change agents to predetermine the conclusions (goals, decisions, action plans, etc.) that they believe are the "right" answers. The distinction between focusing on intentions and focusing on goals is elusive and important. It is the difference between engaging and manipulating. Change intentions articulate the aspirations of the change without dictating how they will be achieved. Organizational goals are specific aims of the organization that can be created through the process or set through more traditional means. It is a leap of faith to let go of "I have the answer" and trust the wisdom in the room. Those who take that leap are frequently surprised that the creativity, commitment, and effectiveness far exceeds what they thought possible.

- *Be bold.* The pragmatic reason for boldness is simple: Given the investment of time and effort, the bolder the initiative, the greater the potential return. There is a subtler and perhaps more important reason to be ambitious. Interrupting current patterns with a call to something big inspires involvement and sustains commitment, particularly when the work gets tough. With a bold, clear intention in hand, you don't need to have answers to get started. In fact, you are better served by letting go of the need for immediate answers and focusing on inviting the people of the system in to find what best serves the organization or community.

Now that you have compelling outcomes, ask the second follow-up question, "If all of these outcomes are accomplished, in one sentence, what will be different in your/our world?" The answer to this question gets at the heart of the purpose for change. It is the culmination of the outcomes.

If done well, you will have a purpose statement that calls people to the work. People throughout the system see themselves in it and they feel compelled to participate: some with enthusiasm and hope, others with fear and skepticism. Regardless, a right purpose creates a visceral reaction and attraction within the various stakeholders and members of the whole system.

With a clear purpose and agreed-upon outcomes, you are now more ready to consider the various methods available. Compare the purpose and outcomes statement to the five dimensions of purpose presented in the Summary Matrix (see chapter 1). For instance, some purpose statements will be more directed toward planning, others toward structuring or improving, and some aim to accomplish all three. Narrow your choices to those methods that seem most similar to your purpose.

Continuing with the Catholic Schools Initiative:

As the leadership, design team, and support staff wrestled with the notion of purpose and outcomes described above, a teachable moment arose one day in planning a specific event. This moment led to a shift in how they approached collaborative design and how they understood the importance of purpose.

A large meeting had been scheduled for principals. The staff described how a study was conducted to target problem areas and key decisions that needed to be made. The data was analyzed, and was to be provided as a report in a two-hour workshop. The intended process was as follows: Welcome, Agenda, Report Results, Identify Problem Areas, and Action Planning. The conversation then moved to an "in order to" discussion. The study was done in order to . . . the report will be presented in order to . . . and so forth. The intentions and real aims of the workshop emerged. The conversation became lively; there was laughter and debate. Meaning emerged; people sensed a deeper connection among everyone in the room. As the conversation continued to focus on outcomes, further discussion on the overall purpose emerged. Needless to say, the actual agenda and much of the original workshop changed—not because the activities were "bad," rather because the purpose and outcomes provided important criteria for choosing how to proceed. "Designing our future together" emerged as a purpose critical to answering the next question.

WHO NEEDS TO BE INVOLVED?

Involvement is about people. The question of "who" helps to define the natural boundaries of the system undergoing change. As boundaries are explored, purpose is further clarified. It is an iterative process in which the emerging web of connections informs where to draw the lines (e.g., functions, intentions, aspirations, interests, geography, etc.) for the type of system and event size. Two aspects—type of system and event size—are useful "people" dimensions for further clarifying the choice of method or methods to use (see the Summary Matrix in chapter 1).

Some methods are more suited for community engagement, while others are more suited for organizational settings. An interesting pattern for many of the methods is to see how they are morphing and adapting to other settings. In addition to the type of system, it is important to consider the sheer number of people expected to participate in the process and the events that occur throughout. Some methods are more suited to very large numbers of people, whereas others are more suited to involving smaller numbers over time. In determining who needs to be involved, consider the following general guidance:

- *Make a clear choice to engage.* The primary aim for involving people is NOT to reduce resistance and create buy-in. These are by-products of a more compelling reason to engage people—wisdom. The people in the system, when engaged, will ensure that the best decisions about the future are made. As a result, people see themselves in the answers that emerge and begin integrating them immediately. That is why breakthroughs from these methods can far outstrip anything that comes from the top down. That said, for many in leadership positions, it is a leap of faith to invite people into conversations regarding substantive decisions. While it's true that transforming a large system requires commitment from people with position power, change can begin anywhere. In fact, if you trace the inspiration for change in many large efforts, you'll find a modest beginning from a person or persons located in a variety of places in the system.

- *Get the right people involved.* Who is affected by the change? Who can influence it? Who brings needed resources? There are two aspects of people to consider: stakeholders and diversity. Stakeholders are those constituents who play a particular role in the system. Diversity refers to the biographical characteristics such as gender, age, and ethnicity. Bringing together broad representation sets the stage for breakthrough. The more creatively the system is defined, the more the potential for wisdom to emerge. Perhaps the most surprising participants are the "wild cards"—the people who seem to have the least connection to the system—because they contribute perspectives and ideas that aren't normally part of the conversation.

- *Bring the spirit of invitation.* People know when they are wanted, when the invitation is sincere. What's important is that the invitation conveys something other than "business as usual" is happening, and there is a choice in participating. The first communication sets the tone for what follows. It is an important opportunity to generate excitement and curiosity, to attract people into a productive adventure. It starts to break habitual patterns, naming publicly the bold intentions and aspirations that you desire people to bring. A great invitation affirms each person's wisdom . . . that they have something important to offer. While there are occasions in which the initial request may involve required attendance, over the life of a change project, contribution increases both in quality and quantity as people experience it as their choice.

Continuing with the Catholic Schools Initiative:

With their purpose and outcomes, a Design Team, a microcosm of the whole, came back together. They were a representative sample of people from across the 95 schools. With the superintendent's staff, they further clarified the purpose and outcomes, and then they discussed who needed to be involved. It became apparent that they were both an organization and a community! First, teachers, priests, and administrators were identified. The more they talked about their purpose, the more their list grew: staff members, students, parents . . . and it continued to grow. What about including superintendents from public schools, local colleges, alumni, city leaders, special-needs parents and advocates, and more? One person on the superintendent's staff would often put his head in his hands with a half smile and say, "It's getting bigger . . . and bigger . . ." You could see the mixture of excitement, wonder, fear, and skepticism. He wanted to know how all these people could work together, make a decision, and actually move forward.

What Conversations Need to Take Place?

With purpose clear and people identified, focus shifts to the nature of the process—how to have productive and meaningful conversations that move the organization or community toward the future it yearns to have. A consistent message from masters of the work is that change is more than an event; it is a journey that unfolds as people come together to create shared meaning and agreements for action. They converge together through events like summits, town halls, meetings, and workshops. They continue the journey by dispersing back into the system to follow through on the work, then coming together again as needed. This is often referred to as "converge-diverge." It is a critical aspect to engagement processes. The benefit of convergence is acceleration. When a critical mass of the people who make up the whole system focus attention together in "real time," becoming aware of their connections, clarifying their aspirations, and agreeing on pathways, there is a fundamental paradigm shift—and collective action ensues.

Process-oriented dimensions that are helpful to consider when selecting a method are the event size, timing (preparation, events, and follow-up), cycle of use, and special resource needs (see Summary Matrix in chapter 1). These dimensions can be framed as basic design questions. In charting a change journey, consider the following general guidance:

- *Take the time needed.* Generally, most clients will ask for this work to be done in fewer days, fewer hours, and small chunks of time for people to meet. In these situations, a simple reminder helps: "Sometimes you have to go slow to go fast." Humans require a certain processing time when addressing ambitious issues. In fact, research confirms this notion. The "Zeigarnik Effect" states that people remember uncompleted tasks better than completed ones. Multiple-day processes rely on this insight, often ending the afternoon with an open-ended task. When participants arrive the next morning, they come with energy and insights that deepen and broaden the work. Don't risk the opportunity for breakthrough by scrimping on the time.

- *Pay attention to the flow.* What is the talk in the environment? Is there room for taking on a challenge in the minds and hearts of the people affected? If a disaster just took place, the first work may require triage. Look for the opening to engagement and then link the change journey to the current situation such that people see how the investment can make a difference or prevent a similar catastrophe in the future. For many complex issues, incredible work has already been done and lots of creative answers identified, yet nothing quite turns into action. In these cases, because the ideas are ripe for harvesting, whole system change methods are often just the ticket to get the work moving.

- *Keep it simple.* Whether it is in the choice of method, the selection of participants, or the specifics of process design, if you are working so hard that nothing gels, it is usually a good indicator that something simpler is needed. It is time to return to the intentions for the project, the task, the issue at hand in order to find a more elegant answer. One way to do this is to start with a blank sheet of paper. Kathie Dannemiller would often sit with a design team that was wrestling with the change plan details. After hours of listening, debating, and working toward consensus, she would take the pages and rip them from the flip chart. She would look at the group and say, "Let's start over with a blank sheet . . . if it was important, it will make it back up here again." It was amazing that this worked so well; often a richer, better perspective emerged leading to the right design.

Back to the Catholic Schools Initiative:

Although hopeful, the question remained, "How can all these people work together, make decisions, and move forward?" It was nearing the end of June 2005. The leadership team in conjunction with a design team determined that they wanted to look five years out with a focus on the immediate 18 months ahead to December 2006. This date was chosen to align with a critical meeting of the Bishop's Education Council. The council finalizes decisions based on recommendations from task forces and committees. The superintendent, along with his staff, decided to bring forth recommendations for the future in a different way than before, a way that incorporated the wisdom of an ever-widening circle of people. In his words, "As we go out into our schools and parishes, we need to include more and more people in the conversation."

As a first phase of the journey, a Catholic Schools Summit was planned and held in November 2005. More than 400 people from 95 schools took two days together and crafted, for the first time, a mission, vision, goals, principles, and action plans for their whole school system. One key decision from the summit was to work within a new configuration—regions. Each region was to address the question, "How can we work together and ensure the future of Catholic schools in our region?" They developed imperatives for their region, imperatives that required significant collaboration. This was historic. When hearing of this new approach, some people were convinced that either the decisions had already been made or that it was far easier and quicker for someone to "just make a decision . . . tell us what to do." However, the intention was to empower community members to craft a new future. The superintendent was committed to making the circle wider by increasing the number of people included.

Throughout the planning of the summit and regional meetings, processes were considered that lent themselves to the planning cycle and involving people within driving distance. In addition, it was necessary to ensure that the methods would work with minimal resources (e.g., a room, microphones, flip charts, handouts, etc.).

As you consider these questions that they faced in the diocese, consider what role multiple intelligences might play in the selection. Multiple intelligences have contributed significantly in transforming the field of education; similarly, we believe that the multiple intelligences framework can help to broaden and deepen our practice. Several people on the superintendent's staff worked with the multiple intelligences and used their knowledge to shape the various activities that were chosen. What we discovered was that emphasizing multiple intelligences can help us diversify our own approaches while tapping into the hidden potential of those participating in the process.

Concluding the Catholic Schools example:

As specific collaborative activities were considered, the emphasis on interpersonal intelligence and logical intelligence were seen as key to bridging divides among schools and finding new ways to relate and work together. Further, people in the school community rarely used data, facts, and analytical tools for understanding the trends and business issues facing them, individually and collectively. It was often mentioned that people were not aware of their school's viability, particularly when the parish subsidized budget deficits. The relationship between financial issues and key demographics (enrollments, profile of students, changes in public schools, etc.) needed to be understood and addressed. The reality of the regions emerged. Activities were chosen that tapped into multiple intelligences: visuals, music, data, questions, listening, drawing, and more.

At the various regional meetings, something special began to emerge . . . HOPE. The shift was beginning. People began to see the big picture of their system; they heard each other, and started coming to their own conclusions. Stories were being told of how people were spontaneously organizing local meetings, using techniques modeled in the process. One participant stated, "I didn't think it was possible. It seemed that we were going sooooo slow at first, getting all these people involved. Well, it was worth being patient, we are now making real progress." There was a different energy, a confidence that they could accomplish a new future together as a whole school system. And, the journey continues.

A Creative Approach to Selecting

As we uncovered the many approaches to change, we heard from a researcher, Raban Daniel Fuhrmann, who developed a useful process design tool—the Meta-Matching-Method (MMM)—to select and adapt a method to a change initiative.[6] In a six- to eighteen-hour deliberative process, the facilitator and client *map, profile, match,* and *redesign.* Here are the phases in brief:

Mapping: Participants draw "mind maps" of the project to uncover the power and interests of the actors. These "quick and dirty" pictures establish an initial collective awareness and solidarity among the team and lead to a common understanding of the case.

Profiling: Participants go further into the details exploring the requirements of the venture in six categories: (1) complexity of topic, (2) complexity of the actors, (3) method's openness, (4) time pressure, (5) resource availability, and (6) degree of commitment needed.

Matching: The profile is compared with the profiles of possible methods. Together, participants decide on the best choice for their situation.

Redesigning: Finally, the chosen approach is then adjusted to the details of the case.

As a meta-tool, MMM helps facilitators and consultants choose and adapt a good fit for their case. It works by profiling the requirements of the initiative and matching it with a performance profile of appropriate tools. In the process, not only is a method selected, but also the stakeholders gain a deeper understanding of their shared assumptions and an increased commitment to the coming venture.[7]

Selecting a Practitioner

Mastery and selection have been the focus thus far. Now, what about selecting a practitioner to support an organization or community in a particular change? How do you ensure there is a good fit? What criteria should be considered? What questions need to be asked?

Selection is a two-way street. Both the practitioner and key decision makers in the system do the selecting. Experienced clients are hard to come by . . . and so are masterful practitioners. It is an important partnership that is more than selling some "thing" or convincing someone to buy services or trying to find the most inexpensive option. Because these initiatives impact whole systems, the potential loss for an inappropriate fit can be wide-ranging—from money and time to reputation and lawsuits. On the flip side, when there is a good fit, the initiative has the best chance for success and further, real transformation can take place. As with any great partnership, there are some basic "yes" or "no" questions to ask. Regardless of who might benefit directly from the answer, it is imperative that both parties address the questions. Is there . . .

A VALUES FIT?

Whether spoken or unspoken, our values guide our behavior. They are visible in the choices we make and actions we take. There are two levels on which to determine if there is a values fit. First, there is the fit with regard to how the change is planned and implemented. Do leadership and other key people in the client system support engagement-based processes? Do they believe in bringing together microcosms of the whole: harnessing the power of the existing diversity and ensuring that all voices are included? How do answers to these questions compare to the practitioner's beliefs about how to best guide change? Second, there is the character fit.

The character of the community or organization can be seen in how it makes choices and takes action. Does it operate in a way that is ethical and consistent with the practitioner's beliefs? Does the organization or community consider the impact of its actions on the world at large? Are its choices and actions consistent with what the practitioner can support? The answers to these questions can be found through asking and, most importantly, through observing. Actions speak louder than words; spend time paying attention, listening, and noticing.

A Competency Fit?

In scoping the change initiative, there are so many variables to track. How does the scope of the work to be done match the competencies of the practitioner? Do the competencies fit this particular community or organization? Is the practitioner confident, and subsequently, is the client confident in the practitioner? To answer these questions, consider the depth, breadth, and nature of the practitioner's experience, the number and type of projects (e.g., size, industry, and length), references, and education (degrees, certifications, workshops, and trainings).

A Style Fit?

There are certain styles of working. Some people and systems are task focused, linear, structured, and time bound . . . while others may be relationship focused, freer, looser, and less time bound—or the style might be a bit of both. Be clear about the style and what combination works best for the partnership. Maybe the system is best served by having a practitioner with a different style. For example, if the system is less structured, it may be better to have someone who is more task focused. In other cases, it may be desirable to have a more "like-minded" fit.

A Cost Fit?

Cost is often a sensitive issue. Fees that consultants charge for change work not only range widely from practitioner to practitioner, but also between venues. It is important to be clear about fees and other costs early in the process. Know what is negotiable and what is not. Many practitioners with vibrant consulting practices donate time or work for low fees in service to communities and nonprofits. There are so many ways to address this issue! Counsel from seasoned practitioners—never let money be the reason not to proceed. Either negotiate a fee structure that works, or find a practitioner that will work with the community or organization. For example, payment can come in many forms—barter, the satisfaction of making a contribution, developing a new technique, and enhancing one's own experience and skills. Bottom line, there are creative ways meet the needs of the practitioner and client system.

A Timing Fit?

This practical question matters because change takes time. And, more and more, whole-system change initiatives are spanning over years versus one-time events. The practitioner may be the best in the business, but if the initiative is one of a long list they are undertaking, it may not get the attention it deserves. While there are always unexpected twists and turns in complex projects, ensure that expectations around time align between practitioner and client.

A CHEMISTRY FIT?

Chemistry is intuitive. If you are taking on a complex, critical initiative, a cocreative partnership depends on the quality of connection between practitioner and client. No matter how rational our process of selection, often it is the intangible element of "Does it feel like a good fit?" that matters most. Is there a sense of fluidity to the conversations? Do agreements come easily? View this as a choice for a long-term relationship. When there is smiling and information sharing in which a genuine regard emerges, it just works.

The Ethical and Moral Case

The methods described here have a track record of success. Each has made a significant difference in the lives of many people. And, just as a knife can be used to cut us free, so too can it be used to cut deep . . . robbing our inspiration and killing our hope. This is not a pretty picture. These methods must be handled with care, and one important rule of thumb is to be sure that you begin with the right intention. It is not easy to define "right intention," but we all know what it is; it's similar to the principle of "do no harm." Broaden this to whole system change and it can be stated as,

Do no harm to the individual nor to the whole.

Often, in this work, there are cases where a person has a specific need that competes with the group's needs, for example, when someone is dealing with an issue and time is limited. The group must move on, yet doing so may harm the individual. This is a tough dilemma.

Our primary responsibility is to develop the mastery necessary for handling such a situation. We must stay present to our own limitations, know when to seek help, and when to stop and say, "I don't know." In these moments, it is important to not fake it. In the Summary Matrix (chapter 1), there is a category of Practitioner Preparation that emphasizes the amount of preparation required for getting started with a method. From this jumping-off point, developing mastery becomes a lifelong journey. If you choose to go down the path of mastery, you are choosing to make an important difference in the world; and in that choosing, you have a duty—an obligation to develop your highest self and master the art of change.

The Path to Method Mastery

As mentioned, selecting a method is the first step to mastery. Here is some advice to consider as you gain mastery of a method. In the next chapter, you will have a chance to learn more about blend mastery and invention mastery.

1. Educate Yourself. Have you done this . . . bought software or some technology, and jumped right into using it only to go back to the user manual to learn the basics? Getting educated is the key to ensuring you develop the healthy habits and conditions for success. Here is a checklist. Be sure you:

- *Learn the History*
- *Speak the Language*
- *Memorize the Models and Activities*
- *Know the Theory and Research*
- *Create a Personal Library*

2. Embody the Values. Values have been emphasized throughout this chapter, and it comes up again here. There are certain core values that guide these methods. Some values are consistent in whole system change work, while others vary with the unique nature of the method. For example, engaging the diversity of voices is common to all the methods, while the specific role of a leader in the process varies. Practice living the values so that you can experience them viscerally. Use your experience of a method's values to guide you in clarifying your personal values for doing this work.

3. Develop a Support Network. Connect with others, both to learn and to live the principle of cocreation. In short, "never work alone." There is a generosity of spirit among the seasoned practitioners of this work, so seek out mentors, communities of practice, partners, or other resources. Often, it is as easy as a call, an e-mail, or an in-person "hello." Don't be shy; ask for help and you will get it. Mentors can bring you in on projects, provide guidance, and connect you to others in the field. Many methods have communities of practice that meet regularly through workshops, conferences, Listservs, blogs (Web logs), and more. The advice is simple: join them. Your support will not come to you; you must take the initiative to build your network and stay connected.

4. Practice, Practice, Practice. The only way to do this work is to do this work. Get started. Read, review case studies, witness it live, participate in a project. One great way to begin is to support a method master for specific events or whole initiatives. Offer to help with the most mundane activities. Even the tedious tasks give you a flavor of the events and the change journey as a whole. You can also provide services for free or for a minimal charge to get experience. Find a place to help and go through the process, from proposing the idea to designing, facilitating, and guiding. For example, offer to take an organization of which you are a member through a planning meeting. These small projects increase your skills and confidence and often lead to larger and larger projects.

5. Act, Reflect, and Learn. As you gain experience, reflect on your actions. Consider the following questions: What did you plan to do? What happened? What did you learn? What will you do differently next time? Learn from the teachable moments. Document all aspects of your projects, workshops, and other experiences. Archive the material so that you can go back and review it at a later time. Keep a journal of reflections on your journey. Journaling helps to integrate new learning and to identify important patterns. Such introspection is a critical skill for anyone doing this challenging work. It is through reflection that you maintain your center, develop your intuition, and advance your mastery.

6. Educate Others. A great way to internalize learning is to develop an educational program or workshop. Sharing information as an instructor provides a different quality of learning, lending itself to meaningful intention and focus. Design models that communicate your message. Put these models into a presentation or, better yet, create an experience that helps others understand the method. Host your program or workshop and listen to their comments. If you have an experience that was special and meaningful for you, write it up and publish it somewhere. Maybe you have devised a variation on a technique, tool, or activity that worked particularly well. Write about it, share it, and learn from how your words and experience help others. The greatest personal growth can come from sharing what we know.

7. Get Back on the Horse. Sometimes you will feel as if you failed. It may be scary, even heart wrenching. You can be certain that you are in the best of company! When dealing with the complexity of human systems, there are *always* glitches. What makes the difference between failure and success is what you do with it. It is a moment in time. What happened is the past; how you react is the present. While earlier advice focused on reflection, the advice here is much simpler. Get back up on the horse and continue on your way. There may be moments when you are not clear about what was to be learned, you may not discern the underlying meaning, and you may be wondering what the heck just happened. All you have to do is "keep on . . . keeping on." It is all part of the journey toward mastery.

Concluding Remarks

Whether you choose to master a method or select someone to guide you through a change initiative, the questions and advice here are intended to save you time and give you the best chance for success. The wisdom of this work is found in the "whole" and the abiding commitment to the democratic principles that bring systems together into that wholeness. Remember, when the system is connected and self-aware, it will have the wisdom necessary to know what to do next. In fact, it can't help itself; the system will act, and act wisely it will.

---

1. Video and other information regarding Morihei Ueshiba can be found at www.aikidojournal.com.

2. John Stevens, *Abundant Peace: The Biography of Morihei Ueshiba, Founder of Aikido* (Boston: Shambhala, 1987).

3. Gary Klein, *The Power of Intuition* (New York: Currency Doubleday, 2004).

4. Billie T. Alban and John J. Scherer, "On the Shoulders of Giants," in *Practicing OD,* edited by William J. Rothwell and Roland L. Sullivan (San Francisco: Pfeiffer, 2005).

5. Steven Cady, from notes and discussion regarding The Catholic Schools Initiative 2010 with the CYSS staff in the Diocese of Toledo, Ohio, 2005. To learn more, go to www.cyss.org and click on Catholic Schools Initiative.

6. The Meta-Matching-Method (MMM) was developed through a research project on "Procedural Approaches to Conflict Resolution" at the Centre for Interdisciplinary Research at the University of Bielefeld in 2002/2003. A transdisciplinary project is building an Internet database with profiles of innovative procedures and methods from the fields of change management and organizational development and public participation and civic deliberation. For more information, contact Raban Daniel Fuhrmann (rabandf@reformagentur.de).

7. Support for the application of MMM is available through several institutions in Germany: ReformAgency for innovative process design (www.reformagentur.de), R+D Network for Procedural Praxis in Politics, Business and Society (www.procedere.org), and the Center for Technology and Society at the Technical University of Berlin (www.ztg.tu-berlin.de/reg001001_en.shtml).

3

PEGGY HOLMAN

Preparing to Mix and Match Methods

Great leaders are identified by their ability to perceive the nature of the game and the rules by which it is played as they are playing it. In other words, the act of sense making is discovering the new terrain as you are inventing it.

—Brian Arthur

A question that often arises when working with whole system change is: Can you use multiple methodologies together? While the simple answer is yes, the practical answer is much more involved. Mastering the art of blending and innovating new practices looks easy on the surface, yet it is a lifetime's work.

The work begins with preparation. Preparation is vital because change work affects people's lives and livelihoods. It is an awesome responsibility to support organizations and communities who wish to engage people in shaping their future. We, as practitioners, do so by creating "containers," energetic and psychic spaces that support people in learning and working well together. Well-prepared containers are grounded in purpose, engage a relevant diversity of participants, and involve mindfully chosen processes and environments that serve the purpose and people well.[1] Such containers "create circumstances in which democracy breaks out, environments in which it just happens."[2] They enable people to take control of their own situations, compelling facilitators and traditional leaders to move more and more out of the way. As projects involve more people and larger systems, the stakes get higher and the choices more complex.

With growing complexity, mixing and matching methods calls practitioners to act with a unique combination of respect, audacity, and humility that comes from being comfortable with oneself. Well-prepared designs for complex situations open to and hold the dynamic tensions between *individuals* and *collectives* and their needs for *reflection* and *action* (figure 1). Blending methods requires skills for sensing into the underlying energies of a roomful of people, an orga-

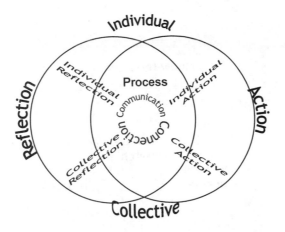

Figure 1. Blend Mastery: The Dance of Dynamic Tensions

nization, a community, or a culture. It involves knowing the principles that inform the individual methods so that resulting designs are an alchemical mix of the individual and collective, reflection and action, such that desired outcomes emerge. At their core, good blends engage people and systems in communications that connect them to ideas, to each other, and to some larger sense of the whole system. Blend mastery is rooted in knowledge and experience in designing processes that creatively use the natural tensions among these forces. The range of skills required is one reason that whole system change consultants rarely work alone. While the challenges preparing for this work may seem daunting, it is extremely rewarding and exciting to learn and grow in this field. For those called to do it, there is really nothing quite like it. And the good news is that there are plenty of smaller, less-complex opportunities for learning the craft.

What's Involved in Mastering the Art of Blending Methods?

Using our own experiences and interviews by Steven Cady's graduate students, ten seasoned practitioners told us about their practices for integrating change processes. We asked them:

- When do you consider bringing multiple methods to a situation?

- How do you decide what to use?

- What do you need to know to blend methods successfully?

Whatever their background, the answers to all three questions were consistent. If you want to mix and match methods, you need to prepare in profound ways. They suggested three forms of preparation (figure 2):

- Know the situation

- Know the processes

- Know yourself

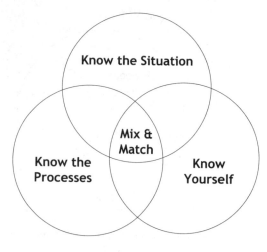

Figure 2. Preparing to Mix and Match

Only then are you ready to mix and match—and perhaps move beyond mixing and matching to fluid creativity in the moment.

KNOW THE SITUATION

While the underlying patterns are common, every situation is unique. Fundamental to the work, whether one or many methods are involved, is getting clear about the desired outcomes, who should participate, and how to engage them. Large group events may be the sizzle, however, the vast majority of the effort happens before anyone steps into the room and continues long after they leave. A clear understanding of the whole situation equips practitioners to determine what method or methods can best serve.

When bringing multiple approaches to the project, many consultants do not always name the processes they use. They start by becoming intimate with the issues and their context—the culture, history, power dynamics, underlying patterns, and dissonances. They seek understanding of the true interests of the people asking for support. They draw people out by asking questions and sharing stories. What is the heart of the situation? Why do they care? This richer, more nuanced understanding creates a strong foundation for exploring possible approaches.

Sense the Energy and Dynamics for Insight into Fit

As important as the practical details of the situation—what's going on, who's involved, and what outcomes they want to achieve—what's unspoken but rather discerned intuitively also informs the practitioner about the fit between situation and methods. Without calling methods by name, simply describing how the work might play out, a seasoned practitioner and client explore the match among need, culture, and approach. It is an art, finding the learning edge where people are not necessarily comfortable but are willing to play. This cocreative dance ultimately leads to choices made from the head and the heart.

One last aspect to remember in any design: The specifics are rarely more than a tentative road map for implementation. Life is sure to get in the way. For many practitioners, that's where the "juice" is—and where opportunities arise for mixing, matching, and process innovation.

A Story: Change in a Complex Context

Follow Chris Corrigan[3] and Lyla Brown, and their process choices to reach an almost invisible community:

In 2005, the federal, provincial, and municipal governments in Victoria, British Columbia, Canada, came together to create an Urban Development Agreement to address inner-city issues including poverty and homelessness. To engage with the urban aboriginal community, we used an appreciative frame to tap and build on assets and we implemented it using ToP's Focused Conversations, Open Space, and World Café. These methodologies were chosen to serve four areas of practice: opening—cracking the veneer for what really matters; inviting—connecting people and drawing them into the process; holding—creating the conditions for emergence; and grounding— aligning resources, and creating and supporting action.

To open, we invited our government clients to invest their hearts, asking, "Why does this engagement with the aboriginal community matter to you personally?" We also asked members of the community what was most important to them, and as a result, we built a substantial amount of Coast Salish cultural protocol and process into our work.

The way you invite Coast Salish First Nations people is very complicated. My partner is of Squamish and Cowichan ancestry and active in traditional venues. She went right to the streets and took her time. One afternoon, she spent two hours sitting with a couple of guys outside the Salvation Army trading songs. After that, she handed them a hundred invitations, and they said, "Yeah, yeah, for sure we'll hand these out." They were our biggest boosters. They went all over, handing out invitations to people and telling them they ought to check out this lady they met who knew all these songs. We also contacted people one on one, asking how their communities wanted to be engaged. Using that information, we structured focused conversations to explore economic, physical and environmental, and social issues.

The first day, two people showed up. With all the work we had done, and all the invitations distributed, we had two people show up. Now, I'm cool with that because we started at zero and we went to two. I'm looking at exponential growth. The government people are looking at sheer numbers, so two people are not a lot with all the time and money we put into this. But we knew that these two people were connectors—advocates for street people—with deep, deep connections in the homeless community. The conversations started with objective questions: "What are the economic issues?" then reflective questions: "Can you tell me some stories about this?" followed by interpretive questions: "What might happen to change this?" and then decisional questions: "If we were to use this process to affect things, what will we do?" The outcome was a list of priorities made from the heart. One idea was "Cedar Village," a cultural precinct like a Chinatown, a living community with economic activity, health centers, and social gathering places.

On the second day of focused conversations, six people came and talked about traditional uses of food—growing food in community plots, harvesting wild foods and importing them from all over Vancouver Island into Victoria. On the third day, we had ten people, and the government sponsors realized that we now had a cadre of community leaders with whom they had not previously worked and who had amazing ideas and commitment. The number one change we achieved was activating previously untapped local leadership.

The practice of holding—creating and maintaining the conditions of emergence—continued as the invitation went out for a community feast and gathering, a cultural tradition. The gathering, which lasted two days, featured an Open Space on the first day, with 100 people participating through the day. The community created its agenda and talked about its issues, moving into planning around issues such as the Cedar Village concept.

The last day, we grounded the work with a World Café, asking the 45 community services and homeless folks who came, "How do we make sure that this work stays off the shelf and that stuff happens?" In the end, a small committee of people volunteered to ensure that ideas would stay alive.

When the Urban Development Agreement was signed, it began a five-year process of getting "stuff" done. Our work contributed a few high-impact, emergent ideas aimed at addressing complex issues: Cedar Village, food production, local governance conversations, and a few other tangible, community-driven, community-owned projects supported by many levels of government. The conversation continues in Victoria within the community and with government partners.

When asked why they selected the specific processes they used, Chris Corrigan responded:

We chose to use these processes for a number of reasons. For the preliminary conversations and the focus groups, the Focused Conversations methodology allowed us to develop a consistent framework for guiding both interviews and focus groups. It tends to work well with a short time period, moving through the four phases of conversation to come to deeper decision points faster. For the community gathering on the first day, we used Open Space Technology to open the agenda to community members. Day two was conducted using The World Café in order to develop ideas that would ensure the community's voice would continue to be heard in the process. We chose World Café over a traditional Open Space action planning process because we were most interested in focused conversation that would propagate ideas quickly throughout the room. We built the day as a feast, and advice that we had from community members caused us to build conscious feast protocol into the day. Food was provided and participants were gifted with blankets for their involvement in the gathering. We opened with a prayer from Elder Skip Dick and opening comments from Chief Andy Thomas of Esquimault, who implored us to take careful notes of what the community was saying and to not let the energy of the gathering wane. We concluded day two with a celebration of the local community, including Métis jigging and songs from Victoria's Unity Drum Group.

KNOW THE PROCESSES

More than any other advice, every practitioner interviewed emphasized knowing the theory and practice of each method as designed before blending anything. What does it do well? How does it work in this situation? How might it blend with other methods being considered? What is your affinity for it? Susan Dupre put it this way:

> Before mixing and blending, live the methods, make sure they are in your bones, your tissues, in the cells of your body so they're not a bunch of activities.[4]

For many practitioners, the principles behind the methods become a life practice. They cease to be discrete processes. As Chris Corrigan said:

> Align who you are and what you are doing with the methods. They will change you if you do them enough. What you're doing is NOT integrating methodologies. Instead you are simply embodying the kind of change you want to see. You come to each situation fresh. If you focus on integrating methods, you've taken your eyes off of what you are doing.[5]

It is a bit like language acquisition. Acquiring a fourth or fifth tongue becomes simpler because there is an intuitive grasp of some deeper pattern. As practitioners integrate more essential practices into themselves, they tap an underlying stream of why things work—the social psychology of emergent systems. From this foundation, it is possible to wisely bring together different processes.

"Living the methods" is a deeply rewarding challenge, like living one's values or sustaining a spiritual practice in the midst of everyday life or immersing yourself in a different culture. Blending them is something of a cross-cultural experience.

Work With the Underlying Principles

Just as learning what another culture values prepares us to be good neighbors, working with the principles that underpin the processes helps practitioners discern the likelihood of a good relationship between them. Principles inform practitioners of the synergies and tensions among methods, supporting them in deducing what might happen when used together—something that is not always easy to predict! For example, practitioner Kenoli Oleari considers the connection between Future Search and Robert Fritz's work:

> Principles give me a framework from which to hang the practical work of design and facilitation. . . . For instance there is an underlying conceptual flow behind Future Search [that] inform[s] the various stages and the progression of the group dynamic. . . . The past-present-future-common ground-action pattern . . . parallels Robert Fritz's patterns for human creativity. . . . Notice that Fritz addresses individual creativity and Future Search addresses community creativity. "Getting" the prin-

ciples can help us make these bridges between levels of development. . . . In all the work we do, things are taking place at all these levels and need to be attended to at all these levels. It is instructive and hugely useful to see the intersections, how principles compare and apply at different levels, and to understand the interactivity.[6]

A Story: Creating the Metalogue Conference

Principle-based blending is a skill to be cultivated. In the beginning, it is an experiment of bringing together different elements that seem to fit based on their underlying principles, and learning by doing. Here's an example of what can happen:

In 1997, Christoph Mandl,[7] Hanna Mandl, and Markus Hauser[8] participated in the 15th Annual International Conference of Organisation Transformation (OT)—the first Open Space conference in Central Europe. The meeting left them wanting a different quality of communication in the community meetings and the workshops. They used their experience as dialogue facilitators, the inspiration from participating in Harrison Owens's OT conference and Juanita Brown's World Café. Joined by three other Austrian consultants—Rudolf Attems, Kuno Sohm, and Josef Weber—they designed and organized a dialogical open space conference, the Metalogue Conference (Metalog-Konferenz), in 1998. (The term "metalogue" originated with Gregory Bateson, describing a conversation where the structure is relevant for the content.)

In a preparatory meeting, as the six consultants shared their experience of organizations transitioning from hierarchy to something not yet clear, the conference topic emerged: "Leadership—Between Hierarchy and . . ." Interesting aspects of this topic like self-organization and complexity management emerged in the large group dialogues and became topics of inspiring workshops. Especially notable was participant feedback on the smooth and unpretentious comanagement by the six consultants. The conference structure—starting with a café atmosphere, plenary dialogues between workshops, and an evening ritual—created a meaningful experience. This highly successful conference resulted in a book published by the organizers and some of the participants writing on their workshop topics. Since then, public Metalogue Conferences have occurred every year and a half on topics like the war in Kosovo, transition times, and spirit in organizations. They are organized by a growing number of consultants and researchers from Austria, Germany, and Switzerland who are part of the metalogikon network.[9]

Metalogue Conferences are also successfully used for consulting to organizations, especially for strategic issues. For this purpose, the conference structure was refined into four distinct phases:

Phase 1: *Setting the tone—conversation in rotating groups*

Phase 2: *Unfolding the structure of the conversation—introducing dialogue principles and holding a large group dialogue*

Phase 3: *Thinking together about the issue—open space workshops*

Phase 4: *Bringing forth the future—a reflective dialogue and then self-organized workshops for next steps*

The first phase is crucial to enhance curiosity and openness. The dialogues foster community spirit and a dialogical attitude in all conversations. The last phase ensures commonly acceptable decisions and personal responsibility for implementation.

This wonderful blend emerged largely because among them, its six creators understood the methods and their underlying principles. It is also a testament to successful cocreative design, modeling the whole system principles it espouses. Successful collaborative design is a sign that blend mastery is present because a key ingredient of the capacity to cocreate is comfort with oneself.

Know Yourself

Some consultants believe that personal maturity, presence, confidence, and the ability to welcome and work with conflict, dissonance, and change are more important than any methodology—that methods are simply the structures through which our essential humanness plays out its power. This can be seen within any community of practice. Some people have special qualities above and beyond their method that make them particularly effective. As you step further out of the supporting structures of a given method into the more fluid environment of mix and match, your personal centeredness, flexibility, and insight become even more important. Many practitioners experience a deep sense of calling to this work. While loving what you do may not be a requirement, once touched by the power of change in whole systems, there is a compelling incentive to continue honing your craft.

Whole system change develops many skills—rational left-brained design, intuitive right-brained sensing; the masculine/yang capacity to set clear intentions, the feminine/yin capacity to let go and move with the flow. The personal capacity for complexity, experimenting with different methods, and having faith and trust in the process and people grows with practice.

Practitioners use terms like flexibility, authenticity, genuineness, and compassion for yourself and others to describe themselves at their best. They talk of being good listeners and observers, being present, using all of their senses, the ability to adjust midstream—to "change the wheels on the car while it's rolling,"[10] to let go of things (e.g., don't get too attached to your design). They describe themselves as tools, part of the process. More wisdom from Chris Corrigan:

> You have to know who you are. The practice of doing this work is the practice of making yourself whole. You can never offer to people something you don't have. And that's not methodologies . . . so really get to know yourself.[11]

Rick Lent eloquently describes his transition from traditional facilitation to the mindful practice of whole system work:

> When I read Productive Workplaces in the late 80's it began to shift the direction of my career and my practice. Several years later I saw Marvin Weisbord facilitate a

group discussion. At one point he did something completely different from what I would have done in that situation. As I watched, I was stunned by the move he made at that point and thought, "I can't believe he did that." From that day, I began to change my whole stance to the consultant's role, revisiting the answer to the question, "What is my role?" away from "providing expertise" and toward "helping the group do what it was ready and able to do." This shift began to affect my work in obvious ways. At the time I was working with another consultant on a client engagement. He told me that he was nervous as he saw me coming to client meetings with a totally different preparation than before. Now, rather than researching a situation and having a report or recommendations, I came with an agenda that engaged the people in the room with the questions that they felt needed to be addressed. I no longer brought new data, new surveys, or new information into the room. I had begun to act from the assumption that with the right people in the room, the necessary information would already be present. Enabling this information to come out would be the value I brought to the client.[12]

Rick's description is a marvelous lens into the journey to mastery: growing past the need to have the answers, to the art of bringing the questions. These are the visible signs of a deeper transition experienced by those who make change their life's work.

Learning to Center and Ground Yourself

Human systems are remarkable in their complexity. No matter how prepared we are, when inviting the whole system to show up and welcoming the conflicts that are an inevitable and a vital part of the mix, it is a given that the unexpected will occur. In fact, because mixing and matching always contains an element of the unknown, the likelihood of the unpredictable increases. How we handle the unanticipated is a measure of mastery: for example, what to do when someone has a heart attack during the opening circle, or how to meet the expectant look on the client's face when she shows you the room that has never held more than 1,500 people and in which almost 2,000 street kids will gather in two days.[13] In the face of such challenges, the capacity for equanimity matters. How do you prepare yourself for the unexpected? It comes through lifelong practice, learning to center deeply in oneself, an ability to call on all aspects of your being—head, heart, body, and spirit—and by staying grounded in the purpose of the work. Kathie Dannemiller counseled Kenoli Oleari:

> You've got to do your own work if you're going to work with groups, or else you're going to be your own client when you're standing up in front of a group and won't be able to serve your paying client like you should.[14]

The ability to stay unattached to outcomes, to be present and in service to the clients—not just those paying the bills, but all who have shown up, entrusting themselves to you—demands that you do your own work. Part of this, according to consultant Kenoli Oleari, is being inviting in a way that brings a person fully forward as we step out of the way (or stand with, not above, them). We fully meet and never become "bigger" (or smaller) than anyone in the room. We understand the huge amount of power standing in the shoes of a facilitator gives us and we don't abuse, fail to acknowledge or deny that power.[15]

A Story: Work With Violent Intergroup Conflict

The power of service is humble, and it empowers the people you're working with. This kind of empowering humility requires developing a very clear and open sense of who you really are. Knowing yourself equips you to ride the waves of the unexpected. Even so, as Susan Coleman[16] discovered, stepping in can sometimes require a lot of deep breathing:

In early 2000, we provided collaborative negotiation and mediation skills training to political representatives from Iraqi Kurdistan as part of a larger capacity-building initiative funded by the State Department and run through the International Conflict Resolution Program (ICRP) at SIPA, Columbia University. The participants were representatives of the PUK and the KDP, the two main political factions, whose competing attempts for political control had resulted in armed conflict. Our job was to design and deliver a five-day skills training in negotiation and mediation, and in the process build an atmosphere of collaboration between the two sides. None of the participants spoke English, and we did not speak either Kurdish or Arabic.

The initial part of the design was straightforward. We had delivered negotiation and mediation training programs for thousands of people around the world, set up a conflict resolution program at the United Nations and at Columbia University, and had run many programs using direct translation. We knew the training could move us toward the program objective, but to create a climate of engagement, with people talking directly to each other in a safe way without a translator required something else. That brought us to Open Space.

When the participants arrived in Ankara, Turkey, on their way to New York, the atmosphere was more than chilly. People sat on opposite sides of the room, avoiding eye contact and all conversation. Group members had lost family in the war between these two sides. For these representatives, this was a paid trip to New York and an opportunity to go to Columbia University, but a passion for reconciliation was not in the air.

The first three days of the program were collaborative negotiation skills training.[17] According to participant accounts and our observations, it was a full, rich, and transformational experience that had some of the following effects:

- *The training mixed the two sides in seemingly arbitrary and face-saving ways to resolve simple conflict issues that deescalated the polarizing tone. People laughed and got playful. We gradually increased the complexity and heat of the issues, ending by role-playing PUK/KDP real-life issues.*

- *Participants' experience in Kurdistan was normalized. Through presentation of theory and reenactment of conflicts mediated in other parts of the world (such as Mozambique), partici-*

pants began to see the predictable phenomenon of adversarial conflict of which they were a part. They also were introduced to the alternative of a collaborative approach—a real eureka to them that such an option even existed.

- *Participants learned models and skills for negotiating collaboratively that they immediately put into practice in the Open Space laboratory that followed.*

On the fourth day, we "opened the space," focusing on the theme "Exploring and Expanding Areas of Cooperation Among Us." To our surprise and definite concern, most of the participants took us literally when we said, "we have breakout spaces, but you are free to go anywhere you like." Indeed they left, and rode the subway from 125th Street to Macy's at 34th Street to shop. That was the most anxiety-provoking moment in the design! A senior representative confronted us: "What's this about?" We calmed him. Holding space sometimes takes nerve.

Why did participants do that? Who knows? Perhaps after three days of intense training, they needed to breathe before they could really talk to each other. Perhaps they just wanted to go shopping. My hunch based on years of cross-cultural work is that the shift from a training run by "professors," however interactive and empowering, to an open space where the responsibility was squarely on their shoulders, was too much in the beginning.

The good news is that everyone also took us at our word when we said, "Wherever you are, whatever you are doing, be here at 4:30 P.M. for 'evening news.' " That's when things started cooking. One by one, participants summoned up the courage to hold our talking "stone," heavy in their hands, and talk to each other about the Kurdistan issues weighing on everyone. The stone, they said, often a weapon of war in Kurdistan, now might be a symbol of peace. The momentum continued through "morning announcements" on the fifth day, to various topic discussions, to an exciting action planning session on the collaborations. Day five ended emotionally with hugging, tears, and singing Kurdish songs. In the program aftermath, through ongoing support from ICRP, the parties created a bilateral conflict resolution center that supports on-the-ground collaboration in many ways including the use of Open Space as a process for high-conflict problem solving.

Did our design work? We could have just done conflict-resolution training. We could have just done an Open Space. It's our view that the combination added real value. Participants gathered for "training" without committing to work the issues. They had a shared experience with low-stress exercises and topics. Important ideas and skills were imparted that could not have been conveyed in Open Space. In Open Space, participants found the passion and responsibility to talk directly to each other about what mattered most. With newly learned skills, and momentum behind them, the space was opened, and held by a neutral third side, as they worked the core conflict issues of their time.

A final note about "knowing yourself." When we first presented the funders of the project with a design that simply said "Open Space" for days four and five instead of the detailed mediation training they expected, they balked. It took a lot of knowing the situation, the processes, and ourselves to have the courage to reassure them that mixing these processes was the way to go.[18]

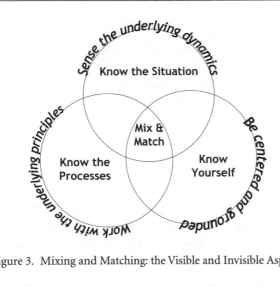

Figure 3. Mixing and Matching: the Visible and Invisible Aspects

Putting It All Together: Lessons in Mixing and Matching

It should now be apparent that mixing and matching methods is the by-product of a complex weave of knowing that encompasses both the visible world of the situation, the methods, and one's own skills and experiences, as well as a deeper knowing that requires sensing energy and dynamics, discerning the synergy among underlying principles, and delving into one's own being (figure 3). Because the field is young, we are still finding our way. When guided by the quality of knowing that shapes successful blending, here are some lessons we have learned so far:

- *Chemistry matters.* Between practitioner and client, method and practitioner, client and method. Sense what is right for you and be willing to say no if it isn't a fit.

- *The client doesn't care what methods are used.* They want their need met in a way that fits their situation.

- *Trust your intuition.* When deciding where to start, bring both your head and heart to the decision. It lessens the confusion among the myriad choices.

- *Take your time.* Add new practices as they feel right to assimilate given the situations you face and your own temperament.

- *Don't be too helpful.* If you solve someone else's problem, they think you are a hero. If you don't, they have someone to blame. Either way, they have missed the discovery that they can do it themselves.[19] Remember, messiness is merely a step on the path to a new coherence.

- *You are not in control.* Anytime you think you are, you are likely to find out the truth the hard way. Think again.

- *Keep it simple.* If it feels like you are working too hard or the answers are not coming, it is time to reconnect with the essential purpose that inspired the work.

- *Do less.* When things get complicated, it is time to step back, breathe, and find one more thing to let go of.

- *Be prepared.* This isn't about memorizing a script, rather, it means being grounded in the practice and centered in yourself. The more centered you are, the more equipped you will be to face whatever happens, whether it is redesigning in the moment or going with the flow.

- *Trust the processes.* Learn to trust the processes you use and, even more important, to trust the larger process that you and they are part of, on behalf of the client and life. Life works through you.

- *Spread the wealth of knowledge and experience.* Let people in on what you know. This generosity of spirit benefits both the students and the overall system. The possibilities of success increase as more people within the system become consciously engaged in creating it in their collective image.

- *Work with partners.* It is a great way to learn. Given the complexity of the work, everyone is better served by multiple experiences and perspectives.

Internalizing these lessons prepares you to move beyond mixing and matching, into the creative flow of inventing process and something more fundamental.

The Next Horizon: Invention Mastery

The metaphors are many: jazz, improvisation, one constant dance, running the river. All of them are a reminder that all is change; nothing is predictable. Developing invention mastery—the capacity to sense into the situation, understand the principles that inform possible approaches, and be present for what's needed in the moment—is a lifelong pursuit. And few of us attempt it alone.

Whole system change is a new field, characterized by cooperation. Partnering with other consultants is a major learning source. Many of the essential practices, Appreciative Inquiry, Dialogue, Future Search, Nonviolent Communication, Open Space, World Café, and others, have vibrant, growing communities of practice. This is no accident, as sharing stories, asking questions, and learning from each other is vital given the complexity of the work. These networks are wonderful and welcoming stops for people wanting to find answers and support. A feeling of abundance, that there is plenty of challenging work for all, is widely held. We are on the leading edge of a shift in how humans organize themselves to accomplish meaningful purpose. Learning together makes us all stronger, better equipped to serve that growing need.

THE ART OF HOSTING MEANINGFUL CONVERSATIONS

As seasoned practitioners from different practice traditions meet and learn from each other, they are innovating not just new methods but new ways of working that create containers for bringing process into the everyday forms that individuals and collectives use to organize themselves for reflection and action. An expression of this shift is the Art of Hosting Meaningful Conversations. Here is their collectively written story:

The Art of Hosting emerged within a Field of Practitioners—friends talking, sharing stories, learning and listening together, wanting to contribute, and asking meaningful questions. The result is a community of people who are called to be hosts, and are called to bring a suite of conversational technologies (Circle, Open Space, World Café, etc.) into play in powerful ways in organizations, communities, families, and all their relations. The work involves teams of practitioners taking collective responsibility for designing practices and creating fields that open the space for imagination, inspiration, love, creativity, learning, and so forth. This inquiry has begun surfacing deeper patterns living below methodologies. It has also given the gift of a fundamental architecture for collaborative and transformative human meetings. It is engaging in questions such as: Where is it that all methods meet, what is the wellspring of design, what are the nonnegotiables in an ever-changing world, and how might our designs support emergence?

The Art of Hosting consciousness engages multiple practices, bringing the insight that to host or teach a practice, you must embrace the deeper pattern of the practice yourself (know the methods), sense the learning edge or "crack" in any given situation to invite the shift wanting to happen (know the situation), and embrace the practice of being present in the moment so as to serve best (know yourself).

For people wanting an immersion into the dynamics of systemic change, the Art of Hosting has much to contribute.[20] The potential of invention mastery, process as an art of living, is still nascent. Still, it offers an intriguing glimpse into possibilities to come. So, bring your questions and your stories. Jump in. You are now part of the river.

A special thanks to Amber M. Linn for capturing the themes of "knowing" in her interview reflections.

1. Definition by Mark Jones (mark_r_jones@worldnet.att.net), Tom Atlee (cii@igc.org), Chris Corrigan (chris@chriscorrigan.com), and Peggy Holman.

2. Seneca Vaught, interview with Lyn Carson, university lecturer, University of Sydney, 2005 (unpublished raw data).

3. www.chriscorrigan.com.

4. Amanie Kariyawasam, interview with Susan Dupre, consultant, Global Visions, 2005. Unpublished raw data.

5. Sue Ellen McComas, interview with Chris Corrigan, consultant, 2005 (unpublished raw data).

6. Kenoli Oleari, personal communication, January 3, 2006.

7. christoph.mandl@univie.ac.at.

8. markus.hauser@ksoe.at.

9. www.metalogikon.com.

10. Andrew Sauber, interview with Tom Atlee, founder, The Co-Intelligence Institute, 2005 (unpublished raw data).

11. McComas, interview with Corrigan.

12. Patti Coutin, interview with Rick Lent, consultant, Brownfield & Lent, 2005 (unpublished raw data).

13. Peggy Holman, "Good Work for 2,000 Colombian Street Kids," 2004, http://opencirclecompany .com/GOOD%20WORK%20FOR%202000%20STREET%20KIDS%20STORY.htm.

14. Oleari, personal communication, January 3, 2006.

15. Ibid.

16. www.colemanraider.com.

17. For a workshop description, see Ellen Raider, Susan Coleman, and Janet Gerson, "Teaching Conflict Resolution Skills in a Workshop," in *The Handbook of Conflict Resolution: Theory and Practice*, ed. Morton Deutsch and Peter T. Coleman (San Francisco: Jossey Bass, 2000).

18. Others vital to this intervention were Andrea Bartoli, Tanya Walters, and Zach Metz from ICRP, and my cofacilitators, James Williams and Ralph Copleman.

19. Thanks to Harrison Owen for this simple but elusive insight.

20. If you want to know more, please meet the stewards at www.artofhosting.org.

4

TOM DEVANE

Sustainability of Results

Well you know you got it if it makes you feel good.
　　　　—Janis Joplin

All too often when a large-scale change effort is nearing its end, some bright-eyed change agent asks, "What shall we do about sustainability of this effort?" It's great to ask the question, but it's the absolutely wrong place to ask it. Dead wrong. We need to stop thinking about sustainability at the end of a change effort, and move it to its rightful place for full, formal consideration—at the *start* of a change effort.

As uncomfortable as it may be to consider, many well-intentioned people often contribute to setting up their organizations and communities for failure. For example, we may consciously ignore things that down deep we know we should pay attention to (*oh, those people in the engineering department won't try to block this change . . .*). Or we may inadvertently miss things that later become important. The good news is that by paying attention to a few key elements at the start, we can dramatically impact sustainability. In this chapter, we hope to move sustainability from "back of mind" to "front of mind." I have included some pragmatic insights into that elusive concept of sustainability and provided some practical tips on how to create conditions that will increase its likelihood. The chapter is organized into the following sections:

- Evidence of Sustainable Change
- Why Sustainability Can Be So Elusive
- Designing Conditions for Sustainability

Evidence of Sustainable Change

How do you know you've got a sustainable change occurring? It's difficult to come up with one sentence that defines sustainability as it relates to large-scale change efforts. Below is a handy checklist of characteristics you can use to assess if a change is sustainable. This can be useful in planning your change effort, in evaluating it midstream, or analyzing what worked and what didn't in a postproject, lessons-learned session. It would be great to have a short, concise, three–bullet point list, but since this is a complicated topic, it calls for a comprehensive approach to defining what we're interested in. When you see the following—hopefully items in all four categories—it's highly likely you have a sustainable change occurring. The four categories of evidence are:

- Direction
- Energy
- Distributed Leadership
- Appropriate Mobilization of Resources

DIRECTION

Direction is the general path forward, with appropriate boundaries that guide what actions people can and can't take. Evidence of direction includes:

- *Belief that the change effort has legitimacy.* For people to commit to a new change and continue to do so, they must believe that it has some legitimacy in the eyes of the organization or community.

- *Cross-functional/cross-group/multistakeholder interests are acknowledged and addressed for the good of the whole moving forward in a common direction.* In an organization or community that has a sustainable change going, even though there are various, often-conflicting interests, people feel they are heard and that they can impact what's happening. This helps them collectively understand, and move forward in the desired direction.

- *Not tightly clinging to a previously designed and implemented solution.* The ultimate "sustainability" of a particular change would be that once it's implemented, nothing about it could be changed. That's obviously not what we're looking for. A sustainable change needs to be adaptive to changing external and internal trends and patterns. The initially articulated direction may need to shift, and that's okay. It is not poured concrete that no one can change, but rather a moving target that continually advances the capabilities of the system to adapt to and influence the external environment. True sustainability needs to be viewed from the context of the greater "big picture" and not viewed narrowly as the sacrosanct recent change that was implemented and cannot now be touched.

ENERGY

Energy is the drive that people have to advance the change initiative. It manifests itself in such ways as people organizing themselves to do continuous improvement, staying/working late, and collaborating across functional boundaries, even though it has no direct benefit to them. Evidence that there is energy in your change effort includes:

- *Gut-level as well as head-level engagement.* To have energy to continuously improve, the affected group of people needs to feel emotionally attached to a particular issue or action plan to improve the current situation. Having a logical understanding is necessary, but not sufficient for ongoing sustainability.

- *Good ideas come from anywhere.* Rather than having good ideas only originate at the top, there need to be mechanisms for good ideas to bubble up from anywhere in the organization or community. Otherwise, widespread enthusiasm and support for the change will dissipate over time, undermining sustainability.

- *People experience genuine opportunities for new, big things to happen.* There are real chances for people to change the status quo, not just window dressing large-group get-togethers. People believe that their voices can be heard without interruption as others suspend judgment, and they *can* make a difference. However, they understand that having a voice doesn't always mean their idea will be accepted, only that they will have a forum for introducing it and having it get a fair discussion.

- *People have some key personal concerns satisfied.* At least one or two critical personal "What's-in-it-for-me?" concerns about the change have been satisfactorily addressed for most people.

- *Appreciation of others' uniqueness as manifested by authenticity and respect toward others.* Unique ideas and capabilities are respected. People are capable of stepping into each other's shoes, even though they may choose not to walk in them for very far. Person A may take an idea from Person B, even though he or she has not typically thought highly of Person B in the past. Such understanding and appreciation where there was none can often unleash incredible amounts of energy for the desired change.

- *There is a thirst for learning.* Research has shown that organizations that learn quickly and have learning-supportive environments have an easier time of implementing large-scale changes rapidly. When people have an opportunity to slake this thirst for learning, everyone wins.

DISTRIBUTED LEADERSHIP

True sustainability requires that people at all levels, in all locations, are authorized to own their own problems and solutions. It also implies that they have the information, skills, and the reward systems to support the new desired goals. Evidence that this is in effect includes:

- *Genuine internal commitment to advancing the change.* Once people are emotionally engaged in the issues around the change, they need to internally have a strong desire to implement the change. Internal motivators (such as a desire to learn or to have an impact) are typically more powerful than external motivators (such as a bonus). When used together, the combination is more powerful than either alone.

- *Better results AND changed behaviors.* To move from the current situation to a dramatically more favorable one, there should be some measurable results as well as changes in the way that people think and behave. However, as Einstein once observed, "All that is important can not be measured, and all that is measured is not important." Key performance variables should be measured in the before and after states to gauge improvement, as well as to designate that the measurement is of a high enough priority to use it. In addition, be on the lookout for formal observations of behavior changes and associated discussions, even though these changes are not quite so objectively measurable.

- *Upward pushback and mutual accountability.* In a well-functioning organization or community, people who do not have formal authority have the ability to confront those in formal authority, particularly if they have a better idea or data to support the challenge. Flowing from this upward pushback principle, mutual accountability is required between those in formal authority and those who do not have formal authority for actions that support the change effort. The combination of great leaders and great followers—and the constant shifting of these roles among people—is the hallmark of effective distributed leadership.

- *The group is not wholly dependent on the top leader for vision or solutions.* Consistent with emerging thoughts on leadership, good leaders don't just articulate a vision and solutions and disseminate them, but actually help people confront the real issues they are facing and help mobilize resources to address them.

APPROPRIATE MOBILIZATION OF RESOURCES

Where sustainability is high, resources—time, people, money, and technology—are mobilized and deployed to places they most benefit the organization or community. Evidence that this is happening includes:

- *The change draws on resources at a rate that matches the availability of resources to support the change.* If critical resources become unavailable, people burn out, or there are too few skilled people to continue the change (e.g., too few people trained in Black Belt skills to carry out a Six Sigma implementation), then the change will falter. It's important to match the demand for the change with its supply for support.

- *When an external or internal consultant leaves, things don't backslide.* People own their own local problems, and solutions to those problems. For this to happen, resources need to be mobilized from the start to conduct a rapid knowledge and skill transfer from external people to internal people. When people outside the group, such as external organization development consultants or internal Six Sigma Black Belts move to other parts of the organization, the local people own the solution and have energy for execution and improvement.

- *People are anxious to move forward based on common ground.* Rather than debate philosophical issues that slow progress, people seek out and expand common ground to move forward (often making initial disagreements irrelevant). They apply effort where there is highest leverage for change (where a small amount of effort yields a disproportionately high benefit).

- *Distributed leadership actions and local initiative taking.* Continuous improvement and effective change implementation occupies a space in most people's heads and hearts after the initial change has been implemented, not just in the heads of organization or community leaders.

- *Communication of important facts, issues, and beliefs.* People know what's happening. In some places, this is done through formal communication plans, while in many high-energy organizations, the word of mouth and the social network are so powerful that formal communication plans are not necessary.

Why Sustainability Can Be So Elusive

There are six factors we've seen that tend to work against having a sustainable solution. Hopefully, you don't see many of these in your organization or community past large-scale change efforts, but they're at least worth thinking about as you proceed through a change effort. The factors we've found are:

- Lack of time

- Lack of money

- Ties to the status quo

- Perceived value of sustainability activities

- The occasional sustainability afterthought

- Change management ignorance, change management bliss

The best way to address all of these is to head off sustainability problems before they occur, and design conditions for sustainability from the start of an improvement effort. However, as a senior vice president of manufacturing for a health-care institution once said to me, "Tom, I live in the real world where those preventive conditions just aren't always possible. What can I do once these problems manifest themselves if I haven't set up sustainability questions at the start?" There are some remedial actions that can jump-start the process. Such perturbations to the system, or management shake-up tactics follow each of the factors below.

LACK OF TIME

Not having enough time is one of the most frequently mentioned reasons for not designing for sustainability. Managers or community leaders want a project implemented by year-end, or competitors are launching their new strategy next quarter, so we have to have ours launched before then. To further complicate matters, many organizations have been reengineered and downsized to very lean staffs, who work hard on completing their technical work tasks, leaving little time for continuous improvement or sustainability. *Management shake-up tactic: Shut down "regular work" for three to four hours each week and provide space for employees to get together and work on change (which, incidentally, should be an aspect of their "real job").*

LACK OF MONEY

Money is another often-cited reason for ignoring sustainability. If change management activities like large group methods are added to the project work plan, then the timeline will no doubt be extended. This means spending more money to get the project done since the resources will be extended out over a longer duration of time. Money can be especially visible if expensive outside consultants are used. For example, on one recent enterprise-wide implementation of SAP software in Colorado, external consultants were charging $4 million per month. When the internal organization development consultant told top management that a design for a sustainable solution would increase the project length by two months, she received a resounding *No* from the steering committee. However, the issue of "We don't have time to do it right, but we have time to do it over" of course reared its persistent head, and the design team ended up battling change resistance for four months after the implementation. *Management shake-up tactic: Each year, dedicate some part of the budget to improvement or change activities, and let teams develop budgets to effectively use that money.*

TIES TO THE STATUS QUO

Many top and middle managers and community leaders have a vested interest in keeping the power base they have built. After years of hard work to get the people, information systems, personal connections, and budgets that they want, they are highly resistant to suggestions reached via a large group method that the organizational structure needs to be flattened and people moved around. *Management shake-up tactic: Move capable people to different parts of the organization to head up areas they are not initially entirely familiar with.*

PERCEIVED VALUE OF SUSTAINABILITY ACTIVITIES

Others still question the perceived value that change activities supporting sustainability might have. Some, who get past the initial hurdle of whether or not it's worthwhile, end up discarding plans because it's thought that the costs outweigh the benefits. *Management shake-up tactic: Publicly reward new behaviors and risk taking that support sustainability.*

The Occasional Sustainability Afterthought

Numerous times we have come in late in the project life cycle, and as the project nears it completion date, we hear some prescient, anguished soul cry out, "Hey, what are we doing about sustainability?" Unfortunately, thinking about sustainability in the last four weeks of a two-year project isn't likely to produce very fruitful results. *Management shake-up tactic: If you haven't planned up front for sustainability, at least get all the stakeholder groups involved in developing a sustainability strategy near the end of the project.*

Change Management Ignorance, Change Management Bliss

Unfortunately, change management ignorance often translates into change management bliss. In many cases of implementing technical large-scale change efforts like enterprise-wide computing or a community-wide initiative, managers or community leaders simply don't know that change management needs to be a component of an overall successful implementation strategy. They see the technical components of their improvement solution (like new computer programs, or new laws) and believe the solution to be so obvious and self-explanatory that absolutely no adjustments of human psyches or behaviors are necessary.

Change-management biases by organizational level or community sector also frequently occur. Many top managers of very large organizations believe that change management just needs to be done for the top two layers of the organization, and the remaining four layers below can just be told what to do and everything will be fine. In a community, the equivalent is assuming that only officials need to be involved, leaving citizen engagement out of issues that affect their lives. Such faulty change foundations cause large improvement projects to fail miserably within about three months of implementation. *Management shake-up tactic: In cases where you can't provide up-front education about the topic, convene discussion forums about change management with internal organization development professionals, external consultants, and other top leaders from similar corporations or communities.*

The content in this section provides some insights into common sustainability problems, and some quick-hit actions that managers can take to try to jolt the organizational system out of complacency and address change issues head-on. However, far better than these knee-jerk, "after the horse is out of the barn" actions is the discipline of designing sustainability conditions into your project from the start.

Designing Conditions for Sustainability Checklist

I had hoped I could boil down all the best global practices for sustainability into eight or so pithy points that would fit on a small laminated card that could be kept in your wallet, purse, or European carryall. However, after extensive research, input from the 95 contributing authors, and personal experiences, I was not able to do so. Not too surprisingly, I found that complex challenges such as large-scale change sustainability require a bit lengthier explanation than might be listed on a one-page laminated card. Below is a checklist, organized by change stage (start-middle-end) to include in your sustainability design process. While many method chapters in part II provide varying tips, this list contains fairly universal principles that are applicable across countries, industries, communities, and nonprofits. The first list in this chapter contained some descriptive *indicators* of sustainability; the following list provides conditions that you, as a leader at any level in your community or organization, can *design* for from the start to ensure you'll get sustainability at the end.

Though up-front conditions are important, conditions for sustainability are constantly being designed throughout a change effort.

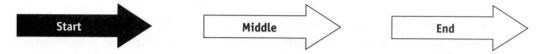

At the start of a change effort, the key high-leverage elements include:

1. *Have a plan and strategy-structure combination to achieve it.* It's important to know where you're headed, so it's essential to have a plan. Ideally, this plan is codeveloped with representatives from the entire system that's affected. Then, there needs to be a structure that's congruent with the plan.

2. *Design early for sustainability.* Don't wait until the end of the project because many buy-in and energizing events need to happen at the start.

3. *Go slow early to go fast later.* It takes a bit more time to get early meaningful involvement, but this helps in terms of shared assumptions, a common understanding, and commitment to joint actions going forward. While it may seem to delay a project at the start, it saves time later because people won't be doing things two and three times, and resisting change, which slows the project down.

4. *Conduct a risk analysis with key leaders, and discuss best- and worst-case scenarios.* Look at potential risks such as budget changes or leadership rotation, and then formulate mitigating strategies for them from the start.

5. *Design to get consultants (external or internal) out as soon as possible, so people can confront their own issues and own the "solution."* Groups need to develop internal capabilities to deal with their own problems, and own them.

6. *Make appropriate investments in long-term improvement.* Those with formal budgetary authority need to commit time, money, and other resources to the sustainability of key organization or community initiatives.

7. *Evaluate systemic issues in the diagnosis and action planning stages.* An organization or community needs to consider structures of key variables, feedback loops, and leverage points for both improvement and breakdown. For example, a newly launched organizational

structure of self-managing, high-performing teams needs existing performance evaluation forms and rewards and recognition schemes modified to favor team behavior over individual grandstanding.

In the middle of a change effort, the key high-leverage elements include:

1. *Design "clearings."* The German philosopher Heidegger articulated the concept of a "clearing" as it relates to people and groups. Just as in a dense forest, in a dense organization, cutting out a clearing makes room for something entirely different to happen. We may not know exactly what will happen, but as with a large group method, we know that we have created the potential for something new.

2. *Meaningfully engage people and increase the circle of participation.* When people can make truly significant contributions (not just recommending the color of their lockers or developing entrees for the cafeteria menu), they start taking ownership and gain commitment. Once an initial group develops a core strategy, continuing to increase that circle of consequential participation creates an organizational energy groundswell.

3. *Clearing people's plates for follow-up.* Leaders need to help mobilize resources to accomplish the desired sustainable change. This often means taking previously assigned tasks off an individual's plate or engaging citizens who are not normally part of the process. This not only is good for the individual's capability to perform what is needed, but also sends a powerful message (by example) to the organization or community of what is important.

4. *Transparent reporting of progress.* It's important to track and report progress of key initiatives and activities to ensure that they are being performed, and get back on track if they are not. Transparency enables a broad view into progress so that people can support each other in accomplishing the work to be done.

5. *Leadership systems with many leaders and role models.* Early adopting formal leaders set the new norms and model them, as well as provide specific expectations and consequences. As more people take responsibility, leadership capacity within the organization or community grows.

6. *Conditions and training for, as well as modeling of, straight talk and harnessing productive conflict.* Straight talk helps cut through the political verbal dances that often occur in organizations or communities. The truth, even difficult news, can be more quickly dealt with than cover-ups and alibis. Managing conflict is an important part of the overall

straight-talk equation. All too often, people fear conflict and consequently avoid it. The truth is that conflict can be useful in moving an organization or community to a better place. Strive to make conflict productive and harness its power.

7. *Design for multiple stakeholders' needs to be adequately addressed, even if they seem to compete.* Large group methods that convene people with various interests and viewpoints are essential to a sustainable solution. Two important contributions of large group methods are: (1) their remarkable ability to uncover breakthrough solutions to the most intractable situations, and (2) their ability to energize people with initially very different stated needs toward a single, shared solution.

8. *Strike the appropriate balance between energy creation (e.g., commitment from a large group event like an Open Space or Search Conference) and tool-enhanced improvement (e.g., Six Sigma or Lean).* The combination of "hard" and "soft" aspects of a change effort can provide both the desire to improve and the capability to improve.

9. *Use more than large group methods to facilitate sustainability.* A solid plan for sustainability requires a combination of large group methods and traditional organization development actions, such as: one-on-ones, one-on-small-group training, one-to-many-with-feedback, and changes to policies and practices.

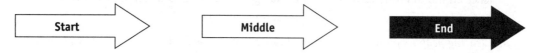

In the wind-down, ending stage of a change effort, the key high-leverage elements include:

1. *Mechanism for follow-up.* A good plan needs great follow-up. Many a large-scale initiative fails because of poor execution, even with a good plan. Powerful implementations of this concept include self-managed teams and active citizen groups. Other strategies include reviews by multidisciplinary steering committees, internal champions with considerable organizational power, CEO attention, and public engagement in a community setting.

2. *Establish clear responsibilities.* Minimizing duplicate activities and ensuring that the unexpected is covered comes through knowing who is responsible for what. This is often done through RACI matrices (a 2×2 matrix of specific responsibilities mapped to each person, with each responsibility stating if the person has primary Responsibility, has Approval rights, needs to be Consulted, or needs to be Informed).

3. *Public commitment to responsibility areas.* As Kurt Lewin researched and demonstrated many years ago, people are more likely to keep a commitment if they make it in a public forum, versus just committing one-on-one to someone, or silently writing personal goals on an piece of paper and not sharing them with anyone. Where practical, in large group methods, strive to include some time for public commitments to continue the work of the group once the session ends.

4. *Track both newly articulated results and behaviors, as well as appropriate follow-up.* A tool developed during the Jack Welch reign at General Electric clearly made a distinction between good and poor results, and good and poor behaviors. Welch was looking to eliminate bullies who intimidated their direct reports into performing at high levels. Welch realized he would need to change behaviors to get the sustainable results he wanted. A critical linchpin to Welch's strategy was to embed the notion of results *and* behaviors into the formal evaluation system, and modify the reward system to encourage behavior changes.

5. *Reinforcement.* Wherever possible, those in formal authority need to reinforce desired new behaviors with monetary means as well as intrinsically motivating means that they have at their disposal. Those people who do not have formal authority or control budgets can use verbal encouragement and support their peers for new behaviors.

6. *Continual external and internal scanning to remain current.* In today's turbulent environment, external and internal situations change so rapidly it's important to establish sensors for monitoring what's happening so plans and structures can be adjusted accordingly.

7. *Learning processes and practices to sustain momentum.* To keep a positive momentum going, it is helpful to institute learning processes (like periodic lessons learned analyses that critically examine what went well versus what might be done differently next time). Organizations and communities that learn quickly will change swiftly and effectively.

In closing, it's important to note that sustainability across the globe still remains elusive for many. The good news is that for those wishing to exert strong change leadership, apply proven principles for sustainability, and develop conditions for sustainability, success is within their grasp. To do this, however, we need to abandon old notions of achieving sustainability. It is less like cramming for an exam the night before, and more like an ongoing building process where new designs are continually added to a strong foundation. What we do up front in a change effort indeed matters a great deal. Winston Churchill once noted, "We shape our buildings, then our buildings shape us." It's the same with our designs for sustainability.

Part II: The Methods

Part II is the heart of *The Change Handbook*. It is the product of numerous hands and the work of highly seasoned change practitioners. Many of the people in this section have devoted their lives to making the world a better place through increasing the capacity of ordinary people to make a substantive difference in their lives, their organizations, and their communities.

We've organized this part of the book into five sections using the overarching purposes of the methods: Adaptable, Planning, Structuring, Improving, and Supportive. Within each section, we open with the "in-depth" chapters organized alphabetically. Following the in-depth chapters within each purpose are "thumbnails," short summaries to give you a taste of the work. Coupled with the quick summaries in Part IV and the end-of-chapter references, you have the means of finding more information about any of these processes.

And now to the heart of the matter . . .

ADAPTABLE METHODS

Adaptable methods are used for a variety of purposes in organizations or communities, including planning, structuring, and improving. This group uses principles and practices that adapt to varying community and organizational needs.

5

DAVID L. COOPERRIDER AND DIANA WHITNEY

Appreciative Inquiry
A Positive Revolution in Change

Be the change you want to see in the world.
—Gandhi

Approaching Problems from the Other Side

Appreciative Inquiry (AI) begins an adventure. Even in the first steps, one senses an exciting new direction in our language and theories of change—an invitation, as some have declared, to "a positive revolution." The words just quoted *are* strong and, unfortunately, they are not ours. But the more we replay the high-wire moments of our five years of work at GTE/Verizon,[1] the more we find ourselves asking the same kinds of questions the people of GTE asked their senior executives: "Are you ready for the momentum that is being generated? This is igniting a grassroots movement . . . it *is* creating an organization in full voice, a center stage for positive revolutionaries!"

Tom White, president of what was then called GTE Telops (with 80 percent of GTE's 67,000 employees), replied with no hesitation: "Yes, and what I see in this meeting are zealots, people with a mission and passion for creating the new GTE. Count me in, I'm your number one zealot." People cheered.

Fourteen months later—based on significant and measurable changes in stock prices, morale survey measures, quality/customer relations, and union-management relations—GTE's whole system change initiative won the ASTD (American Society for Training and Development) award for best organization change program in the country. Appreciative inquiry was cited as the "backbone."

To achieve this stunning shift in organization culture, the team of internal and external change agents asked, "How can we engage the positive potential of all employees toward transforming the company?" We wanted whatever we did to recognize and invite the expression of frontline employee strengths, initiative, and capabilities. We set a goal of creating a narrative-rich culture with a ratio of five stories of positive performance and success to every negative one—to build a vibrant, high-performing, customer-focused culture.

This goal was approached by:

- Training more than 50 internal change agents in Appreciative Inquiry.

- Introducing 800 frontline employees to Appreciative Inquiry.

- Creating a "story center" for sharing "good news" stories.

- Embedding storytelling into existing processes. For example, the annual President's Leadership Award focused on storytelling about the winning employees, their teams, and customer service.

- Adding open-ended questions to the company employee survey and tracking the ratio of positive to negative comments.

- Creating an Appreciative Inquiry storybook as an employee teaching tool.

- Introducing a new partnership model for the unions and company management using Appreciative Inquiry.[2]

Tom White described AI in executive language:

> Appreciative Inquiry can get you much better results than seeking out and solving problems. That's an interesting concept for me—and I imagine most of you—because telephone companies are among the best problem solvers in the world. We troubleshoot everything. We concentrate enormous resources on correcting problems that have relatively minor impact on our overall service and performance. . . . When used continually and over a long period of time, this approach can lead to a negative culture. If you combine a negative culture with the challenges we face today, it could be easy to convince ourselves that we have too many problems to overcome—to slip into a paralyzing sense of hopelessness. . . . Don't get me wrong. I'm not advocating mindless happy talk. Appreciative Inquiry is a complex science designed to make things better. We can't ignore problems—we just need to approach them from the other side.[3]

The Basics

WHAT IS APPRECIATIVE INQUIRY?

AI has been described in a myriad of ways: as a *radically affirmative approach to change* that completely lets go of problem-based management and in so doing vitally transforms strategic planning, survey methods, culture change, merger integration methods . . . measurement systems;[4] as a *paradigm of conscious evolution* geared for the realities of the new century;[5] as the most important advance in *action research* in the past decade;[6] as offspring and "heir" to Maslow's vision of a *positive social science*;[7] and as a methodology that takes the idea of the *social construction* of reality to its positive extreme—with its emphasis on metaphor and narrative, relational ways of knowing, on language, and on its potential as a source of generative theory.[8]

While there are many ways to describe AI—as a philosophy and methodology for change leadership—here is a practice-oriented definition:

> *Appreciative Inquiry is the cooperative, coevolutionary search for the best in people, their organizations and communities, and the world around them. It involves systematic discovery of what gives "life" to an organization or community when it is most effective, and most capable in economic, ecological, and human terms.*
>
> *AI assumes that every organization or community has many "untapped and rich accounts of the positive"—what people talk about as past, present, and future capacities—the positive core. AI links the knowledge and energy of this core directly to an organization or community's change agenda, and changes never thought possible are suddenly and democratically mobilized.*

THE APPRECIATIVE INTERVIEW

At the heart of AI is the *appreciative interview*, a one-on-one dialogue among organization or community members and stakeholders using questions on high-point experiences, valuing, and what gives life to the organization or community at its best, such as:

1. Describe a time in your organization/community that you consider a high-point experience, a time when you were most engaged and felt alive and vibrant.

2. Without being modest, what do you most value about yourself, your work, and your organization/community?

3. What are the core factors that give life to your organization/community when it is at its best?

4. Imagine your organization/community ten years from now, when everything is just as you always wished it could be. What is different? How have you contributed to this "dream organization/community"?

Answers to questions like these and the stories they generate are shared throughout the group resulting in new, more compelling images of the organization or community and its future.

THE POSITIVE CORE

The *positive core* of organizational or community *life* is one of the greatest and largely unrecognized resources in the field of change management today. We are clearly in our infancy when it comes to tools for working with it, talking about it, and designing our systems in alignment with it. One thing is evident, however, as we reflect on what we have learned with AI: Human systems grow in the direction of what they persistently ask questions about. This propensity is strongest and most sustainable when the means and ends of inquiry are positively correlated. The single most important action a group can take to liberate the human spirit and consciously construct a better future is to make the positive core the common and explicit property of all.

By inquiring into its positive core, an organization or community enhances its collective wisdom, builds energy and resiliency for change, and extends its capacity to achieve extraordinary results.

A Working Definition of Positive Change

AI deliberately works from accounts of the positive core. This shift from problem analysis to positive core analysis is at the heart of positive change.

We do not dismiss accounts of conflict, problems, or stress. We simply do not use them as the basis of analysis or action. We listen when they arise, validate them as lived experience, and seek to reframe them. For example, the problem of low management credibility becomes an inquiry into moments of inspired leadership.[9]

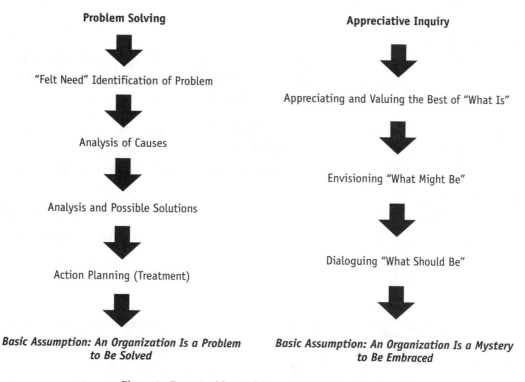

Problem Solving

"Felt Need" Identification of Problem

Analysis of Causes

Analysis and Possible Solutions

Action Planning (Treatment)

Basic Assumption: An Organization Is a Problem to Be Solved

Appreciative Inquiry

Appreciating and Valuing the Best of "What Is"

Envisioning "What Might Be"

Dialoguing "What Should Be"

Basic Assumption: An Organization Is a Mystery to Be Embraced

Figure 1. From Problem Solving to Appreciative Inquiry

With AI, change begins with a rigorous, organization- or community-wide discovery and analysis of the positive core—a "root cause of success analysis." We define positive change as:

Any form of organization change, redesign, or planning that begins with comprehensive inquiry, analysis, and dialogue of an organization's "positive core," involving multiple stakeholders, and then links this knowledge to the organization's strategic change agenda and priorities (figure 1).

THE APPRECIATIVE INQUIRY 4-D CYCLE

The AI Cycle can be as rapid and informal as a conversation with a friend or colleague, or as formal as an organization- or community-wide process involving every stakeholder group. While there is no formula for AI, most change efforts flow through the 4-D Cycle (figure 2). Each AI process is home grown—designed to meet the unique challenges of the community, organization, or industry involved.

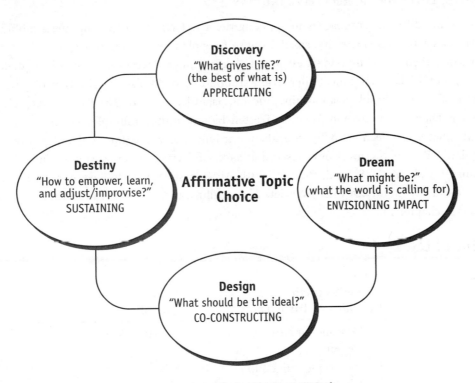

Figure 2. Appreciative Inquiry 4-D Cycle

The four key phases of an AI process are:

- *Discovery*—mobilizing a whole system, multiple stakeholder inquiry into the positive core;

- *Dream*—creating a results-oriented vision based in discovered potential and questions of higher purpose, that is, "What is the world calling for us to become?"

- *Design*—creating possibility propositions of the ideal organization or community, articulating a design capable of drawing upon and magnifying the positive core to realize the newly expressed dream; and

- *Destiny*—strengthening the affirmative capability of the whole system enabling it to build hope and sustain momentum for ongoing positive change and high performance.

At the center of the cycle is Affirmative Topic Choice, the starting point and most strategic aspect of any AI process. AI topics become an agenda for learning, knowledge sharing, and action. They get written into questions for Discovery interviews, serve as seeds for Dreams, as arenas for crafting Design propositions, and for taking action in the Destiny phase.

APPLICATIONS OF APPRECIATIVE INQUIRY

Many different approaches to applying the 4-D Cycle are emerging: mass mobilizing interviews across an entire city; small groups of people interviewing colleagues within their company, then benchmarking best-practices companies; face-to-face interfaith dialogue among hundreds of religious leaders from around the world. Each application liberates the power of inquiry, builds relationships, and unleashes learning. In *The Power of Appreciative Inquiry*, Diana Whitney and Amanda Trosten-Bloom outline multiple "Forms of Engagement" that have been used by consultants around the globe for applying Appreciative Inquiry.[10] Two of the most often used and successful ways to apply AI are Whole-System Inquiry[11] and the AI Summit.[12] The British Airways story that follows is an example of Whole-System Inquiry. A brief overview and an illustrative story of the AI Summit can be found in chapter 14.

Table of Uses

Brief Description	Project Length, Number of Participants	Results
Office of Finance, City and County of Denver Discover and disseminate financial best practices and revenue-generating opportunities across the city	• Mass-mobilized inquiry (2 months) • 200 people trained to conduct 600 face-to-face interviews with city employees, local businesses, and community members • AI Summit (1 day), 100 people • Action teams formed	• Saved $70M

Brief Description	Project Length, Number of Participants	Results
Hunter Douglas Organization-wide cultural transformation	• Whole-System inquiry (3 months) • 900 employees interviewed, 100 customers and community members • Broad sharing of best-practice stories • Small group meaning-making meetings • AI Summit to Dream and Design (3 days), 180 people	• Enhanced employee retention and positive morale • Significant financial savings • Creation of an Appreciative Organization Culture
United Religions Initiative Creation of a global interfaith network dedicated to peace	• Annual 200-person global AI Summits • Regional Summits • Ongoing worldwide Internet dialogue (5 years of inquiry, dialogue, and design)	• Charter signed in 2000 • Current organization of 300 cooperation circles worldwide
Nutrimental Foods Whole-system strategic planning	• AI Summit (4 days), annual summits since, 1,000 people, (all employees, customers, vendors, and community members)	• 200 percent increase in profits, 75 percent decrease in absenteeism

Getting Started With AI

A Case Study at British Airways—A Passion for Service

After two years of significant organizational changes, David Erich, British Airways North America vice president, customer service, realized his job had just begun. It was time to engage employees in improving their lagging survey scores and revitalizing the "Passion for Service" culture. They began a whole system change process using Appreciative Inquiry.

A lot was done well across the 22 customer service stations in North America, yet the best practices were not identified, shared, or replicated. The organization's collective wisdom was like an underground well, full of life-giving potential waiting to be drawn upon and put to good use.

The decision to use Appreciative Inquiry involved a one-day briefing of line managers and organization development professionals and a two-day "core team" meeting. Forty people from all levels, locations, and functions attended this two-day "core team" meeting to decide whether to proceed and set the foundation for the whole system inquiry. The two days included: an overview of Appreciative Inquiry, the selection of affirmative topics, drafting of interview questions, practice interviews, and sharing of best practice stories.

Selecting Affirmative Topics for Inquiry

As the group selected topics, one participant commented, "I see how Appreciative Inquiry can make a difference with people-related issues, but can it be used for technical issues?" Sensing she had a specific issue in mind, we asked her to share it. She said succinctly, "Baggage." Everyone in the room sighed with relief. The paramount issue to the business's well-being was now in the conversation. They explained that when customers' baggage does not arrive on the same flight as the customer, it costs money, time, and goodwill. They shared stories of the wedding dress that didn't make it to the wedding, replaced at British Airways' expense; camping gear that didn't get to the Grand Canyon until the vacation was over; and the daily disturbances of luggage not transferred in time for connecting flights.

We offered the Appreciative Inquiry principle that leads to powerful, strategic affirmative topics, "Given that organizations move toward what they study, what do you want more of?" The response was quick and unanimous—a habitual response: "Better service recovery." We said, "Do we have this right, its okay to lose a customer's baggage as long as you recover it promptly?" The group got the point.

Again we asked, "What do you want more of?" Small groups talked for about 20 minutes. The chosen idea: "Exceptional Arrival Experience." Along with Happiness at Work, Continuous People Development, and Harmony Among Work Groups, the topics for an organization-wide inquiry were defined.

Deciding to Go Forward

Toward the end of the meeting, we posed two questions: "Should this work proceed?" and "What will it take to ensure success?" The first answer was a unanimous yes. The group agreed upon two essential factors for success—"management commitment" and "involvement of the entire workforce." The core team agreed to shepherd the process and signed up for roles that included: conducting interviews, naming and branding the initiative, speaking to groups about AI, writing articles or being interviewed for in-house communications, and serving as their station AI coordinator. A seven-person Steering Team was formed to design, champion, and support the process.

A one-day meeting followed for managers on the Appreciative Inquiry program, branded as "The Power of Two." Core team members shared their enthusiasm for AI and its potential. By the meeting's end, AI was off and flying.

Roles, Responsibilities, and Relationships

Successful change requires commitment from large numbers of people. Our experience suggests that the more positive the focus, the stronger the attraction to participate; and the more likely people are to get involved and stay involved. As table 1 shows, everyone has a role in creating positive change.

	Before	**During**	**After**
Leadership Sponsors and Advisory Team	• Commit to a positive approach to change • Become knowledgeable in AI • Clarify the change agenda • Provide resources	• Champion AI in the organization • Participate—as an equal, essential voice	• Ask: How might we take an AI approach to this? • Lead by discovering and aligning strengths
Core Team	• Become knowledgeable in AI	• Select affirmative topics • Create the interview guide • Determine the interview strategy • Communicate "best" stories	• Use AI as a daily practice
Participants	• Become knowledgeable in AI • Conduct interviews and be interviewed • Review interview stories and share best practices	• Engage in discovery and dialogue • Dare to dream • Design the ideal organization/community	• Integrate AI into existing processes and practices • Create new systems and structures using AI • Practice AI on a daily basis
Consultants	• Introduce AI to the organization • Focus on the "business case" for AI	• Train groups in AI • Support the core team • Facilitate the process	• Assist the organization to integrate AI into daily practices

Table 1. AI Roles and Responsibilities

Conditions For Success

THE LIBERATION OF POWER

For nearly two decades, organizations and communities around the globe have experienced extraordinary transformations using Appreciative Inquiry. Having tracked this success in Nutrimental Foods, GTE, Hunter Douglas Window Fashions Division, and others, Appreciative Inquiry consultants and authors Diana Whitney and Amanda Trosten-Bloom began wondering what created the conditions for AI's success. Why do people get so excited and want to participate with Appreciative Inquiry? Why does participation lead to positive results such as innovation, productivity, employee satisfaction, and profitability? What creates the space for people to be their best at work and for personal transformation? And, what conditions foster cooperation throughout a system of highly diverse groups of people?

They conducted an inquiry into *why Appreciative Inquiry works,* creating questions, holding focus groups, and conducting interviews in several organizations.

Their key finding is that Appreciative Inquiry works by generating six essential conditions that together liberate personal and organizational power. Experiencing the effect on their lives and the world around them, people are permanently transformed. Whitney and Trosten-Bloom named these conditions that unleash human potential the "Six Freedoms."

Freedom to Be Known in Relationship

Human identity forms and evolves in relationship; yet all too often in work settings people relate to another's role rather than to him or her as a human being. Appreciative Inquiry interrupts the cycle of depersonalization that masks people's sense of being and belonging. It offers people the chance to know one another—as unique individuals, and as a part of the web of relationships.

Freedom to Be Heard

A person can listen without hearing or getting to know the other. Being heard is relational, requiring sincere curiosity, empathy, and compassion. It requires an openness to know another's story. Through one-on-one appreciative interviews people come forward with information, ideas, and innovations that are put into action, creating a feeling of being heard, recognized, and valued.

Freedom to Dream in Community

Visionary leadership means unleashing the dreams of people. It means creating organizations and communities as safe places where large, diverse groups of people share their dreams in dialogue with one another.

Freedom to Choose to Contribute

Work can separate us from what matters most or provide a forum for realizing our deepest calling. Freedom of choice liberates power. It also leads to commitment and a hunger for learning.

When people choose to do a project and commit to others, they get creative and determined. They do whatever it takes and learn whatever is needed to do the job.

Freedom to Act With Support

This quintessential act of positive interdependence enables profound contributions and surprising lessons. People know that others care about their work and are anxious to cooperate. They feel safe to experiment, innovate, and learn. In other words, whole system support stimulates people to take on challenges, and draws people into acts of cooperation, bringing forth their best.

Freedom to Be Positive

Today, it is simply not the norm to have fun, be happy, or be positive. Despite the pain, people are swept away in collective currents of negativity. Over and over again, people tell us that Appreciative Inquiry works, in part, because it gives them permission to feel positive and be proud of their experiences.

Appreciative Inquiry works because it unleashes all Six Freedoms during one 4-D Cycle. It creates a surge of energy that, once liberated, won't be recontained. A Hunter Douglas supervisor said, "As people got results, they gained confidence, leading to five times more input, and greater involvement." Appreciative Inquiry creates a self-perpetuating momentum for positive change—a positive revolution.

Principles for a Positive Revolution

AI embodies a philosophy and a methodology that shifts our understanding of human systems and change based upon the following principles:

THE CONSTRUCTIONIST PRINCIPLE

Human knowledge and organizational destiny are interwoven. We are constantly involved in making sense of the world around us—doing strategic planning analysis, environmental scans, audits, surveys, performance appraisals, and so on. To be effective, we must understand organizations as living social constructions. Meaning is made in relationship using words, language, and questions as primary tools of creation.

THE PRINCIPLE OF SIMULTANEITY

Inquiry and change are simultaneous. Inquiry is intervention. The seeds of change—the things people think and talk about, the things people discover and learn, and the things that inform dialogue and inspire images of the future—are implicit in the first questions asked. These questions set the stage for what we "find," and what we "discover" (the data) becomes the linguistic material, the stories for conceiving and constructing the future.

If inquiry and change are simultaneous, it is not, "Is my question leading to right or wrong answers?" but rather, "What is the impact of my question on our lives . . . is it generating conversations about the good, the better, the possible . . . is it strengthening our relationships?"

THE POETIC PRINCIPLE

Human organizations are more like an open book than, say, a machine. An organization's story is constantly being coauthored. Pasts, presents, and futures are endless sources of learning, inspiration, and interpretation—like the endless interpretive possibilities in good poetry. We can study virtually any topic related to human experience, inquiring into the nature of alienation or joy, enthusiasm or low morale, excellence or excess. What we chose to study makes a difference.

THE ANTICIPATORY PRINCIPLE

Our positive images of the future lead our positive actions—this is the increasingly energizing basis and presupposition of Appreciative Inquiry. The infinite human resource we have for generating constructive organizational change is our collective imagination and discourse about the future.

The image of the future guides the current behavior of any organization or community. Inquiring in ways that redefine anticipatory reality[13]—creating positive images together—may be the most important aspect of any change process.

THE POSITIVE PRINCIPLE

Building and sustaining momentum for change requires large amounts of positive affect and social bonding—things like hope, excitement, inspiration, caring, camaraderie, sense of purpose, and joy in creating something meaningful together. The more positive the question we ask, the more long lasting and successful the change effort. The major thing a change agent can do is craft and ask unconditionally positive questions.

In the past five years, the practice of AI has led to articulating additional principles. In *The Power of Appreciative Inquiry,* consultants Diana Whitney and Amanda Trosten-Bloom add three principles they believe essential to successful large-scale positive change: Wholeness, Enactment, and Free Choice. Professors Frank Barrett and Ron Fry in *Appreciative Inquiry: A Positive Approach to Building Cooperative Capacity* add the Narrative Principle as central.

Our experience shows that affirmative language is an extremely healthy and effective approach to change management. A theory of the affirmative basis of human action and organizing is emerging from many quarters—social constructionism, image theory, conscious evolution, athletics, and health care. Taken together, we believe, it is making traditional change management obsolete.

Sustaining the Results

Results generated through Appreciative Inquiry are immediate, often surprisingly dramatic and broad in scope, touching personal transformation, whole-system transformation, and enhancing performance, productivity, and profitability.

We have found that sustained high participation, enthusiasm, and morale, inspired action, agility, and innovation are natural results of becoming an Appreciative Inquiry Organization (AIO). Sustainability depends on consciously and strategically reconstructing the organization's core processes—human resources, management, planning, and measurement in alignment with the AI principles and methodologies.

As AI's principles and methodologies are embedded in daily practices, the capacity to sustain high levels of participation and enthusiasm increases. At one AIO, all meetings begin with an inquiry into "magic moments"—times of extraordinary success among members. Other organizational enactments of AI include annual strategic planning summits, appreciative interviewing as an employee orientation process, appreciative feedback, and affirmatively focused measurement systems.

ROADWAY EXPRESS: MOVING FROM GOOD TO GREAT

For 75 years, Roadway Express has been a leading transporter of industrial, commercial, and retail goods. With services to more than 100 countries, over 300 terminals throughout the United States, and 27,000 people, Roadway is one of the largest less-than-truckload carriers in the nation. Four years ago, Roadway Express launched a bold initiative to drive costs out and to rapidly grow the business by creating an organization with *leadership at every level*—where dockworkers, truck drivers, stackers, and professionals joined with senior management to do annual strategic planning, to learn about the economics and financials of the business, and to create new levels of partnership between the unions and the company.

Roadway held AI Summits throughout its North American operations. When work began, Roadway stock was around $14 per share, rising to more than $40 per share in two years. Beyond stock prices, other measures have steadily improved, including operating ratios, morale, trust, clarity in focus and priority, vision, commitment, and confidence in the future. Much change occurred during an economic downturn, traced to the new culture of engagement fostered by more than 20 Appreciative Inquiry Summits.

Jim Staley, Roadway's chief executive officer, says, "The Appreciative Inquiry approach unleashes tremendous power, tremendous enthusiasm, and gets people fully engaged in the right way in what we're trying to accomplish. It's not that we don't deal with the negative anymore, but the value of AI is that, in anything we do, there's a positive foundation of strength to build on in addressing those problems."

An example is the AI Summit at the Winston-Salem terminal with more than 300 truck drivers, dockworkers, senior executives, teamsters, managers, and customers. A Forbes business writer, Joanne Gordon, participated in the three-day event. Her article captured a vignette from the summit:

Appreciative Inquiry

A team of short-haul drivers came up with 12 cost-cutting and revenue generating ideas. One of the most ambitious: Have each of the 32 drivers in Winston-Salem deliver just one more customer order each hour. Using management data, the drivers calculated that 288 additional daily shipments, at an average revenue of $212 each and with a 6 percent margin, would generate just about $1 million a year of operating costs.

The real story is the momentum's sustainability from AI Summits as a way of life, engaging all the stakeholders in one collaborative planning process (creating thousands of ambassadors and saving time that slower, small group meetings would require), and internalizing high-engagement planning, with in excess of 10,000 people participating in a summit.

Burning Question

BUT—WHAT ABOUT PROBLEMS?

We are not saying to ignore problems. Rather, if you want to transform a situation, a relationship, an organization, or community, focusing on strengths is much more effective. We often work in situations fraught with anxiety, tension, and stress—union-management relations, merger integration, and cross-cultural conflict. Frequently, when we turn people's attention from *what is wrong around here* to *who are we when we are at our best*, conflict turns to cooperation.

Conclusion

To be sure, Appreciative Inquiry begins an adventure. The urge and call to the positive revolution has been sounded by many people and organizations. It will take many more to explore the vast vistas appearing on the horizon.

We are infants in understanding appreciative processes of knowing and social construction. Yet, we are increasingly clear that the world is ready to leap beyond methodologies of deficit-based change and enter a life-centric domain. Relationships thrive where there is an appreciative eye—when people see the best in one another, when they share their dreams and concerns in affirming ways, and when they connect in full voice to create new and better worlds. The velocity and largely informal spread of the appreciative learnings underscore the desire to live and work in constructive, positive, life-affirming, even spiritual ways.

Albert Einstein's words clearly compel: "There are only two ways to live your life. One is as though nothing is a miracle. The other is as though everything is a miracle."

About the Authors

David L. Cooperrider, Ph.D. (David.Cooperrider@Case.edu), is professor and chairman of the Department of Organizational Behavior at the Weatherhead School of Management, Case Western Reserve University. His founding work in Appreciative Inquiry is creating a positive revolution in the leadership of change; helping companies discover the power of strength-based approaches to multistakeholder cooperation. David was recognized in 2000 as among "the top ten visionaries" in the field by *Training Magazine* and, in 2004, received the American Society for

Training and Development's highest award, the "Distinguished Contribution to Workplace Learning and Performance Award."

Diana Whitney, Ph.D. (Diana@positivechange.org), is president of Corporation for Positive Change and a distinguished consulting faculty at Saybrook Graduate School and Research Center. She is a social innovator and pioneer in the emerging field of positive organization change. She is a highly recognized international consultant, a sought-after leadership advisor and a frequently called upon keynote speaker on subjects related to Appreciative Inquiry and Large-Scale Organization and Community Transformation, Appreciative Leadership Development, and Spiritual Cultivation. In 2004, Diana received the Organization Development Network's Larry Porter Award for excellence in writing.

Where to Go for More Information

REFERENCES

Anderson, H., D. Cooperrider, K. Gergen, M. Gergen, S. McNamee, and D. Whitney. *The Appreciative Organization*. Chagrin Falls, OH: Taos Institute Publishing, 2000.

Cooperrider, D., and M. Avital, eds. *Advances in Appreciative Inquiry*. Oxford, UK: Elsevier Science, 2004.

Cooperrider, D., P. Sorenson, D. Whitney, and T. Yaeger. *Appreciative Inquiry: Rethinking Human Organization Toward a Positive Theory of Change*. Champaign, IL: Stipes Publishing, 2000.

Cooperrider, D., P. Sorenson, T. Yaeger, and D. Whitney, eds. *Appreciative Inquiry: An Emerging Direction for Organization Development*. Champaign, IL: Stipes Publishing, 2005.

Cooperrider, D., and D. Whitney. *Appreciative Inquiry: Collaborating for Change* (booklet). San Francisco: Berrett-Koehler Communications, 1999.

Cooperrider, D., D. Whitney, and J. Stavros. *Appreciative Inquiry Handbook*. Euclid, OH: Lakeshore Communications, 2003.

Fry, R. E., F. J. Barrett, J. Seiling, and D. Whitney. *Appreciative Inquiry and Organizational Transformation: Reports from the Field*. Westport, CT: Quorum Books, 2001.

Sampson, C., M. Abu-Nimer, C. Liebler, and D. Whitney, eds. *Positive Approaches to Peacebuidling*. Washington, DC: PACT Publications, 2004.

Srivastva, S., and D. Cooperrider et al., eds. *Appreciative Leadership and Management*. San Francisco: Jossey-Bass, 1990.

Whitney, D., and A. Trosten-Bloom. *The Power of Appreciative Inquiry*. San Francisco: Berrett-Koehler Communications, 2003.

Whitney, D., A. Trosten-Bloom, J. Cherney, and R. Fry. *Appreciative Team Building: Positive Questions to Bring Out the Best of Your Team*. Lincoln, NE: iUniverse, Inc., 2004.

Whitney, D., A. Trosten-Bloom, B. Kaplin, and D. Cooperrider. *The Encyclopedia of Positive Questions*. Euclid, OH: Lakeshore Communications, 2002.

ORGANIZATIONS

AI Commons—http://ai.cwru.edu
> *Articles, Sample Materials, Case Studies about AI*

Case Western Reserve University Weatherhead School of Management—www.cwru.edu
> *Graduate Studies, Research, and Executive Education*

Corporation for Positive Change—www.positivechange.org
> *Change Management Consultation, AI Certificate Program, Appreciative Leadership Development Program, and Keynote Speeches*

Taos Institute—www.taosinstitute.net
> *Conferences, Graduate Studies and Workshops*

OTHER RESOURCE

AI Practitioner (international AI newsletter)—www.aipractitioner.com

---

1. In 1999, GTE and Bell Atlantic merged, forming Verizon.

2. R. Fry, F. Barrett, J. Seiling, and D. Whitney, eds., *Appreciative Inquiry and Organizational Transformation: Reports from the Field* (Westport, CT: Quorum Books, 2002).

3. T. W. White, "Working in Interesting Times," in *Vital Speeches of the Day* 62, no. 15 (1996): 472–474.

4. Ibid.

5. B. M. Hubbard, *Conscious Evolution: Awakening the Power of our Social Potential* (Novato, CA: New Word Library, 1998).

6. G. R. Bushe, *Clear Leadership* (Palo Alto, CA: Davies-Black Publishing, 2001).

7. A. Chin, "Future Visions," *Journal of Organization and Change Management* (Spring 1998); M. Curran, "Appreciative Inquiry: A Third Wave Approach to O.D.," *Vision/Action* (December 1991): 12–14.

8. K. J. Gergen, *Realities and Relationships* (Cambridge, MA: Harvard University Press, 1994).

9. D. Whitney and A. Trosten-Bloom, *The Power of Appreciative Inquiry* (San Francisco: Berrett-Koehler Publishers, 2003), 18.

10. Ibid., 23–49. Chapter 2 provides an excellent overview of the "Forms of Engagement" for applying Appreciative Inquiry.

11. Ibid.

12. J. D. Ludema, D. Whitney, B. J. Mohr, and T. J. Griffin, *The Appreciative Inquiry Summit: A Practitioner's Guide for Leading Large-Group Change* (San Francisco: Berrett-Koehler Publishers, 2003).

13. D. L. Cooperrider, "Positive Image Positive Action: The Affirmative Basis of Organizing," in *Appreciative Management and Leadership*, edited by Rev. S. Srivastva and D. L. Cooperrider (Cleveland, OH: Williams Publishing Co., 1999), 91–125.

6

DICK AXELROD AND EMILY AXELROD

Collaborative Loops

You never change things by fighting the existing reality. To change something, build a new model that makes the existing model obsolete.

—Buckminster Fuller

Making a Difference at Fraser Health Authority

The Collaborative Loops process—an engagement-based approach to organizational change—is making a difference at Fraser Health Authority.

Fraser Health, located on the lower mainland of British Columbia, is responsible for the delivery of all publicly funded acute and community health-care services for the 1.5 million people who live in the largest and fastest growing health-care region in Canada. In practical terms, this means everything from public health issues like immunizations, to end-of-life issues like hospice. In 2001, three separate health-care regions were merged to form this 23,000-person organization, which includes hospitals, clinics, nearly 2,200 physicians, and community health facilities. Fraser works within an annual budget of $1.8 billion.

The Collaborative Loops process brings dissimilar project teams together in a workshop setting to develop their own change processes. Rather than relying on a set methodology, people are freed to develop their own strategies. By providing frameworks and principles, participants are then able to use their own experience to create more effective change. The teams share insights and provide feedback, stimulating innovation and learning. This in turn strengthens the bonds within and among the teams and dramatically improves the organization as a whole. Each team learns to create a Collaborative Loop using the four engagement principles: (1) widen the circle of involvement, (2) connect people to each other, (3) create communities for action, and (4) embrace democracy. How all this occurs is described later in the chapter, but first, let's learn about Fraser Health's experience.

Here is what Susan Good, managing consultant for Fraser Health, has to say:

People in health care experience constant change. Most change methodologies don't engage the people who have the direct knowledge or experience. The result: staff, managers, and physicians often report feeling devalued, disengaged. And we don't get the business results we want.

Engagement values people by honoring their knowledge and experience. People come to work to make a contribution. When they are directly involved in designing and implementing important organizational changes, they are energized and the outcomes are better.

When we create Collaborative Loops, we learn how to create our own change processes. In doing so, we tap into the wisdom of people in our system.[1] Here are examples of projects that were designed and implemented by Fraser Health:

- *Example 1:* The Child Health Initiative team originally thought their purpose was to establish a central place where services such as immunization, vision and hearing testing, and counseling could be provided. To the team, this meant constructing a building that would cost millions of dollars. However, the team came up with an entirely different idea based on feedback from other teams in their Collaborative Loop: Child health services would be provided by a mobile van that cost $150,000. This van would take health services out into the community.

  The team was able to let go of the building idea when they understood that their purpose was not to create a building but to provide health services to children. They got feedback from other teams in their Collaborative Loop that the building would probably go unused most of the time because it would be difficult for parents to bring their children. When the Child Health Initiative team focused on their purpose instead of the outcome, with the help of the other teams in the room, they developed the mobile van idea. Instead of spending millions, they spent thousands.

- *Example 2:* Teams across Fraser Health are using Collaborative Loops to reduce the time it takes to complete the hospital accreditation self-assessment process from six months to a matter of weeks. Accreditation is a bugaboo at any hospital. Everything grinds to a halt as teams work to provide the necessary documentation. The stakes are high: If an accrediting body takes away a hospital's accreditation, the hospital will have to close its doors.

  Normally done by small groups working independently, at Fraser Health, up to 80 participants provide feedback, rate effectiveness, and identify key actions/opportunities in a one-day Accreditation Conference. Key clinicians, physicians, and administrators are all in the same room working together. The results: decreased redundancy and duplication. Even though the self-assessment now involves more people, it takes less than a month, whereas before it took several months.

- *Example 3:* The first project at Fraser Health's Langley Hospital helped long-term care patients become more independent so successfully that Langley decided to implement projects in the maternity unit, licensed practical nurse interface, registered nurse care delivery model, and total hip replacement unit. In the hip replacement project, the length of stay for patients was reduced by 33 percent. Rhonda Veldhoen, a nurse and manager of health services, describes what happened this way:

> The change was amazing—the staff were so pleased to be part of the process. Previously, nurses, physical therapists, and other staff worked independently. It was the "not my job" syndrome. Now they work cooperatively. In the long-term care project, nurses learned that it wasn't just the physical therapist's job to walk the patient; if they were in the room, they could do it too. This results in more satisfying work for staff and shorter stays for the patients.

The Basics

The results in all these examples were achieved by applying three basic ideas (figure 1):

- *Basic Idea 1*—We hold a workshop with dissimilar project teams.
- *Basic Idea 2*—During the workshop, teams work together to create their own change process.
- *Basic Idea 3*—Organizational or community capacity builds when people learn principles rather than methods.

Basic Idea 1

Today, organizations and communities are implementing many changes simultaneously. They are improving their supply chains while installing a performance management system and incorporating lean thinking into the business. Communities are working to improve service delivery and upgrade their schools. These are not isolated events. The teams responsible for these changes need to understand how they impact one another.

Collaborative Loops brings multiple teams together in a workshop to learn how to design and implement their own change strategies. In most organizations, everyone has good intentions, but people work at cross-purposes. By bringing the network together, participants realize that they are bound together by a higher purpose: the overall success of the organization or community. In Fraser Health's case, this meant improved patient satisfaction.

When people interact with those who don't think the same way they do, new options are formed. When people see how others are working, they see what could be done differently in their own work. Everyone's work is enhanced in this creative environment.

Collaborative Loops

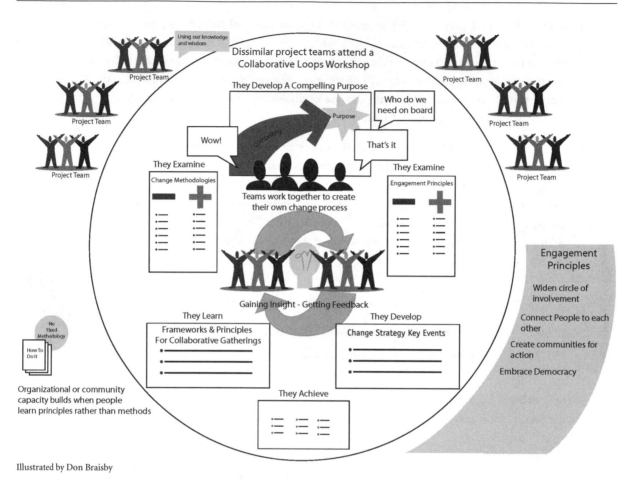

Illustrated by Don Braisby

Figure 1. Collaborative Loops

BASIC IDEA 2

During a typical workshop, teams will:

- Examine the upside and downside of current change methodologies
- Examine the upside and downside of using the engagement principles
- Create a compelling purpose for their work
- Identify whom to include
- Develop the key events that make up their change strategy
- Learn frameworks and principles for designing collaborative gatherings
- Design their first gathering

Let's sample what happens during a typical workshop by looking at how teams identify their purpose.

A Collaborative Loop has a meaningful purpose, but this is usually not the case in the beginning. Most teams responsible for bringing about change don't know what they want to accomplish. They *think* they know it, but when you ask them what they're trying to get done, you get different opinions.

Even if they have a purpose, the purpose they have is less than compelling to them. A nurse might say, "I want to make the emergency room experience more efficient." By exploring why that is important to her, the nurse may eventually realize: "It bothers me when I see patients sitting out there for hours, when we could take care of them sooner. I want patients to get the care they deserve. I want them to be treated with dignity and respect."

Discussions help teams become clearer about what they want to accomplish. Participants come to understand why their project is important to them and to their fellow team members. The nurse and everyone else in the group moves from a textbook understanding (making the emergency room more efficient) to a personal understanding of what needs to be done (giving patients the care they deserve).

In this workshop, in addition to working on the project, they provide feedback to others. People get so much value from having others look at and critique their work that they want to keep working together. One team might hear another team's purpose and say, "I don't even know what you are talking about." This helps them realize that they need to clarify their purpose.

People learn from others, even when they're working on parts of the organization that seem to have nothing to do with them. We advise them to copy ideas that they like and apply them to their own situation. It's not a one-way process where they're giving and not getting anything out of it.

BASIC IDEA 3

Dissimilar project teams come to a Collaborative Loops Workshop wanting to include people, but they don't know how. They want tools. The workshop provides the most practical tool we know—the engagement principles: widen the circle of involvement, connect people to each other, create communities for action, and embrace democracy.

The principles are guides, providing direction, focusing on what needs to be done. Principles are not prescriptions; they don't say what to do, rather, they help decide what to do. For example, say you wanted to build a room addition. If you were following a lighting methodology, the first step would be to open up your lighting handbook. You would look up the lighting standards for a 400-square-foot room and find out that you need a certain number of two-foot-square windows and standard light fixtures. In doing so, you would ignore other ways to make your room lighter, such as picture windows, skylights, mirrors, and bright paint.

If you follow a set methodology, you have only one way to light the room: two windows and one light fixture. If you use principles to guide your actions, many possibilities emerge.

While the engagement principles provide guidance for the overall change process, two other frameworks are needed: the "meeting canoe" and the "little e" engagement principles.

Collaborative Loops

Any change process includes a myriad of meetings, workshops, training sessions, and large group events. Each of these represents an opportunity to engage people in your change process. In Collaborative Loops workshops, people learn to design their own collaborative gatherings using the meeting canoe (figure 2).[2]

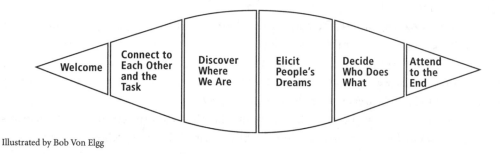

Illustrated by Bob Von Elgg

Figure 2. The Meeting Canoe

The meeting canoe's shape represents a discussion's progress from beginning to end. Conversations begin with a welcome and reach their widest point as participants discover the current state and dream of possibilities. They begin to narrow as decisions are made and the meeting is brought to a close.

The "little e" engagement principles help people decide what happens in each part of the meeting.

Principle	Example
Take time to connect before discussing content.	Ask people what interests them, what is important to them, and why they care.
Engage the whole person through sight, sound, and movement.	Having stand-up meetings or taking a walk shifts energy. Incorporate music and art; they stimulate ideas.
Make the whole visible.	Create a living map of your organization or process. You'll be surprised at what you learn.
Foster curiosity.	Take the opposite side of an issue. Instead of asking people how to make the project successful, ask them how they could make it fail.
Establish creative tension between the current reality and the future.	Create a mind map of current issues facing the organization. Ask people what they want to create in the future.
Take time to reflect.	Take a time-out, go for a walk, or sleep on an idea.
Ask for public commitments to create momentum.	Ask people what they would be willing to do in the next 30 days to move the process forward.

To summarize the basics, Collaborative Loops derive their power not just from the fact that people are able to design and implement successful change processes. They build Collaborative Loops between, among, and within the different project teams and with the people impacted by these changes. Most important, teams take what they learn and apply those lessons to new and different conditions.

Table of Uses

Typical Settings	Issues	Participants	Design and Implementation Examples
One company, one project Multiple project teams focus on a single goal	• Creating a workplace where people feel successful • Implementing a performance management system • Bringing alignment between various change initiatives within the organization	• Members of different project teams that support the overall goal • Up to 20 project teams with a maximum of 10 members per team	• Designed and implemented a series of large group events to deal with the impact of globalization • Designed and implemented the rollout of a global performance management system • Designed and implemented a new employee orientation process
One company, multiple projects (Fraser Health Authority) The different change efforts in the organization develop a change strategy together	• Improving patient satisfaction and safety • Implementing new information technology systems • Redesigning long-term care of mental patients	• Members of different project teams that are working on different change projects • Up to 20 project teams with a maximum of 10 members per team	• Large group events for the accreditation process • Involved employees in improving patient flow through the emergency room • Involved employees in standardizing nursing practices throughout the system
Multiple teams from the public and private sector Each organization sends a team with a specific change project	• Implementing a new call center for city government • Improving claims processing in an insurance company • Preparing students statewide for the twenty-first century	• Members of project teams come from different organizations • Up to 20 project teams, with a maximum of 10 members per team	• Involved key internal and external stakeholders in designing a new call center for city services • Involved school districts, private industry, students, teachers, and parents statewide, in creating a ten-year vision to meet the state's learning goals

How to Get Started

First, you need to arrange a meeting with the sponsors of the project teams you think would benefit from using Collaborative Loops. Typically, we like to work with projects that are in the beginning stages, but we can also work with projects that are already under way. During this meeting we provide an overview of Collaborative Loops and ask the sponsors to examine the upside and downside of participating. Experience shows that a number of sponsors are interested in moving forward.

Once sponsors agree, each clarifies his or her project's purpose, boundaries, and team composition. A robust group, representing different levels and functions and opinions works best.

Next, the sponsors need to meet with their teams and discuss their expectations for the work. Each team's job is to engage the organization in solving a problem. The change effort isn't to be created by some special group. Most teams don't understand this right away; they think their job is to solve the problem and then sell their solution to the organization. Don't worry if they don't get this right away; they will eventually.

Once the project teams have been identified, they attend a Collaborative Loops Workshop. During the workshop, two things happen: The project teams develop their strategy for engaging the organization in the work, and the project team network is built.

Roles and Responsibilities

Now that you know what you have to do in setting up the process, there is also work for the sponsors, participants, and the facilitators.

Good sponsors are active. It's more than meeting with the teams once and then forgetting about them. Periodic progress checks help make sure teams have the resources they need for success. Sponsors need to support the teams throughout the projects and let go when needed.

Sponsors should think about attending a Collaborative Loops Workshop with their teams. Why? Sponsors have ideas about what they want to happen, and those ideas may be essential parts of the plan. Certain information needs to be in the room.

Sponsors must be neither omnipresent nor among the missing. Leaders sometimes try to control a conversation to get the result they want. Other times, they don't want to overinfluence the group, so they don't say anything. When leaders go silent, people get nervous. Sponsors need to be able to give opinions without dictating. They must balance being available to the group and letting the group work on its own.

Participants have a special role in Collaborative Loops. Active participants—people willing to offer ideas, suggestions, and insights—matter. A few contrarians to stir the pot enrich the stew. People are not there just for themselves; they are also there for the network. Skepticism helps; when participants question the content, build on it using their experiences, and decide what is best for them and their organization, the projects succeed.

How do you find participants like this? One great way is to solicit volunteers. You may want to handpick some participants, but volunteers bring their own brand of energy. A combination of personally selected participants and volunteers usually works best. The participants should not expect to attend the workshop and then forget about it; they are required to implement the plans they develop.

Facilitators act as coaches supporting participants in transitioning from dependence on consultants to independence. Facilitators are there to give participants confidence in their own experiences and equip them to get where they want to go. The facilitator's job is not to do the work for participants or to make them fit into a prescribed methodology. In the end, the participants decide what needs to be done. Facilitators provide models, frameworks, experiences, and coaching, painting pictures of what's possible.

Facilitators strive to create an environment where people feel safe to do what they need to do. How do you create such a place? By working with *their* project; honoring *their* experiences. There's no sitting in judgment, no attempts to prove what fits and what doesn't. The goal is to help teams see possibilities that they don't see in themselves and then support them in achieving what they want to do.

Outside facilitators can't do this work alone; it takes assistance from people inside the organization who understand the engagement principles. Training internal people in the concepts, they can support teams during and after the workshop. If participants get in trouble, they know whom they can count on for support. They know that someone will coach them through a tough period. To this end, facilitators need to be available to the groups both during the workshop and on an as-needed basis.

This is a lot to think about; and it's important. No doubt it is clear by now that Collaborative Loops is something you don't use with trivial issues.

Conditions for Success

A meaningful purpose is critical. The work of the project team must matter. It must matter to the organization and to the team members. Team members must be able to articulate why this work is personally important to them not just to the organization.

Team composition is critical to success. You need a robust team made up people with diverse opinions, who have a stake in the outcome, and who possess the ability and authority to get things done.

Post-workshop support is important. After the workshop, a flurry of activity occurs as project teams begin to involve the organization in their work. Once they attend the workshop, your people will feel excited about the change effort, and if sponsors don't support them, they'll feel abandoned and betrayed.

This is an important point. Most leaders underestimate the excitement that is generated and are not prepared to support the teams. The teams that you send to the workshop will need time to meet and the resources to do their jobs.

Collaborative Loops requires courage. It's not enough to say you want people in the organization to be involved in Collaborative Loops or even just to fund the process. At times, the solutions the teams suggest will require taking a stand, like the chief executive officer who refused to pass on increasing health-care costs to employees. Rather, he engaged employees in addressing the issue and implemented their recommendations, such as paying for health screenings, implementing wellness plans, and hiring a nurse to answer employee questions—all of which significantly reduced health-care costs.

The Theoretical Basis for Collaborative Loops

How did all of this come about? Peter Block founded the School for Applied Leadership and asked us, along with Kathie Dannemiller, Meg Wheatley, Peter Koestenbaum, John Shuster, Jamie Schotier, and Cliff Bolster, to join him. The school's basis is to put the organization development skills of consultants in the hands of managers to bring together people from companies, government, and nonprofit organizations. We were teamed with Kathie Dannemiller to teach people how to do large group work.

We decided that the best way to equip people to do large group work was to teach them the underlying principles of what we did with our clients. For us, this meant teaching the engagement principles, which came out of the large group process we created, the Conference Model. What we saw over and over again in the School for Applied Leadership was that teams took these ideas and immediately applied them.

We started using what we learned in the School for Applied Leadership in different organizations. What we discovered about teaching others to create their own change processes eventually became Collaborative Loops.

Collaborative Loops are rooted in three constructs: open systems theory, adult learning theory, and democracy.

- *Open systems theory:* If you change one part of a system, you change the whole system. Living systems require feedback loops to maintain themselves. If you don't get feedback on how you're doing, you essentially die. These ideas play out in Collaborative Loops Workshops as teams give each other feedback. Different groups charged with making change do not operate in isolation. In the workshops, they provide each other feedback—outside information—to stimulate their thinking. This enables people to think differently and produces learning.

- *Adult learning theory:* Adults bring into a learning situation a whole host of experiences, something to be honored. Adults learn by doing, so they learn how to involve people by being involved themselves. Collaborative Loops Workshops are working sessions where people learn how to develop their change strategy by building it in real time. Workshop attendees often say, "Oh, you're doing with us what you want us to do with others." They get it.

- *Democracy:* We want to make change more democratic. Why? Because change becomes more legitimate when those impacted by it are included in its development and implementation.

For us, democracy is sharing information, involving others in decisions, and treating people fairly and equitably. It's a mind-set about the way we work with others. Democracy is always bounded. Without boundaries, there is chaos. Democracy includes rights, rules, and responsibilities. By bringing more people together, our goal is not to create anarchy of the mob; rather, it is to benefit the whole by using the wisdom of crowds.

Democracy is embedded in what Eric Trist and Fred Emery call "minimal critical specifications."[3] We provide people with some core ideas, simple guidelines, and say, "go for it." We don't do for them what they can do for themselves.

Many people discount democracy by taking it to the extreme: "Does democracy mean we have to vote on everything?" For us, democracy is not an all-or-nothing proposition. We ask, "What can we do to treat people better?" "Can we share more information than we did before?" "How can we widen the circle to include more people?" Democracy is not just about voting. It's bigger than that.

By now you must be asking yourself, "If I put all this time and energy into Collaborative Loops, how do I make sure the ideas get implemented?"

How Do I Sustain the Results?

It's actually easier than you think. People sustain the results because they are not looking after someone else's plan; they are implementing a plan that they developed. That is why you don't need elaborate follow-up systems.

People sustain the results because they now have skills to design their own change process. When they meet an unexpected bump in the road, they know how to design alternate routes.

People sustain the results because they know they have support. They are connected to the project leader and to internal resources. They created new relationships during the workshop that help them with their project and make daily work go more smoothly. Teams are not left to flounder. Support is available if they need it.

Learning fairs, initiated by people within the company, help sustain the results. The teams come back together and share what they have learned as they worked on their projects. In these settings, teams learn from each other, pick up ideas, and renew their commitment.

People sustain the results because the culture begins to shift. One of the ways the culture shifts is reflected in the way people talk. Instead of asking how to get people to "buy into our plan," they ask, "Whom do we need to engage to accomplish this?"

People sustain the results because they are successful. Their success is mutually reinforcing, so they want to do more.

Burning Question

In the back of the mind of everyone who participates in Collaborative Loops is this question: Is it worth my time? After all, the projects the participants work on aren't part of their regular job assignment.

What people find out is that their concerns are unfounded. They develop a plan. They have access to more resources. Their team has coalesced around a goal. They're working better together. They walk out feeling energized and supported. They walk out feeling their project isn't so overwhelming. They have a direction. They have new tools. They come in not knowing how or where to start, and they walk out knowing where they're going.

Final Comments

Most other change work involves a set design. With this process, the design is open and the principles are set. It's not that the other processes don't have principles. They do, but their principles guide you in following a set way of working. Here, the engagement principles guide you as you develop your own methodology.

Collaborative Loops is an open architecture. You could put ideas from Appreciative Inquiry, Future Search, or Open Space into Collaborative Loops and you wouldn't be violating anything. They would work.

Participants often say that what they learn in Collaborative Loops workshop is common sense. We agree. Harriet Beecher Stowe called common sense, "The knack of seeing things as they are and doing what ought to be done." Collaborative Loops workshops provide frameworks that enable people to organize what they know about change and use that knowledge to improve their organization or community.

About the Authors

Dick Axelrod (Dick@axelrodgroup.com) and *Emily Axelrod* (Emily@axelrodgroup.com) pioneered the use of large groups for change processes when they cocreated the Conference Model. Collaborative Loops extends this work, providing people with the principles and frameworks to create their own change processes. Dick authored *Terms of Engagement: Changing the Way We Change Organizations.* Dick and Emily, along with Julie Beedon and Robert Jacobs, coauthored *You Don't Have to Do It Alone: How to Involve Others to Get Things Done.*

Where to Go for More Information

REFERENCES

Axelrod, Richard. *Terms of Engagement: Changing the Way We Change Organizations.* San Francisco: Berrett-Koehler, 2000.

———. "Why Change Management Needs Changing." *Reflections* 2, no. 3 (2001): 46–57.

Axelrod, Richard, and Emily Axelrod. *The Conference Model.* San Francisco: Berrett-Koehler, 2000.

Axelrod, Richard, Emily Axelrod, Julie Beedon, and Robert Jacobs. *You Don't Have to Do It Alone: How to Involve Others to Get Things Done.* San Francisco: Berrett-Koehler, 2004.

Beer, M., R. A. Eisenstat, and B. Spector. "Why Change Programs Don't Produce Change." *Harvard Business Review* 68 (November/December 1990): 158–166.

McCormick, M. T. "The Impact of Large-Scale Participative Interventions on Participants." Ph.D. dissertation, UMI Dissertation Services, Ann Arbor, MI, 1999.

Passmore, W. A., and M. R. Faganz. "Participation, Individual Development, and Organizational Change: A Review and Synthesis." *Journal of Management* 18 (1992): 375–397.

Senge, P., A. Kleiner, and C. Roberts, et al. *The Dance of Change: The Challenges to Sustaining Momentum in Learning Organizations.* New York: Currency Doubleday, 1999, 319–334.

INFLUENTIAL SOURCES

Bertalanffy, L. von. *General Systems Theory.* New York: Braziller, 1969.

Block, Peter. *Stewardship: Choosing Service over Self-Interest.* San Francisco: Berrett Koehler, 1993.

Emery, Fred E., and Eric L. Trist. *Toward a Social Ecology.* New York: Plenum, 1973.

Knowles, M. *The Modern Practice of Adult Education.* New York: Cambridge, The Adult Education Company, 1980.

Weisbord, Marvin, and Sandra Janoff. *Future Search: An Action Guide to Finding Common Ground in Organizations and Community.* San Francisco: Berrett-Koehler, 1995.

ORGANIZATIONS

The Axelrod Group—www.axelrodgroup.com

The Learning Consortium—www.tlc-usa.com

OTHER RESOURCES

E-learning program, *How to Make Collaboration Work*—http://axelrodgroup.com/training.shtml

The Collaborative Systems Reader newsletter—http://axelrodgroup.com/newsletter.shtml

1. Susan Good (managing consultant, Fraser Health), interview by authors, November 2005.

2. R. H. Axelrod, Emily M. Axelrod, J. Beedon, and R. W. Jacobs, *You Don't Have to Do It Alone: How to Involve Others to Get Things Done* (San Francisco: Berrett-Koehler, 2004).

3. Eric Trist, "The Evolution of Socio-technical Systems: A Conceptual Framework and Action Research Program," occasional paper, Quality of Working Life Centre, Toronto, Ontario.

Collaborative Loops

7

SANDY HEIERBACHER

Dialogue and Deliberation

All great changes begin in conversation.
—Juanita Brown

Annual Diversity Celebrations

Waterloo, Iowa, a city with a predominantly white population, experienced an influx of Hispanics, Bosnians, and other immigrants in the late 1990s, creating tensions over housing, jobs, social services, and health care. The City of Waterloo Commission on Human Rights, in partnership with the Cedar Valley Diversity Appreciation Team, responded by organizing community-wide "study circles"—multiple small-group dialogues held in different places throughout the community that culminate in collective action based on common ground. Since 1998, more than 2,000 adults and 600 youths have taken part in study circles on racism and race relations, police-community relations, and prevention of youth violence.

Among other things, Waterloo's community dialogue effort has led to annual diversity celebrations that help decrease stereotyping of ethnic groups and neighborhoods, improved cultural competence skills of Waterloo police officers, and increased awareness among teachers and public school administrators of the impact of race on teaching methods and student achievement.

The Basics

Dialogue and deliberation are dynamic processes that can build and strengthen relationships, bridge gaps, resolve conflicts, generate innovative solutions to problems, inspire collaborative action, and more.

Dialogue and deliberation processes provide a plethora of opportunities for people to become more fully engaged in the decision making that takes place in their workplaces, neighborhoods, communities, and increasingly at the national and international levels. The active engagement of people at all levels of a corporation is the backbone of a resilient, successful business, just as the active participation of many people across society is the backbone of a strong democracy.

Dialogue allows people, usually in small groups, to share their perspectives and experiences about difficult issues. It is not about judging, weighing, or making decisions, but about understanding and learning. Dialogue dispels stereotypes, builds trust, and enables people to open to perspectives that are very different from their own.

Deliberation is a related process with a different emphasis; it promotes the use of critical reasoning and logical argument in group decision making. Instead of decision making by power, coercion, or hierarchy, deliberative decision making emphasizes the importance of examining all sides of an issue fairly, collecting and considering the relevant facts, and carefully weighing the pros and cons of various options.

When choices, decisions, or recommendations need to be made, dialogue can lay the foundation for the vital work of deliberation. Engaging in dialogue before deliberation helps ensure that members of a group are open to others' opinions and perspectives, even when they conflict with their own. This leads to a more open and thorough examination of all possible outcomes, resulting in better decision making.

Retaining many of the principles of dialogue throughout the deliberation process also helps ensure that everyone can participate fully and effectively. Establishing ground rules, emphasizing listening, utilizing trained facilitators, encouraging reflection on personal experiences and perspectives—all of these dialogue techniques help ensure that everyone has a real voice.

Another well-known process for grappling with diverse viewpoints is debate. Comparing dialogue and deliberation with debate outlines the interpersonal and political differences between these processes (table 1).[1]

Dialogue and deliberation are increasingly utilized in schools, corporations, government agencies, and communities across the globe to tackle issues and conflicts in new ways that enable people to share power with one another and with community and organizational leaders, instead of ways that leave people feeling overpowered and frustrated; in ways that welcome and validate all perspectives on an issue rather than hearing, once again, from only the most vocal and powerful parties.

People use dialogic and deliberative techniques for public issues ranging from community race relations and school violence to handling nuclear waste buildup or rapid regional development, as well as for conflicts between groups, changes in a workplace, or personal struggles with crises. In organizations, these approaches have been used to address labor-management conflicts and issues crossing organizational boundaries, to explore opportunities in new markets, and in improving relations with key suppliers or customers.

Dialogue and deliberation techniques range from intimate, small-group dialogues to large

Dialogue and Deliberation

Dialogue and Deliberation	Debate
Finding common ground is the goal	Winning is the goal
Participants listen to increase understanding and find meaning	Participants listen to find flaws
Participants are open to being wrong, and open to change	Participants are determined to be right
Participant's point of view is enlarged and possibly changed	Participant's point of view is affirmed
The atmosphere is one of safety; facilitators propose, get agreement on, and enforce clear ground rules to enhance safety and promote respectful exchange	The atmosphere is threatening; attacks and interruptions are expected by participants and are usually permitted by moderators
Assumptions are revealed for reevaluation	Assumptions are defended as truth
There is the possibility of reaching a better solution than any existing solutions	One's own positions are defended as the best solution; other solutions are excluded, and new solutions are not considered
Hold that many people have pieces of the answer and that together they can put them into a workable solution	Holds that there is a right answer and that someone has it

Table 1. Dialogue and Deliberation Versus Debate

televised forums involving hundreds or thousands of participants. A deliberative forum may last two hours, while a sustained dialogue effort can span years. Evolving communication technologies are increasingly used to overcome traditional barriers of scale, geography, and time.

The steps in a dialogic or deliberative program vary greatly depending on the purpose of the program, the process used, and the resources available. Typical steps using *both* dialogue and deliberation include:

PREP WORK

Get to know the issue, the affected stakeholders, and the participants. Prepare participants by providing background materials, issue guides presenting diverse viewpoints, and details on the process.

INTRODUCTIONS

During the event, facilitators introduce themselves and the process. Participants feel welcomed and appreciated, having been prepared for what's ahead.

Establish/Present Ground Rules

Also known as "agreements," ground rules are the backbone of most dialogue and deliberation processes. Ground rules such as "listen carefully and with respect," "one person speaks at a time," and "seek to understand rather than persuade" create a safe space for people with different views and experiences. Adhering to ground rules that foster civility, honesty, and respect is what makes dialogue different from adversarial debate and back-and-forth discussion.

Share Personal Stories and Perspectives

Hearing from everyone at the table is a key principle in both dialogue and deliberation. Dialogue begins by hearing each participant's personal stories and perspectives on the issue, asking "How has this issue affected your life?" rather than "What do you think should be done about this issue?" Stories open people to each other's humanity, engendering trust, establishing a sense of equality, and enabling them to consider the issue from perspectives other than their own. This is especially important when participants have different knowledge or experience with the issue, or when some participants are not comfortable talking about contentious issues in "mixed company."

Explore a Range of Views

Exploring a balanced range of viewpoints is vital in dialogue and deliberation. In groups without a variety of perspectives on an issue, issue guides presenting three or four divergent views are sometimes used so that participants can explore and critique the primary viewpoints—even those unpopular with the entire group. This step prepares them to answer, "Where is the common ground?" and "What should we do about this?"

Analysis and Reasoned Argument

Deliberation is characterized by critical listening, reasoned argumentation, and thoughtful decision making. David Mathews, president of the Kettering Foundation, says that "Deliberations aren't just discussions to promote better understanding. They are the way we make the decisions that allow us to act together. People are challenged to face the unpleasant costs and consequences of various options and to 'work through' the often volatile emotions that are a part of making public decisions." The previous steps lay the groundwork for this difficult step.

Decide on Action Steps or Recommendations

If a dialogue and deliberation process does not transition to action of some kind, participants may feel unsatisfied and frustrated. Participants want to understand how their work makes an impact—or how they can make an impact themselves. The process and purpose shape the form that actions take. Holding more dialogue groups in their workplace or community, making policy recommendations to a chief executive officer or an elected official, and self-organizing to implement their solutions are examples (figure 1).

Illustration by Christine Valenza

Figure 1. The Path to Wiser Group Decisions

These steps support participants in creating the collective wisdom essential for sound, achievable decisions and policies, and the common ground essential for effective, sustainable action.

Table of Uses

Dialogue and deliberation are flexible processes serving a variety of purposes. They can resolve conflicts; influence policy; empower organization or community members to solve a problem; encourage healing after a crime, a crisis, or a layoff; or simply increase awareness of an issue.

Identified by experts in the field, four main "dialogue and deliberation streams"—or ways of utilizing these processes—fulfill four distinct purposes (tables 2 and 3).

Dialogue and Deliberation Stream	Intention/Purpose	Key Features	Important When . . .	Examples of Issues
Exploration	To encourage people and groups to learn more about themselves, their organization or community, or an issue, and discover innovative solutions	Suspending assumptions, creating a space that encourages a different kind of conversation, using ritual and symbolism to encourage openness, emphasize listening	A group or community seems stuck or muddled and needs to reflect on their circumstance in depth and gain collective insight	Strengthening democracy, planning for the future, understanding a community of practice, transforming an organization's culture
Conflict Transformation	To resolve conflicts, to foster personal healing and growth, and to improve relations among groups	Creating a safe space, hearing from everyone, building trust, sharing personal stories and views	Relationships among participants are poor or need to be established. Issues can only be resolved when people change their behavior or attitude, expand their perspective, or take time to reflect and heal	Political polarization, crossing organizational silos, race relations, value based conflicts, healing after crises or trauma
Decision Making	To influence decisions and policy, and to improve public knowledge	Naming and framing, weighing all options, considering different positions (deliberation), revealing common values, brainstorming solutions	The issue is within a single entity's sphere of influence	Budgeting, land use, health care, social security
Collaborative Action	To empower people and groups to solve complicated problems and take responsibility for the solution	Using D&D to generate ideas for organizational or community action, developing and implementing action plans collaboratively	The issue/dispute requires intervention across multiple entities, and anytime collective action is important	Regional sprawl, institutional racism, youth violence, responding to crises, bringing new products to market

Table 2. Dialogue and Deliberation Streams Based on Organizer's Purpose

Dialogue and Deliberation

Exploration	Personal and Group Transformation	Working Through the Issues	Collaborative Action
• Bohmian Dialogue • Conversation Café • Council process • Open Space • World Café	• Public Conversations, Project dialogues • Sustained Dialogue • Victim-Offender Mediation • Web Lab's Small-Group Dialogue	• 21st Century Town Meeting • Citizen Juries • Consensus Conference • Deliberative Polling • National Issues Forums	• Appreciative Inquiry • Future Search • Study Circles

Table 3. Frequently Used Dialogue and Deliberation Methodologies in Each of the Streams

Getting Started

Because dialogue and deliberation programs are used for a variety of reasons, their organization varies greatly. The basic steps for organizing and convening such a program appear in figure 2.

Here are some guiding principles to consider when organizing any dialogue or deliberation program:

INCORPORATION INTO A LARGER ENGAGEMENT EFFORT

Dialogue and deliberation are powerful forms of engagement that motivate participants to stay more informed on issues of concern and increase a sense of connection, even to those with views and experiences different from their own. Isolated dialogue and deliberation processes can make an impact, but are most effective when they are part of a larger engagement effort.

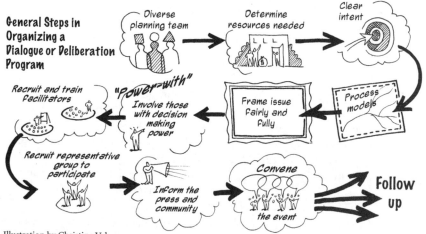

Illustration by Christine Valenza

Figure 2. General Steps in Organizing a Dialogue and Deliberation Program

Dialogue and Deliberation

What is the relationship between the community (or organization, region, nation, etc.) and the topic? What is the culture in terms of engagement in general? Are groups already trying to address this issue? Are others considering dialogue as a way to resolve this conflict? Are there groups or leaders who have supported dialogue or deliberation in the past?

INCLUSIVITY

Effectiveness increases when those with different backgrounds, ethnicities, positions, abilities, education levels, and ages are involved. When planning, recruiting participants and facilitators, and developing background materials—during the program and when following up—inclusivity is a guiding principle.

OPENNESS TO AN UNKNOWN OUTCOME

Setting an intention—improving productivity in an organization, or improving relationships or policy in a community—focuses the work, but defining specific outcomes hinders creative possibilities and sets the process up for failure. Trust that the process enables the participants to reach the best outcome for their organization or community.

COLLABORATION

People are more invested when they participate. Work as collaboratively as possible at all stages of the planning.

TRANSPARENCY

To trust what's happening, people need to see how it works. If labor representatives don't have visibility into the corporation's profit and loss drivers, they may suspect that something is being hidden, and withdraw from the dialogue sessions. If participants do not know who is revamping a state's health-care system, they may suspect that powerful stakeholders (e.g., pharmaceutical companies) are behind the initiative, and distrust its intentions. Open and accessible flow of information about how decisions are made, who is involved, how the process works, and what happens with the results is vital.

Roles, Responsibilities, and Relationships

Dialogue and deliberation programs can be initiated by schools, corporate executives, newspapers, community groups, government officials, activists, student leaders, and others. The key is for the initiating person or group—before going public or making important decisions—to build a diverse coalition representing key positions or groups related to the issue.

Commitment from planning group members is key, especially from those with ties to traditionally underrepresented groups and those with power in the community or organization. Tapping connections to ensure that all groups have a voice and preparing those in power to participate with mutual respect is part of the work.

Trained facilitators are almost always key in a successful dialogue or deliberation program. Although simple, small-group dialogues in coffee shops may require just an hour of phone training, other formats may require a weeklong training or facilitators with substantial experience. A single facilitator may be required for a sustained living room dialogue group on Jewish-Muslim relations, while dozens of facilitators may be needed for an organization-wide dialogue on strategic planning, and hundreds may be recruited for a daylong deliberative event to transform a city's health-care system.

The facilitation role varies greatly depending on the program's purpose and the methodology used. Facilitators may simply keep people on track—making sure participants understand what's happening, keeping the conversation flowing, and ensuring that people's needs are met. More often, facilitators also remind people of the ground rules—when an individual dominates the conversation, for instance. Often, they attend to participants' body language and subtle emotional expressions, to who is and is not speaking, and to emerging themes and areas of agreement in the discussion.

When a dialogue addresses a charged issue, facilitators sometimes reflect the main points back to participants so that the speakers feel heard and understood, and other participants hear the same content from a more neutral (less angry, etc.) voice. The skills for such mentally demanding tasks require adequate training, preparation, and support.

The role of participants also depends on multiple factors. Sometimes they attend meetings or read background materials before the event. They may participate in surveys or polls both before and after a deliberative process. They may rotate facilitation or just come in from the street and rest while talking to a few people about an issue of common concern.

All participants adapt to a new process that may not seem natural at first. They are encouraged to take risks and speak honestly and openly to people they may not know. They are also expected to develop skills in expressing themselves and listening to others in a respectful, civil manner about issues usually argued or debated.

Participants may also be expected to commit to changing their behavior based on what they learned, or they may be encouraged to take responsibility for part of a collaborative change strategy. They may be expected to consider unfamiliar viewpoints in an open, empathetic way, or a logical, thorough way, and they may be asked to make choices based both on values and reasoning.

Conditions for Success

Since dialogue and deliberation processes help people learn more about themselves or an issue (Exploration), resolve conflicts and improve relations among groups (Conflict Transformation), improve knowledge and influence policy (Decision Making), and empower people to solve complicated problems together (Collaborative Action), the keys to success differ based on purpose.

If a deliberative process is helping participants set priorities for their organization or town's budget, for instance, then the managers or elected officials who approve the budget must commit to acting on its outcomes. If a series of dialogues are planned in a workplace to encourage people to talk about issues of mutual concern, involving those in power is less important to success.

There are several conditions for beginning any dialogue or deliberation process:

ADEQUATE TIME TO DO THE PROCESS JUSTICE

Although some processes require just a single two-hour session, most complex issues require multiple meetings over several days—especially if resolving long-standing conflicts or taking action is involved. Match participant, organizer, leader, and decision maker expectations for outcome with a realistic time frame, and be sure participants know what they are committing to ahead of time.

THE LINK TO ACTION AND CHANGE IS CLEAR FROM THE START

Regardless of the program's intent, people should be prepared for how their participation may change things, or change them. Will they influence policy, increase their knowledge, change how they view people different from themselves, take action on the issue? Different processes produce different outcomes, and participants should be told ahead of time what kind of outcome to expect.

ADEQUATE RESOURCES ARE AVAILABLE

Organizations may have lofty goals and enormous passion and energy, but if the resources are not available, their project is at risk. Consider the resources needed before investing in a project. Will you need to rent space or high-tech communication equipment? Will you need to pay or train facilitators? Will you need to pay a consultant, a coordinator, or other staff? Do participants need child care, food, translation equipment, or even transportation? How will you publicize your program, develop and print materials, or support action outcomes?

THE ISSUE IS TIMELY

If an organization is considering entering a new market in the next fiscal year, timeliness means that employees are engaged with plenty of time to impact the decision. On the other hand, a dialogue in October 2005 that is focused on improving race relations should not embrace a theme of "The Aftermath of Rodney King" or "Deconstructing the O. J. Simpson Trial." What is in the hearts and minds of people now? A timely issue helps get people in the door, enlivens the conversation, and increases the likelihood of personal or collective action.

THE PROCESS IS ORGANIZED BY A NEUTRAL PARTY

Ensuring that participants, decision makers, and other stakeholders trust the dialogue or deliberation process is an important but difficult task. Establishing a diverse planning group that shares power helps. If a known environmental activist wants to spearhead a community-wide dialogue on conserving her town's natural resources, for instance, working side by side with loggers and corporations serves the project well.

PARTICIPANTS' NEEDS AND CONCERNS ARE AT THE FOREFRONT

Finally, keep one question in the forefront: "What's in it for the participants?" No matter how important the issue, how impressive the process, and how many human and financial resources are available, people simply will not show up if their hopes and concerns are not addressed.

Theoretical Basis

Although dialogue and deliberation processes are currently enjoying a renaissance and many new techniques have been developed recently, dialogic communication has been used for information sharing and decision making in indigenous cultures for centuries. Deliberation originated when the ability to consider different options rationally developed.

DIALOGUE SCHOLARSHIP

Four prominent scholars impacted dialogue in its current form: Martin Buber (1878–1965), Mikhail Bakhtin (1895–1975), David Bohm (1917–1992), and Paulo Freire (1921–1997).

Martin Buber was a Viennese Jewish philosopher and religious leader whose philosophy of dialogue emphasizes the importance of relationships. Buber held that genuine dialogue is an essential building block of community. The "I-Thou" perspective one has during genuine dialogue—viewing others as people similar to and closely related to ourselves rather than as objects or the means for achieving goals—enables people to achieve a meaningful connection, allowing them to both change the other and be changed by the dialogue.

Russian philosopher Mikhail Bakhtin's theory of "dialogism" emphasized the power of discourse to increase understanding of multiple perspectives and create myriad possibilities. Bakhtin held that relationships and connections exist among all living beings, and that dialogue creates a new understanding of a situation that demands change.

Celebrated Brazilian educationalist Paolo Freire, who is known for his impact in the development of popular education, advanced dialogue as a type of classroom pedagogy. Freire held that dialogic communication allowed students and teachers to learn from one another in an environment characterized by respect and equality. A great advocate for oppressed peoples, Freire was concerned with praxis—action that is informed and linked to people's values. Dialogic pedagogy was not only about deepening understanding; it was also about making positive changes in the world.

The thoughtful experiments of renowned physicist David Bohm sparked the beginnings of a movement toward more dialogic communication and decision making in organizations and businesses. Drawing from quantum physics and the theory of relativity, Bohm posits that individual knowledge is based on limited experiences and assumptions, and that only through dialogue—gaining an understanding of all of the different parts of an issue—can one begin to see the whole picture. Bohm practiced dialogue without facilitation or fixed topics, emphasizing deep inquiry, suspended assumptions, and collective intelligence. Bohmian Dialogue took off when Peter Senge praised Bohm's dialogues as a powerful tool for "learning organizations" in his organization development tome *The Fifth Discipline.*

DELIBERATION SCHOLARSHIP

Although the practice has waxed and waned even in recent history, the ideal of a "deliberative democracy"—that public policy decisions are reached through informed discussion among citizens—has been a basic tenet of democracy since its inception in fifth-century Athens.

Today's emphasis on public deliberation in governance is often traced to two scholars who both advocated for deliberative democracy about 40 years ago, Jurgen Habermas (1929–) and John Rawls (1921–). Habermas advanced the idea of a public world built upon mutual communication and reason. Habermas's concept of "communicative action" emphasizes utilizing all the ways humans think and use language to understand one another and plan for common action.

With his seminal book, *A Theory of Justice,* Rawls revived the idea of basing political thinking and action on moral argument. He held that the moral judgment of ordinary people is essential for good political deliberation. He supported the practice of providing the public with clearly articulated alternative views and options so that people could couple rigorous thinking with personal values to make wise choices.

The current focus on participatory governance arose after decades of devolution and decentralization of policy making and planning from the federal to state and local levels. The burden on communities to tackle contentious, complex social problems and policy issues has grown exponentially, and dialogue and deliberation processes are increasingly recognized by scholars, public officials, and community leaders as effective in addressing these "wicked problems" while strengthening the capacity for future problem solving and decision making.

Public deliberation is a cornerstone of democratic governance, and deliberative practice has long been a subject of scholarly research. A variety of present-day scholars—social capitalists, community developers, public administration theorists, ecologists, and political scientists—support the premise that a new movement toward increased citizen involvement in governance is evolving. They hold that efforts increasing dialogue, deliberation, and collaboration are increasing civic capacity in the United States and abroad; civic capacity that is required when communities take change efforts into their own hands.

These scholars are not alone in paving the way for today's practice of dialogue and deliberation. President Clinton's Dialogue on Race initiative in the late 1990s emphasized the importance of emotional as well as intellectual work—especially when addressing issues of inequality. The pioneering efforts of intergroup dialogue educators have brought social justice education into college classrooms across the country. Experiments in community engagement conducted over the years by organizations like the Study Circles Resource Center, the Kettering Foundation, the Center for Deliberative Polling, and America*Speaks* have exposed thousands of people to the power of deliberative dialogue. Government agencies have instituted policies ensuring public input is factored into their decision-making processes. The implications of recent technological innovations that enable people to talk openly, weigh options carefully, and make decisions together online are just beginning to be explored.

Sustaining the Results

Several strategies can ensure that the benefits of a dialogue or deliberation program are retained.

Sustain the Dialogue

While a single group may meet five or six times and agree to act together, the opportunity for many more groups to experience the process amplifies its effect. Even if hundreds of people participate in a single dialogue and deliberation process addressing racism in their community and transitioning from talk to collaborative community action, racism will not be eradicated. The community can benefit significantly from more dialogue, deliberation, and action.

One way to sustain dialogue is to continually engage on issues of concern. An organization may choose to host a monthly labor-management Bohmian dialogue open to all employees. A public engagement consortium in a metropolitan area may organize Conversation Cafés on political polarization in their city one year, National Issues Forums on health care the following year, and Study Circles on urban development the year after that. The more people become part of the decision-making process, the more they increase their collective capacity to solve their problems, fostering a sense of pride and connection to their organization or community.

Sustain the Action

When a dialogue or deliberation program generates collaborative action, time and resources devoted to supporting action teams and task forces is best included in the planning. Encouragement, support, and advice, as well as fundraising and public relations all support outcomes.

Follow Up on Decisions and Recommendations

For deliberative processes presenting recommendations or consensus decisions to power holders, periodic follow-up with decision makers helps ensure those recommendations were used. Publicizing the recommendations widely increases the pressure for utilizing the results. The benefit to leadership is recognition for taking people seriously. Ensuring participants feel that their time was well spent increases the likelihood that they and others will participate in the future.

Burning Question

One common challenge of dialogue and deliberation programs is ensuring that participants represent the community or organization and the issue being addressed. Convenors must constantly ask themselves, "Who's missing?" and "How can we get them involved?"

Given the barriers that often exist in organizations among departments or functions, across levels of the hierarchy, or between labor and management, and given the deep divides in communities along the lines of race, education, political ideology, religion, economic status, and more, it is nearly impossible for a homogenous planning group to gain the trust and buy-in needed for success.

Reflecting the roles and demographics in your community—race, age, gender, spoken languages, income and education level, political ideology, religion—ensures that, in a way, the entire community is in the room, and that everyone's voice will be welcomed and heard. It also ensures that participants will hear a range of perspectives and learn from the variety of experiences about the issue.

Thinking about who's missing in terms of the issue is also vital. For educational issues, recruit students, teachers, administrators, parents, and community members not directly involved in education. Think about the different viewpoints on the issue, making sure all "sides" are present.

The most important strategy for ensuring representativeness is establishing a diverse planning group, paying special attention to groups whose voices tend not to be heard. Planning group members do not need to be prominent leaders, but they should be people who are respected and well known.

Some Final Comments

To understand dialogue and deliberation, it is useful to distinguish them from debate, advocacy, and mediation. Table 1 contrasted debate with dialogue and deliberation. These processes also differ from advocacy and mediation.

DIALOGUE AND DELIBERATION VERSUS ADVOCACY

When there is a clear outcome in mind from a process, advocating for a position may be more appropriate than engaging people in dialogue and deliberation. Advocacy focuses on a particular goal, while dialogue and deliberation cannot guarantee that participants will come to a particular conclusion.

An activist whose goal is to shut down a nuclear power plant, for example, may find that participants in a dialogue agree on ways to make the plant safer, rather than taking an action that does not meet the needs of the workers at the plant. A common ground solution may not satisfy someone wedded to a specific outcome.

Although dialogue and deliberation can be used among homogenous groups to strengthen relationships and develop action plans, their real power lies in bringing people with divergent views together to learn from each other and find solutions that work for everyone.

DIALOGUE AND DELIBERATION VERSUS MEDIATION AND NEGOTIATION

Mediation is a conflict resolution process in which a neutral third party helps disputants reach an agreement, settlement, or change in relationship. Negotiation can take place with or without a third party. It is characterized by give and take between disputants in a conflict, and leads to agreements often based on compromise.

Dialogue differs from mediation and negotiation in several ways. Dialogue transforms conflicts and is often open-ended, focused more on increasing understanding and developing relationships than on reaching a solution. Dialogue also tends to occur among groups whose conflict is widespread and not specific only to those in the room (e.g., labor-management relations in an organization versus a conflict over a specific grievance, or poor race relations in a community versus a tenant-landlord dispute over parking). Because of this, if a dialogue process leads to action, it is usually focused on fostering change outside of the group as much as on the group members themselves.

A common misconception about dialogue and deliberation is that these processes are "just talk"—that no real action comes from sitting around and being nice to everyone around you. In reality, dialogue and deliberation are powerful processes that mend long-standing conflicts, harness people's collective wisdom, generate innovative solutions to intractable problems, and inspire people to act. Dialogue and deliberation enable people to take action in ways that are informed and effective.

About the Author

Sandy Heierbacher (sandy@thataway.org) is the Director of the National Coalition for Dialogue & Deliberation (NCDD), which brings together those who actively practice, promote, and study dialogue and deliberation. NCDD is a vibrant network of more than 500 people and groups who, collectively, regularly engage and mobilize millions of people across the globe around today's critical issues. NCDD's resource-rich Web site and biennial national conferences are popular hubs for dialogue and deliberation leaders.

Where to Go for More Information

REFERENCES

Atlee, Tom. *The Tao of Democracy.* Cranston, RI: The Writer's Collective, 2003.

Bohm, David. *On Dialogue.* Edited by Lee Nichol. New York: Routledge, 1996.

Constructive Conversations for Challenging Times: A Guide for Home and Community Dialogue. Watertown, MA: Public Conversations Project, 2001.

Constructive Engagement Resource Guide: Practical Advice for Dialogue among Facilities, Workers, Communities, and Regulators. Environmental Protection Agency's Office of Pollution Prevention and Toxics. www.epa.gov/publicinvolvement/pdf/resolve2.pdf.

Ellinor, Linda, and Glenna Gerard. *Dialogue: Rediscover the Transforming Power of Conversation.* New York: John Wiley & Sons, 1998.

Gastil, John, and Peter Levine. *The Deliberative Democracy Handbook: Strategies for Effective Civic Engagement in the 21st Century.* San Francisco: Jossey-Bass, 2005.

Korza, Pam, Barbara Schaeffer Bacon, and Andrea Assaf. *Civic Dialogue, Arts & Culture: Findings from Animating Democracy.* Washington, DC: Americans for the Arts, 2005.

Mathews, David, and Noelle McAfee. *Making Choices Together: The Power of Public Deliberation.* Dayton, OH: Kettering Foundation, 2000.

McCoy, Martha L., and Patrick L. Scully. "Deliberative Dialogue to Expand Civic Engagement: What Kind of Talk Does Democracy Need?" *National Civic Review* 91, no. 2 (Summer 2002).

Saunders, Harold. *A Public Peace Process: Sustained Dialogue to Transform Racial and Ethnic Conflicts.* New York: Palgrave, 1999.

Schoem, David, and Sylvia Hurtado, eds. *Intergroup Dialogue: Deliberative Democracy in School, College, Community and Workplace.* Ann Arbor: University of Michigan Press, 2001.

Yankelovich, Daniel. *The Magic of Dialogue: Transforming Conflict into Cooperation.* New York: Simon & Schuster, 1999.

ORGANIZATIONS

The Co-Intelligence Institute—www.co-intelligence.org

The National Coalition for Dialogue & Deliberation—www.thataway.org

---

1. Table adapted from a paper by Shelley Berman, based on discussions of the Dialogue Group of the Boston Chapter of Educators for Social Responsibility (ESR), and from the Public Conversations Project's much-used "Distinguishing Debate from Dialogue" table.

Dialogue and Deliberation

8

MARIE MIYASHIRO AND MARSHALL ROSENBERG

Integrated Clarity
Energizing How We Talk and What We Talk About in Organizations

> Change *is situational. . . . Transition* is the psychological process people go through to come to terms with the new situation. Change is external, transition is internal.
>
> —William Bridges

Meeting the Needs of Both the People and the Organization

Lovers do it. Families do it. Now organizations and communities are doing it, too, with surprising results. Talking about needs, that is.

Dr. Michael Shafer can testify to that. "We definitely gave voice to our organization needs, creating a palpable cohesion among our team. What we learned about our direction, strengths and challenges served to create our blueprint for the future."

Shafer is founder and executive director of Applied Behavioral Health Policy (ABHP), a team of 27 researchers, evaluators, and trainers at the University of Arizona.[1] An entrepreneurial group, ABHP has raised more than $21 million in grants and contracts since its founding in 1990. Its mission: the treatment of psychiatric and substance abuse disorders.

By the winter of 2004, ABHP's regional reputation had blossomed into national recognition. It is a vital resource for policy makers and behavioral health professionals, as well as community and government agencies. ABHP's heightened recognition, along with forecasts of greater demands for services, led to a sudden boom in workload and number of employees. Just when it needed razor-sharp focus and efficiency the most, it experienced internal communication glitches and lowered morale.

Shafer observed, "Internally, we all wanted to be more efficient with our operations, more productive with our communication. As we grew, our sense of cohesion as a team and our shared values were slipping. The top-down remedies management was implementing seemed to create more of the symptoms we were trying to avoid. We decided to focus on our communication and people first to build our new structure from the bottom up."

In March 2005, ABHP launched Integrated Clarity (IC)™, a high-involvement series of strategic conversations centered around a set of six universal organizational needs. In the first conversation, 95 percent of the team experienced IC through one-on-one interviews, small-group and management team dialogues, or an initial assessment of organizational needs.

The assessment showed that employees ranked meeting "communication" needs the lowest of 20 organizational needs. "Morale" was ranked sixteenth. Low morale and communication inefficiencies hampered and, in some cases, completely thwarted small-group and organization-wide discussions on ABHP's strategic direction.

The second conversation—a one-day Integrated Clarity workshop—was conducted with the entire team. Eleven weeks later, the follow-up assessment showed communication had moved up to sixth, placing it in the top one-third of the indicators. Morale jumped to number three. The overall organizational health score rose 32 percent.

In August 2005, this increased operational energy was leveraged into the third conversation, an all-day strategic dialogue about ABHP's future in the context of the critical organizational needs identified by the IC process. By day's end, the team expressed excitement about clarifying their organizational and people needs. They developed initial strategies for action based on shared values and common direction.

"Yes, this is clear to me now," said a researcher who expressed frustration at the first IC workshop about the organization's lack of clarity over direction and structure. "I know how I can contribute to this. I can see how our structure might change to support our organizational needs."

The Basics

What Is Integrated Clarity?

Integrated Clarity (IC) is a process that helps an organization or community[2] discover and articulate its needs critical to its sustainability in a way that benefits the whole system *and* the people in it. It does this by changing the way people communicate and creates conditions that engage people in a way that is more productive than what most are used to. It is a consciousness and a framework for a process that transforms how and what we talk about. IC provides a missing link for addressing the effectiveness dilemma implicit in the compelling empirical evidence on "dis-ease" in organizations. IC integrates research that shares the idea of empowerment—having power *with* people, not *over* people—into a single framework, bringing together the work of Jim Collins, Kimball Fisher, William Bridges, Jerry I. Porras, and Marshall Thurber (figure 1).

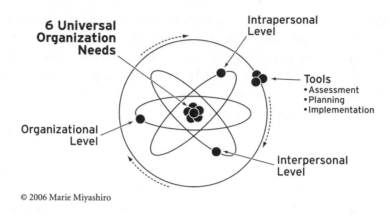

© 2006 Marie Miyashiro

Figure 1. Integrated Clarity Framework

While empowerment is not new, framing it into organizational needs is. IC's framework of six universal organizational needs is: *Identity, Life-Affirming Purpose, Direction, Structure, Energy,* and *Expression.* Productive conversations around these needs provide a solid foundation for helping the organization meet its needs while simultaneously meeting the needs of its people.

Central to the conversations and consciousness of empowerment is a key ingredient—the language model of Nonviolent Communication (NVC)SM, also known as Compassionate Communication. Developed by Marshall Rosenberg, NVC is a language of empowerment. Practicing NVC dismantles our habitual, pervasive way of thinking and speaking that blocks empowerment in organizations, such as thinking or language that includes blame, judgment, guilt, control, and fear.

By introducing a language and consciousness that honor the needs of an organization and the people in it, IC takes out the battle stance, "It doesn't matter what you need, this is for the good of the company" or "It's the company's fault I'm not able to do my job." Instead, it provides a clear and productive forum for seemingly conflicting needs to be equally heard and respected.

There are six steps involved in the Integrated Clarity framework:

1. *Prelude to conversations.* Situation assessment, including a 20-question review of organizational needs.

2. *Conversation: IC overview and meeting people needs.* Learning and living the language of empowerment.

3. *Conversation: meeting organizational needs.* Collective, strategic conversations on identifying, clarifying, and articulating "Source Needs"—*Identity, Life-Affirming Purpose, Direction.*

4. *Interlude: the pause between conversations.* Follow-up assessment.

5. *Conversation: leveraging source needs into planning and implementation.* Collective, strategic conversations on identifying, clarifying, and articulating "Leveraging Needs"—*Structure, Energy, Expression.*

6. *Conversation: the assessment-planning-implementation cycle starts again.* Monitoring and measuring the effects on organizational and people needs using the Organization Needs Dashboard (or Instrument Panel)—an at-a-glance collection of top-line data that encourages participation in organizational conversations.

IC becomes the launching pad for organizations and teams to develop the cultural characteristics that produce empowerment in organizations and people, as documented in organization effectiveness research. As both an organization framework and a collective conversation process, IC operates at all three levels—intrapersonally, interpersonally, and systemwide. IC also works in three ways: as an assessment tool, a planning process, and an implementation mechanism, including NVC as a communication model.

While IC houses the qualities of empowerment under one roof, NVC acts as the day-to-day operational voice of this empowerment consciousness.

IC Empowerment Consciousness

While the "empowerment" movement of the 1980s and 1990s did not live up to what we knew possible, it is a powerful organizational force when it does take root. In fact, many leading practitioners and researchers still believe that "empowerment is the second industrial revolution."[3]

Key qualities of IC empowerment include:

1. *Empowerment* as power with people, not over them; a power that comes from inside of us, our passion and alignment to others and the organization; freely offering what we have in a spirit of contribution (versus control, punishment, guilt, blame, and reward paradigms);

2. *Blame-free environment* of mutual respect, absent of judgment;

3. *Conversation-based operations* characterized by dialogue and debate;

4. *Inquiry-based and iterative*—asking the "right" questions is as important as getting the answers; building on our answers from the last inquiry in a continual refinement process;

5. *Responding to and operating from what we are passionate about,* what's "alive" in us and what we value as an organization;

6. *Capitalizing on the human element*—namely, feelings and needs—in organizational systems rather than tolerating or "managing" them;

7. *Honesty* with each other and about the organizational data, information (including market and business information), and feedback;

8. *Connection* to each other, to the organizational needs, to human needs, and to our markets.

Energizing How We Talk

Most communication in organizations is "dead," and, some would say, not very honest. Speaking and listening nonjudgmentally in the language of NVC transforms every conversation.

It is an invitation into empowerment thinking. NVC develops "our awareness that we are each responsible for our own thoughts, feelings and actions."[4]

This awareness comes from a key understanding and redefinition of "needs." We've been educated to believe that having needs is somehow weak, that needs and feelings are unprofessional and outside the realm of business or organizations.

In truth, all people share the same universal needs, such as respect, choice, trust, comfort, and rest. Understanding this brings us into a universal relationship with each other.

The challenge arises when people confuse needs with requests. For example, a supervisor is actually making a request when she says, "I need you to get that report on my desk by 5:00 P.M." This request is a strategy to meet a need, perhaps a need for efficiency or completion. Confusing needs with requests may be an unconscious, habitual use of the language of "power over people." We might also guess from her choice of words that if the report were not on the desk by 5:00 P.M., there would be punitive consequences. If that's the case, this is not a request, but a demand.

An interesting thing happens when we think someone is demanding something from us. We activate the "demand-resistance cycle." Unconsciously, we hinder productivity by stimulating resistance. This dynamic plays a role in the large number of failed transition efforts (people know someone is trying to get them to "buy in") and operational inefficiencies (ask any manager how much energy it takes to continually "demand" from workers). When requests become the norm and an empowerment consciousness prevails, the data convincingly support significantly increased profits, productivity, and morale.[5]

Jim Collins, author of *Good to Great,* talks about "having the right people on the bus"[6] instead of spending resources to motivate people. If you have to motivate people, he insists, then they are probably not aligned with the team or organization.

The moment we understand the subtle but powerful distinctions that NVC makes clear among needs, requests, and demands, empowerment begins. The four steps of the NVC process can be learned in minutes and may take a lifetime to master:

1. *Make an observation:* What we are observing (objective, concrete, measurable, factual versus interpretation, evaluation, judgment).

2. *Identify feelings:*[7] What is stimulated in us by what we observe (feelings are caused by our needs met or unmet and by our thinking, not by what we observe).

3. *Connect feelings to our needs:* Universal—all people have the same needs (independent of any specific person, event, action, or behavior).

4. *Make requests:* "Would you be willing to tell me if you're able to complete the report and have it on my desk by 5:00 P.M.?" (specific, doable in the moment versus "Can you get it to me right away?").

Using this language of personal responsibility transforms communication in organizations by engendering self-reflection and conscious personal growth. The qualities are consistent with Collins's description of Level 5 Leadership as professional will coupled with personal humility.[8]

He explains how Level 5 leaders develop "under the right circumstances—self-reflection, conscious personal development, with a mentor, a great teacher, loving parents, a significant life experience, a Level 5 boss. . . ."[9] Practicing NVC is one strategy we are confident develops Level 5 leaders.

ENERGIZING WHAT WE TALK ABOUT

At the heart of IC are six universal organizational "needs." Like people needs, universal organizational needs exist for every organization, every team. While NVC provides a language and awareness for human needs, IC provides a language and awareness for organizational needs.

Together, they become a pathway to empowerment. Empowerment, by definition, is a needs-focused solution to our organizational woes, such as workers being:

- value/principles-based versus policy/procedure based,

- self-motivated versus management-controlled,

- purpose/achievement-oriented versus problem-solving, and

- aware of others and the whole system versus focused on themselves and their isolated function.[10]

Research by Fisher, Collins, and Bridges points to the need for self-aware workers, people who can respond to "what is alive" in themselves, coworkers, customers, other stakeholders, and the organization itself.[11] Actions that come out of this connection make up the fabric of empowerment. "Build a culture around the idea of freedom and responsibility, within a framework," Collins says.[12]

IC provides such a framework. By articulating a unified set of organizational needs, IC is a springboard to empowerment. With such a framework, organizations may experience far-reaching results of empowerment like these, cited in the Fisher and Collins research:

- 45 percent lower costs

- 250 percent productivity improvement

- double the revenues and profits

- 50 percent cut in accidents, absenteeism, and sickness

- 3.42 to 18.50 times the general stock market value[13]

With IC as a road map, many of the paradoxical concepts and counterintuitive research findings of empowerment become more readily perceived and easier to apply. See for yourself as you explore our Source Needs: *Identity, Life-Affirming Purpose,* and *Direction* (figure 2).

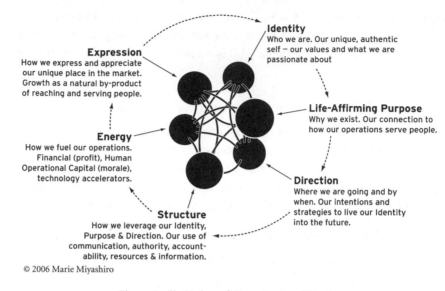

Figure 2. Six Universal Organizational Needs

Identity

The idea of organizational core values and ideology is nothing new. But what have we been doing with them? At best, they are words on the wall for use on special planning occasions. At worst, they are memos in the drawer. Identity invites us into a new kind of organizational conversation. Instead of strategic planning focused on *what we do next*, it becomes a self-inquiry into *who we are*. Collins's discovery of the "Hedgehog Concept"[14] (the intersection among what we are passionate about, what we can be the best at, and what drives our economic engine) is a favorite tool[15] of ours for inquiry into Identity.

Identity is the root need of the six universal organizational needs. When Identity is clear, everything the organization does extends from it. It creates the kind of integrity that Collins calls "fanatical adherence"[16] to our values and what we stand for. "Beliefs must always come before policies, practices, and goals."[17]

Identity also includes whom we invite into our organizations. If we are unclear about our Identity and hire people with values contrary to our authentic and unique organizational self, over time our sense of who we are diminishes. Decisions get made that do not align with our collective self.

Life-Affirming Purpose

"Purpose is the set of fundamental reasons for a company's existence beyond just making money."[18] Empowerment research reveals a pattern in people's answers to the question, "Why do we exist?" Answers are consistently tied to meeting universal people needs and "making life more wonderful."[19] It is this life-affirming quality that can make an organization's purpose an inspiring and powerful guiding force. We live Life-Affirming Purpose; daily operations affirm it.

For example, conversations about Life-Affirming Purpose among a cross-section of employees from Horizon Moving Systems revolved around "providing ease and comfort to people who were in big life transitions—death, marriage, divorce, new job" versus "moving furniture or things." They see themselves helping people through stressful times and are inspired by this.

Direction

"Where are we going and by when?" Amazingly, many organizations have lots of strategic goals that do not point to any future direction. These are organization "to-dos" without a clear intention. They answer the question, "What do we do next?" but not the larger inquiry: "Where do we really want to be?" Direction is a picture of the sights, sounds, and feelings of desired possibilities that is rooted in a deep intention envisioned for our future Identity.

While the Source Needs clarify who we are, the Leveraging needs—*Structure, Energy, and Expression*—catalyze the Source Needs into action. The powerful connection formed by individually and collectively meeting our Source Needs and Leveraging Needs generates the results of true empowerment.

Structure

This need begins with Fisher's empowerment function of authority, resources, information, and accountability[20] as the bones of organizational Structure. We develop Fisher's work with the idea of "perfect balance," equal parts of authority and accountability. To his elegant expression of empowerment, we add communication, the critical ingredient that moves operations throughout the organization. If Structure is the organizational body's skeletal system, then communication is its lifeblood.

Energy

IC reframes profit and workforce morale—often thought of as opposing each other—into a single organizational need of operational fuel. A third key aspect of an organization's Energy need is technology, which accelerates momentum.[21] When we see Energy as a three-legged stool—finances, morale, and technology—the idea that we must choose between profit or people simply disappears.

After reading Marshall Rosenberg's *Nonviolent Communication,* one chief financial officer said she liked it for family or personal use but that "it wasn't appropriate for business use." At the end of an executive retreat with the IC framework, she said, "We have to train every employee in IC, including the language of NVC." The reason she shifted? She grasped that the NVC model's focus on people needs coupled with IC's focus on organizational needs was a direct route to increasing all three aspects of Energy.

Expression

The days of "selling an image" are over. Instead, being clear about our unique Identity and place in the market most effectively connects us with our markets. Expression gives branding and market positioning a voice in the organization's overall framework, not just as the ancillary "sales and marketing" departments of old. The stronger the Identity clarity, the stronger the Expression of that Identity is to customers and other stakeholders.

When and Where Is IC Used?

"Some processes focus on people issues like improving morale or communication while others focus on strategic planning and business aspects," says Valerie Becker, human resources director for Horizon Moving Systems, a 300-employee company. "What's exciting and different about Integrated Clarity is that it addresses both at the same time."

The effectiveness of IC comes from its applicability across multiple levels of an organization (table 1).

Level	Brief Description	Uses
Intrapersonally	what we tell ourselves, our thinking	executive coaching, one-on-one mentoring, self-inquiry and contemplation
Interpersonally	what we tell others, what we think we hear others telling us	conflict resolution and mediation, challenging conversations, personnel reviews, team processes, and operational communication
Organizationally	what we think the data and organizational information is telling us	strategic conversations, providing a planning framework, Organization Needs Dashboard

Table 1. Applying Integrated Clarity to Different Levels

How IC Works

IC increases operational efficiencies by encouraging a blame-free work environment that focuses people on creativity, productivity and learning. To understand the power of NVC in this process, consider the following dialogue between an IC facilitator and Brian Arthur, assistant executive director of Applied Behavioral Health Policy (ABHP). Brian knew the way he expressed his frustrations in the workplace was becoming increasingly counterproductive for his team.

Brian: I came into the office at 8:10 one morning. We open at 8:00 A.M., so I was a little surprised that no one was here. I went into my office and started working. I keep waiting for people to show up. By 8:20, I'm really upset that I seem to be the only one here.

Facilitator: Are you feeling upset because you need consistency around the office?

Brian: That's right. I shot off an e-mail to three key people, told them the time, told them that no one was here and they needed to fix this problem right away. These e-mails haven't worked well in the past, by the way. (laughs)

Facilitator: Are you feeling overwhelmed and need respect?

Brian: No. (pauses silently for about three seconds) I think I was really feeling a bit lonely. Huh. That's surprising to me. I like to come in and get into the flow with others. I also notice that if Mike were here, I probably wouldn't have been upset at all because we would have gone out for coffee. In fact, I'm sure that my need was for . . . (looking at IC Feelings and Needs list) connection. Yes. I like to come in and get connected to people first thing.

Facilitator: Were you feeling lonely and you needed connection?

Brian: Yes. I'm surprised by this actually. (pauses) And now I can see that the e-mail I sent was a strategy to meet my need for connection rather than to address the issue.

Facilitator: With the understanding now of your need for connection, I'm wondering how best to support you. Are there other strategies that would meet your need for connection in the future and meet others' needs for respect?

Brian: I can think of several ways I'd do it differently that would be much more productive. Talking to people in person and explaining what was going on for me would be one much more productive approach, I think.

At the IC team retreat, Brian shared these insights. It was clear that people who had previously judged Brian as "mean" or "angry" now felt a connection with him. Comments at the end of the day and in retreat evaluation forms echoed the power of his sharing. Team tensions eased. One team member suggested that she and Brian have lunch as a way to meet both of their needs for connection beyond the boundaries of work tasks.

By distinguishing between his "needs" and his "strategies," Brian made a profound leap in his processing. He could now see the difference between an organizational strategy—the policy of starting work at 8:00 A.M.—and an organizational need—providing quality service to clients.

By learning to distinguish between needs and strategies as individuals, we are better equipped to apply this skill within the organization. Our chosen strategies meet needs rather than existing for other reasons like, "We've always done it this way," "Everyone else is doing this," or "Gee, I didn't even realize we were doing that." A needs-based approach (as opposed to a strategy-based approach) results in improved relationships, increased productivity, and profits.

Table of Uses

Brief Description	Project Length	Events	Number of Participants
Service Business Developed Source Needs to increase profits, productivity, and morale • Conducted organization health assessment • Facilitated strategic planning conversations • Conducted communication trainings • Designed team meeting models • Restructured executive leadership team • Provided executive coaching • Defined criteria for designing restructured organization	24 months	• Monthly meeting with company-wide management team • 7 strategic planning sessions • Multiple small-group employee trainings • 5 combined communication and strategic planning retreats • 2 large-group meetings • 16–21 sessions at a time	• 15 people • 5–25 people • 30 people • 5–15 people • 300 people • 1-on-1 coaching
Nonprofit and Professional Corporation Merger Facilitated tense negotiations and early transition into new organization structure • Facilitated merger discussions • Determined postmerger organization *structure* and *identity* • Determined financial structure for merger and postmerger operations	6 months	• A series of individual and group discussions with decision makers • Concurrent work groups detailing new structure • Strategic planning session postmerger with large integrated group	• 5 people • 1–3 people • 25 people
State University Provided strategic framework for planning and resource allocations • Articulated Source Needs to unify college in a single direction • Conducted college-wide needs assessment • Provided empathic listening for team members to share loss and fears as well as hopes and plans	13 months	• A series of individual and group discussions with management leaders • Concurrent groups working on different parts of Source Needs • Large group meeting presenting approach and objectives	• 15 people • 1–3 people • 350 people
International Professional Association Assisted board of directors in restructuring the association and programs • Facilitated strategic conversations on *identity, life affirming purpose, and direction* • Developed new program model	2.5 days	• Group meetings with board and committee chairs	• 18 people

Integrated Clarity

Getting Started

For a successful transition, three points are critical:

1. Change is an external event. Transition is an internal psychological experience.[22] Expect to begin with heavily internal and personal work that moves outward to others, ultimately to the whole organization. We believe learning and living IC with NVC as its language model is a fast, effective way to empowerment in organizations.

2. Expect the return on investment in the IC change process to increase over time. The greatest return comes once a critical mass of IC practitioners—people speaking the language of human and organizational needs—is established.

3. Ensure there is a supportive infrastructure for collective conversations, training, assessments, and follow-through required to integrate IC into the system.

Roles, Responsibilities, and Relationships

Since IC is a modeling process, adoption comes more rapidly when people with the most authority—either formal or social leaders—learn and practice IC. Empowerment is a "do as we do" process rather than "do as we say."

Initially, a facilitator or small group of practitioners models the IC language and consciousness, guiding the organization or team in acknowledging and understanding the key distinctions. Facilitator dependence decreases over time as more people internalize the skills and as formal and social leaders within the organization or on the team assume the facilitator's role.

Participants go through three stages of learning IC:

1. Hearing and learning key concepts and making key distinctions;

2. Contemplating, inquiring, and relating concepts to their organization;

3. Practicing and applying concepts.

As participants move through these stages, their decision-making awareness grows from "no or little choice" to optimal choices.

For participant and facilitator alike, with time and practice, IC becomes a way of life.

Conditions for Success

Successfully integrating IC into an organization's culture depends on these factors:

1. A core group of formal and social leaders learning and practicing IC, including the NVC language model.

2. Conscious intention to connect with others is essential for IC to be effective. If treated as a "technique," it can stimulate the opposite of what is desired. If IC is used to "get our way," it disintegrates into manipulation.

3. An organizational investment in collective strategic conversations about its six universal organization needs *before* increasing investments in operations and infrastructure.

4. Emphasizing learning and training. This means devoting about 20 percent of a person's work time to learning:[23] formal classroom training, IC practice groups, on-the-job coaching, mentoring, or team meetings that include learning points. The learning is productive work time because learning happens as work gets done.

5. Developing systemwide standards for other external, non-IC training and coaching—such as technical training—so that there is consistency with the empowerment principles throughout the organization.

Theoretical Basis Table

Theorist/Researcher	Key Theory Elements	Use in IC
Marshall Rosenberg *Nonviolent Communication, Speak Peace in a World of Conflict*	• Needs-focused communication • Universal human needs as separate from strategies • The language of empowerment free of blame, guilt, punishment, reward, shame, and control (Carl Rogers's influence)	• IC adds a universal organizational needs framework to human needs so both can be met at the same time • IC leverages this language as a productivity and strategic planning tool
Jim Collins *Good to Great, Built to Last* (with Jerry I. Porras)	• Level 5 Leadership as "professional will + personal humility" • Hedgehog Concept; Core Values • Big Hairy Audacious Goals • Blame-free environments • Measurable "extraordinary" sustained results in profits	• IC's language model, NVC, provides practical action steps to realizing Level 5 Leadership • IC strategic planning model provides practical action steps to achieve results
Kimball Fisher *Leading Self-Directed Work Teams*	• Empowerment as authority, resources, information, and accountability (ARIA); • Mutual respect among team members • Measurable results on increased profit, productivity, and morale in empowered model	• IC translates elements of empowerment into six universal organizational needs

Theorist/Researcher	Key Theory Elements	Use in IC
William Bridges *Managing Transitions, The Character of Organizations*	• Change as external event • Transition as internal psychological experience • Organization as living entity with personality and life cycles • Feelings as part of transition management	• IC as an intrapersonal process of transition • IC extends the concept of organization as living entity by identifying organizational needs parallel to human needs
Marshall Thurber, Judith Orloff Faulk *International Consultants*	• W. Edwards Deming and R. Buckminster Fuller influences • Transformation of the individual • Enduring human success • Connection among people as the foundation for a productive planet	• IC intention and consciousness based on connection of people to each other • Connection of workforce to a purpose and direction serving humankind

Sustaining the Results

Traditional language works against the empowerment consciousness in subtle yet powerful ways—like drops of water eroding rock, day-in, day-out. At some point, we realize we are no longer in the consciousness of empowerment and wonder why. IC produces sustained results because it infuses the act of empowerment with a supporting language of empowerment.

In our experience, empowerment consciously languaged promises permanent change. As individuals deepen their IC language skills and the organization consciously monitors its progress through the Organization Needs Dashboard, their worldview is never the same.

As Ron Jones, dean of the College of Visual & Performing Arts at the University of South Florida, says about IC, "There's an exciting new energy in our college spreading like wildfire—a clarity about who we are, why we're doing what we do and where we're going in the future."

People take IC out of the workplace, too. They often delight to see the language of NVC impact their personal lives. One woman enthused, "My whole life has changed since learning to make observations!" A business owner reported, "I like what is happening with my employees but let me tell you how this is benefiting my relationship with my 17-year-old daughter."

Burning Question

"How long will this take?" is a frequently asked question about developing an IC consciousness organization. We like to say, "Longer than you're used to and shorter than you think." IC "takes longer than we're used to" because it is not just about changing words. It is also about changing priorities. The important but not urgent work of focusing on needs takes time to learn and practice daily. Reframing time in terms of "getting better as we go" is critical for its success.

What if the needs of the organization conflict with the needs of the person? Remarkably, needs never conflict, only strategies do. For example, a company president wanted to let a worker go because she was not meeting the needs of her position. "I'm confused," said the president. "It seems like this will not meet her needs." With coaching, he realized that this job was a strategy for her, not a need. Her need was for a meaningful job in which she could excel. She was, in fact, miserable in this position. The president talked to their IC-practicing human resources director about this woman's career needs. As a result, the company helped her develop a plan to find the job she really wanted. They did not fire her, after all. She resigned amidst tears of gratitude, hugs, and recommendations for the job that really met her needs. The company then found someone who could meet the needs of the position she vacated.

Some Final Comments

Our wish is that every organization gets crystal clear about its universal organizational needs. We believe when this happens, every worker will experience more ease in finding their seat in an organization that meets their needs. Each organization will draw to it people who are most in alignment with it. The data tells us this leads to more harmony, productivity, and profit in our workplaces. This contributes to organizations picking strategies that meet the needs of society as well.

Simply, we do not have to choose between profit or people. If we ask the question, "Who are we as an organization?" before asking, "What should we do next?" we are halfway home to becoming the kind of organization the research describes as "great," "extraordinary," "lasting," and "visionary."

About the Authors

Marie Miyashiro, APR (Marie.Miyashiro@elucity.com), has consulted since 1985 with Fortune 500 companies, small businesses, nonprofits, universities, and government agencies from across the United States and Asia. Since developing Integrated Clarity and folding in Nonviolent Communication, clients are reporting an invigorated sense of process and increased results. She holds a degree in communication studies from Northwestern University and is accredited by the New York-based Public Relations Society of America. She is president of Elucity Network, Inc., a consulting and training firm. Her book about Integrated Clarity and organizational effectiveness is due to be published in Spring 2008 by PuddleDancer Press.

Marshall Rosenberg, Ph.D. (cnvc@cnvc.org), an international peacemaker, author, and educator, developed the Nonviolent or Compassionate Communication process in the 1960s. His work is taught and used in 35 countries around the world. As founder and director of educational services for the Center for Nonviolent Communication, an international peacemaking organization, his work and NVC's impact is experienced globally. He is the author of the best-selling *Nonviolent Communication: A Language of Life,* as well as *Getting Past the Pain Between Us, We Can Work It Out,* and his newest title, *Speak Peace in a World of Conflict.*

Integrated Clarity

Where to Go for More Information

REFERENCES

"Diverse Business Group Needs to Shape Its Identity." *Arizona Daily Star*, January 17, 2005.

Miyashiro, Marie. *What Leads to Organizational Greatness: Asking "Who We Are?" Before Asking "What Should We Do?"* Keynote address, University of Arizona, College of Fine Arts, Fall Convocation, 2004.

Rosenberg, Marshall. *Nonviolent Communication: A Language of Life.* Encinitas, CA: Puddle-Dancer Press, 2003.

"Workers Help Unlucky Nu Wheel Come Full Circle." *Arizona Daily Star*, June 27, 2005.

INFLUENTIAL SOURCES

Bridges, William. *The Character of Organizations: Using Jungian Type in Organizational Development.* Palo Alto, CA: Davies-Black Publishing, 2000.

———. *Managing Transitions—Making the Most of Change.* Cambridge, MA: Perseus Books Group, 1991, 2003.

Collins, James C. *Good to Great—Why Some Companies Make the Leap . . . and Others Don't.* New York: HarperCollins, 2001.

Collins, Jim, and Jerry I. Porras. *Built to Last—Successful Habits of Visionary Companies.* New York: HarperCollins, 1994, 1997, 2002.

Fisher, Kimball. *Leading Self-Directed Work Teams—A Guide to Developing New Team Leadership Skills.* New York: McGraw-Hill, 2000.

Greenspan, Miriam. *Healing Through the Dark Emotions: The Wisdom of Grief, Fear, and Despair.* Boston, MA: Shambhala Publications, 2003.

ORGANIZATIONS

Center for Nonviolent Communication—www.cnvc.org

For information, workshops, and certification regarding Nonviolent Communication.

Elucity Network, Inc.—www.elucity.com or www.integratedclarity.com

For information, workshops, and certification regarding the Integrated Clarity framework.

PuddleDancer Press—www.NonviolentCommunication.com

For books and materials on Nonviolent Communication.

---

1. ABHP is now located at Arizona State University.

2. Although this chapter is oriented to using IC in organizations, it is also effective in community settings.

3. Kimball Fisher, *Leading Self-Directed Work Teams: A Guide to Developing New Team Leadership Skills* (New York: McGraw-Hill, 2000), 4.

4. Marshall Rosenberg, *Nonviolent Communication: A Language of Life,* 2d ed. (Encinitas, CA: PuddleDancer Press, 2003), 19.

5. Fisher, *Leading Self-Directed Work Teams*; James C. Collins, *Good to Great: Why Some Companies Make the Leap and Others Don't* (New York: HarperCollins, 2001); James C. Collins and Jerry I. Porras, *Built to Last: Successful Habits of Visionary Companies* (New York: HarperBusiness, 2002).

6. Collins, *Good to Great,* 41–64.

7. "Feelings" used here differs from the Emotional Intelligence work by Daniel Goleman that advocates emotional control. See Miriam Greenspan, *Healing Through the Dark Emotions—The Wisdom of Grief, Fear and Despair* (Boston: Shambhala Publications, 2003), 73.

8. Collins, *Good to Great,* 17–40.

9. Ibid., 37.

10. Fisher, *Leading Self-Directed Work Teams,* 18.

11. Fisher, *Leading Self-Directed Work Teams*; Collins, *Good to Great*; William Bridges, *Managing Transitions—Making the Most of Change* (Cambridge, MA: Da Capo Press, 2003).

12. Collins, *Good to Great,* 124.

13. Fisher, *Leading Self-Directed Work Teams*; Collins, *Good to Great.*

14. Collins, *Good to Great,* 90–119.

15. In addition to Collins's Hedgehog Concept, other tools, like Appreciative Inquiry, can be used within the IC framework.

16. Collins, *Good to Great,* 133–139.

17. Collins and Porras, *Built to Last,* 74.

18. Ibid., 76.

19. Marshall Rosenberg, "Getting to the Core of Workplace Conflict," Workshop sponsored by the Oregon Network for Compassionate Communication, Portland, OR, October 11, 2005.

20. Fisher, *Leading Self-Directed Work Teams,* 15–16.

21. Collins, *Good to Great,* 152–153.

22. Bridges, *Managing Transitions,* 3.

23. Fisher, *Leading Self-Directed Work Teams,* 148.

9

Open Space Technology

The times, they are a-changin'.
—Bob Dylan

Three Stories

OPEN SPACE AT WORK

It was a bold experiment, not unlike jumping out of an airplane without knowing if the parachute was functioning. One morning, the Rockport Company, a subsidiary of Reebok International, closed for two days. No shoes were shipped. No orders were processed. The head office was locked.

Except for a skeleton crew left behind to answer the phones, the company's entire workforce gathered in a cavernous warehouse at the distribution center. The president and his senior executives, many of whom questioned his judgment in shutting down a $300M operation, were there. Managers, clerks, supervisors, and dockworkers—350 people in all—milled around uncertainly.

There had been no extensive planning for this day, no agenda set. No one had the foggiest notion of what would happen during the two-day meeting. As the tension built, the consultant stepped into the center of the loosely formed circle and introduced the gathering to Open Space Technology. He told them that this was their meeting and their time. What they did was entirely up to them. He explained a simple procedure: Anyone who wished to do so could step into the circle, write a topic and his or her name on a paper, announce it to the group, and take responsibility for convening a breakout session on the subject. He described four principles:

- Whoever comes are the right people

- Whatever happens is the only thing that could have

- Whenever it starts is the right time

- When it's over, it's over

He told them the one law—the *Law of Two Feet* (if you're not contributing or getting value where you are, use your two feet and go somewhere else). In less than 30 minutes, the meeting was theirs.

"There was a long silence," recalls Rockport's director of distribution. "I thought the meeting had ended right there. With so much of the top brass around, I fully expected that no one would write anything down. But one person rose tentatively, then another, and soon it was like ants going to sugar."

In less than an hour, an energized group had posted dozens of topics: distribution, on-time delivery, customer service, excess raw materials. Many topics were sensitive and had never before been acknowledged as issues of concern, such as women's perceptions of the Rockport environment, eliminating political games, overcoming "we versus they" thinking, and getting rid of paperwork.

At the end of the second day, 66 sessions had been held, creating a sense of camaraderie and purpose. Bringing together sales, production, procurement, and merchandising employees had solved a $4M/year supply chain problem. This achievement was dwarfed only by the new product line that was conceived and prototyped, complete with a marketing and financial plan that launched a new shoe, adding $20M/year in sales.[1]

A Story of Ongoing Open Space

We live in a field of abundance. That was only one of the discoveries made in Spirited Work, an experiment in open space organization that began in 1999 at the Whidbey Institute on Whidbey Island, Washington. Meeting face-to-face four times a year and linked in an online learning environment, Spirited Work was a pioneering experience of emergent organization.

We were an open space learning community of practice. The heart of our practice was the law of Open Space Technology (OST): Take responsibility for what you love. We applied the essential principles of OST: Whoever comes are the right people; Whatever happens is the only thing that could; Whenever it starts is the right time; When it's over, it's over.

To align with the energies of the natural world, we practiced Angeles Arrien's Four Fold Way. (Arrien is a cultural anthropologist who gleaned these principles from her cross-cultural studies of aboriginal people.) We met each season, focusing on that season's practice:

- Winter: Show up and choose to be present;

- Spring: Follow what has heart and meaning;

- Summer: Tell the truth without blame or judgment;

- Fall: Be open, not attached to outcomes.

We organized ourselves according to the patterns of OST—patterns fundamental to human relationship:

- Meet in a circle;

- Begin in silence to listen for the creative spirit;

- Establish a marketplace so individuals can offer whatever they are guided to share—and the emergent field can show up;

- Honor and welcome the "stranger" (or the unexpected!);

- Reflect on our learning;

- Practice dialogic conversation to hear and respect all voices and ways of relationship.

Our company included a wild diversity: corporate folks, educators, artists, writers, musicians, computer wizards, architects, chefs, builders, consultants, students, and preschoolers. The ages of participants ranged from one year old to mid-80s. More than 300 people participated, with a core of about 50 each season. We were from the United States, India, Australia, the Bahamas, Canada, Europe, Taiwan, Israel, Northern Ireland, Ireland, England, Africa, Vietnam, Colombia, and Denmark. We welcomed whoever showed up, whenever they showed up.

Over six and a half years, we experienced individuals transforming, many people taking courageous new steps in their work, their lives, and their relationships. The collective itself transformed. We learned that conflicts signaled something new wanting to happen. By opening to the unknown through asking a question, initiating a conversation in the marketplace, those who cared dealt with the issue on behalf of the whole.

A voluntary circle of "stewards" handled governance. Decisions were made by noticing what was emerging, discerning what served the whole, and taking action. If the response didn't work, someone simply convened a marketplace session and the decision evolved in real time.

Spirited Work functioned as an incubator. People self-organized to work together on projects, research, or long-term conversations and learning. Some of the projects spawned include: Global Citizen Journey; Integral Wellness, a systems approach to health; an international Practice of Peace conference; Radiant Networking; and Journalism that Matters. Books were written: *Breaking the Trance of Scarcity*, *The Power of TED*, and *Spirited Food: A Cookbook for All Seasons*.

Many are now asking: "How do we foster emergent organization?" Our answer from six and a half years of experience is: open space. Live the Law of Two Feet on a daily basis. Organize using OST. That's where the magic is.[2]

OPENING SPACE IN COMMUNITY

In January 2005, under the auspices of the federal government's Urban Aboriginal Strategy (UAS), 275 people met in Prince George, British Columbia, Canada, to address the complex needs of that city's aboriginal community of 80,000 people. They used Open Space Technology to identify priority areas and create a consortium of projects aimed at making a difference in a community riddled with poverty, violence, addictions, and health issues.

However, this was no ordinary gathering. The 275 people included regular citizens, youth, elders, disabled folks, folks with mental illness, the poor and dyslexic, and the rich and educated.

The sponsoring agencies—a loose committee of service providers, government, and local aboriginal groups—set the stage for the success of this event. They decided that the UAS should not be controlled by the existing agencies and organizations. To solicit community leadership, the agencies committed to turning the UAS over to the community. That willingness and openness made a huge difference on the day. In the premeeting, phrases like "we need new ideas to grow" and "supporting community leadership" became touchstones for the media campaign that formed the invitation. The sponsors stated their desire to be completely transparent in how this process was to unfold. They even committed to publishing a summary of the OST results in the local paper. Over three weeks, these messages were repeated in local media with startling results.

The agenda was set within the first hour of the day and the first of 55 discussion groups met on a huge range of issues. By the end of the day, the group had produced a 63-page proceedings document with summaries from 41 groups.

On day two, about 100 people returned to work on projects. People reviewed the previous day's proceedings, space was opened again, and people were invited to post invitations to champion new projects. Participants were asked that passion be tightly bound to responsibility on this day, as they deliberated on how to "get it out of the room."

Project champions came forward from a wide spectrum of experience and background, from poor single mothers to city councilors. Twenty-four project postings were made, and these convened into 19 groups addressing a wide variety of community issues. All of them found support from existing organizations and in just one and a half hours, partnerships were made, action plans drafted, and in some cases, goals, objectives, and visions were written. One group became so close that when they were finished, they stood in a circle for a minute tightly holding hands and prayed together. All of this was self-organizing, all of it happened in Open Space.

Within three weeks of the Open Space event, most of the champions had hosted follow-up meetings and attracted funding sponsors and other resources. By six weeks after the event, the project champions had formed a collaborative decision-making body that would oversee the strategy and make funding recommendations to the federal government.[3]

Frequently Asked Questions

What Is Open Space Technology?

At the very least, Open Space is a fast, cheap, and simple way to better, more productive meetings. At a deeper level, it enables people to experience a very different quality of organization in which self-managed work groups are the norm, just-in-time leadership is a constantly shared phenomenon, diversity becomes a resource to be used instead of a problem to be overcome, and personal empowerment is a shared experience. It is also fun. In a word, the conditions are set for fundamental organizational change, indeed, that change may already have occurred. By the end, groups face an interesting choice. They can do it again, they can do it better, or they can go back to their prior mode of behavior.

WHEN TO USE IT?

Open Space is appropriate in situations where a major issue must be resolved, characterized by high levels of complexity, high levels of diversity (in terms of the people involved), the presence of potential or actual conflict, and with a decision time of yesterday.

PROBABLE OUTCOMES

Depending on the length of time (one to three days), the following are essentially guaranteed: Every issue of concern to anybody in the group will be on the table. All issues will have been discussed to the extent that the interested parties choose to do so. A full record of the proceedings from the discussions will be in the hands of participants upon departure. Priorities will have been recognized, related issues converged, and initial action steps identified. In addition, the people in the organization will have experienced a very different and self-empowering way of working that they take back with them into their organizations. Substantive outcomes have ranged from organization redesign, strategic plan development, and product design, to name a few.

HOW DOES IT WORK?

Open Space runs on two fundamentals: passion and responsibility. Passion engages the people in the room. Responsibility ensures that things get done. An urgent theme or question provides the focus for the event. The art of the question lies in saying just enough to evoke attention, while leaving sufficient open space for the imagination to run wild.

All participants are seated in a circle (or concentric circles if the group is large). I have found that the circle is the fundamental geometry of open human communication; have you ever heard of a *square* of friends? The four principles and the one law that guide life in Open Space are introduced (figure 1). The participants are invited to identify any issue for which they have some genuine passion and are prepared to take personal responsibility. With the issue(s) in mind, they come to the center of the circle, write their issue on a piece of paper, announce it to the group, and post the paper on the wall. When all the issues that anybody cares to identify have been surfaced, the group is invited to go to the wall, sign up for the issues they care to deal with, and get to work. No matter the group size, all this takes somewhat more than an hour. From there on out, the group is self-managing. As the several groups meet, reports of their activities are generated (typically on computers), and at the conclusion (in a three-day event) all issues are prioritized. The "hot" issues are developed in further detail with concrete action as the goal.

THE PRINCIPLES OF OPEN SPACE

Whoever Comes Are the Right People

This reminds people that it is not how many people or the position they hold that counts, rather it is their passion for the subject that is important. So, what happens if nobody comes to your

Figure 1. Elements of Open Space

group? Well, when was the last time you had the time to work on an idea you really cared about? Even a group of one works.

Whatever Happens Is the Only Thing That Could Have

This is a reminder to let go of what might have been, should have been, or could have been. It is in the moments of surprise, large and small, that real learning and growth occur.

Whenever It Starts Is the Right Time

Creativity and spirit don't happen according to the clock; they appear in their own time. Open Space merely reminds us that clocks are human-made constructs and have very little to do with the right time for things.

When It's Over, It's Over

This offers a marvelous way to save time and aggravation. If you get together and it takes ten minutes to do what you wanted, congratulations! Move on and do something else. If, on the other hand, you find yourself deeply engaged in what you are doing, keep doing it until it is complete.

These principles are simple statements of the way things work. While they may appear counterintuitive to some, they are my observations of what always happens when people interact.

The *Law of Two Feet* (or in the case of the differently abled, the law of mobility) says to take responsibility for what you love. This happens by standing up for what you believe. If you feel you are neither contributing nor learning where you are, use your two feet and go somewhere else. The law is fundamentally about personal responsibility. It makes it clear that the only person responsible for your experience is you.

The actual Open Space event lasts from one to three days, depending on desired outcomes. One day allows for the raising and discussion of pertinent issues. In two days, a useful set of proceedings can be generated. With an additional half day, all issues may be prioritized, converged, and brought to a point of action. Shorter times are possible, but with a genuine loss of depth.

LIFE AFTER OPEN SPACE

To the best of my knowledge, no organization comes away unaffected by Open Space. In addition to whatever substantive outcomes may have emerged from the gathering, the "subtle" effects may be even more impactful. At the very least, the organization or community has a new performance benchmark, for all participants now know that endless preparation is not required for useful engagement. Distributed leadership, personal empowerment, appreciation of diversity, even self-managed work groups are all a matter of experience. Of course, the group may choose never to experience all this again, but there is no denying that all of the above took place.

Cost Justification

Since there is virtually no up-front planning or training required (except for theme identification and logistics), and only one facilitator necessary regardless of the group size, costs can range from essentially nothing to whatever the group is prepared to spend for accommodations, travel, and the like. Run these costs against the benefit of doing in two days what had previously taken ten months on a $200 million project, and the justification is pretty clear. Needless to say, not every instance of Open Space produces those sorts of results, but it is not uncommon.

Table of Uses

Brief Description	Project Length	Number of Participants, Time Required
Complex design issue Design an Olympic pavilion to accommodate 20,000 visitors only two months prior to the Olympics.	2 months	35 people, 2 days

Open Space Technology

Brief Description	Project Length	Number of Participants, Time Required
Strategic Planning/Community Building Create a strategic plan for the arts in Washington state through a statewide conversation about the arts. New connections across the arts community were an unexpected benefit.	7 months	1,500 people at 20 gatherings that ranged from 5 to 100 people
Handling High Conflict Brought together 25 Israelis and 25 Palestinians across the political spectrum to explore trust.	1 month	50 people for 3 days
Jobs for Street Kids Bogotá street kids recently out of drug rehab and into a jobs program identified ideas for finding ongoing jobs when they leave the program.	2 weeks	2,100 people (including 1,800 15- to 22-year-olds) for 2 days
Handling layoffs at a large avionics defense plant Plant of 2,400 employees self-organizes to reduce its numbers to 1,600 and completely restructure its operations.	2 months	450 people at 16, 2-day gatherings
Operating an organization in Open Space on an ongoing basis A social service agency transitioned to an entirely self-organizing operational structure. When client load doubled, the increased volume was handled with no added resources, winning awards for leadership and excellence.	Ongoing	100 people; gatherings convened as needed
Supply Chain Management Reorganize airplane door manufacturing at a large airplane manufacturer.	3 days	150 people from the whole supply chain in 2 locations linked by computer

Table of Uses. Continued

Getting Started

When contemplating fundamental change, my first advice is, "If it ain't broke, don't fix it." In short, make sure you really want to take this trip before you start. With specific reference to Open Space, the advice is—if you can find any way other than Open Space to do what you want to do, do it. The reason is simple. With Open Space the good news and the bad news are identical: It works. In Open Space, every group I have worked with becomes excited, innovative, creative, and ready to assume responsibility for what they care about. This all sounds wonderful, but at times for some people, it also sounds like a prescription for going out of control—and they are right. If maintaining control is your fundamental intent, for goodness sake, don't even think about Open Space. On the other hand, if you are prepared to believe in the people, trust them, and acknowledge that in all probability they are the true experts about what needs to be done, then Open Space will deliver—and you can be sure that fundamental change is a likely consequence.

Roles, Responsibilities, and Relationships

Table 1 shows the roles and responsibilities of sponsors, facilitators, and participants before, during, and after an Open Space event.

SPONSORSHIP REQUIREMENTS

The sponsors must be prepared to honor and respect all the participants. This does not mean that every crazy idea generated in the course of the gathering must be implemented, and there will be some crazy ideas. It does mean, however, that the space created must be safe for

	Before	During	After
Sponsor(s)	• Design the invitation • Create the invitation list • Support the logistics • Prepare for postevent support	• Welcome participants • Set the context, focusing the intention • Take responsibility for what they love • Listen and speak authentically	• Support the outcomes • Stay open to where the experience takes the oganization
Facilitator	• Support the development of a good invitation • Work with the logistics team to create the space • Coach leadership on the new ways of working that will emerge in Open Space, beginning the conversation on supporting this spirit	• Open and hold space • Help out with the proceedings	• Support the emergence of innovation and maintaining the spirit of the event • Assist the leadership and organization in working with chaos and self-organization
Participants		• Take responsibility for what they love • Listen and speak authentically	• Follow through on commitments • Bring the four principles and the law back with you

Table 1. Roles and Responsibilities

people to be fully creative and fully themselves. As a matter of fact, groups that I have worked with are rather conservative—whether they are corporations, communities, religious orders, or major political jurisdictions—and collectively they prove to be excellent judges regarding the insanity or applicability of an idea.

Role of the Facilitator

The job of the facilitator is to open the spiritual and practical space in which people can work, and then keep on opening space. Observably, the facilitator has a maximum of 20 minutes "up front" and from that point on, apparently does nothing. He or she will not intervene in any of the groups, or with the group as a whole, unless a Space Invader presents him- or herself. Space Invaders may just be overly enthusiastic participants or (in the worst case) the chairman of the board who is concerned that things are "out of control." Space Invaders take it upon themselves to corral everybody into a single course of action of their design. Open Space is the quintessential "Trust the Group—Trust the Process" sort of thing, and *nobody* has the right to control specific outcomes, so long as they choose to be in Open Space.

Participants' Roles

The simple answer to who participates in Open Space is whoever cares. In practice, the invitation goes to everyone who might care about the answers to the theme or framing question, whether they are from within the organization or from outside. Where the logistics are a challenge, there are a variety of ways to handle the situation, such as limiting attendance to first come, first served or to a certain number from each community affected.

The job of the participants is to be fully themselves. If they are scared, untrusting, or frustrated, so be it—that is the way they are. On the other hand, if they are enthusiastic, creative, and ready for innovation—that is good too. In any case, they are the way they are, and that is precisely the way they should be. Expectations of participants (and that includes everybody including the planning committee, executive staff, and chairman of the board) are that they will show up, and be open to outcomes . . . and then take personal responsibility for ensuring that good and useful things get done. All of this is not the sort of thing that a rousing speech on values and responsibilities is likely to engender, but it seems to take place, almost as a matter of course, in situations where genuine respect is present.

For those who are not able to participate, the proceedings and the people who were there provide the connection to the experience. What happens after that is guided by the passion and responsibility of those who participated and what they bring back with them.

A Word on Planning Committees

Open Space presents a problem to planning committees. There is very little to be done in advance. As a matter of fact, my major effort with such committees is to help them identify what they really care about, shape that into a calling question or theme for the gathering; and help

them understand that after the theme has been determined and the guests have been invited, all the rest is quite simple and straightforward logistics. Rent the hall, arrange for meals, and let it happen. Self-organization does have its advantages.

Conditions for Success

WHEN TO USE OPEN SPACE

Use Open Space whenever the answer is basically unknown, and the only possible hope is that the group, consisting of all those who care, can from their collective wisdom arrive at solutions that no individual or small group can hope to devise.

WHY IT WORKS

Open Space is an evolving mystery. It's simply what people do when they voluntarily organize something. The answers to the question why it works, when and as they appear, will come from what we know, and are finding out, about self-organizing systems.

WHEN NOT TO USE OPEN SPACE

Do not use this method if you wish to remain in total control, at least as we used to understand "total" and "control." Control and accountability are still very much present in Open Space, but the locus of both shifts from the one, wise, all-powerful executive to the participants themselves.

COMMON MISTAKES

Open Space is remarkably forgiving. Indeed, the only way I know to totally mess up the process is to think that you are in charge of it (see above).

Theoretical Basis

Open Space Technology was not the product of careful design. It occurred simply because I was tired of organizing meetings only to discover that participants best loved the coffee breaks, the only part I had nothing to do with. The immediate inspiration was social organization in tribal West Africa, where I discovered that everything of importance and utility occurred in a circle, and all exchange happens via a marketplace of some sort. Every indigenous population I know made the same discovery a long time before I did.

Retrospectively, as we try to figure out why on earth Open Space works, the answers generally come from research dealing with self-organization, complex adaptive systems, dissipative structures, and the like. The associated names are not generally found in the literature of management or even behavioral science, and include the likes of Stuart Kaufmann (biologist), Ilya Prigogene (chemist), and Murray Gel-Mann (physicist)—to name a few. At the level of popularization, we should also include Meg Wheatley and her work presented under the titles of *Leadership and the New Science* and *A Simpler Way*.[4]

Sustaining Results

So you had a great gathering. What do you do next? The answer: Go with the flow. This is quite simple, but perhaps not totally satisfactory. Concretely, this means that in an Open Space gathering, the emergent structure, purpose, and power of an organization will not only reveal itself but will be mapped out in terms of the proceedings and what follows. The "smart money" will support the energy. Where it is strong (coherent and useful), it will provide resources and break down barriers (as in bureaucratic constraints); and where it is weak, don't bother.

The choices of immediate next steps are usually pretty clear and typically are one of three possibilities:

- The actions to be taken are so clear it only remains to do them;
- The actions to be taken are pretty clear, but more information or consultation is required, in which case it is important to set a time by which these tasks will be completed; or
- The issue remains clear as mud, in which case a reasonable next step would be to hold another Open Space, this time devoted exclusively to that issue.

There is also a major opportunity to anchor the new organizational behaviors experienced in Open Space. As mentioned, self-managed work groups, distributed leadership, appreciation of diversity, and self-empowerment, among others, appear as natural by-products of the Open Space environment. Typically, however, these behaviors manifest so quickly and easily that many of the participants will have missed their arrival. For an intact work group, it is very useful to reflect upon the new arrivals. Such reflection should not be confused with standard training programs that previously had sought to engender these behaviors. When a group is already functioning as a self-managed work group (for example), it makes little sense to go back to the beginning with fundamental concepts and practices. We are now dealing with a matter of experience that may be acknowledged and built upon.

Burning Question

Will it work? Answer—Yes. When faced with this question, explain the results:

- every pertinent issue identified,
- all issues discussed,
- reports written,
- priorities set,
- action plans in place.

Don't explain the process. The skeptics won't believe you and the others aren't interested.

Final Comments (Misconceptions)

When many first hear about Open Space, they come away with the opinion that there is no struc-ture and less control. This opinion is totally wrong: there is no *preimposed structure and control.* Such structure and control as is present (and it turns out to be a lot) is all emergent from the people involved, the task they perform, and the environment in which they are operating. In short, it is *appropriate* structure and control—appropriate to the people, task, and environment.

In most cases, people who view Open Space as being out of control with no structure have not actually been in Open Space. Had they been there, they would know what 500 Presbyterians knew after they had gathered to rethink their church. In the process, they created 164 task groups that were self-managed over a 48-hour period, ending with a book of proceedings (350 pages of it) in their hands. All of this was not done by levitation. In short, the level of emergent structure and control is generally of a sort that no planning committee would dare imagine, let alone seek to implement, but it happens and it works. Such is the nature of self-organizing systems.

There also seems to be a notion that Open Space is good only for establishing useful con-versation, with substantive contribution not part of the package. One author even described its sole use as a forum for airing employee grievances. Doubtless, good conversations do take place, and grievances get aired—but substantive output, as in the case of Rockport, is no stranger.

About the Author

Harrison Owen (hhowen@verizon.net), a theorist and practicing consultant, created H. H. Owen and Company in order to explore the culture of organizations in transformation. Somebody once asked him what he did. His response was that he honestly didn't know, but that his intent was to *make human life human.* He has worked in a variety of areas, from the African jungle to the halls of Congress—with large corporations in between. With an academic background and training centered on the nature and function of myth, ritual, and culture, Open Space was just more of what he has always done.

Where to Go for More Information

REFERENCES

Books by Abbott Publishing available at http://www.openspaceworld.com/literature.htm.

Owen, Harrison. *Expanding Our Now: The Story of Open Space Technology.* San Francisco: Berrett-Koehler, 1997.

_____. *The Millennium Organization.* Potomac, MD: Abbott Publishing, 1994.

_____. *Open Space Technology: A User's Guide.* 2d ed. San Francisco: Berrett-Koehler, 1997.

_____. *The Power of Spirit.* San Francisco: Berrett-Koehler, 2000.

_____. *The Practice of Peace.* Circle Pines, MN: Human Systems Dynamics Institute, 2004.

————. *Riding the Tiger*. Potomac, MD: Abbott Publishing, 1991.

————. *The Spirit of Leadership: Liberating the Leader in Each of Us*. San Francisco: Berrett-Koehler, 1999.

————. *Spirit: Transformation and Development in Organizations*. Potomac, MD: Abbott Publishing, 1987.

————. *Tales from Open Space*. Potomac, MD: Abbott Publishing, 1995.

INFLUENTIAL SOURCE

Tillich, Paul. *The Eternal Now*. New York: Charles Scribner's Sons, 1963.

ORGANIZATIONS

H. H. Owen and Company—www.openspaceworld.com

The Open Space Institutes—www.openspaceworld.org
    Currently in Australia, Canada, Germany, Scandinavia, and the United States.

OTHER RESOURCE

Holman, Peggy, producer, and Justin Harris, director. *US West Open Space*. Video. Bellevue, WA: Open Space Institute, 1995.

---

1. Thanks to Srikumar S. Rao, srikumarsrao@cs.com, for the Rockport story.

2. Thanks to Anne Stadler, annestad@comcast.net, for the Spirited Work story.

3. Thanks to Chris Corrigan, www.chriscorrigan.com, for the Urban Aboriginal Strategy story.

4. Margaret J. Wheatley, *Leadership and the New Science: Discovering Order in a Chaotic World*, 3d ed. (San Francisco: Berrett-Koehler, 2006); Margaret J. Wheatley and Myron Kellner-Rogers, *A Simpler Way* (San Francisco: Berrett-Koehler, 1996).

10

MARILYN OYLER AND GORDON HARPER

The Technology of Participation

We are all much more likely to act our way into a new way of thinking than to think our way into a new way of acting.

—R. Pascale, M. Millemann, and L. Gioja

Eradicating Meningitis

Meningitis epidemics occur with predictable regularity in some of the poorest countries in the world. Following a predictable cycle, nearly 200,000 cases were reported in the "meningitis belt" of Sub-Saharan Africa in the last major outbreak, killing and debilitating thousands.

Eradicating this menace is the aim of MVP, the Meningitis Vaccine Project, a unique partnership between the World Health Organization (WHO) and Seattle-based Program for Appropriate Technology in Health (PATH). MVP is supported by the Bill & Melinda Gates Foundation.

In October 2002, MVP used the Technology of Participation (ToP)® methods to create a five-year strategic plan to address the question, "What must the WHO/PATH partnership do as a team by 2007 to successfully deliver on the mission of the Meningitis Vaccine Project?" To create the plan, ten WHO and PATH staff members met for two lively days at MVP's offices in Ferney-Voltaire, France.

The MVP partners followed the classic ToP Strategic Planning sequence: practical vision, underlying contradictions, strategic directions, and implementation. The MVP partners' vision captured the full range of scientific, logistical, and communication complexities they needed to meet. It takes extraordinary effort to invent a safe vaccine, produce it at an affordable price, and immunize nearly 250 million people in settings with hit-or-miss vaccine programs today. Yet that is exactly the picture the MVP team painted as their vision unfolded.

With the bilingual skills of the participants, we were able to use French in some cases to round out the vision, which was largely expressed in English. For example, "It works! It's safe! It's salable! Voila!" captured the vision for the vaccine itself.

Participants identified critical impediments to success. Achieving MVP's ultimate objective would be impossible, they said, unless more staff with critical scientific and business qualifications were added quickly. Surfacing this central obstacle early on led directly to creating a launch activity that made filling needed positions a top priority.

Throughout implementation, participants said, significant attention must be paid to building and sustaining positive relationships with a wide range of governments, businesses, and beneficiaries. One telling part of the vision expressed this last idea succinctly: "All friends count."

Four strategies emerged in the two days, each accompanied by quarterly work plans for 2003. The participants also created a "Level of Effort" chart to estimate allocation of time and resources for each strategy during the five-year period.

"The ToP strategic planning process faithfully yielded a product in the five-year plan itself and built a stronger team in doing so. MVP staff clarified their vision, gained confidence in the prospect of achieving it and identified concrete steps," according to Richard Wilkinson, learning and organization development officer for PATH.

In a Nutshell . . .

The Institute of Cultural Affairs' Technology of Participation (ToP) consists of methods that enable groups to (1) engage in thoughtful and productive conversations, (2) develop common ground for working together, and (3) build effective short- and long-range plans. The institute developed and tested the initial forms of these processes in the early 1960s in a new style of self-help community development called the Fifth City Project on the West Side of Chicago.

In the years since then, these methods have been used in more than 50 countries, in major international social change ventures, in United Nations and World Bank programs, and in hundreds of organizational and corporate change initiatives, adopted as internal processes by government agencies and made part of the staff training systems of international nonprofits.

THE FOCUSED CONVERSATION METHOD

As first born of the ToP methods, Focused Conversation was adapted from a format for engaging groups in serious conversations about art. It has since become one of the most used core processes in the ToP tool kit. It helps a facilitator to maintain a conversational focus on a topic while personally remaining content-neutral. It is designed to maximize the participation of everyone in the group and to bring people out at a new place of awareness at its conclusion.

This method is based on a model of human consciousness that identifies a four-stage progression as the natural flow in a person's thinking process. The acronym that has become widely known as the shorthand for this life process is ORID—Objective, Reflective, Interpretive, and Decisional levels (figure 1).

A facilitator begins by asking questions that elicit what is known—the data—about the topic to be discussed. The questions then invite people to share their initial reactions to the data, both positive and negative, as well as past experiences and associations that may bear on the

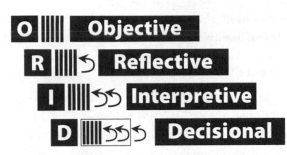

Figure 1. Four-Stage Progression of the Thinking Process

topic. Following this, the questions turn to a consideration of alternative ways to interpret or respond to the data. The final questions allow either individuals or a group as a whole to make a decision about how they will in fact relate or respond to the topic.

THE CONSENSUS WORKSHOP METHOD

This method helps a group form a working consensus, discovering and creating the common ground it needs in order to move ahead. It asks a question that seeks multiple, agreed-upon answers. An example of such a question might be, "What are our foundational values as an organization?" By the end of the workshop, the group will have generated and considered a number of possible answers to that question and come to a point of agreement on several of them.

The five-step process (figure 2) begins by developing the *Context* for asking and answering this question. People then *Brainstorm* individual answers to the question, share these in small teams, and select a certain number to put before the whole group. These are written on cards, posted at the front of the room, and grouped into *Clusters* of related items. The clusters then catalyze a conversation about what to *Name* each of them that provides an agreed-upon answer to the workshop question. When all the clusters have been named, the facilitator leads the group in

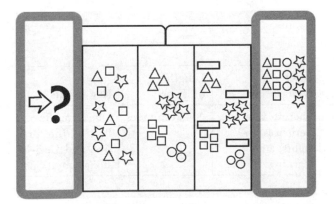

Figure 2. The Five-Step Process of Consensus Workshop

a conversation that confirms its *Resolve* through reflecting together on the experience of reaching this common ground, its significance, and the appropriate next steps.

PARTICIPATORY STRATEGIC PLANNING

Participatory Strategic Planning (figure 3) helps organizations undertake longer-range strategic initiatives, and its companion, the *Action Planning Method*, provides a process for shorter-term project, event, and campaign planning The method begins by creating a shared, positive vision of the group's hopes and desired outcomes (Practical Vision), then looks at the obstacles to the realization of that vision (Underlying Contradictions), identifies a range of possible actions to deal with these obstacles (Strategic Directions), and concludes with a calendar of accomplishments, assignments, and specific next steps for implementing the plans (Focused Implementation). The method also incorporates forms of the Consensus Workshop and Focused Conversation in its process.

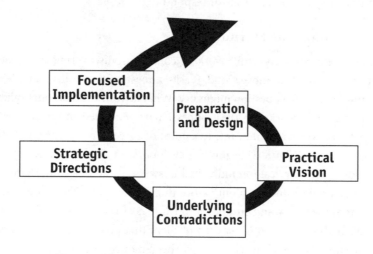

Figure 3. The Participatory Strategic Planning Method

Table of Uses

ToP Method	Typical Setting	Brief Description	Length of Time	Key Events	Number of Participants
Focused Conversation	Team evaluating its past quarter	Sharing data, experiences, insights, and learnings	20–60 minutes	Objective, Reflective, Interpretive, and Decisional questions	Typically 5–25

ToP Method	Typical Setting	Brief Description	Length of Time	Key Events	Number of Participants
Consensus Workshop	Department meeting to decide major sections of an employee handbook	Organize information into agreed-upon categories	1–2 hours	Brainstorming, relational grouping, reaching a consensus on sections	Single group of up to 25; multiple groups
Action Planning	Community meeting to plan annual summer festival	Elicit ideas and develop a plan that has whole group's support	3–4 hours	Vision of Success, Strengths, Weaknesses, Benefits and Dangers, Consensus Workshop, Calendar of accomplishments and assignments	Typically 8–30
Participatory Strategic Planning	Management team needs creative strategies for changing markets, products, customers	Build an agreed-upon road map for future directions that deals with all the realities in the situation	2–3 days	Form a common vision, identify major blocks, innovative actions, new strategies, and an implementation plan	Single group of up to 25; multiple groups up to several hundred participants

What Makes ToP Tick?

The beginning point of the work with any organization or community will often be a Design Conference with a representative leadership or core group from the organization. The intent of the design conference is to create shared understanding of the intention of the program as well as increased buy-in and commitment to the planning effort and follow-through on the actions.

Especially when this is seen as a first step of a longer change process, it is helpful to explore what has happened in the past to bring people to this point. One purpose of the Design Conference is to briefly review the group's history and guiding documents. Are there existing mission, vision, or values statements that provide focus and direction or set parameters for its operations? Has any recent research been done regarding clients, constituents, or market trends?

The Design Conference is in part a discovery process. It helps paint a picture of where the group has been, is now, and hopes to go. Based on this, the leadership and ToP facilitation team can begin to propose and design some next steps in its journey.

Any group process must have as part of its design a carefully thought out purpose or intention—and ToP methods actually call for two of these. The Rational Aim is the focus of a conversation or the practical outcome of a workshop or planning session. It answers people's questions, "Why are we here?" and "What can we expect to have at the end of this session?" An example of a Rational Aim for a Consensus Workshop would be "to establish an agreed-upon set of guidelines for overtime pay."

The second intent is the Experiential Aim, which takes into account the existing mood of the group and the desired impact that the process might have upon it. Formulating this intent helps the facilitator set an appropriate context, modify his or her personal style accordingly, and choose relevant stories, as well as exercises and generally fine-tunes the process. An illustration of an Experiential Aim for the example above might be, "to cut through the suspicions surrounding this issue, so people leave feeling we have a system that is fair to everyone."

At this point, it is time to select the process or processes to be used. It is likely that all the methods described above will be used in a long-term change process, and most events will use a combination of two or three ToP methods. The intended outcome helps give clarity to the choice of methods. Often, Focused Conversation is used when the need is for *shared awareness*, the Consensus Workshop method is used for *shared decision making*, Action Planning is used for *shared action*, and Participatory Strategic Planning is the method of choice when the organization is intending *a fundamental change or innovation*.

The ToP approach is to seek not for some ideal "best" solution or direction, but instead for what a group is actually prepared to say yes to—what in reality it will commit to do. It assumes that what may appear to one person (even the facilitator!) to be a perfect solution is indeed no solution at all if the group as a whole is unwilling to own or act upon it. Any proposed solution must stand up to critical scrutiny and analysis, after which the one that the group will get behind and implement becomes in reality the "best" solution.

George Brewster of Allied Solutions reports:

> Without ToP approaches we could not have gotten through this huge merger process as efficiently or as effectively as we did. Fifteen people in legacy positions came to the table—senior management, middle management, program managers—with real concerns about our capacity to continue to service clients in this new identity. Their work was to help us structure the best business model for the 100 people that work in the field and for our over 2,600 clients. The ToP approaches provided space for the conversations in a structured way that was invaluable.

In starting a change process, the leadership should recognize that the introduction of ToP methods may itself impact the journey of the organization. As people become familiar with these participatory tools and find them effective, they often find themselves wanting to integrate them in various ways into their daily operations. This can require building some new capacities within the organization, and equipping people with participation skills that they can use and adapt in their work. It can even set in motion a gradual change in the organizational culture itself.

Roles, Responsibilities, and Relationships

A few important guidelines or conditions that need to be present for the success of any group considering the use of these methods are:

- The group has the authority or authorization to make substantive recommendations, decisions, or plans at some level about the topics or arenas in question.

- Key stakeholders will be engaged in various ways in the planning or decision-making process, including those whose subsequent support may be essential to its success and those who are expected to implement conclusions or plans arrived at by the group.

- Participants in the process see the need for others' contributions and are willing to make an effort to work together on the matter at hand.

- Leadership is prepared to commit the time and resources required to deal responsibly with the topic—in helping to codesign the process to be used, in sponsoring and enabling the event itself, and afterward in following through with support for the outcomes of the event.

The style of the facilitator is another one of the key factors in establishing a participatory environment. Style goes far deeper than appearance, charisma, charm, and grace. There are very real values, practices, and techniques that enable people to participate in designing their own future. An effective and well-trained ToP facilitator is a living embodiment of the inherent values and principles of participation—a transparent presence that empowers the participants and enables them to get results.

Mutual respect is one of the keys to genuine dialogue. Believing that all the participants have the inherent capacity to understand and respond creatively to their own situation enables a facilitator to encourage authentic self-determination and self-reliance. It also assumes that the group holds the content wisdom, and the facilitator's role is to remain content-neutral and provide the process to aid the group in coming up with its own best solution.

The ToP methods of open inquiry lead to the assumption of individual and collective responsibility. Facilitators assume that everyone is a source of ideas, skills, and wisdom, and every bit is needed. The facilitator receives all ideas as genuine contributions to the process. Respectful questions reveal deeper thinking and enable people to discover their real wisdom.[1]

Conditions for Success

The Institute of Cultural Affairs identifies five foundational values that underlie the ToP methods and are keys to its success in any situation:

1. *Inclusive Participation.* The methods are designed to invite and sustain the participation of all members of a group. We understand that each person holds a piece of the puzzle, and each person's insights help to create a whole picture.

2. *Teamwork and Collaboration.* The Technology of Participation is based on the belief that teamwork and collaboration are essential to get a task done in the most effective, efficient and economical way—and that methods for working together should foster a genuine sense of collegiality among members of the group.

3. *Individual and Group Creativity.* The methods intend to elicit the best of each person's rational and intuitive capacities. By encouraging a dialogue between head and heart, people experience the magic of the whole group's creativity breaking loose.

4. *Action and Ownership.* The group processes have to position a group to fully own the decisions it makes and to take action based on them.

5. *Reflection and Learning.* Time is built into every process for depth reflection and sharing. This confirms both the individual and group resolve and allows for transformation as well as a fuller appreciation of the importance of consensus and collective action.

In addition to these foundational values, there are other keys or conditions for success of the ToP methods:

- ToP methods focus on surfacing things that can unify a group rather than dealing with things that may divide it. Instead of seeking to identify and directly address arenas of disagreement, the methods disclose where a group shares common hopes, perspectives, and objectives.

- ToP methods build on gestalt theory in helping groups identify perceived relationships between data and then decide on the meaning of those relationships. In the Consensus Workshop, all contributions are received and treated with respect. Ideas are not evaluated, nor is the group asked if it agrees or disagrees with any one of them. Instead, the question is where the group sees relationships between different ideas. Once clusters or gestalts of related data have been formed, the group discusses each cluster and determines where it points to an arena of agreement on the issue under discussion.

- In Participatory Strategic Planning (PSP), one thing that helps make the process succeed is identifying the Underlying Contradictions directly following the group's creation of its Practical Vision. Here, people are asked not to think yet of possible steps they might take to realize their vision but instead to identify those things that are blocking this vision from coming into being. Clustering the group's data here and naming the clusters helps people see more clearly what it is that their strategies and actions will need to focus on changing, if their vision is indeed ever to become a reality. An example of a Contradiction might be, "Haphazard fund-raising strategies inhibit program expansion." Once the Contradictions have been named, they become the focus of the group's next brainstorm of possible actions to address them. A group's Contradictions thus become not something "bad," but in effect the very stepping-stones or pathway to the future it seeks.

- A final key to the success of the Technology of Participation is its emphasis on caring for the human spirit of the participants in any process. The natural flow of the methods themselves is designed to honor that spirit. Bringing color, liveliness, warmth, and even some lightness and fun to the serious work that calls people to gather is not simply a nice addition to the process—it is a critical aspect of it. The ways in which ToP facilitators do this are as distinctive and diverse as they themselves, but the understanding of its importance is common to all of them.

Obviously, ToP methods are inappropriate for situations in which leadership has no desire for people to have a real voice in decision making. They are not intended for situations in which people are so locked into preexisting positions that they would prefer no resolution at all to one that would call for them to modify those positions. In situations where people feel that leaders or processes have manipulated them in the past, it may take time and firsthand experience for them to come to trust ToP methods and the facilitators who use them.

The Tap Roots of ToP

The Technology of Participation methods have been cocreated from the beginning. Their initial forms were developed through action research in the fields of community and organizational development. Since the 1960s and the beginning of the Ecumenical Institute, the forerunner of the Institute of Cultural Affairs (ICA), group processes were carefully crafted to achieve certain objectives. The concern was to bring methods and spirit to a wide public. These processes were referred to as "the methods," and at the heart of the methods were phenomenology and existentialist philosophy. The methods emerged out of the practical demands of hands-on efforts at community building and an intense community study and dialogue with the writings of people like Kierkegaard, Husserl, Heidegger, Sartre, Bonhoeffer, Camus, and Ortega. . . . The methods have always served to immerse people in the reality of their own situation and their own depths at the same time.

As the methods developed, they also benefited from the work of other authors: Alex Osborn's work on brainstorming, Olaf Helmer and Norman Dalkey's Delphi Process, and Piaget's writings on Gestalt psychology, for example, have all influenced the Consensus Workshop method.[2]

During the 1970s and 1980s, the ICA and these methods moved around the globe and into many different cultural settings. The methods catalyzed community development efforts, impacted government agencies, and introduced transnational organizations to participatory change processes.

Thousands of ordinary citizens were taught basic consensus formation methods in the 1970s, first around the U.S. Town Meeting campaign and then with the Global Community Youth and Women's Forums. Thousands of Village leaders across the world were taught participatory planning methods as part of the ICA's Human Development Projects and the 55-nation International Exposition of Rural Development. Again, more men and women in corporations and government agencies learned the methods through strategic planning workshops and leadership training seminars in the 1980s. Each of these opportunities provided occasions for refinement and reflection on the methods. In 1989, with the publication of Laura Spencer's *Winning Through Participation*, the methods became known as the Technology of Participation (ToP).

This process of reflection and reevaluation continues to this day. There are 140 active ToP trainers in the United States, with courses offered in 24 cities on a regular basis. They meet annually, stay in touch via e-mail and a Web site, and combine their training of others with their own direct engagement as facilitators. This effort of interchange takes place in many situations for ToP users both locally and nationally as well, and has proven to be a very effective tool for discerning new applications of the methods and sharing effective practices in the established uses.

There are active training systems in ToP methods today in the United States, Canada, Taiwan, Malaysia, Singapore, Egypt, Australia, Belgium, the United Kingdom, Vietnam, and Tajikistan. Course materials are available in English, Spanish, Croatian, French, German, Arabic, Russian, Dutch, Chinese, Portuguese, and Vietnamese.

ICA and ToP methods played a key role during the late 1980s and 1990s in the development of the profession of the facilitator. Much of this was done through helping to bring into being the International Association of Facilitators (IAF) in 1994. The IAF, which now provides a mechanism for the professional certification of facilitators worldwide, continues to offer a vital forum for professional development and the interchange of a wide variety of effective methods in the field of facilitation.

Sustaining the Results

In any planning process, one of the key concerns is how the implementation of the plans will be sustained over time. The excitement generated by the planning event itself can quickly dissipate when people are back in their routine work environments or when conditions change and the plans no longer seem quite to fit the new realities. ToP has built in several components to help groups prepare for success in implementing their plans.

The first component is concluding the planning process with a clear understanding and agreement on the part of the group as to what accomplishments are scheduled for completion during what time frame and which teams are responsible for insuring that each of these happen. In addition, for the initial launch period, usually approximately 90 days, each team will have worked through the very specific steps necessary for each of its accomplishments, with responsible names and dates clearly indicated for each step. The whole group will decide the vital coordination and communication systems for keeping everyone abreast of progress and able to provide support for one another when necessary. When people leave the planning session, they will have a common picture of what is going to happen when, and who is responsible for the different components. This gives everyone confidence that their plans will indeed bear fruit.

This ensuring of successful implementation begins with the Design Conference, where the leadership of the sponsor organization and the facilitation team collaboratively design the proposed planning event. This session deals with many things, one of which is preparing for the implementation of the anticipated plans. It is critical that the leadership understands the implementation will be a journey, and that it will have stages along the way that both the leadership and the larger group need to anticipate and prepare for in advance. ToP helps sponsors consider some guidelines for successfully launching the implementation of a plan, supporting and sustaining its momentum over time, dealing with both normal and unexpected turns of events, and

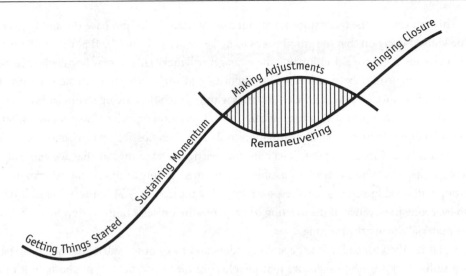

Figure 4. The Implementation Journey

finally bringing unmistakable closure to it (figure 4). Bringing new people onto the implementation teams, acknowledging successes small and large, and building new leadership capabilities make a big difference in a plan's sustainability. Especially important is that the leadership takes seriously the quarterly and annual plan rollover points where teams formulate detailed implementation steps to achieve comparatively short-term milestones.

Frequently, a group's plans call for some new ways of operating and making decisions together. Organizations that use ToP methods for a major planning event often continue to do so as part of the follow-up process. Rather than continually bringing in outside facilitators to lead this ongoing planning, they choose to make facilitative leadership training part of their corporate culture. This results in a shift toward a more participatory mode of operating that can spread throughout the organization.

Burning Question

Can an individual be a content-neutral facilitator of ToP methods within his or her own group, and if so, how? If someone is a member of the group, rather than an outsider brought in for the occasion, isn't he or she personally invested in the group and its decisions and therefore likely to experience a conflict in roles while facilitating a process?

One way to approach this question is to recognize how we all now play multiple roles as a new style of facilitative leadership emerges within modern organizations. Doing so, however, requires that we be clear ourselves and upfront with the group as to the particular role we are playing at any one time. To issue directives or simply tell a group how to resolve an issue may seem an appropriate managerial role—but not for that of a facilitator. As facilitators, we need to bring to the situation ways to engage the wisdom, insights, and commitment of the whole group.

This can call for the facilitator to spell out a set of boundaries and have the ability to articulate the kind of decision that the group needs to make for itself. It may be that this group is being asked to provide input for a decision that the manager will make later. It may be asked for its advice or ideas only, or it may be that it has full authority and responsibility to make decisions here. Groups are most successful when the boundaries within which they are operating are very clear.

There are some practical things we can do when we find ourselves in situations where we play a leadership role or have vital information to share. When possible, it is wise to ask someone else not so invested in the topic to facilitate this particular meeting, so that we can fully and actively participate. When that isn't possible, and we are the source of critical information that the group will need in order to deal responsibly with a topic, it may be appropriate to distribute this to everyone in advance of the meeting or prepare someone else in the group to be the source of this material during the meeting.

What is called for today is a deepening understanding of how leadership and group participation skills work together to ensure that people commit to action. ToP methods seek to contribute to the emergence of new styles of facilitative leadership in almost every arena of human endeavor.

Some Final Comments

We've described above how so much of the development of ToP methods depends upon action research—innovation and refinements coming more from experience in the field than from theory. The Technology of Participation has been fortunate in being able to benefit over the past 40 years from extensive field testing. As ICA expanded its work and the use of these methods around the world in widely diverse social settings, the methods evolved accordingly. The conversational, consensus formation, and planning processes were forced to become equally effective in remote rural villages of India and the corporate offices of Fortune 500 companies. They had to work for people rooted in a Confucian tradition of reserve, respect for authority, and nonconfrontation as much as in one that valued the challenging of authority and freewheeling democratic individualism. The methods had to work with men and women, youth and elders, the illiterate and the highly educated—and they had to be communicable and transferable in many languages.

Thousands of people have had a hand in the development of ToP methods. They have affirmed and helped polish what worked well and suggested ways to improve weaker points in a process. Innovations and adaptations have been shared among the networks of ICA staff and ToP trainers around the world and by legions of individual end users of the methods. As these large or small changes in process occurred, the methods gained greater clarity of focus and the appearance of what some have termed "elegant simplicity." ToP methods deal with the complex realities of our human condition, and increasingly they do so with a process that can be understood and appropriated by people everywhere.

About the Authors

Marilyn Oyler (moyler@ica-usa.org) has coordinated the collaborative development of the nationally recognized Technology of Participation (ToP) facilitation curriculum and national training system offering (ToP) training through a network of 140 trainers to more than 20,000 people all across the United States. She brings more than 25 years of experience in facilitating participatory strategic planning retreats and other organizational change efforts in seven nations with more than 100 organizations covering the private, public, and nonprofit sectors.

Gordon Harper (gharper@ica-usa.org) is an Institute of Cultural Affairs (ICA) senior process consultant and Technology of Participation mentor trainer with more than 30 years experience in facilitating organizational and community development. He has been responsible for the design, curriculum development, facilitation, and training of group processes and leadership formation programs for local communities, government agencies, transnational corporations, and non-profit organizations in 11 countries.

Where to Go for More Information

REFERENCES

Freire, Paulo. *Education for Critical Consciousness.* New York: Seabury Press, 1973.

Nelson, Jo, ed. *The Art of Focused Conversation for Schools.* Gabriola Island, British Columbia: New Society Publishers, 2001.

Spencer, Laura. *Winning Through Participation: Meeting the Challenge of Corporate Change with the Technology of Participation.* Dubuque, IA: Kendall/Hunt, 1989.
   Now in its eighth printing, this how-to book is an indispensable tool for those using participatory methods in organizations and communities. Available in English and Spanish.

Stanfield, R. Brian, ed. *The Art of Focused Conversation: 100 Ways to Access Group Wisdom in the Workplace.* Toronto: The Canadian Institute of Cultural Affairs, 1998.
   This hands-on book explains the Focused Conversation Method, its place in society, how to design and lead conversations with it, and common mistakes in using it—with 100 examples.

———. *The Workshop Book: From Individual Creativity to Group Action.* Gabriola Island, British Columbia: New Society Publishers, 2002.

ORGANIZATIONS

The Institute of Cultural Affairs—www.ica-usa.org

International Association of Facilitators—www.iaf-world.org

---

1. See Wayne Nelson's *Facilitator Style* on www.ica-associates.ca.

2. See Brian Stanfield, "Some Background," *The Workshop Book* (Toronto: New Society Publishers, 2002), 14–20.

SYLVIA L. JAMES AND PAUL TOLCHINSKY

Whole-Scale Change

> *And so, next generation . . . we pioneers are moving to the next learning environment, and leaving this one to you. My assignment to you, before I go, is the following: Stand on the shoulders of the pioneers who went before you . . . honor and learn from us, and then spring into the future with new and robust concepts that will be more than we old-timers ever dreamed of. You are the creative minds of this unfolding Millennium.*
>
> —Kathleen D. Dannemiller (1929–2003)

Covenant HomeCare: The Case for Change

Covenant HomeCare provides comprehensive home-care services within 16 counties in east Tennessee. HomeCare is one of many affiliates of a regional nonprofit health-care system. Prior to the sweeping changes brought by the Federal Balanced Budget Act of 1997, the agency provided approximately 250,000 home health visits annually.

In 2000, HomeCare faced dramatic declines in patient admissions and visits. In October 2000, HomeCare faced a steep decline in Medicare and TennCare reimbursement when changes to the home health services payment system replaced the old reasonable costs-based system. When a new president arrived who was experienced in hospital operations and had a strong belief in systems theory and a formal approach to process improvement, she quickly recognized that the company was in serious jeopardy. Rapid planning and action was necessary for survival. Leadership knew that their core business processes were inefficient and often inaccurate, relying heavily on many rounds of inspections and duplication to accomplish simple tasks. In addition, an employee satisfaction survey pointed to the need for significant change. The survey revealed that employees were neither ripe for change, nor satisfied with their level of involvement in company operations. They did not have a clear vision of where the company was going, nor a strong belief that current leaders could take them forward.

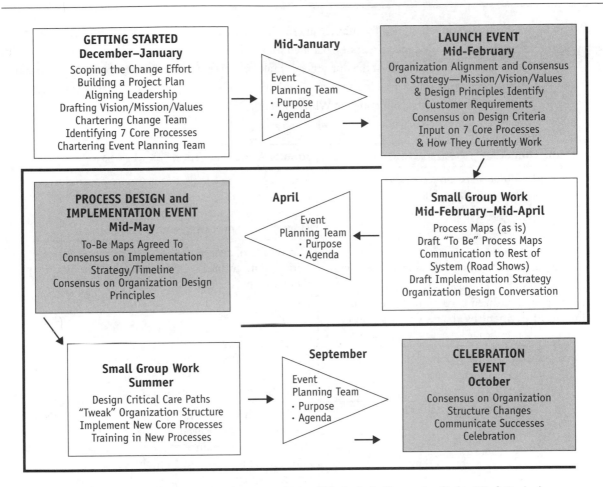

Figure 1. Covenant HomeCare Change Road Map (Whole-Scale Change Applied to Work Design)

COVENANT HOMECARE CHANGE JOURNEY: APPLYING WHOLE-SCALE TO WORK DESIGN

Figure 1 describes the three large group events and the interim small group work that meaningfully involved everyone in the organization in decisions affecting their future and the organization's. The small group work included leadership alignment, event planning, and process redesign. The large group work occurred when pulling together a critical mass of the organization was important. This journey began with small group work to align leadership around the purpose, desired outcomes, and approach for the change. Then a microcosm of HomeCare designed the large group meeting involving all employees, launching the change effort, and giving input to redesign seven processes. The launch meeting's purpose, which the microcosm planning team created, was "To bring together the hearts and minds of all Covenant HomeCare employees so that they became empowered to make changes that determined their future." A second large group meeting, designed by another microcosm of HealthCare, attended by all employees, finalized the newly designed processes, planned implementation, and prepared to align structure with the new work processes. At the third meeting, all employees reached consensus on a new structure and worked through making processes and structure operational. Table 1 highlights Covenant HomeCare's results from applying Whole-Scale™.

Covenant HomeCare's Desired Outcomes	Results Achieved Within Six Months
Reduce a $1.5 million loss projected for the year 2000 to a break-even bottom line in 2001.	The biggest result is that at a time when industry changes caused more than 25 percent to go out of business, and most others struggled to survive, HomeCare is profitable and growing!
Redesign the work: • Identify and redesign core business processes. • Identify top clinical diagnoses for patients and develop standardized care paths for each before fixed payment by diagnosis goes into effect.	The results of redesigning and implementing seven critical, core business processes within six months put them well on their way to their "break-even" goal.
Improve customer satisfaction.	Customer satisfaction improved in all categories and moved from 60th to 70th percentile rankings to 90th percentile rankings in some categories.
Improve employee satisfaction.	Leaders measured both "soft" and "hard" results. In the process, they realized that often the "soft" aspects drive high performance more so than technical skills and knowledge. The next employee survey showed statistically significant improvements in key indicators.
Change the culture of Covenant HomeCare to be one of employee involvement, empowerment, and alignment with strategic goals.	Employees on the redesign teams, seeing their suggestions implemented, signed up to be on implementation teams as well. Before the payroll redesign team's work had been fully implemented, almost all staff readily agreed to utilize electronic deposit for their paychecks when they learned the potential savings that would be achieved. This was quite remarkable considering that some HomeCare staff did not have bank accounts! Leadership viewed themselves as strong champions and sponsors of the change process.

Table 1. Covenant HomeCare's Results

Whole-Scale Change

Frequently Asked Questions

WHAT IS WHOLE-SCALE?

Whole-Scale was born in 1981 when Ford Motor Company, seeking to move its management culture from "command and control" to a more participative style, brought in Al Davenport, Bruce Gibb, Chuck Tyson, and Kathleen Dannemiller to design and facilitate the change. The method that emerged from this initial work has been used for more than two decades and has helped hundreds of organizations and communities around the world. Although each situation is different, the basic direction of Whole-Scale is the same: to help organizations uncover and engage the combined knowledge, wisdom, and heart of their people to meet the challenges of a changing world.

Whole-Scale evolved from "Real Time Strategic Change" (invented by Dannemiller Tyson Associates) and "Real Time Work Design" (invented by Paul Tolchinsky and Kathie Dannemiller). It consists of a series of small and/or large group interactions that enable the organization to shift paradigms, working together to create and integrate all the needed changes. It applies action learning, using Whole-Scale events as accelerators. Through microcosms—groups representing the range of stakeholders, levels, functions, geography, and ideas in the organization—Whole-Scale processes simultaneously work with the parts and the whole of the system to create and sustain change.

Whole-Scale also enables a "critical mass" of the organization to create a new culture *in the moment.* That critical mass then models what the organization can look like, becoming the vehicle for powerful change in the whole system.

WHEN AND WHERE IS IT USED?

Whole-Scale facilitates all kinds of complex systems change, including strategic planning and implementation, organization design, process redesign, merger integration, training, diversity, culture change, technology implementation, and risk/project management. It works well in both the public and private sectors, with groups of ten to several thousand, from the top of the hierarchy through frontline staff, in virtual and/or face-to-face environments. Organizations use Whole-Scale interventions to engage everyone or nearly everyone in creating their organizations (processes and structures), and when a sense of urgency exists, perhaps from a challenging and quickly changing environment. With clear strategy, strong leadership, adequate training, and systemwide follow-through, Whole-Scale processes facilitate rapid systemwide change under many circumstances, and in a wide variety of countries, cultures, and organizations.

A Whole-Scale change project is a complex undertaking that requires a great deal of attention at start-up to ensure later success. Organizations are usually in the midst of one or more change projects as they explore undertaking a Whole-Scale effort. These projects often have different goals, are in different parts of the organization, and are unconnected. Whole-Scale facilitates integration and synergy across these discrepant activities.

A Whole-Scale change project is purpose-driven and includes robust processes that quickly change client systems, preparing them to sustain change by:

- Clarifying and connecting multiple current realities

- Uniting multiple yearnings around a common picture of the future

- Reaching agreement on the action plans that move them toward that future

- Building and integrating the processes, structures, relationships, and shared information that move the organization forward

- Aligning organization leaders and employees so that they implement changes together

WHAT ARE THE OUTCOMES FROM WHOLE-SCALE?

Whole-Scale change outcomes pervade all organizational levels: accelerating change, more immediate results, rapid implementation, and sustained momentum. Every organization differs in how it measures success. Here are some examples:

- New model launched in two years, versus five years previously

- Costs reduced by 34 percent

- Productivity up 20 percent

- Employee turnover rate reduced 53 percent

- Leadership succession plan implemented

- Product delivery time cut over 40 percent

- Sales up from $40M to $50M in first year and $60M in second year of the strategy

- Process cycle time reduced by 49 percent

- Quality the highest at start-up of any new product introduction

- Acquisition integration completed successfully six months ahead of schedule

- Cycle time reduced from 15 to 2 days

- Implementation completed within one year

- Span of control for managers increased from 1:10 to 1:80 people

- Twenty-two departments consolidated to three

- The cost of quality (scrap, rework) reduced from 8.6 percent of sales to 3.4 percent

HOW DOES IT WORK?

The term Whole-Scale describes "wholeness on any scale, as long as it is a microcosm." The power of the microcosm is that it allows stakeholders to see the whole system and work the whole system regardless of the microcosm's size (large or small—the "scale" in Whole-Scale).[1]

Although each situation differs, Whole-Scale helps organizations uncover and engage people's knowledge, wisdom, and heart to achieve strategic business results in their changing world. During small and large group meetings, organizational microcosms create and implement real-time solutions. A Whole-Scale event often involves hundreds of people to get alignment on and breakthrough on key issues. A Whole-Scale journey often involves thousands in simultaneous and integrated change efforts for redesigning processes, structures, technology, skill development, and supporting systems.

At every moment, at least seven models simultaneously guide Whole-Scale work: (1) $D \times V \times F > R$,[2] (2) Action Learning Model,[3] (3) Converge/Diverge[4] for thinking about when to "go whole," (4) any strategic planning model, (5) Star of Success systems model,[5] (6) Data-Purpose-Plan-Evaluate project planning model, and (7) Membership-Control-Goals[6] team formation model.

Once a clear and shared purpose for transformation exists, large group meetings often accelerate and integrate change by aligning people from across the organization. These meetings are always designed by a microcosm called an Event Planning Team. The Event Planning Team and consultants design a Whole-Scale event using a formula for change inspired by Dick Beckhard. The formula, $D \times V \times F > R$, says that if an organization wants systemwide change, they must work with a critical mass of the organization to uncover and combine their Dissatisfaction (D) with how things are. Then they uncover and combine yearnings for the organization they truly want to be—their combined Vision of the future (V). If real change is to happen, the third design element is First steps (F), a combined picture of what people can do differently that *all* believe are

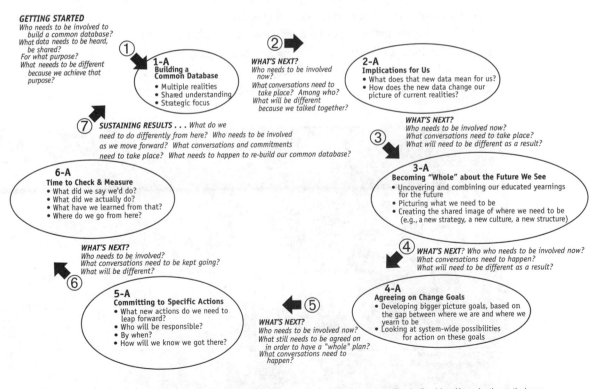

1   This is a point where you might be beginning a systemwide change process and you would (as an Event-Planning Team) be asking and acting on the issues.
2–7 The Event-Planning Team, or some other microcosm group, needs to be asking these questions and acting on the answers to plan the next step.

Figure 2. How We See Continuous Learning in an Organization Using Whole-Scale Processes

right to achieve their vision. Simple math suggests that if D, V, or F is missing, the product is zero, and the change effort will not overcome people's Resistance (R).

The DVF formula describes what an organization does to shift paradigms. If the organization uncovers and combines all three elements, everyone shifts into a new "worldview." They take actions that transform their shared vision into shared realities. Individuals and groups can no longer comfortably keep doing what they were doing. Change has already begun.

Clients help decide which element to address first, but they need to address all three elements eventually to achieve sustainable change. The resistance to change that is inevitably present is a resource telling consultants and leaders what they need to know and where leverage exists to facilitate real change.

The Whole-Scale process is a never-ending journey, a continuing cycle of steps 1–7 (figure 2). Each intervention's design (large or small) addresses steps 1–5. Steps 6 and 7 maintain momentum, promote a learning culture, and inform next steps to sustain the transformation.

People in organizations learn to ask the right questions and to develop a common database from which they create a shared vision. Then they agree on change goals and connect around specific actions. Following Deming's "Plan-Do-Check-Act" cycle gives them results to evaluate. Then the process begins again, tracing an ever-deepening spiral into the mind and heart of the organization.

Figure 3 illustrates the Star of Success systems model. The Star is a practical framework that helps organizations think through systemwide change. Agreeing on what each point of the Star needs to look like ensures focus for moving successfully into the future. The five points collectively correspond to a pattern that, if repeated, leads to repeated successes.

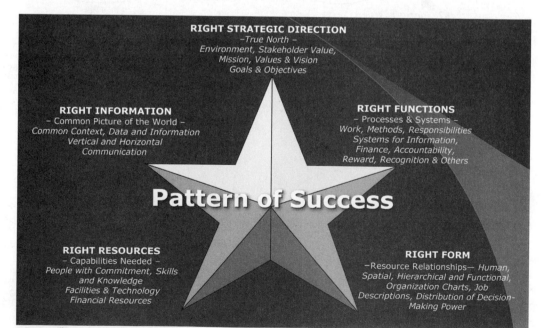

© Dannemiller Tyson Associates

Figure 3. The Star of Success: Guide for Designing the Change Journey

Table of Uses

Whole-Scale works in any type of system, no matter the diverse presenting issues. The following table provides a sampling:

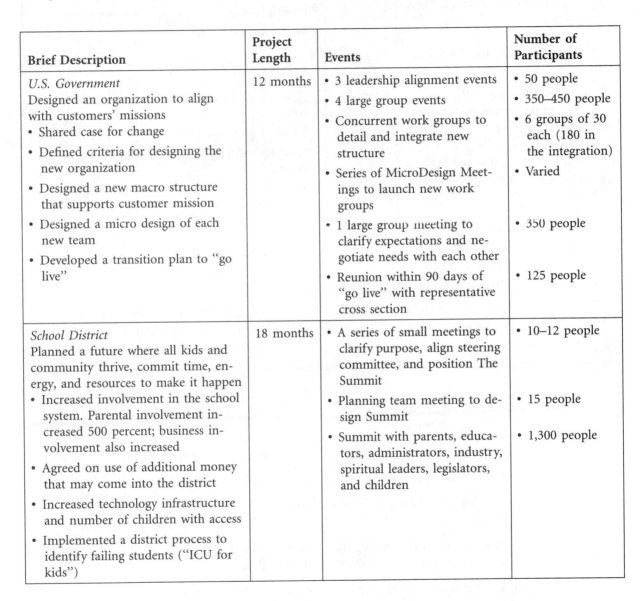

Brief Description	Project Length	Events	Number of Participants
U.S. Government Designed an organization to align with customers' missions • Shared case for change • Defined criteria for designing the new organization • Designed a new macro structure that supports customer mission • Designed a micro design of each new team • Developed a transition plan to "go live"	12 months	• 3 leadership alignment events • 4 large group events • Concurrent work groups to detail and integrate new structure • Series of MicroDesign Meetings to launch new work groups • 1 large group meeting to clarify expectations and negotiate needs with each other • Reunion within 90 days of "go live" with representative cross section	• 50 people • 350–450 people • 6 groups of 30 each (180 in the integration) • Varied • 350 people • 125 people
School District Planned a future where all kids and community thrive, commit time, energy, and resources to make it happen • Increased involvement in the school system. Parental involvement increased 500 percent; business involvement also increased • Agreed on use of additional money that may come into the district • Increased technology infrastructure and number of children with access • Implemented a district process to identify failing students ("ICU for kids")	18 months	• A series of small meetings to clarify purpose, align steering committee, and position The Summit • Planning team meeting to design Summit • Summit with parents, educators, administrators, industry, spiritual leaders, legislators, and children	• 10–12 people • 15 people • 1,300 people

Brief Description	Project Length	Events	Number of Participants
Manufacturing Positioned plant to be the leader in R&D while maintaining quality production • Aligned a 24/7 operation within one week	1 month	• Leadership alignment • Event planning • Series of six meetings	• 12 people • 20 people • 150 each meeting
Global Technology Corporation Implemented new performance management processes: • Strategic alignment • 5,000 managers trained and prepared to implement new processes for acquiring, developing, and managing talent • Performance-driven culture	5 months	• 10 meetings around the world • 3 project planning meetings • Planning meeting for generic event • Series of virtual meetings to customize each Web site	• 500 people • 24–40 people • 20 people • 6 people

Getting Started With Whole-Scale

The first step in using Whole-Scale processes to change an organization is to clearly define the strategic purpose of the effort. Regardless of the "presenting issue" (e.g., strategic alignment and deployment, work design, culture change, technology implementation), the leaders and the consultants must clearly define how the outcomes support the business strategy.

GUIDING PRINCIPLES

Whole-Scale works for any consultant who believes and lives the following principles:

- An organization must understand both its history and its present state to create its future.

- It is impossible for an organization to plan effectively without knowing the future it wants.

- Creating a microcosm of the whole organization enables the larger system to change in real time.

- The wisdom is in the people. When you connect people, they have all the wisdom they need to find the answers. Each person's truth is truth.

- When you listen to the client, listen to see the world they see.

- In order to be of service to my clients, I need to love and respect them even—and especially—when I don't agree with them.

- Whole-system solutions must focus on the interconnectedness of people, processes, and technology.

- People are more likely to support what they help to create.

Roles, Responsibilities, and Relationships

Sponsorship Requirements

It is essential to prepare senior management to function as a leadership team, capable of managing the change process. People yearn for effective leaders, and Whole-Scale processes make those leaders very visible. Leaders communicate boundaries, charter teams to work on changes, provide resources, direction, and support, and oversee implementation of the work between large-scale events. Sponsorship requires involved leaders throughout the process.

An organization's leaders must agree to participate in creating a common database—both by speaking and by listening. The definition of leadership varies by organization: it may include union and management leaders, it may be a project steering committee, an informal group working as change leaders, or a managers' group.

Role of the Facilitator

The consultant's primary role is to guide, monitor, and evaluate the flow of the change processes. Consultants work as a team—two externally and two internally, if available. This combined team collaborates with the leadership team, ensuring they stay connected to what's happening.

A Whole-Scale consultant needs to (1) have a strong customer focus, (2) be able to connect personal wisdom and experience with the client's needs, and (3) partner throughout the transformation process. Whole-Scale consultants must be good strategic thinkers, apply systems thinking principles and characteristics of living systems, and be experienced process consultants. They must be able to embrace conflict and chaos and be able to stay in the situation until the organization has sorted itself out. Organisms need chaos to self-organize their solutions.

In small and large group meetings, the consultant's job is to give clear direction to participants so that they have the conversations required to get the work done. This calls for framing that intentionally unleashes the group's energy and wisdom toward a focused, purpose-driven conversation and then getting out of the way! Throughout these meetings, the consultant is managing complexity and working on numerous levels simultaneously. This requires a selfless ego, curiosity, a tolerance for ambiguity, a pioneer spirit, and stamina!

Role of Participants and Other Roles

Core Team

In Whole-Scale work design, a core team is the working-level linking mechanism from kickoff through implementation. As a microcosm, they help shift the organization by bringing divergent thinking (benchmarking information, possibilities, "straw models," and "out-of-the-box thinking" ideas) to larger groups—other microcosms of the whole system—for convergence. They learn about designing organizations; educate others; support integration of the Whole-Scale change project with other change projects; track task team work; create processes for reconciling task team work into integrated solutions; and ensure that the final design (process and organization) is integrated with the existing organization and its vision, values, and principles.

There is no one "design team" who creates the change, makes the choices. Instead, the core team explores possibilities and engages the critical mass in deciding the new ways of doing business. Sponsorship teams and core teams act as linking mechanisms.

Role of the Event-Planning Team

An event planning team (EPT) is formed to prepare for any Whole-Scale event—large or small. Its members are a microcosm of the planned meeting. The EPT serves as a diagnostic window on the organization. It develops a purpose statement and an event design. Team members provide content expertise, while the consultants provide process expertise. EPT members participate in the event; they join the leaders and consultants in reading evaluations at the end of each day and decide any changes in the next day's design. By their nature, an EPT exists to design a single Whole-Scale session. Each event has a unique EPT.

Role of the Logistics Team

An event is somewhat like a stage drama, and the logistics "czar" is equivalent to stage manager, heading up a team of stagehands, usually one for every 50 people. They work hard, providing a smooth flow, making sure materials are available as needed. Because of the demands of their work, they do not participate in the event. They are often people from other departments or offices who want to learn more about Whole-Scale. They don't need to be a microcosm.

Role of the Participants

People often enter a Whole-Scale process somewhat suspicious and cynical. They have experienced false starts and have lived through numerous seemingly useless change efforts. As people develop a common database, trust builds. They experience empowerment through their journey together, taking appropriate risks and becoming more self-sufficient—as individuals, as teams, and as an organization.

As events unfold, people get to know others in the organization with whom they do not typically interact. They contribute to the common database by sharing their hopes, doubts, fears, and ideas freely, listening to others, and making personal commitments to changed behavior.

Typically, participants sit at round tables of eight to ten people. Each table facilitates itself. Given a handout describing the roles of Facilitator, Recorder, and Spokesperson, each table rotates these roles, learning skills for productive meetings and engaging every voice in difficult, complex conversations.

Conditions for Success

WHY WHOLE-SCALE WORKS

Practitioners of Whole-Scale believe that the wisdom is in the group. The methodology works because leaders who no longer want to command and control find new ways to align and engage large numbers of people with common strategic focus. It facilitates a process of divergent and convergent thinking that brings about change. It works because:

- people are hungry for information,
- it provides the connections with others that people yearn for,
- people at all organizational levels are empowered to be experts on what they do, using and sharing their expertise, and
- "each person's truth is truth" and is part of the whole picture.

COMMON MISTAKES IN THE USE OF WHOLE-SCALE

Common mistakes include the following:

- Not having clear purpose for the transformation and for every intervention
- Seeing Whole-Scale merely as an event, rather than recognizing that each event, whether large or small, motivates long-term change
- Planning or proceeding without the wisdom of a microcosm
- Allowing the leadership of the organization (either union or management) to unilaterally overrule the decisions of a core team or event planning team
- Not building a team within a leadership group so that they are aligned and prepared to be as good as they can be
- Lifting individual processes from Whole-Scale and replicating them as components of good meetings without recognizing the flow of the entire process, thus losing the synergy of what's possible
- Thinking only of "size" instead of focusing on robust processes for getting to one brain/one heart
- Working alone; not partnering with internals

Theoretical Base of Whole-Scale

The bases for Whole-Scale methodology are process consultation, strategy development and implementation, community building, and sociotechnical systems theory. Many of the values and principles come from the Laboratory Method of Learning developed by Ron Lippitt and others at the National Training Labs and from Eric Trist and his colleagues at the Tavistock Institute, who pioneered the Socio-Technical Systems approach to designing organizations.

Whole-Scale Change

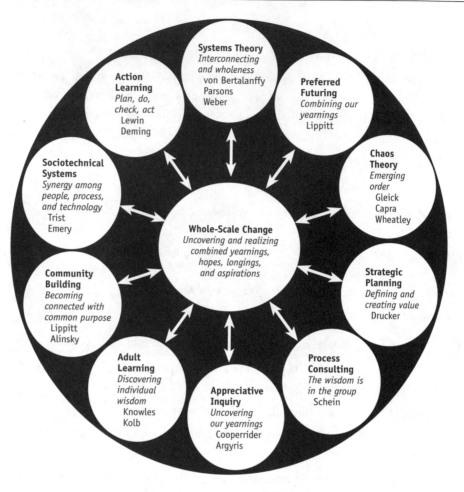

Figure 4. Theoretical Basis of Whole-Scale

More recently Meg Wheatley, Myron Kellner-Rogers, and others have advanced Field Theory, Chaos Theory, and Systems Thinking; and Rick Maurer has reframed resistance in a way that is also very helpful. Figure 4 illustrates how the various elements of Whole-Scale draw from a broad spectrum of research and practice. The figure contains some, but not all, of the theoretical underpinnings of Whole-Scale.

Sustaining the Results

Four principles help sustain the implementation of changes that begin in large-scale meetings:

KEEPING THE SYSTEM WHOLE

In Whole-Scale events, the group remains whole because the microcosms in the room develop a shared picture of the present, the future they yearn to create, and actions to move forward. Once an event ends, the common picture begins to fragment. People return to their "silos," new information emerges, people leave, and new ones arrive. Staying whole in thinking becomes the organization's challenge over time.

Practical approaches to staying whole are: publishing the results and commitments made, creating cross-functional teams to carry out change initiatives, and setting dates to get back together so people can learn from their experiences and decide on next steps. People need opportunities to share their struggles, celebrate their successes, and regularly reconnect to the common database.

Engaging as Many Microcosms as Possible

Sustaining momentum requires re-creating key elements of the large group meeting on a day-to-day basis. As the organization moves forward, it must continue bringing together groups representing the diverse functions, disciplines, levels, and options existing in the organization. New microcosms have to be engaged, such as action teams and implementation teams. Microcosms can convene in large group meetings, checkpoints, deep dives (a series of focused, one-half to one-day meetings, each tackling a specific topic), and reunions. As more people engage in more microcosms, two things happen: (1) you move faster and (2) sustain and create new change energy.

Building Toward Critical Mass

Throughout any Whole-Scale change process, microcosms of the organizational activities create a hologram of the system working together as a whole. The organization must continually expand the circle of involvement. When a critical mass of different microcosms experiences the paradigm shift experienced by event participants, systems change becomes continuous. Constantly expanding sets of microcosms carry the energy to support change.

Keeping the Flame of Change Burning

Energy for sustaining change comes from meaning, hope, and power. Meaning comes from people knowing and seeing themselves in the purpose, direction, and plans for the organization.

Hope comes from knowing that the organization is succeeding in its change efforts, applying its learning as it changes, and achieving demonstrable results. Hope remains alive through measuring the outcomes of change efforts, monitoring and communicating results, and keeping the system whole.

Power comes from actively engaging a critical mass of the organization in the change efforts. Empowering more people instills the capacity in individuals to sustain the change process. Power comes from exercising the ability to influence. Sustaining momentum ensures that people feel powerful about the things that matter to them. Power comes from people knowing that they have impact and can make change happen.

Burning Question

How do you imagine what the journey needs to be when you haven't begun and things are going to change so much? This is a great question because it captures both the complexity and the self-organizing nature of living systems. We begin by working with the clients to identify their purpose and outcomes. Our conversations loosely follow the D×V×F>R flow described earlier to unleash and combine the leaders' yearnings and the organizations' needs and desires. The clients' purpose is their combined responses to, "When you look into the future, what do you yearn to see?"

Road maps (or a good consulting project plan) capture the journey that the client needs to take and provides a moment of comfort that the change will happen. The change road map is initially crafted based on conversations about the desired results from the clients' purpose and their situation:

1. Speed—how fast do they need to move?

2. How complex is the change?

3. How much risk is associated with the change? If it is a high-risk culture, any misstep creates too much distrust. In a high-risk situation, planning might be a month out.

4. What's the minimum critical transformation work to achieve the desired outcomes?

With the transformation purpose and desired results as the strategic beacon, these four factors shape a logically structured path to proceed. Action learning checkpoints inform the system about "what are we learning and now what?"

The road map represents a best guess about what the process needs to look like. It combines the process consultant's wisdom with the journey the clients believe they need to take and the work they believe they need to accomplish. Any good process makes midcourse corrections; that is why we call it action research and action learning . . . it happens consciously and in real time!

Some Final Comments

We are often asked to compare Whole-Scale with other methods of change. The truth is that the approaches are more alike than they are different. Many grow out of the same history, philosophies, and values. We say, "Learn all of them and then create your own—the one that fits you and/or a particular client. We each invented our particular passion in exactly that way. Our clients taught us and shaped our processes, for which we are very grateful!"

About the Authors

Sylvia L. James (sylvia@dannemillertyson.com), partner, Dannemiller Tyson Associates, pioneered Whole-Scale Change in aerospace in the early 1980s. Today, she works globally with complex systems to facilitate healthy change in strategy, merger integration, culture change, and

Whole-Scale Change

organizational design. She is coauthor of books and articles and presents at conferences/workshops around the world. She is passionate about giving people both voice and ways to contribute their wisdom to the organizations and communities where they live and work.

Paul Tolchinsky (pault@pdassociates.com) has been consulting to major companies around the world for 30 years. Paul's focus is on accelerating the rate of change. A pioneer in Large Group Interventions and whole-system thinking, his expertise is designing organizations and Whole-Scale change. Internationally known as a developer of Whole-Scale approaches to change, Paul is author of two books and numerous articles. Featured in works by others, Paul's passion is unleashing the potential and magic in organizations.

Where to Go for More Information

REFERENCES

Bunker, Barbara Benedict, and Billie T. Alban. *Large Group Interventions: Engaging the Whole System for Rapid Change.* San Francisco: Jossey-Bass, 1997.

Dannemiller Tyson Associates. *Whole-Scale Change Toolkit,* 3d ed. Ann Arbor, MI: Dannemiller Tyson Associates, 2005.

———. *Whole-Scale Change: Unleashing the Magic in Organizations.* San Francisco: Berrett-Koehler, 2000.

Dannemiller, K., S. James, and P. Tolchinsky. "Consulting that Unleashes the Spirit." In *The Flawless Consulting Fieldbook and Companion.* San Francisco: Jossey-Bass, 2000.

Eggers, M., S. Kazmierski, and J. McNally. "Unleashing the Magic in Healthcare." *OD Practitioner* 32, no. 4 (2000).

James, S., J. Carbone, A. Blixt, and J. McNeil. "Trust and Transformation: Integrating Two Florida Education Unions." In *The Handbook of Large Group Methods: Creating Systemic Change in Organizations and Communities,* edited by B. Alban and B. Bunker. San Francisco: Jossey-Bass, 2006.

James, Sylvia, and Al Blixt. *Accelerating Strategic Change: Application of the Whole-Scale Approach to Leading and Managing Change.* Vienna, Austria: Learnende Organisation, Institut für Systemisches Coaching und Training, January 2004.

James, Sylvia, Mary Eggers, Marsha Hughes-Rease, Roland Loup, and Bev Seiford. "Facilitating Large Group Meetings that Get Results Every Time." In *The IAF Handbook of Group Facilitation,* edited by Sandy Schuman. San Francisco: Jossey-Bass, 2005.

Kaschub, W. "Employees Redesign HR." *Human Resource Professional* (July/August 1997).

Pasmore, W., and Paul D. Tolchinsky. "Doing It Right from the Start." *The Journal for Quality and Participation* (December 1989).

Tolchinsky, P. "Still on a Winning Streak." *Workforce* (September 1997).

Whole-Scale Change

Tolchinsky, P., and M. Johnson. "A Redesign in the Central Intelligence Agency." *The Journal for Quality and Participation* (March/April 1999): 31–35. Association for Quality and Participation.

Wheatley, M. *Leadership and the New Science.* San Francisco: Berrett-Koehler, 1992.

ORGANIZATIONS

Dannemiller Tyson Associates—www.dannemillertyson.com

Performance Development Associates—www.pdassociates.com

This chapter is dedicated to Kathleen D. Dannemiller, who passed away in December 2003. Kathie coauthored with us the Whole-Scale Change chapter in the first edition of *The Change Handbook*. Kathie's spirit, values, and messages are carried forward in this chapter.

1. Dannemiller Tyson Associates, *Whole-Scale Change: Unleashing the Magic in Organizations* (San Francisco: Berrett-Koehler, 2000).

2. Inspired by Walt Gleicher and Dick Beckhard.

3. Dannemiller Tyson Associates, *Whole-Scale Change*, 12–13.

4. Created by Paul Tolchinsky, adapted from the work of Paul R. Lawrence and J. W. Lorsch, *Organization and Environment: Managing Differentiation and Integration* (Cambridge: Harvard Business School Classics, 1986).

5. Created by Allen Gates, partner, Dannemiller Tyson Associates.

6. Adapted from the thinking of Jack Gibb.

Whole-Scale Change

12

JUANITA BROWN, KEN HOMER, AND DAVID ISAACS

The World Café

In the new economy conversations are the most important form of work.
—Alan Webber, *Harvard Business Review*

What We Know About How Organizations Learn

Several years ago, Meg Wheatley and Juanita Brown, under the auspices of the Berkana Institute, were cohosting a program on living systems. They introduced an innovative approach to large group dialogue, called the World Café. Bob Veazie, an engineer at Hewlett Packard, was among the participants that day. Deeply touched by the experience, here's how he recalls the Café's impact:

> The core question posed for the Café was, "What do we believe we know about how organizations learn?" We had twenty minutes or so for each table of four to explore the question. Then one person stayed at the table and the rest moved to other Café tables, met new people and continued the dialogue. Everyone was very actively involved, the energy and volume were high, and people brought different aspects of what they learned from their last tables to their new conversations. It was very exciting, but very disturbing at the same time.
>
> Something profound happened that day. For those few hours, I experienced something utterly new and yet completely familiar that challenged everything I thought I knew about how the world works. I realized that my organization functions differently from how it looks on the formal organization chart—that underneath those boxes might be more natural conversations than anything that can be formally "managed" in the way we, as leaders, normally think about it. I could see that each day we engaged in conversations around different questions, just like these small table con-

versations in the Café—and that we moved between those "tables" as we did our work. It became clear that the World Cafe wasn't just a classroom experience. This is how life actually works! We just don't ordinarily have the nice tables and the flowers.

I can't honestly say that I knew immediately what the implications of seeing in this new way were for me as a leader. That came later. But that day, the World Café shifted how I saw the world. I started to wonder: If conversations are the heart of our work, then how am I, as a leader, relating to this natural set of conversations going on? Am I contributing to it or am I taking energy away from it? Are we using the intelligence of just a few people when we could gain the intelligence of hundreds by focusing on key questions and including people more intentionally as we did in that World Café conversation? These questions haunted me. My first World Café experience brought up deeper systemic issues that I'm still thinking and learning about to this day.

About a year and a half after his first World Café, Bob was leading a project on reducing the accident rate among 50,000 employees at Hewlett Packard. Using World Café principles, he and his team reduced the company-wide accident rate more than 33 percent by engaging people at all levels in connected conversations about the questions that mattered most to them about safety.

The Basics

What Is the World Café?

Through both our research[1] and a decade of practice, we have come to view the World Café as a *conversational process*, based on a set of *integrated design principles* that reveal a deeper *living network pattern*, through which we coevolve our collective futures.

As a *conversational process*, the World Café is a simple methodology that can evoke and make visible the collective intelligence of any group, increasing people's capacity for effective action in pursuit of common aims. One reason for this is that regardless of the size of the Café, participants experience each conversation at their table as linked and connected to the unfolding conversation in the room as a whole. We have successfully used it with groups from 12 to 1,200. The *integrated design principles* evoke collective intelligence through dialogue. These principles can be used in a plethora of settings, helping people at all levels of a system develop greater collective capacity to shape their futures through conversations that matter.

As a *living network pattern*, the World Café provides a lived experience of participating in a dynamic network of conversations that continually coevolves as we explore questions that matter with family, friends, colleagues, and community. The metaphor of the "World *as* Café," helps us

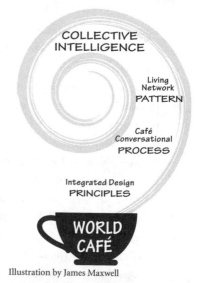

COLLECTIVE INTELLIGENCE

Living Network PATTERN

Café Conversational PROCESS

Integrated Design PRINCIPLES

WORLD CAFÉ

Illustration by James Maxwell

notice these often-invisible webs of dialogue and personal relationships that enable us to learn, create shared purpose, and shape life-affirming futures together.

WHEN IS THE WORLD CAFÉ USEFUL AND HOW DOES IT WORK?

A well-designed Café is useful whenever you wish to access the intelligence and best thinking of groups. Tens of thousands of people on six continents have experienced the World Café in settings as disparate as multinational corporations, small nonprofits, government agencies, community-based organizations, and educational institutions.

In a World Café conversation, four people sit at a café-style table or in a small conversation cluster to explore a question or issue that matters to their life, work, or community. Other participants seated at nearby tables or in conversation clusters explore similar questions at the same time. As they talk, participants are encouraged to write down key ideas on large cards or to sketch them on paper tablecloths that are there for that purpose.

After a 20- to 30-minute "round of conversation" in an initial intimate group of 4 or 5 members, participants are invited to change tables—carrying key ideas and insights from their previous conversation into a newly formed small group. One "host" stays at each table to share with new arrivals the key images, insights, and questions that emerged from their prior dialogue. This process is repeated for several (generally three) rounds and is followed by a harvesting of the dialogue to which all participants contribute.

Given the purpose and design of the Café, the whole process can occur successfully in as little as two hours, while more in-depth explorations may take up to several days. The World Café fosters new connections. Each table and Café round is a self-contained conversation that becomes linked to the larger conversation taking place among all participants. The cross-pollination of perspectives that results is one of the hallmarks of the World Café. As people and ideas become ever more richly connected during progressive rounds of conversation, latent, collective knowledge becomes visible. A growing sense of the larger whole transforms how participants see themselves and their relationships. Collective intelligence grows and evolves, and innovative possibilities for action are brought forward.

Café conversations are designed on the assumption that people already have within them the wisdom and creativity to effectively address even their most difficult challenges. The World Café works because it is based on something we all know how to do—*engage in a good conversation*. It draws on the quintessential processes by which people around the world naturally think together, create shared meaning, strengthen community, and ignite innovation.

The World Café enables leaders in any setting to create generative networks of conversation focused on the questions that are critical to the real work of their organization or community. Given the appropriate framing and focus, Café conversations allow participants to access mutual intelligence in the service of desired outcomes. Those using it often report an unexpected leap in their collective capacity to establish trust, nurture relationships, expand effective knowledge, and create new possibilities for action, even among people with no previous history of working together. Consequently, the World Café and its design principles have immediate, practical implications for meeting

World Café

Illustrations by Sherrin Bennett

In each conversation, individual contributions are focused on questions that matter.

People build on one another's ideas—everyone contributes from their own perspective to create new understanding.

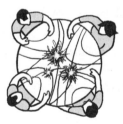

As people make new connections sparks of insight begin to emerge that no one would have alone.

As people share insights between tables, the "magic in the middle" and a sense of the whole becomes more accessible.

The whole continues to evolve into greater coherence—the discovery of collective intelligence.

and conference design, strategy formation, knowledge creation, innovation, and large-scale systems change.

As a metaphor, the "World as Café" helps illuminate a core process that underpins large-scale organizational and societal change. Throughout history, new ideas have been born through informal conversations in cafés, salons, pubs, places of worship, kitchen tables, and living rooms. Major change efforts often begin when the people most affected by an issue simply start talking together. Members of these small groups then share the questions and ideas that touch

World Café

them with others, who do the same. Over time, sometimes quite rapidly, the exploration ripples out and engages ever-larger constituencies in widening circles, stimulating new conversations, creative possibilities, and collective action.

The World Café offers an easily accessible experience of how conversations create shared meaning, which in turn shapes individual and collective behavior. For example, our colleague, Carlos Mota, brought diverse stakeholders together for a World Café in Mexico. High government officials were seated with rural farmers and city-dwelling businesspeople and invited to engage questions vital to their collective future. These diverse voices cross-pollinated their perspectives through multiple rounds of conversation contributing substantially to the direction and focus that Mexico's National Fund for Social Enterprise undertook as a result. Imagine the resulting behavior had the conference been dominated by academic experts presenting papers to a passive audience of government representatives![2]

Table of Uses

Typical Setting	Duration of Project	Number and Length of Cafés	Number of Participants
Conferences of All Types Keynote/plenary or breakout, either as a Café inquiry or combined with a context-setting speaker	Design phase: several weeks or months Conference: from 1–5 days	1 or more plenary or breakout sessions of at least 1.5 (preferably 2) hours, excluding a speaker	20–1,200
School District Teachers and administrators inquiring into improving scholastic performance	Several months to a year or more	Monthly Cafés among various constituencies	20–50 people, depending on scale of system
Consumer Products Company Planning to improve market share, launch new product, and improve operations	Several months to a year or more	5–10 Cafés, 1–2 days each	20–200 people, depending on whose voices are needed at any given Café
Member Associations Discovering what is important to members and engaging them in taking responsibility for what they care about	Several months to a year or ongoing	Cafés distributed throughout the association—some at annual conferences, others at local chapter meetings	Typically 12–100; more during annual conferences
Planning Retreats and Meetings Any situation where people are doing strategic thinking regarding the future	Normal organizational planning cycles	1 or more Cafés as part of the annual planning cycle	Typically 12 to 200 (with some as large as 800)

World Café

Getting Started

The most effective way to plan a World Café is to gather a design team and use the principles of the World Café (see "Conditions for Success," below) in conceiving the event. The first three principles are particularly important for the designers: *Set the Context, Create Hospitable Space*, and *Explore Questions That Matter.*

A strong design team usually involves: skilled Café host(s); the sponsor of the Café (i.e., senior executive, department head, community leader, or credible third party) who will issue the invitation; and the convener of the Café (the person or persons responsible for translating the outcomes of the Café into actionable approaches to daily life and work). These roles may overlap. Other individuals who can make valuable contributions to the design team are those with a sense of the organization's history and those who can voice various stakeholder concerns.

SETTING THE CONTEXT

This is the first design task. Illustrative questions to explore include: What is our purpose in convening the Café? What outcomes do we hope to achieve? What range of perspectives and voices need to be included in the conversation to achieve our goals? Who are the people that embody the necessary knowledge, expertise, and experience? What are the parameters—in terms of time, money, physical constraints, and other operational or strategic factors—that we must keep in mind during the design?

CREATING HOSPITABLE SPACE

This principle begins with the invitation that people receive. Great Café invitations alert people that this is not a business-as-usual meeting. Hospitable space also means attending both to the physical space and to the way people are invited to participate before, during, and after the Café. The impact of the environment on the conversation cannot be overstated. A room set with small tables that seat four or five people produces a profoundly different conversation than one set with tables that seat ten. Likewise, ensuring that natural light, windows, flowers or plants, and refreshments are present creates an atmosphere that nourishes good conversation.

EXPLORING QUESTIONS THAT MATTER

Formulating appropriate questions is more art than science. Each group and each Café is a unique gathering of minds and needs careful consideration when selecting powerful questions that can engage participants in uncovering new insights, knowledge, and innovation. There is no magic formula for crafting questions that matter, but as David Cooperrider[3] has observed, people grow in the direction of the questions they ask. In a Café, questions that are appreciative and that evoke participants' sense of possibility generate more energy and engagement than questions posed from a deficit perspective. Questions that are clear, connected to purpose, and meaningful to participants in practical ways catalyze more creativity than questions that are unfocused, overly general, or abstract. Optimally, the design team spends considerable time in a question discovery phase.

The questions below can help you craft questions for your Café (thanks to Sally Ann Roth of the Public Conversations Project[4]).

- What question, if explored thoroughly, could provide the breakthrough possibilities we are seeking?

- Is this question relevant to the real life or real work of the Café participants?

- Is this a genuine question to which we really don't know the answer?

- What work do we want this question to do? What kind of conversation, meanings, and feelings do we imagine this question will evoke in those who will be exploring it?

- What assumptions or beliefs are embedded in the way this question is constructed?

- Is this question likely to generate hope, imagination, engagement, new thinking, and creative action, or is it likely to increase a focus on past problems and obstacles?

- Does this question leave room for new and different questions to be raised as the initial question is explored?

Careful, up-front design deepens the experience of participants at all levels, and contributes to the likelihood the Café will have lasting beneficial effects.

Roles and Responsibilities

THE CAFÉ SPONSOR/CONVENOR

This is the person or group within an organization or community who authorizes and supports the World Café process. Ideally, the sponsor sees beyond the mechanics of the Café process to notice the power of conversation to surface new insights, coordinate actions, make sense of experience, and bring forth the future—as Bob Veazie did in the opening story. He or she commits to fostering the capacity for "good conversation" in service to the organization or community's larger goals.

THE DESIGN TEAM

The role of the design team is covered in the "Getting Started" section.

THE CAFÉ HOST(s)

World Café conversations are hosted, not facilitated in the traditional sense. Attempting to "facilitate" Café conversations has a deleterious effect on the natural exuberance and generative nature of the gathering. The role of the host is to work with the design team in creating a hospitable space for lively conversation. During the Café, the host is responsible for clearly communicating the details of the process and answering questions related to the "what" and "how" of the Café. He or she is responsible for posing the questions the participants will explore, for making the context of

World Café

	Before	During	After
Sponsor and/or Convenor	Commit to supporting the World Café as a way of accessing the collective intelligence of the group	Participate as a member who holds a piece of the puzzle (not as the CEO, expert, etc.)	Debrief w/design team on lessons learned and how to integrate them into the ongoing concerns of the organization
Design Team	Clarify purpose, invite participants, set parameters, craft questions that matter and coordinate all logistical concerns for successful Café(s)	Participate in the Café(s) as contributing members of the whole	Debrief with Sponsor/Convenor as outlined above
Café Host(s)	Work with design team on all of the above	Host the Café	Debrief Design Team and Sponsor/Convenor
Graphics Professional (when possible)	Integral member of Design Team, when appropriate. Participate in design conversations and record planning efforts	Record the Café and harvest insights	Record any follow-up meeting. Provide formal documentation of Café for collective memory
Participants	If appropriate, provide input on the questions to be engaged during the Café	Talk about what matters to them, using Café Etiquette	Follow up with any action commitments that emerge from the Café

Table 1. Roles and Responsibilities

those questions clear, and for the skillful harvesting of themes, insights, and deeper questions that arise during the Café. The host also helps ensure that the collective knowledge that emerges during the Café becomes visible to the whole group.

A REFLECTIVE GRAPHICS PROFESSIONAL

Whenever possible, graphic professionals map the Café conversation as it is shared in the whole group conversation. Also known as graphic recorders, graphic facilitators, or visual practitioners, they act as the visual cortex of the collective mind of the group. They record voices and create images to reflect key substantive ideas, map previously invisible connections, and illuminate rela-

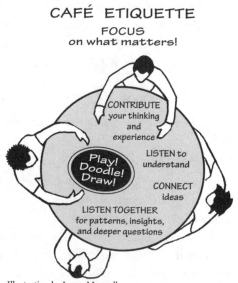

CAFÉ ETIQUETTE
FOCUS
on what matters!

CONTRIBUTE your thinking and experience

LISTEN to understand

CONNECT ideas

LISTEN TOGETHER for patterns, insights, and deeper questions

Play! Doodle! Draw!

Illustration by James Maxwell

World Café

tionships between different perspectives. The maps are valuable records of the Café and create an image of the whole that can highlight both the rich diversity and overall coherence of participants' contributions.

THE CAFÉ PARTICIPANTS

Every conversation has some etiquette associated with it, and the World Café is no exception. Over the last decade, we have evolved a set of practices that link with the design principles to foster the conditions for powerful conversations. Participants use the Café Etiquette to support each other in speaking and listening authentically.

Conditions for Success

In our research, we discovered that the following seven principles, when engaged as an integrated whole, create the conditions that enable the "magic" of Café dialogues to emerge and unfold.

1. *Set the Context:* Clarify the purpose and parameters within which the dialogue will unfold.

2. *Create Hospitable Space:* Assure the welcoming environment and psychological safety that nurtures personal comfort and mutual respect.

3. *Explore Questions that Matter:* Focus collective attention on powerful questions that attract collaborative engagement.

4. *Encourage Everyone's Contribution:* Enliven the relationship between the "me" and the "we" by inviting full participation and mutual giving.

5. *Cross-Pollinate and Connect Diverse Perspectives:* Use the living system dynamics of emergence through intentionally increasing the diversity of perspectives and density of connections while retaining a common focus on core questions.

6. *Listen Together for Patterns, Insights, and Deeper Questions:* Focus shared attention in ways that nurture coherence of thought without losing individual contribution.

7. *Harvest and Share Collective Discoveries:* Make collective knowledge and insight visible and actionable.

In addition to the synergy of engaging the Café principles as an integrated whole, the art of hosting—which involves *invitation, welcoming, offering, and honoring*—is essential to liberating the creative energy,

Illustration by Sherrin Bennett

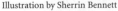

World Café

intelligence, and relational capacity of participants. A skillful host engages participants in "listening for what is emerging" by appreciating how each perspective contributes to an understanding that is larger than any single position could reveal.

Theoretical Basis

The World Café is an emergent process for thinking together focused on creating coherence without control. We first experienced the Café pattern in early 1995 during a two-day dialogue among a group known as the Intellectual Capital Pioneers. Impressed by the power, depth, and innovative quality of these conversations, we asked, "What happened here that fostered such an illuminating conversation?" Reflection on the largely improvised process, and the subsequent research it spawned, resulted in the distillation of the World Café principles and etiquette. The continuing development and use of those principles has given rise to a growing global community of collaborative inquiry and practice.

Today, the community of World Café practitioners includes thousands of people. Juanita Brown's global research and doctoral thesis illuminates the principles underlying the World Café and the many fields of inquiry that are woven into its tapestry of conversations that matter. Juanita addresses both the theoretical and practical bases of the World Café in her dissertation:

> This study calls on the lived experience of a global community of World Café practitioners including line executives, educators and organizational strategists who are using Café learning in a wide variety of cross-cultural community, government and business contexts. It also calls on interdisciplinary insights from living systems and the new sciences, community development, strategy innovation, consciousness studies, dialogue and organizational learning.[5]

Table 2, while not exhaustive, illuminates key fields of inquiry and process domains that inform the theory and practice of the World Café.

Domain of Practice/Inquiry	Representative Authors
Appreciative Inquiry	David Cooperrider, Diana Whitney
Architectural Theory	Christopher Alexander
Biology, Evolution, and Cognition	Humberto Maturana, Francisco Varela
Chaordic Systems	Dee Hock, Tom Hurley
Collaborative Spaces	Michael Schrage
Collective Consciousness	David Bohm, Duane Elgin, Peter Russell
Collective Intelligence	Tom Atlee, George Por, Finn Voldtofte

Domain of Practice/Inquiry	Representative Authors
Communities of Practice	Etienne Wenger
Community Development	Saul Alinsky, Paulo Friere
Complexity and New Sciences	Mitchell Waldrop, Margaret Wheatley
Dialogue	Linda Ellinor, Glenna Gerard, Bill Isaacs
Future Search	Sandra Janoff, Marvin Weisbord
Knowledge Theory	Verna Allee, Leif Edvinsson, Charles Savage
Leadership and Systems Thinking	Peter Senge, Margaret Wheatley
Living Systems	Fritjof Capra, Michael Hoagland, Danah Zohar
Open Space	Peggy Holman, Harrison Owen
Organizational Learning	Chris Argyris, Edgar Schien, Peter Senge
Social Constructivism	Linda Lambert et al., Kenneth Gergen
Strategic Questioning	Marilee Goldberg, Fran Peavey, Eric Vogt
Strategy	Gary Hamel, C. K. Prahalad
Visual Language	Robert Horn, Nancy Margulies, David Sibbet
Wisdom Circles	Christina Baldwin, Charles Garfield et al.

Table 2. Key Fields of Inquiry and Process Domains

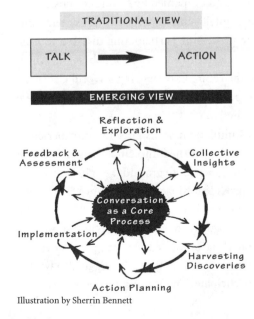

TRADITIONAL VIEW

TALK → ACTION

EMERGING VIEW

Reflection & Exploration
Feedback & Assessment
Collective Insights
Conversation as a Core Process
Implementation
Harvesting Discoveries
Action Planning

Illustration by Sherrin Bennett

Sustaining the Results

The two most critical factors in sustaining the results of a World Café are: (1) a shift in the way the organization and its leaders understand the role of conversation as a core process, and (2) how participants of the Café come to appreciate the centrality of networks of conversation for community/organizational development and well-being.

The traditional view of conversation is suggested by the dictum, "Stop talking and get to work." We now know this reflects a false and potentially fatal dichotomy. As Boston College professor of management Bill Torbert has pointed out: "During the industrial age and the current electro-informational age, we have become technically powerful, but have not culti-

World Café

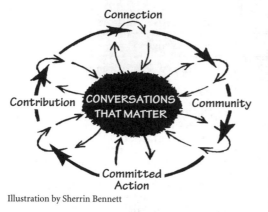

Illustration by Sherrin Bennett

vated our powers of action. People who speak of moving from talk to action are apparently not awake to the fact that talk is the essence of action. We are, in fact, deeply influenced by how we speak to one another."[6]

The organizations that have been most successful in using the World Café are those that have adopted the metaquestion: *"What would it mean for us to see our organization as a living network of conversations focused on our most important questions?"* This was Bob Veazie's breakthrough insight, which resulted in his inviting people throughout Hewlett Packard into transformative dialogues that dramatically improved safety. Through this lens, convening a World Café creates a space for possibility and connection where participants discover a sense of shared meaning, generate new knowledge, establish or deepen trust, and access levels of highly focused creativity that are energizing and exciting. The entire experience fosters a strong sense of shared commitment to and ownership of the outcomes of the process.

The process invites people to focus awareness not just on a given topic, but also on the way in which they speak about that issue. Participants often report a deeper appreciation for the previously unacknowledged assumptions and contexts that shape each other's stance and perspectives.

The experience of intentionally surfacing, honoring, and cross-pollinating diverse perspectives to discover a larger whole is also quite striking for many participants. Moreover, it is an experience that people seek to repeat since it is invariably accompanied by feelings of possibility, excitement, and solidarity. If, as Meg Wheatley posits, "intelligence emerges as the system connects to itself in diverse and creative ways,"[7] then the process of participating in a World Café provides a direct experience of a growing collective intelligence to which all contribute but which is greater than any single perspective or individual in the room. Experiencing a World Café conversation in action also helps individuals make better personal choices about how to participate creatively in the ongoing conversations that shape our lives.

Participation in an effective World Café usually stimulates new insights. In our experience, key insights require at least three key supporting factors to be turned into embodied knowledge: a hospitable space for exploring their dimensions, a set of practices to ground them in daily life or work, and a community of supportive coexplorers to provide feedback and guidance. This highlights, again, the centrality of making conversation a core business process and fostering the development of collective capacities for collaborative dialogue throughout the organization.

As David Cooperrider[8] and Humberto Maturana[9] have pointed out, language does not mirror the world out there, but rather language coordinates our actions. We "bring forth a world" through the networks of conversation in which we participate. The lessons and perspectives of

Maturana's evolutionary biology and Cooperrider's Appreciative Inquiry often come together quite powerfully for the participants of a World Café as they experience the role conversation plays in shaping our collective lives.

Burning Questions

When people ask us about the World Café, their most common question is, "Will it work in our organization?" The answer is "It depends." The World Café is not a panacea for every organizational ill. The Café offers a process for integrating the diverse aspects and participants of an organization or community into a coherent, self-organizing whole, a set of principles for evoking collective intelligence, and a perspective on the central importance of conversation in transforming how we live and work together.

Another question we are often asked is, "How does the World Café relate to other conversational processes?" In our experience, what distinguishes the World Café is the use of Café Etiquette and the conscientious application of all seven World Café design principles. Other processes may feature one or more of the principles and related practices (such as speaking and listening from the heart, or using small tables and timed rounds), but the integrated application of all the principles results in a qualitatively distinct experience capable of delivering the results we have outlined above.

Illustration by Nancy Margulies

The last few years have seen an increase in the cross-pollination of the World Café with other large group processes such as Appreciative Inquiry, Open Space, and Future Search. There is fertile soil to cultivate here. We often get questions on how to integrate various methodologies and, again, the answer is context-dependent. We've discovered that much of the success depends on the experience of the practitioner and his or her willingness to experiment. We welcome these experiments in cross-pollination.

Concluding Comments

Architect and philosopher Christopher Alexander[10] has deeply influenced our thinking. He points out that living systems are made up of wholes at every level of scale—from the individual to the fam-

World Café

ily to complex organizational systems such as towns, cities, and societies. He suggests that life-enhancing improvements arise not from grand plans or edicts from a central authority, but from small acts of collaboration based on a repetition of life-affirming patterns, like the pattern of engaging in conversations that matter. Alexander notes how millions of these tiny acts, carried out locally in any living system, can over time spread their effects to transform the character of the system as a whole.

We invite you to consider that each time you host, convene, and participate in courageous conversations about questions that matter to you (including World Café conversations), you contribute to creating a culture of dialogue that can tap the collective wisdom needed to create a legacy of hope for future generations.

About the Authors

Juanita Brown, Ph.D. (juanita@theworldcafe.com), co-originator of the World Café, collaborates as a thinking partner and design advisor on key change initiatives with senior leaders across sectors—creating and hosting innovative forums for strategic dialogue on critical business and societal issues. Juanita has served as a senior affiliate with the MIT Organizational Learning Center (now Society for Organizational Learning), as a research affiliate with the Institute for the Future, and as a Fellow of the World Business Academy.

Ken Homer (ken@theworldcafe.com) is a World Café host and designer. Ken joined with Juanita and David in 1997 and has been an integral part of the team involved with the evolution of the World Café and its global community. Ken is the webmaster for the World Café Web site and has collaborated on Café designs with the University of California, the Institute of Noetic Sciences, Natural Strategies, Royal Roads University (Canada), Business for Social Responsibility, and a range of other clients.

David Isaacs (david@theworldcafe.com) is president of Clearing Communications, an organizational and communications strategy company working with senior executives in the United States and internationally. He has collaborated with corporate clients including Alaska Airlines, Ericsson, GlaxoSmithKline, Hewlett Packard, Intel, and Sanofi-Aventis. David's nonprofit work has included hosting World Café dialogues with the Shambhala Institute, Kellogg Foundation, and Society for Organizational Learning. He also serves as adjunct faculty for University of Texas San Antonio Business School's Executive MBA program.

Where to Go for More Information

REFERENCES

Alexander, C. *The Timeless Way of Building.* New York: Oxford University Press, 1979.

Brown, J. "Conversation as a Core Business Process." *The Systems Thinker* 7, no. 10 (1996).

_____. *The World Café: A Resource Guide for Hosting Conversations That Matter.* Mill Valley, CA: Whole Systems Associates, 2002.

_____. "The World Café: Living Knowledge Through Conversations That Matter." Doctoral dissertation, Whole Systems Associates, Mill Valley, CA, 2001.

Brown, J., D. Isaacs, and the World Café Community. *The World Café: Shaping Our Futures Through Conversations That Matter.* San Francisco: Berrett-Koehler, 2005.

Cooperrider, D., D. Whitney, and J. Stavros. *Appreciative Inquiry Handbook.* Bedford Heights, OH, and San Francisco: Lakeshore Communications and Berrett-Koehler Communications, 2003.

Holman, Peggy, and Tom Devane, eds. *The Change Handbook: Group Methods for Shaping the Future.* San Francisco: Berrett-Koehler, 1999.

Wheatley, M. J., and M. Kellnor-Rogers. *A Simpler Way.* San Francisco: Berrett-Koehler, 1996.

INFLUENTIAL SOURCES

Adams, M. G. *Change Your Questions Change Your Life.* San Francisco: Berrett-Koehler, 2004.

Atlee, Tom. *The Tao of Democracy.* Cranston, RI: The Writer's Collective, 2003.

Lambert, L., et al. *The Constructivist Leader.* New York: Teachers College Press, 1995.

Levine, R., et al. *The Cluetrain Manifesto: The End of Business as Usual.* New York: Perseus Books, HarperCollins, 2000.

Peavey, F. "Strategic Questioning: An Approach to Creating Personal and Social Change." In *By Life's Grace: Musings on the Essence of Social Change*, 86–111. Philadelphia: New Society Publishers, 1994.

Schrage, M. *Shared Minds: The New Technologies of Collaboration.* New York: Random House, 1990.

Vogt, E., J. Brown, and D. Isaacs. *The Art of Powerful Questions: Catalyzing Insight, Innovation and Action.* Waltham, MA: Pegasus Communications, 2003.

Webber, A. "What's So New About the New Economy?" *Harvard Business Review* (January/ February 1993): 24–42.

Wheatley, M. J. *Leadership and the New Science.* San Francisco: Berrett-Koehler, 1992.

ORGANIZATIONS

Pegasus Communications—www.pegasuscom.com
   Distributor of the World Café book, dissertation, hosting guides, and other materials.

Whole Systems Associates—inquiry@theworldcafe.com
   For World Café and other strategic dialogue consulting. Tel: (415) 383-0129.

The World Café—www.theworldcafe.com
   The best place to go for the latest World Café information, including stories, articles, and hosting resources.

World Café

The World Café Community Foundation—info@theworldcafe.com
> *Nonprofit foundation whose mission is to develop and disseminate World Café and other innovative dialogue approaches for positive futures. Tel: (415) 339-8714.*

The World Café Online Community of Inquiry and Practice—www.theworldcafe.com or www.theworldcafecommunity.net
> *Where World Café hosts share stories, learning, and mutual support.*

The authors wish to extend their gratitude to Tom Hurley for his invaluable help in the creation of this article.

1. J. Brown, with D. Isaacs and the World Café Community, *The World Café: Shaping Our Futures Through Conversations That Matter* (San Francisco: Berrett-Koehler, 2005).

2. Ibid. See chapter 3 for full details.

3. P. Holman and T. Devane, eds., *The Change Handbook* (San Francisco: Berrett-Koehler, 1999).

4. The Public Conversations Project can be reached at: http://www.publicconversations.org.

5. J. Brown, "The World Café: Living Knowledge Through Conversations That Matter" (Doctoral dissertation, Whole Systems Associates, 2001). Available from Pegasus Communications: http://www.pegasus com.com.

6. As quoted in *Leverage Points*, Issue 60, March 25, 2005, published electronically by Pegasus Communications. Archive available at: http://www.pegasuscom.com/levpoints/lp60.html.

7. M. J. Wheatley and M. Kellnor-Rogers, *A Simpler Way* (San Francisco: Berrett-Koehler, 1996).

8. D. Cooperrider, D. Whitney, and J. M. Stavros, *Appreciative Inquiry Handbook* (San Francisco: Berrett-Koehler, 2003).

9. H. Maturana and F. Varela, *The Tree of Knowledge* (Boston: Shambhala, 1987).

10. C. Alexander, *The Timeless Way of Building* (New York: Oxford University Press, 1979).

World Café

13

Ancient Wisdom Council

The first people had questions and they were free. The second people had answers and they became enslaved.

—Native American Wisdom

Way of the Council: Using Universal Intelligences

The CEO of a major telecommunications organization stands in the center of a circle of 500 employees. They are seated in ascending rings of chairs arranged in groups of the eight colors of the rainbow.[1] "We are at a major crossroads in the life of our organization," he begins. "We have a significant opportunity to take this division to a new level. This is not going to happen because of me. It is going to happen because of you. And as a result, I will be able to play more golf." He continues, "I want this company of talented people to become self-directed, self-motivated, and self-organized. You can do it, take over this company! For the next few days, we shall engage each other in council to infuse new life into this company."

This opened an intensive five days with members of the Central and South American division. Using the Ancient Wisdom Council, they restructured and revitalized their organization, adapting to new opportunities and conditions evolving in their field.

During the five-day conference, the employees gathered in ten groups of 50 members. Each group focused on an element of the company's overall program. Within the ten groups, people organized into the eight units of the Ancient Wisdom Council. Called societies, each unit represented an energy of intelligence that contributes to the overall well-being of a balanced, healthy organization or community.

Each group went into their breakout room. They filled the "question basket" with questions or issues about their element's relationship to the organization. They collated the responses into 8 to 16 topic areas and prioritized the topics using the "ten stone" method. This simple pro-

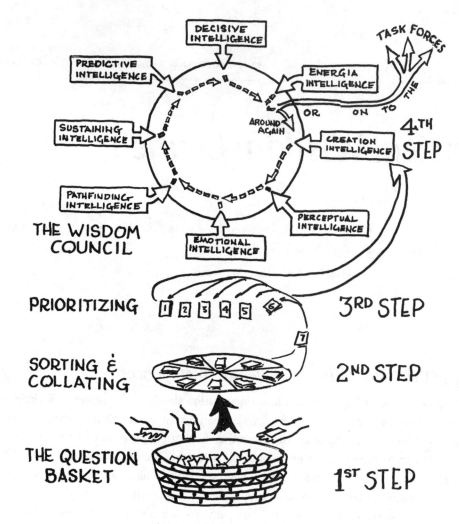

Figure 1. The Steps of the Process

cess expresses the collective's priorities, as each individual places four stones on their first priority, three on their second priority, and so on. Tallying the results sequences the priorities (figure 1).

Each of the ten groups identified six to ten topics for the council process to surface wisdom for change. Topics included: How do we build trust and communication between management and line personnel? What processes can speed response time to client's requests and needs? How can line personnel share their client experience with research and development?

Within each group, one unit held the perspective of one of eight intelligences, seeing through the lens of:

Creation Intelligence—freedom and creativity,
Perceptual Intelligence—present condition and appreciation,
Emotional Intelligence—power and danger,
Pathfinding Intelligence—purpose and direction,
Sustaining Intelligence—maintenance and balance,
Predictive Intelligence—interrelatedness and timing,
Decisive Intelligence—clarity and action,
Energia Intelligence—integrity and vitality.

Exploring through these lenses revealed needed changes in the topic areas. The group's enthusiasm and vitality grew each day, and a strong unity of purpose manifested. During the sessions of council, the CEO visited the different groups, listened, and took many notes. Later, he said, "This is amazing! Why haven't I heard these things before? We need to keep this process going permanently in this division."

At 1:00 A.M. on the third day, the team holding the event met, asking a key question, "What is needed now to start the fire of transformation?" The time we spent that night—asking ourselves how to fly across the void, how to leap into a new time—called us all to our edge. We could all feel it was time for a shift.

The next day, in a room of 500 people, 16 seats in the circle's center remained empty. They were the council seats, reserved for the leaders. We called to the people and asked, "Who will step forward? Who will speak for the people? Who will take responsibility to make the changes we need here?" And we waited.

One at a time, they came from their seats. First a woman, then a man, then another and another until there were 16. They spoke briefly to each other and then stood and spoke one at a time about what they perceived was needed. Then one of them took the microphone and called management to join them. There was silence.

One at a time, the managers came until there were 20. Each spoke to all of us. After the last one had finished, a man in the audience stood and began to chant. He began calling all the people to stand, to step forward, to be part of the change. One at a time, they stood, all 500. They came forward to the center, until all the seats were empty. And the teams of 50 each, gathered once again, recognizing it was up to them to make the changes, to make it live.

What happened? The people accessed their individual and collective voices to contribute their own wisdom, to stand and speak and be recognized for the gifts they brought. A new vitality of collective and individual investment infused the life of the organization.

The Basics

WHAT IS THE ANCIENT WISDOM COUNCIL?

The Ancient Wisdom Council is a deep process that enables participants to step back from the pressures and demands of any situation and open their minds and hearts to listen, to consider, and to source wisdom from deep reflection. It begins with a question that the person, group, community, or team surfaces that affects the well-being of the whole.

The purpose of council is to access the wisdom for addressing an issue or solving deep conflict, allowing the community or group to put their agreement and energy behind new solutions. The Ancient Wisdom Council opens the mind to new thinking by "seeing" through eight different perspectives and accessing the voice and genius of the people. This ancient wisdom is part of many tribal cultures. It was typical for chosen elders of deep integrity to speak for the people, representing each of the perspectives. Part of the training was to speak, not as an individual—with accompanying biases—but for the benefit of the entire group.

Today, council is used by individuals, families, communities, and organizational teams. The only necessary tools, other than understanding the eight perspectives, are the ability to listen deeply, hold respect for the other, and to profoundly care for the integrity of the whole. Those who experience the depth of council find their thoughts expressed by others. Trust deepens, the ability to find collective wisdom is heightened, and the energy for taking a project or new idea to completion is enhanced.

It is important to initiate this process by opening the question, or opening the mind. Hearing from those involved, a question emerges that encompasses the chosen issue. Once clear, those preparing to speak deeply reflect, setting aside personal opinion and looking strictly through the lens of the perspective they represent. Following this, the council begins. Each perspective typically has two speakers, ideally a woman and a man, to share from that direction. They offer their thoughts and recommendations one by one, without interruption on the presenting question.

As input from each intelligence perspective accumulates, agreement takes shape and council recommendations are passed to task forces for implementation. If the first pass around the council does not provide the needed insights and clarity, the question is passed again for deeper reflection.

The universal intelligences and the Ancient Wisdom Council are part of a larger body of wisdom for developing higher states of consciousness.

Table of Uses

Typical Setting	Project Length	Number of Participants
In Schools—Elementary School Staff • To formulate vision • To solve conflict • To bring the community together • To rebuild connectedness	• 2 days • Task force work • 1 day, 2 weeks later	• 50 people: teaching staff, administration, secretaries, and custodians • Implementation teams of 6–9 people • 8 people

Typical Setting	Project Length	Number of Participants
Member Association and Board of Directors • To bring the diverse issues of the member association together • To improve communication and relationships between members and leadership	• 4 days and evenings • 1 month later • 3 days	• 80 people • Follow up with Board of Directors • 20 people
Corporate Setting Venture Capitalist Partners • To implement holistic view decision making • To solve 2-year issue regarding personnel • To improve communication and relationships among partners	3-day working session	12 partners

About the Authors

WindEagle and *RainbowHawk Kinney-Linton* are cofounders and directors of Ehama Institute (ehamainstitute@msn.com). Both are trained keepers and medicine teachers of the Delicate Lodge Teachings, a body of wisdom having its origins in Meso America with Mayan and Toltec cultures. With the staff of Ehama Institute, they have shared these teachings in two-year training programs in the United States and Europe. They have addressed diverse issues through the council process and a variety of other community tools with businesses, community groups, families, and individuals in the United States and Europe since 1987.

Where to Go for More Information

REFERENCES

Carlin, Peter. "How to Make a Decision Like a Tribe." *Fast Company* (November 1995 [premiere issue]): 105.

Kinney-Linton, WindEagle, and RainbowHawk. *Heart Seeds: A Message from the Ancestors.* Minneapolis: Beaver's Pond Press, 2003.

ORGANIZATIONS

DanceHammers—www.dancehammers.org

Ehama Institute—www.ehama.org

Note: The steps of the Ancient Wisdom Council are different from the Center for Wise Democracy's Wisdom Council process defined on page 225 in chapter 18, "Dynamic Facilitation."

1. The colors of the rainbow are a continuous spectrum. In this tradition, the spectrum is divided into eight graduations to correspond to the four cardinal directions and the four marriage points between them.

14

JAMES D. LUDEMA AND FRANK J. BARRETT

Appreciative Inquiry Summit

Great discoveries invariably involve the cooperation of many minds.
—Alexander Graham Bell

Cost, Quality, and Speed at John Deere

A few years ago, the new business unit leader for header manufacturing at John Deere Harvester Works, and Gina Hinrichs, the unit's director of organization development, used an Appreciative Inquiry (AI) Summit to reduce costs, improve quality, and speed up new product cycle time. They took the whole system (wage employees, management, customers, suppliers, dealers, and representatives from corporate—about 250 people) off-site for five days through the appreciative inquiry 4-D process (discussed later in this chapter).

By week's end, the group had launched ten cross-functional strategic initiatives to accomplish their goals. Over the next 18 months, they significantly reduced product cycle time, gained more than $3 million in cost savings, earned millions more in new market share, and transformed relationships between labor and management. Many participants shared that this was the first time they had the opportunity to sit down as equals with management to plan for the future. They talked about how searching for the best in themselves and others validated them and gave them a new perception of the gifts, strengths, and humanity of their colleagues. They said that they learned more and made more progress in five days then they typically do in five years. One participant said that this was the first time in more than 20 years that he had hope for the future.

The Basics

WHAT IS AN APPRECIATIVE INQUIRY SUMMIT?

The Appreciative Inquiry Summit is a large-group method for accelerating positive change in organizations and communities by involving a broad range of internal and external stakeholders in the process.[1] It is typically a single event or series of events (usually three to five days in length) that bring people together to (1) discover the organization or community's core competencies and strengths; (2) envision opportunities for positive change; (3) design the desired changes into the organization or community's systems, structures, strategies, and culture; and (4) implement and sustain the changes and make them work. AI Summits range from 30 to 3,000 people, and include more using online technology. Because of the power of wholeness and democratic self-organizing, the closer summits get to including every member of the system, the more dramatic and sustainable the impact.

BENEFITS OF AN AI SUMMIT

Over the years, we have noticed several positive outcomes from summit interventions, including:

- *Speed:* Summits accelerate change by directly engaging the whole organization in envisioning, designing, and implementing the change.

- *Energy:* AI Summits begin by inviting people into a deep exploration of the organization's "positive core"—its bundle of strengths, assets, capacities, capabilities, values, traditions, practices, and accomplishments that sustains its success. Access to the positive core builds energy and fuels innovation throughout the system.

- *Intelligence:* In any organization, knowledge is fragmented. AI summits connect people to the "big picture" and to other people who have critical information. They see how their individual contribution fits into the "logic of the whole," and they can work smarter, more flexibly, and in support of the entire enterprise.

- *Execution:* As Marvin Weisbord says, people support what they help to create.[2] When people define their own future, they implement with more passion and less resistance.

- *Results:* Summits focus on clear strategic priorities (e.g., market growth, product innovation, culture change, leadership development, customer service, process redesign) and align the whole organization to deliver results.

- *Sustained Change:* For any change to have long-term impact, it must be built into the organization's "social architecture"—its systems, structures, strategies, and culture. Summits sustain change by involving people in designing high-performing systems.

THE AI SUMMIT START TO FINISH

When we refer to the AI Summit process, we include all the activities that occur before, during, and after the actual meeting. As a transformational process involving hundreds or thousands of people, an AI Summit requires thoughtful planning and committed follow-up.

Before an Appreciative Inquiry Summit

Presummit activities take three to four months and include: (1) enlisting active sponsor support, (2) forming a representative planning team, (3) selecting participants, and (4) creating a customized design.

One of the most important activities before an AI Summit is identifying a clear and compelling strategic focus. Positively framed, this focus guides activities during the summit. It is important to avoid framing the task around what's wrong.

Consider this example: "PhoneCo," a global telecommunications company, had experienced a downturn and felt energy and focus were lessening. Company leaders considered a survey to uncover the causes of low morale and lack of enthusiasm. After an introduction to Appreciative Inquiry, the steering group considered this "problem" from an appreciative perspective. They discussed what PhoneCo was like when operating with high commitment and sense of purpose. They discovered that empowered leadership and impacting others' lives through technology were crucial catalysts for high commitment. With this in mind, their summit task became: "Inspired and Passionate Leadership: Transforming the Way People Conduct and Live Their Lives."

During a Typical Four-Day Appreciative Inquiry Summit

Summits are designed to maximize wholeness, strategic visioning, learning, and relating. They require large, arena-type spaces with eight to ten diverse participants clustered in each group. Everyone helps address tasks, also taking responsibility for their own utterances, actions, perceptions, and feelings. Members do not stay in the same groups for the entire summit, but assemble into various stakeholder groups—departmental groupings, customers, suppliers, and others. Although each AI Summit is unique, all are designed to flow through the appreciative inquiry 4-D cycle of discovery, dream, design, and destiny (figure 1).

Day 1: Discovery—discovering and connecting the many facets of the organization's "positive core"—the strengths, assets, competencies, capabilities, values, traditions, wisdoms, and potentials that fuel and sustain its success.

Day 2: Dream—envisioning the organization's future in bold and specific terms.

Day 3: Design—designing the "social architecture" (e.g., strategies, structures, systems, culture, processes, partnerships) to give form to their dreams.

Day 4: Destiny—planning for action. Individual commitments are made, innovation teams formed, strategic initiatives launched, and large-group dialogue promotes organizational alignment. Additionally, the next steps in the change process are launched.

Based on a rendering by Kyle Schimmel

Figure 1. Appreciative Inquiry Summit 4-D Cycle

After an Appreciative Inquiry Summit

Summits generate numerous ideas for action and high commitment, making follow-up important. Action groups often name facilitators or leaders who coordinate group activities and follow-through.[3] In one example from the U.S. Navy, 13 action groups met regularly through virtual teleconference meetings and after six months held a face-to-face meeting. They tracked successes and helped to organize a follow-up summit. Successful teams seek and receive support and involvement from organizational leadership, plan regular meetings with rich communication, and have synergy with their regular responsibilities.

Table of Uses

Organization	Summit Task	Time	Number of Participants
U.S. Navy	Active-Reserve integration	• 1 month to plan • 3 days to conduct • 6 months of follow-up	50 admirals and captains from the active forces and 50 from the reserve
McDonald's	Global strategy for staffing and retention	• 6 months to plan • 3 days to conduct • 3 days follow up	350 regional managers from around the world

Organization	Summit Task	Time	Number of Participants
World Vision	Strategic planning for next 10 years	• 4 months to plan • 4 days to conduct • Ongoing follow-up	150 in person in Bangkok, 4,000 around the world participating online
U.S. Cellular	Culture change	• 2 months to plan • 3 days to conduct • Ongoing follow-up	200 managers from around the central region
K.O. Lee Company	Organization turnaround	• 3 months to plan • 4 days to conduct • Ongoing follow-up	All 30 employees, plus customers and distributors

About the Authors

Dr. James D. Ludema (jludema@ben.edu) is a professor in the Ph.D. Program in Organization Development at Benedictine University and a principal in the Corporation for Positive Change. He is author of many articles and books on appreciative inquiry, including *The Appreciative Inquiry Summit: A Practitioner's Guide for Leading Large Group Change.* Jim is an internationally recognized consultant whose practice focuses on the use of Appreciative Inquiry for large-scale corporate change initiatives.

Frank J. Barrett, Ph.D. (fbarrett@nps.edu) is associate professor of systems management at the Naval Postgraduate School in Monterey, California, where he is also director of the Center for Positive Change. He has lectured and written widely on Appreciative Inquiry, including his most recent book, *Appreciative Inquiry and Organizational Transformation.* Frank has consulted to various organizations including Nike, Boeing, the U.S. Navy, Ford, General Electric, British Petroleum, Nokia, and Johnson & Johnson.

Where to Go for More Information

REFERENCES

Barrett, F., D. Cooperrider, and R. Fry. "Bringing Every Mind into the Game to Realize the Positive Revolution in Strategy: The Appreciative Inquiry Summit." In *Practicing Organizational Change and Development: A Guide for Consultants.* San Francisco: Jossey-Bass, 2005.

Fry, R. E., F. J. Barrett, J. Seiling, and D. Whitney. *Appreciative Inquiry and Organizational Transformation: Reports from the Field.* Westport, CT: Quorum Books, 2001.

Ludema, J. D., D. Whitney, B. J. Mohr, and T. J. Griffin. *The Appreciative Inquiry Summit: A Practitioner's Guide for Leading Large Group Change.* San Francisco: Berrett-Koehler, 2003.

ORGANIZATIONS

Benedictine University's Ph.D. Program in Organization Development (OD)—www.ben.edu/odhome

One of the largest behaviorally oriented management programs in the United States and one of the top-rated graduate OD programs internationally.

Center for Positive Change at the Naval Postgraduate School—www.nps.edu/Academics/CPC

Their mission is to support positive change and Appreciative Inquiry within the U.S. Navy and other government bureaucracies.

Corporation for Positive Change—www.positivechange.org

They apply Appreciative Inquiry for transformation and innovation in business, government, and nonprofit organizations around the world.

1. J. D. Ludema, D. Whitney, B. J. Mohr, and T. J. Griffin, *The Appreciative Inquiry Summit: A Practitioner's Guide for Leading Large-Group Change* (San Francisco: Berrett-Koehler, 2003).

2. M. R. Weisbord, *Productive Workplaces: Organizing and Managing for Dignity, Meaning, and Community* (San Francisco: Jossey-Bass, 1987).

3. F. J. Barrett, D. L. Cooperrider, and R. E. Fry, "Bringing Every Mind into the Game to Realize the Positive Revolution in Strategy: The Appreciative Inquiry Summit," in *Practicing Organizational Change and Development: A Guide for Consultants* (San Francisco: Jossey-Bass, 2005).

15

DICK AXELROD AND EMILY AXELROD

The Conference Model

The world is moved along, not only by the mighty shoves of its heroes, but also by the aggregate of the tiny pushes of each honest worker.
—Helen Keller

Redesigning Three Divisions of a Major U.S. Bank

A major U.S. bank involved employees, customers, and suppliers to redesign three divisions. In each case, hundreds of people participated in a series of two-day conferences where they identified their dreams for the future, examined customer relationships, identified how to improve critical organizational disconnects, and designed new organizational processes and structures.

The results: The Human Resources Division provided better service to its internal customers, the Mortgage Lending Division reduced costs by 25 percent and was named the corporation's Service Center of the Year, and the Home Equity Division saved millions of dollars. The organization went on to use what they learned from their Conference Model® experiences to engage employees in subsequent mergers and acquisitions.

The Basics

The Conference Model (figure 1) engages people in systemwide change through a series of integrated conferences and "walk-thrus" (mini-conferences). Applications include redesigning processes and organizations, developing new cultures, creating team-based organizations, creating organizational futures, and integrating processes and organizational units.

What exactly is a conference? A conference is a meeting of the organization's stakeholders and employees at all levels (including important others from outside the organization such as customers, suppliers, and community members). Conferences can range from small groups of 30 to large groups that number in the hundreds.

Figure 1. The Conference Model

Walk-thrus are mini-conferences that are used to connect people who were unable to attend a conference to the change process by informing them of what happened during a conference and soliciting their feedback. The combination of walk-thrus and conferences creates a powerful platform for change for building commitment and increasing innovation.

The Conference Model is based on three basic ideas:

- *Basic Idea 1:* People support what they have a hand in creating, while a future designed by a few creates unnecessary resistance.

- *Basic Idea 2:* When people understand the system in which they work, they feel empowered to make changes.

- *Basic Idea 3:* It's not enough to hold a large group conference. Use walk-thrus to widen the circle of involvement, thereby including others in the change process.

Basic Idea 1

The Conference Model involves an organization's stakeholders from all levels and departments, as well as customers and suppliers, in large group workshops called "conferences." The model includes three conferences. In the Vision Conference, participants develop vision themes: what they want for the future. In the Technical Conference, participants identify the disconnects in the current organization and the beliefs and behaviors that support organizational success. In the Design Conference, the vision themes, disconnects, and beliefs and behaviors are combined into design criteria for the new process or organization.

Each conference usually lasts two days so people can reflect overnight. When people have time to reflect, they produce better ideas. Conferences are often held several weeks apart. This allows time to take the conference results to the organization and get feedback. We discuss this process further in Basic Idea 3 (the walk-thru).

"Simple commitments" provide a way for people to take immediate action on ideas that emerge during the conferences. Examples include distributing hot towels to hospital patients at the end of each shift to help them feel more comfortable and talking to one's coworkers about supporting the change process. The model flexes to meet client needs. Some organizations have mixed and matched conferences to create their design in as few as two conferences, while others have required more conferences.

BASIC IDEA 2

During the conferences, participants educate each other on how the system works through a series of interactive activities. In the "ropes" activity, for example, people create a visual network representing workplace interactions. They observe that some groups have many ropes, some groups have a few, and some groups have none. When people pull on the ropes, they experience the tugs and pulls in the system.

In "pass the order through" activities, participants depict what happens to an order as it flows through the organization. When you see an order going back and forth between two departments, redundancies become obvious.

As people discuss the beliefs and behaviors that support the current system, shared assumptions are uncovered. Participants identify the beliefs and behaviors that support disconnects in the system and those that need to shift to eliminate those disconnects. During the Design Conference, participants engage in activities that foster innovation. Each group redesigns the organization based on one of the ideas developed in the Vision Conference or the Technical Conference. Next, people join new groups, where they provide feedback on the previously developed designs. New groups are then formed, and participants design the organization or process using the best of all the ideas they have heard.

BASIC IDEA 3

Walk-thrus are one- to two-hour mini-conferences for people who were unable to attend the actual conferences. Participants receive an update of the conference results, participate in one or two activities that were part of the conferences, and give feedback on the conference results. In this way they become an integral part of the change process.

Walk-thrus are critical to success. When dealing with organizations with thousands of people, conferences with hundreds of people are a drop in the bucket. Walk-thrus provide a mechanism for involving the whole system.

We have seen over and over again that walk-thrus generate interest in the change process and more people want to get involved. In one organization, nearly 500 people volunteered to attend a conference after the first walk-thru—an increase of 177 percent. In another organization, 85 percent of the people surveyed said they felt like they could influence the change process.

To summarize, the Conference Model's power comes from its ability to handle issues at increasing levels of depth. With the Conference Model, you create a critical mass for change by integrating conferences and walk-thrus. You can shape the Conference Model to meet your particular circumstances by varying the duration and number of conferences.

Table of Uses

Brief Description	Project Length	Activity	Number of People Involved
Hospital system—five hospitals, 6,000 employees • Redesigned patient care delivery system • Redesigned patient access and flow system • Created patient care and unit teams, consolidated regionalized services, started in-house university, implemented information technology system to support paperless technology	6 months	• 3 conferences • Walk-thrus • 20 design detail teams • 5 implementation teams	• 250 people each • 2,250 people • 8–10 people per team • 8–10 people per team
Insurance company—claims processing • Implemented a process that embedded policy changes in the system for use by appropriate claims examiners • Reduced cycle time by 75 percent; policy changes implemented annually increased from 2 to 186	2 months	1 conference	60 people
Southern Cross University, Australia • Designed a new university • Received broad institutional support for the design • Improved staff-student relationships • Increased school's reputation for customer care and focus • Solicited corporate and student input into course design and delivery	4 months	3 conferences	250 people

About the Authors

Dick Axelrod (Dick@axelrodgroup.com) and *Emily Axelrod* (Emily@axelrodgroup.com) pioneered the use of large groups for change processes when they cocreated the Conference Model. They are both faculty in the University of Chicago's Leadership Arts Program. Dick authored *Terms of Engagement: Changing the Way We Change Organizations.* Dick and Emily along with Julie Beedon and Robert Jacobs coauthored *You Don't Have to Do It Alone: How to Involve Others to Get Things Done.*

Where to Go for More Information

REFERENCES

Axelrod, Richard. "The Conference Model." *Journal of Applied Behavioral Sciences* 28, no. 4 (1992).

———. "Why Change Management Needs Changing." *Reflections* 2, no. 3 (2001): 46–57.

Axelrod, Richard, and Emily Axelrod. *The Conference Model.* San Francisco: Berrett-Koehler, 2000.

Axelrod, Richard, Emily Axelrod, Julie Beedon, and Robert Jacobs. *You Don't Have to Do It Alone: How to Involve Others to Get Things Done.* San Francisco: Berrett-Koehler, 2004.

ORGANIZATION

The Axelrod Group—www.axelrodgroup.com

16

TREE BRESSEN

Consensus Decision Making

> *Democracy is based upon the conviction that there are extraordinary possibilities in ordinary people.*
>
> —Harry Emerson Fosdick

Real-Life Story

It was 1984 and the Green Party was attempting its first large organizational meeting in the United States. More than one hundred activists had gathered for a weekend in St. Paul, Minnesota, to launch the movement. As the hours lengthened, frustrations grew. Well into the second day, as one participant tells it, the group was a "fractious mess," and the term "still birth" was being thrown around to describe what was happening. As this final day drew toward a close, the assembly was stalemated on whether to call a national convention the following year. Many saw the need, but with no resources, no plan, and no organizing team in place, tensions were high and participants were anxious to head home. While there were calls to vote by majority, facilitator Caroline Estes stubbornly persisted in the belief that a consensus solution was possible.

An hour before closing, one experienced activist from the Ozarks suggested that instead of putting on a major national event, energy might better be put toward regional organizing. The idea took hold and was affirmed by the whole of the group. Regional networks were established for the next few years, forming connections that led to the later rise of state chapters. Today, there are accredited Green Parties in 44 U.S. states plus Washington, D.C.

The Basics

WHY USE CONSENSUS?

- *High-quality decisions* based on full access to collective wisdom
- *Builds connection* by replacing competition with cooperation

- *More effective implementation* because full empowerment in the process results in common ownership of the results

HONING DISCERNMENT TO NURTURE EMERGENCE

Consensus is a decision-making method in which all present must agree before action is taken. In this sense, it is a decision-making rule, in contrast to other available decision rules such as autocracy or majority voting. However, as it has grown up in a secular community-based tradition among political activists, residential intentional communities, nonprofits, worker cooperatives, and others, it is also a process and a way of doing business, a method of searching together for what solution will best meet the needs of the group at a given time. Note that this usage of the term "consensus" is distinct from the common usage of the word as meaning "agreement among some broad portion of people involved."

The search for consensus relies on every person in the circle seeking unity. Group members don't need to think the same, have the same opinion, or support the same proposal in a unanimous vote. Rather, what is earnestly sought is a *sense of the meeting.* This is the essence of what the group agrees on, the common ground, the shared understanding or desire. The method is founded on life-affirming assumptions about human nature and is structured to call forth those positive parts of ourselves, weaving into being the "co-intelligence" of the group to meet the needs of the whole.

Consensus may be used as an ongoing decision-making mechanism in standing organizations or communities, or less commonly, among groups gathered to make one-time decisions regarding a task at hand. Key characteristics include:

- Full empowerment of all participants in the decision making

- Deep listening

- Emphasis on continuing to ask questions until unity is reached

- Honoring of dissent as a "piece of the truth" pointing to something the group needs to learn and integrate

- Dynamics of working with all input rather than purely rational analysis (e.g., emotions, intuition, spirit)

- Choice to allocate more time if needed before the decision point in order to ensure maximum support for acting on whatever decision is reached

Canadian Sue Starr describes the Quaker version of the process this way: "My experience . . . is closer to dialogue than debate or discussion, but goes still beyond that. We speak to the 'center' rather than to each other, with spaces of silence between speakers. It is the most respectful way of coming to decisions that I've ever experienced."

How Consensus Works and When to Use It

The process (figure 1) starts with the presentation of an issue or proposal: its history and the goal of the discussion. As the facilitator integrates comments, a sense of group direction emerges. While diverse individuals may start out asserting their positions, as underlying needs and assumptions surface, they are worked with toward synthesis and/or creative breakthrough. Tom Atlee explains, "Consensus process treats the differences between people not as problems, but as stimulants to deeper inquiry and greater wisdom." If the group gets stuck, the issue may be sent to committee, discussed outside the meeting, or set aside for a future meeting. The container is a transformative one, both relying on and leading to individual and group shifts in consciousness.

The process can fulfill any standard organizational function that calls for a decision, including visioning, strategic planning, policy decisions, and budgeting. It can also take a proposal arrived at through other means and search out whether it is acceptable to everyone involved.

Using consensus effectively generally requires a sense of common purpose and training in the method. With practice, organizations can make decisions that are both inclusive and efficient.

Decision Point Options

Once substantial airing of the issues has occurred and every member has made a good-faith effort to find common ground, there are three responses available to each participant at the point of decision:

Agreement

This may range from tolerance ("I can live with it") to zesty enthusiasm. Standards for what level of support constitutes adequate agreement may vary depending on the group and situation.

Standing Aside

This option is invoked due to personal conscience or strongly differing individual opinion. It allows someone who holds a position of dissent to let the group move forward without sacrificing their own beliefs or values.

Blocking

Called "standing in the way" by Quakers, blocking gives an individual authority to prevent the group from taking action if (and only if) the proposal is perceived to be against core values of the group or might jeopardize the group's ability to fulfill its purpose. Inappropriate use of blocking is the mistake that most often gives consensus-based groups a poor reputation; personal values or preferences, no matter how strongly held, are not a reason to block. Anyone considering blocking a decision is obligated to thoroughly explain the reasons and work hard to find an acceptable solution.

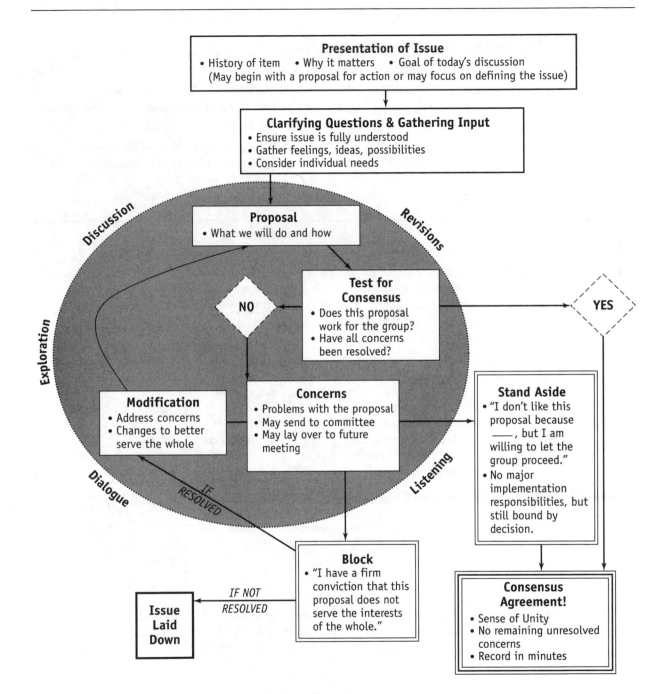

Figure 1. Steps of the Process

The Journey Toward Wholeness

As Mary Parker Follett says, "Social process may be conceived either as the opposing and battle of desires with the victory of one over the other, or as the confronting and integrating of desires. . . . The latter means a freeing for both sides and increased total power or increased capacity in the world." Furthermore, "The time spent in evolving the group spirit is time spent in creating the dynamic force of our civilization. . . . Democracy is the rule of an interacting, interpermeating whole. . . . We have an instinct for democracy because we have an instinct for wholeness."

Table of Uses

Typical Setting	Brief Description	Project Length/ Key Events	Participants
Cohousing Community	Design and adoption of new system for participation and work requirements in the community.	6–8 months 10 committee meetings; 4–8 community meetings	Committee meetings of 3–6 people Community meetings with all members invited, typically 9–45 people
Nonprofit Board	Agreement on new compensation structure as the organization shifts to having more work done by paid staff in addition to the existing volunteer base.	3 quarterly meetings Proposal raised at first meeting, revised at second meeting, and adopted at third meeting.	12 board members
Watershed Council	Development of formal process to assess proposed projects based on scientific management, collaborative process, ecosystem sustainability, and economic diversity.	5 monthly meetings, interspersed with work sessions by smaller task group	50 residents, ranchers, farmers, environmentalists, recreational users, and government representatives
Political Protest	Blockade and disruption of meeting of global governmental agency (WTO, IMF, etc.).	Protest lasting several days. Broad nonviolence guidelines agreed to in advance. Independent decisions by affinity groups of 3–12 people. Coordinated decisions by spokescouncil composed of representatives from 30–50 affinity groups.	10,000+ people

About the Author

Tree Bressen (tree@ic.org) supports a wide variety of organizations in putting their ideals into action via meetings that are lively, productive, and connecting. She teaches practical workshops on consensus decision making, meeting facilitation, and related subjects; facilitates for organizations facing tough issues; and designs large events to maximize dialogue and participation. Her base is in intentional communities—groups that live together and have to deal with each other every day! Tree works on a gift economy basis.

Where to Go for More Information

REFERENCES

Avery, M., B. Auvine, B. Streibel, and L. Weiss. *Building United Judgment: A Handbook for Consensus Decision Making.* Rutledge, MO: Fellowship for Intentional Community, 1981. http://store.ic.org.

Briggs, B. *Introduction to Consensus.* Cuernavaca, Morelos, Mexico: International Institute for Facilitation and Consensus, 2000. http://www.iifac.org.

Dressler, L. *Consensus Through Conversation.* San Francisco: Berrett-Koehler, 2006.

Snyder, M., et al. *Building Consensus: Conflict and Unity.* Richmond, IN: Earlham Press, 2001. http://www.earlham.edu/consense.

ORGANIZATIONS

Seeds for Change (UK)—http://seedsforchange.org.uk/free/consens

Tree Bressen's Group Facilitation Site—http://www.treegroup.info

17

Conversation Café

How do I listen to others? As if everyone were my Master speaking to me his cherished last words.

—Hafiz

Passionate About Intimacy

I'm sitting next to Jerry Garcia at the Grateful Bread coffeehouse. Okay, I'm actually sitting next to a life-size painting of Jerry—so, like everyone else in the café, I am technically alone. Typical, isn't it, in our disconnected world? Ten people, and just one person per table. But tonight is different—it's Thursday evening, Conversation Café time.

Five regulars and three drop-ins arrive, get their tea or coffee and snacks, and settle in. We are engaging in a strangely normal activity. We're talking to strangers. We have followed the first rule of good conversation: showing up. In six weeks of meetings, I've noticed three basic ingredients to the magic of Conversation Cafés: showing up, shutting up, and speaking up.

Showing up is not only arriving in time to talk. It's arriving in soul, ready to engage. Shutting up is about listening deeply. It's having as much curiosity about what others say as about parading out one's own opinions. Speaking up is taking a risk by saying what's real for you. Ah, and there's a fourth rule: "Up." Conversing to enrich everyone. Good conversation has the quality of an infinite game. You play for play, not for winning.

We begin with introductions, saying our names and something about our passions. In this space, we are not our jobs, our complaints, or our manufactured personalities. "I've been on semi-retreat for a long time, trying to understand what is really true for me," says Mara, a slender young woman who looks like a model and knocks us out with her depth of thought.

"I'm passionate about intimacy," says Ed, "How to be it, do it, know it. How to find intimacy among strangers."

The newcomers talk of gardening, politics, and new economic models. They have a special function: variety, surprise. Without this flow of the unpredictable, we could settle in to another ritualized weekly display of opinions—as happens in churches, clubs, and at dinner tables with frightening regularity.

After the introductions, whoever has a topic writes it on an index card. They range from the practical to the esoteric: What does home mean? How can we create community in a city? How do barter networks work?

Today, we select "conversation." Mara starts by raising the question: "Conversation for what?" We explore different purposes of conversation. Some speak; some remain silent. Their very silence is a presence that says, "Go deep. I am listening for your soul."

Now Karina's whole body leaps into animation as she tells us about home in the Deep South. "People talk!" she says. "They connect! They debate! They walk in the evening, gathering neighbors for a movie or a barbecue."

I feel something stirring in me, a combination of fear and gratitude. This conversation is so rich and the more I like it, the more scared I get that it won't happen again. My walls are coming down.

Suddenly Kate, the voice for lighter conversation fare, is crying. "I've been slapped down so many times for being too intense that I just don't risk much anymore."

"Me, too," Mara says. We go quiet. Looking at one another, we realize we just slipped into an uncommon space for virtual strangers. This, then, seems to be the final movement of the Conversation Café, a reflection on the conversation itself, preparing us to separate. There are no promises about seeing each other again. We are all suddenly awkward, a bit like furtive lovers emerging from a motel. We've broken a major taboo, talking to strangers about what matters. We don't say much about what happened, yet we know we're going to do it again—right out in public, with strangers.

What Is a Conversation Café?

Conversation Cafés (CCs) are lively, open, hosted, structured, drop-in conversations in public places—like cafés—among diverse people about our feelings, thoughts, and actions in this complex, changing world (figure 1). Conversation Cafés borrow from two dialogue processes: the talking-stick circle, and inquiry in the tradition of David Bohm and Socrates.

WHEN DO THEY HAPPEN?

Conversation Cafés work best if they are ongoing—weekly, semi-monthly, or monthly at the same location for at least a dozen sessions, allowing the idea of drop-in, quality conversations to grow in a community. Café owners also benefit, as each participant is a customer, encouraged to "pay the rent" by ordering food and drink. CCs are also used at meetings, conferences, workshops, dinner tables, and board rooms to process what they have heard, make meaning together, break down the walls of privilege between "presenter" and "audience" or explore a

Illustration by Nancy Margulies

Figure 1. Drop in to the Conversation Café

key idea. CCs can help citizens with diverse views in times of social/political "stress" to increase understanding.

The CCs are governed by a host, a process, a set of agreements, and a few traditions:

The Host

The host is a full-conversation participant, free to express personal points of view while also paying attention to the quality of the overall conversation.

The Process

Talking Object Round One: Holding the talking object, each person says their name and speaks to the topic for a minute or two.

Talking Object Round Two: Deepening the reflection, each person speaks for a minute or two.

Open Dialogue: Placing the talking object in the middle, it is unnecessary unless someone wants it to claim the next speaking opportunity.

Final Talking Object Round: Each person makes a final comment.

The Agreements

- *Open-mindedness:* Listen to and respect all points of view

- *Acceptance:* Suspend judgment as best you can

- *Curiosity:* Seek to understand rather than persuade

- *Discovery:* Question old assumptions, look for new insights

- *Sincerity:* Speak for yourself about what has personal heart and meaning

- *Brevity:* Go for honesty and depth, but don't go on and on

Two "Traditions"

- No committees will be formed—No to-do lists, collective action planned, or efforts to get everyone to agree on anything.

- No marketing—no causes, candidates, events, or services promoted to other participants.

Table of Uses

Typical Setting	Project Length	Number of Participants	Time Required
A coffeehouse, restaurant, café	Weekly or semi-monthly, ongoing	Minimum 3, maximum 8, plus 1 host per table, occupying as many empty tables as the location has.	90 minutes
A conference, convention, lecture • For small-group dialogue, shifting from being talked at to talking with • To process information being delivered from talking heads	As many times during the conference convention or lecture as conversation is needed	Tables of 6–8; can have one "metahost" who introduces the method to the whole conference, then tables are self-hosting.	30–60 minutes
Board Room, meeting, dinner table—where a few dominate the conversation	One meeting or an ongoing meeting process	Everyone present at the table or the meeting, even if it's more than 8, but no more than 15	As long as it takes for everyone to speak during 3 or more talking object rounds.

About the Author

Vicki Robin (v.robin@earthlink.net) is the coauthor with Joe Dominguez of the national best seller, *Your Money or Your Life: Transforming Your Relationship with Money and Achieving Financial Independence.* She is president of the New Road Map Foundation, an educational and charitable foundation teaching people tools for sustainable living. Vicki served on the President's Council on Sustainable Development's Task Force on Population and Consumption. She is the chair of the Simplicity Forum and is on the Board of the Turning Tide Coalition.

Where to Go for More Information

REFERENCES

Barker, Linda. "Everybody's Talking in Seattle This Week." *Christian Science Monitor*, March 12, 2003.

Brown, J., D. Isaac, and the World Café Community. *The World Café: Shaping Our Futures Through Conversations that Matter.* San Francisco: Berrett-Koehler, 2005.

Hart, Joseph. "Conversation Au Lait: In Seattle Coffee Shops, People from All Walks of Life Talk About What Matters to Them." *Utne Reader* (July/August 2002).

Lappe, Frances Moore. *Democracy's Edge: Choosing to Save Our Country by Bringing Democracy to Life.* San Francisco: Jossey-Bass, 2005.

ORGANIZATION

Conversation Café—www.conversationcafe.org

JIM ROUGH AND DEANNA MARTIN

Dynamic Facilitation

Magic exists. There is a way to help people achieve creative breakthroughs.
—Carissa Lloyd

Gridlock Between Elementary School Parents

Parents at an elementary school had been struggling to address educational issues through the district's established governance systems. At times, the school community found itself in an adversarial gridlock with two sides arguing back and forth. After a particularly challenging experience, a parent group decided to seek a sustained culture of trust and respect through a series of dynamically facilitated meetings.

Over the course of a year, three weekend meetings of 10 to 12 randomly selected parents and faculty members generated unanimous conclusions about issues like communication among parents and teachers, and the need for ongoing dialogue about the philosophy of education and values unique to the school.

Unanimous choices and insights from these meetings, plus the ongoing dialogue they create, now inform how the school operates. Rather than telling faculty and staff what they should be doing, parents are involved, taking actions and sparking outcomes unimagined before the process began. More parents are involved in productive ways. The school principal, a wary participant at the beginning, now recognizes the value that the Center for Wise Democracy's dynamically facilitated "Wisdom Council" process brings to school governance and how these big-issue conversations build community.

The Basics

The best way for a group of people to reach a decision is for them to have a creative conversation with a win/win breakthrough at the end. Then everyone is unanimous about the decision, motivated to implement it, and excited about one another. Most meetings eliminate this possibility. They aim for "decision making," in which logical, orderly progress is achieved. People are encouraged to hold back their passion, stick to the agenda, and try to reach preset goals. This orientation to "managing change" in meetings is good for smaller issues, but it won't work for big, messy, or impossible-seeming issues. Crises are a regular result.

Dynamic Facilitation (figure 1) is an emergent approach to facilitating that helps people address difficult issues creatively and collaboratively, where "shifts" and breakthroughs are the natural result. It is a principled way to elicit a heartfelt, creative quality of thinking known as "choice creating" that generates increased trust, shared understandings, and the spirit of community. In this "self-organizing" environment, breakthroughs become likely. Individual uniqueness and passion, normally seen as liabilities, are valued as assets in the group.

© Jim Rough; rendered by Michael Erickson

Figure 1. The Dynamic Facilitation Process

The dynamic facilitator assures this "self-organizing," edge-of-chaos quality of thinking by avoiding the usual forms of control, like holding people to the agenda or setting guidelines of behavior. Instead, she follows the energy of the participants. She stands in front of a group and helps them determine an issue they all really care about, whether it is solvable or not. Then she helps them to be authentic, speak from the heart and say what is really on their minds. She frames each comment as a new item of data, a concern, solution, or a new statement of the problem. Each comment is then fully heard by group members as one more piece to the puzzle that they all are solving together.

The dynamic facilitator plays an active role, while others can just be themselves. The group diverges and converges around the topics they have identified. The dynamic facilitator captures this story and helps the group notice where they are shifting and progressing. Dynamic Facilitation is well suited to address emotional issues, complex messes, and impossible issues. Because a dynamic facilitator is holding a container of self-organizing energy for people, they naturally think systemically and holistically, seeking the "real" underlying issues and causes. Often their primary discovery is a new understanding of the problem, which comes with a feeling of "empowerment" and the capacity to solve it.

Conclusions are always unanimous. This often happens when everyone "co-senses" what is needed in the situation. Breakthrough insights, shifts of attitude, new levels of trust, enhanced individual capabilities, and a new sense of "we" help make these "co-sensings" possible.

Dynamic Facilitation opens new doors of possibility for large-system change, as was experienced among parents, faculty, and administrators in the school community mentioned earlier. The school's process was part of a new social invention called the Center for Wise Democracy's (CWD) "Wisdom Council,"[1] which uses Dynamic Facilitation to spark a shared, bottom-up vision among all members of a large system of people. The CWD Wisdom Council process is now being used in government agencies, cities, and other organizations to involve everyone in identifying and addressing difficult issues and reaching thoughtful, unanimous conclusions. This new process offers the prospect of engaging all citizens of a city, state, or nation in dialogue to create a unanimous voice of "We the People." As one parent said from his experience in a CWD Wisdom Council session at the school, "Democracy can work."

Table of Uses

Typical Setting	Brief Description	Project Length	Number of Participants/ Key Events
Large system of people, like a government agency or city. A CWD "Wisdom Council" uses Dynamic Facilitation to create a whole-system dialogue.	A randomly selected group is dynamically facilitated to choose issues and address them creatively.	This is an ongoing process, with a new random group every quarter or so.	6–12 participants meet quarterly for 2 half days or longer. They present their results in large group meetings and to everyone in the organization.
Team meetings of employees	Identify and creatively address key issues resulting in employee empowerment, better decisions, and an orientation to quality.	1 hour per week, ongoing	Teams of 6–24 people. Employees address the most important issues, reach unanimous conclusions, share these with management, and take action.
Conflict resolution session for employees and supervisor	A work group has many grievances. A dynamic facilitator helps all to address and resolve their frustrations.	4, 2-hour sessions over 1 month	Involves the entire work group and sometimes others. By the final meeting, the group has achieved a new level of trust and capability.

Typical Setting	Brief Description	Project Length	Number of Participants/ Key Events
Senior or executive leadership strategy sessions	Executives build trust as they create a shared vision and workable strategy. They walk away with actions, plus knowing all the views and how they fit together.	2 half-day meetings, quarterly	Involves leaders and sets a creative backdrop for all operations, like a regular "time-out."

Table of Uses. Continued

About the Authors

Jim Rough (jim@dynamicfacilitation.com) is a consultant, author, speaker, and social innovator. He originated *Dynamic Facilitation*, on which he has been presenting public and private seminars since 1990. Jim also originated the CWD Wisdom Council, a new large-system change approach now being implemented in government agencies, schools, and communities. He is author of *Society's Breakthrough! Releasing the Essential Wisdom and Virtue of All the People.*

DeAnna Martin (deanna@dynamicfacilitation.com) is a dynamic facilitator, educator, and director of the Center for Wise Democracy. She was formerly the director of a statewide nonprofit, Washington Ceasefire; a consultant for public agencies such as Washington's Division of Vocational Rehabilitation and the Port of Seattle; and a program director with nonprofits including the American Diabetes Association and Youth Volunteer Corps. She specializes in conflict resolution, leadership development, communications, training and facilitation, and community organizing.

Where to Go for More Information

REFERENCES

Rough, Jim. *Society's Breakthrough! Releasing Essential Wisdom and Virtue in All the People.* Bloomington, IN: AuthorHouse, 2002.

Zubizarreta, Rosa, and Jim Rough. *A Manual & Reader for Dynamic Facilitation and the Choice-Creating Process: Evoking Practical Group Creativity and Transformation through Generative Dialogue.* Port Townsend, WA: Jim Rough and Associates, 2002.

ORGANIZATION

Dynamic Facilitation—www.DynamicFacilitation.com

Note: The steps of the Center for Wise Democracy's Wisdom Council are different from the Ancient Wisdom Council process noted on page 195 in chapter 13, "Ancient Wisdom Council."

1. For more information on the Center for Wise Democracy's Wisdom Council, visit www.wisedemocracy.org.

19

BIRGITT WILLIAMS

The Genuine Contact Program

The significant problems we face cannot be solved at the same level of thinking we were at when we created them.

—Albert Einstein

Transformational Process

IntraHealth International, Inc., was a newly created nonprofit health-care organization with an inherited legacy spanning multiple countries and cultures. In its 25 years of existence prior to the creation of the new organization, IntraHealth suffered many problems including an ambiguous and ill-defined relationship with the mother institution, lack of clarity, and uncertain congruence between the goals of the organization and those of its host institutions. IntraHealth is also highly dependent on one major donor as the source of its funding.

During its transition from a university-based program to an independent freestanding organization, IntraHealth suffered from a lack of strategic vision and careful planning of its future growth, which led to an atmosphere of fear, mistrust, blaming, and unplanned layoffs. However, the organization had a rich history of quality service delivery in many developing countries, thanks largely to a staff of talented individuals who shone internationally in their respective fields. The new president's dream was to:

- Create a culture of personal leadership, collaboration, high staff morale, and unity behind a common purpose.

- Create an organization capable of supporting multiple projects rather than the singular project of the past.

- Increase productivity and efficient use of resources.
- Shift from "headquarters-centric" to equality among all locations with systems-based work (e.g., finance, human resources) supporting the front line.
- Build on the reputation and strengths of the past.

Keys to successfully meeting these goals included:

- Establishing the will and commitment of the leader.
- Developing the capacity of the senior leader.
- Developing the capacity of his leadership team.
- Developing the capacity of the organization as a whole to lead its own ongoing transformation work.

The leadership team was involved in designing the transformational process. Along with interested staff, the leadership team learned to use the tools and frameworks and participatory meeting methods of the Genuine Contact Program™. Sustaining the new higher level, the organization used the same tools, frameworks, and methods, creating the conditions for ongoing emergence.

What Is the Genuine Contact Program?

The Genuine Contact Program is a holistic approach to change that fosters the shared intention, collective purpose, and vision that drive system innovation and transformation. It provides a blended, synergistic, holistic approach to change and to leadership. It is not about a big quick splash but rather about developing the skills, knowledge, and capacity to sustain the ongoing organizational change necessary to thrive in today's constantly changing, complex times.

This capacity to thrive in changing times is the most important outcome from using this method. The liberating structure and participative architecture creates the space for staff to be responsible, highly creative and innovative, solution focused, and productive. Managers and staff truly understand the degree of freedom that they have within a set of "givens" to do their work. All of their actions and decisions take place within these clear "givens," fulfilling the organizational purpose and achieving its vision, strategic directions, and accompanying strategic goals.

The Genuine Contact Program is used around the world in the private sector, nonprofit sector, development agencies, health and social services, and in organizations of all types. The higher-level organization that results is called a Conscious Open Space Organization.

The Genuine Contact Program navigates transformation of the organization using the Medicine Wheel Tool (figure 1). The process begins in the center of the wheel, and then goes

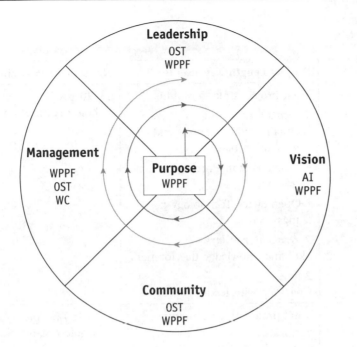

Figure 1. Steps in the Genuine Contact Program

north, east, south, and west. The order is critical to success. During this navigation, purpose, leadership approach, and vision are established, sometimes by the leadership team and sometimes by the whole organization.

While navigating the wheel, participative methods establish the information and commitment needed. Clients choose from a menu of options how to work each segment based on the business's needs. The primary methods used are Open Space Technology (OST), Whole Person Process Facilitation (WPPF),[1] World Café (WC), Appreciative Inquiry (AI), and OpenSpace-Online (OS-Online) Real-time Conference software. When one cycle of the wheel is complete, another cycle begins with every cycle operating at a deeper level. After the initial transformation process, this same Medicine Wheel Tool is used on an annual basis to assist the organization to build its capacity to successfully navigate constant change.

Table of Uses

Description	Project Length/Key Events	Number of Participants
Small, single-location organization responsible to government for community development *Issue:* Improve performance, going from good to great *Results:* Achieved and sustained 5 years later	Total project time: 6 months *4 events over 8 days* • Organization diagnosis and re-generation plan • Whole-Person Process Facilitation and • Open Space Technology meetings *2 events over 6 days* Skill and knowledge development *2 days* Coaching with leader	14–20 people (whole organization involved)
Medium-sized organization in a single location, responsible for national emergency information dissemination *Issue:* Develop vision and strategic directions to guide organization for improved performance despite pending loss of their biggest contract *Results:* Vision and strategic directions now mobilize the organization to find its way in new circumstances (the serious layoff from the terminated contract)	Total project time: 3 months *12 days* • Organization diagnosis and re-generation plan • Whole-Person Process Facilitation • Open Space Technology • Appreciative Inquiry meetings • Strategy mapping *3 events with leadership team* • Diagnosis & regeneration plan • Final strategy mapping *3 events, whole organization* • Whole-Person Process Facilitation • Open Space Technology • Appreciative Inquiry	• 80–120 people (whole organization) • Leadership team of 10 people
Medium-sized, multiple-location health-care organization *Issue:* Transform to culture of personal leadership and unity *Results:* Achieved significant organizational transformation for the organization to thrive in a competitive global market	Total project time: 12 months *40 days* *6 events whole staff* • Whole-Person Process Facilitation • Open Space Technology • World Café	• 80–120 people • Leadership team of 8 people

Description	Project Length/Key Events	Number of Participants
	• OpenSpace-Online Real-time and Appreciative Inquiry meetings *8 events with leadership team* • Diagnosis and regeneration plan • Establishing purpose, leadership approach, vision • Management planning focused on developing liberating structures and a participatory architecture • Leadership coaching • Strategy mapping • Feedback and evaluation *4 workshops for specific skill development*	
Large computer software organization of 10,000 people *Issue:* Establish programs for: • leader development • leadership development • management skills development • organizational capacity enhancement *Results:* Corporate university established as a Conscious Open Space Organization and developed skills to carry on the work over the coming years	Total project time: 18 months *40 days* *6 events whole staff of university* • Whole-Person Process Facilitation • Open Space Technology • World Café • OpenSpace-Online and Appreciative Inquiry meetings *8 events with leadership team of university* • Diagnosis and regeneration plan • Establishing purpose, leadership approach, vision • Management planning focused on developing liberating structures and a participatory architecture • Leadership coaching • Strategy mapping	• 10 people • University leadership team of 4 people to oversee development • Organization leadership team of 50 people

Description	Project Length/Key Events	Number of Participants
	• Feedback and evaluation *4 workshops for specific skill development* *8 events with senior leaders of organization* requiring 17 full days, 16 half days, 14 hours over six months for skill, knowledge, and capacity development	

Table of Uses. Continued

About the Author

Birgitt Williams (Birgitt@dalarinternational.com), in partnership with her husband, Ward, created a holistic approach to business success, the Genuine Contact Program, the International Alliance for Mentoring, Dalar International Consultancy, and Bright Future Holdings. She is one of the pioneers of Open Space Technology and created the concept of the Conscious Open Space Organization. Her background is in cognitive psychology, clinical behavioral sciences, and the healing arts. She has had extensive international experience with a wide range of organizations, challenges, and opportunities.

Where to Go for More Information

REFERENCES

Arrien, Angeles. *The Four-Fold Way.* San Francisco: HarperCollins, 1993.

Genuine Contact Listserv—www.genuinecontact.info.

Holman, Peggy, and Tom Devane, eds. *The Change Handbook: Group Methods for Shaping the Future.* San Francisco: Berrett-Koehler, 1999.

Owen, Harrison. *The Power of Spirit.* San Francisco: Berrett-Koehler, 2000.

Williams, Birgitt Bolton, and Larry Peterson. "Open Space and the Benefits of Accepting Risk and Uncertainty." *At Work* (January–February 1999).

INFLUENTIAL SOURCE

Waldrop, M. Mitchell. *Complexity: The Emerging Science at the Edge of Order and Chaos.* New York: Simon & Shuster, 1993.

Organizations

Dalar International Consultancy—http://dalarinternational.com

Genuine Contact—http://genuinecontact.net

---

1. Whole-Person Process Facilitation (WPPF) is a means of facilitating meetings that taps into the whole person, into intellectual and intuitive wisdom, creating maximum choice and freedom for participants while simultaneously offering a guided facilitation approach. It uses the same principles and law as an OST meeting. For more information on WPPF, visit http://www.genuinecontact.net/mtg_whole_person.html.

20

GLENDA H. EOYANG

Human Systems Dynamics

Too little liberty brings stagnation and too much brings chaos.
—Bertrand Russell (1872–1970)

Real-Life Story

The youth in east central Illinois needed help. In spite of the dogged commitment of schools, health care, youth programs, juvenile justice, parents, and faith communities, children and youth were falling through the cracks. The Lumpkin Family Foundation recognized that change would not come from silos of current services. A systemwide pattern of care and concern was the only way to "help our children reach for the future."

The Human Systems Dynamics Institute, with staff and an advisory team, designed and hosted a two-day Youth Summit. The purpose was to establish the conditions for new patterns of collaboration to self-organize among eight professional disciplines across eight different localities within the region. Borrowing from a variety of methods and techniques, the design focused on shifting conditions for self-organization to encourage new, more productive and resilient patterns of support for children and youth. As a result of the summit, regionwide projects were defined, new relationships were forged across disciplines and locations, and a new energy and optimism were born.

Frequently Asked Questions

WHAT IS HUMAN SYSTEMS DYNAMICS?

Human Systems Dynamics (HSD) is an emerging field of theory and practice at the intersection of complexity and social sciences. We draw concepts, metaphors, and tools from many sciences and areas of mathematics (chaos theory, complexity science, nonlinear dynamical systems, and others) to understand and influence the surprising patterns in teams, organizations, and communities.

HSD represents no single method, tool set, or approach. It provides no step-by-step solutions or surefire answers. We focus on the complex dynamics of human systems that are unpredictable, unique, and surprising by nature. We pose provocative questions and offer ways to see and influence the complex, self-organizing dynamics of human systems.

One tool is particularly helpful as we try to see and influence the patterns that emerge before, during, and after large group events: conditions for self-organizing—the CDE (Containers-Difference-Exchange) Model. Human systems self-organize all the time—a clique forms, relationships develop, niches emerge in the market, and cultural patterns are established. A variety of conditions shape how and when such changes occur. Though the new patterns may appear to be spontaneous, they are responding to conditions that appear naturally in all human systems. HSD describes the three kinds of conditions that shape path and outcome of self-organizing—the CDE Model (figure 1).

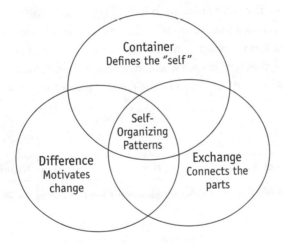

Figure 1. The CDE Model

Containers (C) define the "self" that is to organize. We ask, "What is the emergent pattern that needs to be reshaped?" The container bounds the system and determines what is in or out of the emerging pattern. The two-day time frame and location functioned as containers to help the Youth Summit shift the region toward new patterns of engagement.

Difference (D) provides the motivation for change. We ask, "What are the differences that make a difference?" When everyone is the same, then nothing new is going to be created. Differences also establish the form of the patterns as they emerge. "Local community" and "professional discipline" were the primary differences that influenced the emerging patterns for the Youth Summit. All of our activities and communications were designed to articulate those differences and engage across them to encourage opportunities for creative thought and action.

Exchange (E) connects individuals or groups to each other across their differences. We ask, "What are the connections that need to inform the new patterns?" In Illinois, the exchanges began long before the summit itself. An Advisory Team that represented critical differences in the service-delivery community started the conversation. Focus groups with children, youth, and parents expanded the conversation outside of the two-day container. The press and researchers were invited to participate in the event, to encourage other kinds of ongoing exchanges to perpetuate the patterns that emerged.

These three conditions—CDE—influence how quickly patterns emerge and how distinct the emergent patterns are. A large container, many significant differences, and loose exchanges set the conditions for slow, self-organizing processes with rich but fuzzy results. On the other hand, a small container, a few high-priority differences, and tight exchanges move a group more quickly toward well-defined but perhaps too narrow patterns.

The CDE Model helps us understand and influence patterns as they emerge in teams, organizations, and communities, but they do not let us predict or control change. The natural self-organizing processes of human systems ensure that they will always be surprising!

HSD has been used in a variety of contexts including private industry, government, nonprofits, and communities. It is relevant to a variety of challenges including leadership, team building, large group decision making, human resource management, marketing and communications, training, strategic planning, and facilitation. In each situation, we explore opportunities to shift the underlying conditions to encourage new and more productive patterns across the system as a whole.

Table of Uses

Brief Description	Project Length	Activities	Number of Participants
Culture and Process Improvement *Client:* Human services department in large metropolitan county *Goal:* Establish department-wide approach to sharing client data *Outcome:* Policy defined; project plans created for training, software development, evaluation, process improvement, and forms reform to support implementation of countywide data sharing.	3 months	C: Design team met weekly D: Action Conference explored "myths and realities" of data sharing E: Stated policy and identified strategic areas C: Planning Conference designed project plans for each of the strategic areas	10 people 80 people 30 people 60 people

Brief Description	Project Length	Activities	Number of Participants
Internal Conflict *Client:* Urban school district in major internal conflict *Goal:* Identify and respond to issues that affect performance of students *Outcome:* Specific projects for follow-up, new personal and professional relationships, satisfaction of "being heard" by colleagues and management.	1 month	C: Design team met twice D: Open-space interactions let participants define differences that mattered to them E: Face-to-face conversation shaped new relationships and ongoing reports from teams that self-organized around strategic action	5 people 60 people
Merger and Acquisition *Client:* Mid-sized government consulting firm *Goal:* Respond to the negative effects of an acquisition *Outcome:* Established individual and collective action plans to improve integration	1 day	C: Senior management of acquired company met together D: What do we control, influence, and care about? E: Built shared understanding, plans for action, and ways to communicate with others	2 people in each of 4 engagements

About the Author

Glenda H. Eoyang, Ph.D. (geoyang@hsdinstitute.org) is founding executive director of the Human Systems Dynamics Institute, a network of individuals and organizations developing theory and practice in the emerging field of human systems dynamics. Glenda writes and consults internationally. She uses her extensive knowledge of complex systems theory to design effective organizational interventions, especially in extremely complicated and chaotic situations. Glenda is a talented trainer and has helped hundreds see and influence emergent patterns in human systems.

Where to Go for More Information

REFERENCES

Eoyang, G. *Coping with Chaos: Seven Simple Tools.* Cheyenne, WY: Lagumo Publishing, 1997.

———, ed. *Voices from the Field: An Introduction to Human Systems Dynamics.* Circle Pines, MN: HSD Institute Press, 2003.

Olson, E., and G. Eoyang. *Facilitating Organization Change: Lessons from Complexity Science.* San Francisco: Jossey-Bass/Pfeiffer, 2001.

ORGANIZATION

Human Systems Dynamics Institute—www.hsdinstitute.org

21

RICHARD STROZZI-HECKLER

Leadership Dojo

Knowledge is only a rumor until it's in the muscle.

—Asian proverb

The Largest Pharmaceutical Merger in History

Pharmaceutical giant Pfizer acquired Werner Lambert in 2001, and Pharmacia two years later, in one of the largest mergers in U.S. history. In the midst of these acquisitions, Pfizer also created a new R&D (research and development) business model that included a matrix organizational structure. While immediate attention on the implementation of the new business processes and organization was required, it also necessitated transforming the diverse cultures of these three mega pharmaceutical companies into a single, unified entity. It was as if you were suddenly asked to blend the army, navy, and air force into one high-performing service.

Dr. Nancy Hutson, senior vice president of Global Research and Development committed to building this new business culture. She knew that it would take more than capitalization and a new organizational model to successfully move Pfizer into the twenty-first century—the culture also had to be radically transformed.

The climate in Pfizer was historically competitive, hierarchical, and guarded. Hutson understood that a culture of engagement, authenticity, and trust was needed to make Pfizer both a business success and a place in which people were personally and professionally fulfilled. In short, she wanted everyone to see themselves as leaders, with the skills and sensibility to act accordingly.

The Leadership Dojo was first initiated with the Groton Leadership Team—16 senior leaders who ran the R&D Lab at Groton. We began with two four-day off-site retreats and then took the work to the next level of 150 managers in two two-day conferences. The methodology of the Leadership Dojo was immediately implemented and the participants got real business done while building their leadership skills and a team culture. Dr. Hutson declared, "The Leadership Dojo shifted the culture from one of indifference and infighting to inclusion and colleague engagement."

Frequently Asked Questions

WHAT IS THE LEADERSHIP DOJO?

Dojo is from Japanese and translates to "Place of Training." True to its name, the Leadership Dojo is based in mind/body/spirit practices. The Leadership Dojo is not about watching Power-Point presentations, listening to lectures, or reviewing papers. It's an interactive process that awakens the wisdom of the body. The methodology captures our biological thrust for wholeness to transform organizations into places where people look forward to going and engaging with others. Figure 1 represents the foundational principles practiced in Leadership Dojo programs.

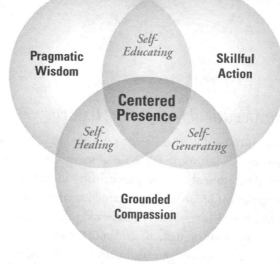

Created by Robyn McCulloch 2005

Figure 1. The Leadership Dojo Model

We stand out from other methods in our emphasis on learning through the body. We get people on their feet and teach them physically how to use their energy to be centered and grounded, to coordinate with others, and extend into the future. We use many practices from the martial arts, specifically Aikido,[1] but they are not martial in the sense of throws or punches. For example, one person will grab his or her partner's wrist. Grabbing the other person is a literal and physical disruption, which is also a rich metaphor of a disruption in the organization. This engages the person's fight, flight, or freeze pattern and in a very direct way, the person being grabbed becomes aware of his or her automatic, conditioned response to change. They center and practice the moves to blend with the change, lead the change, and innovate in the change instead of reacting in a reflexive way.

In mergers and acquisitions, employees tend to take opposing views of the other culture. One of the practices we have them do in their new teams is a simple move from Aikido—turning while standing. They practice this in various configurations with everyone taking part. Coordinating together in movement lessens the grip of their oppositional stance and their inherent biological drive for cooperation is brought to the foreground.

These processes teach the person to take new actions, not just to be "head smart." The learning shifts the story and body of the individuals and therefore the organization. The cost of not including the body in organizational change is increased stress disorders, emotional disengagement, and moods of resentment and resignation. This enormously impacts creativity and productivity. Figure 2 represents the practices, qualities, and actions of an Embodied Leader.

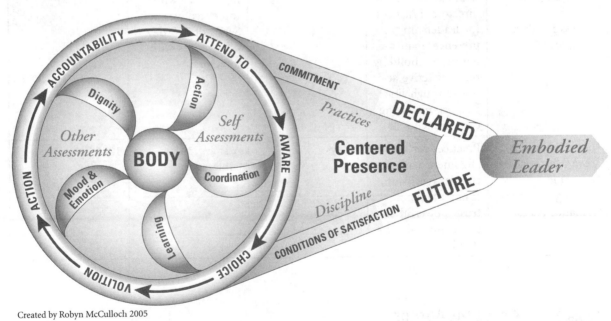

Created by Robyn McCulloch 2005

Figure 2. Developing Leadership Presence

What Are the Outcomes?

There are two things that occur in the Leadership Dojo. First, individuals and teams learn a common language, distinctions, and practices for building trust, listening respectfully to others, generating positive moods, creating a shared vision, managing and fulfilling commitments, having conversations for action, and being lifelong learners. These are all connected to and measured by a return on a business investment. At a deeper level, it allows people to bring their purpose—

what they care about—into their professional life. This creates mature, wise leaders who can act decisively and thoughtfully.

Table of Uses

Typical Setting	Brief Description	Length of Project	Key Events	Number of Participants
Government, Military, and Organizational Change	Practices for leadership presence, learning, taking a stand, trust	6 months	One 4-day conference followed by three 2-day conferences; individual coaching between conferences	25–150 people
Pharmaceutical and Service Organizations Process for developing leaders	Thinking partners with executives for directors: Practices for leadership presence, managing mood, building trust, effective action through linguistics, managing commitments	3 years	Four 3-day meetings a year with top executives Series of 1–3 day conferences with directors	1,500 people
High-Tech and Small/Medium Companies Building high performance teams	Practices for team alignment with company mission, team coherence, trust, powerful assessments, taking a stand	3 days	A single 3-day conference	10–75 people

About the Author

Richard Strozzi-Heckler (richard@strozziinstitute.com) has a Ph.D. in psychology and a sixth-degree black belt in Aikido. He was featured on the front page of the *Wall Street Journal* in 2000 for the groundbreaking leadership program developed for the U.S. Marine Corps. In 2004, he was named one of the top 50 executive coaches in *The Art and Practice of Leadership Coaching.* Strozzi-Heckler has authored six books, including the nationally acclaimed *In Search of the Warrior Spirit.*

Where to Go for More Information

REFERENCES

Strozzi-Heckler, Richard. *The Anatomy of Change.* Boulder, CO: Shambhala, 1984.

————. *Holding the Center.* Berkeley, CA: Frog Publications, 1997.

————. *In Search of the Warrior Spirit.* Berkeley, CA: North Atlantic Press, 2003.

————, ed. *Being Human at Work.* Berkeley, CA: North Atlantic Press, 2003.

ORGANIZATION

Strozzi Institute—www.strozziinstitute.com

---

1. Aikido is a modern Japanese martial art that emphasizes the nonviolent resolution of conflict. It's characterized by blending with the energy of the attacker to neutralize his or her aggression instead of harming the person.

22

MERRELYN EMERY AND DONALD DE GUERRE

Evolutions of Open Systems Theory

We must build a new world, a far better world—one in which the eternal dignity of man is respected.

—Harry S. Truman

Adapting to the Global Economy

When the city of Brandon in Manitoba, Canada, faced a challenging set of competing demands, it turned to the most recent advances in Open Systems Theory (OST). Brandon needed to:

- Maintain its rural values and quality of life while renewing its economy

- Engage its citizens toward participative democracy

Brandon used OST because, while most sectors had expertly developed strategic plans, they were uncoordinated, wasteful, and increasing either citizen apathy or resistance. In the fall of 2001, the city began to create adaptive organizations and governance. They chose a creative mix of Search Conferences (SC), Participative Design Workshops (PDW), and Unique Designs (UD). In 2003, Brandon won the "best place to work in Western Canada" award. In 2004–2005, citizens were selected through the community reference system (see "Search Conference," chapter 35) and engaged in participative strategic planning. Figure 1 shows the social map.

The initial process consisted of:

- Two 1.5-day SCs of 35 participants to the point of deciding a desirable future (strategic goals),

- A 1-day integration event with 10 persons from each SC, and

- A third 1.5-day modified PDW with more than half the original participants to design an organization to do action planning and oversee goal implementation.

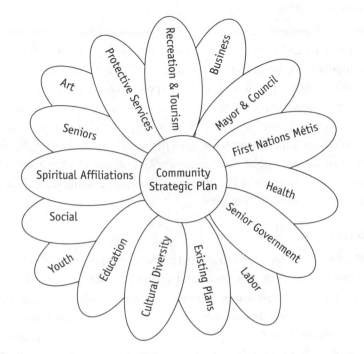

Figure 1. Community Strategic Plan Daisy

The SCs were differently composed, but in the integration event, participants became very excited when they realized that they had agreed to work together across sectors, something never achieved before. Brandon *could* maintain its traditional values and also become the biotechnology center of Canada.

During the final one-day organization design and action-planning meeting, nine self-managed action-planning groups formed around the strategic goals for education, health, socioeconomic development, youth, environment, agriculture, and government. A steering group took responsibility for coordination. They developed a nested series of action plans to implement the goals and prepared to take the work back to the community.

Since then, self-managing groups have refined their plans with widespread support and bright ideas such as the integration of federal, provincial, and municipal government activities. The steering group secured broad citizen support at a Town Hall meeting in the fall of 2005. The city staff team is now announcing new strategic collaborations and citizen involvement through the new democratic organization.

Brandon shows that while OST methods look event-based, they are designed to be a self-sustaining, continuous learning process. The reality-based theory means people grasp it quickly and intuitively. The events are structured to produce high and sustained motivation. There has been no follow-up facilitation. Brandon is shaping its own future.

The Basics: Answers to Frequently Asked Questions

WHAT ARE THE OST EVOLUTIONS?

There are two major evolutions; the two-stage model and unique designs (UDs). Chapters 35 (Search Conference) and 43 (Participative Design Workshop) describe the original methods. The two-stage model is the integration of a Search Conference (SC) and a Participative Design Workshop (PDW) modified specifically for this purpose. UDs are processes that by definition are idiosyncratic to the unique purpose of the work that needs to be done, covering problems as well as puzzle solving. They consist of relevant OST principles and processes rearranged into unique events. These evolutions complement the original methods by providing flexibility to deliver reliable results for virtually any type of work. Since the first edition of *The Change Handbook*, these evolutions have grown fast, meeting the needs of clients and practitioners alike. Understanding these evolutions requires some OST history.

ACKNOWLEDGING THE PROBLEMS

Until 1990, OST practitioners concentrated on developing the SC and PDW for high reliability. There were two problems: The first was that many practitioners struggled to design events that were not strategic planning (addressed by SC) or organizational redesign (addressed by PDW).

The second problem was that some SCs were failing in the implementation phase. Conditions for universal success were not widely understood. Participants often created committees to implement their plans, but committees are bureaucratic structures that sap energy and motivation. SC participants needed to better understand the genotypical organizational design principles and participative democratic structures (see chapter 35).

SOLVING THE PROBLEMS—THE TWO-STAGE MODEL

Merrelyn Emery returned to the theory (figure 2). She discovered that the connection between the two parts of active adaptation—specifically (1) between the system and its environment and (2) within the system—had been lost as the SC and PDW developed as separate methods.

She reconnected the two parts by developing and testing a modified PDW for designing new structures where none existed (communities or new start-up organizations). The PDW modified for design differs from the original in each phase. Early tests including Region 9 of the U.S. Forest Service and the Athabasca Oil Sands in Alberta confirmed that the two-stage model could overcome the implementation problem.

UNIQUE DESIGNS

UDs share all OST concepts and principles. While UDs are by definition one-off events, each UD employs some concepts and steps from the original methods appropriate to its purpose and circumstances.

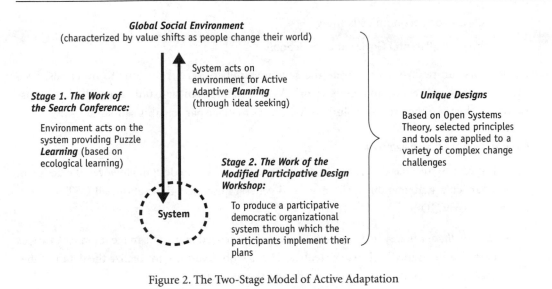

Global Social Environment
(characterized by value shifts as people change their world)

System acts on
environment for Active
Adaptive **Planning**
(through ideal seeking)

**Stage 1. The Work of
the Search Conference:**

Environment acts on the
system providing Puzzle
Learning (based on
ecological learning)

**Stage 2. The Work of the
Modified Participative Design
Workshop:**

To produce a participative
democratic organizational
system through which the
participants implement their
plans

System

Unique Designs

Based on Open Systems
Theory, selected principles
and tools are applied to a
variety of complex change
challenges

Figure 2. The Two-Stage Model of Active Adaptation

A Unique Design is designed backward such that:

- The first step is defining the *outcome*, clearly and precisely.

- The second step is deciding exactly what information the participants will need to accomplish the task. For example, would participants benefit from reviewing the history of the problem? Do they need to analyze the current context in which the problem has reappeared? Each of these pieces of information forms a discrete, participative step of the UD.

- The third step is arranging the required information into a smooth, logical flow of work that delivers the outcome.

Large projects like Brandon involve many unique events such as carefully designed integration events for cohesion.

Examples of UDs include:

- A university internship

- Gaining ISO certification

- Working within new budget constraints

- U.S. Forest Service Economic Action Group

- Reform in Marysville Middle School

- Organizational change in a shoe manufacturer

- Knowledge management in a telecom

- Planning in Groton Community (New York State)

- Sudbury Socioeconomic Planning

- Kahnawake Parental Governance of Schools

Participants can be inside or outside the system. Numbers vary from four to hundreds. Even short meetings can benefit from design work. As the original events are only as good as the preparation for them, so too are the evolutions. OST aims to make participants self-sufficient.

COMMON MISCONCEPTIONS

It is easy to mistake UDs for an "anything goes" approach to design. However, the design of UDs is particularly demanding. There are two general misconceptions about all OST methods and particularly UDs:

- *OST methods are easy to design and manage.* Experienced managers make them *look easy*, as participants immediately work creatively. Casual observers do not realize the depth of theoretical understanding required to produce these effects.

- *OST methods are based on a system of concepts.* Many practitioners are not aware of the incompatibility of OST and some other frameworks. Mixing them can cause confusion, dependency, or resistance.

The rapid growth of these evolutions is a hopeful sign for our democracies.

Table of Uses

Setting	Issue	Outcomes Achieved	Key Events	Number of Participants
National passenger transportation organization, Maintenance Department	Needed to use ISO management system or fail certification	A team structure to deal with certain elements of the ISO system, better training, more efficient use of time and effort in relation to the system, integration of environment, quality, and safety	2-day workshop, including scan of passenger transportation environment, its desirable and probable futures, ISO history and work-flow analysis, and action plans	Managers from across the country
Nonprofit organization with mandate to aid youth in difficulty	Needed to manage within new budget constraints	Development of 12 action plans to be carried out	1.5-day workshop including task environment scan, history, and action plans	All staff and Board of Directors

About the Authors

Merrelyn Emery (me9@grapevine.net.au) has been developing OST methods now for more than 35 years, many of them spent working with Fred Emery. She holds a first class honors degree in psychology and a Ph.D. in marketing. She has worked with innumerable communities and organizations in the public, private, and volunteer sectors. She continues to teach the state of the art of open systems theory around the world.

Don de Guerre (don.deguerre@sympatico.ca) has worked with OST methods for 30 years in both organizations and communities. He is now a faculty member in the Department of Applied Human Sciences at Concordia University in Montréal. He teaches graduates and undergraduates in the domains of human systems intervention and action research, consulting process and skills, organizational design, and small group development. His research is focused on the further development of OST and its methods.

Where to Go for More Information

REFERENCES

Cabana, S. "Participative Design Works, Partially Doesn't." *Journal for Quality and Participation* 18, no. 1 (1995).

de Guerre, D. W. "Variations on the Participative Design Workshop." In *The Collaborative Work Systems Fieldbook: Strategies, Tools, and Techniques,* edited by M. M. Beyerlein, G. Klein, and L. Broedling, 275–286. San Francisco: John Wiley & Sons, 2002.

Emery, F. "Participative Design: Effective, Flexible and Successful, Now!" *Journal for Quality and Participation* (January/February 1995).

Emery, F., and M. Emery. "The Participative Design Workshop." In *The Social Engagement of Social Science: A Tavistock Anthology: The Socio-technical Perspective,* Vol. II, edited by Eric Trist and Hugh Murray, 599–613. Philadelphia: University of Pennsylvania Press, 1993.

ORGANIZATIONS

Centre for Human Relations and Community Studies, Concordia University, Montréal—centreh@vax2.concordia.ca.

For information about training courses and current projects.

Fred Emery Institute, Melbourne—contact AMERIN Pty. Ltd., www.amerin.com.au.

The authors would like to thank Tom Devane for his editorial help.

23

GABRIELA ENDER

OpenSpace-Online Real-Time Methodology

To make the world work for 100% of humanity in the shortest possible time through spontaneous cooperation without ecological offense or the disadvantage of anyone.

—R. Buckminster Fuller

After SARS: Coping in the New Health-Care Normal

In 2003, the Registered Nurses Association of Ontario (RNAO) realized that nurses all over the large province were showing symptoms of "SARS Stress Disorder," which is similar to posttraumatic stress disorder. This understanding prompted the RNAO to organize an OpenSpace-Online® Conference to provide opportunities for conversations by nurses in "real-time" about the theme: "After SARS: Coping in the New Health-Care Normal."

The discussions were rich, informative, and highly productive. The nurses used the conference to share their compelling stories, dialogue about the meaning of their experiences, and to make recommendations about how to effectively manage future outbreaks of diseases like SARS. The extensive OpenSpace-Online documentation of all discussions and results was used by RNAO to plan professional development activities to support nurses and to inform the RNAO's report on the nursing experience with SARS for the Ontario government. In addition, comments from participants indicated that the conference helped nurses with their personal healing journey and enhanced the reputation of RNAO as a health-care leader.

Frequently Asked Questions

WHAT IS THE PURPOSE OF OPENSPACE-ONLINE?

The general purpose of the OpenSpace-Online methodology is to enable organizations to consciously act as "Lifelong Learning Organizations," and to empower interest and work groups to independently cocreate the future for the greater good of society and the whole planet by overcoming the limitations of time and space. Moreover, the purpose of this method is to enable completely new participative collaboration processes to link multifaceted face-to-face and online activities in a highly complementary manner. The completely self-contained Internet method OpenSpace-Online is based on the philosophy of Open Space Technology and on the basic assumption that the best solutions can be found in one's "own system."

The Internet method was developed to encourage respectful, open, and goal-oriented collaboration that enables autonomous, fast, and ongoing work about important questions or issues, priorities, and action steps across distances. This virtually led real-time method is setting new innovation standards for global collaboration and change in business, community, education, health-care, and governmental settings.

WHEN, WHERE, AND HOW IS IT USED?

The easy-to-use conferencing system makes it possible for sponsors and change facilitators to quickly organize and for participants to work together without online moderators in a highly productive and liberated manner. OpenSpace-Online can be used for various goals, themes, and user groups via the Internet or Intranet at any time. It is an excellent approach if "High Passion, High Concentration, and High Play" are desired in order to enable valuable dialogues across distances, and to achieve results and agreements immediately recorded for further work. Once the organizer(s) have defined the scope, objectives, and the title of the OpenSpace-Online event, they are ideally positioned to compose the invitation, and generate interest in it. The method is applied in either time-limited single events or continuing, "endless" team or community processes in worldwide learning and collaboration contexts (figure 1).

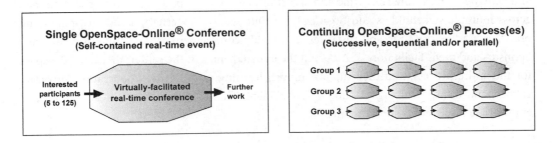

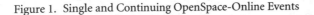

Figure 1. Single and Continuing OpenSpace-Online Events

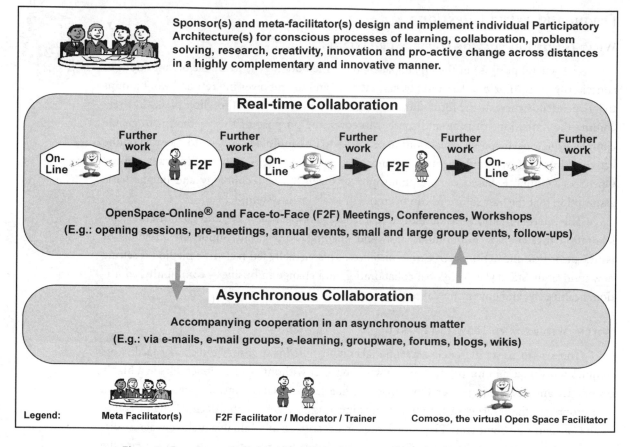

Figure 2. OpenSpace-Online Enables All-Embracing Participatory Architectures

The OpenSpace-Online methodology makes it possible for internal and external meta-facilitators to design individual All-Embracing Participatory Architectures™ (APA, figure 2) consciously linking different participatory communication and collaboration methods, concepts, and activities across time (real-time and asynchronous), across space (face-to-face and online), across multiple stakeholders and organizations (internal and external), across disciplines and branches, and across time and distances in a highly complementary and innovative manner. Sponsors and meta-facilitators of APAs put the human beings in the center; they open the space for the entire process; and they support mutual learning, appreciative cooperation, proactive change, and transparent organizational development. They foster further cocreative work and appropriate implementation of results.

How Does It Work? What Is the Flow or Process?

OpenSpace-Online is a high-encoded (448 Bit) software system that makes it possible for five to 125 persons to work together in real time. The meetings can be scheduled to be from two to eight hours in length. Neither organizers nor participants are required to have prior knowledge or technical expertise. In order to participate, users only need to be interested in the conference theme. Participants use a basic Internet connection on a standard computer that has been loaded with the OpenSpace-Online software (figure 3).

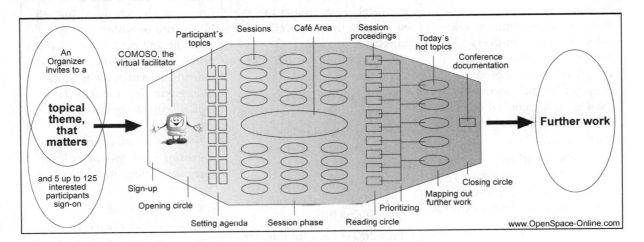

Figure 3. OpenSpace-Online Methodology

The text-based technology guides all participants through successive phases as follows: opening circle, creating a shared agenda, discussing topics in various sessions, café talks and private one-to-one conversations, summarizing the topic sessions, prioritizing topics and planning for next actions or steps, and closing circle. No external online moderator is needed because the virtual facilitator, "Comoso," guides all participants through the conference. The participants themselves are the experts who bring shared interests in the theme, knowledge about various topics, and ideas for new solutions. At the end of each conference, every participant receives an extensive conference book at the press of a button. The report provides an ideal foundation for further work. It contains all generated content, results, arrangements, and contact data made during the meeting. It can be used immediately, in either digital or printed form.

Table of Uses

Typical Setting(s)	Brief Description	Length of Project
Organizations: Professional associations, stakeholder groups in businesses or corporations, colleges or universities, churches, nonprofit or nongovernmental organizations (NGOs), governmental agencies, online communities, virtual teams *Geographic Locations:* Neighborhood or community, town, city, country, province, state, nation, and global network	In general, users around the world share the same desire to address the following: • Working on topics with a decision time of yesterday • Building on the ideas and experience of the "whole system" • Developing, expanding, and evaluating internal and external relations • Supporting the cocreative energy of other online and face-to-face activities • Providing a basis for ongoing, continued work • Fast results and recorded documentation • Easy-to-use online tools, which have to meet high data security • Contributing to conservation of natural resources • Reducing or eliminating travel expenses • Providing alternatives to time and space limitations	Events can be scheduled for 2–8 hours with or without action planning and can include 5–125 people. Different criteria lead to individual event settings (duration, group size, variant). Two typical options regarding length are: • 2- to 4-hour meetings: Most existing work groups or teams regularly meet once a week or monthly • 3- to 6-hour conferences: Mostly public events that involve a varying number of participants

About the Author

Gabriela Ender (contact@OpenSpace-Online.com) invented the OpenSpace-Online Method after 30 years of experience in entrepreneurial management, systems-oriented organizational development, and change facilitation. In 1999, she experienced a strong and very clear vision of a revolutionary, virtually facilitated, real-time meeting methodology. Since 2002, Gabriela and her team have transformed that vision into reality. In 2003, she was the first female entrepreneur, selected by Berlin Partner (Capital Marketing of Berlin) to receive the annual "Founder Award." In 2006, the World E-Gov Forum and PoliticsOnline selected Gabriela Ender and OpenSpace-

Online as one of the Global Top 20 individuals, organizations, and companies having the greatest impact on changing the world of Internet and politics. After three weeks of voting by people around the world, she received the "Top 10 World Changer 2006" Award.

Where to Go for More Information

REFERENCES

Ender, Gabriela. "Having Its Seeds in 'Feeling Good'—Introduction into 'Open Space.'" *Stadt und Gemeinde—DStGB AKTUELL* (2000). German Association of Towns and Municipalities (DStGB), Bonn, Germany.

———. *Real-Time Conferencing Using the OpenSpace-Online Methodology—Results-Oriented Participation via Internet.* Edited by Mario Gust and Dr. Uwe Seebacher. Ottobrunn, Germany: USP Publishing International, 2004. [In German.]

Mavromichais, Carl, "Cyberspace Chat." *Registered Nurse Journal* 15, no. 6 (2003): 25. Registered Nurses Association of Ontario (RNAO), Canada.

Pfützenreuter, Rolf. "The Human Being in the Centre—As Well Across Distances: The OpenSpace-Online Methodology." *Gemeinsinn-Werkstatt.de*, c/o Akademie Führung & Kompetenz Centrum für angewandte Politikforschung (CAP), München, Germany, 2005.

ORGANIZATION

OpenSpace-Online GmbH—The Power of People!—www.OpenSpace-Online.com

24

Organization Workshop

I can see clearly now, the rain is gone,
I can see all obstacles in my way
Gone are the dark clouds that had me blind
It's gonna be a bright, bright sun-shiny day.

—Johnny Nash

High-Tech Entrepreneurialism

Between 7:30 and 8:00 A.M., 50 workshop participants arrived at the conference center nestled among the pine trees in a rural setting. Though the senior executives, middle managers, and frontline workers present had received a preworkshop briefing, there was a high level of anticipation and some anxiety in the room. The California-based H-Tech Company is a 5,000-person high-tech manufacturing organization that was seeking to change its organizational culture. Its target was a culture with more entrepreneurialism, less blame, more individual responsibility, and greater partnership across organizational lines. At 8:00 sharp, the participants were assigned to one of four groups (see figure 1)

- Tops, who had overall responsibility for the organization;
- Bottoms, who were the frontline producers or servicers;
- Middles, who each had responsibility for a Bottom group; and
- Potential Customers, who had projects for the organization and money to pay.

The first exercise lasted the entire morning. Periodically, action halted and members held a Time Out of Time (TOOT). The TOOT's purpose was for people to talk about life in their positions—what was going on in their world, their issues, their feelings (usually a mixture of stress,

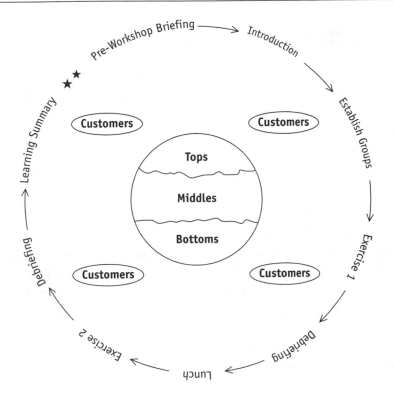

Figure 1. The Four Groups

frustrations, and anxiety), how they experienced other parts of the system, and what their peer relationships were like. The TOOT shed light on what was happening at all levels in this simulated organization; equally important, the TOOT illuminated issues that participants were experiencing in their change efforts back in their real company. For this group, as is almost universal, this was a turning point both personally and organizationally. People recognized that this exercise—which was not constructed as a simulation of their organization—was in fact very much like their organization in the areas of personal frustrations, misunderstandings, and multilevel organizational issues. High-leverage systemic work began here.

Table 1 shows participants' workshop experiences, mirrored in organizational life:

At 1:00 P.M., everyone returned to the conference room and changed organizational positions. As usual in the workshops, ex-Tops who were now Bottoms expressed relief; ex-Bottoms who had become Tops were already feeling the stress and tension of responsibility. (It was a moment of humility for some Bottoms—who had spent energy in the morning criticizing Tops—to find themselves as Tops.) Customers felt separate from the organization. New Middles weren't sure how they felt. Their general sense was that they had no control over what their life would be, and that their experience would depend on the actions of Tops, Bottoms, and Customers.

Position	Condition	Description
Top	Overload	Complex issues not dealt with elsewhere; too much to do with too little time; lots of issues, unpredictable; responsibility for the whole system
Middle	Crunch	Pulled between differing and often conflicting demands and priorities of Tops and Bottoms; pulled apart from each other
Bottom	Disregard	Finding things wrong with their condition and with the system; the sense that Tops or Middles ought to fix things, but don't
Customer	Neglect	Inadequate speed, high cost, poor service coming from the organization

Table 1. Comparison of Participant Experience with Exercise and with Organizational Life

Before proceeding with the second exercise, participants were presented with a strategic framework that helped them see why organizations—despite good intentions and high-quality processes—keep falling into the same old self-limiting patterns. In addition, they were presented with principles and strategies for building healthier, more effective organizations.

The afternoon exercise became a practice field for participants to develop ways out of the common traps present for each organizational space. At the end of the day, participants reported various insights into increasingly successful partnering—both within the organization and with customers—to achieve the organization's overall objectives. At day's close, participants left emotionally charged, eager to bring their new learning back to the workplace.

Four months later, the CEO reported that the initial and ongoing Organization Workshops had dramatic effects on how people interacted, positively affecting performance. Customer satisfaction went way up, and the company significantly decreased new product development time.

The Basics

The Organization Workshop (OW) is a group learning session in which participants experience universal conditions, traps, and dilemmas of organizational life. By learning firsthand about these traps, along with solid theory on avoiding them, participants emerge with concepts, methods, and a common language to improve their interaction in any organization. The result is better partnerships for higher performance.

In the Organization Workshop, participants directly experience the costs of system blindness—the costs to them personally and to the organization—and they experience the organizational power as well as the personal liberation, creativity, and empowerment that come from moving from system blindness to system sight.

Organizations have reported a variety of outcomes, including reduced cycle times, improved quality, lower costs, and higher customer service levels. While the Organization Workshop does not directly address any of these improvement areas, it creates conditions for realizing them through improved system sight.

The Organization Workshop helps organizations become powerful organizational systems—the organization gets what *it* needs, and individuals get what *they* need.

Table of Uses

Setting	Brief Description	Number of Participants	Length of Project	Number and Length of Events
5,000-person high tech manufacturing company	Workshop was tailored to address company-specific issues of increasing entrepreneurship and reducing blame, beginning with a cross-level pilot	50 per workshop	6 months	1-day workshop, repeated 15 times for multiple organizational levels
Pharmaceutical company	Used in conjunction with Search Conference and Participative Design Workshop methods to help organizations reach higher financial performance, operating performance, and intrinsic motivation.	35 per workshop	9 months	1.5-day workshop, repeated 4 times
Software development company	Used as part of leadership development curricula to foster leadership development at all levels	20 per workshop	Ongoing	4-hour workshop, repeated for multiple participant groups

About the Authors

Barry Oshry, Ph.D. (barry@powerandsystems.com), is a distinguished educator and pioneer in the field of human systems thinking. Barry's area of research, writing, and teaching has been the human systems dynamics arising when people are in top, middle, bottom, and customer relationships with one another. He's been exploring with special interest the issue of "middles" in organizations for more than 30 years. Barry's books include *Seeing Systems, The Possibilities of Organization,* and *In the Middle.*

Tom Devane (tomd@tomdevane.com) helps organizations and communities thrive in their respective environments. His diverse background in strategy, Six Sigma, technology, organizational development, community planning, and leadership effectiveness provides for dramatic, sustainable improvement. With BS and MS degrees in finance, Big Six consulting, and industry leadership experience, he founded his own firm in 1988. Clients include Microsoft, Hewlett-Packard, Johnson & Johnson, General Electric, the U.S. Forest Service, AT&T, Honeywell, and the Republic of South Africa.

Where to Go for More Information

REFERENCES

Oshry, Barry. *In the Middle.* Boston: Power & Systems, 1994.

————. *The Possibilities of Organization.* Prudential Station, MA: Power & Systems, 1992.

————. *Seeing Systems: Unlocking the Mysteries of Organizational Life.* San Francisco: Berrett-Koehler, 1995.

————. *Space Work.* Boston: Power & Systems, 1992.

ORGANIZATION

Power+Systems—www.powerandsystems.com

SARAH MACDOUGALL AND CHRISTINA BALDWIN

PeerSpirit Circling
Creating Change in the Spirit of Cooperation

Transformation can occur for the entire human race by the one-time discovery of a bit of knowledge that makes everyone different from that point forward.

—Na'im Akbar

Real-Life Story

In a PeerSpirit training session for the nursing administration of a hospital, 20 leaders and two facilitators met at a retreat facility for a day and a half. Their intention was posted on the wall: "*We gather to find renewed vision for the department and develop support for each other in professional direction.*" Participants were seated in a circle of comfortable chairs. To create a sense of shared space, there was a low table in the center with a mosaic that the group had fashioned at an earlier staff retreat. A tangible center, one of the circle's enduring gifts to modern methodology, acts as an energetic hub that acknowledges the ways a group is more than the sum of its parts. As one CEO explained it, "Something larger than human ego is in the room."

Before any conversation began, four agreements were articulated, establishing expectations of safety and responsibility.

- We honor confidentiality: Personal story is not to be shared without permission;

- We listen with curiosity and compassion, withholding judgment;

- We ask for what we need and offer what we can;

- We practice pauses in action to recenter and focus.

Circle is a social contract: All participants agree to principles of cooperation that set the tone of conversation and govern *how* the group fulfills its intention.

The agreement to pause is activated by a group member who volunteers to serve as "guardian." This person, usually rotating session by session, has authority from the group to make some agreed-upon signal that brings interaction to a halt. This is often a chime or small bell. To initiate pause, the guardian rings the chime. To release pause, the guardian rings a second time and speaks to the reason for calling a rest in action. "We were interrupting each other" or "It seems timely to take a stretch break here."

The circle begins with a round called check-in. Among the nursing leaders, everyone responds to the question, "What led you to this organization and what renews your faith in it?" The pagers and cell phones are off and workday details are far away. People pass a small stone hand to hand to take turns talking. They lean in, speak with heartfelt intensity, and tell a story that moves listeners to nods of recognition, laughter, and sometimes tears. Something happens in this manner of speaking and listening that is a combination of the circle design and the willingness of each person to risk exploring the dreams they have for the place they work.

About halfway round the circle one administrator says, "This is what I've needed—the sense that we are inspired by similar stories and want similar things. When we're back at work, I can imagine listening to each other in a whole different way. So here's my story . . ."

Circle fosters a basis of trust built on honest self-disclosure received respectfully. When a group knows the fundamental stories of its membership, they approach task, planning, and systemic change with confidence that they can think and work together.

As a result of this retreat, these nursing leaders set monthly and annual goals and designed a process of accountability held in circle. They realized that their ability to function as a professional team was dependent on their ability to build trust through integrating story and dialogue into agenda-based meetings.

The Basics

CIRCLE HISTORY

Circle as a form has been with us since the dawn of human culture. Circle is a foundation of human social heritage. PeerSpirit circling, a modern adaptation and innovation of this ancient social and spiritual process, challenges dominant ideologies based on concepts of hierarchy and individualism.[1] Coming into the circle is archetypal. People gather to share wisdom, make collective decisions, and take action for renewal and progress. Circle is the mother of all methodologies.

CIRCLE PROCESS

Prior to coming together in a PeerSpirit circle (figure 1), people intentionally prepare themselves by attending to personal needs. Circle begins by setting the circle space, including establish-

Illustration by Harriet Peterson

Figure 1. The Components of the PeerSpirit Circle

ing a visual center. A check-in connects people, as they slow down and fully arrive. Circle participants then discuss and commit to abiding by PeerSpirit's three principles—rotating leadership, shared responsibility, and reliance on group synergy—and its three practices: intentional speaking, attentive listening, and conscious self-monitoring. They also adopt group norms (agreements) arrived at through consensus.

Someone volunteers to act as guardian of the group energy, paying close attention to group process. The guardian uses some agreed-upon signal to call a stop action to group process, during which everyone pauses and in a moment of silence seeks guidance for what the circle needs next. Within this framework, circle members move into the business or intention of the meeting. Passing a talking piece, a tradition in PeerSpirit circles, ensures that everyone has a chance to speak without interruption. There are times in the circle process when discussion without a talking piece occurs, since some topics are more efficiently addressed using a free-flowing conversation. Intentionally constructing a framework for personal interaction grounded in calling forth the group's collective wisdom or spirit facilitates clear communication. Circle is brought to closure with checkout, a talking-piece round to reflect on what has happened.

CIRCLE TODAY

The circle provides the basis for a culture of conversation in organizations. Principles, practices, agreements (group norms), and other structural components, such as setting intention, using a guardian of the process, and check-in and checkout, comprise the theory that guides the practice of PeerSpirit circling.

The components of circle come alive through their interaction. A clear intention leads to understanding what agreements need to be in place to fulfill group purpose. The center allows diverse opinion, option, and creativity to be figuratively placed for all to consider. By checking in and checking out, the whole group hears what is significant in the learning of each individual. The principles lead to outcomes that cannot be imagined until the process for discovering them is released. The practices develop a conversational culture, which fosters a self-empowering team that can move in coordination within the demands of organizational life.

Table of Uses

Typical Setting	Project Length	Events	Number of Participants
School District Board of Education • Experienced and practiced PeerSpirit circling • Dialogued on critical issues • Came to consensus on how to approach community regarding contentious issues • Established a timeline for their action plan • Committed to continuous, systemic dialogue in PeerSpirit circle	3 days	Weekend retreat	10 board members
School District Teaching Staff Met in PeerSpirit circles to: • build collegiality across grade levels and subject areas • process information on current pedagogy • reflect on implementation of teaching strategies • analyze state testing data • develop and reflect on annual goals to improve student achievement	3 years	Met in small circle groups of 6–8 teachers during 6 half-day sessions each school year	36 K–12 teachers

Typical Setting	Project Length	Events	Number of Participants
School District Leadership Council Met in PeerSpirit circles to: • plan staff development sessions • process feedback from teachers and modify sessions accordingly	3 years	Met monthly during the school year for 2–3-hour sessions	7 teacher volunteer leaders
Health Care Facility Used PeerSpirit process to: • improve communication, especially during emergencies • build a culture of cooperation among administration and staff	6 months	Three 6-hour training sessions	• 5 administrators • 35 health-care workers
Religious Community Learned PeerSpirit methodology to: • create a collaborative culture • renew and sustain current members • investigate ways to increase membership	1 year	Three 3-day retreats	25 community members

About the Authors

Sarah MacDougall, Ed.D. (tenfold@scc.net), is a dedicated educator who investigated the capacity of PeerSpirit circle methodology to transform individual lives and collective group process. Her dissertation establishes a theoretical foundation for the efficacy of PeerSpirit circle process as a means of fostering organizational change.

Christina Baldwin, M.S. (cbaldwin@peerspirit.com), is an innovative facilitator, teacher, and writer. Her studies of group process methodology led to the concepts presented in *Calling the Circle: The First and Future Culture* (Bantam, 1998). She has carried this work throughout North America, Europe, and Africa. She works with organizations in health care, education, religious administration, nonprofit, and association boards.

Where to Go for More Information

REFERENCES

Baldwin, C. *Calling the Circle: The First and Future Culture.* New York: Bantam Books, 1998.

Basic Guidelines for Calling a Circle—http://peerspirit.com/htmlpages/circlebasics.html.

MacDougall, S. N. *Calling on Spirit: An Interpretive Ethnography of PeerSpirit Circles as Transformative Process.* Santa Barbara, CA: Fielding Graduate University, 2005. Dissertation Abstracts International, A66/06, p. 2407 (UMI No. 3178997).

Wheatley, M. J. *Turning to One Another: Simple Conversations to Restore Hope to the Future.* San Francisco: Berrett-Koehler, 2002.

ORGANIZATION

PeerSpirit—www.peerspirit.com

---

1. S. N. MacDougall, *Calling on Spirit: An Interpretive Ethnography of PeerSpirit Circles as Transformative Process.* Santa Barbara, CA: Fielding Graduate University, 2005. Dissertation Abstracts International, A66/06, p. 2407 (UMI No. 3178997).

PETRA EICKHOFF AND STEPHAN G. GEFFERS

Power of Imagination Studio
A Further Development of the Future Workshop Concept

As for the future, your task is not to foresee it, but to enable it.
—Antoine de Saint-Exupery

A Fictional Weather Forecast

An atmosphere of suspense fills the air. We are a group of 80 participants with all of our attention focused on four people in the middle, who are presenting their group results. We witness a fictional weather forecast sometime in the future. Using a picture by an expressionist painter, they explain a satellite image. We learn of training eruptions and competence storms that pour forth like lava. A media Atlantis rises up from the depths and with the help of "Aroma" Computers, Old and New World become networked together, repairing themselves without any help.

One could have heard a needle drop at that moment. The applause for their imaginative, utopian ideas goes on for a long time. Sighs of relief escape from the people who had stepped in the middle of the "6S-4D" Studio (six senses, four dimensions), and they breathe in the lofty atmosphere. Participants who would not have trusted themselves to say anything in front of a large audience suddenly find the encouragement and motivation to do something completely off the wall and ingenious, following their dreams and desires to their hearts' content.

How will the facilitation team bridge the gap to the serious topic at hand? Having jotted down every content-related remark, they now request "translation" of the ideas covering reams of flip-chart paper, using them as a metaphor, describing their hidden meanings. Thus, "competence storms" becomes a mandate for a competence team in a company to track emerging trends. A cardboard bridge is interpreted as creating a meeting place for teams to exchange ideas. A beetle is transformed into a community bus eating up money, demonstrating the idea of cost reduction . . . and the imagining continues.

Frequently Asked Questions

What Is a Power of Imagination Studio?

The starting point for a Power of Imagination Studio—a unique style of Future Workshop—is a serious topic indeed. A studio moderation team acts as a midwife, responsible for the process that shepherds the birth of something new. Participants create the content, the topics, and categories that come into being during the process. Once these are born, the participants are responsible for the ongoing life of the results.

The process works from the belief that the people affected have the capacities they need for change. They are the experts responsible for finding a solution and changing their lives and work environments. External consulting—even trendsetting technical lectures to "prep" participants—is unnecessary. All are treated as equals regardless of position, age, or experience.

A space is provided for a wide spectrum of applications: bringing together different opinions and strengths, awakening slumbering creativity, or supporting self-organization in social groups. Participants mix in different groups and connections, working with questions that matter to them.

The Future Workshop ("Zukunftswerkstatt") originated in the peace efforts of its inventor, Robert Jungk. The Power of Imagination Studio builds on the Future Workshop concept by using the individual and collective shifts that come through creativity.

How Does the Power of Imagination Studio Work?

The theme of the process is established beforehand with the specifics unfolding as participants travel through three phases.

In phase one, participants name their issues and problems, freeing themselves of this burden. *The complaint and criticism phase* brings worry, dissatisfaction, and fears into the foreground so that they can be understood and form the basis for starting anew. This work generates appreciation for the way things are that can move a paralyzed situation symbolically toward the future.

The second phase is the *imagination and metopia phase,* in which "thought landscapes" and ideals are formed. Metopia,[1] derived from the Greek word for "implementable nonexistent place," is an idea about a near future falling under the participants' influence, but not fitting within the horizon of rational analytical thought. Artwork, games, and stories are invented and presented through the use of theatre and the arts. The group selects the most unusual, incomprehensible, and fanciful mental images for the most exciting step of all. The chosen ideas are carefully "translated" into ordinary language. Thus, a bridge fashioned from wood, yarn, and fragments of glass symbolizes improved cooperation, a translation of their desire for greater collaboration as the future they wish to create.

The third phase requires the best of participants' thinking and negotiating skills. In the *implementation and practical phase,* parallel groups work through the chosen themes, clarifying their strengths and intentions and planning their next steps. Good planning is critical, as it gives participants the time to complete a planning instrument that can guide them after the gathering.[2] Periodically, participants review each other's plans, making any necessary corrections to their goal or creating a new one.[3] At the end of the process, creative and sustainable projects exist with established work groups and plans on how to proceed (see figure 1).

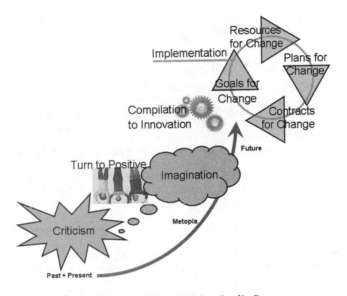

Figure 1. Power of Imagination Studio Process

THE ROLE OF EMOTIONS AND ATTITUDES

This group process works through experiencing "aha's"—surprising insights—and through discovering common dreams. This happens not only intellectually, but also emotionally. Participants become aware that they can change the future, in fact, that they can envision several viable alternatives. They open up creative space together, negotiate agreements on specific steps and changes, and anchor personal interests in common objectives.

Table of Uses

Typical Setting	Time Required	Project Steps	Participants
Organization Improving cooperation between volunteer and full-time workers	6 months	Consulting, conference design, invitation concept, initial talks with the regional head	2 customers + 2 facilitators
		Teambuilding / method design	1 customer + 2 facilitators

Typical Setting	Time Required	Project Steps	Participants
Organization Improving cooperation between volunteer and full-time workers *(cont.)*		Invitation design	25 key customers + 2 facilitators
	3 days	Workshop	130 participants + 8 facilitators
	3 months	Documentation + evaluation	1 customer + 2 facilitators
Specialists from Different Education Associations Developing a training concept for dealing with money/debt	4 months	Half day: initial talks, first workshop, conference design, invitation concept	1 customer + 6 multiplicators + 2 facilitators
	1 day	Second workshop	65 specialists + 3 facilitators
	2 months	Documentation + evaluation	1 customer + 2 facilitators
Department Head and Project Managers of a Consulting Firm Strategy day: security and profile development	2 weeks	Initial talks, topic probe, concept	2 customers + 2 facilitators
	1 day	Workshop	15 managers + 2 facilitators
	3 weeks	Documentation + evaluation	1 customer + 1 facilitator
Residents, City Council, and Politicians District planning in a major urban city	2.5 months	Design with local administration and town residents	2 customers + 2 facilitators
		Weekly half-day mobile office in the district	250 residents + 4 facilitators
	Half day	First workshop (issue definition)	60 residents + 4 facilitators
	2 days	Second workshop (project development)	70 residents + 6 municipal planners + 5 facilitators
	2 months	Consulting/support for 8 project groups	70 residents + 2 facilitators
	Half day	Third workshop (project presentation)	80 participants + 3 facilitators
	4 weeks	Evaluation	10 municipal planners + 4 facilitators

About the Authors

Petra Eickhoff (zukunft-2004@web.de) has her degree in business management (Leipzig) and lives in Cologne (Germany). She is a trainer for business, service, and logistic, professional, and preprofessional development. She is an executive of an association for democratic future design and cofounder of the Future Workshop group, Jena (Thuringia). Her interest is philosophical and political issues about social society after opening of the German Wall. She is certified as an operational trainer and team coach. Topics: Supporting self-organizing groups, strengthening women starting businesses, designing participatory and international conferences.

Stephan G. Geffers (zukunft-2004@web.de) has his degree in computer science (Berlin) and lives in Cologne (Germany). He is a senior consultant for technical and human networking and a cofounder of the Future Workshop facilitators' circle (North Rhine-Westphalia). He worked with the inventors of the Future Workshop, Robert Jungk and Norbert R. Muellert, from 1986 to 1988. He is a certified project manager, and has written reports for federal government, urban authority, and business management. Topics: Technology assessment, environmental city development; media learning, school identity programs; techniques of macro-visualization, and international dissemination of participatory concepts.

Where to Go for More Information

REFERENCE

Jungk, Robert, and Norbert R. Muellert. *Future Workshops—Ways for Reviving Democracy/Use Fantasy to Break Routine and Resignation.* 1st ed., Hamburg: Hoffmann und Campe, 1981; 3rd ed., Munich: 1989. [In German.]

ORGANIZATIONS

Robert-Jungk-Bibliothek fuer Zukunftsfragen (Library of Future Concerns)—www.jungk -bibliothek.at

Publisher of ProZukunft magazine, Robert-Jungk-Platz 1, A-5020 Salzburg, Austria.

Vernetzung von Zukunftswerkstätten—www.zwnetz.de

An invitation to network in everything related to social creativity, engagement, and the participatory and democratic shaping of the future. Platform for ideas about Future Workshop and Power of Imagination Studio.

Conceptual support: Annegret Franz, Axel Weige; translated by Jonathan Mark Dowling.

1. Utopia is defined as an impossible place. A metopia can be implemented as a transition toward a desired state and is always within a field of potential development. [Open Theory Project: "Jetzt erst recht! Auf der

Suche nach einer anderen Zukunft" (Right now: In Search of Another Future), Annette Schlemm, maintainer, 2005.]

2. During the planning cycle, participants decide: (1) their goals; (2) their resources for reaching their goals; (3) the steps of their plan; and (4) their agreements (contract) for implementation.

3. This approach was adapted from Whole-Scale Change (chapter 11).

ROBERT "JAKE" JACOBS

Real-Time Strategic Change

> *I know of no safe depository of the ultimate powers of the society but the people themselves, and if we think them not enlightened enough to exercise their control with a wholesome discretion, the remedy is not to take it from them, but to inform their discretion.*
>
> —Thomas Jefferson

Collaborating Instead of Competing

In New York City, 1.1 million children require care after school, on weekends, holidays, and during the summer. Several city agencies have overseen these critical, yet complex services. They have relied on multiple funding streams. There has been great need for consistent, high-quality care. Collaboration in the past had been low. Out of School (OST) programs in the city have been principally provided by several hundred nonprofit agencies and community-based organizations. Each of these multiple stakeholders has competing needs, since there is a fixed sum of money to allocate. Though all are well intentioned, they have suffered from a lack of alignment. The need to make fast and lasting change has been clear.

During a six-month process, representatives from each of these stakeholder groups met in a series of large group Real-Time Strategic Change (RTSC) events, subgroup working sessions, and leadership team meetings. They realized they shared common challenges. They learned they could better serve the children of the city by collaborating instead of competing. They agreed on a vision, goals, and guiding principles for all OST care throughout the city. Today, city agencies, foundations, and nonprofit service providers have developed a coherent OST system that provides a consistent level of excellent care for the children of New York City.

Frequently Asked Questions

WHAT IS REAL-TIME STRATEGIC CHANGE?

RTSC is an approach that enables people to claim the future they deserve—faster than they ever believed possible. Its focus and methods have evolved in three generations over the past decade:

- *First Generation:* Characterized by a focus on RTSC events. These large group, "roll up the sleeves" working sessions were attended by 10–2,000+ people. The purpose of RTSC at this stage was to build organization-wide alignment, commitment, and action that created lasting change.

- *Second Generation:* Characterized by extending the focus from events to also include the application of RTSC as a way of doing business on a daily basis. Six core principles formed RTSC's foundation—the solid and fixed basis of the approach. The six RTSC principles supported lasting change because they provided guidance in any situation—for change work and for daily work as well.

- *Third Generation:* Characterized by extending the focus from events and principles to also understanding these principles as key polarities. The more effectively organizations manage these polarities or dilemmas, the faster and more sustainable the future they deserve.

WHY DOES IT WORK?

RTSC shines a spotlight on six of these dilemmas that when taken together, enable people to create their future, faster. Each of the RTSC principles manages a specific tension or polarity (table 1).

Principle	Tension/Polarity Managed	Higher Purpose Achieved
Reality as Key Driver	Internal *and* External Realities	Informed Decisions
Empower and Engage	Participation *and* Direction	Clarity and Commitment
Preferred Future	Best of the Past *and* a Compelling Future	Excitement and Energy
Build Understanding	Inquiry *and* Advocacy	Aligned Action
Create Community	Allegiance to Your Part *and* the Entire Organization	Effective Collaboration
RealTime	Planning for the Future *and* Thinking and Acting as if the Future Were Now	Claiming Your Future, Faster

Table 1. The Principles of RTSC

WHEN AND WHERE IS IT USED?

RTSC helps to make big things happen fast. If the situation fits the following three criteria, Real-Time Strategic Change is a path to pursue:

1. Multiple stakeholders have competing needs

2. Aligned action is required

3. Results need to be achieved in radically reduced time frames

HOW DOES IT WORK?

There are three phases to RTSC work: Scoping Possibilities, Developing and Aligning Leadership, and Creating Organizational Congruence. Figure 1 shows how RTSC becomes part of an organization's daily work. Each phase of work leads to desired ways of doing business that ultimately deliver sustained results.

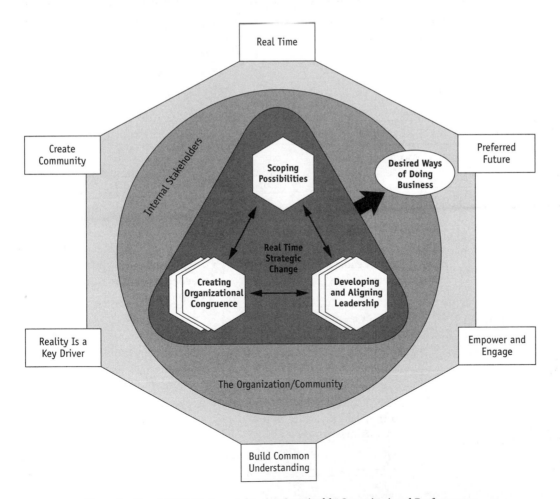

Figure 1. How RTSC Works—Achieving Sustainable Organizational Performance

Scoping Possibilities is about crafting a clear, considered plan for the future. It energizes people with many possibilities for moving forward. This expansive mode complements the focus people require to create a unique pathway that fits their organization's culture, needs, and constraints. For most organizations, creating their own road map is significant evidence of doing business in a new way and symbolizes the power and possibilities of the collective.

Developing and Aligning Leadership is about building leadership competencies and commitment required to succeed. These capabilities can be grown in a number of possible settings: large-scale events, smaller retreats, action learning initiatives, individual reflection and coaching sessions, and training, as well as through daily work with other leaders and the larger organization. These efforts focus on developing a preferred and consistent leadership style, strategy alignment, and a range of skills including leading and supporting implementation of desired ways of doing business.

Creating Organizational Congruence is about engaging the entire organization in developing a solid fit between strategies, actions, processes, systems, practices, and culture. This phase begins with communicating to people the purpose, scope, scale, and plan. Support initiatives for change typically include RTSC events as well as teams, task forces, processes, and methods suited to the particular initiative. Over time, what gets learned in this phase translates into better ways of thinking and acting on a daily basis.

Table of Uses

Typical Setting	Key Events	Number of Participants
Presenting Issue: Mobil's 1,200-person Gulf of Mexico business unit was trapped in a vicious 5-year cycle: Poor performance led to less corporate investment that resulted in fewer growth opportunities that in turn became a cause of its poor performance.	*Scoping Possibilities* • 2-day Retreat to set goals and parameters • 5-day Change Effort Road Map Meeting	• Top management and union leaders (22 people) • Microcosm of the organization (37 people)
Outcomes: • Business unit reorganized around core processes • Return on fixed assets increased 18 percent • Cycle time reductions saved $30 million • Capital spending overage dropped from $70 million to zero	*Leadership Alignment* • 2-day Leadership Alignment Event	• Formal and informal leaders needed for effort to succeed (300 people)
	Creating Organizational Congruence • 3-day "Big Event" to prioritize actions to save the business • 3-day Project Planning Meeting to translate priorities into 6 key business processes	• Entire organization except for skeletal crews to keep wells working (1,000 people) • Representatives from "Big Event" and project planners (40 people)

Typical Setting	Key Events	Number of Participants
• A new business was generating $12M and had led to a 30 percent reduction in a major recurring expenditure • 5 deep-water leases were secured—a first for the business • A culture of mistrust and parochialism was transformed to one of collaboration	• 4 months to complete planning and implementation of changes	• Core team members (50 people) plus relevant others depending on changes to be made (1,200 people)

About the Author

Robert "Jake" Jacobs (rwj@rwjacobs.com) has a 20-year track record helping organizations achieve fast, lasting, systemwide change. His clients have included American Express, Corning, Ford, Home Depot, Marriott, Mobil, PriceWaterhouseCoopers, Shell, and the City of New York. Jake's first book, *Real Time Strategic Change: How to Involve an Entire Organization in Fast and Far-Reaching Change* (Berrett-Koehler, 1994), taught readers the principles and practices of Large Group Engagement. He coauthored his latest book, *You Don't Have to Do It Alone: How to Involve Others to Get Things Done*, which was reviewed in the *New York Times* as "a complete blueprint on involvement" and "the best of the current crop of books on this topic."

Where to Go for More Information

REFERENCES

Jacobs, Robert. *Real Time Strategic Change.* San Francisco: Berrett-Koehler, 1998.

Johnson, Barry. *Polarity Management.* Amherst, MA: HRD Press, 1992.

Weisbord, Marvin. *Productive Workplaces.* San Francisco: Jossey-Bass, 1987.

ORGANIZATION

Robert W. Jacobs Consulting—www.rwjacobs.com

28

CATHERINE PERME AND ALAN KLEIN

SimuReal
Action Learning in Hyperdrive

Where you sit is where you stand.

—Anonymous

Reorganize People

Columbus Regional Hospital wanted to reorganize its medical and administrative personnel around several service lines. The management team was concerned that staff members would see this as a veiled attempt to reorganize people out of their jobs. They wanted real input from their staff and wanted their staff to view this situation from a systemic rather than an individualistic point of view. As a result, they chose SimuReal to help develop several viable alternatives for their restructuring plan.

A cross-functional *Design Team* focused the task for the SimuReal event and created a map of the organization (a bird's-eye view of formal and informal relationships) from which the starting seating plan would be created. Finally, a cross-functional, "diagonal slice" of the organization formed an *Integration Team*. They participated in the event and took the various strategies and ideas generated and refined them into a workable plan.

The participants arrived to find a large room with circles of chairs marked with names of various parts of the organization. These circles would serve as their beginning points. The participants were informed that they had the entire day to work together through three Action Periods, during which they would be free to work on the task in whatever manner suited them. Following each Action Period would be a short Analysis Period, during which the entire group would step back and reflect on what happened, share observations and insights, and make suggestions for the next Action Session.

After the first Action Period, during which the participants tended to stay within their beginning groups, the facilitator called everyone together for Analysis. The facilitator helped the group make connections between the insights of the participants and their behavior, both during the SimuReal and at work generally.

The second and third Action Periods resembled a moving mosaic! Groups formed, unformed, and re-formed as participants broke into different groupings to move the task. The SimuReal event closed with the Integration Team seated in a circle in the middle of the room, with the rest of the group gathered around them. The Integration Team reflected on the day, summarizing what they heard and what they saw as their role in the coming weeks. The result was that the client system was reorganized successfully with very little resistance, dramatically reducing implementation time.

What Is SimuReal?

SimuReal is a large group method that provides a structure for participants to do real work, examine how they do it, and adapt it in real time—all in the course of just one day. It is *not* a roleplay. SimuReal has *real* people doing *real* work in *real* time. What *is* simulated is the organizational structure in the confines of a room. As a result, SimuReal is like action learning in hyperdrive. Participants in a SimuReal event work together, examine how they work, and spontaneously adjust their structure or process to work more successfully.

- To improve current operations, the "psychological" structure of the organization is often included. For instance, if decision making is conducted on the golf course, a small putting green might be placed in the hallway.

- To test-drive new structures or plans, one might simulate the proposed organizational structure. For instance, if the organization is planning to move to a team-based structure instead of a functional approach, participants might be seated together in teams, and asked to do some specific work together.

A one-day *SimuReal* workshop usually includes three stop-action periods, in which participants do real work (action) and then stop to debrief (analysis). The debriefing is focused on what people are noticing about *how* they work and how they contribute to or detract from the task. The goal is to help the organization learn from its experience and determine what to change for the next action period (figure 1).

In advance of the SimuReal, a planning group of six to eight people works with the facilitator for one to two days to decide on the task, the organizational "map," and the process for decision making during the event.

Following up on a SimuReal event is largely based on what occurs during it. However, the planning group can take the initiative by designating an implementation group in advance so that it is clear who is responsible for next steps. After a successful *SimuReal*, participants leave with new awareness, real work progress, and an improved organization or process.

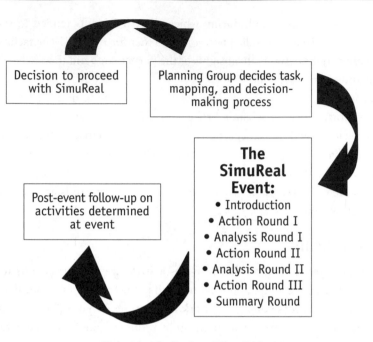

Figure 1. The Basics of SimuReal

What Are the Benefits?

Our experience is that amazing insights have been gleaned simply by *seeing* how the organization works in its "usual" way. People often take advantage of action periods to try new methods or behaviors, and they can see the impact of their changes immediately. SimuReal is a wonderful tool to assist restructuring efforts. If used at the kickoff point, it can identify issues that need to be addressed. If used in a "test-drive," it can show how the new organization might respond to its work challenges, and what gaps exist in the design. Clients estimate that SimuReal helped them reduce implementation time on major decisions or projects by up to 18 months.

Table of Uses

Typical Setting	Elapsed Time	Key Events/Participants Involved
To "test-drive" a restructuring plan before it is implemented. *Example:* School Health Department • Goal: Get staff feedback on a reorganization plan that would significantly change the way school health services are delivered.	1 month	• *Design session:* 2 days with a small group of 8 people who were also members of the Planning Council involved in the redesign. • *SimuReal Event:* 1 day, 125 people. All school health personnel were involved, as well as a handful of principals and representatives of community resource agencies, with whom the school health personnel would have to interface.

Typical Setting	Elapsed Time	Key Events/Participants Involved
		• *Follow-up:* 2-day Planning Council meeting.
When you have a complex, concrete problem or decision to make. *Example:* Psychology Department, Major University • Goal: Decide whether or not to introduce a proposed new doctoral program in Community Psychology.	1 month	• *Design session:* 2 days with a small group of 8 people who were also members of the Planning Council involved in the redesign. • *SimuReal Event:* 1 day. Participants included faculty members; advanced graduate students in each doctoral program, the department chair, and those advocating a specific new doctorate. • *Follow-up:* Within the confines of the normal structure of the department.
To uncover the structural or procedural blocks to solving a problem effectively. *Example:* Clothing Manufacturer • Goal: Decrease the time it takes to move from design to manufacturing of a new product.	1 month	• *Design session:* 1 day, small design team of 6–8 people. • *SimuReal Event:* 1 day. Participants included key professional personnel and managers plus top management staff. • *Follow-up:* 2 permanent, multidisciplinary coordinating committees emerged from the SimuReal Event: (1) Design and Implementation, (2) Manufacturing Review.
When the organization and its management are prepared to engage in self-examination. *Example:* Medical Research Center • Goal: Develop ways to reduce interpersonal and interunit conflicts by dealing more effectively with differences regarding space allocation, use of scarce resources, and other continuing areas of disagreement.	6 months	• *Design session:* 1 day, small design team of 6–8 people. • *SimuReal Event:* 1 day. Participants included senior investigators and staff members of three laboratories; unit chiefs and senior staff members of three hospital-based research groups; center director and administrative team. • *Follow-up:* A new group of laboratory and unit heads formed itself.

About the Authors

Catherine Perme (cathy@cmperme.com) has been facilitating and leading groups and organizations in the process of change since 1978. Her background includes 15 years in line management and leadership positions with IBM and Minnesota state government before starting her business in 1990. Cathy has been studying and applying a whole-system, integrated approach to organizational change since 1995. Along with Alan, she provides shadow coaching and support to organizations and individuals in the use of large group methods.

Alan Klein (alan@klein.net) has worked in a variety of public and private settings as a coach, trainer, consultant, facilitator, administrator, and teacher. Currently, he specializes in the areas of leadership, diversity, team building, and communication. He also provides organizations with support and facilitation in the use of large group methodologies such as SimuReal, Future Search, and Open Space Technology. He was elected to membership in the NTL Institute in 1998 and is currently serving on its Board of Directors.

Where to Go for More Information

REFERENCES

Bunker, B. B., and B. T. Alban. *Simu-Real. Large Group Interventions: Engaging the Whole System for Rapid Change*, 159–167. San Francisco: Jossey-Bass, 1997.

Klein, A. A., and D. C. Klein. *SimuReal: A Large Group Method for Organizational Change.* Columbia, MD: Sea Otter Press, 1997.

Perme, C. M. "Whole Systems Change: A Case Study in the Use of Large Group Interventions and OD Methodologies to Effect Change in a Local School District." *OD Practitioner* 30, no. 2 (1998): 12–17.

ORGANIZATION

Klein Consulting—www.kleinconsulting.com

29

MARTHA L. MCCOY

Study Circles

Democracy needs a place to sit down.
—Hannah Arendt

Helping to Strengthen Local Democracy

In Portsmouth, New Hampshire, public dialogue and collaborative decision making are becoming a hallmark of community life. Over the past several years, community groups and the city have engaged hundreds of residents in "study circles"—small group discussions that take place across the entire community. In the process, people have found their voice, the community's decision-making process has become more democratic, and people have begun to solve critical issues. Through the circles, Portsmouth has addressed bullying in schools, school redistricting, community-police relations, and priorities for the city's ten-year plan.

Portsmouth's study circles began in 2000, when 200 sixth-graders from Portsmouth Middle School and 75 adults discussed bullying and other school safety issues. These circles led to new school policies and a decline in bullying.

A year later, a member of the school board who had taken part in the circles recommended the same process to address a school redistricting issue. Prior attempts to resolve the schools' enrollment and space problems had failed in the wake of bitter public argument. This time, the public had an opportunity for a productive conversation aimed at seeking better answers. The final report from the circles provided new direction for the redistricting plan and resulted in only 65 students being relocated.

In 2002, the city planning board endorsed study circles to generate citizen input for the city's master plan. The program unfolded in stages, involving more than 400 residents in its two years. In the first stage, participants defined what "quality of life" meant to them and recommended ways to sustain it. In the second phase, they identified issues affecting quality of life, discussed what they could do, and made recommendations to the planning board. When the revised plan was released, it was clear that the city had incorporated advice from the circles.

Today, Portsmouth Listens—a study circle organization that involves a range of community groups—is considering how to make deliberation an ongoing part of public life. Table 1 contains examples of action and change that have already occurred from study circle programs in the community.

Changes in individual behavior and attitudes	A participant in a study circle on school redistricting who had consistently opposed tax increases saw the cramped conditions in three schools, heard the concerns and commitment of parents and teachers, and publicly supported a $1.7 million plan for school improvements that entailed a tax increase.
New relationships and networks	After circles on racism, the deputy chief of the police department commented that now when an issue or question comes up, it is easier for someone from the NAACP to simply call him or another officer rather than go through formal procedures.
Institutional changes	After the circles on school safety, new plans included the following student recommendations: cameras on buses, a peer mediation program, and increased adult supervision at school events. Since the plans have been implemented, school bullying appears to have declined.
Changes in public policy	After playing a leading role in organizing study circles on Portsmouth's ten-year master plan and meeting with participants, the planning board used input from the circles to learn residents' priorities. Resulting changes to the plan included approval to purchase ten acres of green space for conservation and rezoning to gear waterfront residences and studios to artists' needs.

Table 1. Examples of Action and Change from Study Circles in Portsmouth, New Hampshire

The Basics

In the study circle process, facilitated, small-group dialogue is at the heart of a community-wide initiative for public dialogue and community change. Community organizing coupled with large-scale small-group dialogue creates opportunities for everyone to have a voice, and links the dialogue to sustained changes in people, in institutions, and in policies.

The Study Circles Resource Center helps communities develop their own ability to organize this process. Many leaders and citizens are drawn to study circles because they provide what's usu-

A study circle . . .

- is a small, diverse group of 8 to 12 people.

- meets together for several, 2-hour sessions.

- sets its own ground rules. This helps the group share responsibility for the quality of the discussion.

- is led by an impartial facilitator who helps manage the discussion. He or she is not there to teach the group about the issue.

- starts with personal stories, then helps the group look at a problem from many points of view. Next, the group explores possible solutions. Finally, they make plans for action and change.

A study circle program . . .

- is organized by a diverse group of people from the whole community.

- includes a large number of people from all walks of life.

- has easy-to-use, fair-minded discussion materials.

- uses trained facilitators who reflect the community's diversity.

- moves a community to action when the study circles conclude.

ally missing in community life. Because the study circle approach combines multisession small-group deliberation with large-scale community change processes, it helps individuals and communities make significant progress in all the "streams" of work approached through dialogue and deliberation—exploration, conflict transformation, decision making, and collaborative action.

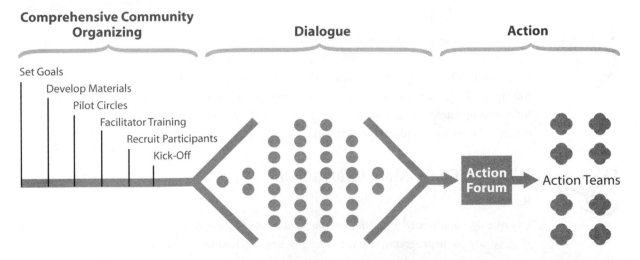

Figure 1. The Study Circle Process

In a large-scale study circle program (see figure 1), many people meet in diverse study circles over the same period of time. All the study circles work on the same issue and seek solutions for the whole community. At the end of the round of study circles, people from all the groups gather in one place to prioritize action ideas that come out of the study circles and begin implementation work. Study circle programs take place in a number of settings—neighborhoods, cities and towns, states, school districts, schools, and college campuses—to address a wide range of social and political issues, such as racism, poverty, police-community relations, education, and growth and sprawl.

Table of Uses

Typical Setting	Brief Description	Project Length	Number of Participants
Study circles are organized in neighborhoods, cities and towns, states, school districts, schools, and college campuses.	Programs take on issues that relate to the concerns and daily lives of many different types of people in the community. Study circle programs often result in: • changes in individual behavior and attitudes • new relationships and networks • institutional changes • changes in public policy	The community organizing process takes several months. The dialogue portion runs 4–6 weeks. The action phase lasts several months. Ideally, communities sustain this cycle as a permanent way to address public issues.	Depending on the size of the community and the scope of organizing, programs engage hundreds, and sometimes thousands, of participants.

About the Author

Martha L. McCoy (martham@studycircles.org) is executive director of the Study Circles Resource Center (SCRC), the primary project of The Paul J. Aicher Foundation, and is president of the foundation. She has made important contributions to the fields of deliberative democracy, community problem solving, and racial justice. One of McCoy's greatest passions is to create close links among these fields. Under her direction, SCRC has helped more than 400 communities organize large-scale study circle programs.

Where to Go for More Information

REFERENCES

Organizing Community-wide Dialogue for Action and Change. A step-by-step guide to organizing study circle programs, www.studycircles.org//en/Resource.39.aspx.

Scully, P., and M. McCoy. "Study Circles: Local Deliberation as the Cornerstone of Deliberative Democracy." In *The Deliberative Democracy Handbook*, edited by J. Gastil and P. Levine, 199–212. San Francisco: Jossey-Bass, 2005.

ORGANIZATION

Study Circles Resource Center—www.studycircles.org

30

Think Like a Genius
Realizing Human Potential Through the Purposeful Play of Metaphorming

You can't teach people anything. You can only help them discover it within themselves.

—Galileo Galilei

Building Wild-Looking Symbolic Models

One of history's greatest inventors, Thomas Edison, once said, "There's a better way. Find it." He meant this in the broadest context of life and not just the visionary acts of every inventor.

One snowy morning at a village mountain retreat in Beaver Creek, 22 veteran venture capitalists, CEOs, and CFOs from Colorado rolled up their sleeves and started building these wild-looking symbolic models that represented their multi-billion-dollar ideas for a whole new telecommunications industry. They didn't just want to be the first to invest in it. They wanted to create it from scratch. In effect, they resounded the noted historians and coauthors of *Civilizations*, Will and Ariel Durant, who said, "The future didn't just happen. It was created."

The focal question posed for this half-day strategic planning session prompted them to reach for their ideals, "Identify the boldest vision of a Shared Network that Centennial Strategic Partners (CSP) can create together which delivers interactive, broadband access faster and better." To rev the creative engines of their collective imagination, the facilitator first told the group, "Define some of the most ingenious models of shared networks that you know exist today. They can be either human-made or nature-made systems." As they percolated on that catalytic assignment, the group was reminded to consider ways they could incorporate this information into their collaborative models.

Over the course of three hours, the four teams were engaged in several interrelated activities that involved: (1) collaboratively creating these imaginative symbolic models; (2) showing and telling the meanings and implications of their models, in order to mine them for fresh insights, discoveries, and innovations; (3) distilling and prioritizing their ideas, as they searched for the big innovations illuminated by their models; and (4) putting together an initial road map to establish a collective goal and identify some practical ways of accomplishing it.

Their models cast the big picture of what this new Shared Network might look like, and how it would work. They also showed what the rich financial benefits would be to each partner, having first identified what each partner in this alliance could potentially contribute, and what the results from their contribution might be under the best circumstances.

As it turned out, it was a profitable day. By morning's end, the group scoped out their initial multipart, multiphase plan that would lead to a multi-billion-dollar payout. Their calculations were based on a myriad of opportunities they envisioned that would advance communications technology.

The expressive, physical models demonstrated that "genuine understanding comes from hands-on experience," to quote Seymour Papert, the twentieth-century mathematician and pioneer of Artificial Intelligence who noted this fact from a lifetime of research on human communication. The models also made evident that *genius thinking is easier done than said*. They also drove home this one inspiring realization: *Genius is everywhere, every day, in everyone, in every way imaginable!*

That's the hallmark of our Think Like a Genius® (TLG) work: Helping people experience the blissful rapture of discovery and innovation.

Frequently Asked Questions

WHAT IS IT?

The Think Like a Genius process provides a better way:

- to brainstorm and express ideas;

- to invent and innovate;

- to create and share new knowledge;

- to solve urgent problems;

- to set and achieve goals;

- and to discover and apply people's creative genius, which enables us all to realize our potential.

The TLG process helps people "give form to" their thoughts, feelings, ideas, knowledge, and experiences by creating symbolic models in response to an important or urgent issue they want to work on. When you make a model, you *show what is on your mind* and make your intangible thoughts as tangible, touchable, and real as possible to help communicate them.

The symbolic models provide the key information and knowledge you need in order to "mine" them for ideas and insights by asking basic, insight-provoking questions. That's how inventions and innovations grow out of these unconscious artifacts of our unbounded creativity and creative inquiry.

Using various common building materials, people are guided to make and explore the meanings of their models in-depth (figure 1). This symbolic modeling activity has been proven to bridge our world of ideas and cultures, engaging people in a whole new type of creative "group think"—one that builds on the diversity of the participants' unique approach to learning, inventing, and innovating. Indeed, a picture *is* worth a thousand words, and a symbolic model is worth a thousand pictures with expressive forms that communicate what words alone cannot.

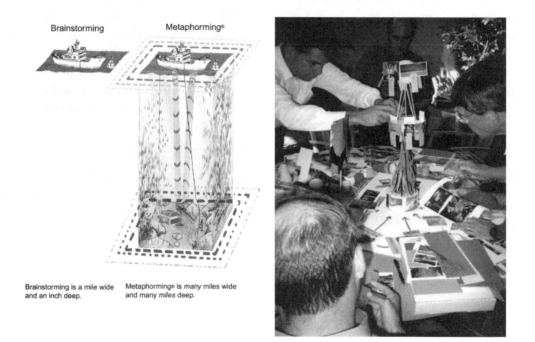

Figure 1. Metaphorming: The Next Generation of Brainstorming Tools

Artists and architects use aspects of Metaphorming (figure 2). when they play with symbolism, signs, stories, visual metaphors, and physical analogies to show their ideas, knowledge, and experiences. Likewise, when scientists and engineers show-and-tell their theories and research, they're using symbolic models of sorts to help themselves and others *see the unseen*, and explain what they're seeing.

As personal as the symbolic models are, they closely link our humanity through their uni-

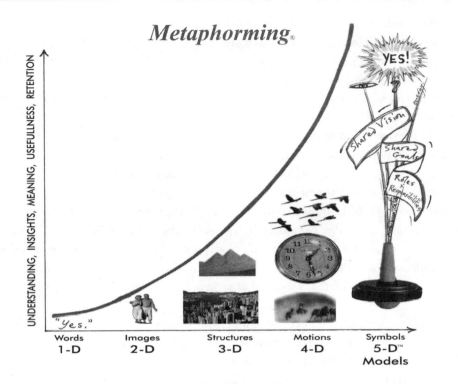

Figure 2. Metaphorming from 1-D to 5-D

versality. Anyone can freely relate his or her life to any given model, which is one reason why they've proven to serve as a kind of global common language in bridging people's worlds, passions, and personal interests.

There are NO value judgments or aesthetic criteria with which to evaluate the "beauty," "importance," "relevance," or "elegance" of your models. Those value-based criticisms merely inhibit a person's prescience, or forethought, and spontaneity.

What is more, there are NO set rules or ways for making a model. There's just *your way*.

In a nutshell, here's the simplest description of the flow and steps of Metaphorming (figure 2):

1. Choose a question you want to model and explore in-depth.

2. Make a symbolic model that expresses and symbolizes your thoughts on the question you've chosen to respond to.

3. Show-and-tell what your model means to you and your team or group.

4. Share it with others, inviting their creative inquiries and interpretations. Then, begin the process all over again entertaining a new question.

How can a bunch of common materials dashed together or carefully constructed into symbolic models possibly change people's lives—even save lives? How can these oddly shaped, forceful objects that grow in the gardens, jungles, and wilderness of our minds hold so much medicinal and curative powers?

The simple fact is: They do. The act of creating and exploring symbolic models have brought families together; helped build communities; enriched cultural and educational programs; increased the wealth and success of companies; and helped envision advanced technology from alternative energy systems to new telecommunications services.

As we see in figure 1, the rapturous faces and body language of Metaphormers (lifelong learners, creators, innovators) suggest that symbolic modeling stimulates the emotional Fun Centers of our whole brains! In those borderless centers, there are no boundaries or limits to experiencing the simple joys of discovery and self-expression. The neuropsychology behind these deep interactions indicates that the intuitive and rational parts of our minds are more entwined than we ever suspected—a fact that's been described by the distinguished neurologist, Antonio R. Damasio, in his path-breaking book, *Descartes' Error: Emotion, Reason, and the Human Brain* (1994).

The Think Like a Genius process builds on the long history of model making. It shows how Metaphorming is connected to creativity, learning, discovering, inventing, and innovating. The History of Civilization, like the History of Creativity, reveals how we are symbol-making creatures. This creative critical thinking process is a natural part of the central nervous system, genes, and communicative powers of every human being.

Table of Uses

Typical Setting	Project Length	Number of Participants
Any environment works. Individuals, groups, and organizations can choose to explore *any* subject, topic, priority, issue, problem, or challenge. Recommend at outset establishing the desired outcomes and tangible results, as well as deliverables.	Session ranges from 3 hours to 3 days. If the purpose is to "journey to the center of the whole organization," that effort takes more time than facilitating a strategic visioning and planning session.	No limit. Facilitated workshops for as few as 5 senior executives to more than 400 people.

About the Author

Todd Siler (tsiler@thinklikeagenius.com) is a visual artist, author, inventor, and consultant, who received his Ph.D. in interdisciplinary studies in psychology and art from the Massachusetts Institute of Technology. In 1986, he became the first visual artist to receive a doctorate from the institute. He was also a Forum Fellow at the 1999 and 2001 Annual Meetings of the World Economic Forum in Davos, Switzerland. Dr. Siler's books include *Think Like a Genius* (Bantam, 1997) and *Breaking the Mind Barrier* (Simon & Schuster, 1990; Touchstone, 1997). He has consulted to IBM, USWEST, Chevron, Chase Manhattan, Nabisco, ING North America, Procter & Gamble, and NTT/Verio.

Where to Go for More Information

REFERENCES

Siler, Todd. "Metaphorming Your Company: Leading with the Next Generation of Brainstorming Tools." In *Leader to Leader*, 15–19. San Francisco: Jossey-Bass, 2002.

_____. "Think Like a Genius Program for Business: Engaging Everyone in an Organization to Think, Learn, Work, and Perform to the Best of Their Abilities Through Metaphorming." In *Organisational Learning for All Seasons: Building Internal Capabilities for Competitive Advantage,* edited by Prem Kumar, 285–296. Singapore: National Community Leadership Institute, 2003.

_____. *Think Like a Genius: The Ultimate User's Manual for Your Brain.* New York: Bantam Books, 1997.

ORGANIZATIONS

Metaphorm !t—www.metaphormit.com

Think Like a Genius—www.ThinkLikeAGenius.com

31

STEVEN N. PYSER, J.D., AND MARC N. WEISS

Web Lab's Small Group Dialogues on the Internet Commons

The bad news: there is no key to the universe.
The good news: it was never locked.

—Swami Beyondananda

Listening to the City—Online Dialogues

After the September 11, 2001, terrorist attacks and the destruction of the World Trade Center, many people had strong feelings about how the site should be rebuilt and how those who died there should be remembered. Some, like relatives of those killed in the attacks, or people who lived, worked, or owned businesses in downtown Manhattan, had a direct, personal stake in the decisions that would eventually be made. However, millions of others, nationally and internationally, felt they had a stake as well.

Although there had been months of forums, hearings, editorials, and letters to the editor following 9/11, something else was needed: a process that would allow a cross-section of the population not just to express their feelings and their opinions, but to offer recommendations based on thoughtful dialogue while probing complex issues and the sometimes-competing ideas held by people of good will.

Two government agencies, The Port Authority of New York & New Jersey and the Lower Manhattan Development Corporation, were responsible for deciding how the land should be used, what memorial ought to be created, and what the area's mix of commercial, residential, retail, cultural, and other uses would be. These agencies recognized the historic nature of the task, and declared that they would seek public input in their decision making. They engaged America*Speaks*[1] to convene "live" meetings with thousands of New York–area residents, and America*Speaks* turned to Web Lab to convene Web-based discussions for people who could not attend the live meetings.

The project, called Listening to the City (LTC), drew international press coverage when more than 5,000 people gathered for a daylong consultation on July 20, 2002. The online dialogues began ten days later, picking up where the "live" meetings left off.

A two-week "asynchronous" discussion, LTC Online used Web Lab's Small Group Dialogue (SGD) technique to allow 808 participants working in 26 parallel discussion groups (with about 40 members each) to log on at their convenience to read and post messages. Responding to discussion materials and questions provided by the planning agencies, participants posted more than 10,000 messages and responded to 32 polling questions. While participants in face-to-face dialogue sessions usually meet only for a short time, LTC Online participants had time to engage each other thoughtfully over an extended period.

Although the process was not designed to produce consensus, strong majority sentiment emerged on several key issues and had a direct effect on the next stage of planning and development. In fact, the guidelines for new designs, the invitation to world-class architects to participate in a design competition, and the final design of the site all reflect many of the citizen recommendations generated during the online dialogues.[2]

How SGD Works

Web Lab's Small Group Dialogues (SGD) are a departure from the norms of online chat and bulletin boards. SGD fosters intimate, high-quality exchanges and a sense of community among participants (figure 1). It employs highly customized proprietary software available for license from Web Lab. By limiting group size and lifespan, SGD emphasizes each member's value, increases accountability, and encourages a sense of belonging and an investment in frequent visits. The result is a structured experience needing little intervention and outcomes unmatched in conventional online dialogue models. These SGD methodologies help to limit the practice of "flaming"—messages that attack other participants—common in many other online conversations and forums.

The SGD tools and technique were developed and refined over several years, through a series of extraordinary discussions about a broad range of social, political, and personal issues. National media organizations, community leaders, activists, government agencies, corporations, consultants, and academics have successfully used SGD and benefited from archived conversations. The technique creates a structure that encourages thoughtful exchanges between people by creating groups of limited size that start together and continue for a set time (usually two weeks). It also encourages participants to start by introducing themselves before launching into discussion about the issues. SGD improves online exchange by making candor more comfortable and disagreement safer.

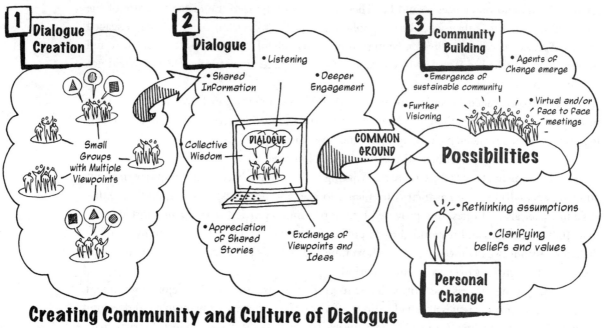

Creating Community and Culture of Dialogue

Illustration by Christine Valenza

Figure 1. Dialogue Creation, Dialogue, Community Building, and Change

SGD Principles

Size—Structure over Clamor

Each participant is assigned to a small group, rather than joining a crowded, anonymous mass.

Time—Investing, Not Driving By

Limited lifespan of each group promotes commitment and provides closure.

Accountability—Listening Rather than Flaming

Emphasis on member bios and member-promoted content drives visibility, a sense of belonging, and self-regulation.

Efficiency—Automation Reduces Moderation

Tracking, administration, and notification system for users and hosts allows cost-efficient community monitoring.

In the summer of 2005, Web Lab was engaged by electronics giant Motorola to develop The Seamless Exchange, a Small Group Dialogue designed to engage thousands of Motorola's employees worldwide in discussions about their company's vision, values, and strategy. During one week of each month between October and December 2005, Motorola employees worked in small groups, discussing the direction, performance, and future success of their company. Their postings were synthesized and best ideas from the groups were presented to Motorola's senior leaders at their annual meeting in January 2006.

Table of Uses

Brief Description	Project Length/Key Events	Number of Participants
Post-9/11 Dialogues on MSNBC .com (Launched November 2001) http://msnbc.weblab.org MSNBC.com readers shared stories and discussed the political, economic, and personal issues facing the nation and the world after September 11.	Participants joined for one-month dialogues, extendable by vote of group. Project ran for four months. Robust asynchronous online dialogue with politically diverse participants. No flame wars.	1,400 participants in 20 discussion groups
First Person Plural (FPP) (Launched June 2004) http://first-person-plural.org A voyage of self-discovery. Hundreds of women of all ages and backgrounds shared stories and explored what they have learned from their breast cancer experiences.	Begun as a 2-week discussion, extended by participant votes for six weeks, then made ongoing. The dialogue is being edited into a book, to be published by William Morrow and Company.	800 women in 21 discussion groups

About the Authors

Marc N. Weiss (mweiss@weblab.org) is the founder and president of Web Lab (WebLab.org), an online laboratory that develops, supports, and champions innovative uses of the Web. A leader in the independent film community since the 1970s, Weiss created the celebrated public TV series *P.O.V.* in 1986 and was its executive producer until 1995, when he began *P.O.V. Interactive.* During his tenure at *P.O.V.,* the series won six Peabody Awards, five duPont-Columbia Awards, and six Emmy Awards.

Steven N. Pyser, J.D. (steve@thedialogue.net) provides dialogue, conflict management, and synergy services to corporations, nonprofit organizations, and educational institutions. He has designed many deliberative forums and served Web Lab as an SGD Fellow, facilitator, dialogue monitor, and report manager/dialogue synthesizer for Motorola's Seamless Exchange. He is Managing Editor of the *Journal of Public Deliberation* and Associate Editor for *Group Facilitation: A Research and Applications Journal.* Mr. Pyser is a faculty member at the University of Phoenix, Philadelphia Campus.

Where to Go for More Information

REFERENCES

Evaluations of the Small Group Dialogue—www.weblab.org/sgd/evaluation.html.

The following references are just a few of the many articles about various dialogues and the technique (*New York Times, Los Angeles Times, Release 1.0, EContent* magazine, *Washington Post, NPR, Wired News,* etc.) available at www.weblab.org/press/sgd.html.

Pyser, S. N., and Figallo, C. "The Listening to the City Online Dialogues Experience: The Impact of a Full Value Contract." *Conflict Resolution Quarterly* 21, no. 3 (2004).

This case study co-authored by Steven N. Pyser explores how an intentional social agreement, called a "Full Value Contract," can help relax skepticism while supporting trust in sustaining full and conscientious participation and community in a purposeful online dialogue.

Smith, Steve. "Keeping a Civil Tongue: Web Lab's Plan to Extinguish Flame Wars." *EContent* (July 2002), www.weblab.org/press/econtent.

Vox Populi. "Online and Downtown." *New York Times,* September 26, 2002, www.weblab.org/press/092602nytimes.

ORGANIZATION

Web Lab—www.weblab.org

---

1. See chapter 41, "The 21st-Century Town Meeting."

2. The final report, incorporating the results of the face-to-face and online discussions, is available online at www.listeningtothecity.org.

PLANNING METHODS

Planning methods help people in communities and organizations shape their future together. These methods set strategic direction and core identity through activities such as self-analysis, exploration, visioning, value clarification, goal setting, and action development.

BILL LENNERTZ

Dynamic Planning and the Power of Charrettes

The foundation of democracy is faith in . . . human intelligence and in the power of pooled and cooperative experience . . . to generate progressively the knowledge and wisdom needed to guide collective action. . . . [E]ach individual has something to contribute, whose value can be assessed only as [it] enters into the final pooled intelligence constituted by the contributions of all.

—John Dewey

Case Study: Transforming a Parking Lot into a Transit-Oriented Village

Prior to the building of I-680, the Walnut Creek area in Contra Costa County, California, was predominantly bungalow and ranch homes nestled among orchards. Residents were either associated with the walnut industry or had relocated from the urban San Francisco Bay area. The arrival of the highway interchange, adjacent to the local Pleasant Hill BART (Bay Area Rapid Transit) station, began to transform what was once a quiet agricultural valley into a regional transportation hub.

In the early 1980s, a specific plan for the 140-acre BART station area was adopted by Contra Costa County, calling for a higher density, mixed-use, transit-oriented community. Since 1986, more than 2,400 housing units, two hotels, offices with more than 4,000 employees, and more than $40 million in major public infrastructure improvements had been built within walking distance of the Pleasant Hill BART station. The accumulation of this development activity increased strain on the once convenient lifestyle of the single-family ranch home neighborhoods surrounding the station area, with the greatest impacts felt due to the increase in traffic congestion.

During the 1980s, a handful of developer-driven programs were proposed for the Pleasant Hill BART station area. These failed attempts were primarily commercial developments with heavy office or entertainment retail uses. The regional market orientation of these projects raised the objections of neighbors, who were concerned by the traffic impacts, and the cities, which were concerned about competition with their own commercial developments. Community members were given limited opportunities to participate in the development proposals, and when they were engaged, there were too few options on the table. It looked to the neighborhood participants as though the heavy commercial and entertainment uses were a foregone conclusion and that their input had no potential impact on the proposal outcomes.

By the late 1980s, many residents of the surrounding neighborhoods believed that any additional development, other than service and residential uses, would push the traffic problem over the edge. This produced a very difficult political environment for the development of the 18 acres of parking immediately adjacent to the station. When the Contra Costa County Redevelopment Agency undertook planning for this redevelopment, they met public resistance on all fronts. It wasn't until they initiated a charrette process that invited local employees, residents, and business owners to help plan the area surrounding the station that any progress was made.

THE CHARRETTE

To plan the Pleasant Hill BART project and conduct the charrette process, a consultant team was selected by a steering committee. The steering committee represented the Contra Costa County Redevelopment Agency, BART, the designated developer, and the neighborhood.

The consultant team held an initial public meeting that sought to take one more step toward reestablishing the trust between the community members and the project sponsors—Contra Costa County, BART, and the developer. During the meeting, community members worked with facilitators in small groups to discuss how the project related to the area and what a vision for the developed site might look like. The consultants then took this input and combined it with the other critical information such as market demand, financing requirements, and site constraints to develop alternative concepts for the site.

A month later, the consultant team of architects, planners, engineers, and economists held a six-day charrette that resulted in a comprehensive plan for the site. Public meetings were held for anyone who wished to attend, and stakeholder meetings were scheduled with neighbors, a technical advisory committee, bicycle and pedestrian advocacy groups, and BART representatives, to name a few. The consultant team worked with all of the input from these meetings and developed alternative concepts. These concepts were brought back to the stakeholders and general public numerous times throughout the week at public meetings and open houses and were revised according to additional input. The consultant team took the refined plans and synthesized them into one comprehensive plan representing the best of all feasible ideas.

THE RESULTS

Over the course of the six-day charrette, the following were all created and refined: form-based zoning and architectural codes; market and financial feasibility analyses; street and transit circulation plans; a plan for pedestrian paths and parks; a transit plan for buses, taxis, and kiss and ride (a designated passenger drop off area); a regulating plan; and illustrative renderings depicting the future state. In the end, the charrette resulted in a comprehensive and detailed plan that met the basic requirements of all parties, ending the deadlock.

In 2002, the board of Contra Costa County supervisors unanimously approved the plan with no attendee speaking in opposition, a rarity for Bay Area development projects. It is notable that in the five years since the charrette, the results have survived the continued scrutiny of community members, ongoing partnership negotiations between the public and private entities involved, and the passing on of the project to a new design firm. Projects are often compromised during the volatile implementation phase, but the plan created during the BART charrette broke ground in 2005 with its original vision in place.

The Basics

The French word "charrette" means "cart" and is often used to describe the final, intense work effort expended by art and architecture students to meet a project deadline. This use of the term is said to originate from the École des Beaux Arts in Paris during the nineteenth century, where proctors circulated a cart, or "charrette," to collect final drawings while students frantically put finishing touches on their work. To quote Andres Duany:

> The charrette is about dynamic balances. It is about principles balanced by process; about the interests of the few balanced by that of the many; about experts being balanced by those who know nothing except how things really should be; about public benefit and private gain. A proper charrette brings into being a collective intelligence and it does this with stunning efficiency.

At the National Charrette Institute (NCI), the core principles of a charrette were used to create the Dynamic Planning process. Dynamic Planning combines the creative, intense work session with stakeholder workshops. It is a collaborative planning process that harnesses the talents

---

An NCI Dynamic Planning charrette is not:

- A one-day workshop

- A multi-day marathon meeting involving everyone all the time

- A plan authored by a select few that will affect many

- A "brainstorming session" that produces a plan but stops short of feasibility testing

and energies of all interested parties to create and support a feasible plan capable of transformative organizational or community change.

While most commonly used for land planning and development projects, Dynamic Planning can be used in various business sectors and is used often to facilitate a comprehensive system change, such as a company reorganization. These projects rank among the most difficult due to their disparate and sometimes contentious group of stakeholders, working within the context of a complex design problem. The most common outcomes of a successful Dynamic Planning process are: new policies, plans, and action programs that are created and implemented by a multidisciplinary team.

How Does Dynamic Planning Work?

Dynamic Planning is a three-phase, holistic, collaborative planning process during which a charrette is held as the central transformative event. Dynamic Planning is designed to assure project success through careful charrette preparation and follow-up.

The Three Phases of Dynamic Planning

Phase One: Research, Education, Charrette Preparation

Phase one of Dynamic Planning establishes the information and people infrastructure for the project (see figure 1). Establishing the information infrastructure includes the identification, creation, and collection of base data necessary to perform the project planning and design during the charrette. Creating the people infrastructure includes identifying and engaging all those who must be involved to produce a feasible outcome that will be supported by the community. This requires early and ongoing collaboration among the project sponsor, the project management team (typically comprised of the managers for the affected functions/departments), those who will be immediately impacted by the project, all relevant decision makers, and potential support-

RESEARCH, EDUCATION, AND CHARRETTE PREPARATION   **THE CHARRETTE**   **PLAN IMPLEMENTATION**

1.1 Project Assessment and Organization

1.2 Stakeholder Research, Education, and Involvement

1.3 Base Data Research and Analysis

1.4 Project Feasibility Studies and Research

1.5 Charrette Logistics

2.1 Organization, Education, Vision

2.2 Alternative Concepts Development

2.3 Preferred Plan Synthesis

2.4 Plan Development

2.5 Production and Presentation

3.1 Project Status Communications

3.2 Product Refinement

3.3 Presentation and Product Finalization

Figure 1. Dynamic Planning Phases

Charrettes

ers and blockers. Furthermore, in order to gain their long-term support, these stakeholders must be treated with respect and assured that their input will have an impact on the outcome. This phase is about becoming "charrette ready," the point at which all of the information and the people are in place. Depending on the project, this preparation process can take anywhere from six weeks to nine months.

Phase Two: The Charrette

The charrette is the transformative event of the Dynamic Planning process. It is a collaborative event that, for complex projects such as land development, typically lasts from four to seven days. Simpler projects take less time. The goal of the charrette is to produce a feasible plan that benefits from the support of all stakeholders through its implementation. A multidisciplinary charrette team consisting of a mix of consultants or experts and sponsor staff produces this plan. It takes place in a charrette studio or meeting place situated in a location central to the project and the stakeholders. During the charrette, the team first conducts a public meeting to solicit the values, vision, and needs of the stakeholders. The team then breaks off to create alternative plans, testing and refining them with the goal of producing a preferred plan. The charrette is organized as a series of feedback loops through which stakeholders are engaged at critical decision-making points. These decision-making points occur throughout the charrette in primary stakeholder meetings and several more public meetings, and possibly an open house. These feedback loops provide the charrette team with the information necessary to create a feasible plan. Just as important, they allow the stakeholders to become coauthors of the plan so that they are more likely to support and implement it. Charrette schedules vary in length according to project complexity. The charrette needs to last at least four days for the simplest of projects, and six to nine days for a complex project, in order to accommodate at least three feedback loops marked by collaborative public meetings.

Phase Three: Implementation

Two major processes follow the charrette. The first is product refinement, during which the charrette team tests and refines the final charrette plan to assure its feasibility. The second is based on a relationship strategy in which the project sponsor continues to work with the stakeholders to maintain their support of the plan. This is done most effectively by involving the stakeholders in the testing and refinement process. The Dynamic Planning process concludes with a post-charrette public meeting during which the revised plans are presented for final public review and input.

Table of Uses

Setting	Brief Description	Length	Key Events	Number of Participants
Community Land Use Plan	*Issue:* How to accommodate community growth and land development *Outcome:* Widely supported community development plans and implementation mechanisms	6–12 months	Ongoing team meetings, including initial project meeting with leadership, early meetings with primary stakeholders 3 key events: • Project visioning meeting at approximately month 2 in the process (1 day) • Charrette midway through project timeline (3–7 days) • Public charrette follow-up meeting at the end of the process (one to two days)	All stakeholders involved at some point in all 3 key events. 45–100s of people. Stakeholders include: public officials, landowners, community members
Land Planning Policies/Codes	*Issue:* How to regulate development so that it reflects a desired community vision *Outcome:* Community-supported policies and codes	9–18 months	Ongoing team meetings, including initial project meeting with leadership, early meetings with primary stakeholders 3 key events: • Community values meeting at approximately month 2 in the process (1 day) • Charrette midway through project timeline (3–7 days) • Public charrette follow-up meeting at the end of the process (1–2 days)	All stakeholders involved at some point in all 3 key events. 60–100s of people. Stakeholders include: public officials, landowners, community members

Charrettes

Setting	Brief Description	Length	Key Events	Number of Participants
Green Building Design	*Issue:* How to design a sustainable/energy-efficient building *Outcome:* Schematic architectural design	6–9 months	• Ongoing team meetings, including initial project meeting with owner/developer, early meetings with end users • Organizational meeting (0.5–1 day) • Workshop (1.5–3 days) • Refinement meeting (1 day)	10–40 stakeholders involved throughout all 3 meetings. Stakeholders include: building owner, tenants, regulatory agency staff
Corporate Reorganization	*Issue:* How to increase productivity and creativity *Outcome:* Corporate reorganization plan and action/implementation plan	3–6 months	• Meeting with leadership • Meetings with management • Company-wide planning meeting • Workshop (2–3 days) • Leadership follow-up meeting • Company-wide implementation meeting	Depends on company size. Leaders involved throughout. All employees involved in workshop and implementation.
Manufacturing Waste Reduction/ Budget Cutting	*Issue:* How to cut costs in manufacturing process *Outcome:* Waste reduction plan	3 months	• Organizational meetings with management and labor leadership • Plantwide workshop (3 days) • Leadership follow-up meeting • Plantwide implementation meeting	Depends on company size. Leaders involved throughout. All employees involved in workshop and implementation.

Table of Uses. Continued

Fundamentals for Getting Started

A Dynamic Planning project can start at any level in a community or organization. The project sponsor can be a leader, such as an elected official or developer, or a core management team, such as planning agency staff. The sponsor may emerge at the neighborhood level with an organization such as a community group. In each case, the project sponsor and the core management team must establish a shared agreement on the definition of the problem. For the project to proceed smoothly, this group must also agree on a shared set of values and operating strategies. Once these agreements are in place, the project management team identifies the primary stakeholders who must be involved to assure project success. The team identifies the relevant stakeholders, what the appropriate involvement will be for each, and a strategy for getting them to participate in the process. A prerequisite for being "charrette ready" is the willingness of these stakeholders to participate consistently in good faith.

The most successful Dynamic Planning projects occur when the people responsible for shepherding the project through planning and implementation share the values that guide the way the project is run and how the stakeholders are treated. The project management team must share the following Dynamic Planning values for a successful process.

DYNAMIC PLANNING VALUES

Community Health

Holistic planning processes based on local values produce solutions that support healthy communities. This is mainly applicable to community land use planning, but the same general value can be applied within any organization. Healthy communities improve the social, economic, and physical well-being of their people, places, and natural environments.

Collaboration

Each individual's unique contribution supports the best outcome. When project sponsors maintain this value, stakeholders are viewed as members of the larger team who have valuable input and who are essential to implementation.

Transparency

Clarity in rules, process, and roles is essential to collaboration. Stakeholders know whether or not a process is genuinely collaborative and any lack of openness will quickly erode their trust in the process.

Shared Learning

Shared learning requires the involvement of stakeholders representing all relevant viewpoints in the decision-making process. Shared learning facilitates new understandings that can lead to changes in peoples' perceptions and positions. Shared learning also reduces costly rework by assuring that the project plan includes the information required to assure its feasibility.

Direct, Honest, and Timely Communication

Collaborative work, based on shared learning, requires frequent communication and feedback between the project sponsors and the stakeholders. These "feedback loops" provide all parties with the reasoning behind decisions and knowledge of how their input affected the outcome.

DYNAMIC PLANNING STRATEGIES

Following are the ten strategies used in the most successful charrettes. These strategies build upon the Dynamic Planning values and should be referred to at every step of the way when designing the process for a project using Dynamic Planning. These ten strategies should be employed in any charrette process.

Work Collaboratively

True collaboration is based on valuing each individual's unique contribution. Therefore, anyone who will be affected by, promote, or block the project is involved early and often.

Design Cross-functionally

Multidisciplinary teams work concurrently to build a feasible solution to community development problems from the onset of the charrette.

Compress Work Sessions

Time compression facilitates creative problem solving by accelerating decision making and reducing unconstructive negotiation tactics.

Communicate in Short Feedback Loops

Regular stakeholder reviews build trust in the process, foster true understanding and support of the product, and minimize rework. A feedback loop occurs when a design is proposed, reviewed, changed, and re-presented for further review.

Study the Details and the Whole

Lasting agreement is based on a fully informed dialogue. Designs at varying scales inform each other and reduce the likelihood that a fatal flaw will be overlooked that could result in costly rework.

Confirm Progress by Measuring Outcomes

By measuring progress through agreed-upon desired outcomes, the transparency of the decision-making process is assured and people can see that the project is being implemented as planned.

Produce a Feasible Plan

To create a feasible plan, every decision point must be fully informed, especially by the legal, financial, and engineering disciplines. The success of a community or organization's work to plan and build together hinges on implementation. Plans that sit on the shelf contribute only to apathy.

Use Design to Achieve a Shared Vision and Create Holistic Solutions

Design is a powerful tool for establishing a shared vision. Drawings help illustrate the complexity of the problem and can be used to resolve conflict by proposing previously unexplored solutions that represent win/win outcomes.

Include a Multiple-Day Charrette

The goal of a charrette is to take a project from a vision to alternative concepts, to a preferred plan, to a developed feasible plan, and on to a final presentation. A minimum of three loops is required to adequately involve all stakeholders in this undertaking. It takes between four and seven days to accomplish this work collaboratively.

Hold the Charrette on or Near the Site

Working on-site fosters participant understanding of values and traditions, and provides the necessary easy access to stakeholders and information.

Roles, Responsibilities, and Relationships

SPONSORSHIP REQUIREMENTS

A successful Dynamic Planning project first requires commitment from the leadership. This includes those who have the power to make decisions that will affect the project's implementation. Stakeholders, people who can provide information critical to the project's success, must also commit. Stakeholders include anyone who will be implementing the plan. *Everyone* must agree to participate in good faith throughout the process.

CHARRETTE LEADERSHIP ROLES

There are two facilitator roles during the charrette: the manager and the meeting facilitator; these roles can be filled by one or more individuals.

Charrette Manager

The charrette manager is responsible for:

- Ensuring that the resources required for an efficiently run charrette are in place. This includes people, data, and equipment.
- The setup and management of the charrette.
- Handling the logistics of the day-to-day charrette organization.
- Managing the drawing production, transportation, and catering.
- Organizing the charrette team.

- Communicating with the public throughout the charrette via the project Web site and the local press.

Charrette Meeting Facilitator

The charrette meeting facilitator is responsible for:

- Organizing and running all major meetings.

- Helping the group focus its energies by staying on task, suggesting methods and processes, protecting all members of the group from attack, and making sure that everyone has an opportunity to participate.

- Assuring that the ground rules are established and agreed upon at the beginning of the meeting and are invoked during the meeting to handle unexpected interruptions.

Charrette Team

The charrette team is the multidisciplinary group of planners, designers, engineers, economists, and the like, working virtually uninterrupted in the charrette studio, taking the project from a cold start to a preferred plan in a matter of days. Each professional is chosen for his or her ability to solve the design/planning problems and complete the required products and documents through an interactive team process in a public setting. The team is most often comprised of consultants, but may also include members of the sponsor's staff, such as public agency engineers and planners. While assembling the team, the charrette manager must consider each individuals' professional skill sets as well as how each person will function as part of the larger team. In short, there must be a balance between talent, personal skills, and ego. Strong ego is often associated with creative talent, but each charrette team member must, in the end, be able to let go and work along with the team for the benefit of the project.

Stakeholder Participants

Charrette stakeholders can be divided into *primary, secondary,* and *general* categories. General stakeholders, most commonly community members, are usually involved in the evening public meetings held at the beginning, middle, and end of the charrette. They may also drop by the charrette studio any time. Secondary stakeholders are those with a keen economic or political interest in the project such as community art organizations, schools, and churches. It is common to hold scheduled meetings with the secondary stakeholders during the first few days of the charrette. The primary stakeholders are those with a strong influence over the project. These individuals hold political, jurisdictional, or economic positions, for example, elected or appointed positions, or they own land nearby. The primary stakeholders must be involved at all key decision-making points in order for the charrette to be a success. These are the people who are most frequently involved throughout the charrette.

Conditions for Success

Dynamic Planning is most useful for projects that have complicated design and/or political issues. This usually includes a large number of designers and stakeholders with possible disparate viewpoints and needs. Dynamic Planning works in these situations because it promotes shared learning and authorship through collaboration in short feedback loops. Dynamic Planning should not be undertaken if primary stakeholders will not participate throughout the process. The following conditions are *common mistakes and pitfalls in executing Dynamic Planning.*

NOT SCHEDULING ENOUGH TIME FOR THE CHARRETTE

Often, first-time charrette sponsors resist holding a charrette for more than three days. When a sponsor has not been through a complete Dynamic Planning process, it is difficult for him/her to understand the benefits of holding a charrette over the course of four to seven days. Sponsors are often concerned about the resources necessary (both in terms of money and time) to complete a lengthy process. However, there are several risks associated with charrettes that are too short. Inevitably, unexpected political and/or engineering challenges that will require extra analysis or meetings will arise during the charrette. If the charrette is too short to accommodate these analyses and meetings, the contentious issues may not be settled. An abbreviated process also will not allow enough time for the charrette team to solve the problem and to produce the final documents in an informative and attractive format for the final presentation. It is a disservice to the project sponsor and all involved not to be able to fully test the preferred plan and create the documents necessary to explain it.

LATE-TO-THE-GAME STAKEHOLDERS

Poor preparation can leave the door open for a small but well-organized group of opponents to undermine the charrette outcome. However, in projects in which potential blockers are identified and engaged early on, they often end up as promoters. Success depends on the charrette team's level of understanding of the opponents' interests and its ability to establish a mutually beneficial relationship.

INCOMPLETE BASE DATA

The charrette is a major undertaking requiring significant resources for its preparation and execution. Once the charrette begins, it is crucial that the necessary resources and base data are readily available for the team to take the project to the level of detail required to assure feasibility. There should never be a time when a team member says something like, "If we only knew exactly where the heritage trees are located then we could precisely plan the location of the main boulevard."

Charrettes

Shortchanging the Implementation Phase

Sometimes, in the interest of controlling the budget, the project sponsor will choose to minimize the involvement of the charrette team during the implementation phase. Often in such cases, team members are called back to the project only when things begin to go wrong. When this happens, the charrette team may find itself in the difficult position of repairing damage caused by poor post-charrette stakeholder communications.

Theoretical Basis

A History of Collaboration

The NCI Dynamic Planning process is rooted in land-use planning. Until the 1960s, public planning agencies or private consultants made many land planning recommendations. People who did not live in the community, working without community input, often made decisions about the future of a community. The civil rights movement and other rights movements that followed, all based on making democracy work for everyone, had an effect on the way public planning decisions were being made. Advocacy planning and community member participation began to take hold. Community design centers emerged to offer low-cost design services to disadvantaged and grassroots organizations.

Community involvement in architecture and planning has persisted and is on the rise today. Conversations about grassroots democracy and collaborative decision making can be heard across disciplines. It has become commonplace and often mandated to include some form of public participation in the planning process.

The Evolution of the NCI Charrette

Dynamic Planning is historically rooted in the collaborative design workshops beginning in the 1950s and 1960s with the Caudill Rowlett Scott "squattings" and Urban Design Associates and the American Institute of Architects Regional and Urban Design Teams (R/UDATs). These early collaborative processes brought the design team to the site to solve design problems quickly and efficiently.

Sustaining the Results

During the plan implementation phase of Dynamic Planning, the project management team works to assure the continued and expanded support of the project as it is guided through adoption and development. This work includes the continued involvement of stakeholders as the charrette team tests, refines, and finalizes the charrette products. The plan implementation phase can be the most volatile part of any project.

The passage of time can be one of the biggest enemies to project implementation. It is preferable that the implementation phase be as short as possible in order to reduce the risks associated with changes in political and regulatory leadership. Dynamic Planning can dramatically shorten the overall project process, but uncontrollable factors such as market changes can cause the plan implementation phase to sometimes last for years. There are multiple challenges to project implementation when the process takes months or years. These challenges may include maintaining the interest and support of charrette stakeholders over a long period of time and educating new stakeholders about the agreements that were forged during the charrette.

People new to a project should be educated as soon as possible, but it is important to use all means available to get agreements completed during the charrette, when everyone is there. If you fail to get an agreement during the charrette, then you will be back to the usual methods of endless meetings. Remember that the charrette is a special opportunity to conclude negotiations.

These potential realities make the work completed during the plan implementation phase all the more important. This work has the potential to create the political and regulatory foundations needed for a project to weather an extended period of approvals and construction. The charrette is also a training session for local community members, staff, and officials who will be in charge of implementing the plan. A successful charrette forges a shared set of agreements on a vision and how to achieve it.

Burning Questions

How Do You Get Leadership to Devote the Time to be Involved?

Whether it is the leadership or the general stakeholder, people must see that being involved may result in a "win" for them. Presenting the project as an opportunity for an individual to achieve his or her win is a way to achieve relevance and assure ongoing participation.

How Do You Get Sponsors to Value the Time It Takes for Proper Preparation?

The best way to get sponsors to devote the resources necessary for the preparation phase is to highlight its inverse relationship to costly rework and waste. Proper charrette preparation is the best way to prevent rework.

What Are the Economic and Political Advantages of a Charrette?

The charrette makes economic sense. Because all parties are collaborating from the start, no viewpoint is overlooked, which allows projects to avoid costly rework. Also, the charrette allows for fewer and more highly productive work sessions, making it less time-consuming than traditional processes. Everyone suffers when a project in which many people have invested time, energy, and money has to go back to the drawing board. The staff or community members suffer because their precious time has been wasted on a plan that sits on the shelf. The leaders suffer because their constituents have one more reason to distrust management. The project sponsor suffers because of the money wasted in planning costs, and in the case of land development, in interest paid. Dynamic Planning continuously strives for the creation of a feasible plan through inclusion and collaboration, increasing the likelihood of a project being built.

Conclusion

The term charrette means various things to various people. To some, it simply connotes a half-day meeting in which people brainstorm and perhaps sketch ideas; to others, the charrette process is synonymous with a multiple-day workshop involving the public. Dynamic Planning charrettes are more than just brainstorming or visioning sessions. They are distinguished from other workshops by their intense, collaborative nature and by their holistic approach, focused on a feasible solution. Dynamic Planning places the charrette in context with a larger, comprehensive planning process that requires extensive preparation and follow-up for plan approval and implementation.[1]

About the Author

Bill Lennertz (bill@charretteinstitute.org) is a leading National Charrette Institute (NCI) charrette facilitator and principal author of the NCI Dynamic Planning curriculum. The NCI is a nonprofit educational institution. We help people build community capacity for collaboration to create healthy community plans. In 1986, as director of the Duany Plater-Zyberk & Company Boston office, and from 1993 to 2002, as a partner with Lennertz Coyle & Associates, Architects and Town Planners, Bill has directed more than 150 charrettes. He has taught at various universities including Harvard, where he received his master of architecture in urban design.

Where to Go for More Information

REFERENCES

National Charrette Institute. *NCI Charrette Start Up Kit.* Portland, OR: National Charrette Institute, 2004.

Race, Bruce, and Carolyn Torma. *Youth Planning Charrettes: A Manual for Planners & Teachers.* Chicago: APA Planners Press, 1998.

INFLUENTIAL SOURCES

Alexander, Christopher, et al. *A Pattern Language: Towns, Buildings, Construction.* New York: Oxford University Press, 1977.

Ames, Steven C., ed. *Guide to Community Visioning.* Chicago: APA Planners Press, 2001.

Cogan, Elaine. *Successful Public Meetings: A Practical Guide.* Chicago: American Planning Association, 2000.

Doyle, Michael, and David Straus. *How to Make Meetings Work.* New York: Berkley Publishing Group, 1993.

Fisher, Roger. *Getting to Yes: Negotiating Agreement Without Giving In.* New York: Penguin Books, 1991.

Jacobs, Jane. *The Death and Life of Great American Cities.* New York: Random House, 1961.

Kaner, Sam. *Facilitator's Guide to Participatory Decision-Making.* Philadelphia: New Society Publishers, 1996.

Rue, Harrison Bright. "Real Towns: Making Your Neighborhoods Work." *Terrain.org: A Journal of the Built and Natural Environments* 11 (Spring–Summer 2002). www.terrain.org/articles/11/rue.htm.

Straus, David. *How to Make Collaboration Work: Powerful Ways to Build Consensus, Solve Problems, and Make Decisions.* San Francisco: Berrett-Koehler, 2002.

ORGANIZATIONS

Charrette Center—www.Charrettecenter.com

Congress for the New Urbanism—www.cnu.org

National Charrette Institute—www.charretteinstitute.org

Place Matters—www.PlaceMatters.com

The Town Paper—www.tndtownpaper.com

U.S. EPA Public Involvement Resources—www.epa.gov/publicinvolvement

---

1. Portions of this chapter have been adapted from *The Charrette Handbook,* forthcoming from the American Planning Association.

MARVIN WEISBORD AND SANDRA JANOFF

Future Search
Common Ground Under Complex Conditions

Nobody can force change on anyone else. It has to be experienced. Unless we invent ways where paradigm shifts can be experienced by large numbers of people, change will remain a myth.

—Eric Trist

Future Search in Action: IKEA and the FAA

Two large systems, each with a complex problem and a myriad of technological, organizational, geographic, economic, and human pressures, discovered creative solutions in a single meeting called Future Search. One was IKEA, a global furniture company, and the other was the Federal Aviation Administration (FAA), a U.S. government agency whose mission is to keep the skies safe. The leadership of both IKEA and the FAA had to make rapid changes in systems too complex for anyone to know all the connections. They chose to bring "the whole system" into one room for three intense days of work that led to unprecedented new directions for each organization. Below we describe the challenges each faced, the people they needed to involve, and the results they achieved. We conclude by describing the principles and methodology that make possible dramatic outcomes in one meeting.

CASE ONE

IKEA, a global furniture retailer, sought to head off a crisis brought on by rapid growth. In early 2003, they had 10,000 products, 1,500 suppliers in 55 countries, 180 stores in 23 countries,

365 million customer visits a year, and 20 more stores on the way. Despite a preference for flat structures, the company over time had centralized its product design, manufacturing management, inventory control, and distribution in Sweden. They were, in the words of their CEO, creating "silos" that made coordination harder and drove up costs in a company famous for high quality and low prices. They chose Future Search as the right planning method because of the congruence of principles with their own. A small planning group hit on the idea of building a Future Search around a single product—the Ektorp sofa—making it a stepping-stone toward redoing the whole system. In March 2003, 52 stakeholders met in Hamburg, Germany. They reviewed the existing system, developed a decentralized design, created a strategic plan, and formed seven task forces for implementation. The plan was developed and approved by the company president and key people from all affected functions, with active support from several customers, in just 18 hours of work over three days.

Participants included the company president; the business area leader for seating products; top staff from product design and development, inventory management, sales, supply and distribution, trading, purchasing, and information technology; finance and retail managers; suppliers from Poland, Mexico, and China; and six Ektorp sofa customers.

They created a flatter organization that involves customers and suppliers from the start in product development, encouraged direct contact between suppliers and stores, and changed central staff roles to resources rather than controllers. IKEA changed the way new products would be test marketed and modified information systems to give everyone greater influence on coordinating and controlling their own work.

A year later, the business area leader reported that the Ektorp had exceeded all expectations, increasing volume, cutting costs, preserving profit margins, maintaining product quality, and reducing prices. The innovations were extended to other products and, by 2005, had far-reaching consequences for the whole company.

CASE TWO

Airspace, FAA's highway system in the sky, is finite. The number of aircraft in the sky is increasing exponentially. By 2004, it was clear to the FAA that, without cooperative solutions among all stakeholders, there was a near certainty of impending aerial gridlock. FAA leaders were attracted to the idea of having all airspace users in the room to look together at the coming crisis. They decided on a Future Search for March 2004, to see whether the parties were willing to make significant course corrections.

Participants included FAA executives and staff, major and regional airlines, the National Business Aviation Association, the Aircraft Owners and Pilots Association, transport carriers, the military, controllers and their union, government agencies, and aviation technologists. The following changes were made:

- A new System Access Plan enabled the FAA to relieve congestion daily based on systemwide data. Flyers would accept short delays and longer routes when this made the overall system work better.

- An "express lane" strategy to be invoked when any airport experienced a 90-minute delay, opening "holes" in the airspace, allowing delayed planes to be airborne instead of waiting hours on the ground.

- Elimination of a decades-old "first come, first served" policy of routing airplanes, enabling controllers to make systemic decisions. Users agreed to "share the pain" of short delays for some to the benefit of the larger whole.

Summary

The systemic changes noted in the cases above were made possible by principles different from those underlying analytic models and expert analysis. In an age of nonstop change—when a system's shape changes like the weather—a short, intense, whole-system meeting may enable results not accessible any other way.

The Basics

Why Future Search? As a society, we have painted ourselves into a technological corner. We have more ways to do things than ever before, yet a lot of what matters to us is not getting done, despite the large sums we spend. We experience high walls between haves and have-nots, experts and amateurs, leaders and followers. In Future Search meetings, we take down the walls. We take control of our own futures. We take back responsibility for ourselves. We discover that we can learn from and work with people from many walks of life.

In a Future Search, we become more secure knowing firsthand where other people stand. We discover resources in ourselves and others that we didn't know were there. We begin to accept our differences—in background, viewpoints, and values—as realities to be lived with, not problems to be solved. We are more likely to let go of stereotypes. New relationships emerge. Surprising projects become possible. Future Search is a simple way of meeting with profound implications for organizations and communities everywhere.

Future Search brings systems thinking to life. The method provides people a way of acting systemically. By uniting diverse parties who *are* each other's "environment," we enable people to experience themselves connected to a larger whole rather than talk about it as something "out there." When people all talk about the same "elephant," putting together their perceptions of the head, tail, trunk, legs, and tusks, they enable actions none thought possible going in.

Too Good to Be True? Data Suggest an Emphatic "No!"

It is against common sense that much implementation would flow from one short meeting of people who have not met before. Nevertheless, unusual, ongoing action has been documented worldwide following Future Searches. We believe that this could not be happening unless Future Search enabled people to use capabilities they already have, skills always there and rarely accessed. Extraordinary results happen when people follow a few key principles.

FUTURE SEARCH PRINCIPLES

- Have the right people in the room—that is, a cross-section of the whole, including those with authority, resources, information expertise, and need;

- Create conditions where participants experience the whole "elephant" before acting on any part of it;

- Focus on the future and seek common ground;

- Enable people to take responsibility for their own learning and action plans.

USES OF FUTURE SEARCH

Future Search helps diverse groups find common ground, develop action plans, build commitment, and plan implementation—all at once. Some examples:

Groups Searching for Common Ground	Specific Use of the Future Search
A 17-year war in southern Sudan had devastated a generation of children when, in 1999, UNICEF invited 40 Sudanese children and 64 adults to address this crisis.	More than 50 schools were established. In June 2000, after UNICEF sponsored a Future Search, 2,500 child soldiers were demobilized back into their villages. By 2002, they numbered 11,000. In 2005, the future that the children had dreamed of in 1999 became a reality when the government of Sudan and the rebel government of South Sudan signed a peace agreement.
Washington State Department of Corrections (DOC)	DOC sponsored a Future Search to create a shared future for corrections in Washington State, including department staff, other government agencies, elected officials, providers from across the state, community groups, and former offenders. They developed cross-agency collaborations to address prevention, intervention, education, health, training, and transition back into the community.
Berrien County in southwest Michigan includes adjoining cities, St. Joseph's and Benton Harbor. After decades of racial tension and economic disparity, they undertook an effort to "Create Interdependent World-Class Communities that Value Diversity and Inclusion."	Nine Future Searches were run. In the first, a cross-section of community leaders created an overarching vision for action. Following were Future Searches for business, communities of faith, community outreach, economic development, education and learning, youth, health care, and government. Three years later, the Alliance for World Class Communities, formed from efforts begun at the Future Searches, was codeveloping a $500 million residential community along the Benton Harbor riverfront.

Groups Searching for Common Ground	Specific Use of the Future Search
The Alliance for Employee Growth and Development (a nonprofit venture of the Communications Workers of America, the International Brotherhood of Electrical Workers, and AT&T)	The alliance empowers AT&T workers displaced by technology to develop new skills and build their careers. The board—senior executives from the three partners—began running board meetings around the country based on Future Search principles, helping local employers and representatives from government, education, and social services develop action plans to benefit all.
Union officials and senior management at 3M Company's St. Paul area Plant Engineering organization	The Future Search helped forward union and management efforts to improve quality of work life, productivity, and management practice. Living the concept of "Unity Through Partnership" in a Future Search, they produced a joint vision of a workplace redesigned around customer needs and devised ways to include people who did not attend. Plant Engineering union and management undertook a large-scale redesign effort involving hundreds of employees.
Kansas City, Missouri, community members interested in youth empowerment, services integration, funding, regional collaboration, technology, and volunteer youth programs	Implemented a community consensus reached earlier to become "The Child Opportunity Capital." Some key outcomes: Children's Mercy Hospital put young people on boards dealing with oversight; a local Junior League chose youth empowerment as its next community commitment, offering 90 volunteers and a $200,000 activities grant including an annual Future Search involving young people.

THE PROCESS

One conference typically involves 60 to 80 people. We consider 64 an optimum number—eight groups of eight. We run conferences in parallel or in sequence to accommodate more people. The purpose is always joint action toward a desired future for "X"—that is, a community, organization, or issue.

We do five tasks in the approximate time frames, shown below:

Day 1 Afternoon
    Task 1—Focus on the Past
    Task 2—Focus on the Present, External Trends
Day 2 Morning
    Task 2 Continued—Stakeholder Response to External Trends
    Task 2 Continued—Focus on the Present, Owning Our Actions

Day 2 Afternoon
    Task 3—Ideal Future Scenarios
    Task 4—Identify Common Ground
Day 3 Morning
    Task 4 Continued—Confirm Common Ground
    Task 5—Action Planning

The Focus on the Past, Ideal Future Scenarios, and Confirm Common Ground are done in mixed groups, each a cross-section of the whole. The Focus on the Present is done by "stakeholder" groups, whose members have a shared perspective. Common Ground is the business of the whole conference. Action Planning employs both existing and voluntary groups. Every task includes a total group dialogue.

The task sequence and group composition are not optional. These set up powerful dynamics that can lead to constructive outcomes. We experience the conference's peaks and valleys as an emotional roller-coaster ride (figure 1), swooping down into the morass of global trends, soaring to idealistic heights in an ideal future. Uncertainty, anxiety, and confusion are necessary by-products; so are fun, energy, creativity, and achievement. Future Search relies on a counterpoint between hope and despair. We believe good contact with our ups and downs leads to realistic choices. In a Future Search, we live with the inevitability of differences, the recognition that no meeting design can reconcile them, and that people are capable of riding the roller coaster to important new action plans without "more data" or "more dialogue," if they agree to keep working together.

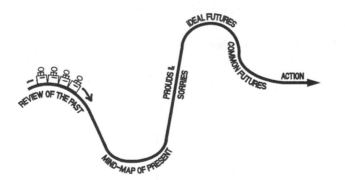

Figure 1. Riding the Roller Coaster

ECONOMIC BENEFITS

In the business world, there is no way to calculate the benefits of Future Search in economic terms. Indeed, these conferences make possible levels of integration not achievable by other means at any cost. At the Hayworth, Inc., Future Search, employees, customers, and suppliers in dialogue with company members discovered and solved a cascading waste-disposal packaging problem. They reduced both cost and environmental impact in a few hours. However, this was only one of dozens of key issues addressed in the Future Search, many of which, such as work redesign, had long-term economic benefits.

Future Searches also generate dollars not previously available. We have seen money flow from haves to have-nots in an eyeblink, as people connect needs and resources. In one conference, a foundation executive offered substantial support for an action plan that he said would not have been funded had it come through regular channels. In an eastern city, the mayor's office offered a community $2 million in public funds that had sat idle for lack of practical plans. A Connecticut school district increased teachers' salaries when the community declared education a major priority. These examples are the tip of a large iceberg that could turn our assumptions about how to assure wise use of money in constructive new directions.

Table of Uses

Typical Settings	Brief Description	Project Length	Key Events	Number of Participants
Organizations, communities, networks, companies, nonprofits, NGOs, schools, colleges, hospitals, congregations, etc.	Any issue where cooperation among diverse parties is critical for ongoing action. *Outcomes:* • Vision, goals, and strategies supported by everybody • Implementation and follow-up plan • High commitment to act by many people • Ongoing unpredictable, constructive outcomes	*Planning:* Three to six months *Meeting:* 16–18 hours, spread over three days. *Follow-up:* Periodic 0.5–1 day reviews, continuing indefinitely	*Planning:* *Minimum:* A 2-day meeting with 6–12 people. *Typical:* A full day followed by several half days and lots of phone calls. *Note:* The big change happens in the planning.	We like groups of 64–72. Future Searches can be run in parallel or sequentially with any number, so long as each group includes people with authority, expertise, resources, information, and need.

Getting Started

In a Future Search, we seek to take that first important step by:

- Getting the "right people" in the room—people with authority, resources, information, expertise, and need.

- Creating a learning environment for participants to experience the whole system before acting on a part.

- Focusing on common ground and future action, treating problems and conflicts as information only.

- Enabling individuals to take responsibility for acting on common ground.

The change begins in the planning. Future Search requires no training, inputs, data collection, or diagnoses. People face each other rather than concepts, expert advice, or assumptions about what they lack and should do. The method involves comparing notes and listening, sometimes to a mishmash of assumptions, misinformation, stereotypes, and judgments rattling around in all of us. Amazingly, it is *not* necessary to straighten all this out to succeed. Commitment builds as we encounter chaos together, hang on despite our anxiety, and come out the other side with some good ideas, people we can trust, and faith in our ability to work together. In short, we uncover buried potential that already exists.

Roles and Responsibilities

	Before	**During**	**After**
Sponsor	• Decide what you hope to accomplish and how Future Search applies. • Know the conditions for success. • Get the right people to join you.	• Be a participant. Share your learnings. • Empower people to act.	• Have periodic review meetings in which stakeholders look at what they are doing, reconfirm common ground, and course correct if necessary. Can include new people. Half day to one day.
Designer/Facilitator	• Help people decide if Future Search will serve their needs. • Help sponsors gather the necessary information, courage, and resources to proceed.	• Manage tasks and time. Keep purpose front and center. • Encourage self-management and responsibility.	• Facilitate a review meeting six to nine months after the conference.

Future Search

	Before	During	After
		• Stay with the uncertainty until people decide what they will do together. • Help people resolve the struggle between old patterns and new paths.	
Steering Committee	• Frame the conference task. • Get the "right people" in the conference. • Set the planning time horizons.	• Participate.	• May or may not continue to organize follow-up meetings.
Participants	• Agree to come and stay the whole time.	• Take ownership of their past, present, and future. • Confirm shared values and principles. • Seek common ground. • Develop action plans based on the common ground. • Share leadership.	• Take responsibility to follow through with plans.

Roles and Responsibilities. Continued

SHIFTS IN ORGANIZATIONAL POWER AND AUTHORITY

During the Future Search conference, participants work as peers to build an information base, communicate what they learn, make decisions, and plan next steps. Afterward, there may or may not be formal changes in power and authority throughout the organization or community. Such changes would depend on the nature of the action plans and implementation strategy.

Conditions for Success

Our conference design embodies a set of mutually reinforcing criteria:

- Practicing the Future Search principles;
- Attending the whole meeting;
- Meeting under healthy conditions;
- Working across three days (i.e., "sleeping twice");
- Taking responsibility publicly for follow-up.

To help people act boldly and creatively, we have to get out of the way. Therefore, we do not strive to reduce complexity to a few manageable issues, to resolve disagreements, or to solve long-standing problems, nor do we give people management models for organizing their varied perceptions. Instead, participants engage in a series of open dialogues on where they've been, where they are, and what they want to do. Future Searches often include total strangers or people with a history of conflict who come with confusing and contradictory information. As they experience each other's diverse agendas, they realize that change means accepting each other where they are in order to go forward together. Those who stay the course find that quick action is inevitable.

WHAT WE CAN'T DO WITH FUTURE SEARCH

Shore Up Ineffective Leaders

We cannot make up for weak leadership. A worldwide religious service organization's lawyer wanted to head off a union drive by disgruntled central staff. A reluctant CEO went along with "legal" advice to sponsor a Future Search that would enable people to devise the workplace they wanted. People welcomed a chance to make their own plans. They were not surprised, though, when the boss acted on none of them. Nor was their attorney surprised when the staff voted in a union to fill the leadership vacuum.

Convince Skeptics to Go Forward

We have had no success "selling" Future Search to people paralyzed by worry about losing control. One troubled corporate giant planned to put thousands of people through a training event staged by a prestigious business institute. To the staff's proposal that the company substitute Future Searches—on the theory that people could get the company out of the box if given a chance—top management turned a deaf ear. They opted for expert training. Nothing new happened. Having two years to "transform the culture or die," they gave up on their way after a year. Several departments ran successful Future Searches, but the company continued its downward slide and later was sold to a rival.

Reconcile Values Differences

We don't know how to reconcile intractable values differences through Future Search. When people disagree about deep-seated religious, ethical, or political beliefs that they hold sacred, a Future Search is unlikely to help them reconcile their ways of thinking. In a school conference, people brought up highly charged feelings about sex education. The differences between those who did and did not want particular curriculums were fierce, deeply felt, and long-standing. The parties believed each other to be wrong. At the same time, they agreed on a host of other goals, such as better use of school facilities and more involvement of parents in learning and teaching. They found that they could not reconcile their moral values in this forum, but had a priceless chance to make progress on matters of benefit to all if they cooperated.

Change Team Dynamics

We can create new dynamics quickly only if we bring together a *new* group and give it a *new* task. Systems expert Russell Ackoff pointed out long ago (1974) that systems change only in relation to the larger systems of which they are a part. That explains why peer-only events—training, T-groups, team meetings—have little effect on the larger system. This seems to be true even when the narrow group does a broad task, such as "scanning the environment." Therefore, our guiding principle is always the "whole system" in the room.

Theoretical Basis and Historical Roots

Future Search is based on theories and principles derived from decades of action research into effective group problem solving and planning. Our main sources of inspiration come from parallel innovations on both sides of the Atlantic. One inspiration comes from Ronald Lippitt and Eva Schindler-Rainman's large-scale community futures conferences held in North America during the 1970s. Another is the pioneering work of Eric Trist, an Englishman, and Fred Emery, an Australian, in developing the Search Conference (hence, the name *Future Search*). From Lippitt and Schindler-Rainman, we learned to get the whole system in the room and focus on the future, not on problems and conflicts. From Trist and Emery, we learned the importance of thinking globally before acting locally, and of having people manage their own planning (Weisbord et al., 1992). We share with all of them a commitment to democratic ideals and their embodiment of the "action research" tradition of the famed social psychologist Kurt Lewin (Lewin, 1948).

PEOPLE, WHOLE SYSTEMS, AND PLANNING

We see Future Search as a learning laboratory for getting everybody involved in improving their own system. It is not the complete answer to anything, yet the principles apply to many kinds of meetings and change strategies. Our society has hardly begun to explore what we can do when diverse parties work on the same task despite their differences. Future Searches enable people to experience and accept polarities and to bridge barriers of culture, class, age, gender, ethnicity, power, status, and hierarchy by working as peers on tasks of mutual concern. The Future Search process interrupts the human tendency to repeat old patterns—fighting, running away, complaining, blaming, or waiting for others to fix things. And it gives everyone a chance to express their highest ideals.

Instead of trying to change the world or each other, we change the conditions under which we interact. *That* much we can control, and it leads to surprising outcomes.

In Future Search, major systemic changes occur in the planning. A diverse group of six to ten people meets periodically from a few days to a few months. They agree on a task and invite a spectrum of stakeholders. They also accept a novel set of conditions, for example, meeting for 16 hours over three days, skipping speakers and expert input, putting off action until near the end, and working interactively. In a meeting structured this way, people discover new capabilities no matter what agendas come up. This opens the door to new, unpredictable, highly desired, and long-lived cooperative action that is a high order of systems change.

We don't work to improve relationships among people or functions. Rather, we set up conditions under which people can choose new ways of relating. We don't abstract out social issues (e.g., diversity, trust, communications, collaboration) from economic and technical ones. We are unlikely to run a conference on "the future of diversity in X." Rather, we'd propose that a diverse group of people explore together what kind of X they want to live and work in. Whatever people's skills, education, or experience, they already have what they need to engage in this process. As facilitators, our main job is to maintain boundaries of time and task and to make sure that all points of view are supported.

SHARING THE WORK

Ours is an encounter with the whole—self, community, and organization. We do not provide an expert systems analysis. Instead, we set up a situation where people experience themselves in action as part of a larger whole. They talk over issues they have not raised before with people they have never met. They take responsibility for matters previously avoided or ignored. They dramatize ideal futures as if they have actually happened, thus anchoring them in their bodies. They identify what they *really* want. They voluntarily commit to actions made possible only because of the other people in the room.

Our procedures evolved while working mainly with people who can read and write. However, the underlying principles do not require literacy. The work could be done entirely with spoken and/or symbolic communication. The results have been repeated in many cultures and in culturally diverse groups all over the world.

Sustaining the Results

The most worrisome aspect of planning is implementation. No process, however comprehensive, guarantees action. Still, we have seen more plans implemented from Future Search than any method either of us has used in 30 years. People act quite apart from whether or not they had a good time, liked the facilitators, collected handouts, resolved their differences, or felt that they had finished. Nor is success a function of how complete an action-planning format we use. People find ways to carry out their plans if they have clear goals, the right people are in the room, and they take the whole ride together. Action requires people who understand and believe in their plans and trust each other enough to join in new steps. We think Future Search fosters understanding, belief, and commitment.

What factors contribute to sustainable results? We believe periodic review meetings that bring together stakeholders from the original conference and other interested parties provide a simple, congruent way to keep action planning fresh, connected, and relevant. What happens after a Future Search depends largely on what people sign up to do. No sign-up, no action. We do not know how to get other people to do things they don't want to do. Future

Search theory holds that we get more implementation when we attend to each stage of the process, giving people ample opportunity to engage each other, create an umbrella of shared values, commit publicly to action steps they believe in, and get together regularly to share what they are doing.

Burning Questions

DO WE HAVE TO INVITE ALL THOSE PEOPLE?

We strongly urge it, if you want to succeed.

DO WE HAVE TO STAY TOGETHER THAT LONG?

Many people have tried, to their regret, to shorten this process. Two and a half days seems to be the minimum time to get lasting changes that were not possible before, despite numerous other meetings.

CAN'T WE DROP THE PAST AND GET TO ACTION PLANNING SOONER?

If you move too fast, you are less likely to get the hoped-for commitment and implementation. We believe action planning goes quickly when people find common ground. If they move sooner, they use action planning time to work out their differences, thus reinforcing the belief that more time is needed.

WHAT IF PEOPLE CAN'T PUT IN THE TIME OR GET "THE WHOLE SYSTEM IN THE ROOM"?

We apologize for not being able to help. The only way to have "change" is to do something you never did before.

WHY ARE YOU SO RIGID?

We love success too much to give up on it.

Some Final Comments

We see Future Search as a building block of theory and practice for a house that will never be finished. Practitioners are infusing Future Search principles into everything they do, and enriching this process with many other perspectives. We cannot contrast what we do with other processes because we believe that processes that hold to the principles of inclusion, dialogue, discovery, and responsibility for action are independently valuable. The roller-coaster ride is inevitable in human affairs. Conceptual schemes and meeting designs come and go. The business of muddling through life's ups and downs together strikes us as a universal process. We believe Future Searches are good for us and good for society. We hope this work enables thousands of constructive action projects everywhere.

About the Authors

Marvin Weisbord and *Sandra Janoff* are codirectors of Future Search Network, an international service nonprofit and coauthors of *Future Search: An Action Guide,* 2nd edition (2000). They have trained more than 3,000 people worldwide in using Future Search.

Marvin Weisbord (mweisbord@futuresearch.net) was an organization development consultant from 1969 to 1991, with business firms, medical schools, and hospitals; a partner in the consulting firm Block Petrella Weisbord; and a member of NTL Institute. He is a fellow of the World Academy of Productivity Science and author of *Organizational Diagnosis* (1978), *Productive Workplaces* (1987), *Discovering Common Ground* (1992), and *Productive Workplaces Revisited* (2004).

Sandra Janoff (sjanoff@futuresearch.net) co-developed an experimental high school from 1974 to 1984 and ran workshops in Pennsylvania schools on alternative practices in education. She also was a staff member in Tavistock conferences sponsored by Temple University in Philadelphia and the Tavistock Institute of Human Relations in Oxford, England. She is coauthor with Yvonne Agazarian of "Systems Thinking and Small Groups" for the *Comprehensive Textbook of Group Psychotherapy* (1993). She has consulted to communities, international agencies, and corporations around the world.

Where to Go for More Information

REFERENCES

Weisbord, Marvin. *Productive Workplaces.* San Francisco: Jossey-Bass, 1987.

Weisbord, Marvin, et al. *Discovering Common Ground.* San Francisco: Berrett-Koehler, 1992.

Weisbord, Marvin, and Sandra Janoff. *Future Search: An Action Guide to Finding Common Ground in Organizations and Community.* San Francisco: Berrett-Koehler, 1995.

INFLUENTIAL SOURCES

Agazarian, Yvonne. *Systems-Centered Therapy for Groups.* New York: Guilford Press, 1997.

Berman, Maurice. *Coming to Our Senses: Body and Spirit in the Hidden History of the West.* New York: Bantam Books, 1990.

Buzan, Tony. *Using Both Sides of Your Brain.* New York: Dutton, 1976.

Lawrence, Paul R., and Jay W. Lorsch. *Organization and Environment, Managing Differentiation and Integration,* research assistance from James S. Garrison. Boston: Harvard Business School Press, 1986.

Lewin, K. *Resolving Social Conflicts: Selected Papers on Group Dynamics.* Edited by G. W. Lewin. New York: Harper & Row, 1948.

Sheldrake, Rupert. *The Presence of the Past: Morphic Resonance and the Habits of Nature,* repr. ed. Rochester, VT: Park Street Press, 1995.

OTHER RESOURCES

Discovering Community. Livonia, MI: Blue Sky Productions. (800) 358-0022.

A video of the Santa Cruz Community Future Search on housing.

Search for Quality. Livonia, MI: Blue Sky Productions. (800) 358-0022.

A video of the Haworth Furniture Manufacturing Future Search.

Weir, John, and Joyce Weir. *Self-Differentiation.* Livonia, MI: Blue Sky Productions. (800) 358-0022.

ORGANIZATION

Future Search Network—www.futuresearch.net; 4700 Wissahickon Ave, Suite 126; Philadelphia, PA 19144; (800) 951-6333, fsn@futuresearch.net

CHRIS ERTEL, KATHERINE FULTON, AND DIANA SCEARCE

Scenario Thinking

Futurism is the art of reperception. It means that life will change, must change, and has changed, and it suggests how and why. It shows that old perceptions have lost their validity, while new ones are possible.

— Bruce Sterling

Real-Life Story

Herman Miller, the office furniture maker, is one of the most influential U.S. design firms of the past half-century. In late 2000, members of the company's Future Insight Group worked with Global Business Network, a consultancy specializing in long-term thinking, to develop a set of scenarios on the future of work and the workplace. The original goal was to identify emergent market opportunities. This initial scenario project went well, but with one small problem: By the time the team was ready to roll out the results and start exploring new innovations, the bottom had fallen out of the office furniture market. In one short year, the company—like others in the industry—saw a 40 percent drop in revenues, resulting in a shift in attention to survival mode.

By 2002, as the team was looking for additional ways to leverage the work, using the scenarios with customers emerged as an opportunity. As a "B2B" business, the majority of Herman Miller's revenues come from big companies that need to outfit large workplace facilities. Before making purchases, these major clients like to meet first with key executives to discuss emerging trends affecting workplace design and productivity—resulting in a steady stream of visits to Herman Miller's headquarters in Zeeland, Michigan. Even in the depths of recession, these customers expect Herman Miller to deliver on its long-standing reputation for fresh thought leadership.

In order to engage key customers in dialogue about their workplace strategies and emerging needs, Herman Miller customized a two-hour scenario process (dubbed the "kaleidoscope"

experience). Beginning with a polished video presentation, the kaleidoscope experience serves three important purposes: It demonstrates the quality of Herman Miller's thinking on the workplace of the future; it provides Herman Miller with a continuous stream of new, innovative ideas for future possible products and services, created by the company's own customers; and it helps to deepen relationships with key customers by creating an accelerated and shared learning experience. To date, dozens of large corporate customers have been through the kaleidoscope process.

"We decided to do scenario work as a platform for thinking creatively about new product development," said Maryln Walton, of Herman Miller's Future Insight Group. "What we did not anticipate was that this work would also have benefits for our sales and marketing efforts, and would have a wider impact on how people in the company think about the future more generally." The success of the kaleidoscope process underscored the value of helping organizations develop their own capacity for engaging others in scenario thinking. In many ways, Herman Miller's creative use of scenario thinking is emblematic of the ways the scenario tool kit has exploded in use beyond its original application as a strategic planning application for the oil industry. Today, scenario thinking tools and approaches are routinely applied toward a broad range of uses in a variety of industries and with diverse groups, large and small.[1]

The Basics

Scenarios are stories about how the future might unfold for our organizations, our issues, our communities, and even our world. Importantly, scenarios are not predictions. Rather, they are provocative and plausible stories about diverse ways in which relevant issues outside our immediate communities and organizations might evolve and interact, such as the future political environment, social attitudes, regulation, and the strength of the economy. Because scenarios are hypotheses, not predictions, they are created and used in sets of multiple stories—usually three or four—that capture a range of future possibilities: good and bad, expected and surprising. Finally, scenarios are designed to stretch our thinking about the opportunities and threats that the future might hold, and to weigh those opportunities and threats carefully when making both short- and long-term strategic decisions.

Ultimately, the point of scenario thinking is not to write stories of the future. Rather, it is to arrive at a deeper understanding of the world in which your organization or community operates, and to use that understanding to inform your strategy and improve your ability to make better decisions today and in the future. At its most basic, scenario thinking helps communities and organizations order and frame their thinking about the longer-term future, while providing them with the tools and the confidence to take action soon. At its finest, scenario thinking helps communities and organizations find strength of purpose and strategic direction in the face of daunting, chaotic, and even frightening circumstances.[2]

Scenarios can be applied in a wide variety of organizational and community settings. Scenarios have been used with groups of all shapes and sizes—to frame intimate strategic conversations among boards and executive committees, to build the capacity of hundreds of employees to adapt to an uncertain and changing environment, and even to catalyze broad-based dialogues about better futures across entire countries. The scenario process has been used extensively with corporations and nonprofits, government agencies, and diverse multistakeholder groups. Scenario thinking has catalyzed national, regional, and local community-based change, and it has been used to connect actors from around the world to engage in strategic conversations around issues of shared interest, ranging from the future of climate change to AIDS.

The most common applications of scenario thinking typically fall into four broad categories: (1) alignment and visioning, (2) setting strategic direction, (3) catalyzing bold action and innovation, and (4) accelerating collaborative learning. Of course, these applications are not mutually exclusive. Most scenario thinking efforts are driven at the outset by a single application, such as decision making or organizational alignment, and result in multiple overlapping outcomes.

ALIGNMENT AND VISIONING

Scenarios can be used with multistakeholder coalitions and single organizations to create a shared vision and increase alignment around a desired future or strategic direction. This is a powerful application because scenario thinking often results in a deeper and shared understanding of the complexities of problem solving—the potential opportunities, barriers, allies, and pitfalls. When working with a diverse group, this shared understanding can help divergent voices find common ground and collaborative solutions for the future.

SETTING STRATEGIC DIRECTION

Scenarios can be used for various levels of strategy development: making a decision on a specific strategic issue; setting a high-level strategic agenda; creating the platform for an ongoing strategic conversation; and assessing risks and opportunities by exploring how complex factors could create very different environments that you might have to navigate. In addition, you can use scenario thinking to test your current strategy, theory of change, or vision in multiple possible futures beyond your control, rehearsing what you would need to do to succeed in different environments—positive, negative, and unexpected.

CATALYZING BOLD ACTION AND INNOVATION

Scenario thinking can be used to get your organization unstuck, catalyzing bold action and innovation. It does so by rehearsing diverse and provocative future possibilities—both desirable scenarios that you would like to help create and profit from and dark scenarios that generate a sense of urgency. Looking across a range of futures often enables organizations and communities to identify new opportunities and threats, and envision innovations that capture opportunities and mitigate threats.

ACCELERATING COLLABORATIVE LEARNING

Scenarios can serve as a powerful platform to collaboratively explore a topic of common interest that organizes what is known and surfaces what is unknown and uncontrollable. An important result of such collaborative learning is to challenge assumptions by introducing new perspectives and new knowledge, leading the group to discover as yet unimagined solutions.

Table of Uses

The following table illustrates the variety of settings in which scenario thinking can be used to facilitate a range of different outcomes.

Setting	Brief Description	Length	Key Events	Number of Participants
Financial services company trying to better understand potential impact of emerging technologies and consumer behavior on the market for investment services	Developed strategic insights that prevented company from overinvesting in growth during the peak of dot-com speculative bubble; initiated new product development	4 months	Interviews with key stakeholders, internal and external; 2-day scenario development workshop; drafting of scenario narratives; 2-day scenario implications workshop; development of strategic agenda	Senior management team and strategic planning group (totaling 16 participants) took part in interviews and scenario workshops
Foundation developing an education program strategy	Incorporated perspectives of diverse public education stakeholders into foundation strategy development process; framed foundation strategy within broader strategic agenda for national education reform	3 months	Similar process as above, with more extensive interviewing and research components	10 interviewees; 25 workshop participants, 10 internal to the foundation and 15 external
Network of technology leaders working in a common region	Developed a coordinated vision for creating an approach to regional technology development; catalyzed innovation in individual organizations and identified synergies across organizations	6 months	Interviews with key observers of the regional technology environment; day-long large scenario development workshop; several workshops to identify implications with smaller subsets of participants; ongoing coordinated strategy development among technology organizations in the region	30 interviewees; 130 participants in scenario development workshop

Scenario Thinking

Setting	Brief Description	Length	Key Events	Number of Participants
Staff of environmental nonprofit	Collaborative learning to build sensitivity to changing circumstances	1 month	Close consultation with steering committee to design customized learning process; circulate survey to all staff members; conduct day-long scenario thinking workshop	6 steering committee members; 500 participants in scenario workshop

Getting Started

Pierre Wack, a planner for Royal Dutch/Shell in the 1970s and the originator of scenario thinking as it is commonly used today, described it as a discipline for encouraging creative and entrepreneurial thinking and action "in contexts of change, complexity, and uncertainty." Scenario thinking achieves this promise because of three fundamental principles: the long view, outside-in thinking, and multiple perspectives.

THE LONG VIEW

Scenario thinking requires looking beyond immediate demands and peering far enough into the future to see new possibilities, asking, "What if?" Such a long-term perspective may seem tangential to an organization's more immediate pressures, but doing so enables you to take a more proactive and anticipatory approach to addressing deep-seated problems; see both challenges and opportunities more clearly; and consider the long-term effects and potential unintended consequences of actions that you might otherwise take.

OUTSIDE-IN THINKING

Most individuals and organizations are surprised by discontinuous events because they spend their time thinking about what they are most familiar with: their own industry or immediate context. They think from the inside—the things they can control—out to the world they would like to shape. Conversely, thinking from the outside in begins with pondering external changes that might, over time, profoundly affect your work—a seemingly irrelevant technological development that could prove advantageous for service delivery, for example, or a geopolitical shift that could introduce unforeseen social needs. Outside-in thinking can help organizations port ideas across industry silos to overcome the artificial boundaries resulting from narrowly focused industry mind-sets, and thus, anticipate and prepare for "surprising" eventualities.

Scenario Thinking

Phases of Scenario Thinking

The scenario thinking process starts by exploring external developments, both in the broad contextual world and in your working environment. Only after you've created scenarios about the external environment do you consider implications for your individual organization or issue. The following diagram illustrates a framework for outside-in thinking. The inner ring refers to your organization or the specific issue at stake. The middle ring is your immediate working environment and the outer ring is the contextual environment, which encompasses broad driving forces such as social values, geopolitics, and technology (figure 1).

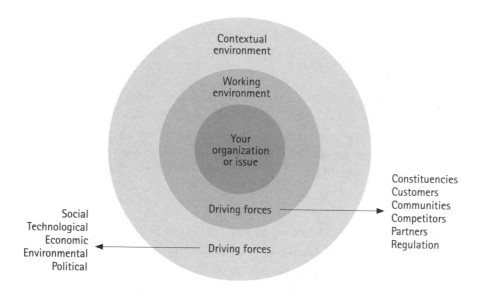

Figure 1. Outside-In Thinking

Multiple Perspectives

The introduction of multiple perspectives—diverse voices that will shed new light on your strategic challenge—helps you better understand your own assumptions about the future, as well as the assumptions of others. When one is working with passionate convictions, it is easy to become deaf to voices you may not agree with. However, consciously bringing these voices to the table exposes you to new ideas that will inform your own perspective and could prove extremely helpful in your effort to see the big picture of an issue or idea. The scenario thinking process creates a powerful platform for multiple (and often divergent) perspectives to come together. The result is an expansion of an organization's peripheral vision—you see new threats and opportunities that you otherwise may have missed.

Over the years, a basic process has emerged that serves as a foundation for most scenario thinking exercises. The process has five phases: orient, explore, synthesize, act, and monitor (figure 2). Just as scenario thinking can be used toward many different ends, the basic process can be

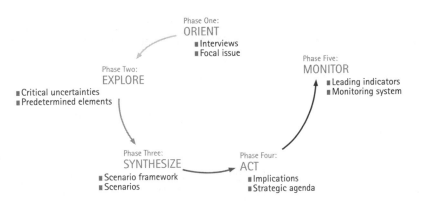

Figure 2. Phases of Scenario Thinking

modified in countless ways to better meet your desired outcomes. In some cases, a few of the phases are abridged and extra time is allocated to other phases. In other cases, a more radical departure from the basic process may be appropriate.

PHASE ONE: ORIENT

The goal of phase one is to clarify the issue at stake. The process begins with learning more about your challenges, and the underlying assumptions that you and others in your organization/community—decision makers, in particular—hold about the nature of those challenges and how they will play out in the future. The most effective and efficient way to surface these assumptions is to conduct structured interviews with key decision makers and other important stakeholders. Once you have learned more about the nature of your challenges, issues, and underlying assumptions, you are ready to frame the focal issue or question that will orient the remaining phases of the scenario thinking process.

PHASE TWO: EXPLORE

In this second phase, you explore the many driving forces that could shape your focal issue, including forces within your immediate working environment like regulatory shifts and changes in your customer base, as well as broader developments—social, technological, economic, environmental, and political. The point of brainstorming a list of driving forces is to look beyond the pressures that dominate your work and mind on a daily basis and seek out those forces in the outside world that could have an unexpected impact.

PHASE THREE: SYNTHESIZE

In phase three, you synthesize and combine the driving forces that you have identified to create scenarios. Start by prioritizing your driving forces according to two criteria: (1) the degree of importance to the focal issue or question, and (2) the degree of uncertainty surrounding those forces. The goal of prioritization is to identify the two or three driving forces that are most important to the focal issue and most uncertain. These driving forces are your "critical uncertainties," and they will be the foundation of your scenario set.

There are a number of different approaches to developing a scenario set. The most common is to picture your critical uncertainties on two axes that frame the poles of what seems possible in your time frame. For instance, a group working in health care might cross an uncertainty about the financial and regulatory environment with an uncertainty about the pace and distribution of technological development to create a scenario matrix. Try to envision the four scenarios created by this matrix. What if the financial and regulatory environments are favorable toward a freer market in health care, and technology develops and spreads at a fast and even pace? This could be a world with a highly automated and efficient infrastructure for managing and administering health care with broad array of choice and a relatively weak safety net. As you try to envision each of the four possible scenarios, ask yourself: Do the combined critical uncertainties produce believable and useful stories of the future? The scenarios should represent a range of alternative futures, not simply a best, worst, and most likely world (figure 3).

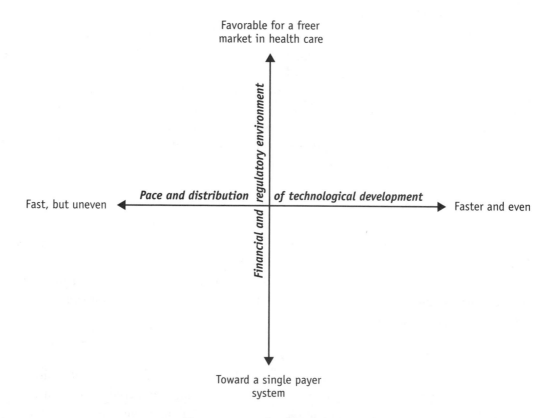

Figure 3. Example of Scenario Matrix

PHASE FOUR: ACT

In phase four, you use your scenarios to inform and inspire action.

The test of a good set of scenarios is not whether, in the end, they turn out to portray the future accurately, but whether they enable an organization to learn, adapt, and take effective action. After you've developed your scenarios, imagine—deeply imagine—living and working in each one. Ask yourself: What if this scenario is the future? What actions would I take today to prepare? You can then analyze the implications that surfaced in all scenarios. Are any of the implications valid in all scenarios? Are there significantly different implications in each scenario? Do these differences highlight any strategic choices that you will have to address? The patterns and insights that emerge from the scenario implications will help you set strategic priorities and catalyze action.

PHASE FIVE: MONITOR

In this last phase, you create mechanisms that will help your organization track shifts in the environment and adjust its strategy accordingly. This can be achieved by creating an ongoing dialogue process to identify and track leading indicators—signs of emerging change—that will tell you if a particular scenario is beginning to unfold, causing some implications to rise in importance and some uncertainties to evolve into certainties.

Roles, Responsibilities, and Relationships

The following descriptions of roles and responsibilities capture how many scenario thinking processes are structured.

SPONSOR

The sponsor is someone with support of decision makers and credibility across all levels of the organization or community. The sponsor is deeply involved through all steps of the formal process and beyond, building broad-based ownership for the output and keeping the strategic conversation alive in the organization or community.

INTERNAL PARTICIPANTS

Internal participants include representatives of key stakeholders in the organization or community. Many of them are interviewed during the initial "orient" phase. They collaborate in a workshop setting to develop the scenarios and identify implications during the explore, synthesize, and act phases. Some internal participants are often recruited (or volunteer) to engage in the follow-on monitoring phase and to lead the implementation of actions that emerge from the process.

EXTERNAL PARTICIPANTS

External participants are creative thinkers who contribute new and sometimes controversial perspectives to the scenario thinking process. They can be integrated into your scenario process in a variety of ways: through interviews in the orient phase, by participating in the scenario development, and/or by providing feedback on your scenarios once developed. The best outside participants are highly creative, skilled at pattern recognition, and comfortable with challenging their own perspectives.

FACILITATOR

The facilitator works in close collaboration with the sponsor and core team to shape and manage the overall process. In addition, it is the responsibility of the scenario facilitator to push the group to think longer term, surface blind spots, and consider a broader range of uncertainties in the external environment. In most cases, the scenario facilitator will also conduct some interviews, analyze the interview input in order to suggest potential focal issues, customize the design of the scenario development and implication workshops, and lead follow-on strategy conversations.

LOGISTICS COORDINATOR

The logistics coordinator is involved in all phases of the formal process. Responsibilities include coordinating interviews during the orient phase; securing meeting space for convening internal and external participants in the explore, synthesize, and act phases; and supporting the sponsor's efforts to secure and coordinate participation of internal and external participants.

CORE TEAM

The core team shepherds the scenario process from beginning to end, and executes scenario development work outside of the facilitated large group process, like conducting interviews, researching driving forces, and drafting scenario narratives. The core team should be limited to four or five members, including the sponsor, scenario facilitator, the logistics coordinator, and one or two others with strong research, writing, and strategy skills.

Conditions for Success

In order to truly internalize and act upon the insights and implications that come out of a scenario process, your organization or community must be very motivated to learn, and ultimately willing to change. Your scenario thinking effort will enable learning and change if the following are true:

- *You are open to hearing multiple perspectives and challenging commonly held assumptions.* By introducing multiple perspectives on the future, the scenario-thinking process can challenge commonly held assumptions and help align your organization's (or community's) perspectives on the future with the changing environment.

- *You are positioned to change in a meaningful way.* The organization/community needs to have some impetus for change, internally or externally driven, in order to make the scenario learning meaningful and, ultimately, to act on these insights. The impetus for change often comes from a strategic issue that does not have a clearly defined solution and that is important enough to catalyze action—like the need to address new forms of competition. The call to change can be driven by either crisis or opportunity, or by both. According to scenario thinker and writer Betty Sue Flowers, "People should have a sense of urgency even if things seem to be pretty good. My sense of urgency doesn't come from impending crisis; it comes from a need to be prepared for anything, including opportunity."

- *You have a well-positioned leader for the process.* In order to make the learning—and subsequent action—stick, there needs to be a credible, facilitative leader who can build support and sustain excitement for the process. That leader must advocate for a way of strategic thinking that, if executed well, can produce considerable change. It's equally important that there be clear ownership of the output—a person or group who will take responsibility for acting on ideas generated during the process.

- *You are willing to commit the necessary resources—time and money.* Like any strategy development effort, scenario thinking demands time and money. Because insights from scenario thinking are developed through extensive reflection and dialogue, senior decision makers must be ready to commit significant time and attention to the effort. That said, the amount of resources required need not be huge, simply commensurate with the scope of your ambition.

- *You have a clear, and realistic vision of success.* As with any strategic intervention, it is critical you enter into the scenario process with a reasonably clear and credible set of objectives and desired outcomes. Once you have identified your primary objectives, you can customize the scenario thinking process to maximize impact around these stated objectives.

Decision Tree

The decision tree depicted below (figure 4) can be used to determine whether scenario thinking is an appropriate tool for addressing your challenge or problem. As always, when skillfully facilitated and in special circumstances, there are exceptions to the logic outlined here.

In summary: Your situation is ideal for scenario thinking if:

- You are dealing with a strategic issue and the solution is unclear.
- You are working in a highly uncertain environment.
- There is leadership support for the scenario thinking process.

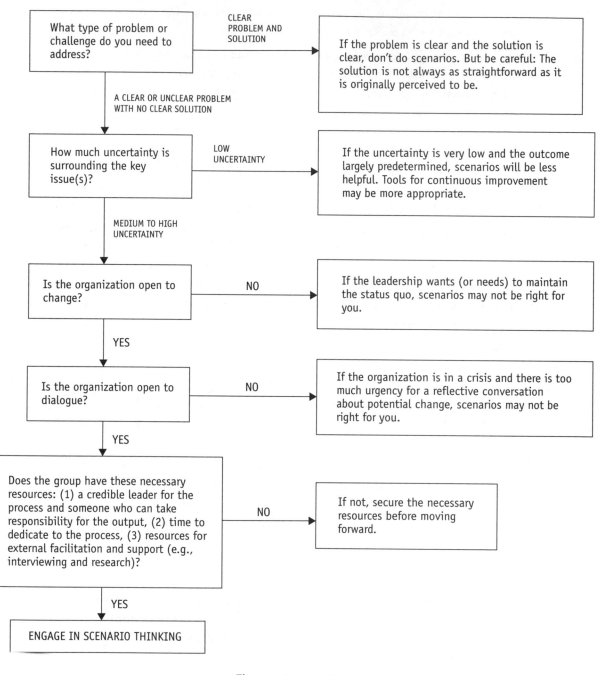

Figure 4. Decision Tree

- Your organization is open to change and dialogue.

- You can attract the resources necessary for a successful initiative.

Theoretical Basis

The idea of scenarios—telling stories of the future—is as old as humankind. Scenarios as a tool for strategy have their origins in military and corporate planning. After World War II, the U.S. military tried to imagine multiple scenarios for what its opponents might do. In the 1960s, Herman Kahn, who played an important role in the military effort, introduced scenarios to a corporate audience. In the 1970s, Pierre Wack, a strategist at Royal Dutch/Shell brought the use of scenarios to a new level. At Shell, Wack realized that he had to get inside the minds of decision makers in order to affect strategic decisions—and scenarios could enable him to do so. Wack and his team used scenarios to paint vivid and diverse pictures of the future so that decision makers could rehearse the implications for the company. As a result, Shell was able to anticipate the Arab oil embargo, and then again anticipate and prepare for the dramatic drop in oil prices in the 1980s. Since then, scenario thinking has become a popular tool for the development of corporate strategy in numerous industries.

The codification and spread of scenario thinking was accelerated in the late 1980s, with the founding of Global Business Network, a network of corporations, scenario practitioners, and provocative long-term thinkers across multiple disciplines. In the early 1990s, there were successful experiments using scenarios as a tool for civic dialogue around large intractable issues, such as the future of South Africa at the end of apartheid. Around the same time there were also public-sector efforts to use scenarios as an economic development tool, most notably by the Dutch and Scottish governments. With the growth of the nonprofit capacity movement in the 1990s, scenario thinking began to extend more rapidly into the U.S. nonprofit sector and into civil society around the world. In recent years, scenarios have been increasingly used to help corporations anticipate and embrace rapid technological and geopolitical change, catalyze product innovations, and manage risk. From its early use in the late 1960s to today, scenarios have evolved from cutting-edge practice to a mainstream part of the corporate strategy tool kit.

Sustaining the Results

The scenario thinking process is often defined as a discrete series of workshops that facilitate group collaboration. During the workshops and immediately after, participants are opened up to the range of challenges and opportunities that the future may bring. They can come out of the process with great momentum and enthusiasm to embrace newly defined opportunities. They may also emerge feeling overwhelmed by the amount of change and adaptation that is required of their organizations, their communities, and themselves. If the scenario thinking process ends with the last workshop, once the organizational implications are identified, it is natural for participants to go back to old behaviors and file away the recommendations surfaced.

In order to ensure follow-through and retain the benefits, it is important to approach scenario thinking as both a process and a posture. It is a process through which scenarios are developed and then used to inform strategy. After the process itself is internalized, scenario thinking becomes, for many practitioners, a posture toward the world—a way of thinking about and managing change, a way of exploring the future so that they might then greet it better prepared. Internalizing the scenario process requires: (1) a system for incorporating the fundamental principles of scenario thinking (taking the long view, outside-in thinking, and embracing multiple perspectives), and (2) dedicated leaders who can marshal resources and support for such a system, and build ownership for the process outcomes, shepherding them from recommendations to strategic priorities to action.

Burning Questions

The most frequent—and most difficult—questions that tend to arise relate to precision and evidence. How can one be sure that the right scenarios have been developed? What indicators illustrate the effectiveness of the scenario thinking process? Such questions are seeking clear answers; yet, at its best, scenario thinking surfaces better questions, which lead to a better understanding of the system in which an organization or community is operating. Scenario thinking is an ongoing learning process. As such, there are better scenario sets, but no "wrong" scenario sets; furthermore, the process typically yields many new insights, but few measurable indicators of effectiveness. As Arie de Geus, one of the pioneers of scenario thinking, once explained: "Scenarios are stories. They are works of art, rather than scientific analyses. The reliability of [their content] is less important than the types of conversations and decisions they spark."

Similarly, Pierre Wack pictured scenario thinking as part of an iterative learning process (figure 5):

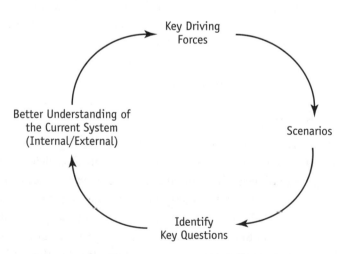

Figure 5. Scenario Thinking: An Iterative Learning Process

Some Final Comments

Scenario thinking is often confused with strategic planning. Strategic planning is a discipline for helping your organization achieve its desired impact; the strategic planning process identifies the priorities and corresponding actions that will help your organization fulfill its mission and succeed. Scenario thinking facilitates and strengthens the strategic planning process by keeping it alive and responsive to the changing environment.

By using scenario thinking to inform your strategic planning, you can turn a discrete activity into an organizational behavior. Unlike many strategy development efforts that are designed around the creation of a strategic plan, scenario thinking is an ongoing, collaborative process. It results in deep organizational learning and, ultimately, in the ability to change in response to both challenge and opportunity.

While a strategic plan can be a great tool to keep an organization on track and the process for developing the plan can spark fruitful conversations, the plan itself can quickly become obsolete. This is because a strategic plan is more fixed than fluid, and the corresponding planning process is more linear than dynamic. While the production of a fixed plan may result in organizational decisions, those decisions are often difficult to convert to actions—especially if the behavioral changes necessary to implement these decisions are not also addressed. Scenario thinking, in contrast, creates a platform for an *ongoing* strategic conversation—it is more a process than an endpoint, and identifying and confronting behavioral barriers to change are inherent to that process.

About the Authors

Chris Ertel (Chris_Ertel@gbn.com) is cohead of Global Business Network's (GBN) consulting practice. Since joining GBN in 1997, Chris has led or worked on about 50 long-term strategy projects related to education, regional development, and the consumer goods and financial services industries, among others.

Katherine Fulton (Katherine_Fulton@monitor.com) is a senior practitioner at Global Business Network, a partner of Monitor Group, and president of Monitor Institute, the primary vehicle through which Monitor applies its assets to complex social problem solving. She coauthored with Diana Scearce GBN's 2004 publication, *What If? The Art of Scenario Thinking for Nonprofits.*

Diana Scearce (Diana_Scearce@monitor.com) has led scenario processes and training courses for organizations across sectors since 1998. Diana developed a passion for scenario thinking during her tenure at Global Business Network. She is currently a consultant with the Monitor Institute.

Where to Go for More Information

REFERENCES

Scearce, Diana, and Katherine Fulton. *What If? The Art of Scenario Thinking for Nonprofits.* San Francisco: Global Business Network, 2004.

Schwartz, P. *Art of the Long View.* New York: Doubleday, 1991.

Shell International's Global Business Environment. *Scenarios: An Explorer's Guide.* London: Shell International, 2003.

Van Der Heijden, Kees. *Scenarios: The Art of Strategic Conversation.* Chichester, UK: John Wiley & Sons, 1996.

Wack, Pierre. "Scenarios: Shooting the Rapids." *Harvard Business Review* 63, no. 6 (1985): 139–150.

————. "Scenarios: Uncharted Waters Ahead." *Harvard Business Review* 63, no. 5 (1985): 72–79.

INFLUENTIAL SOURCES

Kahane, Adam. *Solving Tough Problems: An Open Way of Talking, Listening, and Creating New Realities.* San Francisco: Berrett-Koehler, 2004.

Kelly, Eamonn. *Powerful Times: Rising to the Challenge of Our Uncertain World.* Upper Saddleback River, NJ: Wharton School Publishing, 2006.

Meadows, Donella. "Chicken Little, Cassandra, and the Real Wolf: So Many Ways to Think about the Future." *Whole Earth Review,* Spring 1999.

Ogilvy, James. *Creating Better Futures: Scenario Planning as a Tool for a Better Tomorrow.* New York: Oxford University Press, 2002. An exploration of the ethical dimension of scenario planning—our ability as humans to imagine and realize better futures.

Senge, Peter, Art Kleiner, Charlotte Roberts, Richard B. Ross, and Bryan Smith. *The Fifth Discipline Fieldbook: Strategies and Tools for Building a Learning Organization.* New York: Doubleday, 1994.

ORGANIZATION

Global Business Network—www.gbn.com

1. The material in the remainder of this chapter draws heavily on a guide to the scenario thinking process written by Scearce and Fulton, *What If? The Art of Scenario Thinking for Nonprofits* (2004).

2. Note on terminology: This methodology is called interchangeably scenario planning and scenario thinking. We prefer to use the term "scenario thinking" because the action of "thinking," as opposed to "planning," conveys an ongoing discipline as well as a time-bound process.

Scenario Thinking

Search Conference

The reasonable man adapts himself to the world;
The unreasonable one persists in trying to adapt the world to himself.
Therefore, all progress depends on the unreasonable man.

> —George Bernard Shaw

Real-Life Story

Microsoft management wanted their newly formed product unit to accomplish three major objectives by the end of their planning retreat. They wanted:

- A strong, targeted strategic direction for their selected niche market,
- All members of the division to understand the key business, and
- Solid action plans that its members would be committed to implementing.

The strategic foundation this group constructed would plot the business course for penetration into its selected market over the next five years. Senior members of that business unit selected the Search Conference (SC) method to help them achieve their objectives. An SC was particularly appealing to Microsoft for four reasons:

- Time pressures in the industry made it imperative that Microsoft develop a solid, comprehensive strategy as quickly as possible.
- Microsoft's strong, action-oriented culture demanded not only a solid strategy, but also a set of tactical implementation plans to ensure that people knew exactly how to implement the plan.

- Alignment of all in the group was extremely important because of high levels of personal independence and initiative.

- People needed to get on with their jobs of developing products as quickly as possible; Microsoft wanted the entire planning process to occur in less than three days.

Executives believed the planning method that best met their business objectives was an SC. We conducted the SC at a resort far from day-to-day pressures. On the first day, the group developed a shared understanding of the external forces affecting the world economy, their industry, and their business group. They also explored the critical Microsoft historical events that would shape how they interacted with their external environments and other Microsoft units. Then they conducted a brief analysis of their new organizational unit and how it had been functioning in its short existence. The group continued until 9:30 P.M.

On the second day of the SC, the group articulated two sets of future possibilities for the organization:

- how it would be ideally positioned in the marketplace over the next three years if they could implement anything it wanted; and

- how it would most likely be positioned in the marketplace over the next three years if it took minimal proactive planning steps and allowed itself to be subjected to external market forces.

The discussions were heated at times, based on varying opinions about the current state of the business and the likely interplay of external forces in the future. However, there was little actual conflict, because the group members were all working toward a common goal and striving to understand the varied perspectives that each person brought to the table. The second day, they worked until 11:30 P.M. with the same energy level they arrived with. Though they hadn't planned such a late night of work, several issues arose that led them to choose to work late to ensure a large block of time for action planning the final day.

On the third day, the members finalized their strategy and developed action plans to implement it. As they left, they all remarked on the "tremendous feeling of accomplishment" they felt. They became leaders in their market.

The Basics

WHAT IS A SEARCH CONFERENCE?

A Search Conference (SC) is a participative process in which a group of people develops a set of strategic goals *and* tactical action plans that they will later implement. Any group of people—a corporation, government agency, community, or an industry (henceforth referred to as a system)—might use a Search if they need to create a plan for the development of their system. Searches may also be conducted around issues of national or regional importance.

SCs work best with groups of 20–35 people. The duration is usually two days and two nights. Fred Emery and Eric Trist conducted the first Search in 1959. They are custom designed for the realities of each individual system. Large complex systems can use a series of Searches with an integration event at the end.

WHEN TO USE A SEARCH CONFERENCE

- Strategic planning and the basis of policy making

- Creation of new systems to manage emergent or neglected issues

- Rationalization of major conflicts within a strategic planning context

In large systems, an SC may be conducted to address issues and opportunities for a variety of purposes for different parts of the system or for the entire system. Some organizational examples are listed below. Large geographical communities may be divided into suburbs or neighborhoods.

PROBABLE OUTCOMES

There are three types of outcomes associated with a Search Conference:

Type of Outcome	Example
Visible outputs	• A well-articulated set of goals expressed as the most desirable, achievable future, and an associated timetable for realizing that future • Coordinated action plans for achieving the goals • A community of people who have learned how to actively and adaptively plan
Shared learning process, understanding, and motivation	• Learning about the environment by all participants with shared insights about external forces affecting the system • Common commitment to implementing the plan through having taken responsibility for their future goals • Shared knowledge about the past, present, and future conditions and opportunities • A common set of ideals that overcomes more superficial differences

Type of Outcome	Example
Communication	• Environment for exchange of ideas with openness in all areas • Common language to interpret external and internal events and conditions • Reduced/eliminated consciousness of status, rank, and influence • Critical thinking and challenging of assumptions before implementation.

Specific outcomes for an SC vary greatly, and depend on its stated purpose. Community examples include economic development with a clean environment, a redesigned road and traffic system, and a viable health system.

How It Works

Figure 1 shows the key elements of the open system and the interrelationships of those elements. Open systems theory states that all systems have permeable boundaries and are, therefore, open to their environments. Some systems may also have a relevant "task environment," one lying between the social field and the system, as above. Simply stated, open systems theory asserts that for a system to be viable over time, it needs to:

• constantly scan the relevant environments for changes that might affect its viability, and

• actively adapt to new information it receives in such a way that it also influences those environments.

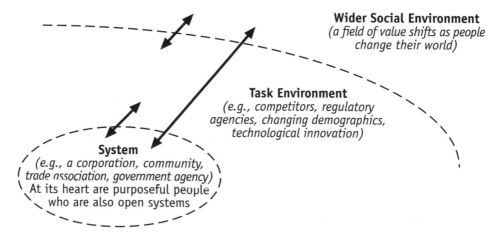

Figure 1. The Open System

Contemporary case studies of organizations such as IBM, Sears, and Compaq also demonstrate the importance of adapting in a *rapid* way, or at least in a timely enough way that it doesn't cost billions of dollars to turn the organization around. Turning IBM around cost $8 billion.

Open systems theory says that the system and environment *operate together* to help shape and determine the future of both. That is, they do not evolve independently of each other, but rather they coevolve. In addition, open systems theory holds that the system and its environment are governed by laws, and that these laws can be articulated. In a Search, participants implicitly discover these laws and use them to plan for the future of their system and the environment.

THE PROCESS

Since the SC is based on open systems theory, the key elements of the work are the system, the environment, and integrating what is learned about these into action plans to produce an active adaptive system (figure 2). The process is, therefore, integrated learning and planning. Diffusion is an essential distinguishing characteristic of a Search because without effective diffusion, any time spent developing strategic plans is virtually worthless. In a Search, the participants develop action plans in such a way that their implementation includes effective diffusion of the goals and their underlying ideals. This strategy diffusion is an important element of performance for world-class systems.

The picture of a funnel is an apt analogy because at the start of a Search, participants consider all possibilities and gradually home in on their focus and best bets. They start broadly from

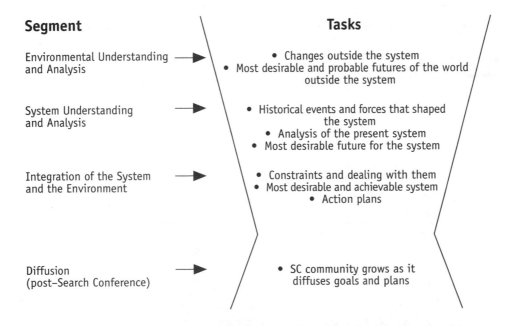

Figure 2. Search Conference Schematic Framework (Real Searches May Vary Greatly)

the possible implications of changes in the social field, and as the Search progresses, they gradually narrow their focus to a set of specific ends and the means to achieve their future as an adaptive system that influences its surrounding environments.

The SC is a community-building event, not a small group event. Any small group work must be integrated in large group plenary sessions to become community property. Integration includes the process of rationalizing conflict so that the common ground is crystal clear.

COST JUSTIFICATION

A cash flow analysis is usually impossible and not recommended as they are suitable for evaluating resources to be applied to a particular problem, but a Search is *not* a problem-solving event. It can, however, get you a long-term future to which the people in your system are committed. How much is this worth? What will be the cost of letting your system drift in an unpredictable environment?

A discussion about this subject usually entails some of the following:

- The presenting symptoms

- What the system needs in terms of a strategic perspective

- Discussion about what's currently missing that the Search Conference could provide and what the Search Conference involves

- Details of the benefits, and what it's like to conduct participative strategic planning instead of relying on a few individuals who currently develop strategic plans and impose them

- A critical evaluation of whether or not a Search Conference is the appropriate method

Table of Uses

Specific examples of Search Conference use include:

Setting	Brief Description	Project Length	Number of Participants
Software developer	Develop strategic and tactical action plans for a strategic business to penetrate selected market niches	2.5 days for SC, 6-month implementation of plans	24
Telecommunications company	Develop common strategic and tactical direction for two newly merged, dissimilar departments	2.5 days for SC, 10-month implementation of plans	35
U.S. government agency	Sustain community development after regional loss of a $200 million tax base	2.5 days for SC, 14-month implementation of plans	28

Setting	Brief Description	Project Length	Number of Participants
Colorado mountain community	Search for common ground and develop plans for diverse regional interests including education, gambling, commercial zoning, farming, and recreation	2.5 days for SC, 1-year implementation of plans	32
Pharmaceutical company	Increase patient supply of life-saving drug by increasing interdepartmental collaboration between production and quality departments	2.5 days for SC, 5-month implementation of plans	34

Getting Started

FUNDAMENTALS TO CONSIDER

It's important to start this section by saying that conducting an SC does *not* necessarily result in a transformational path of upending change for the entire organization. It does, however, represent a fundamental change in the way that most systems do strategic planning. For systemic structural change, please refer to the chapter on Participative Design Workshops (PDWs). Often, PDWs are used after SCs to effect such change.

A number of things need to occur before an SC. A good checklist of essential pre-SC activities would include:

- Decide exactly what the system or potential system is
- Elaborate a purpose statement if required
- Determine what each participant needs to know before attending
- Do research to acquire this information if it is not available
- Determine who needs to be involved and develop an invitation list
- Educate people about the conference, its purpose, content, and method
- Design the Search
- Do logistics and schedule the conference facilities.

Strategic planning Searches for organizations usually consist of senior management, those who get paid to take responsibility for the health and direction of the organization. Other participative events or unique designs (see chapter 22, "Open Systems Theory Evolutions") may be required before and after the organizational Search. For other Searches, we recommend use of the

Community Reference System, a nonbiased procedure through which systems choose their own participants. It ensures that all required knowledge of the system is in the room.

The one overriding *guiding principle* is that the Search Conference is an opportunity for people to start taking more control over their affairs and their destiny. Every aspect of theory and practice is geared to this end.

Roles, Responsibilities, and Relationships

Different types of Searches may or may not have sponsors and/or a planning group, and their roles and responsibilities will vary depending on its nature and purpose. Specific roles and responsibilities that are typically associated with the facilitator(s)—who are called SC manager(s)—and participants appear in table 1, below. We purposely avoid the word "facilitator" and instead use the term "manager." There are two good reasons for this. Some, not all, facilitators are wedded to traditional roles. We make a clear distinction between these sets of "traditional" facilitator behaviors and what an SC manager needs to do.

First, SC managers do not act as helpers or counselors, which imply that they become involved in the content or work of the conference. The underlying assumption is that the participants are dependable adults who are capable and willing to take responsibility for their future. There is, therefore, a strict division of labor where the participants do the work and the SC manager ensures that the participants have the very best learning environment and process within which to do that work.

Second, we don't want participants to think of the SC manager as a traditional facilitator. This can encourage dependency. It is always useful to check expectations at the beginning of the event.

	Specific Roles and Responsibilities		
	Before the Search	**During the Search**	**After the Search**
SC Sponsor (may not be applicable)	• Assess appropriateness of an SC as planning mechanism • Announce and demonstrate to the organization (system) importance of SC • Agree that neither the sponsor, or any other group within the organization, will unilaterally overturn or discard the results of an SC	• Refrain from using positional authority to dominate discussions and decisions • Provide input as necessary in areas in which participants have minimal "big picture" knowledge which the sponsor, by virtue of its position, may hold	• Ensure time for participants to work on action items from the SC • Check that planning groups are holding each other accountable for executing the agreed-upon post-SC action steps • Demonstrate leadership in the new paradigm of strategic planning and learning

	Specific Roles and Responsibilities		
	Before the Search	**During the Search**	**After the Search**
SC Manager	Work with person(s) in the system to think through all aspects of purpose, preplanning, and design, for example: • Development of participant list • Need for participative meetings • Design the series of participative meetings • The planning horizon • Any research needs • Education of participants and others about purpose and method • Draft design • Appropriate logistics	Manage all aspects of the learning environment and process, for example: • Juggle time and tasks • Provide crystal clear, simple task instructions • Determine small group composition • Use rationalization of conflict process during integration • Watch for and prevent negative group dynamics • Design "on the run" where required	• None
SC Participants	• No roles, participants not yet identified at this stage, except perhaps person(s) with whom SC manager is liaising, below	• Provide content expertise • Learn about the environment and system • Plan the future of the system to influence the environment	• Follow-up on commitments made in the SC, that is, implement the plans
SC Planning Group	• Assess appropriateness of an SC as planning method • Educate themselves and others about the importance of the SC for their situation • Do Community Reference System if required • Negotiate all agreements relevant to successful work and implementation	• May or may not be participants	• They assume the roles assigned to participants (shown above)

Table 1. Roles and Responsibilities

Search Conference

SHIFTS IN ORGANIZATIONAL POWER AND AUTHORITY

The SC is not designed to shift power and authority. *During* the event, participants operate in a peer-to-peer mode, which means that no one has a "one-up" position—"see no stripes, wear no stripes."[1]

After a Search, the action plan groups should maintain their democratic structure, which means no committees or project teams with a manager (because there would be two levels of management). Therefore, these groups represent an informal change if the organization has a bureaucratic structure, but if it already has a democratic structure, it would represent no structural change.

Conditions for Success

WHEN TO USE THIS APPROACH

The following conditions are necessary for a successful SC:

- The community (of whatever type) or management has demonstrated that the SC is important

- Pre-SC work is comprehensive and thoughtful—an SC is only as good as its planning

- All essential knowledge about the system is in the room to provide the pieces of the strategic planning puzzle

- Participants are in the system and know they are responsible for implementing the action plans

- SC managers know their theory and the principles of good practice

- During and after the SC, there is a democratic structure in place to implement the action plans.

WHY IT WORKS

This method works because:

- it is based on a unique combination of solid concepts within an internally consistent framework (see the "Critical Underlying Theory and Research Base" section of this chapter), and

- it has been developed over 45 years.

DON'T USE THIS METHOD IF . . .

- The conditions for success listed above are not present.

- The purpose is to find a means to an end (problem solving), not creating the ends themselves (puzzle solving). That is, if the problem is something like, "Which technology will most increase productivity?" don't use the Search. If the purpose is genuinely open-ended and something like, "What business should we be in?" then it is appropriate.

- Your organization already has a set of strategic goals and your people are already committed to monitoring and understand external change. In such a case, go directly to a Participative Design Workshop (see chapter 43).

COMMON MISTAKES

Well-run SCs stick to the principles. Table 2 shows the three general categories of mistakes:

General Category	Mistake	Example
Improper Use	• An SC is used for problem solving or decision making • Senior management wishes to create buy-in for an unpopular cause	• The firm wants to decide where to locate a new plant • The CEO wishes to convince people that downsizing is necessary. This assembly of people might give the false appearance of a collaborative decision by all.
Inadequate Participant List	• All the knowledge of the system is not present in the SC • Some participants (called "stakeholders") cannot be responsible for implementing action plans • Outside experts are invited to kick off or participate in the SC.	• Knowledge of R&D is not present when the firm's future depends on technological innovation • Customers are invited to an organizational SC • Management guru Peter Drucker is invited in to talk about the future of knowledge work at the start of an SC (better to have him give his views before the SC begins)
SC Follow-up	• There is lack of education and agreement beforehand about what will be involved • There is a failure to educate about genotypical organizational design principles and/or to put modified PDW at end of Search	• Groups are not given time for implementation and they continually postpone their follow-up actions. • A community sets up committees to implement action plans.

Table 2. Common Mistakes

Critical Underlying Theory and Research Base

The SC has a comprehensive theoretical base. Table 3 lists the key ones and their use.

Theorist/Researcher(s)	Key Theory Elements	Use in Search Conference
Fred Emery and Eric Trist	Open systems theory (figure 1) and original SC were used to merge two giants in the aircraft industry.	SC is the translation of the open system into content and process.
Fred Emery	• Genotypical organizational design principles • Set of human ideals and ideal seeking	The organizational structure of the SC is based on the second design principle, that is, responsibility for outcome and implementation belongs to participants. Creates conditions for ideal seeking, productive work, high-quality products, and commitment to these.
Fritz Heider, James J. Gibson, and Fred Emery	• Ecological Learning—the ability to directly extract meaningful knowledge from the world around us.	This process is used throughout the SCs so they do not require literacy or education. It builds confidence in perceptions, experience, self, and others.
Fritz Heider, Theodore M. Newcomb, and Solomon Asch	• The $\frac{A-B}{\backslash X/}$ model of influence and change and the conditions for effective communication within it.	SCs bring those (A+B) who share a purpose or mutual concern (X) together and includes all of the conditions for most probable success.
Wilfred Bion	• Outlined the dysfunctional assumptions that groups can make and the creative working mode (W)	SC is designed and managed for (W); there is no emergence of these assumptions such as to fight, passively resist, or be irresponsible.
Philip Selznick	• Distinctive (unique) competence	Used in 1959 as the basis of current system analysis. It is sometimes used today, but is often replaced by more comprehensive analyses.

Theorist/Researcher(s)	Key Theory Elements	Use in Search Conference
Fred Emery	• Rationalization of conflict and search for common ground—stage 1 ("recentering the conflict") and stage 2 (separating agreements from disagreements).	We begin outside the focus of any probable disagreement (stage 1). Any disagreements are acknowledged, thoroughly discussed, and if real, are coolly put on a "disagreed list" (stage 2). We then work on the now precisely defined common ground. There are always more than enough common goals to continue collaborative work.
Sylvan S. Tomkins	• The primacy of the emotions in human motivation and behavior.	Conditions for energizing feelings of excitement and joy are built into SC.
Fred Emery and Merrelyn Emery	• As above, plus years of research and development.	With dedicated others, these researchers brought open systems to a high level of reliability.

Table 3. Theoretical Basis

Sustaining the Results

The conditions for sustainability are built in if the two-stage model of SC plus modified PDWs is followed (see chapter 43). When people work in structures where they are responsible for coordination and control and the other elements are integrated, they want to make it happen.

IMPACT ON ORGANIZATION'S CULTURAL ASSUMPTIONS

Culture is normally defined as the systems of assumptions and behavioral conventions that govern the lives of those who see themselves as part of a particular group. It is a product of people *and* environment, and people behave differently when they are in differently structured environments. This is why many express surprise when people do not behave as expected in Searches. They cooperate and work together rather than competing or dominating. They have more energy and motivation. If the conditions are sustained over time, these "new" behaviors become the accepted pattern.

Burning Questions

Organization Question: Why would our organization want to assemble 25 to 35 people to participate in a planning process? There are probably only about three to four people who really know the business; why shouldn't they just do it?

Answer: When the larger group of people get together for planning purposes, several things happen that don't necessarily happen when three people get together:

- Participants realize that there is more knowledge of the business spread through the organization than assumed, and this diversity of knowledge makes discussions about the future possibilities much richer

- Participants begin to understand each other's assumptions and perspectives

- The capacity for strategic thinking is disseminated beyond just a handful of people

- People working together in the SC increases the coherence of the organization into the future

- There is energy for implementation of the action plans because there is joint ownership of the plans that the participants developed

- This energy makes dissemination of the strategy content quicker and easier

Community Question: Our urban planning council met last month. They determined what needs to happen for the community over the next eight years, so is there really a need for a Search Conference?

Answer: A Search Conference can bring a community together and provide the spark for the development of additional issues, as well as the energy to implement the plans they develop for these issues. It can bring the people and their council closer together.

Some Final Comments

Table 4 summarizes what is distinctive about SC to illustrate more clearly what an SC is and what it is not. The combination of these characteristics is the source of the high-leverage potential for an SC.

Search Conference

In a Search we . . .	Because our research and experience have shown that . . .
assume that participants/clients are responsible adult human beings who want to learn and create their own futures. Managers do not facilitate groups or intervene in the content. Participants learn how to be self-managing, active, adaptive planners.	the relationship of SC manager and participants needs to be "adult to adult" rather than "parent to child" so that participants are active planners of their futures rather than dependents.
expect that when people are working on a task of mutual concern, some disagreements will occur. We use the rationalization of conflict.	when people do task-oriented work about shared purposes, they can acknowledge differences and work toward outcomes based on common ground.
discuss any conflict, and sort it into that which is really agreed and disagreed.	a few serious disagreements do not prevent people working together.
structure the event on the second design principle for ideal-seeking, positive emotions, energy, and motivation.	the organizational design principles have very powerful effects on human behavior.
seek to develop a strategic plan and set of actions that the entire group owns and implements. All group work is integrated and becomes community property.	precisely agreed common ground is essential for commitment to strategic direction and wise use of scarce resources.
spend roughly one-third of the time on action planning.	workable action plans must be carefully coordinated with goals.
use a coherent and internally consistent body of theory.	different approaches do not always mix, producing confusion and frustration.
focus on the extended social environment first and most importantly, as to ignore it can leave the system vulnerable to value shifts in such things as markets or use of technologies.	the external environment is more powerful than any system.
design in the conditions for effective communication and manage accordingly.	totally open, public dialogue and acknowledgement that we are all human and live in the same world are critical to developing trust and a realistic, workable plan; lots of "aha's" happen under these conditions.
elicit ideals as the basis for a most desirable future. Integration of environmental and internal constraints ensures this future is also realistic. We do not use projections from the past, as this can miss major changes that are just around the corner.	the ideals unite and motivate people. Ideals override value differences.

Table 4. Summary of Differences from Other Methods

Search Conference

In a Search we . . .	Because our research and experience have shown that . . .
are focused first on most desirable futures that emerge from puzzle solving, not problem solving	our unpredictable environment demands new ideas. People are frustrated with trying to solve yesterday's problems.
begin and finish with total task orientation. We do not use "ice breakers."	when people come together around purposes of mutual concern, they don't want time-wasting activities.
ensure that each plan encompasses the individuality of the system and its people.	people have no commitment to plans in which they cannot recognize themselves.

Table 4. Continued

About the Authors

Merrelyn Emery (me9@grapevine.net.au) has been developing open systems theory (OST) methods for more than 35 years, many of them spent working with Fred Emery. She holds a first-class honors degree in psychology and a Ph.D. in marketing. She has worked with innumerable communities and organizations in the public, private, and volunteer sectors. She continues to teach the state of the art of open systems theory around the world.

Tom Devane (tomd@tomdevane.com) helps organizations and communities thrive in their respective environments. His diverse background in strategy, Six Sigma, technology, organizational development, community planning, and leadership effectiveness provides for dramatic, sustainable improvement. With B.S. and M.S. degrees in finance, Big Six consulting, and industry leadership experience, he founded his own firm in 1988. Clients include Microsoft, Hewlett-Packard, Johnson & Johnson, General Electric, the U.S. Forest Service, AT&T, Honeywell, and the Republic of South Africa.

Where to Go for More Information

REFERENCES

Bradshaw, C., J. Roberts, and S. Cheuy. "The Search Conference: A Participative Planning Method That Builds Widespread Collaboration." In *The Collaborative Work Systems Fieldbook: Strategies, Tools, and Techniques,* edited by M. M. Beyerlein, C. McGee, G. D. Klein, J. E. Nemiro, and L. Broedling, 43–56. San Francisco: Pfeiffer, 2002.

Cabana, S. "Participative Design Works, Partially Doesn't." *Journal for Quality and Participation* 18, no. 1 (1995).

Cabana, S., F. Emery, and M. Emery. "The Search for Effective Strategic Planning Is Over." *Journal for Quality and Participation* 18, no. 4 (1995): 10–19.

de Guerre, D. W. "Action Research as Process: The Two Stage Model for Active Adaptation." *Ecclectica* 4 (2002), http://www.ecclectica.ca/issues/2002/4/.

_____. "Variations on the Participative Design Workshop." In *The Collaborative Work Systems Fieldbook: Strategies, Tools, and Techniques,* edited by M. M. Beyerlein, G. Klein, and L. Broedling, 275–286. San Francisco: John Wiley & Sons, 2002.

Emery, F. "Participative Design: Effective, Flexible and Successful, Now!" *Journal for Quality and Participation* (January/February 1995).

Emery, F., and M. Emery. "The Participative Design Workshop." In *The Social Engagement of Social Science: A Tavistock Anthology: The Socio-technical Perspective*, Vol. II, edited by E. Trist and H. Murray, 599–613. Philadelphia: University of Pennsylvania Press, 1993.

Emery, Merrelyn. "The Evolution of Open Systems to the 2 Stage Model." In *Work Teams: Past, Present and Future*, edited by M. M. Beyerlein, 85–103. Amsterdam: Kluwer Academic Publishers, 2000.

_____. "The Power of Community Search Conferences." *Journal for Quality and Participation* 18, no. 7 (1995): 70–79.

_____. *Searching: The Theory and Practice of Making Cultural Change*. Philadelphia: John Benjamins, 1999.

_____, ed. *Participative Design for Participative Democracy*. Canberra, Australia: ANU/CCE, 1993.

Emery, M., and R. Purser. *The Search Conference: A Powerful Method for Planning Organizational Change and Community Action*. San Francisco: Jossey Bass, 1996.

INFLUENTIAL SOURCES

de Guerre, D. W. "The Co-Determination of Cultural Change Over Time." *Systemic Practice and Action Research* 13, no. 5 (2000): 645–663.

_____. "Democratic Social Engagement." *Innovation Journal* 10, no. 1 (2005).

de Guerre, D. W., and H. Hornstein. "Active Adaptation of Municipal Governance: An Action Research Report." *Innovation Journal* 9, no. 1 (2004).

de Guerre, D. W., and M. M. Taylor. "Participative Design and Executive Coaching." *International Journal of Knowledge, Culture and Change Management* 4 (2005): 513–521.

Emery, Merrelyn. *The Future of Schools: How Communities and Staff Can Transform Their School Districts*. Lanham, MD: Rowman & Littlefield Education; Toronto: Oxford University Press, in press 2006.

_____. "The Search Conference: Design and Management with a Solution to the 'Pairing' Puzzle." In *The Social Engagement of Social Science: A Tavistock Anthology: The Socio-Ecological Perspective*, Vol. III, edited by E. Trist, F. Emery, and H. Murray. Philadelphia: University of Pennsylvania Press, 1997.

————. "The Six Criteria for Intrinsic Motivation in Education Systems: Partial Democratization of a University Experience, Partial Success." In *Educational Futures: Shifting Paradigm of Universities and Education*, 309–334. Istanbul: Sabanci University, 2000.

Paton, John, and M. Emery. "Community Planning in the Torres Strait." *Journal of Quality and Participation* 19, no. 5 (1996): 26–35.

Purser, R. E., and S. Cabana. *The Self Managing Organization: How Leading Companies Are Transforming the Work of Teams for Real Impact.* New York: The Free Press, 1998.

Trist, E., and H. Murray, eds. *The Social Engagement of Social Science: A Tavistock Anthology: The Socio-Technical Perspective*, Vol. II. Philadelphia: University of Pennsylvania Press, 1993.

ORGANIZATIONS

Canadian Institute for Research and Education in Human Systems—cirehs@sympatico.ca
> *For information about training courses and current projects.*

Centre for Human Relations and Community Studies, Concordia University, Montreal—centreh@vax2.concordia.ca
> *For information about training courses and current projects.*

Department of Applied Human Sciences, Concordia University, Montreal

Fred Emery Institute, Melbourne—contact AMERIN Pty. Ltd., www.amerin.com.au

The Modern Times Workplace—www.moderntimesworkplace.com

The Vaughan Consulting Group—www.vaughanconsulting.com/pdw.html

---

1. This admonition causes confusion for some senior managers. They ask, "There are some things that I know about the business that the other participants don't. Does that mean I need to remain quiet?" The answer is an emphatic "No!" There will always be a disparity in depth of knowledge and experience among participants. (This disparity, in fact, is one of the factors that actually makes SCs so successful as a planning process. We need diverse perspectives from the system to do robust action planning for the system.) The issue is when and how these senior management ideas are introduced. Leaders with positional authority should introduce their information at the appropriate times as other pieces of data for the group to consider—not as edicts from upper management. During the Search, the leaders need to discuss issues in democratic, instead of autocratic, mode.

GILBERT STEIL, JR., AND MAL WATLINGTON

Community Summits

The community stagnates without the impulse of the individual. The impulse dies away without the sympathy of the community.

—William James

Focusing Funding on Worthy Causes

Early in the new century, leadership at the United Way of Rhode Island (UWRI) became aware that their potential for positive community change had become diluted over time. Funding an ever-increasing number of worthy causes had reduced the allocation to each to a level that precluded major impact. Realizing this, they sought ways to focus their funding, while minimizing the political fallout expected from more selective resource allocation.

In 2003, UWRI decided to sponsor several Community Summits to decide community priorities for three focus areas: Solutions for Children, Youth, and Families; Helping People in Crisis; and Building Adult and Neighborhood Independence. Following each of the summits, participants were invited to join an Impact Group that continued the work of setting and assessing progress on community priorities.

In the fall of 2003, UWRI developed participant invitation lists for the summits, carefully balancing stakeholder participation representative of the focus area and geographic representation from all parts of the state of Rhode Island.

Two summits were held during the winter of 2004, with more than 300 participants braving a blizzard to show up for the first one. At their conclusion, participants identified and showed support for a short list of community priorities providing the foundation for UWRI Board funding consideration and the work of Impact Groups. Of the 700 summit participants, 300 became active in Impact Groups. Many were still active 21 months later.

In October 2005, UWRI held a celebration at the site of the summits, featuring news and successes from summits to Impact Groups to the first-ever open grant process. What began as a hopeful model for change was given life through the summits, and is now the accepted means for funding high-impact social change in Rhode Island.

Frequently Asked Questions

WHAT ARE COMMUNITY SUMMITS?

A Community Summit is a 15-hour planning meeting for a broad spectrum of stakeholders, defined by a focus issue, who come together to agree on a specific course of action. They are our intervention of choice when a vision for a desirable future is already in place (or latent) and the work that needs to be done is the targeted allocation of limited resources in the most effective way.

WHAT HAPPENS AT A TYPICAL COMMUNITY SUMMIT?

The picture below outlines a two-day Community Summit (figure 1). On Day 1, participants assemble in a large room and are seated at tables of eight, where they actively engage acknowledged experts on the focus issue, who help set the context for the meeting.

Photo by Pamela Murray.

Figure 1. The Community Summit Process

Once there is sufficient shared context, participants are divided into five or six smaller groups, which may have 64 to 72 participants. These groups are focused on a specific subdomain of the focus issue, for example, *violence and crime* as a subdomain of *building adult and neighborhood independence.*

Next, individual stakeholder groups—for example, *defense attorneys* in *violence and crime*—articulate their collective historical experience, assess the current state of their subdomain, and describe their wishes for the future. In broad communities (e.g., Rhode Island), this may be the first time that members of a stakeholder group have worked together. Their work is captured in a display, used in the next step.

Participants are regrouped into mixed tables. These "learning teams" inspect the work produced by each stakeholder group in turn, led by the learning team member representing the stakeholders who created the displays. Day 1 normally ends in the middle of this process.

On Day 2, participants return to their breakout rooms, complete the work of the learning teams, and collectively develop and post "well-formed" goals. New interest-based teams form around tables to flesh out the goals, develop action steps, and work toward agreement on which goals and actions will emerge from the room as final output.

Following goal selection, participants create posters describing the goals and action steps, and post these along with those from other rooms in a large gallery. All participants pass through the gallery and indicate their preferences. Their stated preferences become a starting point for focusing community resources on well-supported, high-impact projects and programs after the summit. The summit closes with a celebration, and an invitation to participate in the work to follow.

Many variations are possible, especially the tailoring of goal creation and action planning to the needs of the community or organization. When possible, we spread the Community Summit over three days, beginning with lunch on the first day and ending in the early afternoon of the third day.

What Must Exist to Make This a Viable Option?

Community Summits are designed for situations where the critical mass of participants is in the range of 130 to 2,000. They work well when the critical issues facing the community have been discussed in various forums, but real action has been slow in coming. They work well when there is an understanding that decisions must be made about how to invest limited resources, and people are ready for those decisions to be made. They require a client willing to trust the wisdom of the whole system that is assembled. It's important that participants understand that much work will need to be done following the decisions made at the summit.

How Much Does It Cost?

The cost varies considerably, but the key expenses are: food for participants; space rental; consulting fees for two lead consultants for planning, design, and training of other summit team members, and facilitation; materials; documentation (written, still photos, video); and publicity. United Way of Rhode Island held its Community Summits in a 1920s dance hall and made ample use of volunteers.

Table of Uses

Brief Description	Project Length	Activities	Number of Participants
Large Statewide Charity Organized a broad community to allocate funds and take specific action on 3 focus issues • Identified groups and individuals across the state who represented the communities defined by the issues • Affirmed latent visions of the future • Planned specific courses of action • Organized Impact Groups to allocate funds in an open process	6 months	• 2 board retreats • Collaborative summit design • Training of facilitation and logistics teams • 3 large group events • Impact group meetings—ongoing	• 20 people • 10 people • 25 people • 350 people • 200 people
Coalition of Diverse Advocacy Groups Found a path to concerted action in pursuit of a shared goal • Affirmed a latent vision held by all • Projected a probable future • Created multiple actions supported by resources available within the coalition • Made specific commitments to joint action	2 months	• Defined membership in the coalition • Event planning • Summit meeting	• 3 people • 2 people • 32 people

About the Authors

Gilbert Steil, Jr. (gilsteil@gilsteil.com), principal of Gil Steil Associates, is an organization and management consultant specializing in the development of strategies, plans, and designs through the engagement of whole systems and their key stakeholders.

Mal Watlington (malw@citysquareconsulting.com) is president of City Square Consulting, Inc., a firm specializing in human capital and business performance strategy, competitive analysis, and organizational change.

Where to Go for More Information

REFERENCE

Alban, B., and B. Bunker. "Special Issue on Large Group Interventions." *Journal of Applied Behavioral Science* 41, no. 1 (March 2005).

INFLUENTIAL SOURCE

Surowiecki, J. *The Wisdom of Crowds: Why the Many Are Smarter Than the Few and How Collective Wisdom Shapes Business, Economies, Societies, and Nations.* New York: Doubleday, 2004.

ORGANIZATION

Community Summits—www.gilsteil.com/communitysummits

GILBERT STEIL, JR., AND MICHELE GIBBONS-CARR

Large Group Scenario Planning

The revolutionary idea that defines the boundary between modern times and the past is the mastery of risk: the notion that the future is more than a whim of the gods and that men and women are not passive before nature.

—Peter L. Bernstein

Real-Life Story

Keeping air traffic moving efficiently while preventing midair collisions is a lot more vital and imperative than deciding on computer software standards for the next decade. So it came as no surprise in February 2003 that the Chief Information Office (CIO) of a large aviation administration was falling behind on its commitments to an "Enterprise Architecture." Making things more difficult was the fact that all of the operational information technology departments—the groups that would implement any new strategy—lived within fairly autonomous divisions of the agency. Their autonomy was based on some excellent reasons: the critical real-time nature of controlling national airspace, heightened security needs in an era of increasing terrorism, and the rising sophistication of cyber attacks. At the same time, the agency was about to face the implications of an Electronic Government Initiative, begun at the highest level of government, to increase productive use of electronic technology while simplifying the applications that already existed.

The main tool available to the CIO was the CIO Council, a cross-functional team that dealt with standards and strategies for the management of technology for the future. If there was to be change, every member of the CIO Council needed to be in enthusiastic agreement.

A two-day off-site meeting was planned for March 2003. Success would entail: a clear understanding of how the agency's enterprise architecture would serve its divisions; the identification of specific areas of collaboration across divisions; and a set of principles to be employed in those collaborations.

The ability to agree was being limited by considerable uncertainty in the environment in which the agency had to operate (not within the agency itself). Would the demands for airspace continue to climb or would terrorism and the use of the Internet for business meetings lead to a decline? Would higher levels of government impose their own architecture on the agency? Would the needed platforms and other technology exist in time?

The heart of Large Group Scenario Planning is the characterization of four plausible future worlds *outside* the client system for which there is supportive data in current trends, and which are starkly different from each other. The CIO Council meeting began with a brainstormed list of trends in the government outside the agency, and in the world outside the government. Next, the resulting trends were divided into those that could be predicted and those that could not. The council then selected the two unpredictable trends that were the most important, which in traditional scenario planning are called the *critical uncertainties.*

One of the two critical uncertainties chosen was airspace demands, which could drop as larger aircraft came available and jet fuel price climbed, or which could rise dramatically as small jets became cheaper and as the economy supported a resurgence in single-engine pleasure aircraft. The other big uncertainty had to do with IT reform at the broader government level. Would the government impose new standards on all agencies in the short-term future? Or would the Electronic Government Initiative focus first on application simplification and issues with little impact on the agency's enterprise architecture?

A matrix of these two critical uncertainties led to four possible future worlds:

1. *Pressure and Conflict:* If the combination of strong requirements for the Electronic Government Initiative and high airspace demands occurred simultaneously.

2. *President's Agenda:* if the airspace demands dropped in the context of strong requirements for the Electronic Government Initiative.

3. *Mission Focus:* If Electronic Government was focused elsewhere while airspace demand soared.

4. *Agency Opportunity:* If neither airspace demand nor strong requirements to comply with Electronic Government became a reality in the five years ahead.

The CIO Council went on to grapple with probable and desirable futures for the agency, in the context of the four possible worlds. And then in that shared understanding, they began their work on areas of collaboration. The planners were unstuck, and the next year was characterized by successful collaborative work across the agency.

Frequently Asked Questions

How Does Large Group Scenario Planning Differ from (Traditional) Scenario Planning?

The first generation of large group interventions, based on developments in social psychology between 1946 and 1990, changed forever how we think about participation in decision making within our organizations and communities. With these new tools, we discovered how to structure inclusive and effective interventions that utilize the wisdom of 35 to hundreds of people representing whole systems meeting face-to-face. Scenario Planning (chapter 34, "Scenario Thinking") also dates from the mid–twentieth century and is a unique and valuable tool for thinking about the future. Large Group Scenario Planning brings the rich tool of traditional scenario planning into the family of social psychology–based interventions, where whole systems meeting in real time can use scenarios to enhance their planning for the future.

WHAT VALUE DOES SCENARIO PLANNING ADD TO LARGE GROUP INTERVENTIONS?

The use of Scenario Planning in large group interventions adds the discipline of careful thinking about the world in which the client organization or community will live. It precludes the risky assumption that the future will be an extrapolation of the past and present. The goal is not to create an accurate picture of tomorrow, but to challenge assumptions and expand perspectives so that better decisions about the future can be made in the present. The power of scenarios is that they take competing ideas—a variety of perspectives and interests that may clash—and considers them in a way that makes everyone face up to those aspects of future possibilities to which they may have to respond (see figure 1).

Activity Flow for Large Group Scenario Planning
(32 - 256 participants)

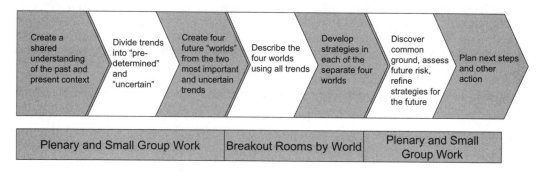

Figure 1. LGSP Activity Flow

Large Group Scenario Planning (LGSP) provides an answer to the question: How should an organization or community plan long-term strategy in the face of significant uncertainty about the future of the world in which that organization or community must live?

LGSP is based on the work of traditional scenario planners Schwarz, Ogilvy, Ringland, Schoemaker, and van der Heijden, who pioneered the development of several different but plausible views of the future as a way of setting direction when the character of the future environment is in doubt. LGSP compensates for the natural tendency of an organization or community to think of the future as an extrapolation of the present and the past, which in uncertain times can be a serious blunder. See chapter 34 for a fuller discussion of traditional scenario planning.

Table of Uses

Typical Setting	Brief Description	Project Length	Number of Participants
Government Agency	• Critical uncertainties identified • Strategic planning accomplished in face of uncertainty	4 months	Planning—6 LGSP session—40
Graduate School of a Major University	• Critical uncertainties identified • Strategic planning accomplished in face of uncertainty	6 months	Planning—20 LGSP session—128

About the Authors

Gilbert Steil, Jr. (gilsteil@gilsteil.com), principal of Gil Steil Associates, is an organization and management consultant specializing in the development of strategies, plans, and designs through the engagement of whole systems and their key stakeholders. Gil holds degrees in mathematics from Case Institute of Technology and in organization development from The American University.

Michele Gibbons-Carr, Ph.D. (phnxmgc@aol.com), is an organization consultant specializing in the area of organizational change and transformation, strategic planning, and use of large group interventions to initiate vision-driven change. Michele holds degrees in psychology from the Pennsylvania State University and in clinical psychology from Boston University, where she also studied organization development.

Where to Go for More Information

REFERENCES

Schwartz, P. *Art of the Long View.* New York: Doubleday, 1991.

Steil, Gilbert, and Michele Gibbons-Carr. "Large Group Scenario Planning." *Journal of Applied Behavioral Science* 41, no. 1 (March 2005).

INFLUENTIAL SOURCES

Fahey, L., and R. Randall. *Learning from the Future,* New York: Wiley, 1998.

Schoemaker, P. *Profiting from Uncertainty.* New York: Free Press, 2002.

ORGANIZATION

Gil Steil Associates—www.gilsteil.com

JACKIE STAVROS, DAVID COOPERRIDER, AND D. LYNN KELLEY

SOAR
A New Approach to Strategic Planning

With our dreams and aspirations we find our opportunities!
—Sue Ebaugh

Real-Life Story

Faced with mounting challenges for profitability as a Tier 1 automotive supplier, a program manager used SOAR™ to create a strategic planning process. He recalls:

> Orbseal Technology Center relocated to Michigan to form a closer working relationship with customers. I was confident SOAR would create a strategy to drive growth.
>
> I wanted to do an inquiry into our values and strengths to discover what we do best and to imagine the best possible future by creating a guiding vision statement. We needed a documented direction and purpose to allow for a deeper understanding of our core strengths and to design strategic initiatives for growth. We didn't need to identify weaknesses—we knew these. We needed to be innovative and inspire others to action—to SOAR!

This decision was unanimously supported by his team. The VP traveled from headquarters to be part of this strategic planning event. This approach made the VP curious about how the three divisions would work together.

PHASE ONE: INQUIRY

During this phase, the Orbseal team identified four areas to explore: adaptive processes and people, dedicated employees, positive environment, and strong product core.

Phase Two: Imagine

They created the following:

- *Values:* dedication, flexibility, creativity, team spirit, and continuous communications
- *Vision:* To be a diverse and global leader providing best-in-class engineering; noise, vibration, and harshness (NVH); sealant; and adhesive solutions with unsurpassed sales and service.

Phase Three: Innovate

Strengths and opportunities were developed into meaningful aspirations. The team engaged in dialogue about initiatives, markets, strategies, structure, and processes. Two strategic statements were created:

- We are hardworking, flexible employees who design, sell, and service cost-effective and innovative engineering, NVH, and sealant solutions that are value added to our original equipment manufacturers (OEMs).
- We provide a safe, positive environment conducive to creativity that attracts and retains best employees.

These became part of the center's strategy—the "how"—to achieve measurable results. Then, the team produced a tactical plan with action-oriented activities.

Phase Four: Inspired

The team identified its aspirations to drive them to results. This phase encompassed shared dialogue on the best way to implement and sustain a collective sense of purpose—mission statement and attainment.

The VP left with an objective to complete the SOAR approach with the 400 employees at the corporate office. He stated:

> The process went beyond my expectations because three divisions became boundaryless and came together to co-create the future. Everyone was heard and everyone has a stake. Now we have a strategic action plan to best move forward.

A team member shared his feelings about SOAR:

> I've been with Orbseal for one year and this allowed me to openly share what I believe we can be! It was nice to hear that others have similar aspirations. I feel connected to this team.

Today, a continuous improvement mind-set now drives the culture at Orbseal.

The Basics

WHAT IS SOAR?

SOAR is an innovative, strength-based approach to strategic planning and invites the whole system (stakeholders) into the process. This approach integrates Appreciative Inquiry (AI) with a strategic planning framework to create a transformational process that inspires organizations to SOAR.

The SOAR framework goes beyond the original AI 4-D model[1] to link the concepts (figure 1). This framework, using AI principles, transforms the traditional strategic planning SWOT model (Strengths, Weaknesses, Opportunities, and Threats) into SOAR and accelerates the strategic planning efforts by focusing directly on those elements that will give life energy to the organization's future. The AI Principle of Relational Awareness builds dynamic and sustainable relationships among stakeholders.[2]

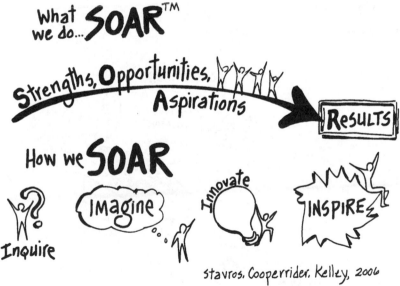

Illustration by Nancy Margulies

Figure 1. SOAR: What We Do and How We Do It

WHEN AND WHERE IS SOAR USED?

SOAR can be used whenever the strategic planning process is done to complete environmental scanning; revisit or create organizational values, vision, and mission; formulate strategy, strategic plans, and tactical plans; and bring about transformational change. This framework has been used in for-profit and nonprofit settings: education, manufacturing, service, health care, automotive, pharmaceutical, and banking at the corporate and strategic business unit level. The first clients to use SOAR in their strategic planning efforts were Roadway, Tendercare, Textron Fastening Systems, Positive Change Corps, Utah Education Association, and CASE University.

What Are the Outcomes?

SOAR has been used in four-hour to three-day planning sessions. Participants learn to:

- identify the positive core of the organization (strengths and opportunities)
- obtain clarity of values, vision, and mission to align with initiatives, strategies, and action plans
- plan, design, and facilitate a whole-system strategic planning session
- identify measurements that drive performance

Participants have achieved improved results in:

- productivity and sales
- communications—continuous and open

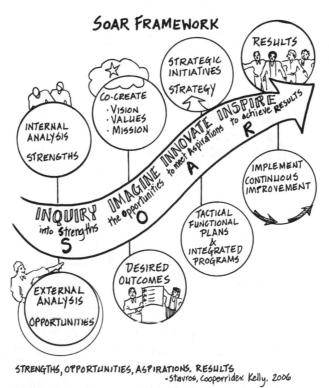

Illustration by Nancy Margulies

Figure 2. Summarization of SOAR

- morale and attrition rates

- goal attainment

How Does SOAR Work?

To achieve a strategic impact, this approach integrates AI, Dialogue, and the whole systems approach with a framework that builds upon an organization's positive core to SOAR. By focusing on *Strengths* and *Opportunities*, organizations can reach their *Aspirations* (desired outcomes) with measurable *Results* by:

1. *Inquiring* into strength and opportunities;

2. *Imagining* the best pathway to sustainable growth;

3. *Innovating* to create the initiatives, strategies, structure, systems, and plans; and

4. *Inspiring* action-oriented activities that achieve results (figure 2).

Table of Uses

Setting	Project Length	Participants/Time
SOAR Planning Sessions Corporate/department level • Strategic Inquiry • Imagine the Future • Innovate Strategy, Structure and Plans • Inspire to Implement Plan	2–4 times/year Annual Complete to-one or team interviews	10–400 people 2–3 days • 2–4 hours • 2–4 hours • 2–4 hours • 1–2 days
Higher Education Completed environmental scan Identify vision, mission, and initiatives for campuswide strategic plan	1-day kickoff launched	125 people 4 hours
Manufacturer—completed Balanced Scorecard to align with strategic initiatives	Yearly—review quarterly	40 people 1.5 days
Statewide Education System—stakeholders created strategic and tactical plan with accountability systems	Ongoing—Meet one to three times/year	40–200 people from 2 to 2.5 days
Health Care—facility strategic renewal plan	18 months	Core Team—10 people; 76 interviews in 6 weeks

About the Authors

Jackie Stavros (jstavros@comcast.net) is professor at Lawrence Technological University. She coauthored *Dynamic Relationships: Unleashing the Power of Appreciative Inquiry in Daily Living* and *Appreciative Inquiry Handbook*. Her clients include: ERIM International, Tendercare, General Motors, and Girl Scouts USA.

David Cooperrider (dlc6@po.cwru.edu) is professor and director for Business as Agent World Benefit (BAWB) at CASE University. He coauthored *Advances in Appreciative Inquiry: Constructive Discourse in Human Organizations* and *Appreciative Inquiry Handbook*. His clients include: Roadway, Green Mountain Coffee Roasters, United Nations, and GTE.

D. Lynn Kelley (lkelley@textron.com) is responsible for enterprise-wide global programming in Six Sigma and Integrated Supply Chain at Textron University.

Where to Go for More Information

REFERENCES

Stavros, J., D. Cooperrider, and L. Kelley. "Strategic Inquiry with Appreciative Intent: Inspiration to SOAR!" *AI Practitioner: AI and Strategy* (November 2003).

Sutherland, J., and J. Stavros. "The Heart of Appreciative Strategy." *AI Practitioner: AI and Strategy* (November 2003).

INFLUENTIAL SOURCES

Cooperrider, D., D. Whitney, and J. Stavros. *Appreciative Inquiry Handbook*. Bedford Heights, OH, and San Francisco: Lakeshore Communications and Berrett-Koehler Communications, 2003.

Stavros, J., and C. Torres. *Dynamic Relationships Unleashing the Power of Appreciative Inquiry in Daily Living*. Lima, OH: Fairway Press, 2005.

ORGANIZATION

Dynamic Relationships—www.dynamic-relationships.com

---

1. The model is Discovery, Dream, Design, and Destiny. Visit AI Commons: http://ai.cwru.edu.

2. This principle calls us to be reflective and actively engaged to move a system forward in a positive direction. For more information, visit: www.dynamic-relationships.com.

39

CHRIS SODERQUIST

Strategic Forum

Tell me, I forget.
Show me, I remember.
Involve me, I understand.

—Ancient Chinese proverb

Real-Life Story

In March 2005, a nationally known health-care provider wished to develop a long-term strategy for delivering dialysis services. The dialysis system is notoriously hard to manage due to a wide variety of factors: high expenses (both operating and capital investments), technologically sophisticated processes requiring a variety of staff skills, burnout and rapid turnover of nursing staff, and patient scheduling conflicts. Also, dialysis is often the result of a progressive disease that saps the strength and morale of patients and staff. Further, Medicare regulations dictate a treatment regimen that medical professionals consider less than ideal—so to provide exceptional service usually takes the organization into the red. In addition, with the surge in adult onset diabetes that is expected to result from an increasingly aging and obese population, there is the potential for demand to overwhelm capacity in the near- to midterm.

Over the course of three months, an external consulting team interviewed the staff (physicians, nurses, and administrators) to identify the major issues (many mentioned above) and examine the historical trends, as well as projected future trends. Because it was clear the stakeholders held vastly different assumptions about the future, as well as what were optimal treatments, the consulting team suggested a Strategic Forum (computer simulation model) where physicians, nurses, and administrators were provided a practice field to:

1. Understand future population scenarios
2. Explore different treatment strategies

3. Observe implications of treatment strategies on population, staff, and expenses

4. Test the ability of process capability to facilitate the efficacy of strategies

During the Strategic Forum, participants were amazed to see a wide discrepancy in assumptions about future patient dynamics, as well as the wide variety of desired treatments. In particular, physicians were more likely to suggest innovative treatment strategies, while administrators and nursing staff—who understood the financial and staffing implications—saw a more tempered approach to migrating to innovative strategies. The resulting conversations brought the entire stakeholder group onto the "same page" regarding optimal treatments *and* how to systemically orchestrate a strategy to implement. The staff is now in an ongoing process of revising the computer simulation (and map shown in figure 1) to include insights generated from the forum—they are in a continuing process of learning regarding the dialysis system.

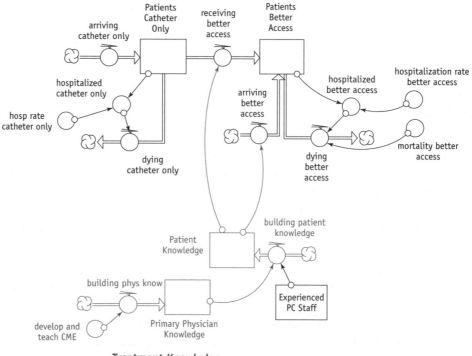

Figure 1. A Section of the Forum Map

The Basics: Answers to Frequently Asked Questions

WHEN IS A STRATEGIC FORUM APPROPRIATE?

Although it works well for a variety of strategic (even tactical) issues, it is especially suited for issues where the future is filled with uncertainty, where multiple scenarios are likely to occur, and where there is little data to understand how the current system works. In addition, it's ideal in organizations where there are contentious debates about multiple strategies because the highly experiential process (system mapping and computer simulation) helps to "cool off" the personality focus and get the group to concentrate on the issues.

How Does a Forum Work?

A forum works by helping the group apply a different paradigm to the development of their mental models of how the system works. This paradigm leads them to:

- Look at the issues as long-term (behavior over time) patterns rather than events
- Develop an operational mental model using a visual language that reduces ambiguities and forces rigorous thinking/testing
- Use computer simulation as a way to test the usefulness of the mental model

What Should I Know About Mapping and Simulation?

Mapping is used to synthesize the implicit mental models of stakeholders into an explicit visual representation. Simulation software translates those maps into something a computer can use to test out "what ifs" regarding the synthesized mental model. The mapping methodology used in a forum relies upon the more sophisticated (and operational) language of stocks and flows. This language better represents time delays, leading indicators, bottlenecks, and unintended consequences—increasing the likelihood of identifying appropriate levers and timing for pulling those levers—than the more commonly employed causal loop mapping methodology. It also enhances mental simulation of how the group believes the organization/system works.

How Do I Know What Should Be Included in the Forum Maps/Models?

All models (whether mental or those turned into computer maps/models) are developed using a particular lens of what we value—what we think is important to understand, or what performance we wish to develop or improve. Although organizations can build forum models focusing on the *performance measure du jour,* they would be well advised to use a systemic or integral framework for what to include. The Balanced Scorecard (chapter 50) framework (Financial, Customer, Business Processes, and Learning & Growth) provides an excellent and systemic frame of what to include—how to develop measures in each of those areas. Other frameworks worth mentioning include Triple Bottom Line frameworks or Ken Wilber's Four Quadrant framework.

If I Were Interested in Delivering a Forum, What Are the Steps I'd Need to Follow?

1. Identify the issue as something requiring a systemic understanding
2. Locate a competent system dynamics practitioner

3. Assemble a multidisciplinary team (internal and external) to understand the issues and how the system works

4. Develop simple maps and ask for rapid feedback across stakeholder groups to assess usefulness of map

5. Build and test the model(s) with a core team of stakeholders

6. Create learning objectives and learning environment for forum

7. Implement forum and generate list of next steps

8. Don't shelve the models/maps! Rather, use them in an ongoing process of updating the key assumptions in the models/maps, and hold annual forums to evaluate current applicability of model and strategy to the organization.

What's the Long-Term Impact of a Forum on the Organization?

Once an organization implements a forum, strategic discussions tend to become more in line with a systems-thinking paradigm. Leaders begin to ask: What are potential unintended consequences? Is there internal consistency with the strategic objectives? How will this unfold over time—is there some way to better orchestrate implementation? If we are achieving objectives, what are leading indicators that will help us assess this sooner?

Table of Uses

Typical Setting	Brief Description	Project Length	Key Events	Number of Participants
All types of organizations have used the Strategic Forum. Examples include: • health care • manufacturing • high-tech • nongovernmental organizations (NGOs) • defense • government (national and local)	Issues that have: • proven intractable historically • multiple stakeholders who must buy in to implement • several likely futures • complex interrelationships • an accelerating pace of change	2–6 months	Assessment and Interviews (1–4 weeks)	5–20
			Mapping and Modeling (2–8 weeks)	5
			Development of Forum Materials (2–4 weeks)	5
			Strategic Forum Event (1–2 days)	5–30
			Implementation (2–6 months)	The organization

About the Author

Chris Soderquist (chris.soderquist@pontifexconsulting.com), president of Pontifex Consulting, helps individuals, teams, and organizations in building capacity to develop strategic solutions to complex issues. With his extensive experience in Systems Thinking/System Dynamics, group facilitation, communication skill development, and statistical/process analysis, he integrates the "hard stuff" and the "soft stuff" for effective, actionable solutions. Representative clients include: Boeing, Dow Chemical, WW Grainger, Hewlett-Packard, Merck, MnDOT, NASA, Nextel, Northrop Grumman, Sustainability Institute, and the World Bank.

Where to Go for More Information

REFERENCES

Kaplan, R., and D. Norton. *The Strategy-Focused Organization.* Boston: Harvard Business School Press, 2001.

Richmond, Barry. "The Strategic Forum: Aligning Objectives, Strategy and Process." *System Dynamics Review* 13, no. 2 (1997).

Soderquist, C., and M. Shimada. *Operational Strategy Mapping: Learning and Executing at the Boeing Company.* Waltham, MA: Pegasus Communications, 2005.

INFLUENTIAL SOURCE

Wilber, Ken. *Introduction to Integral Theory and Practice: IOSBasic and the AQAL Map.* Boulder, CO: Integral Institute, 2003.

ORGANIZATION

Pontifex Consulting—www.pontifexconsulting.com

40

DAVID SIBBET

Strategic Visioning
Bringing Insight to Action

One of the more difficult lessons to learn is to recognize current reality as it now is, which often is different from what you think it is supposed to be or how you want it to be.

—Robert Fritz

Real-Life Story

The Save the Redwoods League (SRL) is a California-based organization committed to preserving some of the oldest—and tallest—organisms on the planet. SRL has a long and successful history of preserving old-growth redwoods since its founding in 1918. Although skillful in its efforts, the league had never developed a formal strategy, and external factors began to make the need more evident. The election of a new board president and appointment of a new executive director—combined with growing public misperception that its mission had largely been accomplished—led the league's directors to undertake a process to chart a course for the next five years. It was important to them that the process lead to a strong consensus among key stakeholders, resulting in a compelling vision linked to actionable strategies, and that the process be able to handle the complexity of the issues.

SRL chose a Strategic Visioning process, a highly visual method that uses large graphic templates to guide people through the different perspectives needed to do good strategy work. The league process involved three one-day sessions with key stakeholders over three months. League staff, board, and council members and other stakeholders participated. A key step was creating a graphic history of SRL, understandably important to everyone concerned. This was analyzed to better understand the guiding principles and processes that had served it best over the years. The Strategic Visioning process then took everyone through a graphic review of the current environment, a mapping of current strengths and weaknesses and opportunities at SRL, and some in-depth visioning about the future. This culminated in identifying specific initiatives and game plans.

The process incorporates many methods from traditional strategic planning, but uses large Graphic Guides (wall-sized templates) to capture and organize information. This allows everyone to visualize what they are saying, and to develop a panorama of charts that support taking a systems-level view. This was unexpectedly important for an organization with many members formally trained in ecosystems thinking and management. The imagery also supported more robust visioning in the projective parts of the process.

The process brought the group to agreement on three key initiatives, and an overall game plan (figure 1).

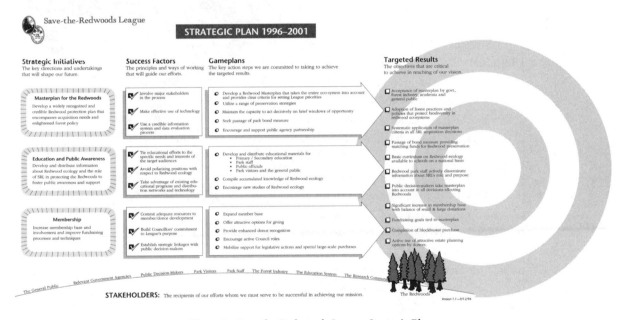

Figure 1. Save the Redwoods League Strategic Plan

SRL's purpose, guiding principles, and strategic initiatives were then integrated in a graphic depiction of the organization's vision that notably enhanced the league's ability to relate its vision to others (figure 2).

The vision and game plan provided the organization with a clear and compelling framework for its efforts. The documents were touchstones for direction setting and frequently referred to at board meetings, committee meetings, and annual board and council meetings to help chart their progress. By the end of a five-year period, nearly all of the original objectives had been accomplished, and the league undertook another round of Strategic Visioning. This second round involved more people, a full gathering of an advisory council with many notable environmental experts. The earlier success helped directly in gaining trust.

Frequently Asked Questions

What Is Strategic Visioning?

Strategic Visioning as a term arose among planning professionals because "planning" in a traditional sense—creating a precise blueprint for moving forward—is not possible in a dynamic social and economic environment. Combined with a strong, shared vision that catalyzes learning and innovation, it can work; thus, "Strategic Visioning."

Strategic Visioning integrates two additional methodologies—large-scale group process and graphic facilitation—making the process robust and customizable for nearly any kind of organizational planning, from teams to entire enterprises.

By working with large-scale graphics and being attentive to the frames and metaphors involved in strategic communication, Strategic Visioning complements traditional, analytical planning. It achieves a holistic integration of the intuitive, emotional, intellectual, and physical, creating a framework for effectively involving diverse stakeholders.

Figure 2. Save the Redwoods League

Strategic Visioning's seven steps fall into three major phases: *Developing Hindsight: Embracing Current Realities*, *Projecting Foresight: Evolving a Shared Vision*, and *Bringing Insights to Action: Executing in the Present*. It is best illustrated in figure 3, which shows the whole flow, shown against the background of a meeting room with charts.

Think of the top of the diagram as representing overview and intuition, and the bottom as the ground of practical reality. The process systematically connects these levels, resulting in a creative tension that catalyzes action. The process also connects the past, future, and present perspectives. The figure eight reminds users that Strategic Visioning requires repeated rounds of work, each one deepening insight and strategic learning. This conceptual model becomes the orienting frame for a design team when developing initial planning offsite meetings, cascade processes that involve large numbers of stakeholders, and review processes downstream as implementation begins. Each of the

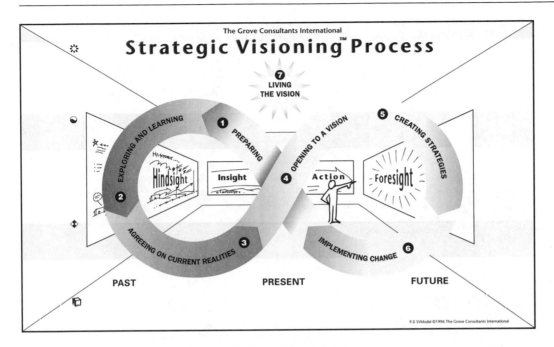

Figure 3. The Strategic Visioning Process

steps is accompanied by a set of customizable Graphic Guides that visually frame the work of that step, two examples of which are shown in figures 4 and 5. Figure 4 shows a Context Map for environmental scanning; and figure 5, called "Five Bold Steps," is for mapping the shared vision and key strategies. There are 18 Graphic Guides in the system that can be sequenced in different ways, depending on the duration and complexity of the planning process.

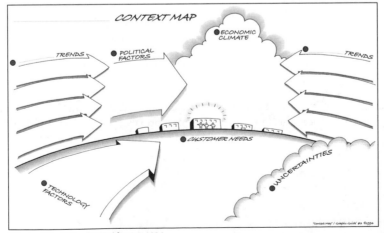

"Context Map"/Graphic Guide #3 © 1996

Figure 4. Context Map

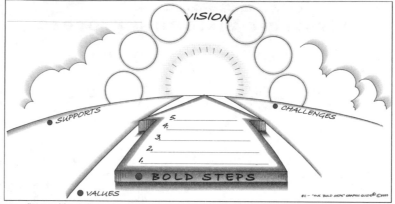

#11—"Five Bold Steps" Graphic Guide® © 1997

Figure 5. Five Bold Steps for Mapping

Table of Uses

Typical Setting	Key Events	Time	Number of Participants
Board Planning Retreats Revisit the vision and strategy of a nonprofit or business.	Usually covers the following: • Graphic history • Context map: Look at current environment • SWOT analysis[1]: Agree on internal realities • Visioning • Strategy formation	2 days	8–20
Team Action Planning Get clear on team goals, roles, tasks, constraints, and game plans.	• Chartering; goal clarification • Team building • Graphic game plan • Road map	1 day or a series of half days	5–15
Annual Planning Align divisional vision and goals to organizational mission and goals; determine strategies and road maps.	Usually covers the following: • Graphic history • Industry structure map: Look at current environment • SWOT analysis: Agree on internal realities	3–6-month process, with many meetings	5–15, plus related consultants and experts

Typical Setting	Key Events	Time	Number of Participants
	• Portfolio analysis • Visioning • Agreeing on strategies • Road map • Value proposition development • Strategy map		
Large-Scale Change Processes Evoke and implement a new direction for an organization, community, or region.	Involves a series of meetings, the initial ones of which look like Organizational Strategic Visioning (SV). The visioning parts are extended with dialogue, groupware, and other tools integrated with the graphic template work.	6 months–years	100s; focus on key stakeholders and informal leaders
Personal Strategic Visioning Come to grips with a new career direction.	Involves working through a series of graphic templates derived from SV for groups.	1–2 days total	1–2; may involve a counselor

About the Author

David Sibbet (www.davidsibbet.com) is an organizational consultant who, since the early 1980s, has facilitated strategy and visioning sessions around the world for large and small organizations. He is a master of graphic facilitation, process design, and experience-based learning for leadership. David is founder and president of The Grove Consultants International, an organization development consulting firm focused on visualizing change. He is a central author for The Grove's tools for managing group process.

Where to Go for More Information

References

The Grove Consultants International. *Strategic Visioning Process Model, Overview and Leader Guides for Corresponding Graphic Guide Templates.* San Francisco: The Grove Consultants International, 1996–2004.

Sibbet, David. *Best Practices for Facilitation.* San Francisco: The Grove Consultants International, 2002.

Sibbet, David, and Ed Claassen. *Team Leader Guide: Strategies & Practices.* San Francisco: The Grove Consultants International, 2004.

INFLUENTIAL SOURCES

Dannemiller Tyson Associates. *Whole-Scale Change: Unleashing the Magic in Organizations.* San Francisco: Berrett-Koehler, 2000.

Porter, Michael. *Competitive Strategy: Techniques for Analyzing Industries and Competitors.* New York: The Free Press, 1998.

ORGANIZATIONS

David Sibbet—www.davidsibbet.com

The Grove Consultants International—www.grove.com

---

1. SWOT analysis is a process sometimes used in strategic planning. SWOT stands for strengths, weaknesses, opportunities, threats.

CAROLYN J. LUKENSMEYER AND WENDY JACOBSON

The 21st Century Town Meeting
Engaging Citizens in Governance

Never doubt that a small group of thoughtful, committed people can change the world. Indeed, it is the only thing that ever has.

—Margaret Mead

A Real-Life Example

Washington, D.C., has a long and well-documented history of problems in government management, resulting in residents highly distrustful of, and disconnected from, decision makers. In 1999, Mayor Williams launched a process to renew people's faith in government and involve them in changing the status quo. During a seven-year partnership with America*Speaks*, the mayor's office held a series of "21st Century Town Meetings," through which more than 13,000 residents (including 1,500 young people) deliberated about the city's spending priorities and made recommendations for change. Residents came to these forums with concerns about safety, education, youth, housing, and government responsiveness, among other issues. Their efforts bore fruit:

- Millions of dollars in the city budget were reallocated to address citizens' priority concerns;
- New community-based governance mechanisms were put in place, including enhanced oversight measures;
- A new role for youth in the district's policy development process was codified.

Frequently Asked Questions

WHAT IS IT AND WHAT IS ITS PURPOSE?

The 21st Century Town Meeting™ is a public forum that links technology with small-group, face-to-face dialogue to engage large numbers of people—up to 5,000 at a time—in deliberations about complex public policy issues. Through a combination of keypad polling, groupware computers, large-screen projection, teleconferencing, and other technologies, these forums enable people to simultaneously participate in intimate discussions *and* contribute to the collective wisdom of the whole.

The 21st Century Town Meeting helps people resolve differences and find common ground. When polls indicate the public might reach consensus on an issue, even if politicians cannot, the process is particularly effective. Several features of the model accomplish this: recruiting a diverse and representative group of "general interest" citizens who aren't representing stakeholder positions; focusing on shared values before addressing issues and priorities; using trained, small-group facilitators; allowing for anonymous polling; paying careful attention to group dynamics and seating plans; and providing access to nonpartisan experts.

The 21st Century Town Meeting creates a level playing field on which citizens can authentically engage with each other in policy and planning discussions that are directly and transparently linked to key decision makers and real governance processes. While the model has most often been used to impact government decision making, it is also successful in nongovernmental contexts.

WHAT ARE THE OUTCOMES FROM A 21ST CENTURY TOWN MEETING?

By convening thousands of people at a time, a 21st Century Town Meeting shines a very public spotlight on important policy concerns, which cannot be ignored by decision makers. As a result, the model achieves significant results. For example:

- Nearly 1,000 people from the six counties that make up the Chicago metropolitan region made sure their priorities shaped a regional plan that focused on transportation, land use, and economic and community development.

- One thousand Britons produced a clear road map for changing their country's health-care system and secured a commitment from Prime Minister Tony Blair to implement their priorities.

- More than 1,000 citizens of Mecklenburg County, North Carolina, crafted a priority agenda for their community's children that influenced local budgeting and service delivery.

HOW DOES IT WORK?

A 21st Century Town Meeting engages citizens, decision makers, and other stakeholders (e.g., advocates, community-based organizations, or representatives from affected businesses or industries) over many months, both preceding and following a large-scale event. While the center of the process is the daylong town meeting, preparatory work is intensive, including careful issue and material development, as well as extensive stakeholder and community engagement (see figure 1). These tasks are described by example below.

Figure 1. Steps in the 21st Century Town Meeting

Issue and Material Development

In 1998, a national discussion on Social Security reform engaged more than 45,000 Americans across the country. The issue was highly visible at the time—President Clinton had featured it in his State of the Union address, and it was the subject of numerous congressional proposals. While the public had great interest, there wasn't a clear consensus on policy direction. All of these factors made the issue "ripe" for large-scale citizen engagement. To maintain credibility while developing the agenda and content for a national discussion, an advisory board was formed that brought together Republicans and Democrats, representatives from conservative and liberal think tanks, unions, the American Association of Retired Persons (AARP), and others. The issue and material development for the national discussion were overseen by this diverse group.

Stakeholder and Community Engagement

In 2002, in the aftermath of 9/11, there was much discussion about how redevelopment of the World Trade Center site would be responsive to the diverse groups impacted by the tragedy. The 21st Century Town Meeting brought New York civic and political leaders together with more than 5,000 people to address this question. One of the many engagement challenges for this initiative was to bring in those who were marginalized in the redevelopment efforts. For example, to ensure inclusion of undocumented immigrants who held low-paying jobs in and around the towers, special arrangements were made for them to register without providing names and addresses. In the end, 10 percent of the participants in "Listening to the City" were undocumented immigrants.

Following extensive preparatory work, the 21st Century Town Meeting proceeds through four stages:

- *Setting the Context.* Beginning with a welcome from sponsors, and brief comments from key political leaders, participants answer demographic questions using keypad polling.

- *Clarifying Values.* Before deliberation on key content, there is a "values discussion" that lays the groundwork for prioritization of ideas and concerns.

- *Developing Recommendations.* Participants engage in small, diverse table discussions led by trained facilitators. Networked laptop computers at each table serve as electronic flip charts to record ideas and send them to a "Theme Team," which identifies commonalities and presents them back to the assembly for modification and voting done with individual, handheld keypads. The "back and forth" between small- and large-scale dialogues occurs as often as needed to develop recommendations.

- *Reporting Out.* By the end of the meeting, the Theme Team drafts a preliminary report detailing keypad voting results and the shared agenda. Every participant, decision maker, and journalist receives the report upon leaving.

What Are the Critical Success Factors?

The four critical success factors for using the 21st Century Town Meeting model are: (1) making sure every voice is in the room; (2) getting decision makers involved from the beginning and committed to acting on outcomes; (3) providing sufficient scale to compel attention; and (4) ensuring transparency and immediacy of results.

Table of Uses

Typical Setting	Key Events, Outcomes	Number of Participants, Locations
Policy, planning, or budget development linked to governance processes in the United States and abroad. Examples: • Social Security policy • Health-care policy • Regional growth • City budgeting • Recovery and rebuilding after tragedies such as 9/11 or natural disasters	21st Century Town Meeting lasts one full day or part of a day. Over 6–12 months, the following preparation takes place: • Issue development • Decision maker, stakeholder, and participant engagement • Materials creation • Media engagement • Event planning	• 100–5,000 participants Depending on meeting size • 5–40 staff • 20–500 volunteers

Typical Setting	Key Events, Outcomes	Number of Participants, Locations
Planning, visioning, or agenda development for nongovernmental organizations such as universities, associations, or collaboratives (e.g., National 4H Council, the National Conference on Citizenship, Colorado College, the American Camping Association).	Outcomes include policy changes, reallocation of resources, development plans, etc.	Locations have included: • *Cities* (e.g., Washington, DC; San Francisco; New York; Birmingham, UK; Brussels, Belgium; Perth, Australia) • *Counties* (e.g., Hamilton County, Ohio; Charlotte, DeSoto, and Hardee Counties, Florida) • *Regions* (e.g., northeast Ohio, metropolitan Chicago) • A nation as a whole or multiple nations

About the Authors

Dr. Carolyn J. Lukensmeyer (CJL@americaspeaks.org) is the founder and president of America-Speaks and its international arm, Global Voices. Prior to this, she served as consultant to the White House chief of staff, as deputy project director for management of the *National Performance Review,* as chief of staff to Governor Richard F. Celeste of Ohio, and as an independent consultant. Lukensmeyer earned a Ph.D. in organizational behavior from Case Western Reserve University and completed postgraduate training at the Gestalt Institute of Cleveland.

Wendy Jacobson (wendy.jacobson@verizon.net) is an independent consultant specializing in policy research and analysis. She is a 1997 Annie E. Casey Foundation fellow, and holds an MSW from the University of Georgia and a BA from Yale University.

Where to Go for More Information

REFERENCES

Links to a range of published resource and reference materials on the 21st Century Town Meeting and large-scale citizen engagement work in general can be found at: www.america speaks.org/resources/library/as/pubs/index.htm.

Goldman, J. *Millions of Voices: A Blueprint for Engaging the American Public in National Policymaking.* Washington, DC: AmericaSpeaks, 2004.

Lukensmeyer, C., and A. Boyd. "Putting the 'Public' Back in Management: Seven Principles for Planning Meaningful Citizen Engagement." *Public Management.* Washington, DC: International City/County Management Association, 2004.

Lukensmeyer, C., and S. Brigham. "Taking Democracy to Scale: Creating a Town Hall Meeting for the 21st Century." *National Civic Review* 91, no. 4 (2002): 351–366.

ORGANIZATIONS

America*Speaks*—www.americaspeaks.org

Global Voices—www.globalvoices.org

*America*Speaks' *international arm.*

STRUCTURING METHODS

Structuring methods organize the system to create the desired future. They rely on an effective plan and result in redefined relationships among people and redesigned work practices.

42

Community Weaving

Unless local communal life can be restored, the public cannot adequately resolve its most urgent problem, to find and identify itself.
—John Dewey

Good Neighbors

Community Weaving emerged from the experiences of a small group of neighbors who created their own social support system. It was sparked by a mother's desire to meet the needs of her children and thrive. Frustrated by the way local agencies treated her—as if she was broken and needed fixing—she gathered her neighbors together and started a social support network. After cutting through a lot of red tape to hold gatherings at a local school, the neighbors invited school parents and staff to participate. Everyone pooled their resources, shared stories, and invited speakers from local agencies to address topics impacting their lives. They learned about local resources, developed new skills, and supported one another. This created a synergy that attracted more parents and neighbors from the surrounding area. The families agreed to be "Good Neighbors," pool their resources, support one another, and abide by the "Steps to Excellence." The Steps to Excellence were guidelines on how to strive for excellence in one's life for the betterment of the whole group. They shared knowledge and resources, taught each other new skills, and did special projects to improve conditions in their community. Over time, they felt like a family.

Everyone made their own unique contribution by organizing or attending educational and recreational opportunities, and spearheading change initiatives in the community. Good Neighbors wanting to provide one-on-one support to those referred into the network by local agencies were trained as "Family Advocates." The group published and distributed a monthly newsletter to keep each other informed of their accomplishments and included a calendar of upcoming activities. The newsletter was posted throughout the community so others could get involved and participate in activities.

In February 1993, the group developed partnerships with organizations in the community, formed a board of directors, and founded a nonprofit 501(c)3 organization called the Family Support Network (FSN). The organization was established to overcome the barriers they encountered as an informal group. The nonprofit status transformed the group into a legitimate, sustainable entity, enabling it to collaborate with other organizations and to receive grants and tax-deductible contributions.

Over the next three years, the FSN grew to more than 400 Good Neighbors and Family Advocates across five states and was featured in articles on the front page of the *Seattle Times* on March 2, 1996, and February 8, 1997. This brought national attention to this grassroots effort, and Good Neighbors from across the country registered their resources and engaged with neighbors who shared common interests or lived nearby using Web-based technology developed by volunteers. Those who did not have access to computers contacted FSN Community Weavers, who helped them access resources, activities, trainings, and their neighbors.

The individual capacity of the Good Neighbors grew in direct proportion to the human and tangible resources made available by all other Good Neighbors and FSN Partners on the FSN Web site. Good Neighbors tapped the FSN Resource Treasury for the resources they needed to help themselves and others, and used the network to find jobs, housing, cars, and to tap into great ideas. Assistance was freely given and the knowledge and insight gained from the experiences transformed FSN volunteers into leaders, pioneers, role models, mentors, and change agents in their communities. Many received awards and recognition for their accomplishments and continue to give back to their communities.

Frequently Asked Questions

How Does Community Weaving Work?

The Family Support Networks and experiential learning communities emerge from Community Weaving practices. Partnerships with organizations representing the diversity of the community are established. Partners recruit staff, employees, clients, students, parents, and members as participants who pool resources and make their own unique contributions to a collective effort striving for the common good. Everyone has free and easy access to one another, resources, and opportunities to engage and serve.

Community Weavers learn Community Weaving practices and principles from Master Weavers, who share their stories and teach them how to use the tools, techniques, and technology to grow their own social support networks in their schools, churches, neighborhoods, organizations, and businesses. Good Neighbors who share similar passions or common interests combine resources and create furniture warehouses, child-care co-ops, clothing exchanges, and community gardens. Those who enjoy the outdoors and recreational activities organize rafting trips, campouts, ropes courses, barbeques, softball games, paintball competitions, and vision quests.

Community improvement projects are organized using FSN technology to spearhead change initiatives, such as shutting down crack houses, responding to disasters, organizing block watches, raising funds for neighborhood beautification and revitalization projects, and starting up new businesses.

Local organizations such as the American Red Cross, Public Health Department, schools, churches, businesses, and a variety of civic, social service, and youth organizations are recruited as FSN Partners and provide free space for activities, access to speakers and educational materials, as well as free trainings to FSN volunteers. FSN partners train staff as Community Weavers who utilize the resources of the FSN to better meet the needs of their clients.

WHAT ARE COMMUNITY WEAVING WEBS OF SUPPORT?

Cultivating diverse and meaningful relationships is at the core of Community Weaving. It occurs among individuals, within communities, and across states, as the following examples illustrate:

- The Emergency Service staff of the Seattle King County American Red Cross placed victims of disasters into the homes of Good Neighbors who were trained as Family Advocates. Child Protective Services (CPS) used FSN volunteers to mentor parents and supervise visitations of children in foster care when there was a shortage of staff to supervise the visits.

- A local hospital called a Community Weaver instead of Child Protective Services when a single mother abandoned her colicky baby in an emergency room because she was overwhelmed and at her wits' end. An example of how a web of support is interwoven in this scenario is illustrated by this story. The hospital connects the young mother to a Community Weaver who assesses the situation over the phone. The Community Weaver matches the young mother to an FSN Family Advocate volunteer living nearby who is a retired nurse, loves to garden, and is feeling lonely and depressed. The Community Weaver asks her to provide respite care to the single mother by babysitting. This gives the retiree a sense of joy and great satisfaction. While babysitting, she notices the empty lot next to the mother's home and discovers it is for sale. She taps the FSN Resource Treasury to connect with someone who knows the ins and outs of community gardening, and they approach an agency that writes a grant to purchase the vacant lot and start a community garden. The nurse now is doing what she loves, and the young mother brings her children over to help in the garden and visit with her friend, whom they call Auntie M.

- "Operation Safe Havens" is another large-scale Community Weaving illustration that includes four FSN volunteers and local agencies. An FSN volunteer initiates Operation Safe Haven in an effort to provide transitional housing to evacuees displaced by hurricanes Katrina and Rita. The Community Weaver living in Seattle screens the families offering transitional housing and conducts background checks. The Community Weaver living in Austin, Texas, works with local shelters and matches evacuees looking for transitional housing with host families in Seattle. Organizations in Austin, such as the Red Cross and Salvation Army, give families the resources needed to cover transportation costs to get to their new homes.

Companies, organizations, and associations use Community Weaving to link employees and members together to foster creativity and innovation in a fail-safe environment. This results in increasing individual and community capacity and productivity. The model can be utilized as a system of support that extends beyond the walls of the organization and can serve as an employee/member-run assistance program. Engagement and participation increase when people feel valued and have access to resources to take care of their own needs.

These various applications of Community Weaving demonstrate the power of connectivity, level of ingenuity, and commitment people are willing to make to serve one another. These are examples of how Community Weaving taps into grassroots initiative and functions interdependently with organizations to foster innovation and manifest good works. All the materials developed for these special projects are made available free of charge at www.communityweaving.org. This makes it easy to access the materials and technical support to replicate efforts in other communities to address similar situations.

The data collected about the activities of FSN volunteers provides indicators of accomplishments, self-sufficiency, and gaps in services. This information is published in *FSN Updates* and distributed to leaders at all levels of the community. The updates provide valuable information to base decisions on how to best serve the community. *FSN Updates* is a tool used to identify administrators, public officials, and policy makers who are responsive to the needs of the community.

Weaving the Fabric of Community (Outcomes and How It Works)

Community Weaving fosters a vibrant grassroots web, which builds and bridges social capital between individuals, among group members, and across community systems (figure 1). The result is an intricate patchwork of conscientious citizens functioning interdependently with one another and formal systems, in order to mend the tears in the social fabric caused by fragmentation and shifts in the cultural, economic, and political climate. Given time, the beneficent presence and dynamic activity of Community Weaving changes the culture of community and transforms lives.

Community Weavers are the key to building and bridging social capital to weave a grassroots web of support. This new web of volunteers provides a system of support to catch those falling through or out of formal systems. The skills and insights gleaned from serving others raise social consciousness and reweave the shredded fabric of community. Partnerships between grassroots and formal systems create opportunities for cooperation and teamwork. This interdependent web of relationships instigated by Community Weaving strengthens the social fabric of community and creates space for creativity, innovation, authenticity, and living democracy.

Community Weaving

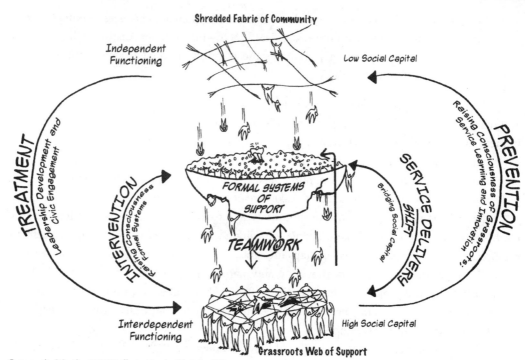

Community Weaving © 2005. Illustration by Christine Valenza.

Figure 1. Weaving the Fabric of Community

The cohesiveness of the community is strengthened as formal systems and the grassroots function interdependently to solve problems impacting the health and welfare of communities. This fosters resiliency to enable individuals, groups, organizations, and whole communities to thrive.

The Web-based database tracks data detailing the interconnections and interactions. The Community Weavers document the innovations made to improve lives and conditions in the community, as well as the efforts to fill gaps. This information is exchanged among all Community Weavers, enables them to coordinate efforts and compensate for changes by tapping the creative potential of participants and empowering them to solve problems.

Core Beliefs and Guiding Principles

Core Beliefs

- Giving and receiving are equal because both are needs and both are gifts.

- People working together create a synergy that increases the community's capacity to identify resources and solve problems.

- Community as a whole has everything it needs to thrive.

- Lives are enriched through the sharing of diversity and experience.

- Individuals and community issues can be addressed through collaboration and shared resources.

- All individuals have the right to identify their own needs and be supported to choose their own solutions.

- Everyone deserves respect and the right to confidentiality and privacy.

- Everyone has unlimited potential for development beyond their presently perceived capabilities.

Guiding Principles

- Everyone has something to offer

- Everyone is welcome to participate

- Treat others the way you want to be treated

- Take responsibility for what you care about

- Experiment with new ideas

- Be open to outcome

- No blaming or judging

- Reflect on experience

- Apply insights to new endeavors

- Pass on the gift of experience

COMMUNITY WEAVING CHANGE DYNAMIC

The change dynamics of Community Weaving (figure 2) raises consciousness and enhances functioning of individuals and systems by fostering creativity, innovation, and cooperation resulting in an increase in productivity. There are two causes for engagement in Community Weaving. A lower-consciousness response is a reactive response to internal needs within the givers or receivers. Those operating at a higher level of consciousness view challenges as opportunities to initiate change and find satisfaction contributing toward the common good. To improve community functioning and increase levels of productivity, participants experience the process of change through:

- Action

- Interaction

- Insight

- Integration

- Actualization

- Change in behavior, thinking, and beliefs

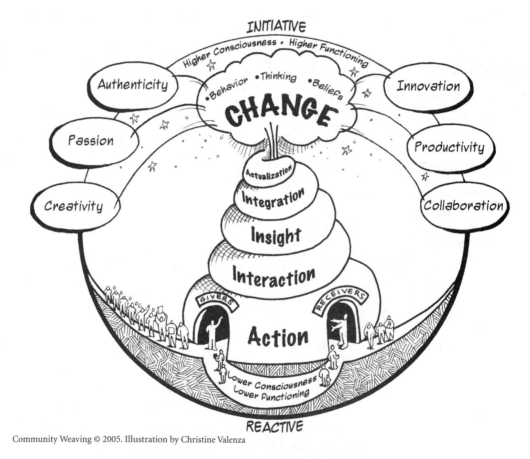

Community Weaving © 2005. Illustration by Christine Valenza

Figure 2. Community Weaving Change Dynamic

Table of Uses

Typical Setting	Timeline	Implementation Steps	Number of Participants
Community-Wide • Create thriving communities by tapping abundance of grassroots resources to increase individual and community capacity.	Month 1	*Phase I* • Meeting with organizers to define purpose for social change initiative and identify Community Coordinator and Master Weavers who facilitate trainings.	• Varies
• A social change approach that fosters interdependent functionality among the grassroots, public, and private sectors.	Month 2	• Train Master Weavers and Coordinator, who design Community Summit. *Phase II*	• 2–5 people
	Month 4	• Community Summit to launch project, recruit partners, clarify expectations, get buy-in and survey community readiness.	• 300 leaders and 700 citizens
• Weave a web of support for families and create more cohesive communities.		• Establish coalition of stakeholders that meet monthly, representative of the diversity of the community.*	• 100 leaders
• Incorporate participatory democracy practices within existing systems of governance to increase citizen involvement and engagement.	Ongoing Month 5	• Recruitment of Community Weavers *Phase III* • Train Community Weavers (CWs) who are connected into national CW network.	• 30–50 people
• Build and bridge social and human capital to foster innovation, self-sufficiency, and free enterprise.	Month 6	• Train Family Advocate (FA) Trainers • 1-day Community Readiness Workshop	• 2–5 CWs • 500 people
• Increase resiliency and protective factors to reduce chemical dependency and crime.		• 1-day Strategic Planning Session with organizers and coalition. • Integrate Technology *Phase IV*	• 100 stakeholders and CWs
• Mobilize volunteers in community service learning activities to increase skills, raise awareness of social issues, and foster empathy and understanding for others.	Month 7 Ongoing	• Recruit and engage volunteers using Web-based technology to pool and inventory resources. • Master Weavers conduct series of CW trainings throughout the community.	• 1,000+ volunteers • 20/training
	Month 8	• Recruit and train Family Advocate volunteers in series of trainings.	• 200–300 volunteers
• Generate relevant data to guide public policy and hold leadership accountable for decision making.	Ongoing	• Community Weavers meet monthly to coordinate recruitment efforts, brainstorm, and exchange ideas.	• Varies

*Existing coalition, corporation, or agency may administer project and assume fiscal responsibility.

Typical Setting	Timeline	Implementation Steps	Number of Participants
• Foster emergence of new leadership at all levels of community. • Foster informed, responsible, and responsive citizenry to enhance system of care.	Ongoing Month 12	• CW & FA reps meet with coalition to review progress, schedule specialized trainings, negotiate needs, fill gaps, and plan community-wide event. *Phase V* • Event to recognize achievements, award outstanding service, highlight successes, identify barriers, explore challenges, and envision the future.	• 3CWs and 3 FAs, and Coalition • 2,500+ participants
Organization (Single-Site) (Schools, churches, agencies, associations, companies) • Affect change in culture • Optimize productivity • Create fail-safe environment to experiment with new ideas • Improve motivation • Foster emergence of leaders • Reduce absenteeism due to illness • Increase retention • Attract new participants and customers	Month 1 Month 2 Month 3 Month 4 Month 5 Ongoing Month 6 Ongoing Ongoing Month 9	• Meeting with management. • Project team to plan event(s) • Organizational event(s) • Integrate technology • Train Community Weavers (CWs) • Train Family Advocates (FAs) Trainers • Pool and inventory strengths and assets of participants using Web-based technology. • Recruit and train Family Advocates • Community Weavers meet monthly • Community Weaver reps meet with management • Event to honor volunteers, recognize and award outstanding service, highlight successes, identify barriers, and envision the future	• Participants vary • 5 people • Varies in size • Ratio 1:100 • 3 CWs • Target 50 percent participation • 20/training • Varies • 2 CWs, 2FAs, and management • Organization-wide
Disaster Preparedness and Response • Educate and engage citizens in disaster preparedness. • Mobilize trained volunteers as first responders.	Month 1	• Meet with Emergency Management Director(s) at all levels of community • Strategic planning session with Emergency Management personnel	• 2–5 people • 10 people

Table of Uses. Continued

Typical Setting	Timeline	Implementation Steps	Number of Participants
• Create and educate social support system. • To bolster relief efforts, create pool of human and tangible resources to tap into in the event of a disaster.	Month 2	• Identify and train Master Weaver(s) • One-day work session with leaders of local volunteer organizations.	• 1–3 people • 20 leaders
	Month 3	• Identify Community Weavers from each volunteer organization. • Integrate technology *(Optional)*	• Varies
	Month 4	• Train CWs	• 25/training
	Ongoing	• Recruit and engage volunteers	• 1,000+ volunteers
	Month 5	• Recruit and train Family Advocates	• 200 volunteers
	Ongoing	• Organizations cross-train volunteers	• Varies

Getting Started

Community Weaving fosters experiential learning communities to enhance the innovative capacity of individuals to affect change in whole systems. An experiential learning community is one that learns continuously and transforms itself. Community Weaving is a whole system-learning framework that offers insight on many different levels. Learning occurs through self-reflective practice, interactions with others, and new ways of engaging with systems, resulting in shifting social consciousness. A sign of success is when conversations among participants include reflective dialogues to help each other make meaning out of their experience. Community Weaving measures success by increased levels of confidence, self-esteem, initiative, productivity, and engagement. When individuals are able to correlate their presence in the moment from insights learned from past experience, they are more apt to recognize opportunities. In fact, they can actually manifest opportunities through recognition of possibilities. Instead of seeing what they need or don't have, they have a heightened awareness of the presence of what is or what could be. As participants integrate experience with knowledge through dialogue and interactions, it impacts the way they view themselves, others, and the world. Empathy emerges, resulting in the manifestation of possibilities they never knew existed before. This is the ultimate condition for success.

GRASSROOTS, GROUP, AND ORGANIZATIONAL INITIATIVES

Community Weaving is implemented by trained Community Weavers who use the materials, tools, and technology to increase individual and group capacity through recruitment of Good Neighbors, tapping their passions, engaging them in service activities, and weaving them into an experiential learning community (figure 3).

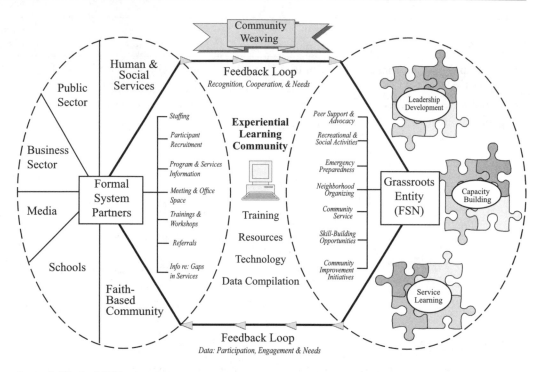

Community Weaving © 2006

Figure 3. Community Weaving Framework

COMMUNITY-WIDE INITIATIVES

Implementing Community Weaving at the community level can be accomplished in two ways:

1. In a bottom-up approach, staff or community volunteers are certified as Community Weavers and start implementing Community Weaving by recruiting participants and building partnerships with diverse organizations in the community. This approach does not require buy-in or coordination of community systems. The downside of this approach is it does not have the synergy of a collective action for a community change initiative. It takes longer to build trust, legitimacy, and momentum.

2. For a community-wide change initiative, collaborative partnerships representative of the diverse cultural sectors of the community are formed. Together with an experienced Master Weaver, who has insight into the process, a strategic plan for implementation is designed. This requires three to six months of preparation before Community Weaving commences and involves education, surveying community readiness, and identifying and training Community Weavers. The sponsoring organization completes a Community Weaving application that indicates purpose to implement Community Weaving, and iden-

tifies initial stakeholders. A strategic plan is developed with a Master Weaver detailing roles and responsibilities for raising awareness, developing partnerships, setting up administration, recruiting participants, and conducting a Community Readiness survey. A contact person coordinates these preparations and identifies who will be trained as Community Weavers and where they will be stationed. Communities with experience in Asset-Based Community Development appreciate the concrete steps used in the Community Weaving model. It puts theory into practice with the tools and technology to support it.

Community Weaver Certification Training

Community Weavers learn the theories and practices that underpin the methodology. They learn the dynamics of system change and how to foster conditions to evoke change by employing Community Weaving principles and practices.

Coalition Building

Organizing a collaborative partnership of committed stakeholders who represent the diversity of the community builds a solid foundation that sustains the effort. If a coalition already has experience working on community improvement initiatives, including administrating grants, this is ideal.

Family Advocate Recruitment and Training

Family Advocates are participants engaging as leaders; role models and mentors who learn skills to provide direct support services in a safe and confidential manner. All Family Advocates must pass background checks.

Coalition Partners

Coalition members representing various aspects of the community empower Community Weaving by providing financial support and access to resources.

Community Coordinator

The Community Coordinator oversees implementation of CW initiatives, develops partnerships, and raises community awareness.

Do's and Don'ts

Do . . .	Don't . . .
Engage everyone who wants to be involved	Exclude people from participating or engaging
Encourage participation of disenfranchised citizens	Mandate or obligate participation

Do ...	Don't ...
Use technology to stimulate interactions	Rely on technology to do all the work
Plan, prepare, and educate	Plan outcomes
Create space for emerging ideas and action	Restrict flow of ideas by rules or discount them
Support ideas and encourage participation	Discard ideas when enthusiasm is attached to them

Roles, Responsibilities, and Relationships

COMMUNITY WEAVER

Community Weavers are trained volunteers and staff, representative of the broad spectrum of community who create interconnected social support systems at all levels of community. They recruit, train, and engage participants to interact with others in the community (or organization) using Web-based technology, and strive to build and bridge social capital across systems.

GOOD NEIGHBOR

Good Neighbors comprise the majority of participants. They are part of a growing collective of caring citizens, volunteering to serve others and pooling their resources in the Resource Treasury. Good neighbors engage with others in the network and organize social, educational, or recreational activities to build relationships and expand social networks. In some circumstances, they commit to volunteering a specified number of service hours in their community.

FAMILY ADVOCATE

Family Advocates are volunteers trained to provide peer support services to those requesting assistance. They are viewed as leaders and change agents in their organizations and communities. They must pass a background check. Commitment to volunteer a specified number of service hours is requested of Family Advocates to satisfy funding requirements.

PARTNERS AND SUPPORTERS

Partners and supporters are individuals, community organizations, agencies, and businesses who contribute cash, time, expertise, services, and equipment. Partners and supporters are welcome to serve as coalition members in community-wide Community Weaving initiatives.

COMMUNITY COORDINATOR

Community Coordinators oversee large-scale implementation and are responsible for administration, public relations, marketing, and building collaborative community partnerships.

Conditions for Success

Any project or initiative involving change requires preparation, planning, and awareness of what to expect and how to negotiate change. Resistance to change is natural and often triggers a response. These responses open gateways for new insights and opportunities. Resistance played an instrumental role in the development of Community Weaving practices. As obstacles were encountered, they were viewed as opportunities to creatively address issues impeding progress. With this in mind, the conditions for success of Community Weaving are:

- Desire to function in ways that foster innovation and creativity;

- Engaging individuals to take responsibility for what they care about;

- Supporting new initiatives instigated by those tapping into their passions;

- Engaging Community Weavers who are passionate and committed to contributing to the common good; and

- Incorporating Community Weaving practices into policies and procedures.

COMMUNITY READINESS

Communities must be readied to embrace this transformative community-building approach. The keys to community readiness are a desire to change, a willingness to participate, and openness to outcome. Kent Roberts, founder of the Civility Center and author of *Community Weaving*, offers the following insight and provides indicators for community readiness.

> If we are serious about improving communities, we must be aware of the local community context and the readiness of that context for change. Even the best strategies will not be successful unless the community environment has a culture of acceptance for new ideas. Conversely, if we have a context of readiness, then anything we do will have a higher probability of success. The correlation between the probability of success and the readiness of the community cannot be over stressed.
>
> In order to assess the readiness of a community, we must determine its ability to confront the conditions that inhibit growth and development. We must ask questions like: Are individuals open to the possibilities of change? What is the relational trust within the community between individuals and its institutions? Do people treat each other with dignity and respect? Where are the opportunities for open, safe, and civil dialogue? Can we accept others' differences and build upon what we share in common? Answers to these questions begin to determine the readiness level of the community. Understanding the concept of readiness is the first step to increasing the collective capital of that community.
>
> Before we start, we must internalize the importance of why we are entering into this complex area of work. We should encourage the community to ask itself: Why

must we commit to working together differently? Are things really that much different than in the past? Why can't we just go our separate ways and still be members of the same community? If a community can't truthfully answer these questions, it will never succeed. Understanding "the why" is more important than figuring out "the how." The need to commit to this effort is paramount to the future of the community.

If we want communities and organizations to change their behavior, we must change their context and their readiness level for change. If the contextual culture of the community does not change then nothing really changes. Often we want to implement new ideas but we don't recognize the level of readiness for them. When our ideas fail, we are discouraged and lose energy. There was nothing wrong with the idea; the community's level of readiness was not strong enough to support the initiative. As we begin to work together differently, we must recognize the present context and correlate our efforts to fit the degree of readiness for change. You don't teach a child to run before it can walk. The same principle applies as we start our collective journey in making our communities better places in which to live, learn, work, play and pray.

Theory Base

Theorists/ Researchers	Theory	Key Aspects	Application	Outcome
Margaret Wheatley	Self-Organization	Creating conditions where systems self-organize	Creating the space and conditions for self-organizing to occur in many ways on many different levels	• Community system reorganization • Engaging in new ways • Tapping innovation • Increased productivity
David Kolb	Experiential Learning	Experience as the source of learning and development	Gaining knowledge and experience through interacting with others	• Increased knowledge and understanding of self and others. • Developing interpersonal skills • Applying knowledge in new ways to increase learning.

Theorists/ Researchers	Theory	Key Aspects	Application	Outcome
Peter Senge	Learning Communities	Service combined with learning adds value to each and transforms both	Lifelong learning in interactive learning community of people who share common purpose. Dialogues promote inquiry, reflection, and experimentation	• Raises awareness of self and others • Develops leadership • Fosters social and civic engagement • Embrace possibilities • Builds confidence and self-esteem
Robert Putnam	Social Capital	Social interactions build individual and community capacity	Engaging participation to create opportunities for civic engagement, social interaction, and learning	• Individual engagement • Pooling resources • Mutual sharing and learning • Building and bridging social capital
Nan Lin	Social Networks	Social networks are fostered by relational ties	Creating conditions for social interaction to foster relationships that evolve into social support systems	• Face-to-face interactions • Social support networking • Increase in resiliency • Increase in protective factors
Don Beck and Ken Wilber	Spiral Dynamics Integral	Evolution of consciousness	Participants experience an increase in understanding of self and their relationship in the world around them	• Engage on many different levels • Raises understanding of self • Raises collective consciousness • Higher level of functioning

Community Weaving

Theorists/ Researchers	Theory	Key Aspects	Application	Outcome
John McKnight and Jody Kretzman	Asset-Based Community Development	Citizen-centered community development based on existence of assets	Individual strengths and assets are tapped to increase community capacity and mobilize citizen engagement	• Participant-driven efforts • Citizen's voice is heard • Increased community capacity • Collaborative partnerships

Theory Base. Continued

Sustainability

The essentials to sustaining Community Weaving are:

1. Establish a corporate entity to create legitimacy, or affiliate with existing group or organization;

2. Recruit Community Weavers who are passionate and committed to weaving community;

3. Train staff as Community Weavers to employees in community weaving activities;

4. Integrate Community Weaving practices into policies and procedures;

5. Incorporate fail-safe conditions that foster innovation;

6. Document results and make materials easily accessible to others for replication;

7. Make efforts self-supported through entrepreneurial enterprises, contributions, and training fees.

Burning Questions

The burning questions people ask usually are about money and liability: How much does something like this cost? How can it be sustained? Who is liable if someone gets hurt or if property is damaged?

Saving lives is priceless. Initial investment for implementation and training is minimal. The beauty of this approach is that existing staff can be certified as Community Weavers to implement Community Weaving practices in local schools, churches, businesses, organizations, or neighborhoods by attending a three-day training session or by completing online Community Weaver Certification training and participating in conference calls. A Community Weaver spends an average of ten hours a week recruiting, weaving, and engaging volunteers using cutting-edge, Web-based technologies. Due to the wealth of human and tangible resources generated by their activities, the group, organization or company employing them reaps multiple benefits. These benefits include: cross-training and skill-building workshops available to staff and those they serve; a social support system of trained volunteers committed to caring and sharing resources; and a means to self-organize and initiate change initiatives to improve conditions in the workplace and in communities. The result of these benefits increases individual and community capacity, empowers people to act on their own behalf; reduces stress and burnout; and fosters cooperation, which enhances productivity and improves retention. Community Weaving is sustained as the duties of the Community Weavers are integrated into job descriptions at the various levels of the organization and in diverse community sectors.

The Good Samaritan Law blankets most volunteer activities, as long as there is verbal consent from the person receiving services. All participants, whether they are practitioners or receivers, must consent to adhering to policies and procedures, acknowledge the Civility Pledge, and agree to release of liability prior to participating in Community Weaving activities.

Final Thoughts

In a time when gauging success is based on measurable outcomes, research is necessary to determine those outcomes. This approach has yet to be scientifically researched to qualify as a best practice and for the benefits that come with the distinction.

About the Author

Cheryl Honey (cheryl@communityweaving.com), Certified Prevention Professional; president, Excel Strategies, Inc.; and founder, Family Support Network, International. Cheryl pioneered Community Weaving practices from her grassroots experience growing Family Support Networks. She received recognition from the Asset-Based Community Development Institute and the Institute for Civil Society for her innovative approach to building individual and community capacity. Cheryl graduated from Antioch University Seattle in transformative community building and human services.

Where to Go for More Information

REFERENCES

McKnight, John. *The Careless Society: Community and Its Counterfeits.* New York: Basic Books/HarperCollins, 1995.

McKnight, J., and J. Kretzman. *Guide to Capacity Building.* Chicago, IL: ACTA Publications, 1996.

Putnam, R. D. *Making Democracy Work: Civic Traditions in Modern Italy.* Princeton, NJ: Princeton University Press, 1993.

Roberts, K., and J. Newman. *Community Weaving.* Muscatine, IA: National Civility Center, 2003.

Solo, Pam. "Beyond Theory: Civil Society in Action." *The Brookings Review* 15, no. 4 (Fall 1997): 8. www.brookings.edu/press/REVIEW/FALL97/SOLO.HTM.

Solo, Pam, and Gail Pressburg. "Beyond Theory: Civil Society in Action." In *Community Works: The Revival of Civil Society in America*, edited by E. J. Dionne, Jr., 81–87. Washington, DC: The Brookings Institution Press, 1998.

Community Weaving

INFLUENTIAL SOURCES

Follett, M. *Creative Experience.* New York: Longmans, Green and Co., 1930.

————. *The New State.* New York: Longmans, Green and Co., 1920.

Kolb, D. A., I. M. Rubin, and J. Osland. *Organizational Behavior: An Experiential Approach to Human Behavior in Organizations.* 5th ed. Englewood Cliffs, NJ: Prentice-Hall, 1991.

Kretzman, J., and J. McKnight. *Building Communities from the Inside Out.* Chicago, IL: ACTA Publications, 1993.

Senge, Peter. *The Fifth Discipline: The Art and Practice of Community Organizations.* New York: Doubleday, 1990.

Wheatley, M. J. *Turning to One Another: Simple Conversations to Restore Hope to the Future.* San Francisco: Berrett-Koehler, 2002.

Wilber, Ken. "An Approach to Integral Psychology." *Journal of Transpersonal Psychology* 31, no. 2 (1999): 109–133.

ORGANIZATIONS

Center for Effective Collaboration and Practice—http://cecp.air.org

FSN (Family Support Network) Approach Recognized as Promising Practice.

Community Weaving—www.communityweaving.org

Excel Strategies—www.excelstrategies.us

Provides training in Community Weaving.

Family Support Network, International—www.familynetwork.org

Special thanks to Kent Roberts, who kindly lent his expertise and the notion of Community Weaving to this methodology. Kent and his colleague, Jay Newman, coauthored a community building handbook entitled Community Weaving.

43

MERRELYN EMERY AND TOM DEVANE

Participative Design Workshop

We must be the great arsenal of democracy.

—Franklin Delano Roosevelt

Real-Life Story

Cyclone Hardware P&N Tools manufactures products for the building and engineering indus-tries. The company began to encounter serious problems as imports reduced P&N Tools' market share. Management downsized the workforce, initiated four-day weeks, and reduced capital expenditures.

Internally, quality, production times, and operating costs were not competitive. Manage-ment believed reducing the hierarchy from five levels would improve cycle times and reduce costs through faster decision making. They also realized they would need a structure that encouraged motivation and responsibility from employees at all levels.

Their first attempt using a Sociotechnical Systems (STS) approach foundered because apart from the design team, the workforce didn't feel ownership. Representation is not the same thing as participation.

As it happened, P&N Tools had previously been introduced to the concepts of Participative Design Workshops (PDWs); subsequently, all employees participated in a series of PDWs. The final design contained three levels of function without supervision and in which the manage-ment team concentrated on productive work. All goals were aligned with the business strategy.

The business results were extraordinary:

- Equipment utilization improved by 30 percent in three months.

- Stock levels were successfully built up prior to Christmas shutdown, even though teams only had a 1,200-hour window for 1,600 hours of work.

- A year later, a third production shift was added because of increased product demand attributed to higher quality and customer satisfaction.

In addition to the impressive business results, other changes in the way the workforce worked together became strikingly evident (table 1).

Teams Now Have	Instead of
responsibility for handling and scheduling back orders	waiting for orders
daily information about stock levels	monthly reports
responsibility for minor maintenance on machines	downtime, waiting for maintenance
become multiskilled	one skill per person
requested Total Quality and Just In Time tools to increase performance	"Its someone else's job"
spontaneous ideas for improvement	staying silent and apathetic

Table 1. Changes in Workforce Behavior

These results have been sustained and this experience is not unique. Similar results have been obtained from 1971 and from such different organizations as Microsoft, Weyerhaeuser, Hewlett-Packard, Karadoc Winery, and the Federal Judicial Court System of the United States.

The Basics

WHAT IS THE PARTICIPATIVE DESIGN WORKSHOP?

The PDW is one of several open systems methods that help organizations or communities get on top of their unpredictable environment. The other methods are covered in chapters 22 (Evolutions of Open Systems Theory) and 35 (Search Conference). In a PDW, participants bring into being a structure that leads to increased levels of responsibility and motivation to achieve their strategic intent. At the end of a PDW, participants know how to sustain performance improvement. There are two forms of PDW, one for redesign, and one for designing a structure where none exists, for example in a Greenfield or start-up organization or community. The differences between the PDWs for redesign and design are discussed in chapter 22. This chapter concentrates on the PDW for redesigning existing structures.

A PDW is a highly structured and participative process in which people redesign their own organizational structure from one based on the first genotypical organizational design principle to one based on the second, as described below. It is a comprehensive process during which they also design a set of measurable goals, training requirements for the new design, and other necessities such as how they will cooperate with other groups. These are subsequently negotiated with others before final agreement. Any organization—a corporation, government agency, or association—can use a PDW. A community may use a modified PDW to design itself an organization structure (see chapter 22).

The first PDW was conducted in Australia in 1971. It was devised by Fred Emery to replace the method experts used in the 1960s (STS). This old method evolved from the early 1950s to provide experimental proof that there was an alternative to autocracy in the workplace. It was not suitable for everyday use or to educate people about what is involved in designing DP2 (the second genotypical design principle, described below) organizations. The PDW, therefore, is a method to bring into being organizational forms that have been successfully tested over long periods of time.

THE TWO GENOTYPICAL ORGANIZATION DESIGN PRINCIPLES

The two genotypical design principles were discovered during the Norwegian Industrial Democracy Project (1962–1967). They're called "genotypical" because like DNA, they determine the most fundamental aspects of organizational shape and characteristics. These principles differ in the nature of the redundancy used in an organization. Organizations cannot survive without some redundancy, but there are two distinct ways of obtaining it. The first design principle (DP1) is called "redundancy of parts" because there are more people in the organization than it can use at any given point in time. In DP1 structures, people are replaceable parts. Its critical feature is that responsibility for coordination and control is *not* located with people who are actually doing the work. Therefore, DP1 produces a supervisory hierarchy where some have the right and responsibility to tell others what to do and how to do it. Terms associated with this principle include "command and control," "autocratic," "bureaucratic," and "master-servant relationship."

The second design principle (DP2) is called "redundancy of functions" because flexibility is gained by building into each individual person more skills and functions than he or she can use at any point in time, and certainly a lot more than would typically be associated with a single job description. The most critical feature of DP2 is that responsibility for coordination and control *is* located with people who are actually doing the work (see figure 1). Therefore, DP2 produces a flat

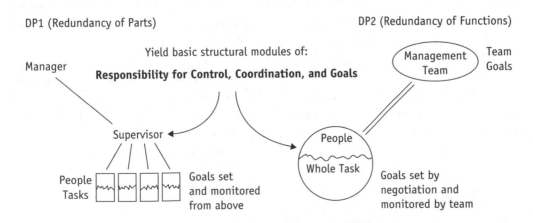

Figure 1. The Organization Design Principles

hierarchy of functions based on self-managing groups where relationships between all groups—both laterally and vertically—entail negotiation between peers. Terms often used include "high performance," "democratic," and "self-directed."

DP2 structures should not be confused with the "you can do what you like" approach, which is called "laissez-faire." Laissez-faire is seen today in DP1 structures where the supervision and management is so loose that it approximates a lack of structure. DP2 structures are highly regulated, as each group contracts to meet a comprehensive set of measurable goals covering every aspect of its day-to-day work. These are all negotiated to ensure that collectively they meet the organization's strategic goals. As the team goals control the work of the teams, so this network of interconnected goals ensures tight control within the organization.

In the PDW, participants are briefed on the design principles and their effects. One of the major effects is on the "six criteria," a set of psychological requirements people have when attempting to do productive work. They are well established and extensively researched. These criteria are:

1. Elbow room, autonomy in decision making

2. Continual learning, for which there must be (a) the ability to set goals, and (b) accurate and timely feedback

3. Variety

4. Mutual support and respect

5. Meaningfulness, which consists of (a) doing work with social value and (b) seeing the whole product or service

6. A desirable future

These requirements are the intrinsic motivators and are closely tied to the design principles. DP1 structures work against the six criteria as well as deskilling over time. Short-term increases in motivation are gained by increased pay, but for sustained high scores on the six criteria, a DP2 structure is a necessity. The design principles also affect other features of interpersonal relations such as the quantity and quality of communication and personality differences. As research continues on these principles, the more powerful they are seen to be.

The overall organization chart looks something like that in figure 2. Every level of the flat hierarchy is composed of self-managing groups, each of which does productive work and negotiates changes. The double lines indicate relations between equals with two-way communication and initiation of negotiation. They do *not* signify reporting relationships in the traditional sense of the term (i.e., who reports to whom, and who supervises whom).

Table 2 summarizes the key distinctions between DP1 and DP2 organizations.

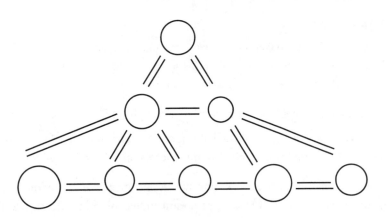

Figure 2. DP2 Structure

	In an Organization Based on ...	
	Design Principle 1	**Design Principle 2**
Basic Performance Unit	Individuals with a supervisor	Self-managing group
Overall Organizational Design	A hierarchy of personal dominance; superiors have the legal right and responsibility to tell subordinates what to do and how to do it	A nondominant hierarchy of functions where all relationships are between peers who negotiate; every functional level does productive work only
Responsibility for Coordination and Control	Is held by successive levels of supervisors and managers	Is held by self-managing groups at every level of the functional hierarchy
Type of Redundancy	Redundancy of parts: People are replaceable parts	Redundancy of functions: People are knowledgeable assets
Quality of Work	Is the direct responsibility of supervisor or specialized quality control section	It is the responsibility of groups doing the work and built into explicit, monitored goals
Specialized People or Sections (e.g., R&D)	People with specialized skills are also treated as replaceable parts; specialized units often fail to coordinate work	If training or legalities prevent full multiskilling, coordination is still shared by the group, but control rests with individual specialists
Requirements for Productive Work	Usually ignored; designs typically work counter to these requirements	The design of the organization specifically addresses the six criteria

Table 2. Comparisons of Structures Based on the Two Design Principles

WHEN TO USE A PDW

PDWs are used when management realizes that high productivity and profit today and into the future depends on the cooperation of staff that is gained by treating them as people, not machines. That is, PDWs are used when top management wants to:

- see increased commitment and responsibility throughout the organization, and

- have an active, adaptive organization that can rapidly reorganize itself in response to changing environmental conditions, and also influence its outside environment.

Embarking down this path of changing the design principle is obviously not a simple, tweaking kind of change program. There are profound and far-reaching effects. Selecting this path requires serious consideration because when the design principle is changed, most existing organizational systems must also be changed, including that of pay and classification. Such fundamental change also demands changes in roles and responsibilities for *all* members of the organization.

PROBABLE OUTCOMES

The primary outcome of one or a series of PDWs is a redesigned, self-managing organization (figure 2). There are other outcomes that occur as a direct result of the PDW:

- Higher productivity and quality because each team has a comprehensive set of measurable goals that collectively further the organization's strategic goals

- Increased responsibility and commitment because all members of the organization are treated as responsible adults

- Reduction in infighting and turf battles, as each team has an agreed-upon identity and area of work, and interfaces with other groups are clearly defined

- Increase in multiskilling because people share goals and work, and the organization has moved to a skill-based pay system

HOW A PDW WORKS

PDWs can be used very flexibly. Small organizations as a whole or sections of larger organizations can redesign their structures in a long day, or over several sessions. Many different parts of a large organization can simultaneously redesign at the same time. Many organizations are not rich and cannot afford to pay overtime for example, to a whole off-shift crew. Therefore, a small "deep slice" team[1] may attend the workshop and then take the *process* back to the others so that everyone is involved in analysis and redesign. Numbers can, therefore, vary widely.

For larger organizations, a series of PDWs will be carefully designed, starting at the lowest level of the organization, and finishing with the senior management team. We start at the bottom for reasons explained later in this chapter.

In a small organization, the design can be of the whole organization. Large organizations are broken into natural sections of the existing structure. Table 3 represents general PDW flow for a section.

PDW

Segment	Tasks
Introduction	• Participant introductions, if required • Senior management/union overview
Analysis	*Briefing 1: DP1 and Its Effects* • Participants score themselves on the six criteria for productive work in their section • Participants identify skills held in the section • Reports and analyses
Structural Redesign	*Briefing 2: DP2 and Its Effects* • Participants draw the work flow and current organizational structure • Participants then redesign the structure, *not* the work flow • Reports
Practicalities for Success	*Briefing 3: Requirements to Make the Design Work* • Participants draft a comprehensive set of measurable goals for each team and the section • Participants decide on the training required for start-up (from the skills matrix) • Participants decide what else is required for the design (e.g., mechanisms for coordination with other groups, technological changes) • Participants draft career paths for the section based on skills held • Participants show how the design improves scores on the six criteria

Table 3. Participative Design Workshop Flow

The PDW manager gives comprehensive briefings about the design principles and their consequences so everybody has this knowledge for the future.

Variations of PDWs include: conducting PDWs in parts separated over time, multiple teams designing different sections, and multiple teams designing the same section. In large organizations where teams have redesigned section by section, management holds its PDW to design the management structure and integrate the existing redesigns into a coherent organizational design.

COST JUSTIFICATION

Increases in productivity and quality arising from change to the second design principle (DP2) have been consistently measured since the early 1950s using normal organizational statistics such as quantity, wastage, accident, and error rates.

Despite this consistent history, this structural change is not for everybody. Some people put their belief in autocracy and their comfort level with the status quo above the need for increased performance.

Table of Uses

Brief Description	Project Length	Number of Participants and Outcome
Software development firm starting up a new venture wanted a high-participation structure for fast, high-quality decisions.	2 days	40 people designed self-managing structure that was instrumental in capturing 68% of their target market in 2 years.
Data mining firm was seeking to decrease report production time and delight customers.	3 days	55 people redesigned 6 departments into one organization of high-performing teams. Report production decreased time by 50%.
Electronics assembly firm wanted to dramatically increase product quality and customer satisfaction levels.	2.5 days	80 people redesigned a structure the reduced customer failures by 45% within 14 months.
Postapartheid South African quasi-government lending agency sought to extend offerings of government services while increasing profits.	2 days per site for 26 sites over 4 weeks	1,300 people formed corporate and branch high-performing teams that developed numerous new products for emerging market segments. Within 18 months, revenues doubled with the same number of staff.

Getting Started

FUNDAMENTALS TO CONSIDER

PDWs require certain conditions for success and sustainability. For unionized enterprises, the union should be involved right from the first discussions. The basic conditions are:

- For all legally constituted organizations where responsibilities are encoded into contractual documents such as duty statements or job specifications, a decision must be made by the relevant authorities that the organization or large autonomous subsection will legally change its design principle. This must be enshrined in some agreement that is binding though some reasonable period of time. *If the design principle is not legally changed from DP1 to DP2, then it is still legally DP1. Everyone will soon realize this, and nothing will actually change in the long term.*

- For unionized enterprises, guarantees usually need to be in place that no one will regress in terms of pay and conditions and that no one will be laid off as a direct result of the process.

- There must be at least "in principle" formulas and plans for such matters as fairly sharing the increased productivity, and finding productive work for people whose levels of the existing hierarchy have been designed out.

- An agreement for a new, more flexible pay system must be in place, whereby people are paid for skills held, not for a job. Changing the design principle alters career paths that are based on movement up the hierarchy.

- Everyone must be educated about the change and its effects through prebriefings about the concepts and the process.

- First-line supervisors and middle management need a special session prior to the PDWs because transfer of responsibility for coordination and control from supervision to productive groups can be threatening. They may need reassurance that opportunities will be provided for them to design themselves creative new work.

For those looking for a proven way to move from a DP1 to a DP2 structure, conducting a series of PDWs for every large section of the structure is a high-leverage, systemic process. For people who still believe that command-and-control methods work in today's rapidly changing world, we wish you success and suggest that you avoid PDWs like the plague.

Guiding Principles for Using the Method

The guiding principles for using PDWs are as follow:

- There is a binding agreement that the entity (large enough to have the autonomy to change the genotypical design principle) will move to DP2.

- No designs will be imposed. Everyone in the organization participates in analysis and detailed design of his or her section.

- The process is educational. Everyone gains conscious conceptual knowledge about the design principles and how to use them.

- Those who work in a section redesign their section. As long as the design is genuinely DP2, the workers in it will continue to improve and redesign it because it is *theirs*.

- Use trained and experienced PDW managers. They must know the theory, give briefings, answer questions, and recognize non-DP2 designs.

Roles, Responsibilities, and Relationships

Role of Top Management

Before the PDW, top management is responsible for the following:

- Sitting down with the unions, if present.

- Making it crystal clear to everyone what type of structures they are moving from and to.

- Clarifying that a strategic change has been decided and is not negotiable.
- Ensuring that everyone has a clear vision of strategy for the future.

Top management (and/or senior union representation) is usually not present throughout an entire PDW unless it is a smallish organization or the PDW is for a senior management group. However, during a PDW:

- The CEO should open the workshop, returning later to hear the reports.
- Relevant managers should be on hand if questions arise about the reality of the change or about information that groups might need to finalize a design.

After the PDW or series of PDWs, the strategy level (the top level of the organization that makes strategic decisions and develops organizational policy) has the responsibility to:

- ride the boundary between the enterprise and the environment, disseminating knowledge of relevant environmental change, and updating strategic plans and policies; ensuring the overall financial health of the enterprise through investments, and so on.
- ensure conditions are right for the new structure to succeed.

ROLE OF THE PDW MANAGER

We use the word "manager" instead of "facilitator" because PDW management excludes much conventional facilitation in running groups. PDW managers have a totally "hands-on" role to produce:

- workable DP2 designs for the new organizational structure, and
- an enterprise whose members hold conceptual *and* practical knowledge to redesign for active adaptation to the changing environment.

PDW managers are responsible for giving accurate briefings, assuring participants' understanding, challenging designs, and suggesting alternatives when required.

ROLE OF PARTICIPANTS

Before the PDW, the participants must attend prebriefings. During the PDW, they redesign the structure of their section, and design in the practicalities that will ensure the design works. Afterward, they work within the new structure, redesigning and improving as conditions warrant.

Conditions for Success

WHEN TO USE THIS APPROACH

We've discussed why and when to use this approach and what conditions above are necessary to get started. Long-term success depends on this preparatory work and these conditions.

WHY IT WORKS

This method works because:

- It is based on a well-established and unique combination of solid theories (see the "Critical Underlying Theory and Research Base" section of this chapter).

- DP2 creates the structures that provide for individuals to be treated as people. When people hold responsibility for coordinating and controlling their own work and can use their human abilities for learning, thinking, and planning, they respond with responsibility, motivation, and creativity.

- The PDW was designed by the same person (Fred Emery) who discovered the genotypical design principles after years of research on people, social systems, and how to create organizations fit for people to work and live in. It has been continually refined over a 35-year period to ensure that when followed, it is a highly reliable method for making this change.

WHEN NOT TO USE THIS METHOD

Do not use this method if:

- The conditions for success listed above in the "Getting Started" section are not present.

- Your objective is just one or two high-performance teams or teams just at the operational level. This process is intended to redesign the *entire organization*. The design principles do not mix within an organization.

- Senior management is unsure that it's the best strategic direction. This effort must *not* be posed as a "pilot" or any type of experiment, because people will not take it seriously.

However, if management is simply unsure about the method, an "educational PDW" can be run, and a technically accurate simulation is also available from Amerin Consulting. The only difference between an educational and a real PDW is that no guarantees are given that the results of the educational PDW will be implemented.

COMMON MISTAKES

Most mistakes are avoided by education. Some common mistakes in the use of this method are shown in table 4.

PDW

PDW

Common Mistake (and Likely Result)	Reason for the Mistake	Remedy
Asking employees if they want a DP2 organization (*this decision is not their responsibility*).	Executives are trying to model participation, but only top management has the authority to make this decision.	Do research and decide. Inclusivity is covered by education and participation in redesign.
Not committing to a binding agreement to change the design principle (*people realize the announced change is phony and nothing will change*).	The most important reason is lack of understanding of the reality and power of the design principles.	Educate top management thoroughly up front and don't hold PDWs until the conditions are in place.
Not committing to change the compensation and reward system (*dissatisfaction will rise rapidly*).	Some can resist. However, compensation and reward changes are necessary for economic justice, and everybody must understand why.	Build compensation and reward system changes into the agreement. Hire a professional career path designer to use drafts from the PDWs and integrate them to fit the new structural form.
Mistake multiskilling for changing the design principle (*multiskilling does not produce increased motivation and proper use of increased skills*).	Multiskilling is fashionable and relatively easy. DP2 structures both motivate and encourage multiskilling.	Change the design principle first and follow with a pay-for-skills-held system. Then people also have a financial incentive to increase the depth and breadth of their skills.
Having team leaders for "self-managing groups" (*people realize that only the name changes, that responsibility has not shifted*).	There is no understanding of the design principles and a corruption of the term "self-managing group."	Change the design principle and ensure that all understand the concepts. Leadership and lead roles will move around the group as required.
PDW manager confusing DP2 with laissez-faire or corrupting the PDW (*performance and scores on six criteria go backward*).	PDW manager doesn't know the theory and practice. The PDW is not a "touchy-feely" or human relations–based approach to organizational change.	Learn the theory and practice. Choose PDW managers who can show you DP2 designs and hard-data outcomes from previous work.
Designs being implemented before goals are agreed, essential training done, and so on (*performance and scores on six criteria become lower, and there is a risk of accidents from lack of training*).	There is haste and confusion between DP2 and laissez-faire. Without measurable goals, the design is laissez-faire and the results are worse than those from DP1.	Don't implement designs until everything is in place.

Table 4. Common Mistakes

Critical Underlying Theory and Research Base

As Kurt Lewin once noted, "There is nothing as practical as a good theory." To build a sustainable organizational structure in which people are intrinsically motivated to implement the strategy and continually improve performance, the Participative Design Workshop draws upon solid theory from a wide variety of research venues over the past 70 years.

Theorist/Researcher	Key Theory Elements	Use in Participative Design Workshop
Kurt Lewin and others	Discovered effects of democratic and autocratic climates and "laissez-faire"	Climates now known to be produced by structures. PDW manager must recognize and reject autocratic and laissez-faire designs.
Eric Trist and Ken Bamforth, and others	Birth of sociotechnical systems	These researchers began the work that ultimately led to the PDW.
Fred Emery	Characteristics of open sociotechnical systems as a subpart of open systems theory	This work builds on more than 50 years of research on "open jointly optimized sociotechnical systems," now called systems with DP2 structures.
Fred Emery	Genotypical organization design principles	PDW provides conscious conceptual knowledge of these principles and how to design and implement structures based on the second of them (DP2).
Fred Emery and Einar Thorsrud	The six criteria that constitute the third, human dimension of organizational success—what people require for productive work.	People assess the six criteria for productive work in their current structure and then design a structure that improves their scores.
Fred Emery, Einar Thorsrud, and others	Development of previous method (STS) used to establish scientific proof of the efficacy of DP2	PDW replaced STS because it was designed for diffusion. Proof was accepted in 1969 that there was an effective alternative to autocracy at work.
Merrelyn Emery	The "two-stage model" of active adaptation (see chapter 22)	This researcher modified PDW for design (e.g., to have a PDW follow the Search Conference to complete an organization's active adaptation).

Table 5. Theory Base

Theorist/Researcher	Key Theory Elements	Use in Participative Design Workshop
Fred Emery and Merrelyn Emery	As above, plus years of associated R&D	With dedicated others, these researchers brought open systems to a high level of reliability.

Table 5. Continued

Sustaining the Results

ADVICE FOR RETAINING THE BENEFITS ACHIEVED

If there is an agreement and the designs implemented are genuinely DP2, the conditions for sustainability are built in for the life of the agreement. When the agreement is up for negotiation, anyone who wants to revert to DP1 has to convince all parties to do that, which will be difficult.

IMPACT ON ORGANIZATION'S CULTURAL ASSUMPTIONS

Culture is normally defined as the systems of assumptions and conventions that govern the lives of a particular group. These usually implicit rules of behavior are largely determined by the structural relations between people—those governed by the design principles. When the design principle is changed, a whole new system of behaviors comes into play: cooperation rather than competition, motivation rather than passivity and carelessness. Over time, these behaviors become established.

Burning Question

Why would I bother changing the design principle when I can currently afford a pay increase to boost my employees' commitment?

Your employees' commitment after a pay increase lasts for only a short time, after which everything returns to normal and you have to increase the pay again. Changing the design principle ensures that your organization will enjoy a long period of high commitment with increasing innovation and productivity.

Some Final Comments

Table 6 summarizes what is distinctive about PDW to clearly illustrate what PDW is and what it is not.

Participative Design Workshop	PDW Does Not
• Is based on open systems theory that specifies an environment, produces active adaptation to that environment, and uses environmental knowledge to make change. Messengers do *not* get shot.	• Rely on closed systems; no environment is specified, so organizations ignore it. Messengers can get shot when they convey news of environmental change.
• Assumes people are purposeful, responsible, want to learn, and can change their environments.	• Assume that most people need direction from above or help to be responsible and purposeful.
• Deals with genotypical material. Does not rely on words such as "teams," but deals with hard legal realities of structural relationships. Is sustainable.	• Deal with phenotypical (superficial) material such as communications and interpersonal relationships. People feel good in the short term.
• Transfers conscious conceptual knowledge and know-how of the design principles for sustainable, active adaptation to all. Reduces dependency.	• Neglect to transfer conceptual and practical knowledge for future use. Can produce dependency.
• Produces motivation to sustain changes.	• Produce only short-lived change or resistance to change
• Produces energy and creativity for innovation.	• Produce more cynical and apathetic people without the energy to change anything.

Table 6. Summary of Differences from Other Methods

About the Authors

Merrelyn Emery (me9@grapevine.net.au) has been developing opens systems theory (OST) methods now for more than 35 years, many of them spent working with Fred Emery. She holds a first-class honors degree in psychology and a Ph.D. in marketing. She has worked with innumerable communities and organizations in the public, private, and volunteer sectors. She continues to teach the state of the art of open systems theory around the world.

Tom Devane (tomd@tomdevane.com) helps organizations and communities thrive in their respective environments. His diverse background in strategy, Six Sigma, technology, organizational development, community planning, and leadership effectiveness provides for dramatic, sustainable improvement. With BS and MS degrees in finance, Big Six consulting, and industry leadership experience, he founded his own firm in 1988. Clients include Microsoft, Hewlett-Packard, Johnson & Johnson, General Electric, the U.S. Forest Service, AT&T, Honeywell, and the Republic of South Africa.

Where to Go for More Information

REFERENCES

Bradshaw, C., J. Roberts, and S. Cheuy. "The Search Conference: A Participative Planning Method That Builds Widespread Collaboration." In *The Collaborative Work Systems Fieldbook: Strategies, Tools, and Techniques,* edited by M. M. Beyerlein, C. McGee, G. D. Klein, J. E. Nemiro, and L. Broedling, 43–56. San Francisco: Pfeiffer, 2002.

Cabana, S. "Participative Design Works, Partially Doesn't." *Journal for Quality and Participation* 18, no. 1 (1995).

Cabana, S., F. Emery, and M. Emery. "The Search for Effective Strategic Planning Is Over." *Journal for Quality and Participation* 18, no. 4 (1995): 10–19.

de Guerre, D. W. "Action Research as Process: The Two Stage Model for Active Adaptation." *Ecclectica* (2002), http://www.ecclectica.ca/issues/2002/4/.

———. "Variations on the Participative Design Workshop." In *The Collaborative Work Systems Fieldbook: Strategies, Tools, and Techniques,* edited by M. M. Beyerlein, G. Klein and L. Broedling, 275–286. San Francisco: John Wiley & Sons, 2002.

Emery, F. "Participative Design: Effective, Flexible and Successful, Now!" *Journal for Quality and Participation* (January/February 1995).

Emery, F., and M. Emery. "The Participative Design Workshop." In *The Social Engagement of Social Science: A Tavistock Anthology: The Socio-technical Perspective*, Vol. II, edited by E. Trist and H. Murray, 599–613. Philadelphia: University of Pennsylvania Press, 1993.

Emery, Merrelyn. "The Evolution of Open Systems to the 2 Stage Model." In *Work Teams: Past, Present and Future*, edited by M. M. Beyerlein, 85–103. Amsterdam: Kluwer Academic Publishers, 2000.

———. "The Power of Community Search Conferences." *Journal for Quality and Participation* 18, no. 7 (1995): 70–79.

———. *Searching: The Theory and Practice of Making Cultural Change.* Philadelphia: John Benjamins, 1999.

———, ed. *Participative Design for Participative Democracy.* Canberra, Australia: ANU/CCE, 1993.

Emery, M., and R. Purser. *The Search Conference: A Powerful Method for Planning Organizational Change and Community Action.* San Francisco: Jossey Bass, 1996.

INFLUENTIAL SOURCES

de Guerre, D. W. "The Co-Determination of Cultural Change Over Time." *Systemic Practice and Action Research* 13, no. 5 (2000): 645–663.

———. "Democratic Social Engagement." *Innovation Journal* 10, no. 1 (2005).

PDW

de Guerre, D. W., and H. Hornstein. "Active Adaptation of Municipal Governance: An Action Research Report." *Innovation Journal* 9, no. 1 (2004).

de Guerre, D. W., and M. M. Taylor. "Participative Design and Executive Coaching." *International Journal of Knowledge, Culture and Change Management* 4 (2005): 513–521.

Emery, Merrelyn. *The Future of Schools: How Communities and Staff Can Transform Their School Districts.* Lanham, MD: Rowman & Littlefield Education; Toronto: Oxford University Press, in press 2006.

_____. "The Search Conference: Design and Management with a Solution to the "Pairing" Puzzle." In *The Social Engagement of Social Science: A Tavistock Anthology: The Socio-Ecological Perspective*, Vol. III, edited by E. Trist, F. Emery, and H. Murray. Philadelphia: University of Pennsylvania Press, 1997.

_____. "The Six Criteria for Intrinsic Motivation in Education Systems: Partial Democratization of a University Experience, Partial Success." In *Educational Futures: Shifting Paradigm of Universities and Education*, 309–334. Istanbul: Sabanci University, 2000.

Paton, John, and M. Emery. "Community Planning in the Torres Strait." *Journal of Quality and Participation* 19, no. 5 (1996): 26–35.

Purser, R. E., and S. Cabana. *The Self Managing Organization: How Leading Companies Are Transforming the Work of Teams for Real Impact.* New York: The Free Press, 1998.

Trist, E., and H. Murray, eds. *The Social Engagement of Social Science: A Tavistock Anthology: The Socio-Technical Perspective*, Vol. II. Philadelphia: University of Pennsylvania Press, 1993.

ORGANIZATIONS

Canadian Institute for Research and Education in Human Systems—cirehs@sympatico.ca

For information about training courses and current projects.

Centre for Human Relations and Community Studies, Concordia University, Montreal—centreh@vax2.concordia.ca

For information about training courses and current projects.

Department of Applied Human Sciences, Concordia University, Montreal

Fred Emery Institute, Melbourne

The Modern Times Workplace—www.moderntimesworkplace.com

The Vaughan Consulting Group—www.vaughanconsulting.com/pdw.html

The authors thank Peter Aughton of Amerin, Australia, for the use of the P&N Tools case study and Don deGuerre of Concordia University for his suggestions and help in editing.

1. A "deep slice" team covers each level of the existing hierarchy in the section and as many different functions and skills across the section as possible. Do not allow PDWs to be used with only one level of the existing hierarchy at a time, or with a single-function section, as the designs will be inadequate.

44

JEREMY TEKELL, JON TURNER, CHERYL HARRIS,
MICHAEL BEYERLEIN, AND SARAH BODNER

Collaborative Work Systems Design

Never tell people how to do things . . . they will surprise you with their ingenuity.

—General George S. Patton, Jr.

 ## Creating New Forums for Dialogue

Although the automotive glass plant had made great strides in improving its culture to create an environment that fostered excitement about the work and pride in the company, management was struggling with taking their improvements to the "next level." They discovered Collaborative Work Systems (CWS) Design and sent a group of managers and operators to a workshop to learn more about it.

In the workshop, they looked at their organization's support of collaboration through the results of the accompanying assessment tool and were able to spend time together discussing what they thought the results meant. Having managers and operators working together brought more perspectives into the discussion and opened a dialogue between them that didn't exist before. Together, they identified some major issues and created plans to address them.

A new change leadership team comprised of a cross-section of the organization was formed to lead the way in creating a long-term strategic plan. The goal was to move toward collaboration as a means of achieving business results while building on their healthy culture and integrating their LEAN manufacturing initiatives. This change leadership team took great strides to work with all levels of the organization to bring in their perspectives to the change plan.

CWS Design helped the plant create new forums for dialogue and a long-term plan for change that will lead the plant toward excellence for many years to come.

The Basics

WHAT IS CWS DESIGN? WHAT IS THE PURPOSE OF THE METHOD?

CWS Design guides those leading the change effort through a holistic design process that creates the framework for successfully changing the organization to support collaboration and improve business results. Figure 1 provides a visual overview of the method.

CWS Design helps change leaders take a systemic approach to change by applying a strategic change model and using assessment to help decide where they are and where to they want to be in their change effort.

People at all levels of the organization are enabled to work together to design and lead change. This allows all areas of the organization to have a voice in the process, which promotes a sense of ownership.

The method is grounded in sociotechnical systems theory as well as decades of compre-

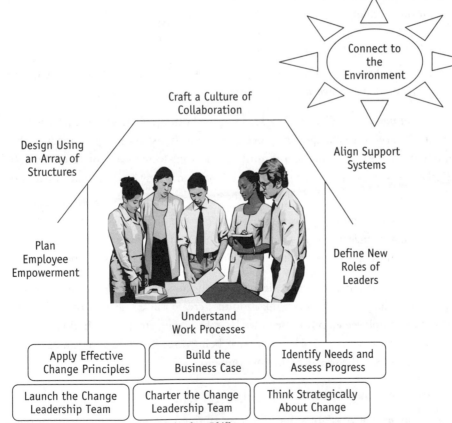

Beyerlein and Harris, 2004; reprinted with permission from Pfeiffer.

Figure 1. Collaborative Work Systems Design

hensive research on collaborative environments in the workplace combined with practical use and validation in the field.

WHEN AND WHERE IS CWS DESIGN USED?

This method is appropriate for organizations looking for greater flexibility around their work, those that are looking to incorporate a mixture of individuals and teams, and those currently using teams. It may be used in conjunction with existing initiatives as well as a starting point for change. The focus is on using collaboration to achieve results.

WHAT ARE THE OUTCOMES FROM USING CWS DESIGN?

Groups come away with an understanding of the broad elements of the organization involved in supporting collaboration, a shared awareness of the strengths and concerns in their organization, and real plans to implement change. The accompanying assessment tool provides a baseline measure of support of collaboration and can be repeated to determine progress. Participants build on their organization's previous successful change work and create a long-term framework for future change.

HOW DOES CWS DESIGN WORK?

CWS Design is organized around 13 critical success factors of collaboration (see figure 1). These factors are divided into two major categories:

1. *Create a Foundation for Change.* The bricks at the bottom of the model examine the "process" of organizational change. The process of change is just as or more important than the content of change. Any change effort must have a strong foundation for success. Each of the critical success factors acts as a brick in the foundation. If any brick is weak, the foundation will crumble and sacrifice the integrity of the entire structure.

2. *Align the Organization to Collaboration.* The house and sun represent the "content" of the organizational change necessary to support collaboration. Redesigning the framework of the organization to support collaboration should improve both business and people results.

The work is in the center of the model because business reasons should be the "anchor" of any change effort. The pieces of the organization that create the framework of the building are culture, structure, employee empowerment, leader roles, and systems. The building framework must be constructed to meet the needs of the work being done inside it, and be able to adjust to the changing demands of the weather (the environment).

WHAT IS THE FLOW OR PROCESS?

Organizational change is not a linear process, so there is no prescribed order or one right way to develop and support collaboration. CWS Design allows change work to begin or continue building on previous efforts where it is most appropriate for each organization.

Table of Uses

Setting and Description	Project Length	Events	Number of Participants
Automotive Parts Manufacturer • Made "go" decision on change effort • Creation and development of change leadership team • Big-picture planning of change effort • Development of plans to generate shared leadership • Design of implementation plan • Development of internal resources to facilitate the change effort	1.5 years	• Workshop for managers and operators to "scout" possible changes • Workshop for change leadership team to come together and make initial plans • Workshop to develop internal resources • Multiple working sessions for the change leadership team to develop and implement change plans • Series of events to share with and gather input from organizational members	• 8 people • 10 people • 2 people • Varied • Varied
Chemical Processing Plant • Cooperation of union and management in change initiative • Mapping of desired organization structure and subsequent actions • Development of plans to generate shared leadership • Creation of design teams to implement the change effort	2 years	• Workshop for union/management leadership group to determine the desired state and initial plans • Workshop for design teams to develop implementation plans for the change effort • Multiple working sessions for detailed implementation work	• 8 people • 30 people • Groups of 10–20
Animal Health Products Manufacturer • Education and development of a cohesive steering committee • Design of new organization structure • Creation of empowerment plan • Development of a comprehensive set of training materials to develop new teams • Development of internal facilitators to deliver the training • Creation of a comprehensive plan for support systems development that coordinated with empowerment plan and leader transition	2 years	• Series of workshops for steering committee • Weekly sessions to develop training system • Monthly sessions to develop support systems • Series of training sessions to develop cross-functional teams	• 8 people • 6 people • 4 groups of 8–12 people • Varied

About the Authors

The Collaborative Work System Design Group (CWSDG, workteam@unt.edu) consists of *Dr. Michael Beyerlein* (Center for Collaborative Organizations), *Dr. Sarah Bodner, Dr. Cheryl Harris, Jeremy Tekell, Jon Turner,* and *Sydney Weinman-Barcus.* The group, located in Dallas–Fort Worth, Texas, strives to unleash the power of collaboration through research and consultation with client companies. Members of the group approach collaboration as practitioners, consultants, researchers, and scholars.

Where to Go for More Information

REFERENCES

Beyerlein, M., D. Johnson, and S. Beyerlein, eds. *Advances in Interdisciplinary Studies of Work Teams.* Vol. 9, *Team-Based Organizing.* Oxford: Elsevier/JAI Imprint, 2003.

Beyerlein, M., C. McGee, G. Klein, J. Nemiro, and L. Broedling, eds. *The Collaborative Work Systems Fieldbook: Strategies, Tools, and Techniques.* San Francisco: Jossey-Bass/Pfeiffer, 2003.

Beyerlein, M. M., and C. L. Harris. *Guiding the Journey to Collaborative Work Systems: A Strategic Design Workbook.* San Francisco: Pfeiffer, 2004.

Nemiro, J., G. Klein, C. McGee, and M. Beyerlein. *The Collaborative Work System Casebook.* Denton, TX: Center for Collaborative Organizations, 2006.

ORGANIZATION

Center for Collaborative Organizations (University of North Texas)—www.workteams.unt.edu

45

WILLIAM A. ADAMS AND CYNTHIA A. ADAMS

The Whole Systems Approach
Using the Entire System to Change and Run the Business

Change is the law of life. And those who look only to the past or present are certain to miss the future.

—John F. Kennedy

A Privately Owned Enterprise

Carlson Companies, Inc., a privately owned, family enterprise, has more than 190,000 employees in 50+ countries providing services in travel, hospitality (hotels and cruises), marketing, and the restaurant industry. Top company leaders include second- and third-generation family members of founder Curt Carlson.

For 65 years, Carlson operated as a holding company with six distinct business units managing more than 16 brands, including Radisson Hotels and Resorts, Country Inns and Suites, TGI Friday's, Carlson Marketing Group, Carlson Wagonlit Travel, and Regent Seven Seas Cruises. In 2003, Carlson leaders strategically chose to move from a holding company to an integrated operating company focused on the customer, as illustrated in table 1.

The changes have impacted every area and system of the organization. Since the official kickoff in February 2003, Carlson has realized substantial enterprise-wide and business unit results. December 2007 is the date for achieving a fully transformed organization, resilient and positioned to thrive over the next 65 years.

As Jay Witzel, CEO of Carlson Hotels Worldwide observed, "We've created a culture accus-

From	To
1. Product centric	1. Customer (relationship) centric
2. Working for a silo (BU/Function)	2. Working for Carlson
3. Silo approach	3. Optimize at the Enterprise level (T-Management)
4. Lack of trust in other groups/learned apathy	4. Trust and partnership between groups; assume positive intent
5. Opting out/everything is optional	5. WED (We Encourage Debate) and WEA (We Expect Alignment)
6. Fund everything/everything is important	6. Prioritization/vital few
7. Task-driven reward for activity	7. Outcome-driven reward for tangible results
8. Anecdotal decisions	8. Fact-based decisions
9. Cost-driven	9. Value-driven
10. Ad hoc	10. Operational and process discipline
11. Complacency	11. Sense of urgency; speed to market and agility
12. Holding company	12. Operating company

Table 1. Carlson Companies, Inc., Moving to an Integrated Operating Company

tomed to change. Continuous change will be the methodology of the day. Long-term success means continuous change."

Frequently Asked Questions

WHAT IS THE WHOLE SYSTEMS APPROACH? WHAT IS ITS PURPOSE?

The Whole Systems Approach (WSA)ˢᵐ is a framework for effectively weaving multiple organizational change initiatives into a well-designed, highly effective, coherent whole. The purpose of WSA is to achieve organization-wide change and large-scale employee engagement, buy-in and results through enhanced leadership, and employee commitment and accountability.

The name itself—whole systems—goes to the heart of the approach. Every system within the organization is evaluated, created, modified or redesigned and then integrated and aligned. By filtering each system through the WSA framework, organizations can ensure the various parts are connected in a thoughtful, consistent manner to support employee engagement, effective leadership, and peak performance levels. Every stakeholder—including employees, vendors, management, contractors, and customers—is involved in the process.

WHEN AND WHERE IS THE WSA USED?

The WSA framework is particularly valuable when:

1. A need to fundamentally change or transform is evident;

2. A number of existing efforts require integration into a comprehensive whole;

3. Large-scale engagement/commitment of all constituencies is desired;

4. A new organizational focus is required;

5. A new possibility could potentially yield significant value or enhanced capability; and

6. Current efforts lack speed, results, or broad ownership.

WHAT ARE THE OUTCOMES FROM USING THIS METHOD?

The WSA framework focuses on:

- increasing leadership effectiveness,

- large-scale engagement

- creating changeable organizations, and

- producing exceptional business results.

Grounded in practicality, the WSA is centered on what works. When the blinders come off and people develop a sense of ownership, contribution, and significance, enthusiasm and heightened motivation become contagious.

As Al Pino, COO of First Security Information Technologies, Inc., observed, "I have never experienced anything so natural, tiring, rewarding, difficult, and, at the same time, energizing in my life. I feel very close to this work. It has created many opportunities for me. I find satisfaction in knowing I have expended everything I can for the values in which I believe." Pino likened his organization to an elephant on an invisible chain. "Once we let go of our limiting beliefs, new possibilities were evident in every area of our organization."

Companies investing in the WSA can expect to:

- accelerate the speed of change implementation,

- stimulate cooperation, engender commitment, and reinforce teamwork,

- generate organizational-wide ownership of efforts with all stakeholders,

- produce results that could not have been accomplished using traditional methods,

- develop organizational self-reliance and resiliency for sustaining a thriving organization, and

- achieve successful fundamental change and corporate reinvention.

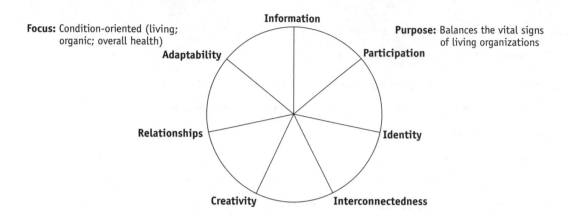

Focus: Condition-oriented (living; organic; overall health)

Purpose: Balances the vital signs of living organizations

Information

Participation

Adaptability

Identity

Relationships

Creativity

Interconnectedness

Figure 1. Conditions of Thriving Organizations. Leadership is responsible for creating and maintaining the conditions that allow the organization to thrive.

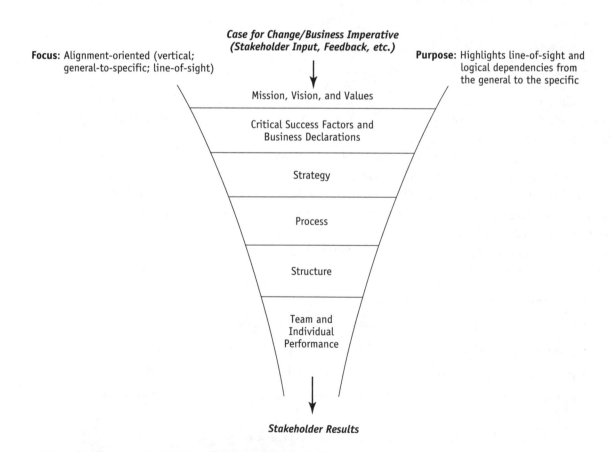

Focus: Alignment-oriented (vertical; general-to-specific; line-of-sight)

Case for Change/Business Imperative (Stakeholder Input, Feedback, etc.)

Purpose: Highlights line-of-sight and logical dependencies from the general to the specific

Mission, Vision, and Values

Critical Success Factors and Business Declarations

Strategy

Process

Structure

Team and Individual Performance

Stakeholder Results

Figure 2. Alignment Model. Line of sight is achieved by aligning the organization from organizational identity (mission/vision/values and strategy) to team and individual results.

How Does WSA Work? What Is the Flow or Process?

This approach is centered on three core models and a systematic process, as shown in figures 1 through 4.

Through experience, we have found the application of these models within the context of the Phases of Transformation to be the most effective means of planning for and implementing transformation, from inception through implementation to running the business. The beauty of this approach is that any change methodology, small or large in scale, may be incorporated under the WSA umbrella.

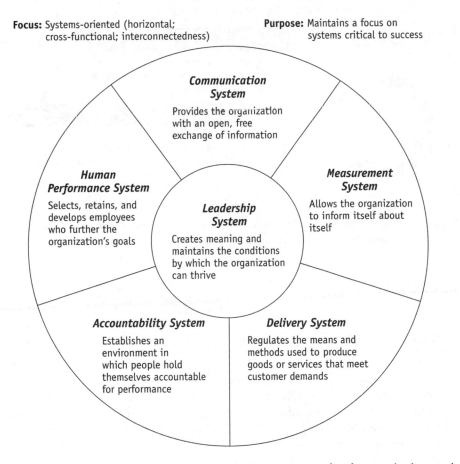

Focus: Systems-oriented (horizontal; cross-functional; interconnectedness)

Purpose: Maintains a focus on systems critical to success

Communication System
Provides the organization with an open, free exchange of information

Human Performance System
Selects, retains, and develops employees who further the organization's goals

Leadership System
Creates meaning and maintains the conditions by which the organization can thrive

Measurement System
Allows the organization to inform itself about itself

Accountability System
Establishes an environment in which people hold themselves accountable for performance

Delivery System
Regulates the means and methods used to produce goods or services that meet customer demands

Figure 3. Six Systems of Organizational Effectiveness. Six Systems ensures that the organization continues to be healthy and that changes are sustained.

Set the Stage

- Establish case for change
- Establish vision
- Build capacity to lead change
- Build infrastructure to drive change

Change the Business

- Communicate/engage employees
- Skills, incentives, resources and action plans
- Design new processes, systems, and behaviors
- Build new infrastructure for the organization
- Execute project implementation plans

Transition

- Program management
- Adopt newly designed processes and systems
- Stop old processes and behaviors

Run the Business

- Sustain key elements of the new organization
- Continuously improve the new organization
- After action reviews
- Course corrections
- Learning and feedback

Communication

Figure 4. Whole System Phases of Transformation. Four phases provide the process framework for transforming an organization and sustaining the changes once they are made.

Table of Uses

Typical Setting	Brief Description	Project Length	Key Events	Number of Participants
Senior leadership effectiveness assessment and development sessions, team effectiveness meetings, forums and retreats	Developing top leadership (L1–L3) into the most effective leadership team they can become; the need for change is clearly understood and articulated	Design and deliver a series of sessions over 18–36 months	Needs assessment, design, delivery, evaluation, and ongoing validation and reinforcement	Number can range from a low of 30 to a high of several hundred in larger organizations; participation is limited to the top 3 leadership levels

Typical Setting	Brief Description	Project Length	Key Events	Number of Participants
Transformation work planning sessions and Result Focus and Alignment (RFA)	Integrating and aligning major multiple change initiatives within the organization to maximize the results enterprise-wide	Develop the strategic vision and work plan within 2 weeks–several months	One-on-one and large group interviews and information gathering	Leadership and other organization members and external constituencies
Organizational readiness and whole system assessments	Resolving confusion regarding the underlying causes of corporate ineffectiveness	Complete the assessment within 2 weeks–several months	Review and research readiness criteria	Snapshot view of the organization that includes gathering data from all constituencies
Strategic planning process and planning sessions	Working with the existing strategic process and plan; redesigning and creating, if necessary, a process	A year with ongoing work over 18 months	Sessions typically last from several hours to several days with monitoring conducted quarterly during the RFA sessions	Top 3 executive team levels and engaging the entire organization

About the Authors

William A. (Bill) Adams (William.Adams@maxcomminc.com), with more than 30 years of leadership experience, coaches and develops CEOs, presidents, and their teams to create a compelling vision and lead large-scale change and cultural transformation. His clients, Fortune 500 corporations to venture-capital start-ups, represent diverse industries. Coauthor of *The Whole Systems Approach: Involving Everyone in the Company to Change and Transform Your Business,* Bill holds an MS in interpersonal and organizational communication.

Cynthia A. (Cindy) Adams's (Cindy.Adams@maxcomminc.com) primary talent is in guiding clients through all aspects of cultural and systems transformation, including work redesign, large-group conferencing, organizational development, continuous improvement, and customer service enhancement. Coauthor of *The Whole Systems Approach: Involving Everyone in the Company to Change and Transform Your Business,* she has worked with clients including GOJO Industries, Ameritech, and Michigan Consolidated Gas. She holds an MS in organizational management.

Where to Go for More Information

REFERENCES

Adams, Cindy, and W. A. (Bill) Adams, with Michael Bowker. *The Whole Systems Approach: Using the Entire Organization to Transform and Run Your Business.* Provo, UT: Executive Excellence Publishing, 1999.

Maxcomm's *Whole Systems Approach to Changing and Running Your Business Guide.* Salt Lake City, UT: Maxcomm, Inc., 1999.

A comprehensive "how-to" manual documenting the entire changing and running the business process from a Whole Systems Approach perspective. The purpose of the guide is to create "a world of work where people thrive."

INFLUENTIAL SOURCES

Gerstner, Louis V., Jr. *Who Says Elephants Can't Dance?* New York: Harper Business, 2002.

Kaplan, Robert S., and David P. Norton. *The Balanced Scorecard: Translating Strategy into Action.* Boston, MA: Harvard Business School Press, 1996.

Wheatley, M. *Leadership and the New Science.* San Francisco: Berrett-Koehler, 1992.

ORGANIZATION

Maxcomm, Inc.—www.maxcomminc.com

IMPROVING METHODS

Improving methods increase effectiveness and create operational efficiencies in such areas as cycle time, waste, productivity, and relationships. Basic assumptions of how the organization works often stay the same, while breakthroughs are achieved in processes, relationships, individual behaviors, knowledge, and distributive leadership.

46

PATRICE MURPHY, CELIA KIRWAN, AND RONALD ASHKENAS

Rapid Results

All life is an experiment.

—Ralph Waldo Emerson

Two Stories

ACCELERATING COMPANY GROWTH

In 2002, Avery Dennison's CEO, Philip Neal, and the company's president, Dean Scarborough, were searching for new ways to accelerate organizational growth. With revenues of just over $4 billion and more than 20,000 employees around the world, this maker of adhesive materials enjoyed enviable profitability levels, but had grown less than 10 percent over the past two years. Plus, the company's pipeline of new initiatives was mainly long-term, with payoffs at least two to three years out.

Neal and Scarborough decided that they had to find ways of growing more quickly using products and technology that the company already possessed. Three divisions in the Cleveland, Ohio, area were selected for a pilot experiment using the Rapid Results approach. In the pilot, the divisional managers identified 14 growth opportunities and assigned each one to a cross-functional team. Each team was then given the challenge of achieving a measurable new business result within 100 days—with the prospect that the innovation might offer much larger gains in the future.

The results achieved in this 100-day period were remarkable. One team designed and developed a product solution previously considered "impossible"—and got customer approval at a very good price. Another team closed within 50 days on a sales target that had been sched-uled to come in over the course of 12 to 15 months. A third team not only developed certain automotive components that they would supply, but also started acting as a kind of coordinating broker—integrating the contributions of a number of other suppliers for a critical product line for one key customer. The customer solved an urgent problem, and the team more than doubled sales of Avery Dennison components in that customer's product line.

Late in 2002, the company's top managers traveled from California to Ohio to hear teams report on their 100-day experiences. In addition to the impressive results, team members talked enthusiastically about how much they had learned—and the exhilaration of generating a real success. CEO Neal later described the meeting as one of the best days in his career.

Neal and Scarborough immediately decided to expand the process across the company. Using the Rapid Results approach, $50 million in additional revenue was realized in the first full year from dozens of projects that utilized existing products, technologies, or customer relationships. From 14 initial U.S.-based projects, the program quickly grew to 500 projects worldwide, involving thousands of employees, generating more than $150 million in less than two years.

RAPID RESULTS IN INTERNATIONAL DEVELOPMENT

In 2003, with the scourge of HIV/AIDS sweeping across Africa, Dr. Saleh Meky, minister of health for the tiny country of Eritrea, knew he was racing against the clock to prevent a health disaster in his country of 4.5 million citizens. Although a five-year plan was in place to prevent the spread of the disease, Dr. Meky was not satisfied that the pace was sufficient.

Based on advice from the World Bank, Dr. Meky worked with a consultant to launch six Rapid Results teams in the central region of Eritrea. Each team set a truly ambitious goal—a result that would achieve a significant and measurable gain on one priority HIV/AIDS prevention theme in the five-year plan. However, instead of five years, each project goal needed to be achieved in 100 days or less.

Projects touched various components of the five-year plan, including school-based education, home care, and engagement with critical groups such as commercial sex workers and truck drivers. For example, one of the projects focused on one region aimed to increase the use of voluntary counseling and testing services (VCT) by 25 percent and achieving an 80 percent positive satisfaction rating from users, all within 100 days.

By project end, the weekly number of clients visiting VCT facilities in Asmara had leapt by 80 percent and the trend continued to rise. User exit questionnaires developed as part of the Rapid Results Initiative also showed a consistent 95 percent level of satisfaction with the quality of the VCT service.

To achieve the result, the team tried innovations such as opening three new VCT sites, training five additional counselors, distributing Rapid Test kits, procuring some new equipment and furniture (videos for waiting rooms, for example), and putting in place a systematic tracking and monitoring system. The team noted that these developments—and the result—were accomplishments they would never have thought possible before the rapid cycle project.

The other five initial projects had similarly positive results. At a two-day workshop held at the end of the 100-day project cycle, Dr. Meky was so impressed by the results and enthusiasm of those involved that the projects were scaled up and expanded to tackle additional challenges, and dozens of additional projects were launched in other parts of the country. Since 2003, more than

10,000 people have been involved in Rapid Results projects to combat the spread of HIV/AIDS in Eritrea—helping the country limit increases in the infection rate.

The Basics About Rapid Results

The Rapid Results approach is a powerful way to "jump-start" major change efforts. It enables change leaders to achieve ambitious goals by stimulating action, experimentation, and learning in the pursuit of dramatic results in critical focus areas. Rapid Results projects are used as the essential building blocks for large scale and long term transformation.

Rapid Results projects can be undertaken singly or in combination, according to the scale of the overall change effort. Such projects have clear attributes—they are:

- *Results oriented*—work is focused on achieving tangible, measurable, bottom-line results (instead of activities, preparations, or recommendations)
- *Fast*—project duration is 100 days or less
- *Exciting and experimental*—fosters innovation and learning
- *Stimulating*—participants gain new insights on implementation challenges and risks
- *Empowered*—teams set their own goal, and are expected to actively pursue it with considerable latitude
- *Cross-functional*—teams draw together people who have frontline knowledge of the challenge at hand
- *Visible*—projects are actively supported and valued by an explicit sponsor commission

When Rapid Results Should Be Used

The Rapid Results approach should be used when change efforts need to be unstuck, accelerated, and injected with a sense of urgency—and where it is necessary to engage and empower various stakeholders in the process. Since the Rapid Results approach is modular, it can be used either project by project or, by launching many projects simultaneously, as a vehicle for large scale change.

Rapid Results should *not* be used when there is a "preordained" solution to the challenge at hand, since this dissipates the characteristic empowerment and excitement mentioned above.

Probable Outcomes

Rapid Results projects have a dual focus on achieving results *and* generating learning and insights into the process and dynamics of change in the organization. Each project is designed as a mini–organizational development effort, both for individual and for team learning about change.

Teams typically meet or exceed their Rapid Result goals. In those instances where teams are not fully successful in achieving their goal, the team's experience is treated as a rich source of learning and insight, enabling future teams to focus in more productive areas.

How Does It Work?

The life cycle of a single Rapid Results project is shown in figure 1. Rapid Results projects follow a similar rhythm regardless of their duration. First, there is a short period in which change leaders, project sponsors, and facilitators work together to define areas for focused effort. This could conceivably spring from earlier strategy development work using methods such as Open Space (chapter 9), WorkOut (chapter 58), or Future Search (chapter 33), or be based on urgent and compelling priorities facing the organization. Sponsors define an executable challenge for each team, providing guidance as to where a result is needed, and helpful intuition regarding the territory for discovery.

A major insurance business faced last quarter results well below plan. The CEO challenged seven senior managers to each launch a Rapid Results initiative that would deliver an extra surge of profitable growth by year-end—and lay a foundation for stronger performance in the next year. Each manager commissioned a team to deliver a measurable result within 60 to 100 days.

The sponsors, team leader, and team members are brought together at a formal launch event, usually lasting one day, at which they carve out their own goal and shape a work plan for

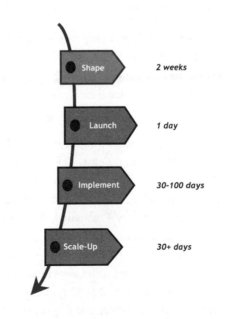

© RHS&A 2006

Figure 1. Phases of Rapid Results Cycle

achieving the result. The critical distinction here is that the team *sets its own goal* at a level that is challenging enough to stimulate innovation and experimentation. We use the "gut test": The goal should create a slight feeling of anxiety as to how it will be accomplished. If the team is relaxed and confident that the goal is readily achievable using the current system, then it is not enough of a stretch. By encouraging the team to *push itself* into its own discomfort zone, ownership of the challenge and commitment to change is located with the team.

> In one line of business, the sponsor called together a team in one office, to find a way to reduce non-value-adding administrative work and significantly increase the amount of business being quoted. Having laid out the challenge, he left the room. The team of underwriters, technicians, and support staff spent four hours deciding how to simplify the work flow, and quantifying how much more business they would aim to handle as a result. A facilitator encouraged them to aim high. At the end of the day, they reviewed the goal with their sponsor, calibrating their own perceptions against his, but ultimately basing their goal of increasing quotations by 30 percent on their own instinct about the challenge ahead.

After the launch meeting, the team is in the driver's seat during the implementation phase that lasts 30–100 days. There are at least two major review points where the teams report on progress and results. Halfway through the projects, the teams meet for a midpoint review to check for traction against goals and team learning. At project completion, teams have a final review to report and celebrate final results, share the team's learnings, and share their ideas to sustain results over time.

> The Rapid Results team held monthly review sessions with the sponsor and facilitator, reporting out on progress in streamlining the work flow, occasionally asking for help, and tracking the production volume that was now being achieved. By the end of the project, they had transformed their work flow and exceeded their goal by another 50 percent.

Once the team's work is done, sponsors and change leaders consider the scale-up opportunities, taking into account the team's insights. This can include turning fresh attention to a related challenge or a new issue thrown up by the team, extending the experiment to other locations or customer segments, or "snowballing" the best practice insights to other work groups for adoption or further development and discovery. Frequently, Rapid Results projects also reveal crosscutting or supporting activities (such as training or system enhancements) that are needed across locations, which are commissioned as part of the overall portfolio of system changes.

Major organizations and communities have built large transformations on a foundation of many Rapid Results projects, spun out of large group events such as WorkOuts, knitted together in waves or as an inverted pyramid where one project spawns multiples.

> The Rapid Results team formally reported their innovations and results, sharing the new forms and checklists they had created. Other offices immediately started to

adopt some of the changes. A few months later, the sponsor coordinated calls between all the offices to encourage uptake and further improvement. By year-end, most of the innovations had been scaled up, and all offices were sharing their improved results monthly.

Table of Uses

Setting/Challenge	Example of Initial Project	Large Scale Impact	Number of Participants/ Length of Project
Avery Dennison U.S. producer of pressure-sensitive materials; office products; and various tickets, tags, labels, and other products • Increase revenue growth from existing products	Launched 14 Rapid Results projects across 3 divisions.	Impressive early results led to global use of Rapid Results teams generating $50 million of new sales in the first year with $150 million in the second year.	Grew from 14 to 500 projects involving 2,000 employees within 2 years.
Eritrean Ministry of Health, Africa • Combat the spread of HIV/AIDS	6 initial projects in central region of Eritrea included teams focused on: increased use of voluntary counseling and testing centers (VCT), increasing use of female condoms among commercial sex workers (CSWs), school-based HIV/AIDS prevention program.	Annual goal of 12,000 VCT in the central region of Eritrea, considered ambitious in March, was shifted upward to 15,000 in June after the first round of Rapid Results initiatives (RRIs). The end-of-year results fell just short of 20,000 users after 3 rounds of RRIs.	Projects in Eritrea have involved about 10,000 people over 2 years.
Grupo Industrial Saltillo Large Mexican conglomerate of automotive, industrial, and consumer products • Change Acceleration Process (CAP+) to improve manufacturing performance	Reduce cost of top 4 common materials (safety supplies, pallets, packing materials, chemicals) by 25%.	Realized cost synergies of $2 million in the first year from this corporate procurement project. Other projects undertaken in 4 other areas resulted in faster sales growth, new products introduced earlier, quicker start-up of new facilities, and significant cost savings.	This corporate-wide effort took place over a year with more than 250 people involved in teams and steering committees. Also created and trained an internal consulting group of 12 to sustain and expand the CAP+ process to other operational areas.

Rapid Results

Setting/Challenge	Example of Initial Project	Large Scale Impact	Number of Participants/ Length of Project
MeadWestvaco U.S.-based global packaging, paper, consumer and office products, and specialty chemicals company • Acquisition integration	In 1999, Westvaco announced the first of several acquisitions to expand and transform their business. Used Rapid Results teams as a means to quickly integrate and achieve desired synergies.	A succession of smaller acquisitions knitted into the larger corporation with Rapid Results projects enabled swift execution during Westvaco's merger with Mead in 2002.	In the course of 4 acquisitions and the merger of MeadWestvaco, dozens of teams worked on integration planning and execution that produced hundreds of millions of dollars (more than $325M in the merger alone) in cost reductions and revenue growth. The integration teams over a period of 3 years engaged hundreds of people in carrying out the work.
Zurich/Eagle Star British division of Swiss financial services company • Transform financial performance and corporate culture	In the first year, more than 30 WorkOut sessions launched more than 100 Rapid Results projects that produced measurable savings in excess of US$10 million.	Rapid Results projects facilitated rapid and successful integration of Zurich and Eagle Star's different cultures. The project's accountability and results-focus has strengthened the company's monthly and quarterly business reviews and built a sustained focus on achieving short- and long-term financial success. Company actuaries verified savings from the projects to be in excess of $100 million over four years with overall company performance shifting from significant losses to strong and sustained profits. UK CEO Patrick O'Sullivan has successfully "exported" the program to other parts of the Zurich organization with significant results.	Over the first year—hundreds of staff were involved, as well as dozens of internal facilitators. By year 4, more than 3,000 staff members were involved in at least one of these sessions. 300 people were trained as internal facilitators, and another 50+ more as skills designers of these efforts.

Table of Uses. Continued

Getting Started—The Fundamentals

The ability to calibrate the change effort to organizational appetite (starting small, scaling up from demonstrated success) is one of the greatest strengths of the Rapid Results approach. If the readiness for change is small, start with local efforts based on a few projects that demonstrate the potential for change. The tangible, valuable result—plus the enthusiasm and energy that emanates from successful teams—become the fuel for scaling up into a larger effort. Stoking the fire in this way offers better payoff than trying to negotiate up front for the big commitment of resources, emotional energy, and organizational time needed to launch a huge change effort.

Paradoxically, this works so well because the Rapid Results approach leverages the stability of whole systems to create cells for experimentation and innovation, below the radar screen and without the risks associated with shifting the entire system simultaneously. Once Rapid Results experiments have proven their worth, change can be scaled-up across the whole system from a position of demonstrated value, rather than from a position of faith and guesswork.

GUIDING PRINCIPLES

There are nine guiding principles that underpin both the Rapid Results approach and individual projects:

1. Focus on a transformational challenge

2. Carve out a stretch goal

3. Organize around short-term time horizons

4. Pinpoint clear accountability for results

5. Drive experimentation and discovery

6. Execute in a planned and disciplined fashion

7. Assess learning throughout

8. Design methods for the next round

9. Scale-up

DESIGN MODELS

Typically, Rapid Results projects adopt one of five designs (table 1).

Rapid Results Project Design	Sample Business Goal	Possible Rapid Results Goal
1. *Performance Improvement:* Improve one dimension of performance to learn how to achieve similar improvement on other dimensions.	Increase the satisfaction of customer Q served by 3 of our divisions.	Reduce the cost of service calls to the customer in one location by X% in 100 days by coordinating both the sales and service processes of the three divisions.
2. *Strategic:* Do a small-scale demonstration of how to enter a new market, open a new line of business, or move in some other major strategic direction.	Provide a new type of security service to office buildings.	Prepare a description of a new service plan and get 2 customers to add it to a test basis for the months of June and July.
3. *Model Week or Month:* Go after a specific level of performance for a week or a month, without making any commitment to continue to achieve that level.	Reduce errors and reprocessing in customer invoices.	During October, reduce the error rate in customer invoices from 5% to less than 1%.
4. *Process Redesign:* Map and redesign one part of a larger process, to demonstrate how more ambitious redesign can be done.	Increase profitability through reducing the cycle time from order to delivery to payment.	In plant X, reduce the time from when a customer receives a shipment until customer is billed from an average of 13 days to an average of 4 days within 100 days.
5. *One-Location Pilot Test:* Select one location to demonstrate and test a method intended for all locations.	Increase major account sales.	Increase major account sales in London office by 30% in 100 days.

Table 1. Five Rapid Results Project Designs

Roles, Responsibilities, and Relationships

The key roles and responsibilities are shown in figure 2.

Sponsorship needs to come from a senior-level manager who is prepared to place a "demand" upon a team—a challenge to achieve improved organizational results. This should always be captured in a written sponsor statement.

In large scale change, a senior-level manager can sponsor a portfolio of Rapid Results projects—with other senior managers acting as champions for individual project teams. The sponsor works with the champions to decide how the overarching business challenge or strategic plan can be carved up into a portfolio of Rapid Results projects. Again, the sponsor communicates the context, the challenge, and the expectations for results *in writing*, to ensure that a consistent message is cascaded to teams by champions.

	Change Sponsor	Team	Facilitator
Shape	• Select an opportunity/focus area for team • Designate team leader and select team • Clarify challenge in written note to team • Align key stakeholders		• Work with sponsor to help define challenge to team • Prepare sponsor and team leader for launch event • Agree with team leader how to work together during the launch event and beyond
Launch	• Attend start of launch event to clarify challenge • Return to close launch event, review goal and challenge work plan	• Review data • Set team's Rapid Results goal • Develop a work plan to achieve the goal	• Facilitate team through goal setting exercise and action planning
Implement	• Attend periodic reviews • Remove implementation hurdles for team • Help distill team learnings • Help plan for sustainability of results	• Implement steps in plan • Track progress and adjust as needed • Prepare and present at periodic reviews • Document learning	• Assist team during implementation team meetings • Help team prepare for reviews
Scale-Up	• Conduct wrap-up workshops to celebrate success and share learning • Support changes required to assist sustainability • Organize "next wave" Rapid Results projects	• Involvement in/coaching of the next generation of teams	• Work with sponsor to identify how results/learnings from previous projects impact the overall strategic context

© RHS&A 2006

Figure 2. Roles and Responsibilities

We have worked in organizations where one sponsor is from management, the other from a labor union. This works when there is joint commitment to results from both management and labor.

Facilitators working with Rapid Results teams need to be focused on results, support innovation and learning, foster execution, communicate effectively, influence appropriately, and be able to demonstrate adaptability.

Conditions for Success

WHY RAPID RESULTS WORKS

Rapid Results projects work because they:

- Begin with action and results, not preparations
- Strengthen grassroots implementation capability, building capacity and confidence

- Test large scale change in low-risk ways

- Drive accountability lower in the organization—so that someone beyond management is lying awake at night thinking about what it will take to accomplish the result, and how to bring all the necessary elements together

- Are designed to replicate, in a calm and systematic way, dynamics that naturally arise during crisis—such as clear sense of purpose, sense of urgency, collaboration across boundaries, and freedom to experiment. We call these the "zest" factors.

What's the ROI of Rapid Results?

The return on investment (ROI) of Rapid Results projects is twofold: financial and developmental. Projects typically yield confidence-building payoffs, process innovations, and the learning and development that expand everyone's capacity to manage change. These outcomes set the stage for expansion and acceleration of progress. As each project is completed, it serves as a building block for larger-scale change. In most organizations, the results achieved in the first few Rapid Results projects more than pay for the investment in the entire effort. In fact, this rapid payoff has spurred some management development units that use the approach to consider themselves as profit instead of cost centers.

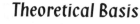

Theoretical Basis

The Rapid Results approach draws on diverse theoretical foundations:

- Kurt Lewin taught us that the best way to change a system is to actually try tweaking it.

- Robert H. Schaffer has shown that adults learn best when actively engaged in the experience, consistent with David Kolb's adult learning theory. We learn best by actually experiencing what it feels like to touch, see, smell, and live a small piece of the big result we are trying to achieve.

- Goal-setting theory explains the power of a sharp, clearly defined goal.

- Social identity theory illuminates how creating collective ownership among team members increases the odds of success, even of an ad hoc effort.

The insights of the Rapid Results approach are also born out by the empirical research of many scholar/practitioners, such as John Kotter and Dan Cohen, and Michael Beer and coauthors.

Rapid Results Approach Challenges the Conventional Wisdom

The Rapid Results approach challenges conventional wisdom in three ways. First, we believe that involvement for involvement's sake isn't enough. We say that change in organizations is strongest when built on a combination of cultural changes *and* actual results. Second, the Rapid

Results approach turns the "begin with preparations and wait patiently for results" paradigm upside down and begins at once with results. Managers do not need to wait for the final consulting report, or the full analytical market study. They can begin with actions that often yield more learning than any report or study. Finally, we don't believe that a large scale change effort must involve the whole organization in a lock-step system transformation. Consistency is the enemy of creativity and social discovery. Conventional wisdom often holds that short term is "bad." We say that short-term successes, built on local, small-scale, rapid-cycle efforts, can be the fuel for learning and large scale change.

HISTORY OF CREATION

The Rapid Results approach was originated by Robert H. Schaffer and the firm he founded (RHS&A) in the early 1960s. It has been documented in hundreds of articles and more than a dozen books. Over four decades, the approach has been validated by an international practice community including major corporations, government agencies, nonprofit organizations, and development agencies.

Sustaining the Results

The results and learning from a portfolio of Rapid Results projects are embedded in an organization through attention to three dynamics: sustainability, expansion, and scale-up.

Sustainability refers to the capacity to maintain the particular result achieved during a rapid-cycle project, in that area. As each project progresses, the team is asked to recommend any shifts that will be needed to lock in its result for the longer term. It might require training, systems changes, formal process redesign, or targeted communication. For example, a Rapid Results team in a hospital operating room (OR) that has reduced the average time to prepare the room between patients by 20 minutes would ask itself what is needed to maintain that standard after the intense effort of the rapid-cycle project is ended.

Expansion refers to a team's capacity to take the learnings from one project and leverage these into a bigger or related effort in the same domain. Examples include a team agreeing to take another crack at an even better result on the same issue, or picking a related issue that could not be fully addressed in the previous project. In the case of the hospital OR team, this could mean trying to reduce turnaround time by another ten minutes, by targeting administrative errors or doctor delays.

Scale-up refers to the capacity to take the result achieved by a particular team and replicate it more broadly across the organization. A result in one unit, segment, or region or with one customer is used to stimulate similar results elsewhere. In our hospital example, this could mean taking what was learned in one OR and trying to replicate the result on every shift and in every OR across the hospital system. This requires a careful balance between constantly reinventing the wheel and simply rolling out a solution in a command-and-control manner. The ownership of the goal and the opportunity for innovation remain core dynamics of change,

Rapid Results

even when a work team is being asked to adopt and build upon the ideas and learnings from a Rapid Results team.

IMPACT ON AN ORGANIZATION'S CULTURAL ASSUMPTIONS

The cultural shifts that arise from the Rapid Results approach are most noticeable in a few key mantras that play out in the organization:

- *The wisdom for change lies within.* Communities develop stronger capability to drive change when people realize that outside experts are not needed to make major change happen. We have noticed that in communities and countries facing development challenges, traditional "big-fix" programs often stumble because of a lack of grassroots implementation capability. Using rapid-cycle projects, the "target population" ceases to be a target and becomes a driver for change, building its own experience of successful implementation.

- *No more excuses.* Rapid Results projects often smash organizational myths that serve as convenient excuses for lack of improvement. Teams often start with a conviction that a particular cause outside their control (such as a systems issue) lies at the root of their problems. However, the discovery process often uncovers many root causes that the team can control, empowering the team to bring its full creativity and ownership to bear on the challenge. As Avery Dennison's Dean Scarborough put it: "The 100-day deadline drove an incredible amount of creativity. When people hit obstacles, they did not come to management for help. They . . . did what they had to do to get over the obstacles. They took some risks."

- *Do it, just do it.* As more rapid-cycle projects are carried out, there is more of a "go for it" feeling throughout the organization. Out of big, amorphous goals, short-term targets are set. Team accountabilities are specified. Work plans are developed. As projects succeed, participants absorb the learning and move on to more ambitious and sophisticated undertakings. Additionally, as implementation capability expands, so does the organization's capacity to master its strategic direction. The culture of the enterprise begins to shift even though the focus is on tangible results—not cultural change.

- *Make tomorrow start today.* Achieving rapid-cycle results enables organizations to shift to a faster, empirically based approach to strategic direction setting. Again, Scarborough argues that the Rapid Results approach "allows you to test big strategic concepts very quickly and in a very focused way. . . . If you go out and test the idea in a small-scale 100-day way, you have some real solid data. We have been able to implement certain strategies much more quickly this way."

Burning Question—Doesn't This Simply Exploit Low-Hanging Fruit?

While there is nothing wrong with accomplishing easy goals, the Rapid Results process helps people to carve up difficult, seemingly insurmountable challenges into achievable chunks. Each

Rapid Results project should make a significant contribution toward achieving an urgent, compelling objective. If the Rapid Results goal can be accomplished easily—if it does not need the combined efforts of a team—then it is not worth the investment of the entire team's time and effort. The collective "gut test" should confirm that the team is aiming for a significant step-up in performance.

Some Final Comments

KEY DIFFERENCE BETWEEN RAPID RESULTS AND SIMILAR METHODS

Teams and task forces are commonplace within most organizations. However, most such teams are held accountable for little more than activities or recommendations. Rapid Results teams are held accountable for achieving results through innovation, and for extracting learning and insights along the way. Taken together, these elements build confidence and capacity to manage further change.

COMMON MISCONCEPTIONS AND CONFUSION ABOUT THIS METHOD

The belief that a short-term focus is always bad. This universally accepted "truth" of organization management is exposed as fiction by the success of Rapid Results. This myth is the legacy of too many panicky, short-term moves that have damaged companies—like cutting R&D or eliminating customer services. We have discovered that short-term thrusts can be powerfully beneficial if they are executed intelligently and if they are designed as stepping-stones toward major strategic gains. Short-term thrusts are bad only if they are poorly conceived or poorly executed.

About the Authors

Patrice Murphy is a senior consultant at the Stamford-based management consulting firm of Robert H. Schaffer & Associates (RHS&A). *Celia Kirwan* is a consultant and *Ron Ashkenas* is a managing partner of the same firm. This chapter reflects the beliefs, work, and insights of the authors and their colleagues. RHS&A consultants collaborate with clients from around the world to accomplish dramatic bottom-line improvements and bring about far-reaching change. We developed, practice, and teach the high-impact consulting mode, whereby modest consulting inputs can be leveraged by clients to catalyze significant results. The authors can be reached at info@rhsa.com or through RHS&A's Web site at www.rhsa.com.

Where to Go for More Information

REFERENCES

Matta, N., and R. Ashkenas. "Why Good Projects Fail Anyway." *Harvard Business Review* 81, no. 9 (September 2003): 109–114.

Schaffer, R. *The Breakthrough Strategy.* New York: Harper Business, 1988.

————. "Demand Better Results—And Get Them." *Harvard Business Review* 69, no. 2 (January/February 1992): 80–89.

Schaffer, R., R. Ashkenas, and Associates. *Rapid Results! How 100-Day Projects Build the Capacity for Large-Scale Change.* San Francisco: Jossey Bass, 2005.

Schaffer, R., and H. Thomson. "Successful Change Programs Begin with Results." *Harvard Business Review* 70, no. 1 (January/February 1992): 79–89.

INFLUENTIAL SOURCES

Beer, M., R. A. Eisenstat, and B. Spector. "Why Change Programs Don't Produce Change." *Harvard Business Review* 68 (November/December 1990): 158–166.

Beer, M., and N. Nohria, eds. *Breaking the Code of Change.* Boston: Harvard Business School Publishing Corporation, 2000.

Kotter, John P., and Dan S. Cohen. *The Heart of Change: Real-Life Stories of How People Change Their Organizations.* Boston: Harvard Business School Publishing Corporation, 2002.

Smith, D. *Taking Charge of Change: 10 Principles for Managing People and Performance.* New York: Perseus Books Group, 1997.

ORGANIZATION

Robert H. Schaffer & Associates—www.rhsa.com

RONALD D. SNEE, PH.D.

The Six Sigma Approach to Improvement and Organizational Change

Six Sigma is quickly becoming part of the genetic code of our future leadership.

—Jack Welch

The Supply Chain and Biopharmaceuticals

For a major U.S. biopharmaceutical manufacturer, it was the best of times and the worst of times. Though approval for their new blockbuster drug was expected in nine months, the company's manufacturing and quality assurance processes were not ready to manufacture product and generate required FDA (Food and Drug Administration) documentation in a reliable, repeatable fashion (McGurk 2004). Another company product already in production had historically suffered from supply problems. For both the old and new drug, the creation and review of "batch records" was also a major problem. These records, required by corporate standards and government regulations, track important steps in the manufacturing process. Failure to keep accurate batch records can result in high inventory costs, a potential plant shutdown, and delays in shipments of lifesaving drugs to patients awaiting treatment.

The stakes were enormous and the organization was at loggerheads. The manufacturing organization blamed Quality Assurance (QA) for inconsistencies in the records and the long delays in completing them. QA insisted that manufacturing should get the records right the first time instead of simply throwing in lots of undigested data and expecting QA to find the incon-

Phase	Six Sigma Principles and Tools Helped . . .
Define	• Clearly identify the problem to be solved and associated financial impacts
Measure	• Understand the process through various measurement tools
Analyze	• Analyze data to determine root causes of problems
Improve	• Develop and test potential solutions
Control	• Sustain the gains by developing control plans to monitor key performance variables

Table 1. Six Sigma's DMAIC Methodology

sistencies and correct mistakes. Meanwhile, the clock was ticking toward approval of the new product, and problems persisted with the existing product.

The manufacturer decided to address the poor performance of its batch records review process—and the underlying organizational issues—through Six Sigma's powerful problem-solving methodology: Define, Measure, Analyze, Improve, Control (DMAIC) (see table 1).

In the *Define* phase of DMAIC, management created a cross-functional team of ten people drawn from operations, quality assurance, and documentation, and reached agreement on what success of the project would look like: a reduction of 50 percent in review time of the batch records for the two products in six months.

In the *Measure* phase, the project team mapped the batch record process and identified key measurement points that allowed them to track review cycle times through a complicated network of participants (the lab, operators, supervisors, manufacturing, quality assurance, and investigators reporting out-of-spec incidents).

In the *Analyze* phase, the team tracked and analyzed each of the subprocess cycle times and overall cycle time. In addition, the analysis uncovered the root causes of errors in the records, which was the other critical-to-quality (CTQ) criterion besides cycle time. The team identified five areas that needed to be addressed: lack of expectations and targets for the overall process and subprocesses, a single reviewer, lack of feedback through metrics, lack of training, and problems with the records themselves.

In the *Improve* phase, the team worked with management to develop target cycle times for each step in the process, set up a system to report progress on the targets, initiate training, create backup reviewers, and restructure the review process to focus more on exception resolution than routine data gathering. These improvements reduced cycle time by 55 percent for one of the products and by 36 percent for the second product, freed up $5.2 million in inventory, increased customer satisfaction, saved $200,000 in cost of capital, and achieved additional savings through reduced floor space and handling costs.

In the *Control* phase, the team initiated a continuous improvement process to manage and improve cycle time, reduce errors over time, and sustain the gains already made. In addition, management planned future evaluations of subprocess cycle times in order to look for further improvements.

This example illustrates a number of key features and advantages of Six Sigma. It begins with the premise that improvement happens project by project. Its methodology entails a carefully sequenced set of steps; it relies on rigorous empirical observation as well as statistics, and it seeks not merely to correct individual "defects" but also to get at the root causes of variation in processes and fix them once and for all. Moreover, though it involves manufacturing processes—which Six Sigma is best known for improving—the project actually focuses on a business process, indicating Six Sigma's wide applicability to *any* work process.

In this case, as in other successful implementations, the methodology can help overcome organizational silos and intramural conflict, create an organization-wide culture of quality, and disseminate training and the tools widely among employees, creating a permanent capability for continuous improvement and a training ground for future leaders of an organization (Snee, "Can Six Sigma," 2004). Within one year, the site went from a conflict-ridden, process-challenged facility to one that won the company's global award as a model of improvement.

The Basics: Answers to Frequently Asked Questions

WHAT IS SIX SIGMA?

Six Sigma methodology arose at Motorola more than a quarter of a century ago as a statistically based, process-focused method of eliminating defects in manufacturing processes. It subsequently flourished at Allied Signal and achieved legendary status at General Electric (GE) under Jack Welch. GE, expanding the notion of "defect," recognized that Six Sigma could be applied not only to ailing manufacturing processes but also to any subpar process, enabling the company to drive relentlessly toward a goal of "zero defects" across all of its business processes. Millions of dollars of bottom-line savings resulted. Six Sigma moved quickly beyond manufacturing to administration, finance, business processes, new product development, and supplier performance—becoming the characteristic approach to quality and continuous improvement of organizations as diverse as 3M, Johnson & Johnson, Home Depot, J. P. Morgan, Chase & Co., Dupont, and W. R. Grace. Six Sigma continues today as a well-known approach to process and organizational improvement (Snee and Hoerl 2003, 2005).

Based on the scientific method and utilizing statistical thinking and methods (Hoerl and Snee 2002), Six Sigma builds on quality improvement approaches developed earlier. It seeks to find and eliminate causes of mistakes or defects in business processes by focusing on process outputs that are critically important to customers. Six Sigma projects also often focus on improving productivity, process yields, production rates, and process downtime. As a result, process performance is enhanced, customer satisfaction is improved, and the bottom line is impacted through savings and increased revenue. It is a strategic approach that works across all processes, products, and industries—and it is a significant catalyst for ongoing organizational change.

Six Sigma is also a measure of process performance. The methodology utilizes "process sigma" as a measure of process capability. A six-sigma process has a defect level of 3.4 parts-per-million (ppm) opportunities and a three-sigma process has a defect level of 66,807 ppm (Harry

Six Sigma

1998). In many instances, a six-sigma process is considered world-class. Today, the performance of most processes is in the three- to four-sigma range.

The ability to produce products and services with only 3.4 defects per million opportunities yields a Six Sigma process. Of course, a Six Sigma level of performance should not be the goal for all processes. Some processes, such as airline safety, require a higher level of performance. For other processes, a lower level of performance may be acceptable. The appropriate level of performance is determined by a business decision that balances the cost of attaining the higher level of performance versus the benefits of a higher-performing process. Further, as customer needs and competitive pressures change over time, the appropriate process sigma level may change accordingly.

WHAT ARE THE DISTINCTIVE CHARACTERISTICS OF SIX SIGMA?

There are at least four critical elements that, when combined, make Six Sigma a distinctive, highly value-added approach to organizational improvement:

1. *Six Sigma places a clear focus on getting bottom-line results.* In properly run Six Sigma programs, no improvement project is approved unless the bottom-line impact has been identified. Six Sigma initiatives have been known to produce average bottom-line results of >$175,000 per project and as much as $1 million per year per full-time Six Sigma practitioner.

2. *Six Sigma integrates the human and process elements of improvement.* Six Sigma emphasizes human elements like teamwork, customer focus, and culture change as well as the process aspects of improvement such as statistical process control, process improvement, and design of experiments.

3. *Six Sigma sequences and links the improvement tools into an overall approach.* The five-phase DMAIC improvement process—Define, Measure, Analyze, Improve, Control—sequences and links key improvement tools proven to be effective in improving processes. DMAIC creates a sense of urgency by emphasizing rapid project completion, typically in three to six months.

4. *Six Sigma provides a unique leadership development tool.* Companies such as Honeywell, GE, DuPont, 3M, and American Standard require that managers achieve Six Sigma Green Belt (GB) certification and in some instances Black Belt (BB) certification for management promotion. These companies realize that the job of leaders is to help the organization move from one paradigm of working to another. Changing how we work means changing our processes. By providing the concepts, methods, and tools for improving processes, Six Sigma provides leaders with the strategy, methods, and tools for changing their organizations—a key leadership skill that heretofore has been missing from leadership development.

WHEN AND WHERE IS SIX SIGMA USED?

Across almost all major industries, the pressure to improve to the point of achieving flawless execution—every time—is relentlessly increasing. From financial services to telecommunications, executing on customer service has become one of the few remaining differentiators for products that are largely commodities. In consumer goods, giant merchandisers like Wal-Mart and Target continue to pressure suppliers to improve their performance year after year—or lose business. In the life sciences, with an unprecedented number of blockbuster drugs coming off patent and little in the pipeline to replace them, excellence in manufacturing has taken on more importance than ever. Identifying, investigating, adjudicating, and correcting manufacturing deviations costs pharmaceutical companies millions of dollars each year in reduced capacity and increased labor, inventory, and good manufacturing practices (GMP) compliance problems. In manufacturing generally, where Six Sigma originated, continuously improving manufacturing processes remains a critical imperative.

Within any of these organizations and in any area of the business, Six Sigma can be usefully applied to improve virtually any kind of processes, whether they are manufacturing, financial, supply chain, or customer service. The key is simply to recall the great insight from GE—that Six Sigma can be applied to any process that results in defects or faults, whether the defects or problems are in products, services, or transactions.

WHAT TOOLS ARE USED?

The broad use of DMAIC as an overall framework for improving existing processes adds predictability, discipline, and repeatability to improvement projects. Along with Define, Measure, Analyze, Design, Verify (DMADV; Creveling et al. 2002) for the development of new products and processes, DMAIC can constitute the improvement infrastructure of the organization, linking and sequencing the required tools regardless of their source. Sources can include Lean, which seeks to eliminate various forms of waste through such concepts as just-in-time manufacturing; and Total Quality Management (TQM), which seeks to integrate all organizational functions to meet customer needs and organizational objectives, as well as other improvement tool sets. It's worth remembering, however, that the tools don't make improvements; people do.

Table of Uses

Organization	Project Length	Key Events	Number of Participants
Specialties Chemicals and Materials Company • Main businesses are catalysts, construction materials, coatings/sealants, and silica/absorbents • Sales $2 billion/year • Plants are in the United States, Canada, and Europe. Training done both in the United States and in Europe	30 months	• Executive Workshop • 3 Champion Workshops • 3 waves of Black Belt (BB) in 1999, 2000, and 2001 • 6 waves of Design for Six Sigma (DFSS) training begins 11/01 • Green Belt (GB) training in the United States begins 02/01	• 32 top executives • 15–22 Champions per workshop • 15–25 BBs per wave • 15–20 persons per wave • 15–25 persons per wave

Organization	Project Length	Key Events	Number of Participants
• Goal is to improve productivity and increase growth • Strategy—Top down deployment led by the CEO. Projects reviewed monthly. CEO reviews initiative quarterly • Bottom Line savings: $26M in 2000 and $50M in 2001 • Work reported here is for 1999–2001; Six Sigma Initiative continues		• Process Operator training begins 06/01 • Advanced BB Training 02/01	• 10–15 operators per wave • 20–25 BBs
Manufacturing Facility • Plant is a supplier to pharmaceutical and food industries • 120 employees • Goal was bottom-line savings of $1M/year, increased plant capacity, and improved teamwork • Initiative was led by plant manager • Mentoring sessions held with the GB biweekly • First 10 projects produced $1.7M in savings • Deployment was slow and deliberate by design	3 years	• Plant Leadership Workshop in 08/01 • BB Training 2002 • Champion Workshop 2003 • GB training 2003 • GB training 2004	• 10–12 top managers • 1 BB • 10 managers • 10 GBs • 6 GBs
Project Budgeting Process Improvement • Director of project budgeting process for a clinical trials operations of a pharmaceutical	9 months	• Steering Team Workshop • 3 Champion Workshops • 2 Organizational Awareness Training Sessions	• 10 senior managers • 8–10 Champions per workshop • 100–150 persons per session

Table of Uses. Continued

Organization	Project Length	Key Events	Number of Participants
company desires to increase the forecasting accuracy of the project budgeting process as well as increase the speed of the process and reduce the wasted time involved • Strategy—train 14 employees as GBs to get the needed process improvements now and in the future. GBs were located both in the United States and Europe. Training was done both in the United States and Europe • Mentoring sessions held with the GBs biweekly • Steering Team reviewed projects monthly • First six projects identified $2.2M in wasted effort and cost avoidance savings		• GB Training	• 14 GBs trained

Getting Started

Organizations considering whether to initiate a Six Sigma program have a broad range of choices that range from large-scale deployment across the entire company through a comprehensive, all-embracing Six Sigma structure; to divisional, business unit, or departmental programs; to limited, small-scale pilot projects. However, total deployment may be beyond the budget and resources of some companies. On the other hand, initially confining Six Sigma projects to a single pilot project, or one area, risks quarantining it to the area it is in and eventually killing it. The key phases of deployment and DMAIC projects are summarized in figure 1.

By instituting Six Sigma projects in widely disparate areas, leaders can signal the entire organization that they are serious about it—it's not just for those folks over in manufacturing or Quality Assurance (Snee, "With All Deliberate Speed," 2004). For example, you might choose an operational process, a customer-facing process, and a business/managerial process, each in a

Major Deployment Phases

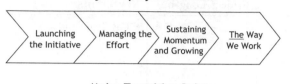

Major Transition Points

From Business as Usual to a Six Sigma Approach	From a New Launch to a Long Term Initiative	From THE Initiative to AN Initiative	From an Initiative to a Normal Part of the Job

Individual Project Methodology: DMAIC

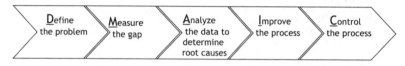

Figure 1. Six Sigma Deployment and Methodology

different department, for initial Six Sigma projects. Moreover, having projects in disparate areas prepares the way for widespread and rapid propagation of Six Sigma later.

There are basically three different types of deployment: Full top-down deployment involving the whole organization, a single location such as a plant, and a process or function such as finance. Other examples of Six Sigma deployment can be found in Snee and Hoerl (2003, 2005).

Once a program—of whatever size—has been established, individual project teams should, in the early stages of improvement, harvest the "low-hanging fruit": correct obvious problems with a process, fix broken measurement systems, and ensure the consistency of process inputs, whether raw materials in manufacturing or data in nonmanufacturing processes. Work should also be streamlined through the reduction of complexity, waste, and non-value-added work. The later stages of improvement focus on optimizing and controlling processes by improving value-added work steps, shifting the process average and reducing variation around it, improving process flow, and reducing cycle time—in short, finding the "operating sweet spot."

Roles, Responsibilities, and Relationships

Six Sigma creates an infrastructure of permanent change agents who lead, deploy, and implement improvement projects. Borrowing terminology from the martial arts, Six Sigma programs train and mobilize practitioners known as Champions, Master Black Belts (MBBs), Black Belts (BBs), and Green Belts (GBs), each with differing roles and responsibilities in individual projects and in ongoing continuous improvement (see table 2).

This infrastructure of quality-conscious people, determined to make improvement stick and thoroughly trained in how to do it, provides the organization with a significant advantage

Participant	General Responsibilities
Corporate Management	Create strategy and goals, define boundaries, provide resources
Unit Management	Establish project selection criteria that support strategy, select project Champions, and approve projects
Project Champions	Ensure proper project setup, regularly monitor progress, and remove barriers to success
Black Belts	Deploy Lean and Six Sigma methodology and tools, deliver process improvements and financial benefits, and access formal power structure as needed to remove barriers
Master Black Belts	Develop, coach, and counsel Black Belts and Green Belts and focus on mission-critical projects
Green Belts	Lead Six Sigma projects at the local level and assist in improving a process as a member of a team that is guided by a Black Belt
Functional Support Groups	Provide data and expertise for improvement, identify improvement opportunities, serve on project teams, and take local responsibility for process execution and improvement

Table 2. Roles, Responsibilities, and Relationships

Six Sigma

over competitors with a less rigorous and systematic approach to improvement and organizational change.

Conditions for Success: The Path to Organizational Change

One of the most frequently encountered obstacles to the success of Six Sigma programs is the "Six Sigma won't work here" attitude, especially in nonmanufacturing organizations. To overcome that attitude, it is critical to obtain some quick wins and, as additional improvements and benefits materialize, the organization's culture will change (Kotter 1996). Deployment should take place rapidly, with attention to critical elements of the launch, but without obsessive worry about defining every detail of the deployment. Taken together, the fundamental elements of Six Sigma deployment provide a path to organizational change that comes not as a result of the deployment but as a result of the benefits that Six Sigma produces, reinforcing its value and weaving it into the organization as *the* way to work. These key deployment elements, their significance, and their pitfalls include (Snee and Hoerl 2003):

- *Strategy and Goals:* Senior management sets the overall vision for Six Sigma deployment, chooses where to initially deploy Six Sigma, develops one- to two-year goals, including financial targets, and communicates the goals widely. Failure to state goals in financial terms often indicates a management team that is not serious about Six Sigma.

- *Process Performance Measures:* These measures, such as quality, delivery, and cost, define what's important for success and are used to select projects. Such measures provide strategic focus areas for the initial projects; and if all initial projects affect the measures, then the organization will have significant, tangible results when they are completed. The chief pitfall here is selecting each project independently rather than choosing projects on the basis of their relation to common, strategic measures of success.

- *Project Selection Criteria:* The process metrics are used to develop a set of more specific criteria for selecting projects. These may include such criteria as savings per project and expected time to project completion. Such criteria also communicate to the wider organization what types of improvement are important.

- *Project Identification/Selection System:* In a Champion Workshop, initial candidate projects are put in a "project hopper" (list of projects) and prioritized for assignment to a Black Belt or Green Belt. In the first wave or two of projects, the focus should be on hard, bottom-line results, because nothing goes further to establish the credibility of Six Sigma. In later phases of deployment, a permanent system is established to identify potential projects, prioritize them, and put them in the hopper so that there is a continual stream of fresh projects. Ultimately, the hopper should be managed as a "project portfolio," the composition of which matches the improvement and financial needs of the organization.

- *Deployment Process for Leaders:* A list of initial Champions is developed in an Executive Workshop. At an ensuing Champion Workshop, Champions develop the list of initial projects, as well as a list of candidate Black Belts to lead them. The pitfall here is selecting the Champions and Black Belts before identifying the specific projects they will lead, increasing the likelihood that important projects will be overlooked.

- *Roles of Leadership and Others:* Although there are generic job responsibilities for Champions, BBs, GBs, and so forth, leadership can tailor the roles for a specific function or business (see Table of Uses).

- *Curricula and Training System:* An overall training system is a must for each of the Six Sigma roles and, at launch, there must be a training schedule for the first wave of Black Belts. The pitfall here is undertaking a wave of mass training, which is usually ineffective and has little lasting impact. Instead, there should be a well-thought-out system that identifies the training needs of the roles and puts them together in a sustained way to continually satisfy training needs in the most efficient way.

- *Project and Six Sigma Initiative Review Schedule:* An effective review schedule involves short, usually 30-minute, weekly reviews by the Champion and monthly reviews with functional leaders, local management, or business leaders, as appropriate. Regular reviews show management's commitment and provide timely feedback to keep projects on course. The entire Six Sigma deployment should be reviewed quarterly by the appropriate corporate or business unit leaders. Failure to review the overall progress of the initiative at this level can slow the momentum of the Six Sigma effort and fail to detect if the initiative is bogging down.

- *Project Reporting and Tracking System:* This system documents the results of the projects and provides management with valuable information. A formal system isn't required during initial deployment, but it will ultimately maintain a record of all Six Sigma projects, generate managerial reports that include financial results as well as nonfinancial information such as number of projects in progress and completed, time to completion, status, and so on. The tracking component of the system documents the financial benefits of closed projects. The pitfall here is establishing an insufficiently rigorous tracking system that cannot provide accurate and credible results.

- *Audit System for Previously Closed Projects:* This system audits the financial and process performance impact of the improvements and the control plan of previously closed projects to ensure that the benefits of these projects are still being achieved. Failure to audit the control plan can lead to the improvements eroding over time.

- *Reward and Recognition Plan:* Human Resources should develop a reward and recognition plan that ensures the acquisition and retention of the best possible candidates for Six Sigma roles. Failure to reward Six Sigma roles in a way that attracts top performers to them can seriously undermine the long-term prospects for success.

- *Communication Plan:* A thorough communication plan, enacted through various media, is essential to support a Six Sigma initiative, especially in nonmanufacturing organizations that may harbor false impressions about the applicability of the approach. Leadership must clearly communicate why they chose to deploy Six Sigma, how it applies to the business, and where they expect it to take the organization both in business and in cultural terms. The pitfall here is setting unreasonable expectations. It is preferable to make more sweeping statements only after significant results are obtained.

Experience has shown that all of these elements of deployment are important. Paying insufficient attention to any of them can seriously limit the effectiveness of a Six Sigma program and leave the organization stuck in old, less-productive ways of doing business.

Theoretical Basis

From the long historical perspective, Six Sigma has its roots in the Industrial Revolution and the division of labor (Snee, "When Worlds Collide," 2004). In the late nineteenth and early twentieth centuries, Frederick W. Taylor introduced scientific management, initially grounded in time and motion studies and standardization of tools and procedures. In 1924, Walter Shewhart introduced control charts. In the 1930s, Shewhart and W. Edwards Deming developed the improvement approach known as PDCA (Plan, Do, Check, Act). All of these methods were developed in response to the need to reduce high variation in production processes.

Joseph M. Juran, who as early as 1928 had already written a pamphlet entitled "Statistical Methods Applied to Manufacturing Problems," made many contributions to the field of quality management. He was the first to incorporate the human aspect of quality management in what came to be known as Total Quality Management (TQM) and promoted such indispensable tools as Pareto charting and the project-by-project approach to improvement.

The ideas of Shewhart, Deming, and Juran were adopted extensively in Japan and began the revolution in quality. In the 1980s, Motorola executives, touring industrial sites in Japan, witnessed how the Japanese had achieved exemplary quality through the application of statistical tools—and Six Sigma was born. Developed throughout the 1980s by Motorola, it was adopted and famously expanded by GE to include any type of process. At the same time, TQM, just-in-time (JIT) manufacturing, Kaizen, Business Process Reengineering, Benchmarking, Lean Manufacturing, and other improvement methodologies were also developing and spreading to organizations all over the world. Today, Six Sigma encompasses the best practices from all of these methodologies.

Six Sigma has had a particularly fruitful relationship with Lean. Lean is based on the premise that work almost always involves waste: of correction (the quality of the worst component), overproduction, overprocessing, conveyance, inventory, motion, and waiting. Lean seeks to eliminate these various forms of waste through such concepts as just-in-time manufacturing. However, Lean does not address the effects of process variation, which Six Sigma, with its data-driven, rigorously statistical methods, can uncover and eliminate. In addition, Six Sigma is ideal for solving complex, multidetermined problems whose root causes are unknown. Often, Six Sigma and Lean are applied either concurrently or consecutively in an approach known as Lean Six Sigma (Snee 2005).

Six Sigma also fits well with ISO 9000 quality management systems and with the Baldrige Criteria for Performance Excellence. The key to their integration is the recognition that all three are process focused, data based, and management led. Six Sigma methods of project selection, reviews, and reporting can also be very effective in turning opportunities identified by a Baldrige assessment into sharply focused, high-impact projects that lead to lasting improvements.

Sustaining the Results

Six Sigma has a formal step in the DMAIC process—the control phase—that is specifically designed to implement controls that prevent improved processes from reverting to their previous levels of lower performance. Management reviews of projects—weekly by Project Champion and monthly by the management team—keep projects on track and also help ensure that the projects continue to generate benefits. At the level of the overall Six Sigma initiative, leadership undertakes quarterly reviews that monitor the progress of each of the elements of the deployment plan and, in particular, the contents of the project hopper.

The system for auditing the financial and process performance impacts and control plans of previously closed projects ensures that completed projects continue to generate the benefits that their improvement produced. If the audit finds that the benefits have eroded, action is taken to revisit the project, regain the benefits, and establish a more effective control plan. Moreover, having a cadre of people trained in Six Sigma ensures that the same disciplined, repeatable methodology will be brought to every project.

From the point of view of organizational development, one of the strongest spurs to maintaining momentum and sustaining the gains comes from the effect that the achievement of significant, measurable benefits has on the culture. People like to succeed, and when they get tangible results, they are eager to repeat the process. That is the simple but powerful principle of culture change underlying Six Sigma: Culture change doesn't produce benefits; benefits produce culture change.

Burning Questions: Project Selection

After the question of how to sustain gains, the burning question both for those who are new to Six Sigma and for those with ongoing programs is how to select projects. The high-level characteristics of a good Six Sigma project, in any area of application, include:

- Clear connection to business priorities and links to strategic and annual operating plans
- The potential to provide a major improvement in process performance and a major financial improvement
- A reasonable scope and a doable time frame of four to six months
- Clear quantitative measures of success, with the baseline measures and the goals well defined
- Clear importance to the organization
- The wholehearted support of management

A Final Word

Six Sigma isn't immune to criticism. It's sometimes said, for example, that Six Sigma offers little that is new or innovative in the way of tools. It's certainly true that many of the techniques of Six Sigma have been borrowed from TQM, Lean, and other quality and improvement programs. However, Six Sigma combines the tools with a disciplined methodology, teaches people when to use them, focuses on bottom-line results, and rigorously and successfully establishes a more effective way of working. Moreover, the insistence on "newness" is misplaced. The true test of an improvement methodology is a proven track record and, after a quarter of a century, it's safe to say that Six Sigma has passed with flying colors.

About the Author

Dr. Ronald D. Snee (Snee@TunnellConsulting.com) is a Tunnell Consulting principal in the Performance Excellence Practice, which offers Six Sigma, Lean Six Sigma, and other improvement approaches. He has authored numerous books and articles on process improvement and quality. Having begun his continuous improvement career at DuPont, Dr. Snee has been honored with the Shewhart and Grant Medals, and the Hunter and Brumbaugh awards. He also served on the Malcolm Baldrige National Quality Award Criteria Team.

Where to Go for More Information

REFERENCES

Creveling, C. M., J. L. Slutsky, and D. Antis, Jr. *Design for Six Sigma in Technology and Product Development.* Upper Saddle River, NJ: Prentice Hall, 2003.

Harry, Mikel J. "Six Sigma: A Breakthrough Strategy for Profitability." *Quality Progress* (1998): 60–64.

Hoerl, R. W., and R. D. Snee. *Statistical Thinking—Improving Business Performance.* Pacific Grove, CA: Duxbury Press, 2002.

Kotter, J. P. *Leading Change.* Boston, MA: Harvard Business School Press, 1996.

McGurk, Thomas L. "Ramping Up and Ensuring Supply Capability for Biopharmaceuticals." *BioPharm International* (January 2004): 38–44.

Snee, R. D. "Can Six Sigma Boost Your Company's Growth?" *Harvard Management Update* (June 2004): 2–4.

———. "Six Sigma: The Evolution of 100 Years of Business Improvement Methodology." *International Journal of Six Sigma and Competitive Advantage* 1, no. 1 (2004): 4–20.

———. "When Worlds Collide: Lean and Six Sigma." *Quality Progress* (September 2005): 63–65.

———. "With All Deliberate Speed: Weaving Six Sigma into the Fabric of the Organization." *Quality Progress* (September 2004): 69–71.

Snee, R. D., and R. W. Hoerl. *Leading Six Sigma—A Step by Step Guide Based on the Experience with General Electric and Other Six Sigma Companies.* New York: FT Prentice Hall, 2003.

———. *Six Sigma Beyond the Factory Floor: Deployment Strategies for Financial Services, Health Care and the Rest of the Real Economy.* Upper Saddle River, NJ: Pearson Prentice Hall, 2005.

Welch, Jack, and John Byrne. *Jack: Straight from the Gut.* New York: Warner Business Books, 2001.

Welch, Jack, with Suzy Welch. *Winning.* New York: Harper Business, 2005.

ORGANIZATIONS

American Society for Quality—www.asq.org

Tunnell Consulting—www.tunnellconsulting.com

48

MARCIA HYATT, GINNY BELDEN-CHARLES, AND MARY STACEY

Action Learning

Knowledge must come through action.

—Sophocles

IT and Strategic Change

Canadian Tire is one of Canada's largest retailers, with more than 37,000 employees. In 2001, the IT division was struggling. "When I inherited IT our reputation was poor. We just weren't delivering," says Andrew Wnek, senior vice president and CIO. "We quickly looked for ways to create strategic change."

Wnek realized the 50 middle managers held the key to changing the culture and improving performance. He initiated Action Learning to "develop leadership while working real issues." Managers were assigned to cross-functional teams, which met monthly over three eight-month blocks. They shared complex, real work challenges with their peers, who provided coaching using Action Learning methods. Presenting managers returned to work with high-leverage actions to implement. In the following months, they provided a progress update to the team.

"Two years later we have an organization that's performing much better," notes Wnek. Individual leaders are more confident, strategic thinkers who are able to challenge assumptions; the management team has stronger relationships and a richer pool of actionable cross-functional knowledge. The result has been an ability to influence the organization and achieve desired change. Ninety-one percent of managers say Action Learning breaks down silos and increases cross-functional teamwork. Eighty-one percent say it is a worthwhile investment in leadership. In a relatively short period of time, a new culture has taken hold in IT. "The business believes that IT is of value and Action Learning is a major contributor to this," says Wnek.

The Basics

Action Learning is a structured change method that engages leaders and teams in a repeated cycle of reflection and action. Research demonstrates that developing the capacity to "learn as you go" is key to organizational success. Action learning builds change leadership in organizations through:

- A focus on complex challenges for which participants have accountability for action

- Groups that meet over a period of time to learn and apply actions

- A questioning process that uncovers assumptions which are guiding current actions within the organization

Action Learning "sets" were first introduced in Great Britain in the 1940s by Reginald Revans. Small groups of people met regularly to coach each other through real work issues. The insights gained were turned into action plans, and updates were provided at subsequent meetings. The method has evolved over 60 years of use in communities and organizations around the world.

Action Learning works because it taps the natural way people learn from experience. It develops the essential skills for seeing patterns, thinking creatively and coaching through questioning. Organizations whose leaders have these skills get better business results.

There are two types of action learning: peer coaching and team learning. Peer coaching is used when peers from different functional areas or professionals doing similar work meet to reflect on challenges for which they are individually accountable. Team learning creates a forum for an intact team to reflect on a shared challenge. Choosing which type of action learning to use depends on the strategy and change goals of the organization. Some groups may include both types.

When and Where Is Action Learning Used?

Action Learning is used globally with peer leaders and project teams to:

- Support large-scale change

- Develop strategic leadership

- Build cross-functional teamwork

- Address complex business problems

What Are the Outcomes from Using This Method?

Action Learning achieves multiple, integrated outcomes:

Individual	Team	Organization
• Cross-functional knowledge and a big-picture perspective • Strategic thinking and action	• Stronger peer relationships • Team commitment, creativity, and flexibility	• Observable improvements in business results • Accelerated strategic change

Individual	Team	Organization
• Coaching support for individual development • Awareness of strengths and development needs	• Productive discussions that lead to more strategic and focused action • Higher-quality team outcomes	• Solutions to complex organizational problems • Greater ability to innovate

How Does It Work?

Action Learning engages participants in a repeated cycle of reflection and action. The Action Learning Framework (figure 1) delineates the stages of inquiry they go through to effectively apply the learning cycle over time. Above the "waterline" questions clarify the situation. Below the waterline questions uncover the current frame, explore other perspectives, and help participants reframe the situation and prepare to take more strategic action. With each cycle, deeper understanding of the situation occurs, and ever more strategic actions are taken. The greater the change needed, the deeper the learning required.

For example, a cross-functional group of regional VPs in a Fortune 100 financial company met monthly for one year to accelerate learning and streamline operations. Here is a snapshot of one member's experience:

Bob had the following situation: "My offices don't work well together. How can I get everyone on the same page?" The group questioned Bob to help him explore his approach. Bob assumed he

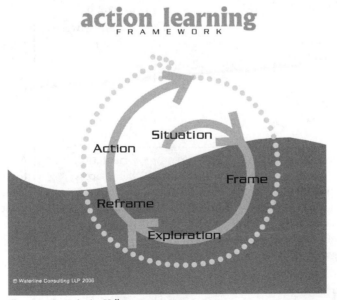

Illustration by Katherine Heller

Figure 1. How Action Learning Works

needed to standardize processes across offices. Through peer questioning, he realized there might be a better way to approach his situation. With this awareness, he met with office managers to help them focus on their regional goals. He then made a point to recognize success stories to spur cross-office learning. As a result, Bob minimized resistance, and his managers shared best practices and supported critical standardization.

Action learning is a powerful tool for change. It has been used to accelerate the implementation of new work designs; improve customer satisfaction, shift culture, and build change leadership. Millennium Pharmaceuticals Inc. initiated Action Learning groups to build leadership bench strength, increase cross-company communication, and to build action learning into their operations. Peer groups of directors, women leaders, Chinese scientists, supervisors, and administrative assistants gathered for a year. The length and frequency of meetings were varied by group. Evaluations showed they achieved their objectives.

Table of Uses

Typical Setting	Brief Description	Length of Time	Key Events	Participants Involved
Peer Coaching	• Peers coach each other on individual challenges to surface assumptions and take strategic action • Used to build cross-functional knowledge, develop leadership, and to address complex challenges.	Minimally groups meet over 6–12 months; some have met for years	• Orientation to the process • Minimum of 4 coaching sessions; 3–8 hours in length • Action between meetings	Leaders and professionals who are either: • from different functions or • do similar work or • are on the same team. Minimum 3 members, maximum 10
Team Learning	• Teams reflect on a shared project; assumptions are surfaced and new insights applied between meetings • Used to accelerate a strategic change or address complex challenges	Teams meet periodically through the duration of their project	• Orientation to the process • Clarifying the reflection questions • Team reflection • Action between meetings	All stakeholders of the team or key leadership of the project

About the Authors

Marcia Hyatt (marcia@waterlineconsulting.com) and *Ginny Belden-Charles* (ginny@waterline consulting.com) are partners at Waterline Consulting LLP. In the past 15 years, they have introduced hundreds of Action Learning groups to deep-learning methods for transformational change. Their clients include American Express, Millennium Pharmaceuticals, AERA Energy, the City of Minneapolis, and St. Paul Travelers. Marcia has an MA in adult education from the University of Minnesota; Ginny has an MSOD from Pepperdine.

Mary Stacey (mary.stacey@contextconsulting.com) is with Context Management Consulting, Inc. In 2004–2006, Context's Action Learning programs were named by Canadian Tire Corporation, The Conference Board of Canada, and the Atlanta-based Information Management Forum as best practice in leadership development and strategic change. Mary holds an MA in organizational leadership and learning from Royal Roads University.

Where to Go for More Information

REFERENCES

Belden-Charles, Ginny, and Marcia Hyatt. *Waterline Action Learning Handbook.* St. Paul, MN: Waterline Consulting LLP, 2004.

Marquardt, Michael. *Optimizing the Power of Action Learning: Solving Problems and Building Leaders in Real Time.* Palo Alto, CA, Davies-Black, 2004.

McGill, Ian, and Anne Brockelbank. *The Action Learning Handbook: Powerful Techniques for Education, Professional Development and Training.* New York: RoutledgeFalmer, 2004.

Pedler, Mike. *Action Learning in Practice.* Hampshire, UK: Gower Publishing, 1997.

ORGANIZATION

Waterline Consulting—www.waterlineconsulting.co

49

CHARLES PARRY, MARK PIRES, AND HEIDI SPARKES GUBER

Action Review Cycle and the After Action Review Meeting

Leadership and learning are indispensable to each other.
—John F. Kennedy

Real-Life Story

Green Mountain Coffee Roasters (GMCR), named one of the "Best Medium Sized Companies to Work for in America," wanted to increase its operational performance discipline—to learn rapidly from success and breakdowns alike.

Formal After Action Reviews (AARs) were conducted in two linked projects—a major expansion of the distribution center and an equipment acquisition. These AARs cascaded upward through the three levels doing the planning and execution: line operators, project leaders, then senior management. Successful practices and areas for improvement were identified and informed the next phases of the distribution center project, engineering improvements, and in further rounds of adding automation equipment.

Today, through the initiative of various leaders, Before Action Reviews (BARs) and/or AARs are used in the performance review process, hiring, finance, a major CRM project, managing response to regional blackouts, and helping the Corporate Responsibility team generate greater impact. GMCR has a bias toward learning throughout projects and ongoing work, rather than waiting for end points. Continuous Learning Director Pru Sullivan reflects: "BARs and AARs require discipline and rigor to actually make them work. They also give people a way to learn and take responsibility when things don't go as planned—and to learn, take responsibility and to celebrate when things go well."

Frequently Asked Questions

WHAT IS THE AAR/ARC? WHAT IS ITS PURPOSE?

The After Action Review (AAR) is a meeting that provides a feedback loop between intended and actual results in a team setting. Paired with a short Before Action Review (BAR) meeting, it functions as the heartbeat of a cycle that brings leading, learning, and execution together in service of sustaining success in a changing environment.

This cycle, known as the Action Review Cycle (ARC), has been used to accelerate leader development, improve operational performance, build an accountable learning organization, shape rapid transformation, and as a competitive strategy (agility).

WHAT IS UNIQUE ABOUT THIS METHOD?

A central challenge facing most organizations today is that their baseline reality has shifted from "stability with exceptions of change" to "change with exceptions of stability." For these organizations, change management and interventions based in the "unfreeze-change-refreeze" paradigm no longer fit the situation, and tend to produce oscillation.

To sustain excellence in the face of changing conditions, the ability to learn and adjust must be a core competence—individually and organizationally. The ARC is a proven means to build this right into how work gets done.

WHEN AND WHERE IS THE ARC USED?

It is unfortunate that the word "After" in the term "AAR" contributed to many adopters of the U.S. Army's innovation missing a key fact—that any one AAR meeting is one part of a self-correcting feedback system for leaders, and *not* a one-time, postmortem review. Not only is it too late in a postmortem to change the result, the recommendations produced in such meetings are rarely implemented.

The ARC (BAR-Action-AAR) rhythm places "bookends" before and after important units of action (figure 1). Once established as normal practice, BAR and AAR meetings are short and disciplined. The best use is building the cycle into projects and repeating operational activities that will pay back the investment of time in innovation, alignment, and rising standards of performance.

WHAT ARE THE OUTCOMES FROM USING THE ARC?

The local-level outcome is leaders and teams that are agile-minded and empowered in facing change, and ready to achieve their intended results. BARs build the habit of briefly pausing to articulate and align on the plan before going into action. Articulating intent (task, purpose, end state, and metrics) helps sort out means from ends. This in turn builds alignment and enables adaptability. It also sets the stage for the AAR to follow. By comparing intended and actual results

BAR: Before Action Review	**A**	**AAR: After Action Review**
Focus: Alignment and readiness for effective action	**C**	*Focus: Accountability and actionable insights*
What are our intended results and metrics?	**T**	What was our intent and plan?
What challenges can we anticipate?	**I**	What were the actual results?
What did we/others learn in similar situations?	**O**	What caused these results and any gaps?
What will make the biggest difference?	**N**	What will I/we sustain and improve?

Figure 1. ARCs Place Bookends Before and After Important Actions

in the AAR, assumptions are tested against pragmatic data from execution. Once established, this feedback cycle makes learning inescapable and accountability visible (figure 2).

When the ARC is widely adopted throughout a whole organization, the outcome is twofold:

First, a culture of accountability (figure 3). In order to produce this, senior leaders must:

- Vigorously maintain a clear line of sight across levels, from vision through to execution—and back;
- Expect teams to continually improve performance in their core work;
- Assure current data is used by leaders at each level to show intended versus actual results;
- Assure the regularity of leader-led ARCs until they take root—when people see them as unavoidable, momentum shifts.

Second, an agile organization (figure 4). Without an integrative process such as the ARC at the team and interteam level, hiring, training and rewarding individual leaders for agility will not produce an agile organization—such individual-centric approaches may in fact produce gridlock. Organizational agility is an emergent quality arising from building blocks such as discipline around shared understanding of intent and regular candid conversations about results. Such cultural norms undergird the likelihood that aligned, agile action will emerge during periods of crisis or unexpected opportunities.

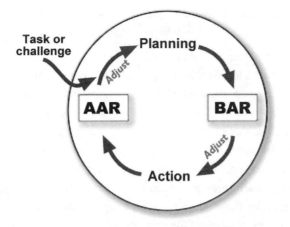

Figure 2. Action Review Cycle (ARC)

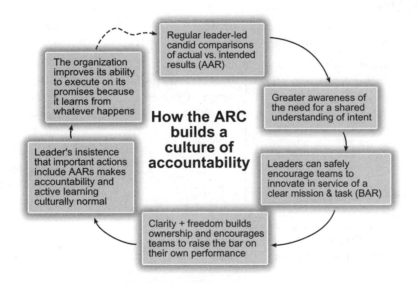

Figure 3. How the ARC Builds a Culture of Accountability

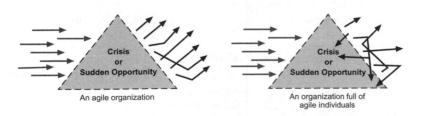

Figure 4. ARCs Shape the Conditions for Organizational Agility to Emerge

How Does the ARC Build Change Readiness and Agility in an Organization?

In a stable environment, organizations often find that separating the functions of leading, learning, and execution is efficient. However, in today's turbulent environments, that separation often becomes a barrier to agility because it interferes with accountability and unity of action. The frequency of disciplined BAR and AAR conversations build an orientation toward anticipating and adapting to changing conditions.

The ARC brings leading, learning, and execution together wherever the organization's work gets done. Gradually, the stovepipes previously separating leading, learning, and execution blur. Leaders lead the learning. Teams learn through execution. Execution within changing conditions becomes a mark of effective leadership and empowered teams. Hubris gives way to humility. Together, these dynamics shape the conditions for organizational agility to emerge—and for the organization to continue to thrive in changing conditions.

Table of Uses

Settings and Participants	Core Work Challenge	Event/Project Specs	Outcomes
Energy company—senior executives and specialist teams (15)	Improve the process for major capital allocations	Initially, 2 half-day sessions on a successful merger facilitated by 2 consultants	• Streamlined process and a template for future capital projects • Major savings in several deals • Proactive stance in preparing for possible challenges such as a hostile takeover attempt
Nuclear plant—management and operator teams (100).	Cut time and cost of maintenance outages	Built review cycles into existing outage procedures	Five iterations reduced average duration 80%, injury 40%, cost 20%
Coffee roaster—New England plant team leaders (15)	Response to power outages—unpredictable periodic events requiring the coordination of many teams	Initial 3-hour session led by plant manager	Plant manager can now promise future outages will be invisible to customers
Society for Organizational Learning—corporate, research, and consulting professionals (25)	Improve alignment and collective impact of the membership	Align participants with design team, anticipate and track action between meetings	• Step change in being focused on what really matters • Grounded the organization's purpose and values in real work through time

About the Authors

Charles Parry, Mark Pires, and *Heidi Sparkes Guber,* together with Dave Flanigan, Joe Moore, and Marilyn Darling, pooled their original research on best practices in organizational learning and broad experience leading military, nonprofit, and corporate organizations in order to provide pragmatic support to leaders who are facing the challenge of building their organization's desire and skill in embracing change—so that organizations can continue to thrive in today's dynamic environments. Their shared mailbox is contact@signetconsulting.com.

Where to Go for More Information

REFERENCES

Darling, Marilyn, D. Meador, and S. Patterson. "Cultivating a Learning Economy: After Action Reviews Generate Ongoing Value for DTE Energy." *Reflections—The SoL Journal on Knowledge, Learning, and Change* 5, no. 2 (2003).

Darling, Marilyn, and C. Parry. *From Post Mortem to Living Practice: An In-depth Study of the Evolution of the After Action Review.* Boston: SR&C Publications, 2000.

Darling, Marilyn, C. Parry, and J. Moore. "Learning in the Thick of It." The High Performance Organization (special double issue). *Harvard Business Review* (July–August 2005).

Parry, Charles, and M. Darling. "Emergent Learning in Action: The After Action Review." *The Systems Thinker* (October 2001).

ORGANIZATION

Signet Research & Consulting, LLC—www.signetconsulting.com

Balanced Scorecard

Managing strategy is synonymous with managing change.
—Robert Kaplan and David Norton

Handling Bags

Think about the following Southwest Airlines baggage handler, then ask yourself if you want to change your organization to have performance measures that support your organization's goals. When asked, this baggage handler responded clearly and quickly about his performance measures to load baggage:

1. Quickly, so planes depart on time, helping to ensure passenger happiness and repeat business.

2. Carefully, so baggage is undamaged, saving money and helping to keep our customers happy.

3. Correctly, so baggage gets to the correct destination, keeping passengers happy and saving the cost of tracking and delivering lost baggage.[1]

We asked numerous senior executives to survey their employees to determine if they knew how they contributed to organizational goals and strategy. Most said they did not need to survey because they knew their employees did not have a clear idea on how they contributed to the organization's goals and strategies. Many said even those who reported directly to them did not understand the strategies for achieving the organizational goals. Some found performance measures that were contradictory to the organizational goals and strategies. Their employees were not all rowing in the same direction. Some of their employees were not even in the same river.

When executives ask their direct reports the following, they are dumfounded to find out how little knowledge their employees have of organizational strategy: What are the organization's goals and strategies? How does your function contribute to those goals and strategies? Which of your performance measures relate to our goals and strategies?

Frequently Asked Questions

What Is the Balanced Scorecard?

The Balanced Scorecard is a powerful change framework to implement strategy by translating it into understandable objectives that drive behavior and performance. It is an excellent way to engage multiple people in moving the organization forward.

This change management tool helps everyone understand how they contribute to organizational goals and strategies, helps change performance measures to the correct level of detail to be meaningful, and aligns performance measures with organizational goals and strategies.

Scorecards:

- Help employees provide input to strategy
- Communicate strategy so everyone understands how they impact strategy
- Align employees so everyone is working in the same direction
- Help employees decide which processes are strategic to achieving strategies and goals
- Change monthly financial statements from historical and control-oriented to future-oriented that employees can act upon
- Link operating and capital budgets
- Change employees' analysis from just tactical to include strategic.[2]

Scorecards change the focus from just financial to four perspectives of measures. They communicate organizational goals and strategies into terms managers and frontline employees can understand and act upon. Frontline workers can actually help shape strategy once they know what it is and understand how different parts of the business interact. Based on strategy, people in all departments set local execution and improvement goals and get a shared sense of organizational direction. All levels have continuing input to strategy through new lenses of aligned goals.

Scorecards show:

- Short- and long-term goals
- Leading and lagging indicators
- Internal and external performance measures
- Financial and nonfinancial measures
- Quantifiable Outcome Measures and subjective Performance Drivers[3]

When and Where Is It Used?

Scorecards are used to better communicate strategy and align employees so everyone is focused on its execution. Executives, middle-level managers, and frontline workers use it. Large organizations and small companies use it.

In deciding to implement, ask yourself, is it important:

- Everyone is rowing in the same direction?
- Everyone understands how they support strategies?
- To change so local performance measures support strategies?

What Are the Outcomes of Using the Balanced Scorecard?

Scorecards clarify strategy for employees and executives; align strategy, critical success factors, and key performance indicators; coordinate target setting with strategy; make changes so strategy is everyone's business; and tell executives and employees if the strategy is working.

Scorecards focus on nonfinancial and financial factors. Organizations say their most important asset is their people. Scorecards make visible those measures that relate to people and their growth and learning. It gives frontline workers a better chance to communicate their findings to senior management so that either the strategy can be changed or the way the organization executes the strategy is modified.

How Does It Work? What Is the Flow or Process?

The Balanced Scorecard[4] suggests starting with Vision, Mission, Values, and Strategy. These should be related to four perspectives: Financial, Customer, Business Process, and Growth and Learning.

Scorecard creation often starts with financial goals. Then ask: What customer measures will help us achieve those financial goals? What business processes do we have to excel at to satisfy our customers so they will buy in a profitable way? Where do we need to expand and teach people, processes, and systems so we can effectively execute our processes that will satisfy our customers so we can achieve our financial goals? Scorecard creation goes from Financial to Growth and Learning. Scorecard use goes the other way, from Growth and Learning to Business Processes to Customer Measures to Financial Results. This is an iterative process:

Financial ⟷ Customer ⟷ Business Process ⟷ Growth and Learning

Scorecards are powerful change tools because if an organization focuses on Growth and Learning of its people and systems, its Business Processes will improve. If employees improve the right business processes, they will satisfy their customers, and if employees satisfy their customers, then they should achieve financial goals.

Middle managers and frontline employees like it because they now know that if they achieve their performance measures, the organization will achieve its goals. They understand what their focus should be. Their local performance measures become their connection to strategy. Strategy becomes everyone's business; it is transparent to everyone.

A high-level example of the scorecard process is shown in figure 1:

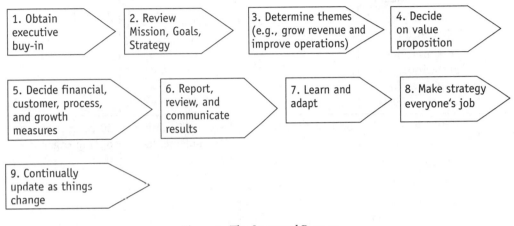

Figure 1. The Scorecard Process

Table of Uses

Typical Setting	Issues/Outcomes	Project Length	Key Events	Number of Participants
Provider of meeting services	• Unfocused • Different executives have different priorities • Executives modified strategy, and agreed to performance measures • This increased firm value	4–5 months	4 executive meetings to set direction; followed by firmwide participation	8–10 to set direction; then employees and managers decide changes

Typical Setting	Issues/Outcomes	Project Length	Key Events	Number of Participants
Nonprofit organization	• Executives not focused • Mostly in reactionary mode • Staff not sure what to focus on • Organization given focus and staff now knows where to focus	1 month	Executive seminar; scorecard meeting, rollout	Executives and employees
Military	• Staff not sure where to focus • Strategy unclear • Revised strategy • Organization now understands where to focus	Several months	Executive training; self-implementation	20 people, entire buying organization
Pharmaceutical	• Initiating key strategy changes • Market mandated new ways of thinking and delivery • Executives want to insure people are personally involved in making changes to their work areas aligned with market	4 months	3 days to set direction; 4 months rest of organization	25 set direction; 100% set local goals and input future strategy

Table of Uses. Continued

About the Author

John Antos (john.antos@valuecreationgroup.com) heads up the Value Creation Group. He is a former CFO and controller. Clients include Amtrak, Baxter Healthcare, Blue Cross Blue Shield, Boeing, Discover Card, Nationwide Insurance, and the U.S. Postal Service. He is the author of numerous articles and books.

Where to Go for More Information

REFERENCES

Kaplan, R., and D. Norton. *Alignment: Using the Balanced Scorecard to Create Corporate Synergies.* Boston: Harvard Business School Publishing Corporation, 2006.

_____. "Balanced Scorecard—Measures that Drive Performance." *Harvard Business Review* (January/February 1992): 71.

_____. *Balanced Scorecard: Translating Strategy into Action.* Boston, MA: Harvard Business School Press, 1997.

_____. "Putting Balanced Scorecard to Work." *Harvard Business Review* (September/October 1993): 134.

_____. "Using Balanced Scorecard as a Strategic Management System." *Harvard Business Review* (January/February 1996): 75.

ORGANIZATIONS

Balanced Scorecard Collaborative—www.bscol.com

Value Creation Group, Inc.—www.valuecreationgroup.com

1. Example from our seminars.

2. Balanced Scorecard seminar created by John Antos and Steve Peacock.

3. Ibid.

4. Robert Kaplan and David Norton, *The Balanced Scorecard* (Boston: Harvard Business School Press, 1996), 9.

MARGARET CASAREZ

Civic Engagement
Restoring Community Through Empowering Conversations

We are what we think. All that we are arises with our thoughts. With our thoughts, we make our world. . . . What we think, we become.
—Buddha

"I'm Homicide"

This chilling introduction was, in fact, the first step in establishing an unlikely connection for a common purpose of positive change. The speaker was a young, streetwise tough, part of a group of 70 inner-city youths. In that meeting hall, "Homicide" and his peers were there to engage in dialogue with a community group a generation older than they. The process was set in motion with the disarmingly simple yet powerful question, "What don't they get about us?" Within a few hours, these kids, once resigned to a future of futility in a community for which they had no use and wanted no place, found that asking different questions would lead to choices that could reframe their role in that community—choices of accountability and leadership participation rather than victimization and alienation. They had something important to say, and in finding their voices, they would find themselves. They committed to continue the conversations that they would convene.

Frequently Asked Questions

Civic Engagement Series (CES) creates an interpersonal synergy that has the power to restore community. CES was designed by Peter Block, initially evolving through his community initiatives in Cincinnati, now applied across the country. Together, "A Small Group," offered the opportunity to hear his unique perspective on the change process he created. In a conversation, Peter Block stated:

> The question that trumps all others is whether we want a future noticeably distinct from the past. Every change effort has to confront this question, for if all we want is continuous improvement, small next steps, or to become more efficient or effective, then we all have the problem solving tools to achieve this. The tools that follow are for those situations where a shift in paradigm, or fundamental way of operating is needed. Authentic change occurs when we change the conversation, have conversations we have not had before, and when these conversations hold the power to create an alternative future. The task of the change agent is to convene and to name the debate so that this can happen. This is done through questions and the structure and intent of questions that have the potential to create an alternative future is what is outlined here.

The key to this process is the convening of the group and the conversations that it sparks, because they are the empowering polar opposites of typically impotent grumbling and powerless

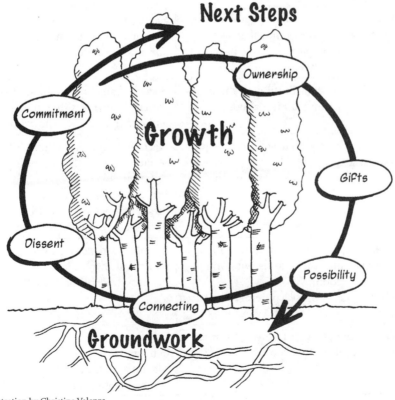

Illustration by Christine Valenza

Figure 1. Civic Engagement Three-Step Process

complaint. When an order to attend a meeting becomes an *Invitation* to gather, problems can give way to *Possibility*. When the accusatory pointing finger turns inward in *Ownership*, and resignation is replaced with lively *Dissent*, empty promises are avoided and true *Commitment* is ultimately achieved. There is forward momentum toward next steps where harping on inadequacies and shortcoming gives way to identification and celebration of capacities as *Gifts*. This three-step process is based on three main objectives the convener seeks to satisfy, in stages, within the civic engagement gathering (figure 1).

Each step involves the asking/answering of powerful questions (table 1), relating to Con-

Powerful Question	Subquestions	Primary Action
Connecting	• Why are you here today? • What do you need to get out of this session to make it worthwhile for you? • What is your intention/purpose for this meeting?	• Begins the transformation of bystanders into engaged, accountable citizens • Challenges individuals to create an alternative future
Possibility	What is the crossroads you are at? What are the possibilities that would bring meaning, purpose, and passion to wherever you show up?	Begun as individual statements that eventually lead to the envisioning of community potentials
Ownership	What is your contribution to the problem you are complaining about?	Become cause rather than effect Determine what value and meaning will occur when we show up
Dissent	What is the "no" that you are postponing? What is the "yes" that you no longer mean?	Declaring "no" is the antidote to lip service; "no" is the beginning of commitment Brings to awareness the habits, behaviors, anxieties that would tend to undermine possibilities/outcomes
Commitment	What are you willing to declare for your own life (that travels with you into every room)? What is the promise you are willing to make?	Establishes next steps that the participants will own Promise that brings about changes
Gifts	What is the gift you received from another person in this room?	Reinforces individual contributions and benefits from the experience Maximizes strengths, uncovers potential contributions and commitments

Table 1. Powerful Questions

necting, Possibility, Ownership, Dissent, Commitment, and Gifts, which engage the individual in a focus of their attention toward a group purpose. The order can vary depending upon the sensitivities to a certain topic and/or the tolerance for risk of those assembled, or as a function of the familiarity of group members.

This method has the ability to impact the process of the group, and the awareness and perspective of the individuals that comprise it, effecting the sort of systemic change that is most powerful and abiding. The effectiveness of the Civic Engagement Series can best be shown through the apparent shift of paradigms for the participating groups. Generally, the level of engagement rises with increased ownership for outcomes. The measurement is a simple one for all past participants: Is the climate electric and engaged with powerful questions? Are people clear and committed around purpose? Is there a palpable difference in the way they engage? To answer the inevitable question about social capital, the tangible proof for civic accountability is in the *pride of the general citizenship.*

Table of Uses

Brief Description	Project Length	Number of Participants
Various Community Groups Seeking to maximize the empowerment and focused effort of Civic Engagement, regardless of group size or historical setbacks.	• The entire length of each project is 2 weeks with 2 Key Events consisting of 3 half-hour sessions This project continues in an expanding and cyclical fashion with participants going out on their own and setting up further meetings and discussions • Goes as long as there is someone to invite people together and participation	15–200 people
Government Organizations The potential for enlightened restructuring of bureaucracies mired in red tape. A new context for interaction of the government and the governed.		
Corporations Companies embracing a corporate culture that aspires to a sense of community.		

About the Author

Margaret Casarez, M.O.D. (Bowling Green State University) (magcasarez@fuse.net) specializes in executive coaching and emotional intelligence. Her accreditations include HayGroup certification and study/implementation of Whole Scale Systems change with Kathleen D. Dannemiller. She is the founder of the UNbound Consulting organization and leadership development consultancy, and the designer of The Peace Model and its workshops focusing on discovering opportunity in the face of individual and group conflict situations. Margaret is a member and convener of Peter Block's "A Small Group" for civic engagement.

Where to Go for More Information

REFERENCES

Block, Peter. *Stewardship: Choosing Service over Self-Interest.* San Francisco: Berrett-Koehler, 1993.

————, ed. *Civic Engagement and the Restoration of Community: Changing the Nature of the Conversation.* Fanwood, NJ: Designed Learning, 2005.

McKnight, John. *The Careless Society: Community and its Counterfeits.* New York: Basic Books/HarperCollins, 1995.

Pharr, Susan J., and Robert D. Putnam, eds. *Disaffected Democracies: What's Troubling the Trilateral Countries?* Princeton, NJ: Princeton University Press, 2000.

Putnam, Robert D., with Robert Leonardi and Raffaella Y. Nanetti. *Making Democracy Work: Civic Traditions in Modern Italy.* Princeton, NJ: Princeton University Press, 1993.

ORGANIZATION

A Small Group—http://asmallgroup.net

52

The Cycle of Resolution
Conversational Competence for Sustainable Collaboration

Covenantal relationships induce freedom, not paralysis. A Covenantal relationship rests on shared commitment to ideas, to issues, to values, to goals. . . . Words such as love, warmth, personal chemistry are certainly pertinent.

—Max DePree

Developing Conversation Skills

Gail Johnson is the executive director of Sierra Adoption, a nonprofit transforming lives of foster children through finding permanent adoptive families. Thousands of children are trapped in the California foster care system, out of reach of adoptive families. More than half of foster youth who come of age without a permanent family are homeless, in prison, or dead within two years. Gail's success recruiting and preparing families to adopt children with disabilities often ended in the frustration of being told such children were "unadoptable." Because of Gail's work, California no longer considers any child unadoptable!

In 1999, Sierra was engaged in a federally funded partnership with the Sacramento County agency that was referring children to Sierra. The working relationship had fallen apart. Gail wanted to resolve long- and short-term conflict, get beyond mistrust, and forge a high-performance team. Few believed the partnership could be salvaged, let alone become a high-performance team. Using the Cycle of Resolution, the conflicts were resolved and a working agreement was structured in a short period of time. That agreement was the foundation for a healthy, productive partnership with a new vision of sustainable collaboration. In the first year following the intervention, 109 "unadoptable" children were placed in permanent families.

Change happened because the conversational process of the Cycle of Resolution forged a shared vision and a high-performance team that enabled the realization of Gail's vision of "unadoptable" children with real homes.

Frequently Asked Questions

How Does the Cycle of Resolution Work?

This change model provides a set of principles and conversational protocols that provide a road map for difficult conversations people often avoid. They are reluctant to engage because they do not have a map to navigate through difficult conversations. They do not know how to get into, through, and out of the dialogues. The Cycle of Resolution leads to an "agreement for results" that serves as a map and project manager to desired outcomes. The premise of the method is that:

> The effectiveness of any collaboration and any organization reflects the quality of the relationships that constitute the enterprise; and, the relationships reflect the quality of agreements among the participants. The goal of the interventions is sustainable collaboration and a "culture of agreement and resolution" where everyone has the same vision, the same path to get there, and the same tools to keep them on track.

The first part of the process is developing an attitude of resolution—enrolling people through the realization of just how large the huge cost of conflict really is and understanding that most conflict is not about bad intention—most conflict is structural, a function of different individual characteristics, needs, and outcomes. Different needs and the lack of clear explicit agreements lead to conflict. Few people have ever learned what to speak about when they want to prevent conflict and collaborate effectively. They do not have the map to solid "agreement for results," the basic building blocks of collaborations and organizational culture. The ability to engage in such a dialogue requires some basic traditional communication skills (self-awareness, listening, and emotional intelligence), a desire to embrace the principles that make up the "attitude of resolution," and knowledge of the conversational steps.

Another key premise is that no matter how good the agreement on the front end, conflict will arise because of changing and unforeseen circumstances, incompleteness, and personal challenges. Besides crafting good agreements, an important aim of the intervention is to "normalize" conflict so that people will not remain emotionally triggered—they internalize the skills and temperament to get through the "white water" that is challenging them on the way to the skill and goal of reaching more effective agreements. The long-term goal is the realization that when disagreements occur, a fight does not have to follow—you just need a new agreement. When an organization, or a collaborative partnership of any kind, embraces the cyclical process—the Cycle of Resolution—there is little drain on productive capacity; they realize the empowering align-ment resolution and agreement brings.

The key aspects of the method include:

1. Understanding the Costs of Conflict:

   - *Direct Cost*—The cost of professional help

   - *Productivity and Opportunity Costs*—lost time and diminished productive capacity

   - *Relational and Continuity Costs*—The real cost of replacement

   - *Emotional Costs*—The immeasurable drain

2. Cycle of Resolution (figure 1):

   - *Attitude of Resolution*—mind-set and principles for engagement

   - *Telling the Story*—everyone sharing how they see the situation

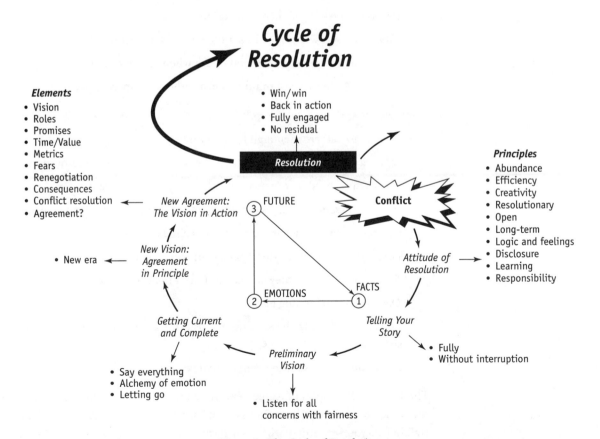

Figure 1. The Cycle of Resolution

- *Preliminary Vision*—what might be fair and take care of everyone's concerns
- *Getting Current and Complete*—a structured way of processing emotions
- *Agreement in Principle*—the broad-brush new vision for the future
- *New Agreement*—the details of the new vision and road map
- *Resolution*—back in action, with no constraints on full engagement

3. Ten Essential Elements of "Agreements for Results":

- *Intent and Vision*—a picture of the desired outcome
- *Roles*—who is responsible for what
- *Promises*—what people will do
- *Time and Value*—how long and what will each person receive
- *Measurements of Satisfaction*—the metric that measures success
- *Concerns, Risks, and Fears*—what's creating fear of moving forward
- *Renegotiation*—the ability to make changes
- *Consequences*—what is the loss if the vision is not achieved
- *Conflict Resolution*—the method to use when conflict occurs
- *Agreement*—meeting of mind and heart, the assessment of trust

4. Principles of the "Attitude of Resolution":

- *Abundance*—there is enough for everyone
- *Efficiency*—what is the quickest, most effective way to get to resolution
- *Creativity*—the ability to meet in a shared space and invent
- *Fostering Resolution*—does the communication process encourage resolution
- *Openness*—full disclosure of facts and feelings
- *Long-Term Perspective*—the opposite of winning today
- *Respecting Feelings*—they are real and need to be accommodated
- *Disclosure*—no holding back
- *Learning*—allowing the shifting of positions as you learn each other's perspective
- *Responsibility*—resolution cannot be delegated

5. The Law and Principles of Agreement: A detailed set of guidelines flowing from the basic law that "Collaboration is established in language by making implicit (talking to yourself about what you think the agreement is) and explicit (discussing the agreement with others) agreements."

6. Laws of Manifestation: The power of our thinking and engaging brings our vision into being. The clearer our thoughts and agreements, the more powerful the results will be.

Table of Uses

Typical Setting	Brief Description	Time	Key Events	Number of Participants
Close relationships	• Conflict • People are stuck • No win-win • No commitment	1–3 days	• Education • Facilitation	Entire system
Project teams	• No Agreement • No joint vision • No road map • No communication	Practice	• Facilitation • Education	5–12
Partners	• Can't partner • No partnership • No covenant	6–8 weeks	• Education • Facilitation • Practice	2–5
Senior team	• Lack collaboration	6 months	• eLearning	5–12
Boards	• Stuck • No connection • No covenant	6–12 months	• Education • Facilitation • eLearning	5–12
Departments	• No unified vision • No covenant • No teamship	3–6 months	• Education • Facilitation • eLearning	5–50

About the Author

Stewart Levine (www.ResolutionWorks.com) creates agreement and empowerment in challenging circumstances using his conversational models to create "Agreements for Results." Clients include government agencies, nongovernmental organizations, and Fortune 500 companies. *Getting to Resolution* was an Executive Book Club selection, featured by Executive Book Summaries, named one of the 30 Best Business Books of 1998, and called "a marvelous book" by Dr. Stephen Covey. *The Book of Agreement* (Berrett-Koehler, 2003) has been called "more practical" than the classic *Getting to Yes* and named one of the best books of 2003 by *CEO Refresher* (www .Refresher.com). Levine is an instructor for the American Management Association.

Where to Go for More Information

REFERENCES

Levine, Stewart. *The Book of Agreement: 10 Essential Elements for Getting the Results You Want.* San Francisco: Berrett-Koehler, 2003.

————. *Getting to Resolution: Turning Conflict into Collaboration* (Russian, Portuguese translations). San Francisco: Berrett-Koehler, 1998.

Resolutionary Thinking Newsletter. www.ResolutionWorks.com.

ORGANIZATION

Resolution Works Online—www.ResolutionWorks.com

For information about ResolutionWorksOnline, a new eLearning program, contact Stewart Levine: ResolutionWorks@msn.com or (510) 777-1166.

53

Employee Engagement Process

Our work in the world is to change the nature of the conversation. . . .
A conversation of ownership and possibility is the antidote to blame.

—Peter Block

Global Pharmaceutical Distribution

The distribution network of a global pharmaceutical firm was beginning a three-year journey to achieve a new strategic vision. Its improvement framework covered: quality, service, costs, and people/culture. While the first three areas had metrics in place, people/culture did not. The Employee Engagement Process was selected not only to quantify people/culture but also to evolve the culture itself toward greater engagement and shared responsibility.

The process began by educating managers, preparing them for a more open environment in which they shared information more freely and heard employee feedback without emotional resistance. This presurvey work was an important part of the change process. Once the managers were ready, the McCormick Employee Engagement Inventory (MEEI) was distributed to all 1,000 members of the Distribution Centers. Results were compiled but not analyzed and returned to managers and staff together in a series of site-specific "all hands" meetings. At these meetings, managers and frontline employees sat in mixed groups, first making sense of the data, then forming work groups to discuss team strengths and challenges, and finally planning implementation of suggested changes.

On the "strength" side, the team discussed that most employees—management and non-management alike—felt real meaning in their work. They had a line of sight to the customer and knew that their role in distributing medications around the globe was of critical importance. They were able to "see from the whole." On the "challenges" side of the equation, employees felt somewhat isolated from corporate, somewhat stagnated, and that the support they gave each other was clearly lacking. Suggestions that arose from work included a process for job rotation, self-imposed norms to eliminate site gossip, a process to better communicate company benefits to remote locations, and life-management courses to support employees with work-life issues.

Many of management's preconceived priorities turned out to be quite different from what came out of the meetings. Both management and employees moved past a mind-set of "blame" to one of joint ownership, seeing from the whole and solving the problems together. One lasting outcome of the work was a cultural shift in the site's management team. Center headquarters staff saw that the process positively impacted site safety, union avoidance, employee performance, attendance, and morale. The MEEI survey methodology has since been adopted for other company surveys, profoundly shifting how survey data is shared and used as an impetus for change across the organization.

Frequently Asked Questions

What Is the Employee Engagement Process?

The McCormick Employee Engagement Inventory (MEEI), which is at the core of the process, is a 35-question instrument with content validity. Engagement—defined as *a personal state of authentic involvement, contribution, and ownership*—is characterized by seven scales:

Scale	Desired State
Communication	Feels informed
Customer Relationship	Sense of customer ownership
Job/Role	Role clarity and confidence
How I Do My Job	Personal initiative
Goals and Outcomes	Goal confidence
Work Climate	Open and trusting culture
Leadership	A "leader-full" organization

How Was the Employee Engagement Process Developed and How Has It Evolved?

When developed in 1999, the MEEI was a radical departure from traditional survey methodologies. It resulted from the personal frustration of Fortune 100 company employees of more than 12 years with both the survey's content and process. Every two years, all employees completed an extensive survey on workplace issues such as satisfaction with supervisor, pay, and other external factors. It excluded issues of substance, such as the impact of "my voice at work" or "finding meaning in my work" in relation to the whole. We would either see no survey results or we would see no action resulting from the survey. Frustrated with the lack of connection between the survey and any apparent change, the MEEI and the Employee Engagement Process sought to shift both the nature of the questions and how results were distributed and used. Thus, the Employee Engagement Process marries a survey that quantifies workplace culture with the employee as the locus of control with a process that is transparent, collaborative, employee driven, and action oriented. This process turns survey results analysis and action planning over to employees and managers through whole-system feedback and action meetings. Responsibility is spread across employee groups to create a more engaged workplace. The survey process catalyzes meaningful results and a real opportunity for engagement.

The MEEI survey instrument grew out of extensive research conducted for my Ph.D. I had been intrigued by the impact of high-participation methodologies like Future Search and the Conference Model on successful change initiatives. The first version of the MEEI sought to measure this impact. The scales and the questions were developed through analyzing focus group and interview data gathered from people who had participated in one or more large group organizational change initiatives. The seven scales are the apparent differentiators in successful change initiatives. For example, participants' perceptions of the "big picture" and that "my voice is heard" both correlated highly with their ratings of the initiative's success. Over time, the survey evolved to measure employee engagement not just during a change initiative, but generally.

Research performed in 2002 by the Philadelphia Area Human Resource Planning Group linked MEEI results to productivity, consistently showing that the better-producing units also had higher engagement scores.

How Does the Employee Engagement Process Work?

The Employee Engagement Process is similar to traditional survey methodology in that it follows the basic steps of survey localization, survey administration, and results compilation. It varies from traditional methodology in the transparency of the process; the content of the survey itself; the level of education prior to, during, and after the survey administration; the fact that results compilation is an important beginning rather than an end; and the systemwide involvement in action planning and implementation. The process:

- Supports managers in becoming more open to giving employees voice,
- Models a new way of working together, and
- Places change in the hands of employees (including managers) rather than in the hands of Human Resources or management alone.

Through individual analysis, group discussion, and action, people become more informed and accountable for their workplace. They learn that there isn't a "them" that will make changes, but that they can make changes together. Figure 1 summarizes the process.

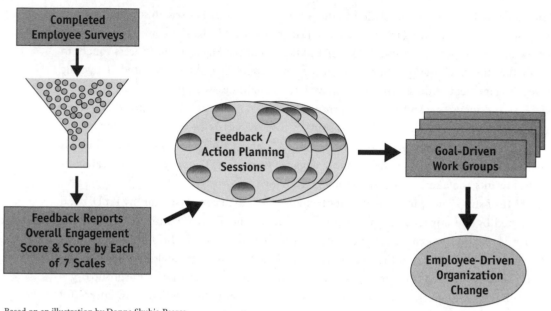

Based on an illustration by Donna Skubis-Pearce

Figure 1. Employee Engagement Process

The process works particularly well in settings like manufacturing, health care, and education, in which the sense of ownership of frontline workers is particularly important and where it's important to capture the knowledge of these employees. This empowerment is reinforced over and over again in the Employee Engagement Process.

Table of Uses

Setting	Project Length	Key Events	Number of Participants
Pharmaceutical Shifting the culture from strictly top-down to more collaborative	12 months (to be repeated after 1 year)	• Completion of survey by each participant • Compilation of survey results/report by Data House and consultant team • Whole team meeting at each of five sites (largest team split into 2 meetings)	• 750 people • Data House and 2 consultants • 6 groups of approximately 50 each

Setting	Project Length	Key Events	Number of Participants
Health-Care System Administered survey to multiple hospital units in a large health-care system. Compared engagement measures of most productive entity to others to establish correlation between engagement and productivity. Most productive unit also most engaged. Worked to increase engagement in all entities as a way to a more productive and healthy work environment.	>6 months	• Administered surveys to most productive entity and a number of other hospital units • Results of all units shared with every hospital • Work teams developed action plans to increase engagement in various hospitals • Target to increase productivity in less-productive units	• 500+
Child Care Survey a number of schools in a for-profit child-care system. Sought to compare level of engagement with productivity. The ultimate goal is to increase staff retention.	>6 months	• Survey staff of most productive school and other schools	• 100+

About the Author

Marie McCormick, Ph.D. (Pmccg@aol.com), has led successful organization development consulting practices for the last ten years. For more than ten years prior to consulting, she held a unique blend of line and staff positions in a Fortune 100 company as it navigated the challenges of operating in an increasingly competitive and deregulated business environment. Her education and experience in the areas of psychology, operations, education, finance, marketing, and management provide her with a broad background and knowledge base to help her clients become more successful.

Where to Go for More Information

REFERENCE

McCormick, Marie T. "The Impact of Large Scale Participative Interventions on Participants." Doctoral Dissertation, Temple University. *Dissertation Abstracts International*, 1999.

INFLUENTIAL SOURCES

Block, Peter, ed. *The Flawless Consulting Fieldbook and Companion: A Guide to Understanding Your Expertise.* San Francisco: Jossey-Bass/Pfeiffer, 2001.

Oshry, Barry. *Seeing Systems: Unlocking the Mysteries of Organizational Life.* San Francisco: Berrett-Koehler, 1995.

Whyte, David. *The Heart Aroused—Poetry and the Preservation of the Soul in Corporate America.* New York: Doubleday, 1994.

ORGANIZATION

InSyte Partners—www.insytepartners.com

Creating profound change through work on the individual and systems levels.

WOLFGANG FAENDERL

Gemeinsinn-Werkstatt
Project Framework for Community Spirit

Enough words have been exchanged; now at last let me see some deeds!
—Johann Wolfgang von Goethe

Tolerance in Frankfurt

In 2002, projects dealing with intercultural cooperation, tolerance, and prevention of violence in the community of Frankfurt/Oder were unproductive. People from the different projects perceived each other as rivals rather than partners. They were exhausted and the public did not support the subject of tolerance. A small group of volunteers from various organizations arranged a preparatory meeting with a Gemeinsinn-Werkstatt consultant (Phase 1) to initiate a participatory process for dealing with the issue (figure 1).

ACTIVATION PHASE (PHASES 2–4)

Parallel, relevant stakeholders (Phase 2), essential cooperation partners (Phase 3), and interested people became involved. This helped to gradually integrate the participants' needs, visions, and abilities to pursue the common goal. A growing team of consultants, evaluators, and facilitators coming from adjoining initiatives and institutions applied various methods (e.g., Appreciative Inquiry, Open Space) to pursue the common goal. The highlight was the "activation forum" (Phase 4), a three-day large group event in the spring with 45 people covering all generations, cultures, and social groupings: "Learning *from*, creating *with*, and engaging *for* each other."

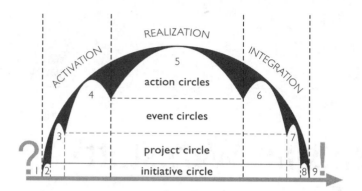

Figure 1. The Gemeinsinn-Werkstatt Phases

REALIZATION PHASE (PHASE 5)

Different self-organized action circles were established, and during the summer, they profited from the networking experience and the methodological know-how, as well as from the organizational support of the project circle. Assistance from regular meetings, large group events, information markets, research activities, mediation offers, interactive web modules, method trainings, and the like, enhanced information exchange and cooperation. Thirteen projects were carried out, such as public relations and supervision groups, a publication (presented by the academy for seniors), an international youth meeting, and even a successful singing ensemble.

INTEGRATION PHASE (PHASES 6–9)

Six months later, during Thanksgiving, another gathering with 40 people took place. The "integration forum" (Phase 6) invited all participants to reflect upon, present, and celebrate their results. This phase announced the well-deserved recreation for both the project circle (Phase 7) and the initiative circle (Phase 8). The self-dependent action circles were able to pursue their individual processes and even develop their own Gemeinsinn-Werkstatt beyond the given project time (Phase 9).

SUSTAINABLE DEVELOPMENT OF NETWORKING

The Gemeinsinn-Werkstatt created a new and sustainable network between various organizations with people still meeting regularly (figure 2). The institutions began to specialize, giving recommendations to each other and improving the quality of the programs. Common petitions and events, mutual information about financial resources, and advice became daily practice. People in Frankfurt/Oder became more aware of tolerance activities, and the process also had a positive effect on the project teams and their private relations.

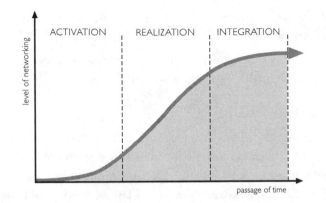

Figure 2. Development of Networking

Frequently Asked Questions

WHAT IS THE SPECIFIC NATURE OF THE METHOD?

The Gemeinsinn-Werkstatt is a "space for voluntary participation." It offers a project framework in which many different people *want* to, *like* to and *can* accomplish different activities related to a common urgent issue. To create a suitable atmosphere, the voluntary participation process uses numerous methods, which are selected and developed with the participants. The framework of the Gemeinsinn-Werkstatt consists of three parts (figure 3):

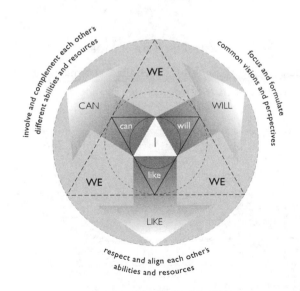

Figure 3. Motivation Model

- *Gemeinsinn Concept:* A practical research project develops the principles of social consciousness, social abilities, and social engagement.

- *Project Procedure:* A transparent process design with flexible elements of consulting, management, and large group methods in a building block system.

- *Support Network:* Process consultants support participation processes and public events, offering training and further developing the methodology.

WHEN AND WHERE IS IT USED?

The participation approach has been employed in various contexts and with a wide range of issues. Educational and social sectors, public initiatives, organizations, associations, and corporations along with economic and scientific fields cooperate according to the principles and methods of the Gemeinsinn-Werkstatt. Projects can last from six months to three years, and involve all interested people—going beyond hierarchies, generations, and interest groups; that is, a real investment in civic engagement.

WHAT ARE THE OUTCOMES FROM USING THE METHOD?

Those who appropriately involve others have much to gain. Gemeinsinn-Werkstatt offers structures to optimize this exchange: It does not have ONE project manager but MANY. Participants can expand their methodological repertoire, may use their knowledge for further enterprises, and apply their individual strengths and resources for the benefit of all. The surplus of this procedure is the triple-win effect, which can be considered "Gemeinsinn" (community spirit): Win for oneself, for other partners, and for the larger community.

$$1^1 + 1^1 + 1^1 < (1 + 1 + 1)^{1+1+1}$$

HOW DOES IT WORK? WHAT IS THE FLOW OR PROCESS?

As shown in the example of Frankfurt/Oder, the Gemeinsinn-Werkstatt proceeds in nine steps. It also offers a project structure to coordinate the allocation of tasks in cooperative pro-

TASK-AREAS	TASK-FIELDS			ROLES
TOPIC	decision	communication	documentation	PARTICIPANTS
ORGANIZATION	funding	supply	design	ORGANIZERS
METHOD	consultation	evaluation	moderation	FACILITATORS
EDUCATION				

Figure 4. Three Areas of Responsibilities

cesses. Figure 4 shows three areas of responsibilities (task areas) with three further task fields each. This offers both transparency and options for participation over time. Volunteers can choose a role according to what they can, like, and want to do.

Table of Uses

Typical Setting	Project Length	Key Events (Phases from Figure 1)	Number of Participants (According to the "Exponential Three")
The Gemeinsinn-Werkstatt is a procedure for all people who want to improve their present situation and to achieve greater objectives together. Areas for community-spirit processes: • facilitation networks • communal and social work • political and voluntary engagement • youth work and school development • educational and science projects and initiatives • innovation at traditional institutions • organizational and corporate development The Gemeinsinn-Werkstatt is a project framework that helps in • dealing with complex issues in a structured, motivated, and self-organized way,	Between 6 months and 3 years, depending on the issue	1. Starting point (1–3 consultative meetings ranging from 30 minutes to 3 hours)	1–8 people (initiators)
		2. Clarifying talks (1–3 meetings ranging from 90 minutes to 9 hours)	3–26 people (initiative circle)
		3. Planning sessions (3–9 meetings ranging from 90 minutes to 3 days)	9–80 people (project circle)
		4. Activation forum (1 large group event lasting 3 days)	27–2,186 people (event circle)
		5. Realization phase (agreed numbers of meetings, workshops, large group events, etc., lasting from 3 weeks to 3 years)	81–open number of people (action circles)
		6. Integration forum (1 large group event lasting from 1 to 3 days)	27–2,186 people (event circle)
		7. Reflecting sessions (1–3 meetings lasting from 90 minutes to 3 days)	3–80 people (project circle)

Typical Setting	Project Length	Key Events (Phases from Figure 1)	Number of Participants (According to the "Exponential Three")
• finding many partners for networking, and • realizing sustainable solutions to issues.		8. Final talks (1 meeting taking between 90 minutes and 3 hours)	3–26 (initiative circle)
		9. Results (1 consultative meeting 6 months later, taking 30 minutes to 3 hours)	1–8 (initiators)

Table of Uses. Continued

About the Author

Wolfgang Faenderl (faenderl@gemeinsinn-werkstatt.de) was born in Munich, and he was awarded a Master of Arts degree in social sciences in 1990. He also has additional qualifications in systemic therapy and various large group processes. Between 2000 and 2004, he was a scientific coordinator of research and development projects for "Gemeinsinn" at the Centre for Applied Policy Research (CAP) at the Ludwig-Maximilian University of Munich in cooperation with the Bertelsmann Foundation. Since 2004, he has been a counselor, facilitator, and research fellow for participation processes in association with the CAP.

Where to Go for More Information

REFERENCE

Faenderl, Wolfgang. *Beteiligung übers Reden hinaus—Gemeinsinn-Werkstatt: Materialien zur Entwicklung von Netzwerke* ("Participation Beyond Mere Talking—Gemeinsinn-Werkstatt: Material for the Development of Networks"). Guetersloh, Germany: Bertelsmann Foundation, 2005.

ORGANIZATION

Gemeinsinn-Werkstatt—www.gemeinsinn-werkstatt.de

For workshops and network activities. The booklets and the building block system of methods are available to all, in German and increasingly in English.

Best thanks for editing support to: Daniel Song and Michael Pannwitz, Jr., Maren Schuepphaus, and Antje Gerike, as well as to the Bertelsmann Foundation.

JASON MAGIDSON

Idealized Design

You've got to be careful if you don't know where you're going because you might not get there.

—Yogi Berra

Idealized Design of the Academy of Vocal Arts

In 1997, the management of the Academy of Vocal Arts (AVA), a small, premier opera training school based in Philadelphia, decided to engage the entire organization in an idealized redesign of the institution. There was no crisis, only a desire to make it the best opera school in the world.

At the time, a few things were holding AVA back. Bold ideas were being discussed, but not widely, so they were not getting the support required for implementation. There was no shared vision of what the stakeholders wanted the organization to become. The school was overreliant on a small number of benefactors. Well-known graduates did not stay connected with the school. The school was not well known outside of the opera world.

Idealized Design kicked off with an all-day session involving 48 stakeholders, including students, faculty, staff, alumni, board members, benefactors, and management. The participants were divided into four teams of mixed stakeholders. The teams were instructed to pretend that AVA had been destroyed the night before and they were to design their ideal from scratch. The idea is to get them to focus on what they *want* rather than getting caught up in what *already exists*. During the first two hours, they generated a list of bulleted statements or "specifications" about the ideal AVA. In the next hour, they began creating a design that would bring about the specifications.

After lunch, the subteams presented their designs to each other and then went back into their subteams to go into more detail and to incorporate aspects of the other teams' designs that they liked. The designs were subsequently synthesized. In the following months, a core team added additional detail and planned implementation.

AVA implemented many aspects of the overall design. Five years later, AVA repeated the Idealized Design process, updating their earlier design with what they had learned from its implementation.

In addition to attracting the very best students, the design was directed at producing well-attended performances, increasing public awareness, and attracting more people to opera by holding more performances in more locations. Students were to receive enough financial support to eliminate distractions from money worries. The design also included measures to engage alumni in the school.

The design included a state-of-the-art facility with individual training rooms, soundproof practice areas, a large area for building scenery, and a performance theater. At the end of the kick-off session, people unanimously agreed that to realize this facility, the academy should buy the building next door—doubling the facility size. AVA subsequently approached the owner, who agreed to sell. One benefactor was so inspired that she contributed $2.5 million for buying and renovating the building.

The design called for attracting more of the best students by: engaging the media to make more potential students aware of the academy; having faculty, staff, and students attend a variety of opera performances scouting for talent (which they began doing); providing financial support; and providing challenging performance opportunities.

To generate media coverage, AVA invited prominent alumni to participate in its performances, which attracted newspaper and radio attention. A local radio station began broadcasting AVA's performances. National Public Radio profiled AVA and a student who had debuted at New York's Metropolitan Opera.

AVA's Idealized Designers realized that media exposure and alumni participation were not sufficient for attracting the best students. New York's Metropolitan Opera, a strong competitor for potential students, was paying students who participated in their apprentice program. Idealized Design helped AVA realize that they would need to offer at least full tuition plus cost-of-living stipends. AVA's increased media exposure enabled it to attract additional funds for fellowships and cost-of-living stipends for almost half of its students. Also, to convince potential students that going to AVA was more attractive than the Met's apprenticeship program, the academy had to offer more prominence in its performances. The new message was that AVA would support student development while moving them more rapidly into starring roles.

Because of their involvement in Idealized Design, the participants "owned" the design and became strong advocates for its implementation. Their enthusiasm was evident to financial supporters, who helped double AVA's endowment.

AVA demonstrates Idealized Design's application in the nonprofit sector. Idealized Design has been applied in many other situations, including the design of enterprises, products, processes, services, facilities, communities, and systems. Such examples can be found in a new book entitled *Idealized Design* (Ackoff, Magidson, and Addison 2006).

Idealized Design: The Basics

Idealized Design is a powerful method for generating "discontinuous improvement"—that is, breakthroughs. Participants pretend that whatever existed was destroyed last night and they are starting from scratch in designing what they ideally want today. One of the key characteristics of Idealized Design is that it begins at the end—the state desired today—and enables people to work backward, thus removing many apparent constraints, mostly self-imposed.

Idealized Design can be used in both crisis situations and where managers want what they are managing well to become even better.

Outcomes of Idealized Design include breakthrough ideas, quick wins, and ideas that improve efficiency. Additional benefits include strong commitment to implementing, improvements in morale and productivity, and empowerment.

Idealized Design starts with initial kickoff sessions (see figure 1) ranging from a half day to two days depending on the complexity of what is being designed (simple product—half day; redesign of organization—two days). Follow-up sessions, held over subsequent weeks or months, involve creating a design that will bring about the desired properties or "specifications." The design is circulated to a wider audience for input on how it can be improved. A completed design is then settled. Implementation planning takes place in parallel.

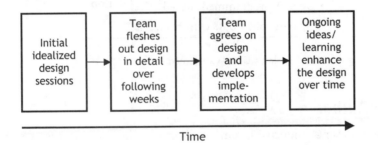

Figure 1. Idealized Design Steps in Initial Kickoff Session

Table of Uses

Setting	Project Length	Key Events/Number of Participants
Nonprofit Organization Opera school wanted to become best in world.	• 1 day • 2 weeks	• 1-day kickoff, 48 people • Working team formed • 6 people on core design working team • Design document developed

Typical Setting(s)	Project Length	Key Events/Number of Participants
	• 6 months–1 day every 2 weeks	• Planning/governance team of 8 • Implementation planned and executed
Department Creates a New IT System for Employee Use New system helps procurement department save millions of dollars annually	• 0.5-day Idealized Design sessions held for the development of the first procurement system (for spend analysis) • 12 weeks • Prototype iteratively developed and reviewed • 90-minute prototype review and feedback sessions • 14 weeks • System programmed, tested • System rolled out, with training	• 40 people (4 sessions with 10 people) • Core design team of 5 people formed to lead prototype development • 45 people involved in design review and enhancement • 40 people • 3 programmers, program manager, and a 2-person review team from the business function

Table of Uses. Continued

About the Author

Jason Magidson (jason@productwish.com) is director of innovation processes at GlaxoSmith-Kline, where he has applied Idealized Design with employees and suppliers. For more than 20 years, Jason has engaged end users—the source of most innovations—in product, service, and system design. Jason has written for publications including *Harvard Business Review* and is coauthor of the book *Idealized Design* (2006). Jason received a PhD from the Union Institute and University.

Where to Go for More Information

REFERENCES

Ackoff, Russell L., Herb Addison, and Jason Magidson. *Idealized Design: Creating an Organization's Future.* Upper Saddle River, NJ: Wharton School Publishing, 2006.

Magidson, Jason. "Shifting Your Customers into 'Wish Mode': Tools for Generating New Product Ideas and Breakthroughs." In *The PDMA Toolbook 2 for New Product Development*, edited by Paul Belliveau, Abbie Griffin, and Stephen M. Somermeyer. Hoboken, NJ: John Wiley & Sons, 2004.

Magidson, Jason, and Gregg Brandyberry. "Putting Customers in the 'Wish Mode.'" *Harvard Business Review* (September 2001).

ORGANIZATIONS

Ackoff Center Weblog—www.ackoffcenter.blogs.com

ProductWish.com—www.productwish.com

56

The Practice of Empowerment
Changing Behavior and Developing Talent in Organizations

The core of the matter is always about changing the behavior of people. In highly successful change efforts the central challenge is not strategy, not systems . . . but changing people's behavior.

—John Kotter and Dan Cohen

Building Partnerships—Overcoming Barriers

Bob Franco, vice president of the Global Talent Division at American Express, tells his story about a successful application of the Practice of Empowerment:

> A key challenge in institutions is how to move individuals to higher levels of performance, specifically when it involves building partnerships within complex organizational systems. Our team had been working under circumstances that in many ways prevented their ability to achieve our mission—there were barriers such as lack of access to critical information or key partners, and limited experience—creating results in a politicized environment.
>
> The highly effective empowerment tools helped produce significant, measurable and sustainable behavior change within our team. This process helped us separate the circumstance around us charged with a disempowering "pathology," and helped us focus our own personal accountability toward what we can accomplish and what we are ultimately capable of attaining. After a deep assessment of our organizational

culture and challenges, this process enabled us to build our consulting skills, leverage our collective talent and create business results.

The results were a clearly defined value proposition and an ability to be successful despite any organizational barriers. This process moved us away from the crippling power of "problems" to a new power—one inside us, one focused on what we want to create. Through this work, this team now has daily practices focusing on their vision. We are empowered!

Frequently Asked Questions

WHAT IS THE PRACTICE OF EMPOWERMENT?

The Practice of Empowerment is the process of enabling individuals to adopt new behaviors that further their individual aspirations and that of the organization (see figure 1). It is based on 25 years of research and practice and has been applied by hundreds of change practitioners in organizations throughout the world.

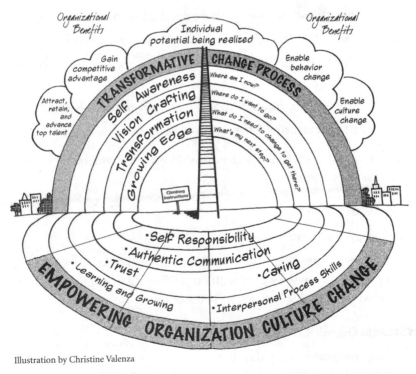

Illustration by Christine Valenza

Figure 1. The Practice of Empowerment: Changing Behavior and Developing Talent in Organizations

EMPOWERING THE SPACE

In order for Bob's group to adopt new behaviors and develop their talent, a learning and growth culture first had to be established. Many change interventions assume that an organization's learning and growth capacity is inherent. They neglect to see if the cultural ingredients are present, and because they rarely are, the organization's ability to achieve the desired behavior change is limited.

Using the analogy of nature, for new seeds to take root, they need fertile soil. Fertile soil in an organization is a learning and growth culture. To create this type of culture requires that a set of practices be established, which I call "empowering the space." An empowered space enables individuals to feel safe and trusting enough to risk true growth. The six practices described below are experienced during the training, and then the group is assisted in establishing them in their work culture.

- *Self-Responsibility:* Individuals take responsibility to make their job, team, and organization the way they want them to be.

- *Authentic Communication:* Individual communication is open, honest, and transparent.

- *Trust:* Individuals feel safe enough to try out new behaviors and take risks.

- *Learning and Growing:* Individuals are encouraged to work on the real behaviors they need to change.

- *Interpersonal Process Skills:* Protocols and skills are learned to resolve interpersonal issues.

- *Caring:* Leadership demonstrates tangible concern for individuals.

With the groundwork for behavior change in place, the empowerment model provides the overall transformation strategy.

EMPOWERMENT MODEL

Shift from Pathology to a Vision

Where we place our attention is what we create. Shifting our focus from what doesn't work to what can work motivates us to take action. It's the difference in planting a garden from focusing on removing weeds to envisioning flowers in full bloom.

Shift from Static to Organic Growth (Growing Edge)

Many of us view growth as a static process. There is a place to get to and I'm either there or not. Until I get there I'm frustrated or discontent, and when I get there my growth is over. The natural world provides an alternative model for growing. If a tree is alive, it is always growing. The place where this growth is coming into existence is its growing edge; it is the place of greatest aliveness. Similarly, we feel our greatest aliveness at our growing edges.

Integration of Self-Awareness and Behavior Change

Many growth processes assume that if we are aware of something, we will do it. The focus is on increasing self-awareness. While awareness increases our self-knowledge, it rarely leads to a change in behavior. On the other hand, we can set a goal for something we want, harness our wills to achieve it, and then discover that it wasn't really what we wanted. We did not have enough self-awareness.

EMPOWERMENT METHODOLOGY

The four-part empowerment methodology activates this transformational strategy and provides the operating system for behavior change.

- *Self-Awareness*—Increases knowledge to determine what is desired. (Where am I now?)

- *Vision Crafting*—Translates knowledge into a compelling vision. (Where do I want to go?)

- *Transformation*—Identifies and transforms limiting beliefs with vision adjusted as needed. (What do I need to change to get there?)

- *Growing Edge*—Uses directed thought to mentally seed next growth step. (What's my next step?)

The process culminates in an individual intention statement and image that represents the next place of growth around the desired behavior or outcome.

Let's go back and follow Bob through this process. As a result of a series of guided exercises around each of these four steps, he and his team were able to adopt the behavior of self-responsibility, and move from being victims within a dysfunctional organization to being at cause for how they wished it to be and choosing a different possibility.

First, Bob went through a *self-awareness* exercise. He discovered he was going through the motions and had lost a lot of passion for his consulting and leadership. As he went through the *visioning exercise,* he saw it was possible that he and his team could develop a more robust skill-set that could more effectively serve their clients. He realized that rather than being trapped, he could rise above the dysfunctional system if he could increase the capability of his team.

However, when Bob came down from the mountaintop, he saw that this achievement would not be easy. Were he and his team up to it? Would his clients participate? He then went through a *transformation* exercise in which he identified and turned around these limiting beliefs.

His *growing edge* was believing in his team and being willing to engage in this transformation process. In the past, Bob had needed to lift everyone by the force of his vision and will. As each team member revealed his or her growing edges, it became clear that they were developing the capacity to do this on their own.

Bob translated his growing edge into this intention statement: "I help my team build our consulting skills and leverage our collective talent to create business results. I lead and am led by an empowering team who knows what it wants and gets it!"

A support system of coaching calls and master classes were established to help sustain the behavior changes.

Organizational Change Intervention

- *Step 1:* Interview leadership to determine behavior changes and talent development strategy.
- *Step 2:* Assess culture on six practices to determine its capacity to change behavior.
- *Step 3:* Establish metrics and design empowerment intervention.
- *Step 4:* Pilot program.
- *Step 5:* Iterate, stabilize, and scale.

Table of Uses

Brief Description	Project Length	Number of Participants, Time Required
Behavior change and talent development in Global Talent division of American Express	1 year	15 senior internal consultants, 3-day workshop with follow-up coaching and support system
Dozens of public-sector agencies and nonprofits use a variation of this model for citizen behavior change around environment, health, safety, and community development issues	2–5 years	Thousands of individuals and hundreds of neighborhood groups participate in 4–8 meetings around various topics facilitated by trained volunteer leader

About the Author

David Gershon (dgershon@empowermentinstitue.net), founder and CEO of Empowerment Institute, is a world-renowned expert on empowerment and behavior change. He is the author of nine books, including the best-selling *Empowerment*, which has become a classic on the subject. He is currently writing *The Practice of Empowerment: Changing Behavior in Organizations and Society*. He codirects the Empowerment Institute Certification Program, which specializes in transformative change coaching, training, and design. He has lectured on his behavior change and empowerment methodology at Harvard, MIT, and Duke, and served as an advisor to the Clinton White House.

Where to Go for More Information

REFERENCES

Empowerment Institute Certification Program. www.empowermentinstitute.net/files/Cert_Program.html.

Training program to change behavior at personal, organizational, and societal levels,

Gershon, David, and Gail Straub. *Empowerment: The Art of Creating Your Life As You Want It.* New York: Delta, 1989.

A classic on personal empowerment. Provides underlying approach used in the organizational behavior change work.

INFLUENTIAL SOURCES

Allen, James. *As a Man Thinketh.* Philadelphia: Running Press, 1989.

Maslow, Abraham. *Toward a Psychology of Being.* 2d ed. New York: Van Nostrand Reinhold, 1982.

ORGANIZATION

Empowerment Institute—www.empowermentinstitute.net

57

SUSAN DUPRE, RAY GORDEZKY, HELEN SPECTOR, AND CHRISTINE VALENZA

Values Into Action

Two sides to every question, yes, yes, yes . . .
But every now and then, just weighing in
Is what it must come down to . . .

—Seamus Heaney

The Parliament of the World's Religions

Is it possible to bring together the world's preeminent religious leaders, as well as other global leaders and citizens, to commit to take action with their own communities to address critical global issues? This question moved the Council for a Parliament of the World's Religions to sponsor the development of Values Into Action (VIA) for the International Leader's Assembly at Montserrat, Spain, July 4–7, 2004.

This event unfolded over three days, with 400 invited participants—from diverse cultures, geography, ages, stations in life, and socioeconomic levels. During the Assembly participants considered the following four issues: (1) eliminating external debt burden on poor countries; (2) supporting refugees worldwide; (3) creating access to safe, clean water; and (4) overcoming religiously motivated violence. Participants worked in small groups and in plenary to seriously explore these issues and build relationships with one another and between faith traditions. The meeting culminated in individuals making commitments to simple acts for positive change in the lives of people impacted by these issues.

Three hundred individual commitments were collected from participants in this conference. Another 200 individual commitments were made during four initial pilot conferences held in Israel and Kenya, and the open-participation assemblies held as part of the program of the Parliament of the World's Religions in Barcelona, July 7–13, 2004.

The results continue to unfold: Participants in an executive leadership program built schools in Kenya and dug wells in Kenya and India; church communities visit an international airport's welcoming facilities to help upgrade the services available to refugees as they enter the country, and Muslim and Jewish students meet at Hebrew University in Jerusalem to heal religious and cultural divides.

The Basics

VIA is a question-based meeting process where a diverse group of people explore together their connections to a local or global issue, and make personal commitments to act on behalf of those impacted by the issue. The questions turn people first to one another and their own experiences with the focus issue, then to the issue's complexity and dynamics. This exploration creates a deeply personal understanding, and momentum for individual action and community change (figure 1).

Working in small groups, individuals explore the focus issue through a few questions:

- Why do they care about the focus issue?

- How do their most deeply held values and convictions motivate them to take positive action?

- What examples of positive efforts are already being taken to bring about change for people affected by the issue?

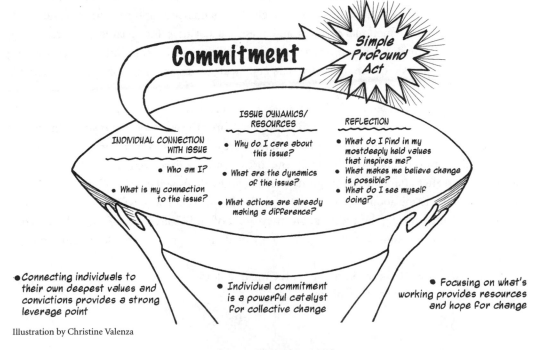

Illustration by Christine Valenza

Figure 1. Values Into Action

- What commitments to action will individuals make to engage members of their own community to make a difference on behalf of those impacted by the issue?

VIA engages the motivations and commitments of the *individual* within the context of a large group meeting. The large group acts as a resource and sounding board for individuals to better understand the issue, their relationship to the issue, and their desire to make a difference.

Three principles form the foundation for this meeting process:

- Individual commitment is a powerful catalyst for collective change.

- Connecting individuals to their own deepest values and convictions establishes strong leverage for change.

- Focusing on strengths and on projects that are already creating positive change generates ideas for new initiatives and hope for continued change.

We have found the use of experts in the issue and graphic artists recording the proceedings to be particularly valuable in the cross-cultural, multistakeholder settings in which we've worked. We use the term "experts" in a broad way. Toward the start of the meeting, we ask several individuals affected by the issue to share their stories with the entire gathering. These presentations put a "human face" on the issue. In order to gain a more nuanced understanding of the issue's complexities and dynamics as the meeting proceeds, academics/practitioners give brief presentations, followed by small group conversations to further explore the issue. These presentations help participants establish a rich assessment of the issue based on its history and evolution over time.

Graphic recorders work with pastels on eight-foot banners to capture in images and words the ideas, associations, emotional rhythms, and questions that arise during large group reporting. In addition, individuals work with the recorder to capture their ideas in images. The resulting multicolored graphics cross linguistic barriers and create a rich reminder of both the ineffable and the expressible.

We developed this approach focusing on individual action, rather than on gaining common ground for collective action, for several reasons. First, those attending this meeting would not likely meet again. In addition, many would not have easy access to travel or communication, making joint projects unlikely. Finally, in our organizational development practices, we have observed how, after attending a large group meeting, individuals will engage others in their local community or organizational department in collective action. The seeds for such individual action are planted during the meeting, but they don't often become part of the collective discourse during the meeting. Sometimes, these individual projects become the foundation for systemic change.

Subsequent applications have shown the methodology to be quite flexible in terms of the time required and number of people involved.

Table of Uses

Brief Description	Project Length	Key Events	Number of Participants
International World Religious Leaders Assembly Designed VIA for diverse groups of world leaders from all religions and other institutions around the world, resulting in 500 commitments to action that led to significant change on four critical global issues.	12 months	• 4 planning meetings • 4 design meetings • Tested the methodology with 4 large group events, one focused on each issue, in various parts of the world where the issues have local significance. • One 3-day large group meeting with world leaders at Montserrat • 4 large group meetings, one focused on each of the four issues, at the Parliament of World Religions	• 15 people • 50 people • 100 each issue meeting • 450 people • Varied (50–100 each issue)
Community Peace Building Conference Adapted VIA to support a 1-day conference resulting in 250 commitments to act.	4 months	• 3 design meetings to integrate VIA into whole program design • One 1-day large group community meeting • Various meetings before and after to build capacity of community leaders to use the process locally	• 10 people • 400 participants • 45 people each meeting

About the Authors

Helen Spector (helen6451@aol.com), *Ray Gordezky* (ray-g@rogers.com), and *Susan Dupre* (sus dupre@aol.com) consult to industry, public agencies, nonprofits, education, and communities. They adhere to a solid but fluid set of "large group system change" principles and use these to create innovative methodologies and designs that make it possible for diverse groups (15–1000+) to work together to determine what they want to do collectively and individually and how they're going to do it.

Christine Valenza (www.christinevalenza.com) is a seasoned graphic facilitator experienced in bringing visual and graphic support to large-scale change processes. The authors frequently collaborate on projects, as they did for the Parliament, and also work with other talented consultants from around the world in an expanding network of whole system change consultants.

Where to Go for More Information

Reference

Dupre, Susan, Ray Gordezky, and Helen Spector. "World Religions Engage Critical Issues." In *The Handbook of Large Group Methods: Creating Systemic Change in Organizations and Communities*, edited by B. Alban and B. Bunker. San Francisco: Jossey-Bass, 2006.

Influential Sources

Cooperrider, D., and D. Whitney. *Appreciative Inquiry: Collaborating for Change* (booklet). San Francisco: Berrett-Koehler, 1999.

Schell, J. *The Unconquerable World: Power, Nonviolence, and the Will of the People.* New York: Henry Holt, 2003.

Weisbord, Marvin, and Sandra Janoff. *Future Search: An Action Guide to Finding Common Ground in Organizations and Community,* San Francisco: Berrett-Koehler, 1995.

Organizations

Council for a Parliament of the World's Religions—www.cpwr.org

Values Into Action—www.valuesintoaction.net

58

RON ASHKENAS AND PATRICE MURPHY

WorkOut

I have never failed to see a marked change come over the entire organization . . . as soon as the members felt they were accorded recognition as rational beings and to be consulted on matters of common interest. . . . The operative, if encouraged to think, will soon effect great savings in the work at which he is more of an expert that anyone else.

—H. Fitz John Porter

WorkOut at Work

When the state of Connecticut's Department of Transportation (DOT) needed to make urgent improvements to customer service while at the same time reducing head count, the commissioner was unsure how to proceed. After all, the kinds of changes that were needed would require strong collaboration between traditional civil service managers and a unionized workforce—a relationship that had been uneasy for many years. After considering a number of approaches, he decided to try General Electric's (GE's) WorkOut process, especially since he could access some of GE's own in-state consulting resources to help. Shortly thereafter, 40 people—from maintenance workers to managers, from different levels and functions of the DOT—came together for two days and were asked to brainstorm ways to streamline work, increase productivity, and improve customer satisfaction. At first they were reluctant and suspicious, but after some initial hesitation, these highly unnatural teams began sharing their mutual frustrations and, with the help of facilitators, identified dozens of ways to take out unnecessary work and dramatically improve the way the DOT provided service. At the end of the WorkOut, the teams consolidated their thinking into specific recommendations that they presented to the commissioner and other senior managers at a "town meeting." Much to everyone's surprise, instead of getting polite "thank-yous" for the many ideas, they were engaged in a thoughtful discussion of every recommendation, followed by an immediate "yes or no" decision from the commissioner. Moreover, virtually every recommendation was approved—to loud applause. The recommendations included:

- A faster, simpler process for granting permits and rights;
- A radical approach to night maintenance to speed repairs and minimize traffic delays; and
- Fewer sign-offs for major documents and letters.

Having received the go-ahead for action, each team that had presented an idea was then empowered to get it implemented over the next few months. Their success, individually and collectively, was the beginning of a turnaround in both the DOT's productivity and its labor-management relations.

The Basics

WorkOut is a change process originated at GE in the late 1980s to bring together large groups of people to eliminate bureaucracy, improve critical processes, and strengthen customer relationships. It is a method for engaging employees across levels and functions in a rapid effort to get results, while also transforming the organization's culture. WorkOut is summarized in figures 1 and 2.

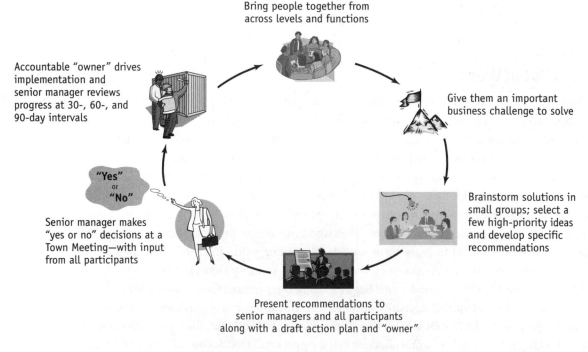

Figure 1. WorkOut Steps Summarized

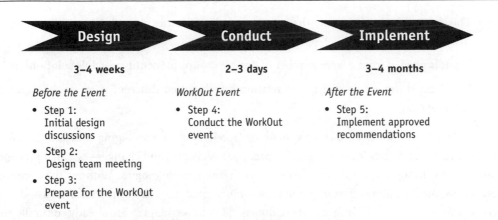

Figure 2. WorkOut Timeline and Phases

Key distinguishing characteristics of WorkOut include:

- A drive for simultaneous operational and cultural change;

- Focus on clear, visible, and measurable results;

- Facilitation of honest and open communication between diverse groups both inside and outside the organization;

- Emphasis on quick action and the achievement of goals in a few weeks or months;

- Accelerated senior management decision making, requiring "yes/no" decisions that are immediate and public;

- Engagement of people across organizational boundaries; and

- Empowerment of frontline people to implement approved recommendations.

WorkOut at its best can create fundamentally new relationships between managers and employees, between functions or departments, and between customers and suppliers. In most organizations, these relationships often range from uncomfortable to confrontational, fraught with tensions, misunderstandings, and missed opportunities. WorkOut creates a structured forum where people from these different groups can sort through these dynamics and align themselves around common goals and mutually developed actions. In almost every WorkOut session, there is a magic moment when people see each other in a new light and make connections that strengthen the organizational fabric. For example, when employees see previously distant or detached senior managers struggle and squirm with real-time, public decision making, taking input and really listening, the effect can be electric—whether an idea is approved or not. Given these characteristics, WorkOut is an effective change strategy when:

- There is urgency for immediate decision making and rapid implementation;

- The improvement opportunity cuts across different functional groups, business units, branches, or regions;

- The change challenge is somewhat complex, and root causes and solutions are not immediately obvious;

- Input is needed from a large number of diverse groups to identify possible solutions; or

- Paradigm shifts are needed in the relationships between different parts of the organizational system.

WorkOut is also effective as a precursor or "accelerator" of a Six Sigma effort. At GE, WorkOut helped to create a culture that valued speed, fast decisions, and change—essential preconditions for the more analytical and rigorous Six Sigma methodologies. Without these cultural conditions, the Six Sigma effort might have become bogged down in unnecessary data and paralyzing perfection. Instead, Six Sigma at GE flourished because people were already culturally conditioned to work in teams, examine processes, challenge traditional ways of doing things, and move into action. In other organizations that have started with Six Sigma, WorkOut has sometimes been introduced afterward as a way of speeding up Six Sigma projects and pushing them beyond analysis and into decisive action.

At the same time, WorkOut is not a panacea, and may not be appropriate for your organization when the main objective is to get buy-in to decisions that have already been made. Also, it may be inappropriate when management is unwilling to make immediate decisions and launch immediate action, or when the goal is a reduction of staff.

WorkOut has generated substantial results in a wide array of organizations:

- WorkOut at GE produced millions of dollars in savings and revenue enhancements across all of their businesses, while making the company faster, simpler, and less hierarchical.

- Zurich Financial Services used WorkOut to turn around its insurance operations in the United Kingdom over a four-year period—generating $75 million in verified bottom-line savings and tens of millions more in qualitative benefits such as improved customer service and productivity.

- Dozens of WorkOuts at Armstrong Industries over two years helped produce $30 million in savings.

- New Hampshire Power and Light used one WorkOut to improve line crew utilization rates—producing an estimated $1.5 million in annualized savings.

- WorkOuts in the African country of Eritrea engaged community constituents to help stabilize the rate of HIV/AIDS infection. (For more on this case, see chapter 46, "Rapid Results.")

Table of Uses

Setting	Brief Description	Number of Participants	Project Length	Key Events
Hong Kong Publishing Company	Cross-functional team challenged to reduce costs and increase subscription rates in Asia Region	35	5 months	One 2.5 day WorkOut
Israeli Software Firm	High potentials given key business challenges—such as consolidating a data center without affecting services; reducing corporate costs	30	4 months	One 3.5 day WorkOut
European Electronic Products Distributor	Regional sales teams charged with increasing revenue in a slow-growth environment	40 in each of three regions	1 year	Three regional 2.5 day WorkOuts
Mexican Manufacturing Conglomerate	Integration of corporate acquisitions—and then ongoing cost reduction	20–50 in each session (multiple sessions)	2 years	Multiple 2.5 day WorkOuts
Telecommunications Company in United States	Company-wide business process transformation. Issues ranged from reducing network outages to speeding repair time for handsets	30–60 in each session (multiple sessions)	1.5 years	Multiple 1- to 3-day WorkOuts (held for every major business process)

About the Authors

Ron Ashkenas is a managing partner and *Patrice Murphy* is a senior consultant with Robert H. Schaffer & Associates, a global management consulting firm based in Stamford, Connecticut. Ashkenas was part of the team that developed and implemented WorkOut at GE, and is coauthor (with Dave Ulrich and Steve Kerr) of *The GE Work-Out,* with Murphy as a contributing author. Ashkenas and Murphy can be reached at info@rhsa.com.

Where to Go for More Information

REFERENCES

Ashkenas, Ron, and Matthew McCreight. "Work-Out and Six Sigma." In *Rath & Strong's Six Sigma Leadership Handbook,* edited by Thomas Bertels. Hoboken, NJ: Wiley, 2003.

Ulrich, Dave, Steve Kerr, and Ron Ashkenas. *The GE Work-Out: How to Implement GE's Revolutionary Method for Busting Bureaucracy and Attacking Organizational Problems—Fast!* New York: McGraw-Hill, 2002.

Welch, Jack, and John Byrne. *Jack: Straight from the Gut.* New York: Warner Business Books, 2001.

ORGANIZATION

Robert H. Schaffer & Associates—www.rhsa.com

SUPPORTIVE METHODS

Supportive refers to practices that enhance the efficacy of other change methods, making them more robust and suitable to the circumstances and participants. They are like spices in a meal, enriching methods to satisfy the unique tastes of the client. They weave into and often become permanent elements of other methods.

59

NANCY WHITE AND GABRIEL SHIRLEY

Online Environments That Support Change

A computer terminal is not some clunky old television with a typewriter in front of it. It is an interface where the mind and body can connect with the universe and move bits of it about.

—Douglas Adams

Washington State Public Health Nursing Directors

The Washington State Public Health Nursing Directors (PHND) are the state's front line of public health communication, responsible for disseminating information and assisting in implementing public health policy for issues ranging from a West Nile Virus outbreak to possible chemical or biological attacks. They receive regulatory information from the federal and state levels and help regional health districts and hospitals develop policies, procedures, and readiness plans for public health emergencies. To be in a state of heightened preparedness is to live constantly on the leading edge of change. It's a busy job.

The nursing directors meet face-to-face and via teleconference periodically to exchange information, ask questions, and discuss best practices. In the 1990s, they used an e-mail Listserv to help bridge the communication gaps between face-to-face meetings, to ask questions, and share useful practices from their day-to-day work. It was both a success and a failure.

Practices were shared by some and read by others, but there was no common space where the group's wisdom was collected for future reference. They could communicate as a group instantly across hundreds of miles, engaging in their own time to accommodate busy schedules. Still, multiple simultaneous conversations created confusion, like ten people having ten different conversations all at once!

When the challenges of the e-mail list outweighed the benefits, the group looked for alternatives. They chose a Web-based discussion service providing multiple organized conversations, with different subgroups participating in each conversation. All conversations were accessible to anyone. "Flash conversations" (quick, easily started conversations) were created for a quick response to urgent issues.

When health districts share information, nurses, doctors, lawyers, and administrators save time. In autumn 2004, during a flu vaccine shortage in the United States, larger health districts used immunization clinics to vaccinate patients while using the situation as an emergency preparedness drill for a small pox epidemic. Smaller health districts did not have the resources to conduct the drill, but learned from their colleagues' experience through the Online Environment.

Because PHND's Web environment is private, their conversations sometimes include "venting sessions" about, for example, new policies from above. The online setting is a pressure release valve, providing a place to commiserate, as well as time for reflection and for carefully developing responses. As a result, face-to-face meetings are more productive and less emotionally charged.

The Basics

What Is an Online Environment?

It is a technologically mediated "place" using the Internet to be together, to work, to share information, and to have conversations. It can be one tool, like e-mail, or many tools including discussion spaces, instant messaging, file sharing, and collaborative white boards. Anyone with Internet access can use Online Environments.

Online Environments are increasingly multimodal. Originally text based, today's environments integrate audio, visuals (including video), and text, creating a rich communication medium. While some social gestures, such as body language, are lacking in some online environments, new gestures are emerging. Online presence indicators combine with other benefits, such as reflective space and centralized group memory, to create a rich environment. As technologies evolve, we naturally integrate online and off-line experiences into one coherent experience, utilizing the richness of all media.

At their best, Online Environments provide a platform to identify, connect, and engage diverse groups of people and information, creating the possibility of a new kind of collective action. They bridge time and distance, providing opportunities to discover useful questions, answers, and perspectives. Conversations emerge and stories are told. They offer transparency of both process and content, creating a record for reflection, study, and action. They provide a medium for accelerating and sustaining change.

Three Perspectives for Considering Online Environments for Change

Why include online elements in change? How might they be of value? These "snapshots" reflect a continuum of potential uses. They can be mixed and remixed, and often overlap. Con-

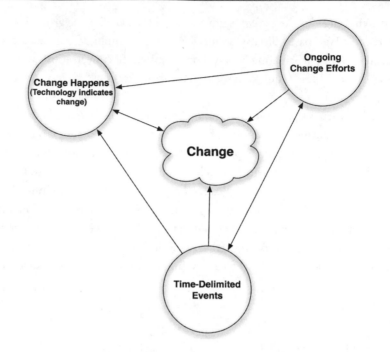

Figure 1. Three Perspectives for Online Environments for Change

sider them an introduction to the many possibilities in a rapidly emerging domain. As you read them, think about the human interactions first and the technology second. Figure 1 illustrates the three perspectives.

Supporting Time-Delimited Events

Online Environments can support change efforts that include significant events, such as an Open Space gathering or Appreciative Inquiry Summit, or they can be used for closing events and evaluation/reflection activities. Groups can be colocated or distributed.

Online Environments support events in several ways:

- *Planning and Preparation:* Dispersed Organizing Teams plan the event, recording key plans, interviews, research, action items, and assumptions in a centralized location open to all. As team members are added, they can review history or search it when questions arise. Transparency comes naturally, with all interactions captured in an "online record."

- *Registration and Logistics:* Online registration can centrally gather logistical needs.

- *Relationship Formation:* Registration can end by inviting participants to a pre-event Web-based conversation to introduce oneself and learn about other participants. Members can share contact information, experiences, needs, and the like for use during the change process.

- *Information Dissemination:* Background materials provide an opportunity for participants to arrive with shared knowledge.

- *Distributed Participation:* Sometimes some people can't join face-to-face events due to distance, cost, or schedule. Online Environments enable a variety of distributed participation strategies. Some "tune in live," others extend the event over time for increased interaction and absorption.[1]

- *Event Artifacts:* Activities recorded in a variety of ways—audio, video, photographs, graphic recording, transcriptions, commitments, stories, notes, presentations, and so forth can be shared online for all participants to continue their work after the event ends.

- *Extend Change Beyond the Original Event:* Online Environments can be a place to share results, network with other change efforts, and create action plans, task forces, and work groups.

---

e/merge 2004

Started as a face-to-face conversation in December 2002, e/merge 2004 (http://emerge2004 .net) promoted online communities and online collaboration in South Africa, particularly for curriculum development and innovation in education. "We may as well run an online conference about online collaboration, we thought! The idea was born, with some enthusiastic organizational partners," recounts Tony Carr, one of the key organizers. Here are some of the highlights Tony captured about the e/merge conference:

> Online conferences are a new feature on the southern African landscape, so we couldn't make any assumptions about participants, the technology, or bandwidth. We needed participation to be as easy as possible to show the value of online environments.
>
> The e-learning and blended learning community in southern Africa is relatively small, so we encouraged networking and communication among researchers, practitioners, and technologists. We tried to balance presenter participation (in an unfamiliar medium) with traditional standards of academic rigor, creating peer-reviewed publication opportunities.
>
> Lastly, we hoped to ease staging future online conferences by distributing the software platform under an open source license.
>
> A key to participation was attention to the "Warmware"—40 presenters and 15 support roles (some with multiple people playing a role).
>
> We analyzed participation in several ways, showing activity ratios of 80–20 or 70–30, i.e., 30% of participants generated 70% of the activity. A core group drove discussion and created a vibrant space, with a larger group of readers.

The event's energy catalyzed ongoing interactions in the newly formed network.

The analysis exemplifies some of the hidden potential of online events. We can measure active participation by number of "posts." We can understand passive (reading) participation by page views. We have not yet measured the impacts of active or passive participation. We hear stories of the value of participating via reading, often derogatorily called "lurking." In fact, this "legitimate peripheral participation" is very powerful.

Lessons learned:

- Start with purpose and intended participants before planning the technology

- Consider how you will measure and evaluate your event for future work

- Seek to understand the invisible: the impact of participants who read but don't reply[2]

Supporting Ongoing Change Efforts

Change rarely happens in an instant, or in a single event. Online Environments can sustain the process from a variety of perspectives, some similar to the "event" perspective.

- *Information Sharing:* Collecting data, sharing documents, and posting schedules is quick and inexpensive with online tools.

- *Ongoing Communication:* "Talking" over time via online discussion tools, instant messengers, chat, and voice over IP (VOIP), allows conversations to continue among the entire group, or subsets working on aspects of the change initiative.

- *Subgroups When Not Everyone Is Online:* Sometimes only a portion of the people involved are, or need to be, online. A planning or leadership group may find Online Environments useful for coordination and process transparency.

- *When the Change Connects to a Larger Network:* Nothing exists in a vacuum. Often, organizations working on change interact with others in a larger system. Online Environments "show a face to the world" in an efficient manner, benefiting from the larger network's knowledge. Doing some or all of a change effort "in public" online enhances access to those networks.

Spirited Work

From 1998 to 2005, a community of practice comprised of diverse professionals met for three days, four times a year. The group's purpose: to explore integrating work and spirit through practicing Open Space principles in daily life. The group, *Spirited Work*, became a laboratory for practicing the skills for living gracefully amidst constant change—as individuals, as a community, and within the myriad organizations we represented.

It quickly became clear that connection between face-to-face gatherings would benefit the community. An Online Environment was created. A planning group managed logistics online as a virtual team, individual members announced activities and projects, and there was even a play space to write collective poems and share stories. Over time, work groups formed around specific projects, using the Online Environment to inform others of their needs and progress. Individual members carried learning into their organizations, extending their practice from four times a year to daily life.

The stories of Spirited Work's impact poured in over the years, and were shared via the Online Environment: How Open Space principles were used to negotiate a contract with the Pentagon. How partnerships were gracefully created and dissolved through careful attention to passion and responsibility. How initiatives created new organizational structures, journalism that matters, and opportunities for U.S. citizens to work with Nigerians and Burundians to improve their local communities.

By 2005, the community had inspired so many members to live their lives more purposefully, to change their organizations, create new initiatives, to follow passion with responsibility, that there came a time when the gatherings were no longer needed. The community followed the Open Space principle—"When it's over, it's over"—had a big celebration, then archived the Online Environment.

Lessons learned:

- Storytelling can be very powerful online

- Create space for experimentation and discovery

- Archive old material and conversations so the group's history is available but not in the way

Change Happens: Technology as Influence on Existing Efforts and Practices

Change starts from a tiny spark, even a technological spark.

Using new technology sometimes (perhaps often) represents a social system's implicit desire for change. Consciously, it may be "improving customer support" or "producing better widgets" or "creating better channels of communication between functional areas." Someone gets a bright idea about helping the situation by using technology. "Wouldn't it be great if the manufacturing team could see the design team's work earlier in the process? Hey, we could set up a Web site and store designs in progress, inviting manufacturing folks to look and comment."

In these situations, technology can change behavior and communication patterns, increase trust, agility, and productivity, without a formal "change effort." It encourages existing conflicts to emerge when creative tension may benefit a process: "What are you guys doing?!! Don't you know that doing it that way means reworking these other pieces? But if you do it this way . . ."

Technology shifts can provide fertile ground for pilot change projects, return on investment (ROI) studies, and early success stories. A few questions in a discovery session can uncover the story of change in progress: "What groups have implemented new technologies in the past two years? What motivated them? How has technology changed their behavior?"

New technology does not automatically imply that "change is happening." There are many examples of technologies enforcing "the way things need to be." Consider what motivated the change and its impact.

Seeds of Change in the Caucasus

A small international nongovernmental organization (NGO) received a grant to develop "online communities for NGOs and small/medium enterprises (SMEs)" to increase connections and stimulate growth and innovation in the former Soviet Republics of Azerbaijan, Armenia, and Georgia. For cost and political reasons, face-to-face was not an ongoing possibility. Two of the countries were in a territory dispute.

The agency had little online community experience. Paul Lawrence, working in isolation in Azerbaijan, went on the Web to seek advice and information, and found an international network working in online interaction. They quickly offered knowledge and support. From the start, Internet connections were key to leveraging resources nonexistent in the geographic area.

Paul brought in his Georgian and Armenian counterparts. They recruited local and regional knowledge to inform ongoing work, creating a trusted network "knitted together" with online tools. The initial small SME project came and went, but the network continued.

This informal "community of practice" began influencing the organization and shaping other projects. Ideas were tossed around online. Perceptions around communication, collaboration, and international development were challenged and shifted. Sometimes it created friction, disturbing the status quo. Distributed and isolated field staff grew stronger, supporting each other online in their learnings, no longer dependent on headquarters. Through Internet supported communications, they increased their capacity daily.

From the international online group, a seed grew into a multicountry community for field staff. This strength enabled the small NGO to win funds for successful online interaction projects around community volunteerism, preventing domestic violence and school connectivity in the southern Caucasus—programs they could not have done without changing their own practice. Small seeds . . . large trees.

Lessons learned:
- We learn by doing

- Online tools can disrupt the status quo and stimulate change

- Online tools can span boundaries that are challenging to cross face-to-face due to time, distance, cost, or even politics

When to Use It

Large-scale change methodologies construct a container for collective activity that can be supported, accelerated, and sustained using Online Environments . . . if the conditions are right. If the conditions aren't good, the Online Environment may distract from the purpose. If you know more about change methods than technology, talk with others who can help bridge the gap.

Here are some starting points. Is it possible to do this change process entirely face-to-face? If so, how compelling is the motivation for adding an online component? How does it add value? Consider these questions, and if there are no compelling reasons, don't go online!

Logistical Reasons

- Are participants separated by time or distance?

- Is there a need to create and nurture networks and communities over time and distance?

- Is there an event that would benefit from online support—before, during, or after?

- Are the cost or other factors of gathering face-to-face a barrier?

- Is the process going to last a long time where records, ongoing conversation, and information sharing will be useful?

- Will an Online Environment increase participation and access? Will it enable inclusion of more diverse voices than if there was no online option? Is this a desired outcome?

- Is there complexity that would be supported with a variety of interaction and recording options (i.e., are there needs for information exchange, conversation, relationship building, project tracking, and the sharing of artifacts like text, images, audio, and video)?

- Is there a need for transparency? Records of the interactions? How much transparency is useful?

- Are there special participant requirements that lend themselves to online interactions (communications needs, culture, etc.)?

- Are there people working in multiple languages or second languages that would benefit from "slowing down" the conversation to allow time for reflection?

Motivation and Methodology

- What motivates those who would use the technology? What are the demotivating forces?

- Is there a tangible and visible expansion of potential by going online?

- Will key stakeholders be willing to lead through action online?

- Will the motivation for connecting be stronger than the perceived barriers to using technology? This will be influenced by the technology used—so keep it as simple and intuitive as possible.

- Is there sufficient support and will to overcome technological and access barriers?

- Is there a need to support peripheral participation (people who "listen, read, watch" but may not be actively involved in the core processes)?

- Is there a need for privacy (suggesting boundaried, password-protected Online Environments)?

- How important is individual identity and personal voice versus collective identity and collective voice? (Identity evolves differently online.)

- Is increased transparency/visibility an opportunity or a threat?

PROBABLE OUTCOMES

Going online influences outcomes somewhat, but well-crafted interventions are about the change initiative, not the technology. Until people have experience and comfort with online tools, expect both interest in and resistance to technology. Beyond technological resistance, the transparency of the Online Environment highlights and even magnifies other types of resistance, including to change itself. This is one way Online Environments accelerate change. The joke is that our warts look even bigger online.

The environment can seem less warm and human to some, or so complicated that others feel disconnected. If you adopt Online Environments, helping people feel welcome and comfortable is critical.

If the initial group is successful, or transformed by its online experience, it influences future interactions. The change effort may reach other areas of the organization more quickly.

Successful online interactions can affect:

- *Relationship Building:* Broader "line of sight" and access to more people via online directories and interactions expands networks and deepens relationships.

- *Knowledge Building:* The old adage "two heads are better than one" is made visible by access to diverse knowledge and perspectives, building the overall group knowledge and enhancing group memory.

- *Increased Transparency:* Online records and open, traceable processes, where people see what is going on, support trust.

- *Participation—Direct and Peripheral:* Online Environments foster direct engagement and learning through observation.

- *Flattened Hierarchy:* Many-to-many access and communication means fewer layers of hierarchy are needed.

- *Finding a Safe Space:* Working out anxieties online can bring an enhanced quality of presence to face-to-face interactions.

- *Heartbeat That Beats Beyond a Face-to-Face Meeting:* The enormous energy of a face-to-face meeting creates a ripple effect that can be extended online.

Table of Uses

Here are some common change activities and how Online Environments can support them:

We Need	Consider These	Effort/Cost	Outcomes
Relationship Building			
In distributed initiatives • Prior to a face-to-face meeting • One-on-one support • "People finding" • Occasional check-in	• Online people directory, photos • Online introductions • Identify topics of interest • Instant messaging for one-on-one • E-mail groups for occasional check-ins	• Effort: medium • Cost: low to medium	• People connect • Build relationships • Fast trust • Increased comfort
Content			
• Share documents • Carry face-to-face artifacts forward • Prepare face-to-face materials • Share content between online/face-to-face	• Web-based file library (Internet) • Document repository (Intranet) • Discussion forum to comment on documents • Audio/video streaming server	• Effort: low • Cost: low to high	• Content easy to find • Fewer distractions • Focus on communication • Better use of historical assets • Group memory
Coordination			
• Coordinate planning • Prepare for a kickoff event • Project management • Task work • Change incubator	• Telecons (teleconferences), screen sharing • Shared calendar, white board • Discussion forum, file library • Web project management tools • Private spaces, invitational spaces	• Effort: low to medium • Cost: low to medium	• Builds team energy • Fast access to information • Increased transparency • Increased accountability • Increased agility • Builds trust

We Need	Consider These	Effort/Cost	Outcomes
Conversation			
• Planning • Share learning • Connect remote participants • Input from stakeholders • Meaning making • Evaluation	• Discussion forum • Online library with comments • Story collector • Audio/video streaming • Event reporters with blogs (Web logs) • Photo gallery • Live chat	• Effort: medium • Cost: medium to high	• More effective face-to-face time • More inclusive events • Informal knowledge sharing • Idea generation • Stakeholders more engaged

Table of Uses. Continued

Getting Started

Whether all online, or coupled with an existing off-line effort, the Online Environment is integral to the overall change effort. Here are nine interrelated elements to consider:

PURPOSE

Purpose drives everything. Be sure it is clear, understandable, and has clearly identified goals. Focus on change purpose first. NEVER adopt technology just because you can.

METHODOLOGY

Select a change methodology that fits your needs, preferences, and culture; then work on the technical or social architecture.

ACCESS

Assess the technological landscape—computers, internet connections, skill, and comfort of your audience—to determine what technologies to evaluate. Consider potential resistance to online approaches and cultural barriers that might be exacerbated online (i.e., beliefs about transparency, formality, etc.) to inform the design and implementation.

ARCHITECTURE: TECHNOLOGICAL AND SOCIAL

With purpose and methodology clear, access assured, design the technological and social architecture. These two interrelated strands evolve together.

Technological Architecture

Many change facilitators do not feel comfortable choosing and deploying technology. That's okay. Do not use technology if you are strongly resistant. Put your energies elsewhere.

Selecting a suitable technical platform can be bewildering given the many options. An experienced partner who understands social systems, change efforts, and designing Online Environments helps.

Social Architecture

Once the technology is chosen, "prepare the space." Online Environments for change generally begin with a minimal yet sufficient structure to orient participants. They "open the door" to possibilities, inviting participants to bring their thoughts, opinions, and issues. It is comfortable and feels immediately useful because issues people care about are discussed. Here are design decisions that help "open the door":

- What's public and what's private? Make sure people know what can be "seen" by whom.

- Provide space for informal social interactions, especially for people who will not meet face-to-face. Discussion topics for introductions, social banter, and games help people get comfortable online.

- Create a compelling invitation. This is key to overcoming fear of technology or sense of "yet another thing" to do.

- Provide content and information. Making background information available increases comfort for some participants.

- Structure an "on-ramp" into the space. Start with minimum tools and content areas to prevent overwhelm, and add new areas as needed.

- Balance control and emergence. Structure provides a safe transition to the Online Environment. Choices support emergent needs and directions. Both are required, and balancing them is an art.

FACILITATION

Facilitation glues the other pieces together, bridging the gaps between process, technology, content, and experience. Plan time and activities for people to get comfortable. Help participants learn new tools and processes. Do a short telephone orientation and walk-through, answering questions and relating them to the purpose at hand.

Consider who will facilitate; with a global group, recruit from different time zones for broader coverage. Cofacilitators help discern meaning in a text world, checking with each other when not sure how to interpret a response.

ITERATION, ADJUSTMENT, AND EVALUATION

This framework has all the ingredients to start. One additional piece is particularly relevant online: Iteration. Online Environments and tools are fairly "plastic." Tweak and adjust them in small, easy-to-tolerate increments. Solicit feedback, watch interaction patterns, and constantly improve the environment to serve your purpose (figure 2).

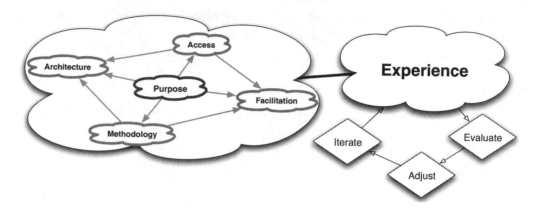

Figure 2. Be Prepared to Iterate and Evolve Over Time

GUIDING PRINCIPLES FOR THIS APPROACH

Online Environments reflect and amplify what is already present in a group, both positive and negative.

If groups are open to change, an Online Environment accelerates it by increasing the density of connections and flow of information/conversation among people.

The environment requires flexibility to grow and change with the participants' changing needs. Flexible technology, flexible design, frequent redesign, agility to switch technologies quickly, or some combination of all of these is a must.

Roles, Responsibilities, and Relationships

SPONSORSHIP REQUIREMENTS

As in off-line efforts, sponsor commitment gives participants confidence that their efforts are recognized. Having sponsors who are open to supporting what emerges from the group's activities is vital. Unique to the Online Environment, where interactions are recorded, is comfort with transparency. There is no place to hide!

Beyond the invitation, direct sponsor participation depends on the project. Their participation is often as a catalyst and role model. If they are technology shy, support their learning.

WHAT QUALITIES AND SKILLS MAKE A GOOD FACILITATOR?

Online facilitation[3] encompasses face-to-face expertise, plus comfort and skill with technology. Often the facilitator supports the group processes, and serves as tech support and tool trainer. They often model online processes unfamiliar to a group, such as sociability in a foreign environment—"talking" with people they can't "see."

Competencies include:

- Modeling the basics of social interaction online—responding appreciatively, asking clarifying questions, commenting, and continuously inviting participants to share their hopes, ideas, and visions for the future.

- Modeling the use of the tools and processes.

- Providing or referring people to technical assistance.

- Weaving together conversations from different "spaces" online, or cross-linking them for greater visibility and synergy.

- Working with misunderstandings that happen more easily online.

PARTICIPANTS AND OTHER ROLES

The key role for participants is to show up and be present—bringing hopes, desires, ideas, and inspirations. Showing up takes visible and invisible forms—active engagement/posting or passive listening/reading. Both are valuable. Build trust explicitly online, as people often rely on face-to-face cues.

Participant expectations depend on the design and intention of the process. Generally showing up, introducing themselves, raising issues of importance, and engaging in topical conversations, decision-making processes, and ongoing team activity are involved.

Conditions for Success

WHEN YOU WOULD USE THIS APPROACH

From the convenience and speed of electronic communication to support for a complex initiative that spans space and time, solutions can be simple or elaborate. Think of throwing a party. Sometimes setting out the cheese and crackers is enough. Other times an elaborate table with a multicourse meal and paired wines is required. Context is everything.

WHY IT WORKS

Designing and executing based on the context is a condition for success. However, there is a caveat: Online Environments and interaction are still new. We don't know all there is to know. Sometimes it doesn't work. Do not use this method if there is no technology support. Be prepared to be surprised. Don't use it when the purpose and value is less compelling than the barriers of using technology.

When it does work, there are a variety of reasons. It creates a "common now"—a space where time and experience is preserved for group interactions regardless of time zone. It provides opportunities to express divergent ideas simultaneously and converge them via collective processes. Reflective thinkers are often more comfortable online than face-to-face, feeling more engaged and valued. A common space for group activity forces the issue of organizing collective information for historical access. Search features provide a method to find gems that previously were lost forever.

Theoretical Basis

HISTORY OF CREATION

The history of Online Environments for change sits in the evolution of online communities,[4] computer-supported communication, and distributed group work (teams). From early experiences of scientific and academic networks, Usenet, the early online e-mail, and Web-based online communities, to today's sophisticated mix of tools and approaches, online interaction continues to grow in complexity and variety. It evolves on two complementary but not always congruent axes of technology development and process innovation. As more off-line change processes adopt technology, new combinations are emerging, including tools designed for specific processes. Through lessons learned from the early work of Peter and Trudy Johnson-Lenz (www .awakentech.com), Lisa Kimball (formerly of www.metanet.org, now www.groupjazz.com), and Doug Carmichael of www.metanet.org, to the recent work of WebLab (www.weblab.org) and America*Speaks* (www.americaspeaks.org), the landscape continues to change. New processes, springing out of the affordances of technology, promise yet more innovation.

CRITICAL UNDERLYING THEORY AROUND ONLINE COMMUNICATIONS

A large body of theory and research underpins online interaction technologies and practices for change efforts. It has spawned "Internet Research," spanning many disciplines, from sociology and anthropology to the cognitive sciences. Two primary areas inform work in online interaction environments: computer-mediated communications research and online group research (virtual teams, online communities, online learning, and network theory).

SOCIAL INTERACTION ONLINE

For example, trust is formed and withdrawn differently online, influencing group interactions. Relationship formation follows different paths online, more easily forming "loose bonds" and more slowly forming tighter bonds and relationships.[5] Identity—or more accurately, the small slices of identity we share online—affects our interactions.

The body of research is young, and early conclusions are situated in specific contexts that may not generalize to other online interactions. There are conflicting conclusions about the absence of face-to-face contact. Even a quick scan shows the need for more research. The studies are small and few track what happens in distributed groups mixing online and off-line or the role organizational culture plays.

EXPERIENCE

Individual learning and communication styles affect online experiences, particularly when working in only one modality, such as text. Those not comfortable reading on a screen, for example, are significantly disadvantaged. For aural learners, audio (podcasts, videos) enhances their experience. Knowledge of the different preferences is important in designing Online Environments. Virtual team research informs us about group experience, including processes for negotiating interdependent tasks in a change effort.

ATTENTION

The concept of "continual partial attention," coined by Microsoft researcher Linda Stone,[6] indicates that often we pay less attention to various electronic communication streams because we are paying attention to more than one at a time, or we are splitting our attention online and off-line. Think of listening to a phone call and reading e-mail or participating in an online meeting and a family member interrupts you. This partial attention can rob the end results of fullness. In contrast, electronic communication puts more in our line of sight, allowing new connections, insights, and innovation. New technologies for combining tools and content add opportunity and complexity. We don't yet understand how this affects our attention.

Finally, research is blossoming around the sociopolitical aspects of online interaction, including the "digital divide." This research examines complexities of who has access and control of online technologies, and how technology and its underlying values influence online interaction, coloring the application of Online Environments to change efforts.

Sustaining the Results

If your Online Environment begins with visioning, consider expanding it to accomplish daily work. Long-term and near-term work spaces within the same Online Environment can inform each other.

Alternatively, use an event model where the Online Environment is always available but is actively used periodically.

Another approach is archiving your Online Environment once it has accomplished its goals, keeping it available for reference. Officially closing an environment may reinforce positive experiences and a desire to "do it again one day."

Burning Questions

Three types of burning questions are common:

1. *Most frequent:* "Isn't online a poor second to face-to-face?" Online interactions can augment face-to-face and enable connections where face-to-face isn't possible. Here is a reframe of the question: "Isn't connecting and communicating around change essential—any way we might get it? How do we create the best possible Online Environments and interactions?"

2. *More an assumption than a question:* "Since it is online, it is free and fast, right?" It is rarely free and almost never fast. Human communication takes time and attention, regardless of the environment. Time is used differently online, complementing our personal schedules. But it still takes time. The cost can be far less than flying 30 people to a city and staying in a hotel for three days. Still, software, design, training, and facilitation have a cost.

3. *Finally, the most challenging and ongoing question is how to get individuals and groups to par-ticipate.* The emerging answers address the first question about "poor second" to face-to-face. When people have a meaningful online experience, the first question goes away. The challenge is designing and deploying online interactions that capture deep attention, meet real needs, and connect people with warm, electronic communications.

Some Final Comments/Possibilities for the Future

Online interaction environments are in their infancy. Our skills at successfully communicating and working within them are new. This is a rapidly evolving domain with new tools literally emerging daily, along with creative applications of human processes designed for online use.

Some technological developments like wikis (easy-to-create Web pages that can be edited by any user), blogs (Web logs), and communal resource sharing may support bottom-up self-organizing, unlocking doors. The emergent creative "hacking" of images from services like www.flickr.com may tap our visual interaction skills. Podcasting and vodcasting for easy online audio and video brings the warmth of voice and nuance of body language. Graphic facilitation, which has so enriched off-line facilitation, is beginning to blossom online. Some Web services even allow people to create and configure their own tools without knowing a computer language.

Imagine this: Nongovernmental disaster relief workers are facing a crisis. Scattered across the world, they mobilize with images, data, tools, and the critical conversations that quickly make meaning, chart a course of action, and respond. Geographic positioning systems track their work and provide critical feedback so that the system as a whole quickly adjusts as new patterns, resources, and scenarios emerge. Questions from the field flow to a "global brain bank" and are answered within minutes or hours, rather than days or weeks. Support surrounds an isolated relief worker through communication channels embedded in her mobile phone, which also translates in six languages so she works in context with those around her. And her partner, 3,000 miles away, gets to say "good night" every night . . . online.

These visions do not diminish the incredible warmth we share as humans who gather face-to-face. This is not an issue of "replacing warm communication with cold." It is twofold: finding our warmth and humanity online, and identifying the mix of online and off-line, enabling people to achieve their goals and fulfill their potential. Embracing the mix of perspectives moves us forward in making wise choices in a world that needs all the wisdom it can get. No technology surpasses a hug, or a shared meal. Rather, it prepares us for finding still more connections that create change.

About the Authors

Gabriel Shirley (Gabriel@bigmindconsulting.com) is an entrepreneur and consultant working at the convergence of leadership development, human potential, emergence, and technology. He has designed online collaboration technologies and consulted with start-ups, NGOs, and Fortune 50 companies to further their change efforts through the appropriate use of technology. He is the founder of BigMind Media, where he designed the BigMind Catalyst online platform and Big-Mind Consulting, where he currently works as an independent consultant. Gabriel's personal change effort is to inspire people . . . to live their dreams, to be more productive than they knew was possible, and use business as an opportunity to improve the human condition. Online Environments are one medium he uses to accelerate that process.

Nancy White (nancyw@fullcirc.com) is a leader in the field of online facilitation and online interaction design. She works in the nonprofit, organizational, and business spheres helping people connect and achieve their goals online and off-line. She has a particular interest in online collaboration and connection for people who would otherwise not be able to work together due to time, distance, and resources. She writes, teaches, and speaks about online interaction strategies and online facilitation, encouraging development of the practice in a wide range of settings. Nancy founded Full Circle Associates. She actively chronicles developments in online interaction through her blog (www.fullcirc.com/weblog/onfacblog.htm) and Web site (www.fullcirc.com).

Where to Go for More Information

REFERENCES

Barab, Sasha A., Rob Kling, and James H. Gray, eds. *Designing for Virtual Communities in the Service of Learning.* Cambridge: Cambridge University Press, 2004.

Lipnack, J., and J. Stamps. *Virtual Teams: Reaching Across Space, Time, and Organizations with Technology.* New York: John Wiley, 1997.

Rheingold, Howard. *The Virtual Community: Homesteading on the Electronic Frontier.* Reading, MA: Addison-Wesley, 1993.

Schuler, Doug. *New Community Networks: Wired for Change.* New York: ACM Press, 1996.

Smith, Mark, and Peter Kollock, eds. *Communities in Cyberspace.* New York: Routledge, 1999.

INFLUENTIAL SOURCES

Hock, Dee W. *Birth of the Chaordic Age.* San Francisco: Berrett-Koehler, 1999.

Mohr, Bernard, and Jane Magruder Watkins. *Appreciative Inquiry—Change at the Speed of Imagination.* San Francisco: Jossey-Bass/Pfeiffer, 2001.

Owen, Harrison. *Open Space Technology: A User's Guide,* 2d ed. San Francisco: Berrett-Koehler, 1997.

Senge, Peter, Otto C. Sharmer, Joseph Jaworski, and Betty Sue Flowers. *Presence: Exploring Profound Change in People, Organizations, and Society.* New York: Doubleday, 2005.

Sheldrake, Rupert. *The Presence of the Past: Morphic Resonance and the Habits of Nature.* Rochester, VT: Park Street Press, 1995.

ORGANIZATIONS

BigMind Consulting—www.bigmindconsulting.com

Full Circle Associates—www.fullcirc.com

OTHER RESOURCES

Methods for Change—http://methodsforchange.com

Nancy White's Online Community Toolkit—www.fullcirc.com/community/communitymanual .htm

Open Space Institute (USA)—www.openspaceworld.org/cgi/wiki.cgi?OpenSpaceInstituteUSA

Sample of a wiki.

---

1. Blending face-to-face and online is one of the more complex deployments. All virtual or all face-to-face is easier!

2. Jean Lave and Etienne Wenger, *Situated Learning: Legitimate Peripheral Participation (Learning in Doing: Social, Cognitive & Computational Perspectives)* (Cambridge: Cambridge University Press, 1991), http://emerge2004.net/osn_presentation/emerge2004_files/v3_document.htm.

3. For more, see www.fullcirc.com/community/facilitatorqualities.htm and www.fullcirc.com/community/onlinefacilitationbasics.html.

4. Howard Rheingold, The Virtual Community, www.rheingold.com/vc/book/.

5. M. Chayko, *Connecting: How We Form Social Bonds and Communities in the Internet Age* (Albany: State University of New York Press, 2002).

6. Cited in Thomas Friedman, "Technology Backlash," *San Juan Star,* January 31, 2001, p. 23.

SARAH HALLEY AND JONATHAN FOX

Playback Theatre

You try to cross over into that part of you that's always there but is only alive when you're playing.

——Dwike Mitchell

Sharing Personal Experience

Imagine a stage with two chairs off to one side, a combination of wooden boxes and simple colored fabrics center stage, and a variety of musical instruments on the other side. The occasion is a staff recognition dinner, with about 100 staff members from affiliated nursing homes and senior centers in the audience. The actors, conductor, and musician enter in a way that evokes the artistic and ritual feeling of a theatrical performance.

The performers begin as themselves, with a song, and an introduction that models the self-disclosure and public sharing that is a necessary component of Playback Theatre (figure 1). The conductor, who acts as a kind of master of ceremonies, sets the stage by welcoming the audience and saying a few words about what Playback Theatre is and what people might expect in the next hour or so. The conductor then begins to invite audience members to tell short moments, feelings, and experiences that are played back by the actors and musician. The process continues— the conductor asks questions, audience members respond, and then actors embody the story on stage.

The conductor invites longer stories in which the teller sits onstage next to the conductor for the interview and enactment. One person after another tells about how demanding the work is and how thin they are stretched. The actors act out the feelings. Then the conductor asks, "Why do you do the work you do?" A woman comes to the teller's chair. She tells how she has grown up in the city, on a block where there were many older people. As a child, she had thought of them all as her grandparents. So it seemed natural for her to care for older adults as a profession. As the

Illustration by Christine Valenza

Figure 1. What Playback Theatre Looks Like

actors portray the teller as a young girl with her older neighbors, the love between them is palpable. There are many moist eyes in the audience. After the story, the atmosphere in the room changes. There is a sense of vision present and a feeling of renewal. The performance ends with reflection of the stories and themes present as integration.

What Is Playback Theatre?

Playback Theatre is an improvisational theatre form that takes personal stories told by participants, in the moment, and turns them into compelling theatre. It gives the storyteller and the group a chance to see the story from a different perspective. Because the story is embodied, it provides group members with the opportunity to experience the story and access a greater depth of empathy, transforming the listening from an "intellectual exercise" to a whole-body experience.

THE VOICE FOR THE COMMUNITY

Because of Playback Theatre's effectiveness in building community and its inherent valuing of all voices, it can play a key role in organizational change efforts. This is especially true for any organization looking to develop a more effective team culture, greater openness and transparency in management, and more participatory leadership at all levels.

TYPICAL OUTCOMES

In the many different settings for Playback Theatre—which include public, semipublic, and private gatherings—Playback Theatre's outcomes are similar. Dialogue occurs through the public sharing of stories. One story leads to another, connections are made between people, and awareness of differences between people and their life experiences are also brought out. Compassion, empathy, and greater understanding are frequent outcomes. At times, a sense of "everything is fine" can be replaced with a more realistic view, one that honors the current contradictions and existing conflicts, building individual and system capacity to live with ambiguity, which is necessary in any significant change process. Specific outcomes that can be built into a Playback Theatre event include:

- Surfacing critical issues, especially during a change process

- Celebrating successes and endings

- Energizing and clarifying vision, getting back to the heart and meaning of work

- Kicking off event to build energy and buy-in

- Building team cohesion, increasing intimacy and trust

- Bringing depth to data that has been gathered during an organizational assessment, and giving direction for additional data gathering that may be necessary

- Increasing openness and transparency in an organization, especially during a change process

- Breaking norms of indirect/underground communication, bringing conflict out into the open, giving permission for resistance to be openly expressed, and providing people with a chance to see and be seen at a deeper level

- Providing public forum for people to grieve, process, move

- Bringing out the "underheard" or minority voices in a community or organization

EVERY STORY IS IMPORTANT

A key guiding principle for Playback Theatre is a kind of democracy or inclusion, in which all stories and tellers are seen as important. During a Playback Theatre event, the faciliator, or conductor, is always tracking who has told and who has not, as well as patterns in the tellers (like race, gender, and organizational role). The conductor uses that awareness to invite those tellers and stories that have not yet been heard.

Playback Theatre is culturally respectful and adaptable; its motivation is an impulse toward healing and positive change; it operates on both individual and group levels; it is an unfolding process rooted in the moment that is highly spontaneous and trusts in nonlinear movement. It draws on the aesthetic, creative capacities of participants; sees inherent value in play; and it requires a ritual container that is created by the forms and presense of the performers and conductor.

Playback Theatre draws inspiration from the idea of the small community, in which everyone is known to one another. Its brand of storytelling improvisation conforms to characteristics of traditional societies where cultural ceremonies were intimate, communal, redressive, and attuned to the environment (see Fox 1994). From the theory of J. L. Moreno, originator of group-focused role-play approaches, such as sociodrama and psychodrama, it takes the idea that every individual is endowed with a capacity for creativity and spontaneity and can contribute to positive group life. Playback Theatre is also informed by the ideas of the Brazilian educator, Paulo Freire, whose concept of critical consciousness suggests the identity clarifying power of personal story. Freire also emphasized the importance of listening, of an open-ended, democratic process of research.

The result of these influences for Playback Theatre is an approach that truly trusts participants' input. Playback theatre teams perform with no script whatsoever; they come ready to listen; they put their artistic skills and humanity to the service of the tellers. Playback Theatre also has the sense of a "theatre of neighbors," quite different from the anonymous urban feel of modern theatrical performance. Finally, it is an essential aspect of the Playback Theatre approach that the theatre be constructive. Art alone is not enough. This theatre is not simply entertainment; it has an educative purpose.

Frequently Asked Questions

What If No One Wants to Tell?

Usually, if troupe members have done their homework and prepared adequately, including designing the opening of the show to meet people where they are and warm them up to the process, people are open to telling. And if there is some reluctance to tell, then the conductor needs to go back and continue to warm the group up with easy-to-answer, "safe" questions. If no one tells, it is a clear signal to the facilitator that people are either not warmed up enough, or there is not enough safety in the group. One way to address this is by inviting people to talk to another person (dyads) about a structured question or topic. Then the conductor can invite someone to tell a short moment/feeling, or even ask a specific question that he or she is sure some people will be able to answer yes to, for example: "Is anyone experiencing mixed feelings about the change the company is going through, like hopeful and worried?"

What If Someone Goes Too Deep, and Is Emotionally Affected to the Point That He or She Is Overwhelmed or Too Exposed?

In our experience, individuals and groups have an innate wisdom that guides them to tell at a level they can handle. If deep feelings emerge, the conductor is trained to help the teller and group process their feelings and use the situation as a learning moment for the whole group.

What If the Group Does Not Tell the Stories We Want Them to Tell—Stories That Are "Off Topic"?

Stories that might seem "off topic" or superficial are often rich with relevant metaphors and themes, and can become a vehicle for truth to emerge. The following is an example from a performance Sarah Halley did with participants from a variety of Fortune 500 learning organizations. The theme of the gathering was about how to integrate a successful, out-of-the-box initiative by a small subdivision of a large corporation into the larger organization, when the sense of being new and different was an essential component of the initial success. At one point in the performance, a man came to the teller's chair and he wanted to tell the story of Goldilocks and the Three Bears, from Goldilocks's perspective. Typically in Playback Theatre, the teller tells a personal story that is true for him, but there was something about the genuineness with which he presented the story that moved the conductor to go with it. One theme that emerged in the enactment that resonated strongly with the group had to do with the courage it takes to put yourself in a situation in which you are vulnerable and out of your element. And we were left with powerful questions to ponder—Why did she wander out into the woods alone, and where were her parents? Where did her confidence come from? Was this a case of neglectful authority? Was it a story about the drive to take "the road less traveled," which cannot be tamed by authority? What did the bears represent? In the end, this simple and irrelevant story was anything but that.

An Inappropriate Story

If we meet every story with respect, and trust there is some message of relevance to the group, then no story is truly inappropriate. Playback Theatre is based on the premise that anyone's story has meaning and it's our job to bring out the meaning. At one conference, a woman told a story about having different lovers in different cities. Partway through, Sarah realized that the woman had been drinking, and she was using the teller's chair in part to make a public invitation for someone to "pick her up" that night. Sarah did her best to be as brief as possible during the interview process, and the actors brought out the range of feelings in the story. After the story, Sarah made a "metastatement" about the challenges of being away from home for work reasons. She asked who else in the room travels regularly for work, and many hands went up. She then asked for other feelings about traveling and being away from home. In effect, she built a bridge between her story and the group by making explicit the shared concern/issue that she believed others could connect with.

A Racist Story

We use the term "racist" because we hear that often, but there are a myriad of attitudes and behaviors that could be substituted. There are a number of interventions we might try in the case of a racial story. We might use inquiry to ask questions that get at why the person feels the way he or she does. We might ask how he or she thinks the target of the oppression felt. We might make a metastatement to the audience that brings in some sort of larger social context, or provides a piece of historical information many people may not know. We work to accept the teller and his or her truth, while at the same time acknowledging that there are other ways of seeing the story.

We will also work for brevity and hand the story over to the actors as soon as possible, knowing the actors are trained to use their craft to bring out the feelings of all the people in the story and they will complete the intervention in their enactment. They will work to humanize both the teller and the person who has been the target of the oppression. They will also look for a way to bring in the larger social context. Once the story is done, the teller will have a chance to speak. We might ask if the teller was surprised or learned anything by seeing his or her story. If we sense there is a lot of energy in the audience, we might invite audience members to talk in dyads about how the story impacted them, and how it connects to their lives. We might then ask for feelings—not about the teller, or the teller's story, but for a feeling of how the story, or a moment in it, connected to their own personal experiences. We might even ask, in the next story, for a time when someone felt targeted for being different. In Playback Theatre's service of helping a community get to a deeper dialogue, the story told by the racist can be both confronting and helpful.

Table of Uses

Brief Description	Project Length	Key Events	Number of Participants
Public performance Open performance with or without a theme.	1 evening	1.5-hour open performance	• Audience of 15–300 • Team of 4–5 actors, a musician, and a conductor
Residential college preparatory school With a mission to serve orphaned children and children living in poverty, in the beginning stage of a change initiative that will mean a significant expansion of the school and number of students served. Existing staff (teachers, house parents, support staff, counselors) with varying levels of buy-in to the expansion plans mandated by the board.	3 weeks	6 performances Each performance is part of a 3-hour event with a segment on the past, the present, and the future. The Playback Theatre portion is a 1-hour show on the present situation.	• 50–60 staff members from all areas of organization attend each performance. • Team of 3–4 actors, a musician, and a conductor

Brief Description	Project Length	Key Events	Number of Participants
Biannual regional sales force meeting of a major airline Assess performance, strengthen working relationships between representatives in different geographic regions, and strategize for the future.	Single performance	1.25-hour performance on the morning of the first day of the weekend retreat, to kick off the meeting.	• 30–40 sales representatives in audience • Team of 3–4 actors, a musician, and a conductor
Off-site residential training facility Professional training with participants from business and educational sectors who are practitioners of Neuro-Linguistic Programming (NLP). Advanced train-the-trainer on presentation skills offered by well-established NLP training organization.	7-day training, into which Playback Theatre workshop time is integrated daily.	1.25-hour Playback Theatre session at the end of each training day	• 80 participants

Getting Started

Playback Theatre is an interactive process. Whether performance or workshop, it begins by warming participants up to each other, to their own stories, and to the Playback Theatre method. The amount of needed container building—that is, structure and boundary setting to ensure safe sharing—depends on who is in the room and the specific objectives of the event.

In a workshop run by a facilitator without an acting team, the steps are different, but the goals are similar. The workshop begins with a variety of activities designed to build connection, safety, and spontaneity. Additional skills like active listening and improvisation are practiced. At some point, personal storytelling is introduced, and participants become performers for each other's stories. At the end of the workshop, there is a closing process that includes reflection on the takeaways.

Playback Theatre is particularly valuable where an infusion of creative energy is needed, or as a memorable way to bring people together and strengthen the community. This includes kick-off meetings, situations in which the group is in conflict and could use some "aerating," where increasing trust and risk taking is necessary for success, or where there is some significant loss that the group needs to acknowledge and mourn in order to move on.

Playback Theatre

Roles, Responsibilities, and Relationships

FACILITATION

The facilitator for a Playback Theatre performance or workshop is the Playback Theatre conductor. The conductor guides and frames the process from beginning to end. Playback Theatre is a highly facilitator-dependent method, and the conductor's role requires a great deal of skill to accomplish well.

The cornerstone of the conductor's training is a thorough understanding of group process, including the stages of group development; how to adequately warm up and close a group; diagnostic and intervention skills; thinking on one's feet; and a strong sense of ritual—that is, a heightened sense of aesthetic form and presence. In addition, the conductor must be skilled in using the Playback Theatre method, understand what forms to use where, how to invite a teller, and make sure the actors know what they need. Finally, the conductor also needs to be a bridge between the organization and the acting troupe, understanding the issues and cultures of both. The conductor training is extensive, and we would refer anyone who is interested in learning how to be a Playback Theatre conductor to the School of Playback Theatre.

Acting teams need to have performing skills along with the ability to listen to and hear the deeper levels of a story. The performers also need to know the culture of the audience. It needs a skilled conductor, and the right context.

Actors need to show depth and humanness of every character, regardless of how "one-sided" the teller might be. Actors need to use the content of the story to bring out its social dimension. By social dimension, we mean the factors that are related to the social, historical, and political setting and cultures present in the story—factors that, when embodied and given voice, can both enrich the teller's experience of the story and open up levels for others in the group to connect the story to their own experience.

Conditions for Success

OPENNESS AND TRUST

Because Playback Theatre is naturally interactive, it will only work if people are willing to tell their stories. There are always some people who are comfortable talking in front of groups and are willing to self-disclose. This fact does not diminish the need to meet the group where it is and intentionally build on opportunities for trust to develop, so that *all* audience members will at some point feel safe enough to offer a piece of their story. The beginning portion of the performance or workshop is designed to gradually increase the level of risk in sharing, so that participants are incrementally warmed up to telling longer stories. How this is done depends on the specific outcomes of the event, and how connected the group is initially.

Some basic level of trust is necessary for Playback Theatre to be effective, and it is the responsibility of the Playback Theatre practitioner to evaluate the existing conditions and proposed context to insure there is the potential to build enough trust to ask for public sharing of stories. There are certain situations where Playback Theatre is not appropriate because it is not safe to share anything personal.

In public performances and events such as professional conferences, the majority of audience members are unknown to each other. If the performance has a theme, people will have some affinity or desire to explore the theme, which means they may arrive more warmed up or ready to tell. In the case of an existing group, there may be norms in the group that limit what is shared. For example, if trust has been previously damaged in a group, the stories shared initially might not be very deep or risky (which would be appropriate). Increasing the trust level is a basic outcome of all Playback Theatre events.

The most basic requirement of participants is an openness to participate. Not all group members need to have the same level of openness. As long as there is some openness, the Playback Theatre process can be effective. The process itself can help increase openness in more resistant group members.

One example of this kind of opening is a performance we did in a church on Christmas Day during a dinner for homeless and poor people in the community. Sarah observed an initially disengaged man in the back of the room as he slowly opened up to the performance. He moved his seat about three times until he was in the front row, and when we ended, he enthusiastically jumped up and hugged each of us for coming. I couldn't help but think that if we had passed each other on the street that morning, we would never have greeted each other that way, and it was the human sharing of stories that created that opening.

Theoretical Basis

THIRTY-YEAR HISTORY

Playback Theatre was founded in 1975 by Jonathan Fox and colleagues in the Hudson Valley of New York State. From the start, we experimented with a variety of community applications. We brought Playback Theatre to schools, festivals, organizations, and community centers. We started to travel internationally in 1980. At the same time, we began to offer training in the method. In 1990, in response to the growth of Playback Theatre around the world, the International Playback Theatre Network (IPTN) was founded. Service trademarks reside in the hand of this nonprofit association; Playback Theatre is not a franchised business. Rather, it tries to apply to its own professional community the same generosity of spirit needed by performers on the stage as they enact stories of a local community. Every few years, an international conference brings Playback Theatre practitioners together. Gatherings have been held in Sydney, Australia; Olympia, Washington; Perth, Australia; Rautalampi, Finland; York, England; and Shizuoka, Japan. In 1993, Jonathan started the School of Playback Theatre, of which Sarah is a core faculty member. The school offers comprehensive training for Playback Theatre and enjoys a diverse student body from about 25 countries. Its Libra Project is dedicated to bringing Playback Theatre training to regions needing to rebuild civil society. The school also works with institutional partners to bring the method to organizations and groups.

Playback Theatre has been compared to psychodrama and theatre of the oppressed (TO), created by Augusto Boal, a student of Friere's. Like Playback Theatre, both methods value a non-scripted approach. However, there are significant differences. In contrast to psychodrama, Playback Theatre does not position itself in the therapeutic domain, even though it is grounded in the concept of constructive change. Unlike TO, Playback Theatre does not begin with any assumptions of what a particular audience's "oppression" might be, but trusts that the members of a group, through the medium of their personal stories, will always raise issues of importance to them. TO looks for solutions, but Playback Theatre enactments do not. Playback Theatre stories instead engender shared perspectives and deep dialogue. Psychodrama, TO, and Playback Theatre are fully allied in a commitment to voicing truth, which can take courage because powerful forces—personal, social, and political—often urge us to suppress the real story. We believe it is positive and necessary to face the truth of a situation in order to creatively imagine the future.

Sustaining the Results

Measuring shifts in spontaneity, listening, creative thinking, and degree of cohesive community is not easy. As a largely supportive method, the partnering consultant is largely responsible for guiding the organization through the change process and building in measures of success. We have found, over and over, that a single playback event can become a powerful keystone metaphor for the kind of collaborative and responsive teamwork that many organizations strive to cultivate.

The positive outcomes from Playback Theatre are enforced by more than one performance—spaced sometimes up to a year apart—so that participants integrate deeply the experience of openness and creativity that playback promotes. There have been some organizations that have initiated an in-house Playback Theatre performing group comprised of diverse employees, thus guaranteeing sustainability.

It's hard to say exactly why Playback Theatre works as well as it does. It has a universality and accessibility that has helped it spread to more than 50 countries around the world. It is simple on the one hand, and rich with metaphor and meaning on the other. It taps into a deep need for people to been seen, validated, and part of a community. And it carries with it the power of storytelling to heal and transform.

Burning Question

What Commitment Is Necessary?

Commitment on the part of higher-ups needs to include seeing value in play and creative activity and rewarding instead of penalizing participants for their openness (even if they are not in agreement with the content of what has been shared). Leaders must be committed to working with process as well as task goals in their team. Over time, if senior management can demonstrate its openness, others will follow. By the same token, some form of reasonable follow-up needs to be built into the system over time, so that everyone shares some responsibility for making the changes that are needed.

Parting Remarks

Playback Theatre is an action method and a boundary-crosser, spanning the fields of theatre, psychology, oral history, and conflict resolution. It works because people are eager to tell their stories. When members of a group are willing to share honestly their different perspectives on an issue and see them embodied on the stage, evidence indicates that Playback Theatre has led to permanent positive change in organizations.

About the Authors

As an undergraduate, *Jonathan Fox* (jonathanfox@hvi.net) studied oral composition at Harvard, focusing on preliterary epics. His MA is in political science, which he earned in New Zealand while on a Fulbright Fellowship. He spent two years in the Peace Corps in Nepal learning the culture of preindustrial village life. Immersed in the experimental theatre at the beginning of the 1970s, Jonathan also studied psychodrama. All these strands led to Playback Theatre, which has been his principal focus since 1975.

Sarah Halley (sarahhalley@gmail.com) has traveled from engineering to organic farming to education to social change work to the performing arts to team building, diversity training, and organizational change work. The red thread that connects them all is a passion for learning, a deep reverence for the interconnectedness of all beings, and a commitment to making the world a better place—all of which are expressed through her Playback Theatre work.

Where to Go for More Information

REFERENCES

Coles, Robert. *The Call of Stories.* Boston: Houghton Mifflin, 1989.

Fox, Jonathan. *Acts of Service: Spontaneity, Commitment, Tradition in the Nonscripted Theatre.* New York: Tusitala, 1994.

————, ed. *The Essential Moreno: Writings on Psychodrama, Group Method, and Spontaneity.* New York: Springer, 1988.

Fox, Jonathan, and Heinrich Dauber, eds. *Gathering Voices: Essay on Playback Theatre.* New York: Tusitala, 1999.

Salas, Jo. *Improvising Real Life.* 2d ed. New York: Tusitala, 1996.

INFLUENTIAL SOURCES

Arrien, Angeles. *The Four-Fold Way.* San Francisco: HarperCollins, 1993.

Freire, Paulo. *Education for Critical Consciousness.* New York: Seabury Press, 1973.

Playback Theatre

ORGANIZATIONS

International Playback Theatre Network—www.playbacknet.org

School of Playback Theatre—www.playbackschool.org

OTHER RESOURCE

Tusitala Publishing—www.playbacknet.org/tusitala

NANCY MARGULIES AND DAVID SIBBET

Visual Recording and Graphic Facilitation
Helping People See What They Mean

The soul never thinks without a mental image.
—Aristotle

Some Stories

As Meg Wheatley, Myron Rogers, and Frijof Capra presented their views on chaos, complexity, and self-organization, author Nancy Margulies stood to the side with four easels and recorded the complex ideas they presented (figure 1). These colorful maps were then posted in the room for people to review. During each three-day session, Margulies produced 20 to 30 maps, or Mindscapes. The participants found them helpful for reviewing and clarifying the theories and applications presented. A small black-and-white booklet was photocopied and handed out the last day of the conference. Participants reported that the visual record enabled them to better comprehend new concepts, review them, and share the ideas with others.

In another setting, Margulies recorded visioning sessions for Xerox Business Services. She asked the participants to envision the future, share their ideas with a partner, and ultimately draw images that reflected their vision. The images were then posted and studied. Margulies suggested visual metaphors that pulled the elements together in a coherent whole. She then drew a mural using the images people had created. A small version of the same Mindscape was used in publications within the division. Margulies always leaves space on a vision and strategy map that asks, "What is missing?" and "Where do you see yourself in this picture?" In this way, the document is not completed by one group and imposed on another but is a work in progress that

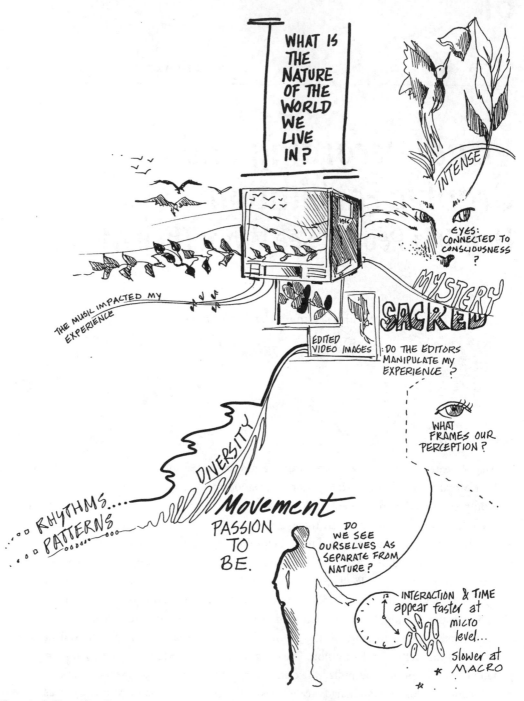

Illustration by Nancy Margulies

Figure 1. The Nature of the World

invites additions and changes. Employees at all levels of the organization added their thoughts. They reported that this invitation to participate included them in a process that previously felt like it was more of a directive than an invitation.

When faced with a need to explore possibilities for change at the level of an entire society, Margulies uses visual mapping to clarify issues and record visions of the future. As this book goes to press, groups across the nation are gathering to explore the possibility of humanity consciously evolving in response to the breakdown of our institutions. If widespread disillusionment due to corporate scandals and governmental failure in response to natural disasters represent evidence of a chaotic system reaching a bifurcation point, then what might be next? What higher-level order might emerge? The map in figure 2 captures these reflections and invites further conversation.

A team at Hewlett Packard's LaserJet Division was charged with presenting the results of

Illustration by Nancy Margulies

Figure 2. Possibilities

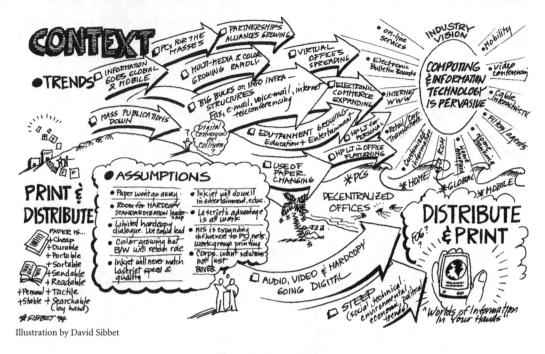

Illustration by David Sibbet

Figure 3. Context Map

three months of research on possible new $2 billion businesses to their top management. Two prior task forces had not been well received, and the group of seven was worried. During three face-to-face meetings, author David Sibbet helped the team develop a set of murals to use instead of computer projector slides. Their purpose was to create a panoramic display environment supporting real story telling and involving top management rather than pushing information at them. To further assure their involvement, the murals were created in a conference room close to the executive's offices several days before the meeting.

On sheets of 4 × 8-foot paper, the team developed a project history, a chart showing all the resources interviewed, a context map (figure 3), a vision mural, and several Graphic Gameplans using a template that includes room for illustrating objectives, resources, strategies, success factors, and challenges (figure 4).

The final session was a workshop with the team leader and another knowledgeable colleague making final content decisions. Another team placed the information in the templates, and then Sibbet worked with a person who checked details on the final murals.

The top management couldn't stay away from the steamy conference room; they were in there kibitzing the whole time, looking at murals in various stages of development. When the final report came, they entered a room with the first four murals up, and they revealed the game plans one at a time. Each team member played a part in presenting. It was a celebration rather than a confrontation. Everyone already knew the main ideas and they were excitedly experiencing the full panorama in a real thinking fiesta—a perfect balance of push and pull.

Graphic Facilitation

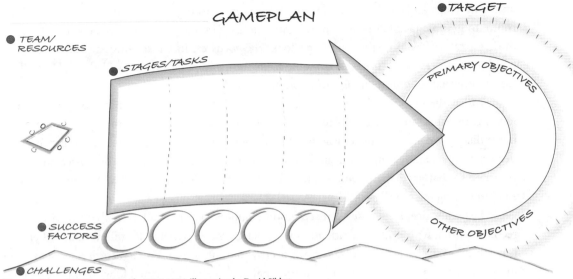

"Graphic Gameplan"/Graphic Guide #12 © 1996; illustration by David Sibbet

Figure 4. Graphic Gameplan Template

The presentation was so successful that the top management asked to have their next strategy meeting facilitated graphically, as did the group managers one level up. The members of the team were eventually assigned to some of the big ideas, which were actually implemented!

The project demonstrated the tremendous power of graphic facilitation and the simple templates that unlocked this power for people who can't draw well, but who can think spatially and visually.

Frequently Asked Questions

What Are Visual Recording and Graphic Facilitation? When Are They Used?

Visual recording and graphic facilitation are part of a growing body of practice using real-time illustration of words and images to help groups work together and communicate more effectively. The methods have roots in the way designers have always worked, using sketches, diagrams, and imagery to try out new thinking, present possibilities, make sense of complexity, and remember rich amounts of information. Organizations in rapidly changing environments now use visual recorders and graphic facilitators for retreats, planning sessions, team projects, dialogue sessions, problem solving, community building, strategic thinking, and knowledge creation. Educators and trainers use the methods to deepen learning. The applications are extensive and inspiring.

At a recent conference of the International Forum of Visual Practitioners, formed in the mid-1990s, attendees generated some 30 different names for practitioners in this field. Practitioners range from people visualizing presentations off to the side of a group, the results of which animate breaks and final reports, to visual recorders working with facilitators in front of the room, to graphic facilitators and consultants who use graphics as an integral, cocreated display during strategy sessions. In general, persons who focus on just recording are called visual or graphic recorders and those who combine facilitation and recording are called graphic facilitators. However, the combinations and variations are rich.

All of these approaches use images along with written words to capture conversations, ideas, comments, and presentations. Some simply use colorful symbols to highlight ideas and make displays of words more engaging. Others use artistic renderings as well as well structured display formats along with words and phrases. In all cases, the material is organized while it is recorded so that participants who study it see connections and patterns that may not have been evident during the event itself.

Listening deeply is a key and common component across all forms of practice. Good recorders listen with undivided attention for metaphors and patterns that illuminate. Often, the unspoken or implied is as important as the overtly communicated. Visual recorders learn to listen on several levels at once. When people realize that they are being listened to with full attention, it inspires them. To use a phrase coined by Philip Henderson, recorders are "motivational listeners."

Here are some predictable outcomes from working in this fashion:

1. *Increased Participation and Engagement:* Interactive visualization invariably increases involvement and participation. The human mind is a pattern-seeking organ. Incomplete, emergent patterns are the most fascinating. As people see their actual words and imagery reflected faithfully, they come alive and contribute more. In addition, imagery has a deep, resonant impact on people beyond its surface meaning.

2. *Group-Level, Big-Picture Thinking:* Systems thinking requires visualization because of its complexity. Visual recording and graphic facilitation use big pictures literally, and make it possible for groups to expand their thinking well beyond norms for other media. Making ideas visible, using both words and images, means that we are making our very process of thinking visible. Often we attempt to solve problems without a conscious awareness of our own process. Visually mapping means that our ideas and mental models now exist on paper—outside our brains, where we can explore them in greater depth.

3. *Increased Memory and Continuity:* People remember what happens at meetings with much higher rates of retention when they use working visual displays and evocative imagery. Within meetings, the posted charts provide continuity by supporting persons who drift in their attention. Reproduction afterward greatly increases chances for retention and follow-through. Since the reproductions are exactly what people saw being drawn in real-time, memory is supported directly. Another benefit of visual recording is its value to those for whom English is not a first language. Rereading charts and studying the maps is truly helpful.

Table of Uses

Typical Setting	Time	Key Activities	Number of Participants
Café Dialogues Asking questions that matter; fostering engagement and insight.	1.5–4 hours	2–4 rounds of small group talk, often using table graphics, bracketed by large group discussion, recorded on large charts	15 to 100s
Teaching and Workshops Supporting learning and retention	1–8 hours	Usually broken into hour segments, each recorded distinctly	Up to 50
Team Planning and Project Reviews Getting alignment on outcomes, roles, rules, and progress	0.5-day meetings in multi-month contexts	Series of meetings involving chartering, team building, goal setting, project planning, and progress reviews	5–15
Web Conferences Support ongoing project work	1–2 hours	Introduction, agenda, and series of topics—supported by simple graphic templates, word recording, or tablet PC drawing	5–12
Retreats Building relationships and dealing with important turning points	1–3 days	Usually involve 4–8 different sessions, each supported with different kinds of graphics	6–25
Design Workshops Innovate and generate new ideas	1–2 days	Usually includes rounds of brainstorming using cards, visualization, prototyping, and media	15–30
Launch Events and Celebrations Get everyone aligned on new plans and acknowledge contributions	1–2 days	Usually speeches by leadership, catalytic speakers, and small group work—each supported with different kinds of graphics	100s
Strategic Visioning Work through analysis of environment, organizational strengths and weaknesses, decide on priorities	1 day to 6 months	Predictable series of visualization activities: • Histories • Context mapping • SWOT* analysis • Visioning • Strategy formation • Game planning • Portfolio adjusting	6–12 per facilitator; can combine in large processes of 100s

*SWOT analysis is a process sometimes used in strategic planning. SWOT stands for strengths, weaknesses, opportunities, threats.

Graphic Facilitation

Typical Setting	Time	Key Activities	Number of Participants
Large Group Visioning and Planning Get the whole system in the room to resolve complex issues	2–3 days	Almost always a flux between large and small group work, with visual recording and facilitation supporting both	100—1,000s
Change Management Providing images and metaphors that open people to potential in the new directions	Short- or long-term change	Series of sessions work key leadership through frames, critical stories, and imagery	Team to whole communities

Table of Uses. Continued

Getting Started

Graphic facilitators and recorders can be used in all phases of change initiatives. They can act as thinking partners when planning an event. Recorders can also help large groups interact and think together more effectively. Graphic recording can also be combined with coaching.

Successfully applying visual recording and graphic facilitation to a group change process means involving the graphic practitioner from the initial planning stages. When graphic facilitators sit on design teams and offer suggestions, they help think through the agenda and decide which graphic formats are best for each aspect of the design. Often graphic professionals have experience with a variety of organizations, initiatives, and graphic formats, and can provide valuable content input to help shape the event's success. Being graphic means being explicit. When outcomes, agenda, roles, and rules can be visualized, it means they are clear to meeting designers and probably will be to participants.

There are some unique logistical aspects to recording. Using large displays requires big expanses of flat wall or the equivalent. It's possible to make portable walls out of large sheets of plywood or foam-core poster board that rest on easels (two per board). Getting this equipment and setting it up requires some work from the sponsoring organization ahead of time. Some recorders use flip charts in lieu of large displays.

Roles, Responsibilities, and Relationships

A graphic facilitator leads groups toward agreed-upon outcomes, usually with participation and ownership from all involved while staying neutral regarding outcomes. The facilitator is responsible for collaborating with meeting sponsors and presenters and agreeing on the formats used for each piece. During discussion, the facilitator uses the displays to catalyze thinking. Facilitation can be separate from recording or combined for smaller groups.

A recorder can do a great deal during a meeting to help a facilitator keep things on task by titling displays so they communicate outcomes, numbering clearly to support sequence, color coding and emphasizing in overlays when points become clear, or even providing verbal summaries of the charts to help people understand what they have come up with.

One of the values of graphic displays is having all ideas recorded on one sheet without devaluing any of them. Each person can see their ideas recorded and notice their relationship to the contributions of others.

Digital images of the graphic record can then be used for printed booklets, Web sites, or presentation software. Teams with ongoing meetings can pull out old charts or load digital images into Web conference software and continue almost as if there were no gap.

Conditions for Success

Visual recording and graphic facilitation can strongly support both the planning and implementation phases of group process. This is where clients perceive real value from displays making sense out of what occurred and what ideas showed up.

Imagery can also be used very effectively for inspiration and learning that is less bottom-line oriented. These applications demand more from the practitioner in flexibility and sensitivity. During dialogues, for example, when a recorder is quietly receptive and well paced, it honors speakers and enhances deep listening.

Since visual and graphic recording integrate both imagery and structured display, it combines linear and nonlinear processing styles of the brain in very useful ways. Success lies in the integration of elements—a proper space for display, good planning of the agenda and graphics, open listening and support for everyone being heard, and an overarching intention to actually understand and make sense out of what is occurring.

Theoretical Basis

Extensive literature on the importance of visualization to thinking underlies this work. Some 80 percent of our brains are dedicated to processing visual information. Pattern finding is basic. Whether or not we are visual, auditory, or kinesthetic learners, everyone uses imagery for recall and their eyes to perceive nuances—to drive, watch movies, use computers, and navigate. Studies in twenty-first century literacy are concluding that visual thinking is a core competency that everyone needs to develop.

In the growing science of complexity, a large preponderance of the advances have come through visualization of dynamic systems and literally seeing the patterns in complex systems such as weather, commodities, urban growth, consumer behavior, and planes in the air.

Reflecting Patterns in Nature: In the 1970s, David Sibbet worked with Arthur M. Young and his Theory of Process study group to look at visualization as a process rather than just a pattern. Out of this theoretical work evolved the Group Graphics® Keyboard (figure 5), a description of the seven archetypal patterns for visually displaying information, organized from simple to complex.

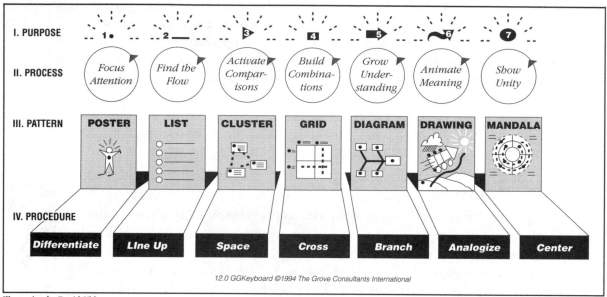

Illustration by David Sibbet

Figure 5. Group Graphics Keyboard

This grammar lies at the heart of The Grove Consultants International's approach to teaching graphic facilitation and visual literacy, and has been tested worldwide since 1976.

Bob Horn, inventor of Information Mapping in the 1970s, has tracked the theoretical basis of this field and summarized his findings in Visual Language (see "Where to Go for More Information"). Edward Tufte and Saul Wurman both have written extensively with regard to information architecture and information design, noninteractive applications of visual thinking that are very helpful for displaying information. Since visualization is so protean, it is increasingly hard to know just where the edges of this field lie.

HISTORY OF VISUAL RECORDING AND GRAPHIC FACILITATION

Real-time visualization methods find their upstream tributaries in the work teachers do on blackboards and what engineers and designers do on white boards. Many of the early practitioners of graphic facilitation were on the West Coast of the United States, where graphic facilitation had its start as a formal process discipline. The West Coast is rich in design professionals. Interaction Associates (IA), formed in San Francisco in 1969, was a pioneer in professionalizing facilitation that used recorders integrally. IA founders David Straus and Michael Doyle were both architects.

David Sibbet, a next-door neighbor of IA in San Francisco, pioneered the systematic use of large displays in facilitation and the development of formal training in graphic facilitation in the

1970s. He was inspired by the work of Geoff Ball, an engineer turned consultant who worked at Stanford Research Institute (Now SRI); Joe Brunon, a former architect also working at SRI; and Fred Lakin, an information artist from Stanford University. For five years, Sibbet experimented widely with all forms of visual recording and graphic facilitation as a way to get Coro Fellows in Public Affairs to make sense out of their field internships and projects. This became the basis of a full-time graphic recording and facilitation consulting and training practice in 1977 and eventually The Grove Consultants International.

Nancy Margulies developed Mindscaping as a way to support teaching and learning, as well as a system for recording and facilitating business conferences. She began recording business meetings in 1984 with clients dedicated to making changes in their organizations. As one of Peter Senge's "Fifth Discipline" consultants, she applied visual note taking to the five disciplines. Her more free-form, artistic style of recording and workshops has inspired one branch of visual practitioners. Her books for teachers and students bring visual recording and Mindscaping into classrooms and counselors' offices.

THERE ARE MANY OTHER INFLUENCES

Tony Buzan, based in the United Kingdom, popularized mind mapping in the 1980s and 1990s—with software now available that supports the process. A German process called Metaplan formalized elaborate use of different shaped cards in planning. Disney developed storyboarding as an interactive visualization practice that has its adherents. Jim Channon, as an army briefing officer, created Advanced Visual Language and currently innovates with adventure learning applications. The Total Quality Movement used visualization of data integrally with TQ groups and problem solving.

The 1990s saw another rapid expansion of the field in applications to Future Search, Appreciative Inquiry, and The World Café (see chapters 33, 5, and 12, respectively). All incorporate graphic recording as an aspect of their design.

In 1995, San Francisco Bay area graphic recorders Leslie Salmon-Zhu and Susan Kelly founded an association of visual practitioners. In 2000, the International Forum of Visual Practitioners (IFVP) became an official association, hosting annual conferences for its members, and a Web site that provides lists of practitioners, samples of their work, and resources.

Sustaining the Results

Visual recording and graphic facilitation is unique in having a very tangible output that directly supports follow-through.

Graphic facilitation challenges the notion that committees and groups are clumsy, unintelligent instruments and that meetings are generally unproductive. Visual records tap into and enhance group intelligence in direct ways. A key to sustaining this impact is to understand the truly empowering effect of deep listening and respect for groups, as well as being able to see patterns and processes. Visualizing taps the generative power of groups like few other processes, and is the reason that cutting-edge design firms like IDEO use it integrally to help create cultures of innovation for their clients.

Graphic records enable people to keep the feeling as well as the content alive after the event. People who are not able to attend an event can be brought up to speed by reviewing the visuals with someone who was there. Two people can't read a written document while discussing it, yet they can be literally on the same page looking at a graphic. The visuals are often reprinted in newsletters, on Web sites, and displayed in office hallways.

The growth of graphic recording and graphic facilitation has changed the work cultures of companies. It is becoming a movement in its own right.

- Graphic facilitation is now a frequent feature of high-tech planning. At a turnaround for National Semiconductor, use of large-scale graphics and graphic facilitation resulted in a 95 percent worldwide recognition of their vision among an employee base of 23,000.

- In education, many teachers and teacher support centers use a wide range of graphics to support the profession and to learn advanced note-taking skills.

- Change process and innovation labs that use graphic facilitation are springing up in organizations like the U.S. Navy, Hewlett-Packard, Procter & Gamble, and Agilent Technologies.

- Organizations inspired by Peter Senge's work on the learning organization have created the Society for Organizational Learning and use graphics integrally in thinking about systems.

- America*Speaks*, a large-scale change organization facilitating huge gatherings of citizens around issues like rebuilding New York City and rebuilding the Gulf region now uses groupware and graphics integrally in its forums.

- In Europe, a Future Centers network is using graphics and other creative media to support Future Center planning and innovation activities in facilities that have been inspired by knowledge capital work.

Burning Questions

The questions people ask of this method often have to do with its interface with other work processes, such as the growing world of online communications and virtual work. These problems are disappearing as digital photography helps link these worlds. Tablet PCs (personal computers) and Web conferencing software now allow for online visualization.

Other questions revolve around what will be done with the graphics. People ask,

"How can we preserve and use this document? Can it be accessible digitally?" The answer is, "Yes, thanks to modern technology."

"Will this work in other settings such as a sales/motivational event or an executive development program?" Yes, these settings lend themselves well to graphic recording because any time

Graphic Facilitation

that people need to retain new information and be motivated to review it, visual representations can enhance the experience.

"We usually publish written notes as a way to document our meetings. Do we still need them?" Our clients most often use graphic representations as the sole document but in some cases, traditional notes accompany the visual maps because the client requires a word-for-word document as well as one that captures key ideas.

A frequently asked question by clients experiencing visual recording and graphic facilitation is, "Can we develop the internal capacity to visually record our meetings and special events?" The answer is, "Yes." Some 20 percent of people get through school and still enjoy drawing, but practically everyone consumes increasingly sophisticated visual information on TV, movies, and computers. Everyone can learn to draw the simple graphics used by visual recorders if they are convinced of the value and are willing to practice (figure 6).

Illustration by Nancy Margulies

Figure 6. Visual Recorders

For those interested in developing this expertise in their organizations, there are a growing number of workshops available that directly teach graphic recording and graphic facilitation. Both Margulies and Sibbet have successfully trained many thousands of people. (See their Web sites and that of the International Forum of Visual Practitioners in "Where to Go for More Information.")

Most professionals in this field develop solid recording skills working with facilitators before they combine the roles, but some adept at graphics jump right in and get great results. Most organizations have people who would make excellent graphic facilitators if given a chance.

Graphic Facilitation

Some Final Comments

There is a huge difference between a graphically facilitated meeting and one run with graphic presentation software. The former creates a panoramic, cocreated visual environment at a speed that people can absorb and remember. The latter pushes fire hoses of information out that are hard to scan and remember as a system. Therefore, visual practitioners increasingly ask what we would give up if we focused on becoming faster and more transactional. Would we be losing or helping our ability to think ahead and appreciate the context and implications of actions? We value human interaction and an approach to change efforts that allow reflection and time to listen to all voices and points of view.

Meg Wheatley, a business author and articulate spokesperson for the power of emergence in human system, puts it most eloquently when she reflects on her collaboration with Nancy Margulies and her respect for the field of graphic recording:

> When reviewing Mindscapes created in our dialogues and meetings, ideas that I'd forgotten leap off the page. Moments of learning or tension or laughter in the group come vividly to mind. The range of faces and feelings comes back into focus.
>
> We couldn't have dealt well with the richness, the challenge, and the wonder of the concepts we were exploring in new science without these Mindscapes. As they went up on large wall charts, we saw the individual ideas and, more importantly, their interrelationships. We could literally see what we were trying to understand—the systemic nature of life.
>
> I can't imagine learning how to think systemically without some sort of visual imagery, without seeing the system swim on the page, flowing onto the next page. I can't imagine remembering the complexity of concepts without seeing them up on a large chart. . . . once the words and shapes are on the page, they are there for us to remember.

About the Authors

Nancy Margulies (www.NancyMargulies.com) began developing her visual recording technique in 1984. Her books and videotapes are popular in several countries. Nancy collaborated for many years with Meg Wheatley, author of *Leadership and the New Science.* Other activities include working with President Clinton and his cabinet and the Dalai Lama. She facilitated workshops and strategic planning in Australia, New Zealand, Israel, Switzerland, Turkey, South Africa, and India. She is one of the developers of The World Café.

David Sibbet (www.davidsibbet.com) began his work as an organizational consultant and information designer in the mid-1970s. He works in both public and private sectors on projects in Europe, North America, and Asia and is an acknowledged master facilitator and expert on visual language. David is founder and president of The Grove Consultants International in San Francisco, a full-service organization development consulting firm and publishing company focused on visualizing change.

Where to Go for More Information

REFERENCES

Hanks, Kurt, and Larry Belliston. *Draw! A Visual Approach to Thinking, Learning and Communicating.* Los Altos, CA: Crisp Publications, 1992.

Horn, Robert. *Visual Language: Global Communication for the 21st Century.* Bainbridge Island, WA: MacroVU, 1998.

Kaner, Sam. *Facilitator's Guide to Participatory Decision-Making.* Philadelphia: New Society Publishers, 1996.

Margulies, Nancy, with Nusa Maal. *Mapping Inner Space.* 2d ed. Chicago: Zephyr Press, 2002.

Margulies, Nancy, with Christine Valenza. *Visual Thinking: Tools for Mapping Your Ideas.* Bethel, CT: Crown House Publishing, 2005.

Sibbet, David. *Graphic Facilitation: Transforming Group Process with the Power of Visual Listening.* San Francisco: The Grove Consultants International, 2006.

_____. *Principles of Facilitation and Best Practices for Facilitation.* San Francisco: The Grove Consultants International, 2002.

ORGANIZATIONS

The Grove Consultants International—www.grove.com

International Forum of Visual Practitioners—www.visualpractitioner.org

Nancy Margulies—www.NancyMargulies.com

Graphic Facilitation

WARREN LIEBERMAN

The Drum Café
Building Wholeness, One Beat at a Time

"Umuntu ngumuntu ngabanutu" meaning . . .
A person becomes whole through their interactions with other persons . . .
I am because we are.

—A Zulu proverb

Who Is Going to Play All Those Drums?

We walk into the conference room, tired and unmotivated after a long, tough financial year. The underlying tension and rivalry between departments has dominated the company this year, and the communication between employees is poor. We expect the same annual conference and have few expectations of change.

This year is different. When we arrive at the venue to find a circular arrangement of hundreds of chairs and a drum placed in front of each one, we all ask the same question: "Who is going to play all those drums?" Before long, the answer becomes clear: We are—a group of 200 accountants with absolutely no musical skills.

As the drumming team starts to beat a simple, powerful rhythm, the music gradually takes hold of us and, tentatively, a few brave individuals start beating away on their drums. The music becomes infectious and soon everyone is tapping their drums. At one point, our marketing manager gets carried away with the energy in the room and leaps into the middle of the circle for a quick dance to the wild applause and cheers of his colleagues.

Then, without saying a word, the facilitator gets up, teaches the group simple drumming rhythms, and starts to orchestrate the group with a repertoire of body language signals, bringing the 200 entry-level musicians into perfect harmony.

For an hour, we are engaged in a cooperative activity that leaves us feeling energized, exhilarated, and unified. We feel surprisingly motivated and ready to share ideas and work as a team. Funny how after just an hour of drumming together, my company feels more like a community.

Frequently Asked Questions

What Is the Drum Café?

The Drum Café brings interactive drumming to mergers, product launches, conferences, road shows, year-end functions, incentive breakaways, and other corporate events to bridge gaps and understanding among different groups (diversity, multiculturalism, etc.). Venues vary widely, from traditional conference centers or intimate settings in nature to massive sports and performance arenas.

What Inspired the Drum Café?

The Drum Café was born not long after Nelson Mandela became president of South Africa in 1994. This was a time of ambivalence, a period of joy, fear, and hope, where many people anticipated bloodshed and war. With 11 official languages, cultural differences, and a history of a minority that had held power for decades, South Africa needed to undergo a radical change. Under the guidance of President Mandela, bloodshed and war were averted, and South Africa was transformed rapidly and profoundly into a "rainbow nation," which brought together cultures, races, and communities under a unified banner.

The Drum Café took Madiba's[1] philosophy as the core of its approach and during South Africa's time of transition, it brought the message of cohesion and unity to hundreds of companies across South Africa. The Drum Café facilitated communication and cooperation between black and white, male and female, old and young. It taught how to bridge the gap between the old and the new, and to foster understanding and friendship between employees from vastly different cultural backgrounds.

How Do We Work and What Are the Outcomes?

Prior to any event, client and consultant explore the factors affecting the organization and its key goals. This understanding is used to shape the process to address these issues.

On the day of the event, a team of facilitators and musicians collaborate to teach the group simple drumming rhythms. The group is taught to play the same bass rhythm and to listen to one another. As the session progresses, the music gradually becomes more harmonious and the team is transformed into a percussive orchestra. The analogy between an orchestra and wholeness provides perspective into the synergy between individual and team. Figure 1 is a visual representation of a Drum Café session.

Following a Drum Café experience, participants are often more open to taking in new information and concepts. This experience fundamentally alters participants' perceptions of what can and cannot be achieved and lays the foundation for organizational change. Because the

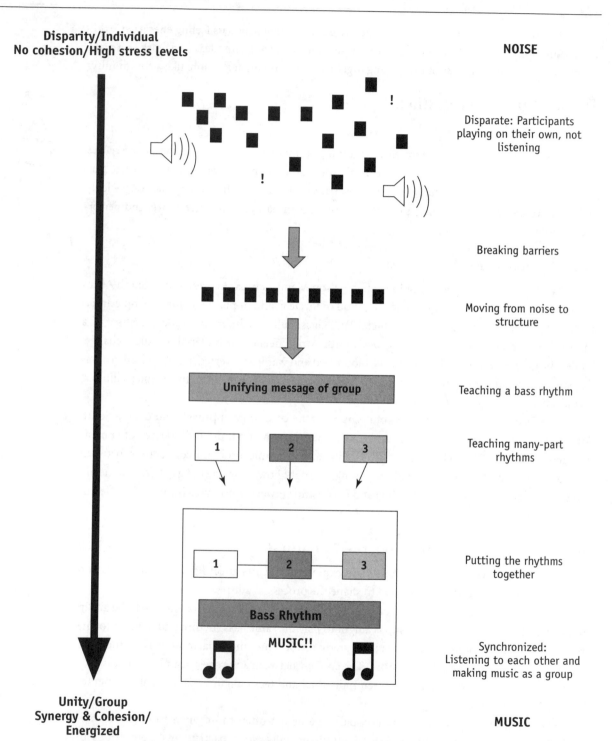

Figure 1. Creating Unity Through Music

learning is hands-on rather than taught, participants can extrapolate their learnings and draw insightful analogies based on the principles of music and drumming.

One manager talked of being allowed to "let her hair down" in front of her employees. She explained how at work she had struggled to create bonds with her employees because her managerial position had kept her distant. She reported that after the Drum Café experience, her relationships had significantly improved and there was a much more relaxed atmosphere in the office, which has been of great benefit to her team's performance.

Table of Uses

Typical Setting	Brief Description and Results	Time and Participants
Connecting Diversity Usually at client premises, conference centers, or under a tree.	• Participating in an exercise of communication, effective listening skills, and the power of a truly synchronized organization promotes the power of nonverbal communication. • Feelings of isolation and dissent disappear, as the drumming experience bonds every participant into a motivated and unified whole.	• 60–90 minutes • 10–500 people
Conflict Resolution	• With the proliferation of negative interaction between individuals and teams, the handling of conflict is often very difficult. • Drumming together helps break down barriers to create a more effective and harmonious environment.	• 60–90 minutes • 2–200 people
Road Shows, Conferences, and Workshops	• A series of shows delivered around the country when unveiling new vision, mission, and values of company. • It can draw people together, celebrating success and ensuring that the delegates leave feeling invigorated and motivated.	• 10–90 minutes • Up to 100,000 people

About the Author

Warren Lieberman (warren@drumcafe.com) graduated with a degree in physics and applied mathematics at the University of Cape Town and also attained a BSC with honors in electrical engineering. He started the Drum Café from his home in 1995. Warren recently produced and directed the Off-Broadway hit *Drumstruck*. He also published a book on traditional music in

South Africa—*The Drum Café's Traditional Music of South Africa* by Laurie Levine. Warren has also produced two CDs of African traditional music and fusion music. He is currently developing a traditional African orchestra that uses only traditional African instruments (such as Kudu horns, cow horns, and marimbas).

Where to Go for More Information

REFERENCES

"Bongos in the Boardroom: Companies Go to Extremes to Foster Teamwork." *The Detroit Business News*, February 14, 2004. www.drumcafe.com/articles/Bongos%20in%20the%20 boardroom%20Companies%20go%20to%20extremes%20to%20foster%20teamwork%20 -%2002-14-04.htm.

"Drum Sessions Protect Employees from Burnout." *Reuters*, February 19, 2004. www .drumcafe.com/articles/Yahoo_drum_article.htm.

"Drumming Up a Happier Workplace." *BBC News World Edition*, February 20, 2004. www .drumcafe.com/articles/BBC/BBC_News.stm.

Laurie, Levine. *Traditional Music of South Africa.* Johannesburg, South Africa: Jacana Publishing, 2005.

ORGANIZATION

Drum Café—www.drumcafe.co.za/www.drumcafe.com

---

1. In South Africa, "Madiba" is an affectionate nickname for President Nelson Mandela.

BRIAN TATE

JazzLab
The Music of Synergy

Everything we do is music. Everywhere is the best seat.
—John Cage

Making Your Own Music

A large group of participants enters a ballroom. Rather than taking their usual seats, they form two large concentric circles around the perimeter of the room. They are about to become musicians for the rest of the morning. Following a brief introductory talk on how to make music (breathe, stay loose, jump in, have fun), rhythm and groove are quickly established with clapping and rapping, growing magically from a single pattern to two parts, and then to four parts. Then comes the moment everyone has been anticipating: playing the rhythm instruments they have made themselves from instructions sent prior to the event. Shakers, drums, scrapers, bells, and woodblocks are readied for the debut of the "artistic, mystic, synergistic mass rhythm orchestra." Within minutes, an entire room full of self-described nonmusicians is in the groove and having a great time. Everyone is discovering a new way of listening, getting "in synch," experiencing diversity in action, and creating organizational synergy—where the whole is indeed greater than the sum of its parts (figure 1). They are now musicians for life.

What Is JazzLab?

JazzLab is an exciting, enlivening, hands-on experience, using music making as a way to transform your organization. From an hour-long workshop to a daylong intensive, participants become musicians, composers, conductors, and improvisers—and no musical experience is required! It emphasizes working together, having a great time, and making music that sounds wonderful. JazzLab uses music making to address vital organizational questions such as:

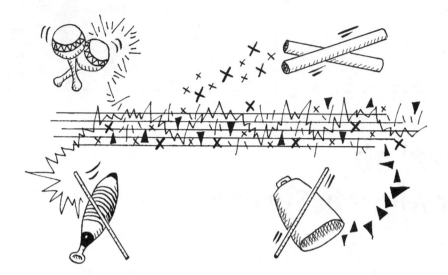

Figure 1. Combining Instruments and Rhythms Creates Synergy

- How can we listen and communicate better?

- How can we create effective teams yet still retain autonomy?

- How can we better foster creativity and innovation?

- How can we encourage diversity?

- How can we create effective structures, but not be bound by them?

- How can we think better on our feet?

How Does JazzLab Work?

JazzLab is based on the premises that:

1. Everyone is musical, whether they know it or not.

2. Making music is an excellent metaphor and training tool for whole-system thinking.

3. Rhythm and percussion are quick, easy, and effective ways for people to make music together.

JazzLab begins with clapping and keeping a simple beat. A single, shared pattern divides into two, then into four parts. Voices are brought into the mix with a rap song in four parts. Then the rhythm band is formed, with each group of instruments given their own part. Participants then get to conduct or play in an improvised symphonic "movement" with the large ensemble. Smaller groups are then formed, with participants creating and performing their own original compositions. Finally, "improv trios" are formed, where three players sit facing each other with an array of instruments and create a two-minute free improvisation on the spot.

The Four Elements of Music

The foundation of JazzLab is rooted in four primary elements of music, all of which interact simultaneously. As participants begin to feel these elements flow together, it becomes apparent that they are also the foundation of a holistic, healthy, and vital organization.

1. *Listening: Deepening and widening your listening.* Our average listening span in conversation is remarkably short, yet while playing music, we can listen deeply for long periods of time. Making music provides a framework for deep listening, the foundation of all effective interaction.

2. *Being "in synch": Getting in the groove.* Following a common beat together is akin to having a common purpose and vision. Not everyone needs to play the same part or play the same way, but hearing and synching up to that common beat is essential. Once the group is unified this way, effort and struggle can then relax into groove and flow.

3. *Diversity: Having everyone's contribution matter.* In life, we tend to naturally gravitate to the familiar—those who look, act, and think like ourselves. In music, however, we naturally seek out variety and diversity. Every part is important. The wider the mix of instruments, the more interesting texture and overall sound. A mix of skill sets, personalities, and backgrounds usually makes for a wider knowledge and innovation base.

4. *Synergy: The whole is greater than the sum of its parts.* Synergy as a concept can be difficult to grasp. In music, however, we can instantly hear and experience the power of synergy. Listen to the rhythm section of a band—the keyboard, guitar, bass, and drums all have interesting parts by themselves, but when they come together, something wonderful is created that surpasses the mere combination of parts.

Improvisation: The Final Frontier

The essence of jazz is improvisation, a concept that often frightens people. Yet, every day we are improvising all the time. We call it conversation. Think about it: You may have an opening line to initiate a conversation, but after that you respond to each other on the moment, building on what is being said, and creating a dynamic exchange. That is improvisation! Another way to look at day-to-day improvisation is in how you "play" your day. You may have a structure to your day, but chances are you will make many additions, revisions, diversions, and other changes that are appropriate to your situation. That too is improvisation, and it is what gives life and meaning to the structures around it. In JazzLab, musical improvisation demonstrates powerfully that we can trust our intuition—that improvisation does not lead to anarchy and chaos, but rather allows for new structures to emerge, structures that are dynamic and alive.

Table of Uses

Brief Description	Number of Participants	Time Required
Experiencing Rhythm and Music Establishing rhythm and the four elements of music through clapping and spoken rhythm. Introduction of instruments and how to play them, creating the mass rhythm band, and playing a piece together.	Up to 2,000	60 minutes
Composing Music Improvisational conducting with the large group to establish non-rhythmic musical ideas, then breakout groups of 6–8 collectively compose/rehearse an original piece of music and perform it for the others.	Up to 50	90 minutes
The Art of Improvisation Introduction to improvisation, setting up a workshop space for three musicians, and inviting participants (up to three at a time) to create 2-minute free improvisations. Concludes with mass group structured improvisational piece.	Up to 50	60 minutes
The Theatre of Improvisation Everyone is divided into two large groups with a hierarchy of positions of leadership. Each group creates and performs a musical play in the style of Kabuki theatre using actors, musicians, and a chorus.	Up to 60	90 minutes

About the Author

An award-winning composer as well as an accomplished and versatile musician and facilitator, *Brian Tate* (btate@axion.net) attributes the success of his multifaceted career to a love of working with people and a passion for the arts. Brian received his Bachelor of Music degree from the University of British Columbia and went on to further music studies in London, England, and Toronto. His love for music of many kinds has led to a diverse career that includes orchestral and choral conducting and performance; West African drumming; jazz piano and vocals; musical theatre; and composing music for film, television, stage, and the concert hall. As a facilitator in the area of business and education, Brian takes the elements of creativity, process, chaos, and discovery found in the performing arts and transforms them into powerful, interactive group experiences toward developing leadership, authenticity, innovation, and systems thinking.

Where to Go for More Information

REFERENCES

Davis, Miles. *Kind of Blue.* CD-ROM. Sony, 2000.

Nachmanovitch, Stephen. *Free Play: Improvisation in Art and Life.* Los Angeles: J. P. Tarcher; New York: St. Martin's Press, 1990.

Nisenson, Eric. *The Making of* Kind of Blue: *Miles Davis and His Masterpiece.* New York: St. Martin's Press, 2001.

Suzuki, Shunryu. *Zen Mind, Beginner's Mind.* New York: Walker, Weatherhill, 1970.

ORGANIZATION

Brian Tate—www.briantatemusic.com

JAMES HAUDAN AND CHRISTY CONTARDI STONE

The Learning Map Approach

If a picture is worth a thousand words, a metaphor is worth a thousand pictures.

—Author Unknown

PepsiCo and the Revolution on Beverage Street

Imagine you are a route driver for PepsiCo's North American team. The company employs approximately 35,000 people, the vast majority of whom are route drivers—just like you. Everyone in your region receives an invitation to the annual company-sponsored town hall meeting. What runs through your head? You probably think, "Why is management doing this? It is a waste of time. I have work to do. Can't I just do my job?"

The day arrives and you enter a room set in round tables to accommodate the hundreds of people in your area. For years, you normally sat with a group of your buddies at the back of the room. Not today. You are directed to a table with a mix of eight to ten people from different roles and levels of the organization. "This ought to be interesting," you think to yourself.

A poster the size of the table is flipped over. It has bright-colored data, charts, figures, and pictures. The interesting thing is that this poster brings to life a story centered around the theme of "A Revolution on Beverage Street." You learn that for the next few hours all of the groups will be using the large posters—called Learning Map® visuals—discussion questions, and some exercises to share observations and learn together. You discover that the market for carbonated soft drinks is not growing, and you examine trends about pricing pressure, soda consumption by age group, and the growth of other drink options such as water, tea, and private-label products. The figures that catch your attention are those about the decline in soda consumption as people get older. When you look at the forecast for this trend, it doesn't look good for your core four products—Pepsi, Diet Pepsi, Slice, and Mountain Dew. When your group examines the informational graphic showing growth in water, tea, sports drinks, and fancy new-age beverages, one of the other drivers at the table comments, "The company needs to add new products if we want to continue to be successful." You find yourself agreeing.

The group concludes the discussion on the first Learning Map module, and a second poster is placed on the table. This one depicts the entire Pepsi-Cola work process. The core steps are all there—including forecasting demand, negotiating deals with customers, product processing, loading the trucks, delivering product, and settling the route. Proudly, you recognize that of the eleven steps, drivers are responsible for those at the heart of the process. As group members read through the questions and share their observations, you learn that you touch more of the process than you ever recognized before. Others at the table with different responsibilities begin to observe how you all work together to take care of the customers. The group talks about how each person, in his or her specific role, can make a difference. The session concludes with people sharing their observations and conclusions.

Why would Pepsi do something like this instead of the standard PowerPoint road show? As described above, these modules combine a table-sized poster, which uses a visual metaphor, with open-ended Socratic dialogue questions, data, learning activities, and small group interaction. This process helped Pepsi North America effectively engage its entire workforce, and resulted in increased business acumen, as well as improved understanding of the system, interrelationships, and personal roles within the organization. Pepsi's own pre- and post-meeting assessments show improved understanding of critical issues and commitment. This process helped effectively launch the organization's strategy to become a "Total Beverage Company." Demonstrating Pepsi's success in deploying this strategy, reports as of December 2004 indicated that 82 percent of Coke's global volume was in carbonated soft drinks, while 65 percent of Pepsi's North American beverage volume came from carbonated soft drinks.

The Basics: Answers to Frequently Asked Questions

The Root Learning Map methodology, pioneered by Jim Haudan and Randall Root, has become a benchmark for engaging and connecting employees to business strategy (figure 1). The methodology is dialogue driven and discovery based. The approach is typically used to help people understand the drivers of change (the "why"), the specifics of the change (the "what"), and how they can connect and contribute.

Because of the visual nature of Learning Map modules, they are particularly helpful in creating shared understanding across diverse cultures. The modules can be designed to be led by trained facilitators from within the organization, or to be self-facilitated if that works best for the company's culture. Facilitators don't need to be professional trainers or subject matter experts. Modules are rolled out in groups of eight to ten people, who can come from a natural work team or may represent a mix of levels and roles. The rollout plan and group composition is determined by the company's goals and objectives as well as its operating structure.

Outcomes for organizations using the Learning Map methodology range from increased

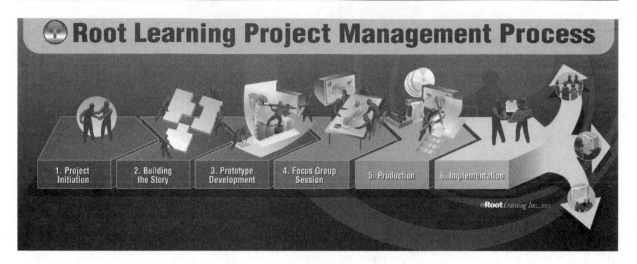

Figure 1. Steps to the Learning Map Process

knowledge and understanding to improved performance and business results. Clients determine the outcomes and success measures that are important to them, such as levels of employee engagement and improved business indicators. The power of the methodology is in creating conditions for people to come to their own understanding of complex issues. It is important to use maps in environments where leaders are willing to share information and engage employees. There is a five-step process used to develop a Learning Map module:

1. Project planning and kickoff:

    •   Project goals and key milestones are determined.

    •   Roles and responsibilities are reviewed.

2. Building the story:

    •   Content is gathered from subject matter experts.

    •   Learning outlines are built and validated.

    •   Key data points are determined and provided.

3. Prototype development:

    •   High-level concept sketches are created and feedback is incorporated.

    •   Concept sketches are developed to higher levels of details.

    •   The visual, learning outline, dialogue questions, and learning exercises are developed to a prototype level.

    •   Focus group test sessions are held.

    •   Revisions are made and finalized.

4. Production of materials:

- Facilitators are trained.

- Materials are translated, if necessary.

- Final materials are produced and distributed to locations.

5. Implementation:

- Modules are rolled out in a manner designed to meet company objectives and operating structure.

- Measurement and assessment is conducted, if desired.

Table of Uses

Brief Description	Project Length	Key Activities
• *"Big picture" issues:* Changing customer expectations, competition and new markets, shifting technologies. • *"Financial acumen" issues:* Sources of revenue, cost components, critical financial measures, drivers of financial performance. • *"Customer value" issues:* Customer needs, performance attributes, best practices. • *"Process" issues:* Redesign, internal supplier relationships, process improvement, cycle-time reduction, improving service levels.	Average project time: 2 months, determined by customer needs, level of content definition, degree of alignment-building and engagement required	1. Project initiation, 1 day–2 weeks 2. Building the story, 1 day–2 weeks 3. Prototype development, 5 days–3 weeks 4. Production 5. Implementation

About the Authors

James A. Haudan (haudanj@RootLearning.com) is chief executive officer of Root Learning and a cofounder of the Learning Map technology. He leads the firm's growth and the creation of a global client network. He has researched, developed, tested, and implemented a host of customized, enterprise-wide learning initiatives in areas that include global manufacturing, retailing, insurance, pharmaceuticals, health care, information technology, biotechnology, utilities, aerospace, transportation, and education. Jim is a frequent presenter at industry conferences, including the American Society for Training and Development, the HR Forum, and at global leadership conferences for Fortune 2000 companies. Root Learning has twice been recognized as one of the Best Small & Medium Companies to Work for in America.

Christy Contardi Stone (contardi@RootLearning.com) is director of marketing at Root Learning. She leads a team focused on building Root's brand and generating growth opportunities for the business. In her ten years at Root Learning, Christy has held various leadership positions, including building two of the company's five industry-focused consulting practices, and key account management for retail and health-care clients in the Fortune 1000, including Sears, Toys'R'Us, Baxter Healthcare Corporation, and Merck. The Sears project, which Christy helped lead, was featured in the *Harvard Business Review*.

Where to Go for More Information

REFERENCES

Huselid, Mark, Brian Becker, and Richard Beatty. *The Workforce Scoreboard*. Boston, MA: Harvard Business School Press, 2005.

Quinn, Robert. *Building the Bridge as You Walk on It*. San Francisco: Jossey-Bass, 2004.

Yury, Boshyk, ed. *Business Driven Action Learning*. New York: St. Martin's Press, 2000.

ORGANIZATION

Root Learning—www.rootlearning.com

65

CHARLES J. PALUS AND DAVID MAGELLAN HORTH

Visual Explorer

Art [is] the attempt to wrest coherence and meaning out of more reality than we ordinarily try to deal with.

—Peter Vaill

Crate and Barrel

Crate and Barrel's cross-functional Internet Team is meeting for two days to cocreate a shared vision for Web-based innovation over the next five years. A key frame for the meeting is Appreciative Inquiry, with a desire to celebrate recent successes, as well as to appreciate and explore diverse perspectives among team members about what the future may look like. The challenge, however, is how to begin such a conversation in a way that, per the culture of Crate and Barrel, is both serious and productive as well as celebratory and fun. Thus, the meeting opens with more than 200 images (diverse, engaging, provocative) from Visual Explorer (VE) spread out around the room on the floor and tables. Team members browse the images with this instruction in mind: "Walk around the room and each of you choose one image that represents what innovation looks like from your perspective" (figure 1). The team then engages in a form of dialogue, with each of the chosen images being put in the middle in turn. *Each* person examines and describes *each* image for what it literally contains, as well as the meanings and metaphors it evokes. The differences and similarities in what each person sees among all the images is both surprising and illuminating—and dramatically heightens the awareness that one's point of view colors one's perceptions. Profound insights overlap with laughter. For the rest of the meeting and afterward, several pictures and metaphors for what innovation means keep recirculating.

Figure 1. Differences and Similarities in Perceptions Are Explored

The Basics

Visual Explorer (VE) is a method used to produce a dialogue rich with images and metaphors—and thus fresh ideas—while exploring similarities and differences in perceptions and perspectives. The Visual Explorer product consists of a loose-leaf deck of 224 color images printed on 8.5 × 11-inch heavyweight paper. The images are quite diverse in content, cultural context, and artistic media (photography, painting, sculpture), and have been selected for their ability to connect literally and (especially) metaphorically with a wide variety of topics.

VE is typically used when a group is exploring a complex challenge. The first phase in any such exploration is to see the challenge in depth from a variety of perspectives. VE allows group members to illustrate and articulate their various points of view using vivid metaphors and imagery. The critical contribution of VE is that the images themselves are tangible objects that invite careful attention. Thus, one teammate can examine another's image and say something like "What I notice in this image is . . ." or "If this were my image, it would have another meaning for me. . . ."

VE uses are varied. Some people use VE as a one-time tool; still others tap into its more far-reaching powers for transformation by reenacting the process with a series of groups, and reusing the resultant stories, images, and metaphors as media for cross-boundary dialogues.

The outcomes of a VE session typically include some or all of the following:

- Sharing of perspectives about an issue in a way that leads to synthesis and the construction of new perspectives

- Fresh, memorable metaphors and stories about a complex challenge

- Mutual understanding of emotions, intuitions, and tacit knowledge that might otherwise be left unspoken and unillustrated

- Tangible images that can be reused in paper or digital forms

- Shared understanding about the issue that can help in establishing a vision, making decisions, and creating action steps

- Increased skill in the practice of dialogue

The steps in a VE session typically include:

- Framing of one or more priming question related to a larger issue or challenge. For example: What should be our highest priority as a team? What is the future of our product? What would a good solution look like?

- A few minutes of individual reflection and writing in response to the question(s).

- Participants browse the 200+ images spread out around the room. Each person finds an image (or images) that represents or tells a story about how he or she answers the question(s), or sees the issue.

- A dialogue with the images in the middle. Each person describes his or her own image and what it means with respect to the issue. They also do this for the images chosen by the *other participants* (figure 2)

Illustration by Nancy Margulies

Figure 2. Teammates Examine Each Other's Images

When this initial dialogue with the images is finished, a certain kind of momentum is often present, and it works well for the dialogue to keep going in whatever direction is important to the group.

Subsequently, the most significant images and metaphors can be reused in ongoing creative problem solving, invention, and communication. The images lend themselves to "cascading" to other groups in the same organization, especially if they are scanned into digital media for use in, for example, Intranet sites, PowerPoint shows, and dialogue mapping tools such as Compendium (see "Where to Go for More Information").

Table of Uses

Setting	Project Length	Key Events	Number of Participants
Verizon Senior managers in an action learning process focused on facing and solving complex challenges. *Priming questions:* What is the nature of this challenge our team is facing? What are the root causes? What might solutions look like?	4 months	Teams met over 4 months, with VE used in initial sense making, ongoing problem solving, and in outcome communications.	20 senior managers (4 teams) per cohort
A Regional Hospital Opened their conversations in various ways, bridging leadership at all functions and levels, including shared hopes and fears. *Priming questions:* What stands out for you in our review of this organizational climate data? What creative competencies do you personally bring to our shared work?	6 months	A series of Leadership Team meetings and retreats ranging from the core team to a whole-system group. Digital scans of key VE images, coupled to related stories, are used in multimedia collages for reflection and dialogue.	8 senior leaders in a core Leadership Team; 50 leaders across the system.
A Pharmaceutical Company Cascaded entrepreneurship and innovation to all levels of the organization *Priming question:* What is your role in creating conditions for extraordinary innovation over the next 8 months?	4 months	15 sessions with previous commitment statements and video clips contained in each cascading session as leaders at all levels of the organization visualized their role in innovation.	80 people

About the Authors

David Magellan Horth (horthd@leaders.ccl.org) is a senior enterprise associate at the Center for Creative Leadership. He is president of the Creative Education Foundation. David's background includes 21 years in the computer industry, beginning as an R&D engineer and later as a strategist specializing in creativity and innovation. David describes himself as an artist-in-training. He enjoys drawing, writing poetry, and playing a variety of instruments including African drums, folk guitar, and didgeridoo.

Charles J. Palus, Ph.D. (palusc@leaders.ccl.org), is a senior enterprise associate at the Center for Creative Leadership, and manager of the Connected Leadership Project. His team conducts research on how organizations develop interdependent leadership practices and cultures. Prior to his coming to the center, he was a research engineer for the DuPont Company, and an instructor and program designer for the Hurricane Island Outward Bound School.

Where to Go for More Information

REFERENCES

Palus, C. J., and W. H. Drath. "Putting Something in the Middle: An Approach to Dialogue. Reflections." *SoL Journal* 3, no. 2 (2001): 28–39.

Palus, C. J., and D. M. Horth. "Exploration for Development." In *The Center for Creative Leadership's Handbook of Leadership Development (Second Edition).* San Francisco: Jossey-Bass, 2003.

———. *The Leader's Edge: Six Creative Competencies for Navigating Complex Challenges.* San Francisco: Jossey-Bass, 2002.

———. "Leading Creatively: The Art of Making Sense." *Ivey Business Journal* (September/October 2005). Reprint # 9B05TE05.

INFLUENTIAL SOURCE

Perkins, David. *The Intelligent Eye: Learning to Think by Looking at Art.* Los Angeles: J. Paul Getty Museum, 1994.

ORGANIZATIONS

Center for Creative Leadership, Visual Explorer—www.ccl.org/visualexplorer

Compendium Institute—www.CompendiumInstitute.org

Part III: Thoughts About the Future from the Lead Authors

So, where is all this high-leverage, transformation stuff headed? This book contains a wide variety of methods from different disciplines that help organizations and communities on their journeys to greater effectiveness, intrinsic motivation, healthier societies, and job satisfaction. It seems fitting that after providing you with some wonderful stories about the past and present, we also peer into the crystal ball and give you a taste of what we see unfolding in the future. Since the three lead authors—Peggy Holman, Tom Devane, and Steven Cady—have very different experiences, we each give you a chapter on an aspect of the future (chapters 66, 67, and 68, respectively).

One final note as we look across the variety of high-leverage change approaches emerging today. We believe that these methods are a powerful testament to a revolution in progress. What is truly revolutionary about them is their commitment to participation and systemic change. The chapters in this part speculate on where that heritage is taking us.

66

PEGGY HOLMAN

From Chaos to Coherence
The Emergence of Inspired Organizations and Enlightened Communities

The multitude which is not brought to act as a unity is confusion. The unity which has not its origin in the multitude is tyranny.

—Blaise Pascal

The processes in this book bring out the best in people as they improve their workplaces and communities. The chapters are filled with examples of people discovering:

- Wisdom within themselves,
- Connections to one another,
- Respect for people's differences,
- Power through sharing stories, and
- Capacities for bringing dreams to life.

What is going on? I believe that we are on the leading edge of a shift in how humans organize themselves to accomplish meaningful purpose. The underlying patterns of these processes pave the way for new, highly adaptive and cooperative forms of organization and community that interrupt the ordinary and inspire the extraordinary. Having tasted such mindful, heartful, soulful ways of working and living together, how can we operate this way all the time? In other words: *How can we seed, grow, and evolve inspired organizations and enlightened communities?*

After years of witnessing remarkable transitions from fear, hopelessness, and conflict to renewal, commitment, and action, I perceived a pattern that provides a pathway from chaos to coherence. It has dramatically shifted how I do this work. Two catalytic actions start the process:

- Welcoming disturbances using powerful, life-affirming questions
- Inviting the diverse mix of people who care to explore the unknown

We are just beginning to understand what keeps it growing and evolving.

Seeding the Ground for Inspiration and Enlightenment

Transformational change often begins with looming crisis, fear, conflict, and despair. Sometimes it starts from hope, dreams, desires, and possibilities. Either creates "disturbances" that indicate something new wants to emerge.

Welcoming disturbances may seem crazy or simply asking for chaos. Yet, turmoil is a gateway to creativity and innovation. Just as seeds root in rich, dark soil, so does transformational change require the darkness of the *unknown*. Being receptive to not knowing takes courage. Buddhist nun Pema Chödrön speaks eloquently of this:

> By not knowing, not hoping to know, and not acting like we know what's happening,
> we begin to access our inner strength.

Asking *unconditionally positive questions* at such times can overcome fear, uncertainty, and doubt—questions like these World Café classics: What question, if answered, would serve us all well in this situation? What could our community, our organization also be?

Such questions reframe problems as possibilities, focusing attention on what matters, and bound the territory to explore, reducing the feeling of losing control. They also provide a powerful attractor for inviting the diverse mix of people who care. The greater the diversity, the more divergent the exploration is likely to be. The wider the divergence, the greater the possibility something unexpected will emerge. Travel with me through a real-life example of what can happen:

> In an industry deeply in crisis, where conversations focus on what's broken, with no solutions in sight, 29 journalists from print, broadcast, and new media; mainstream and alternative—editors, writers, bloggers, publishers, educators, funders, community activists, and even a Wall Street analyst—came together drawn by the question: "What does it mean to do journalism that matters?"

Entering the unknown with appreciative questions liberates *individuals* and connects the *collective* to itself. Inviting people to *follow what has heart and meaning* elicits the unexpected. It is a remarkable gift, asking each person to look within his or her own place of mystery. As the journalists quickly discovered, through stories of individual passion, the exploration *diverges* in many directions:

Throughout their time together, the journalists set their own agenda, sharing stories, discovering the myriad interconnections among print, broadcast, and new media. They asked questions that stimulated new ideas—Is journalism without advertising possible? Our companies, ourselves, our journalism: Why are we so pissed off? What can the elders and newcomers in journalism learn from each other?

Paradoxically, as people follow their own call, a new sense of connection to each other surfaces. Differences seem less divisive, more beneficial. By collectively *reflecting* on learnings, the connections to each other grow stronger. And something more difficult to name begins to happen—the same conversations show up no matter the subject. These are the signals of *emergence*, recognizable because they resonate so clearly. People sense a connection to something that defies description, a feeling of being part of a larger whole. This felt sense of emergence has at its core the discovery that what is deeply *personal*, what means most to us individually is also *universal*. The discovery is palpable. The collective comes alive as new ideas and relationships emerge. We experience our *connection* to the "whole" filling us with excitement and energy, as a new coherent clarity emerges. The story continues:

Twenty-nine journalists found kindred spirits as they reconnected with the original impulse to make a difference that drew them to the field. They found others with the same longing for meaningful work; they saw an expanded role in the community, both as outsider witnesses and as storytellers and weavers of healthy communities. Together, they pictured a newsroom based in these ideas:

- *Journalists as conveners of conversations that inform and engage people*

- *Professional and citizen journalists working in partnership*

- *High-tech delivery (Web based, podcasting, etc.) with high-touch sourcing of stories from listening posts in ordinary places: cafés, libraries, schools*

- *An economic model based in local investment*

As they imagined a new way of working, the group came alive. A newspaper editor described the experience:

The conversations were exhilarating and breathtakingly fresh. A picture began to emerge of how the future of journalism might be transformed. Not only could we imagine a new model, we could describe it, and could see ourselves working in it.

Personal and collective meaning *converge* into *coherent, clear intentions*. New ideas, insights, leaders, and structures naturally emerge. *Action* is often swift and effective, focused by clear, collective intention. There is no need to "enroll" others because people enroll themselves, *taking responsibility for what they individually and collectively love*. The threads that connect people weave a powerful web of community. Ideas travel the web, sometimes achieving dramatic breakthroughs. Other times, changes surface months or years later, as they travel the indirect pathways of new network connections. Parenthetically, this network frequently extends to those who didn't attend the event, who "catch" the spirit of the experience, as our journalists discovered.

The ideas were magnetic, providing a glimpse into the emerging pattern of a new journalism and creating a foundation that has attracted others to join the effort. The next step of this adventure was conceived: bringing community leaders, journalists, media educators, and funders together to devise experiments in three communities—urban and rural, depressed and affluent. Months later, the 29 journalists continue communicating electronically, still connected by the power of their experience.

As figure 1 shows, this pattern of emergence moves individuals and the collective from chaos to coherence through:

> appreciative, compelling questions . . .
> that spark divergence into the unknown . . .
> as individuals follow their hearts and the collective reflects . . .
> to emerge connected in new ways that ignite innovative ideas . . .
> and converge into coherent, clear intentions and committed actions.

This pattern contains the seeds for new forms of organization and community.

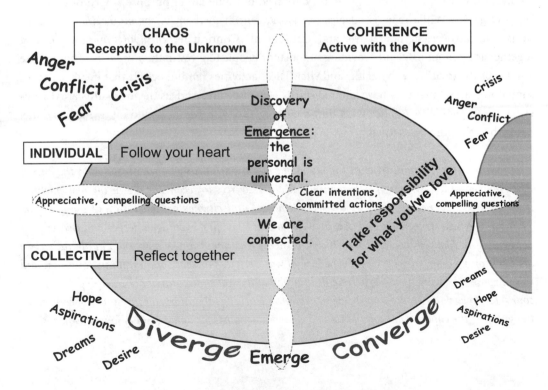

Figure 1. Emergence: Moving from Chaos to Coherence

Nourishing the Seeds of Inspired Organizations and Enlightened Communities

What causes these seeds to grow and evolve? The answer is oddly simple. Do it again! Better yet, do it continually. Ensure your focus not only attends to the visible outcomes—project ideas and plans, new teams, and agreements—but also nourishes the invisible web of community that generated those actions. In the long run, nurturing the human connections ensures ongoing generativity, the continual creation of new ideas, projects, and relationships. Having moved from chaos to coherence, new disturbances—conflicts and dreams—unquestionably arise. It is far easier to welcome disturbance when one knows one is in good company working toward shared dreams!

Shared inquiry into hopes and dreams increases the capacity to invite diversity, let go of answers, and step into the unknown. More equipped to hold dynamic tensions—short-term/long-term, individual/collective, profit/service—while staying connected to each other, inspiration and enlightenment become a way of being, not a destination. The more we embrace our differences, the more our capacity to recognize the opportunities inherent in what makes us uncomfortable grows. With practice, we become more willing, even enthusiastic, to take the vital step into the unknown.

It is the practice of caring for oneself, others, and the whole that weaves and sustains the web of connections. By supporting people in tuning in to personal meaning, sensing a heartfelt connection to each other, and feeling they are held by some larger purpose, a virtuous cycle of support grows. While many strategies can work, central to them is *communication* that connects—narrative rich, interactive, and transparent. Continually *clarifying purpose*, coming together as a *community*, and providing support for people to grow in their *capacity* to contribute also keeps the invisible web healthy and vital. These activities remind people that they are part of something larger, that they have kindred spirits who also care. And, as the journalists are discovering, when people care about what they are doing and with whom they do it, work gets done, even when the going gets tough.

With no formal infrastructure in place, some of the journalists who were inspired by the images that emerged of a new type of newsroom found the resources to reconvene and bring new partners into the mix. Six months later, 22 diverse journalists and citizens gathered around the question, "What is the next news room and how do we create it?" The first evening, a deeper and clearer purpose emerged, sparked by a citizen participant: "This isn't about a new newsroom at all; rather, we are envisioning a new news ecology." The insight was electric. The sense of community forged around this purpose is bearing fruit—experiments in urban and rural communities are emerging. By staying connected to each other, these experiments become a learning laboratory, a community of communities growing the capacity of professional and citizen journalists for a new kind of journalism.

THE CHALLENGE AND THE POTENTIAL OF EMERGENT PRACTICES

Perhaps the most common block to using emergent processes is that it is virtually impossible to know the specific forms outcomes will take. This is because emergence, by definition, involves the unknown. What reduces the risk and increases the likelihood of success is the clarity of intention guiding the work. This powerful combination—direction established with a question that focuses intention, coupled with openness to the unknown—creates a dynamic tension ripe for emergence. While it can be a leap of faith to believe great results come without defining the specific outcomes, if you want breakthroughs, a broad and deep delving into passion and purpose almost always far exceeds any predetermined outcomes. Those who ultimately choose this route often do so because they are stuck, but realize that continuing to act in the same way won't produce the fundamentally regenerative results they seek.

The Evolution of What Emerges

A group's diversity, an event's duration, and ongoing experience shape the nature of what unfolds (table 1). New ideas, relationships, and connections regularly form in short, homogeneous events. Two days and increased diversity can generate breakthrough ideas pursued by self-organized teams. Longer events often provide glimpses of the ongoing pattern of emergent leadership and structures. With multiple experiences, the pattern is internalized. Experiments frequently emerge in self-managed teams in organizations and citizen committees in communities. When embraced as an ongoing practice, people organize themselves following inspiration and commitment. Structures emerge to fit the context. New forms of governance are required when leaders are those who attract followers by taking responsibility for what they love.

Time and Diversity	What Emerges
Less than one day, limited diversity	Ideas and relationships (new connections)
At least 2 days	Special projects (temporary structures and leaders)
Long events (3–7 days)	Glimpses of emergent leadership and structures (temporary experiences of fluid form, fluent leadership)
Multiple experiences	Self-managed teams and committees (new structures, fluent leadership)
Ongoing pattern	Emergent organization/community and governance (fluid form, fluent leadership)

Table 1. The Evolution of Emergence

What Happens When Taking Responsibility for What One Loves Becomes the Norm?

When taking responsibility for what one loves becomes the norm, then the weave of the invisible web remains whole. People care for themselves, each other, and the whole. Individuals consistently follow what has heart and meaning. The collective regularly connects with itself by reflecting together, remembering the meaning and purpose that nourishes the web of community. The resulting coherence supports individuals and groups in taking responsibility for what they love. I think of coherence as "differentiated wholeness" because it exists when there is space for the individual and collective, the inner life and the outer life. Being our quirky, unique selves while staying connected replaces our current cultural tendencies toward conformity, isolation, and group think.

Many of us learned that to care for ourselves is selfish, that sacrifice and compromise are necessary for a working society. In practice, denying our own deep needs seems to generate a shallow egocentricity. People disassociate from a deeply fulfilling connection to themselves. Selfishness and greed result, as individuals and groups protect their own "interests." Society fragments. Feelings of scarcity surface. The web of connections disintegrates and the sense of wholeness is lost.

Contrast what happens when invited to ask oneself, "What is important to me? What do I care about so much that I am willing to take responsibility for it?" Internal attention shifts from ego to center—where head, heart, and spirit connect to guide us. When acting from our center, differences cease to be barriers and become gifts that attract new connections. There is a feeling of abundance, as differences are integrated into new, fuller understandings of ideas and relationships. Oversimplified "us versus them" positions are replaced by a richly nuanced inclusion of differences. A more elegant simplicity is found through a better understanding of the true complexity of our individual and collective distinctiveness. This is truly differentiated wholeness in action.

Leadership emerges everywhere. Individuals, guided by their heads and hearts, act as "free agents." They speak from their full voices. When that voice resonates with others, as if some universal truth were spoken, people follow. What is a leader after all, but someone who speaks a truth so compellingly it inspires others to join him or her? When this opportunity is widely available, a powerful and fluid field of leadership emerges in the collective.

When we collectively take responsibility for what we love, there is an unaccustomed openness in which our connections to each other form a "resonant network." In truth, we are always connected. When we act from inner connection, we open to each other, and that connection is visible. In this web of community, people are more alive and effective, sharing their gifts with each other. They easily find others who care about the same things they do. The tension between the needs of each individual and the needs of the collective dissipate. We are in coherence. If one voice is dissonant, it no longer fragments the group. Rather, with increased capacity to embrace differences, attractive, appreciative questions are framed and insights emerge that are integrated for the good of the whole.

When coherence is sustained, through continually tapping our sense of connection, the ripples are powerful. Newfound trust develops as breakthroughs in ideas, solutions, and relationships support both planned and emerging action. There is a greater willingness to be flexible. A virtuous cycle of ideas, connections, and actions feed into even more exciting ideas, connections, and actions. How might it resolve for the journalists? Beyond their gathering, what new possibilities were sparked by their time together? Here's an imagineering story of where it could lead:

During the three-day gathering of journalists, new connections were made and projects defined. As the community experiments take shape, what might they look like organizationally, how might they affect the communities in which they operate?

Imagine the morning news meeting convened in the local café, open to whoever wishes to participate. The content for Web, broadcast, and print for the day is selected as people reflect together on what best serves the community's needs. Stories are pursued by people taking responsibility for what they love:

- *A citizen journalist hears about a potential conflict between a social service agency and the people it serves. She recruits a professional journalist to investigate with her. Their first step is creating some powerful, appreciative questions to discover what is life-giving in the situation, so that the whole story is told.*

- *A high school student covers the local school board meeting as a community service project. The high school newspaper staff partners with professional journalists. Beginning with school and youth issues, as student skills increase, they cover broader community issues. And, of course, the growing population of young bloggers is engaged in all aspects of this community journalism work.*

- *A musician is listening and composing. He will travel to restaurants, cafés, and street corners singing the news of the day.*

- *A professional journalist has just turned in his series on an emerging community trend in cross-cultural cooperation. Before the new news operation joined the community, there was little interaction among different ethnic groups. As people from the different parts of town met through gatherings convened by the news organization, they got to know each other. They realized knowing more about each other's cultures would lead to greater trust and cooperation. It began with progressive dinners and sharing traditional foods. Now people are visiting each other's places of worship. They're even forming study circles to learn about each other's beliefs. Some were inspired to set up a blog, an online newsletter, and podcasts to increase their reach within and beyond the community.*

- *A graduate student is interviewing several activists, journalists, and politicians about the new movement in "action research journalism," in which investigative journalists team up with nonprofit advocacy and research groups to investigate corporate or governmental abuses of power. Confronting the officials involved with the potential exposé draws them into negotiations to correct their actions. Major deliberations with citizens and other stakeholders are under way to change the systems that make such abuse unattractive or unavoidable. Successful negotiations and deliberations become news stories of successful reform in which everyone wins. The would-be exposé becomes mere background material eclipsed by the narrative of positive change. Commentator Paul Hardey dubbed this growing phenomenon "appreciative democratic blackmail."*

One of the offshoots of action research journalism is that more officials are taking the initiative—before any investigation happens—to deal with difficult moral decisions proactively. They engage journalists in utilizing public dialogues, appreciative inquiries, and community deliberations to work out acceptable—and sometimes thrillingly creative—approaches that are widely reported and credited to the initiating officials.[1]

A feature of the news organization Web site is the "tip jar" button. Both citizen journalists and professional journalists benefit not only from feedback and interaction with their audience but feel acknowledged for a job well done.[2] It has also proven to be a great recruiting tool for attracting citizen journalists.

That afternoon, local journalists meet online with members of two other communities engaging in similar experiments. They've been approached by a new community that wishes to learn from their example. They discuss how to communicate the initial challenge of enticing people to become citizen journalists. After years of being a passive audience, it takes creativity and commitment for people to realize the benefits of getting involved.

The news organization has also just heard from a national broadcast news network that wants to explore a local/national partnership. As market share for national broadcast news continues eroding, networks have a new openness to learn from thriving community news operations. It is a long-awaited opportunity to scale local learning for the national stage.

That evening, the editor and interested news organization employees meet with the citizen oversight board, a self-selected group who come together monthly to ensure that the social, economic, and cultural needs of the community are met. Tonight, they discuss the upcoming annual review, inviting a randomly selected mix of citizens to provide feedback on how well the news organization is meeting the community's needs.

This annual event has worked so well that the local Citizens for a Better Community group is working with the town council and the news organization to convene a similar event for the community. They plan to randomly select 20 citizens for a weekend of facilitated conversation to produce a consensus statement about the state of the community. The journalists will cover the selection process, who these very different participants are (so the community can identify with them), and how they change during their dialogue. Their findings and public discussions will also be covered. With repetition and good coverage, they expect the process to become a powerful way for the community to see itself. Dreams and concerns are voiced in a coherent way that everyone—public officials, institutions, and the public itself—can engage.[3]

On the other side of town that same evening, a citizen journalist is covering a town meeting on waste disposal. With increased trust among the community's many ethnic groups, there is growing confidence that those who show up are acting in service to the whole. This has enabled people to follow the issues they care most about, knowing that others are doing the same on their behalf. This virtuous cycle of increasing trust and creative community engagement mediated by community journalism has attracted national recognition, and a national foundation has just informed the town that they have received an award as one of the most livable communities in the country.

What Worked?

The constant practice of recognizing the potential that is inherent in disturbances and embracing it through asking powerful, attractive questions becomes the conscious way of working. When an issue arises, someone takes responsibility to convene a gathering, inviting whoever cares to address it on behalf of the whole. There is growing confidence that when diverse people follow what has heart and meaning, when they embrace the dynamic tensions that emerge among them, and when they reflect collectively on what unfolds, then unexpected and innovative insights cohere into clear intentions and meaningful action.

My working definition of an inspired organization or enlightened community offers an answer to the often-asked but rarely answered question about transformation: "Change to what—what is it that we wish to become?" This is my answer: A system that consistently achieves what is most important to it, individually and collectively by . . .

> continually increasing its capacity for emergence through . . .
> people caring for themselves, each other, and the whole . . .
> in service to a meaningful purpose.

The practices, experience, and consciousness to do this are growing among us and around us. As more of us engage with the processes in this book, we can see this new way of being together clearly emerging as a vital trend. As the new century unfolds and the illusion of control continues to erode, this capacity for embracing dynamic tensions and stepping into the unknown will increasingly be recognized for its power to nurture emergence and self-organization—and thus it will grow. As this happens, the possibilities become truly limitless.

---

1. Thanks to Tom Atlee (cii@igc.org) for the "action research journalism" examples.

2. Thanks to Nancy Margulies (nm@montara.com) for this idea.

3. Thanks to Tom Atlee for this paragraph.

67

High-Leverage Ideas and Actions You Can Use to Shape the Future

History will be kind to me for I intend to write it.
—Winston Churchill

An organization or community that constantly scans the external environment and subsequently reacts to changes in it is exercising *passive adaptation*. For example, an electronics firm introduces a new product in reaction to a competitor's recent launch, or an inner-city group organizes protests in response to funding cuts for local city parks.

The concept of *active adaptation*, however, is quite different. It espouses that not only should an organization or community react to changes in its surroundings, but it should also be proactive in exerting influence on its external environment. For instance, a software company that seeks to increase the accessibility of computers to all people on the planet, or a town that hosts a planning session to accommodate the incoming biotechnology boom while simultaneously keeping traditional community values. In other words, don't just focus on making local changes; strive to make industry and global changes based on your actions.

This isn't just a chapter about my thoughts on what's coming up in the world so that you can react to it. This chapter provides some practical nuggets that you can use to shape it. Change agents who read the first edition lamented that since they never had the time to research practical change principles, they wanted some pragmatic takeaways. In response to reader feedback, here they are, summarizing key advice in a series of Top 10 lists. This chapter reflects my own personal experiences, and therefore my personal experiential biases on what works and doesn't.

It is by no means intended to be a complete treatment of the subject of change management. And since it's based on my experiences, it goes without saying that this does not necessarily reflect the views of my coeditors. I make some high-leverage recommendations that I have found on my change journey across a variety of industries and communities spanning five continents over 29 years of industry, community, and consulting experience.

Once you grasp some of the key principles and methods for effective change, two huge parts of your success will be attitude and persistence. Let's start with attitude. *Think you can have a positive impact on how your organization or community interacts with its external environment?* You likely can, if you follow some fundamental change principles. *Think you'll need some friends and colleagues to support your change ideas?* Probably. *Think that just a few concerned people can never make a dent in the status quo?* Think again. Anthropologist Margaret Mead, who has studied centuries-old civilizations across the globe, stated, "Never believe that a small group of caring people can't change the world. Indeed, it's the only thing that ever has."

However, a great attitude, wonderful idea, essential change principles, and knowledge of some proven large group methods will only get you so far. Persistence is necessary to drive your idea forward, and to convince others of its value. It can keep you going when others are saying you should give up. It can bring your idea back onto other people's radar screens after it has been wrongly dismissed. And persistence can help you, your company, your community, and perhaps even mankind by successfully bringing an idea to the fore that others had previously rejected, or not even dared to imagine.

One final note on your perceived ability to implement the changes you desire: Don't assume you need to have immense amounts of resources behind you. How many people and how large a budget did Gandhi have behind him before successfully freeing India from the 90-year rule of the British Empire? In 1976, when Steve Jobs sold his Volkswagen van and Steve Wozniak sold his programmable calculator to finance building the first ready-made personal computer in Jobs's garage, was it conceivable that they might change the way people store information, communicate, and calculate? Great things can and do start with a handful of people who have strong intentions—and often limited resources—to initiate a major change and the persistence to see it through.

This chapter is organized into five sections:

- Where People Are Missing the Boat Regarding Large-Scale Change

- High-Leverage Principles for Dramatic, Sustainable Change in the Future

- A Framework for a Multifront Approach to Effective Change

- Simple Quick-Hit Actions

- Moving Forward

Where People Are Missing the Boat Regarding Large-Scale Change

There are some common missteps that I've encountered when people are trying to achieve successful, sustainable change. While all these steps are well-intentioned, in my experience, they have caused serious problems because they've missed critical aspects of the bigger change puzzle. Table 1 lists ten common missteps I've encountered, their implications, and alternative recommendations.

Observation Causing Problems	Implication(s)	Consider . . .
1. Focusing on events as the sole mechanism of large-scale change	Not all change can be accomplished through large group methods. If day-to-day actions and policy changes don't support the effort, then it's unlikely significant, sustainable change will happen.	Pulling a combination of levers to achieve sustainable change in addition to large group methods, such as traditional organizational development practices like coaching, active two-way communications, and aligning formal appraisals and rewards with the change.
2. Getting everyone together in one room and calling it effective large-scale change	People's time may be wasted, consensus is difficult to reach, and people leave the session with a bad taste in their mouths for change.	Inviting only the people that really need to be there. Sometimes this means having representative members of the relevant system of interest that is changing (as with the Search Conference method). Other times, 100 percent participation may be required (as for restructuring events such as Participative Design Workshop).
3. Keeping the existing deep hierarchy	Long-lasting dramatic change will be difficult if the organization does not directly address collapsing a steep hierarchy. Otherwise, problems like slow decision making, turf protection, and entitlement mind-sets tend to persist.	Collapsing the hierarchy into semiautonomous high-performing teams and designing new ways for career advancement, such as job rotations, lateral skill-building assignments, and pay-for-skill compensation schemes.
4. Having a singular focus (hard or soft) on a method or set of methods used	Nonsustainability will ensue if only a "hard focus" (e.g., implementing quality tools) or a "soft focus" (e.g., Dialogue) is pursued.	Combining predominantly hard methods (such as Six Sigma) *and* soft methods (such as Dialogue) to result in dramatic, sustainable change.

Table 1. Ten Common Missteps in Achieving Change

Observation Causing Problems	Implication(s)	Consider . . .
5. Implementing nonsystemic change	Just focusing on one area of a problematic organization or community, such as customer feedback, will produce suboptimal results.	Launching a change program on multiple fronts, including processes, culture change, Human Resource practices, organizational structure, and technology use.
6. Avoiding vs. courting conflict	Opportunities to improve dramatically are foregone, often internal resentment builds, and people feel stifled, fearful of taking improvement steps.	Actively surfacing conflicting viewpoints for discussion in an environment of candor, as espoused by methods such as Action Review Cycle and Dialogue.
7. Summarily silencing dissenters	Ideas from outcast dissenters that may work in the future never make it to the discussion phase. Powerful grassroots leaders don't emerge.	Providing a forum for dissidents to have a voice (not necessarily one that must be followed).
8. Confusing alignment with agreement	If everyone on a team or large group believes they must agree 100 percent on an issue before moving on, the pace of change and resultant improvements will be agonizingly slow.	Explaining, at the start of a group activity, that alignment does not necessarily mean agreement, and that members who are aligned and committed to common goals will support each other moving the group forward on various issues, even if there may not be 100 percent agreement on a decision.
9. Failing to consider the power of internal collective experience brought to bear in planning and problem-solving sessions	Outside experts are brought in, who may or may not add value to the specific local issues faced. This can result in unnecessary delays, sapping of organizational initiative, and excessive reliance on outside resources.	Numerous studies and personal experience have shown that a collection of informed internal people, working collaboratively, often develop higher-quality strategies and solutions than outside experts.
10. Pushing through all large-scale organizational changes solely under the banner of leadership development	Though developing leaders is extremely important, I have seen far too many organizations assume that training many people in skills such as feedback, clear communication, and charismatic projection is sufficient to accomplish successful large-scale change.	Effective large-scale change has a body of knowledge, proven principles, and large group methods that can increase the likelihood of sustainable success. Learn them and use them to supplement leadership development training in intrapersonal and interpersonal skills.

High-Leverage Principles for Dramatic, Sustainable Change in the Future

With today's scarcity of time at work and home, leverage is the name of the game. This section contains principles I have seen that are extremely high-leverage—that is, a moderate amount of effort nets you a substantial benefit. My Top 10 list for what I've seen work across a wide variety of organizations, communities, and geographies is as follows:

PRINCIPLE 1: CHANGE THE OLD LEADERSHIP PARADIGM

Contemporary high-leverage leadership is not so much about having a powerful vision and disseminating it to others so that they can execute it. It's more like having people confront their own problems and then fostering the mobilization of resources to help them achieve their group-defined directions and goals. This is a critical perspective for implementing large-scale, complex changes. Be aware that changing old leadership paradigms is often easier said than done, requiring new training, mind-sets, behaviors, peer support groups, and job rotations to be as successful as possible.

PRINCIPLE 2: ENLIST SOME ALLIES IN ACHIEVING YOUR VISION

After becoming well versed in large-scale change principles and methods, there's a natural tendency to want to apply them immediately. Having witnessed them work just once or twice and seeing the sparks they ignite in people's motivation provides a compelling reason for you to move forward quickly in your organization or community. Just be sure you enlist a coalition of people who understand the theoretical base, and who share your ideas on how traditional approaches to change and leadership need to evolve. The Village People's warning of "No man does it all by himself" is applicable here for men as well as women leaders in the throes of implementing a new vision of effective large-scale change.

PRINCIPLE 3: ESTABLISH A CLEAR RESPONSIBILITY AND ACCOUNTABILITY SYSTEM

Organizations ranging from command-and-control to self-managed teams (and all along the continuum between) all benefit from clear definition of responsibilities and a system that shows poor performance in time to correct it. Having crystal clear answers to questions like "Who needs to be involved in this decision?" and "Specifically, what would that involvement look like?" contribute mightily to organizations and communities achieving even their most aggressive stretch goals.

PRINCIPLE 4: HAVE A GREAT STRATEGY, AND DESIGN A STRONG STRATEGY STRUCTURE CONNECTION TO IMPLEMENT IT

Get the right diversity of experience involved in planning the future. Ensure they address key areas such as product/service offerings, consumer needs, market segments addressed, external sourcing, and distribution channels. Keep in mind that more CEOs are fired for the poor execution of a strategy than for the inability to develop a good strategy. Once a strategy is well formulated using the appropriate diversity of experience, the odds of it being successfully implemented dramatically increase when there is a specific structure designed to support it (not just an adaptation of the current structure to implement the new strategy bullet points). For example, if the organization's new strategy calls for increased closeness to the customer, it would likely make sense to structure the organization into customer service teams instead of keeping a deep hierarchy that is functionally siloed.

PRINCIPLE 5: BUILD A HIGH-PERFORMANCE STRUCTURE

Organizational structures consisting of semiautonomous teams that set and monitor their own goals can create cultures of high commitment and extraordinary performance. Unfortunately, though many top leaders extol the virtues of teamwork in their organization, very few commit to having a formal organizational structure comprised of teams. Many organizations do a good job of resolving the dual nature of work (cross-functional process outcomes for customers and maintenance of functional expertise) through a matrix structure, though often managing a matrix structure is challenging and remains more art than science.

PRINCIPLE 6: CREATE OPPORTUNITIES FOR MIDDLE INTEGRATION

In the course of a large-scale change, or even the subsequent execution stage, middle managers can make or break the success of the change and its sustainability. It's important that the middle managers have an opportunity to gather—without their managers or direct reports—and discuss issues such as boss-subordinate relationships, cross-functional improvement opportunities, communication, interdepartmental handoffs, and people development issues.

PRINCIPLE 7: PRACTICE INTELLIGENT EMPOWERMENT

Identify which decisions might be pushed downward in an organization and accompany those with appropriate information, skills training, and rewards.

PRINCIPLE 8: INSTITUTE COLLECTIVE, GROUP ACCOUNTABILITY (NOT JUST INDIVIDUAL)

When a group of people is accountable for setting and achieving a goal, they have a cadre of built-in coaches, supporters, and coercers that increase the likelihood of achieving a goal. Yes, there is that old adage about "when everyone's responsible no one's responsible," but that argument doesn't hold true in an organization where groups set and monitor goals, and are collectively rewarded or punished based on outcomes.

PRINCIPLE 9: PAY FORMAL ATTENTION TO CULTURE

Culture is something that can and should be managed. This is true in organizations, communities, and nongovernmental organizations alike. Start by assessing culture, either with a formal tool or informal conversations. Then identify the major "from-to" areas, and methods to change ways of thinking and acting required to support the desired state. Take special note of any long-standing policies or practices that are ingrained in the organization and in people's minds.

PRINCIPLE 10: IMPLEMENT FORMAL AND INFORMAL PRACTICES TO COMPENSATE FOR THE NATURAL WEAKNESS OF A SELECTED ORGANIZATIONAL STRUCTURE

As mentioned earlier, the structure of an organization is critical to implementing a change and operating within the new parameters. Because design trade-offs must be made for any implemented structure, every organizational structure will have weaknesses that need to be addressed. For example, structures organized along functional expertise will have some cross-functional blind spots. Alternatively, structures organized by process will have people in teams whose technical skills may begin to atrophy as they focus more on process outputs than on maintaining their technical expertise. Well-planned structures acknowledge inherent weakness and design to strengthen the overall organizational framework. For example, in an organization structured along process lines, there would be "centers of excellence" that periodically meet to maintain skill sets and discuss important matters specific to those members who possess similar skills.

A Framework for a Multifront Approach to Effective Change

Research and personal experience have shown that approaching a large-scale change on multiple fronts drastically increases the likelihood of effective, sustainable change. The Performance Framework model (figure 1) has been used in organizations to plan, monitor, and adjust large-scale change activities for more than 15 years. This model helps leaders plan specific actions for key factors that accelerate sustainable change *and* impact organizational performance. While there is some applicability for communities, most of the model's historical use has been with organizations.

There are three major sections of the Performance Framework:

- *External Environment:* depicts what's happening outside the organization,
- *Six Performance Bases:* represent key performance factors that leaders can influence, and
- *The Energizing Core:* provides fuel for the desired changes.

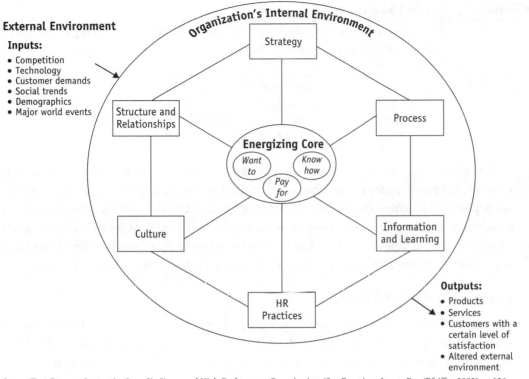

External Environment

Inputs:
- Competition
- Technology
- Customer demands
- Social trends
- Demographics
- Major world events

Outputs:
- Products
- Services
- Customers with a certain level of satisfaction
- Altered external environment

Source: Tom Devane, *Integrating Lean Six Sigma and High-Performance Organizations* (San Francisco: Jossey-Bass/Pfeiffer, 2003), p. 126. Reprinted with permission of John Wiley & Sons, Inc.

Figure 1. Performance Framework

Each of these segments is influenced by the others. Here are explanations of each performance factor "base":

Performance Factor	Brief Description
Strategy	The organization's direction, which delineates its offerings of products and services, markets served, and the channels they use to serve them.
Process	A collection of activities and decisions that produces an output for an internal or external customer. Processes often span departmental or group boundaries. Examples include new product development and order fulfillment.
Information and Learning	Information flow is critical to any improvement effort. It may be transactional information, such as the number of cars going through a toll booth, or it may be tacit knowledge, such as lessons learned from the last new product development launch.
Human Resources (HR) Practices	Policies and activities of the Human Resources function enable certain behaviors, and limit others. Examples include compensation, rewards, recognition, performance appraisals, training, retention, hiring, and firing.

Performance Factor	Brief Description
Culture	The shared beliefs and assumptions that determine behavior. Though typically acknowledged as important, culture is usually not actively managed in large-scale changes.
Structure and Relationships	The formal pattern of how people interact within an organization. Structure is shown by lines and boxes; relationships denote the informal behavior patterns such as degree of collaboration, nature of supervision, and role clarity.

Change leaders can use the Performance Framework as an upfront planning tool to develop action plans for each performance factor, as a statusing tool throughout the project, and as a communication tool to inform the organization about upcoming changes. Organizational performance assessments are often done as a group activity, usually by a cross-functional, multilevel group responsible for initiating the change. More information on using the Performance Framework and accompanying free organizational diagnostics can be found at www.LeanSixSigmaHPO.com.

Simple Quick-Hit Actions

Let's face it, the world often throws you a curve ball. Sometimes you may just step into a mess that another leader has created and you won't have the ability to start a large-scale change effort correctly from scratch. Or you might have a great idea on what needs to be done, but others aren't quite so sure, and these people have the authority to block your efforts. While taking all the steps necessary for successful large-scale change effort from scratch is always the best way to go, this may not be your only option. In the absence of having a perfect plan from the start, here are ten actions that change leaders—at any level—can do:

- Jump-start a change effort and peak interest in the minds and hearts of others who may not have considered a formal approach to change

- Demonstrate early benefits of paying attention to engaging people in change

- Revive a failing large-scale change effort, and then follow up with a larger-scale, more comprehensive approach to change

Even if an organization or community does not move beyond the simple suggestions listed below to a larger, more formal change approach, the following actions can yield significant short-term benefits. Of course, given a choice, to address large gaps, I usually would opt for a well-planned, large-scale approach to change that included large group methods, changes to the performance appraisal process, role modeling by key influencers, and measurement systems that draw attention to desired and achieved results. However, in life, you can't always get what you want, though, in the words of that important English philosopher, immortalized in song, "If you try sometimes, you might find, you get what you need."[1] Many of the tips in table 2 are used as a component within larger large-group-method events, but can also be helpful as stand-alone techniques for increased participation or better decisions.

Quick-Hit Tip	The Concept in Brief	Example
1. Collective assessments	When groups perform simple assessments—such as process mapping sessions or culture assessments—they can gain useful insights and also generate energy for closing the identified gaps between what they aspire to and what they currently are.	An investment bank mapped one of its major cross-functional processes and conducted (1) a culture assessment and (2) a customer satisfaction survey as part of a new focus on the customer effort. Gaps between what was needed and what they had were huge, and they mobilized teams to address the gaps.
2. Simple, visible accountability system	In a group setting, participants identify key interdepartmental handoffs, people publicly make personal performance commitments, establish metrics to assess future performance, and publicly monitor and improve.	Four departments involved in clinical trials at a pharmaceutical company developed a simple accountability system and reduced the time required for clinical trials by 42 percent. Clear definitions of who was to do what and when were instrumental in achieving and sustaining the gains.
3. Conduct a two–flip chart brainstorm and analysis of old behaviors and desired new behaviors	Most often, large-scale change requires specific behavior changes, but unfortunately no one clearly articulates the "from and to" behaviors in one place. Set up two flip charts ("Old Behaviors" and "New Behaviors") and convene a group of people to do just that.	A Midwestern manufacturer of control devices realized that to sustain the quality improvement gains, top management would need to change its behaviors. A cross-functional group from all four layers of the organization convened and brainstormed old and desired behaviors.
4. Build high-performance teams	Form and charter high-performance cross-functional teams to seize opportunities or solve thorny, long-standing problems.	A 200-person high-tech electronics assembly manufacturer chartered two high-performance teams using a Participative Design Workshop approach (chapter 43) to implement a Six Sigma quality improvement approach (chapter 47).

Table 2. Tips for Increased Participation or Better Decisions

Quick-Hit Tip	The Concept in Brief	Example
5. Conduct group-based (1) design, and (2) learning sessions	Getting groups of 15–50 people together to design or learn can yield significant technical benefits, as well as fuel emotional commitment for additional changes. Consider a simple method template, such as Open Space Technology (chapter 9) for quick-hit design and learning sessions.	The venue was a 2-day Open Space session of 120 users and implementation team members of a new enterprise-wide computing system called SAP. The priming question was, "What can SAP do to improve our business and our work lives?" In the session, participants explored system capabilities, user concerns, rapidly achievable benefits, and business process redesign requirements. In addition to addressing technical issues, this generated energy for the implementation.
6. Keep, drop, and create brainstorm	Set up three flip charts and have participants brainstorm what they want to keep, drop, or create when moving forward to address a particular issue.	Three Colorado mountain communities brainstormed and evaluated options to rebuild a shared teen community center that would be constructed the following year.
7. Get middle managers together	Since middle managers face common problems and can often influence the quality of interdepartmental handoffs, periodically convene them to discuss issues and suggestions (without their bosses or direct reports).	Managers at a disk storage assembly company met monthly to discuss issues they were facing regarding: their direct reports, their management, department interfaces, and people development.
8. Gather a concerned group and ask some simple, high-leverage questions that focus on expanding common ground, not differences	Pose questions to the collective group intelligence such as: What's our common ground, and how can we expand it? Can we agree to disagree on this point and move on without it affecting our outcome? What's missing?	During a planning conference for a community of New Age people and ex-military personnel, the issue of "all life is sacred" came up. There was quite a heated debate until the facilitator asked both parties if the issue could be placed on a "Disagree" list and they could move on. They did, and never returned to the issue because it did not impact the plans the community was making.

Table 2. Continued

Quick-Hit Tip	The Concept in Brief	Example
9. Conduct simple collective analysis, solution development, and implementation sessions	Conduct simple collective assessments using a process map and classification of activities as value-added or non–value-added. Also, analyze root cause, which may be as simple as asking *Why?* five times to get at a problem's underlying issues.	A consumer electronics company conducted several simple improvement projects. Their success and enthusiasm spread to other areas and started a process improvement wildfire resulting in plant operating cost reductions of 34 percent and cycle time improvements of 68 percent. The plant manager had to "control" enthusiasm with a prioritization team to ensure people weren't simultaneously on too many improvement teams.
10. Convene a Dialogue session, with no immediate decisions required	Get people together to discuss a topic of interest—often a "hot topic" politically—and agree that no decisions will be made in the meeting, only assumptions and interests will be explored, and action planning sessions will be conducted later.	Senior managers at a service company conducted a Dialogue session (chapter 7) to surface each other's assumptions, options, and objections to a planned upcoming benchmarking study.

Where to Now?

Below are some starter questions to help your organization or community get going or keep going on a successful, sustainable change effort. As we used to say in a Big 6 consulting firm where I worked many years ago, "Good answers cost 25 cents, good questions cost 25 dollars." Inflation has, of course, taken the cost of consulting advice far beyond that figure, but Czech poet Rainer Maria Rilke likewise echoes that sentiment and asserts, "It is not the answers that show us the way, but the questions." Therefore, this chapter closes with a set of questions for you to consider in your change journey. I suggest you pose them to a group of people who have, or who intend to seize authority to make things better in your organization or community. Have deep discussions about these questions in groups of concerned people. Sometimes such discussion sessions might result in decisions, sometimes they may not; either way, it's okay, as long as progress is made. Ultimately, implementation decisions will need to be made, but up front it can be best to surface assumptions, then establish common ground, gain general agreement, and codevelop action plans for moving forward. It may seem that there are simple yes/no answers to some of these questions, but honest dialogue will likely reveal varying degrees of agreement within your potential change group. It will be important to discuss these because your *group's* agreement on an answer will determine your specific path forward. The questions are:

1. Do we trust the skills of people who are not in the top organization or community ranks enough to involve them?

2. Do we trust people's intentions enough to give them a say in matters that affect them?

3. Do we trust that in many cases a diverse group of internal people can come up with exceptional recommendations?

4. Where might teams be used to enhance performance, and how do we ensure they'll be high-performance teams once they are formed?

5. Do we need to change the current culture to support the improvements we're seeking?

6. If top management distributes some decisions and "empowers" people, what organizational and process designs are needed to ensure things don't totally get out of control and go in the wrong direction for the long term?

7. What assistance criteria do we need to think about before we interview potential consultants to help us?

8. What's the appropriate line between accountability and freedom?

9. How do we ensure follow-up after a large group method?

10. What are strategic points where organizations and communities can advance their causes by organizing, conducting, and integrating various large-scale interventions like the ones presented in this book?

---

1. Mick Jagger.

68

STEVEN CADY

Hope for the Future
Working Together for a Better World

When we come together to play and be, we are truly ourselves. When we are truly ourselves, it is wonderful and when we act collectively in that wonder we do transformative work for our community and our world.

—Brad Colby

The sixty-one approaches described in this book are a testament to human ingenuity and the capacity to adapt. The founders and inventors of these methods share three important qualities. First, there is an unyielding commitment to creating a better world through engaging whole communities and organizations. Second, they believe that real wisdom, ingenuity, and know-how emerge through connecting all aspects of the system. Finally, each method is represented by a unique community of practice; advocates applying what they know while learning from, sharing with, and supporting each other. Some of these communities number in the tens of thousands and others are in the hundreds—it's a lot of people.

This chapter is a place for me to share reflections from my experience with all the authors who contributed to this book. It is almost indescribable to express how different I am after seeing the world through their eyes. As I listen to their stories, read their writings, learn their approaches, and reflect, I come away with hope . . . hope for our future.

Early versions of this chapter were sent to various people for review and comments. A dialogue ensued and their feedback has shaped the ideas presented here. The conversation has begun. My desire is to effectively convey the inspirational and practical message that is collectively emerging, an important message with implications for each and all of us.

Hope and Despair

The number of crises and conflicts around the world—economic instability, unemployment, resource scarcity, terrorism, wars, ethnic divisions, oppression, natural disasters, climate changes, and more—is cause for hopelessness and despair. And the research is clear: Focus on the negative aspects long enough and things will only get worse with more blame, shortsighted solutions, cascading harm, and a serious drain of human energy. Positive psychology compels one to ask an important question, "What do we want more of?"[1]

Explore amazing transformations around the world; you will find examples of resilience, innovation, healing, and abundant energy driven by people committed to seeing a better world. The practitioners of the methods in this book, the pioneers and masters, have dedicated much of their professional and personal lives to supporting organizations and communities in realizing their potential. Their stories are here to be witnessed. If we want more, then this is where we need to focus. Tom Atlee captured the spirit and challenge of our times when he wrote,

> I've come to believe that things are getting better and better and worse and worse, faster and faster, simultaneously. And so I've found myself bouncing back and forth between optimism and pessimism. "Things are going to work out well." Or: "There's going to be real disaster!" It's been really exhausting.[2]

Gather Together

Well then, what next? Professionals in our field are naturally focused *outward*. This makes sense when considering their passion and calling. I offer that it is time to focus *inward* as well. In addition to the work we do for a better world, consider what might be possible if we take care of our collective self.

Let's put to practice one of the most common principles to all the methods—get our whole system into a room.

Imagine a place, a house with an amazing garden. Someone is on the roof, shoring up shingles. Another is inside, working on the wiring. There are people in the garden: watering, planting, pruning. There is a fire being put out on the front porch, while out back, someone is putting up a hammock between two trees. Still others are inside, teaching people to play music and dance the samba. They all share something—a desire to support a vibrant place to live. Each person, while making a unique skillful contribution, knows there are others with the same desire. Yet, they really have not talked much, if at all.

In this place, overlooking a golden pond, is an open-air veranda next to a kitchen where the most sumptuous meal is being prepared. A cool breeze flows through the kitchen and veranda . . . a tantalizing aroma begins to swirl around the house, through the garden, and among the woods. The meal is placed out on the veranda. One by one, the people come from all over. They sit and eat . . . conversations begin, connections are made. As time passes, a few people wander together through one of the house's many archways. They sit together and talk, for the first time. Others meander through another archway. They play and share ideas. The conversation is fluid, kindred spirits gathering as a whole, forming small groups, fanning out through the archways like breath bringing oxygen to the lungs . . . back again to the whole, for more food, desserts, and nightcaps. They share, diverging and converging. On this day, in this moment, something different has occurred for each person and the whole place.

When we come together as a community of communities, it is possible to transcend consensus where ideas coalesce into a new coherence; in which people act, taking responsibility for what they love, based on the essential core that emerges. As we gather, it will be important to recognize our individuality and our unique contributions; and, in so doing, we can achieve more than we dreamed possible.

Our networked communities can be like a spinning flywheel. In the book *Good to Great*, Jim Collins describes a large disk about 30 feet in diameter, weighing 5,000 pounds, and mounted on an axle like a "spinning plate." Each push on the flywheel moves it forward an inch, then another inch, and finally a full rotation. Over time, the flywheel spins faster and faster until a breakthrough is reached. Momentum takes over. Collins states,

> Now suppose someone came along and asked, "what was the one big push that caused this thing to go so fast?" You wouldn't be able to answer; it's just a nonsensical question. Was it the first push? The second? The fifth? The hundredth? No! It was all of them added together in an overall accumulation of effort applied in a consistent direction. Some pushes may have been bigger than others, but any single heave—no matter how large—reflects a small fraction of the entire cumulative effect upon the flywheel.[3]

Each of the communities of practice has their own flywheel, and they can bring their momentum . . . their passion to the community of communities. Advances in the whole system methods and cutting-edge technology make such an assembly viable in a new way not possible just a few years ago. Today, practitioners are leveraging their methods by coming together with distance (online) and in-person (face-to-face) tools that facilitate synchronous and asynchronous collaboration (see table 1).[4] Consider, for example, Spirited Work at the Whidbey Institute. Corporate folks, educators, artists, writers, musicians, computer wizards, architects, chefs, builders, consultants, students, and preschoolers have been able to stay connected over a significant period of time. They meet in-person four times a year and incorporate online tools to support their work together on projects, research, or long-term conversations and learning.[5] This example demonstrates an important opportunity reminiscent of candlemakers of yore: Once the light bulb was created in 1879, things would never be the same again.[6] The candlemakers had a choice, whether they realized it or not . . . and so do we.

The collective flywheel can be spun; converging and diverging, adding to the momentum, creating sustainable follow-through. It is through the blending of on-line and in-person tech-

	In-Person	Distance
Synchronous	• Meetings • Conferences • Summits • Classes • Conversations • Flip charts • Hugs and high-fives	• Chat • Webinars • eClasses • Video and phone • Discussion boards • Brainstorm and vote
Asynchronous	• Voting—ballots • Surveys • Suggestion boxes • Group murals and visuals • Bulletin boards • Sign-up sheets • Notes	• Blogs (weblogs) • E-mails • Podcasts and vodcasts • Articles and books • Discussion boards • Surveys • Project lists • Libraries

Table 1. Ways to Spin Our Flywheel

nologies that "follow-through" transforms into "flow." Change becomes a constant source of positive energy supporting the natural rhythm of collaboration.[7]

In addition, we can use our expertise to advance the methods as we do our work. Yes, shape our future with our own tools, and in the process invent whole new ways to support system-wide change. How much further might we go? What might we as users uncover that will inform practice, research, and education? What is our common ground? Let's embrace the possibilities and spin the flywheel with two initiatives:

1. initiate a distance conversation supported with on-line tools, and

2. create a space for an in-person gathering (e.g., a conference).

As this book took shape, the notion of coming together emerged. In fall 2006, a group of people brought the various communities of practice together with online tools. This virtual conversation was designed to flow into an in-person conference at Bowling Green State University in Ohio set for March 2007, and to continue from there. Perhaps even as you read this book a networked community of practice will be making a difference.[8] What follows below are some initial convening questions and ideas to consider.

Claim Our Identity—Our Field

Our identity, in many ways, provides a focal point that enables greater coherence. There is not yet a consensus as to what to call this work. Labels like large-scale change, large group interventions, and large group methods, exist, but there is a wide-open space—a vacuum if you will—in the world that is yet to be claimed. It's time to claim that space intentionally, with the nimble vigor that embodies the wisdom of our field and founders. Marvin Weisbord wrote in his book *Productive Workplaces,*

> What are corporate alternatives to rain dancing on the crest of the third wave? . . . I want to describe an extremely promising method for getting whole systems in one room and focusing on the future—the search conference. Like so many workplace innovations, its origins are traceable to creative extensions of Kurt Lewin's insight that you steer a ship by feedback from outside, not by how the rudder, engines, or crew are behaving. Innovators in both Europe and the United States began extending Lewin's work to larger systems many years ago, responding to the psychological stresses of accelerating change.[9]

We need a clear label toward which to direct our attention and energy. Recent research looking at twenty years of publications in practitioner and scholarly periodicals has shown a consistent use of words like whole, system, change, and transformation.[10] In addition, the notion of the "whole system" is inclusive and connected to our historical roots as seen in Weisbord's words above.

Here are some questions to consider with regard to identity:

- What is our intention? Who are we?

- What space do we claim? How do we want to be recognized?

- What do we want to call ourselves? What label do we choose?

- What is the case that we can make for the value we add; a case that calls people to learn and practice the methods?

- Are we effectively communicating our work and our field to various audiences around the world?

- What is the connection between the value of our field and the public good?

- How can we craft an image that helps the world to find us and get our support?

- How can we make our work more accessible to more of the world?

- What else might you add?

Innovate New Ways

The approaches are evolving, as evidenced by the sheer increase in methods described in this second edition. Since the first edition, the authors have enhanced their approaches, both deepening their practice and inventing new applications. There is a spirit of innovation in the air. Edie Seashore describes how our future can be seen through our invention of new methods and ways for change.[11] And, as we innovate, Kathie Dannemiller[12] and Billie Alban[13] encourage us to build on the shoulders of those who have come before us. Together, they are imploring us to leap forward by taking the methods to new places and embracing new ways of thinking and being.

Consider the following questions:

- What have we learned thus far . . . what do we know?

- What are we yearning to know more about?

- What does the world need right now and what can we innovate to better serve those needs? What can be anticipated?

- What is emerging as our methods take communities and organizations to new heights?

- What happens next when an organization or community embraces the methods, embodies its fundamentals, and develops an advanced sophistication?

- How can we share our learning so that we can accelerate the development of robust approaches?

- How might we blend our in-person practices with online technologies?

- What else might you add?

Advance Theory and Research

There is emerging evidence to support the validity of whole system change methods. One challenge is that the approaches tend to draw from diverse and esoteric domains like small groups, chaos, quantum physics, psychology, biology, education, anthropology, organizational behavior, marketing, theater, leadership, urban planning, sociology, therapy, music, religion, organizational design, art, economics, spirituality, strategic planning, and more. Christopher Worley and Ann Feyerherm conducted interviews with pioneers in the field of organization development and found that

> the most frequently mentioned theme was that the field needed to avoid getting trapped into a reliance on fads and techniques. Almost half of the comments were derisive in tone, including "less prescriptive, faddish people not knowing what they are doing" and "less jumping on every trendy notion that comes along." In addition, this theme also included admonitions to continue using classic design skills and traditional (but effective) processes.[14]

We have such a rich setting for conducting research and developing theory. Through interdisciplinary scholarship we can develop a rigorous research agenda that not only validates what we know, it can provide the impetus for something new in a way that pleasantly surprises a few people.

When considering research and theory, how can we . . .

- gather together the existing knowledge so that we have a comprehensive view of the current state of the research and theory for our field?

- propose intellectually compelling questions?

- build a unifying theory? Is it even possible?

- develop the necessary skills to conduct research?

- use appropriate methods for the research questions we ask?

- make a strong case for the robust nature of methods through encouraging research and theory development as critical to our field?

- differentiate effective methods from fads or gimmicks?

- craft a theory that lends itself to a practice-oriented research agenda?

- What else might you add?

Educate—Educate—Educate

Learning to practice the methods is much more than an intellectual or cognitive exercise. It is a whole "get it in your bones" experience and a key component of a thriving community of practice. As we attract more and more people to this work, they yearn to learn. This can be seen with students—from those beginning their career to those who have been working for many years. They get excited by the possibilities and ask, How can I learn more? Where do I go? What is the best way to gain experience? Who do I talk to? Learning is also important for people living the change. For example, Dick and Emily Axelrod make a case with Collaborative Loops for developing internal capability so that people in the organizations and communities can design their own change process. The key feature of the methods is the focus on engagement principles and less on specific techniques.[15] Such a shift in focus can be seen among many of the methods that exist today.

Some possibilities to consider are:

- What is the best way to tap into the wisdom of the masters and benefit from their expertise?

- What are the most effective learning methods, course designs, and curricula structure for developing competencies?

- How might we use the principles of the methods in the design of curricula and other educational initiatives?

- What role can distance learning play?

- How can mentoring, and other models such as apprenticeship, support learning?

- What about ensuring quality and accountability (e.g., certification, college courses, training, research)?

- How might we support curriculum in K–12 and higher education?

- How can we get this body of knowledge and practice into core curricula such as business, organization development, human resource management, educational leadership, urban planning, political science, law, communication, educational leadership, and management?

- What else might you add?

The Nexus

The ideas and questions posed highlight three perspectives or "hats": those of the practitioner, researcher, and educator. Some people wear one or two of the hats, while others wear all three. Widen the circle. There is also a role for a leader, an activist or change agent that is different from the three hats mentioned. Broaden the circle further to include diverse fields and applications, then go broader still.

One way to think of the intersection is as the scholarship of engagement.[16] True scholarship brings the three main perspectives together to address relevant world issues that contribute to the public good. Interestingly enough, Action Research was an early departure from the expert model that has dominated consulting and academia. Kurt Lewin advocated a partnership among this intersection in order to create new knowledge by experimenting with how to bring about the changes most desired.[17]

Some intersecting questions to consider are:

- What is the community of communities looking to accomplish?

- How can we ask relevant and significant questions collectively?

- How do the perspectives intersect?

- What are ways to ensure that our aims are realistic?

- How can this intersection guide our future work?

- What new possibilities are emerging from our shared experience?

- What criteria shall we use to assess the impact of our methods?

- In what ways have the intersections gone through changes together, informing each other "real-time" along the change journey?

- How can we articulate and use what we are learning and developing together?

- What else might you add?

A Call to Action

We have a unique opportunity and an obligation to create more coherence in order to facilitate progress. If you have been to various conferences, workshops, and symposiums on the change related subjects, you can appreciate how comfortable practitioners and scholars tend to be with keeping things "open-ended." It is time that we take the very principles and practices used to guide our work and apply them to our field.

Several people, wearing the different hats, were asked to review this chapter and provide their advice. The box in this section provides selected quotes that capture the essence of the conversation that has begun. In reading their advice and listening to observations, something subtle emerges. There is concern and consternation, juxtaposed with enthusiasm and inspiration. Regardless, the comments have an important undertone of urgency—a call to action. It's *not* about withdrawing or being nice; it's about "putting a stake in the ground." Wayne Dyer makes an observation that can be related to this sentiment, "change the way you look at things, and the things you look at change."[18] His words are compelling. STOP . . . BREATHE . . . take a look at how we think, how we decide what we want, and what we do to get there. Consider the following adaptation of his words:

If we want to change the world, then we need to change the way we are changing.

The Conversation Has Begun

This virtual conversation is compiled from e-mail exchanges I received just before this chapter went to composition.

Is it really a field? More like an aggregate, a collection, at the moment. It's a bit difficult to brand a disparate collection. A riotous mob is also a large group and they use time honoured methods. The language is wrong and only with good cooperation will a genuine field be developed. I would tap into the power of the collective to identify commonalities and new approaches to meet the challenges of the future.

—Merrelyn Emery[19]

We do not have the time to ponder the questions in longitudinal studies . . . we need purposeful action in service of a different future now. Can you see us letting go of the investment we have in our models to come up with powerful children born of good but not GREAT parents? We each have pieces of the puzzle . . . let's work on the jigsaw.

—Stewart Levine[20]

Embedding practitioner-friendly research methods into the field is another way of advancing the work. I, too, believe that we have much to learn from those who are practitioners, and that will require that practitioners (me included) use some agreed-upon rigor in reflecting on our practice and learning from our work.

—Royce Holladay[21]

I think one interesting issue is where there is cross-over between such things as blended learning, moving between synch/in-person and asynch/distance (using the best of two different models). Or, consider other modality issues: One-to-one or one-to-many, or many-to-many (or even many-to-one, as in traditional research surveys). Also what is the intended use? Exchange of information, education (presentation and group learning), group motivation, research, collective intelligence, play, workflow, planning, change of worldview?

—Jon Kennedy[22]

It's a shame that we have not done more research. Open Space has been used in excess of 60,000 times and 120 countries around the world. If we could collaborate with researchers to explore the concepts of self-emerging systems, that would be great!

—Harrison Owen[23]

It truly takes practice and time out to allow for cycles of reflection and action to move in a positive way forward in building the most dynamic relationships with appreciative intent. Allow yourself to dream and you will discover that destiny is yours to design. This leads to many possible ways of knowing and seeing the world which will impact what the communities can create together.

—Jackie Stavros[24]

Connecting the Intersection highlights the perspectives—the practitioner, leader, researcher and educator hats. Unfortunately, at gatherings of our colleagues people tend to gather only under only one tent. We need to encourage more "web-like" thinking where there is a recognition of the other hats AND acknowledgment that it is perfectly permissible to validate the OTHER hats. We live in a world of abundance. There need not be a hoarder's mentality. Also, it's OK to be vulnerable and admit the educational (or the other hats) are not the panacea. It's much like seeking a surgical consult—the surgeon will recommend cutting. A holistic healer will recommend another type of healing approach. My training is as a trial lawyer. As a practicing attorney, I tried cases. I became a more effective attorney when I embraced the fields of negotiation and alternative dispute resolution. We need to do the same as change agents. Embrace the differences and incorporate the best of the interdisciplinary approaches.

—Steven N. Pyser[25]

The space for us to claim is our incongruence with natural laws. It took humanity's mistakes to reveal that space and we now, today, can see too clearly the consequences of continuing a path askew.

—Steven Mercer[26]

> *I'd be curious to know the common ground of all the communities, that is the propositions that every person—100%—would say "yes" to. Without such a statement of principles and goals shared by all, there can be no "field."*
>
> —Marvin Weisbord[27]
>
> *It is most important to start our conversations with the larger context—"the world as client." We need to make sure we include people from around the world in these discussions. Then, we can consider things like shared principles, research possibilities, the role of technology, and our contribution to the challenges facing the world today.*
>
> —Barbara Bunker and Billie Alban[28]

A different kind of leadership is necessary to bring the field together. It is a collective action in which together we can be that "strange attractor" that broadens the web of connections around what is possible when people are engaged. Something special happening in our world and the more we advance our field, the more the world will benefit. We can do it . . . and we can do it now.

The Nexus for Change

Join the journey. Come learn, share, and explore with other like-minded people.
To get connected, go to: www.nexusforchange.org or www.thechangehandbook.com.

In addition to the people mentioned above that provided invaluable guidance and quotes for this chapter, I would like to thank Dick Axelrod, Juanita Brown, Margaret Casarez, Amanda Day, Jenna Encheff, John Hine, Cheryl Honey, Warren Lieberman, David Sibbet, Kate Siner, Christine Valenza, and Chris Worley.

1. J. E. Gillham, ed., *The Science of Optimism and Hope: Research Essays in Honor of Martin E. P. Seligman* (Radnor, PA: Templeton Foundation Press, 2000). See also M.E.P. Seligman, *Authentic Happiness: Using the New Positive Psychology to Realize Your Potential for Lasting Fulfillment* (New York: Free Press, 2002).

2. Tom Atlee, Co-Intelligence Institute, www.co-intelligence.org/crisis_fatigue.html.

3. Jim Collins, *Good to Great: Why Some Companies Make the Leap . . . and Others Don't* (New York: HarperCollins, 2001), 165.

4. Jon Kennedy and Brian King provided valuable insight for the table to ensure it represented the various tools and technologies available, July 2006.

5. See chapter 9 (Open Space Technology) for more on the Spirited Work example. See also chapter 59 (Online Environments for Supporting Change) for more information on the possibilities for blending online with in-person approaches.

6. Ralph and Terry Kovel, "Light Bulb Set Lamp Designers Free," *The News & Observer* [Raleigh-Durham, NC], July 29, 2006, 12E.

7. Marie Miyashiro, e-mail exchange with Steven Cady, July 2006. See chapter 8 (Integrated Clarity).

8. Find out more at www.thechangehandbook.com.

9. Marvin R. Weisbord, "Inventing the Future: Search Strategies for Whole Systems Improvement," *Productive Workplaces: Organizing and Managing for Dignity, Meaning, and Community* (San Francisco: Jossey-Bass, 1987), 281–282. See also Weisbord's *Productive Workplaces Revisited: Dignity, Meaning, and Community in the 21st Century* (San Francisco: Jossey-Bass, 2004).

10. Steven H. Cady and Lisa Hardalupas, "A Lexicon for Organizational Change: Examining the Use of Language in Popular, Practitioner, and Scholar Periodicals," *Journal of Applied Business Research* 15, no. 4 (1999): 81–94.

11. Edith W. Seashore, closing plenary at Organization Development Network (ODN) Annual Conference, Atlanta, GA, 2000.

12. Kathie Dannemiller, chapter 11 (Whole-Scale Change).

13. Billie T. Alban and John J. Scherer, "On the Shoulders of Giants: The Origins of OD," in *Practicing Organization Development: A Guide for Consultants*, 2nd ed., edited by William J. Rothwell and Roland Sullivan (Hoboken, NJ: Pfeiffer, John Wiley & Sons, Inc., 2006).

14. Christopher G. Worley and Ann E. Feyerherm, "Reflections on the Future of Organization Development," *Journal of Applied Behavioral Science* 39, no. 1 (March 2003): 103.

15. See chapter 6 (Collaborative Loops).

16. To find out more, go to www.scholarshipofengagement.org.

17. Marvin Weisbord, e-mail exchange with Steven Cady, July 2006. See also Steven Cady, "A DIET for Action Research," *Organization Development Journal* 18, no. 4 (Winter 2000): 79–93.

18. Wayne Dyer, *The Power of Intention* (Carlsbad, CA: Hay House, 2004), back jacket cover copy.

19. See also chapters 22 (Evolutions of Open Systems Theory) and 35 (Search Conference).

20. See also chapter 52 (The Cycle of Resolution).

21. See also chapter 20 (Human Systems Dynamics).

22. Jon Kennedy, e-mail exchange with Steven Cady, July 2006.

23. Harrison Owen, e-mail exchange with Steven Cady, July 2006.

24. See also J. Stavros and C. Torres, *Dynamic Relationships Unleashing the Power of Appreciative Inquiry in Daily Living* (Chagrin, OH: Taos Institute, 2005).

25. See also chapter 31 (Web Lab).

26. Steven Mercer, e-mail exchange with Steven Cady, July 2006.

27. See also chapter 33 (Future Search).

28. Barbara Bunker and Billie Alban, e-mail exchange with Steven Cady, July 2006.

Part IV: Quick Summaries

The secret of Zen is just two words: not always so.
—Shunryu Suzuki Roshi

The Quick Summaries provide a one-page-per-method look at key information, including:

- An image of the process
- Purpose
- Outcomes
- When to Use
- When Not to Use
- Number of Participants
- Types of Participants
- Typical Duration
- Brief Example
- Historical Context
- For More Information

The Quick Summaries are organized alphabetically. We've indicated whether the chapter on the process is in-depth or a thumbnail, the overarching purpose of the method (i.e., Adaptable, Planning, Structuring, Improving, Supportive), the chapter number, and its page number.

Action Learning

PURPOSE:

To develop the practices that advance organizational strategy in the midst of complexity by developing essential skills for thinking creatively, coaching through questioning, and finding leverage points for action.

OUTCOMES:

- Increased ability to accomplish strategic change
- Improved cross-functional teamwork
- More strategic and focused leadership
- Ability to address complex challenges

WHEN TO USE:

- Changes in strategy require new leadership behaviors
- Teams are undertaking long, complex projects
- Cross-functional teamwork needs strengthening
- Strategic thinking is needed throughout the organization

WHEN NOT TO USE:

- For refining established processes, roles, and structures
- When the right people are not on the team
- For doing basic problem solving
- Cannot commit to meet over the length of the cycle

NUMBER OF PARTICIPANTS:

- Peer Coaching group: 3–10 people
- Team Learning groups: 3–30 people

TYPES OF PARTICIPANTS:

- Peers from different functional areas
- Leadership teams
- Professionals with similar work
- Intact teams responsible for strategic change

TYPICAL DURATION:

- Orientation: 4–16 hours
- Sessions: Over 6–12 months
- Follow-up: Optional custom design

BRIEF EXAMPLE:

Canadian Tire, one of Canada's most shopped retailers, used Action Learning to create culture change in its IT organization. Ninety-one percent of participants said it increased cross-functional teamwork and broke down silos. The IT organization became more performance oriented and aligned to business priorities.

HISTORICAL CONTEXT:

The Quakers have used a similar method (Clearness Committee) for more than 400 years. Reginald Revans pioneered Action Learning groups with organizations beginning in the 1940s.

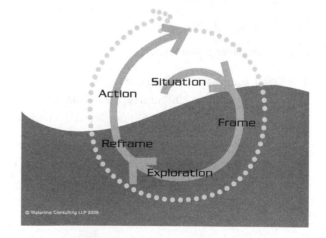

For More Information: Waterline Consulting, www.waterlineconsulting.com

Action Review Cycle/AAR

Thumbnail
Improving Method
Chapter 49
Page 484

PURPOSE:
To continually raise the bar on performance, build a culture of accountability, and sustain success in a changing environment.

OUTCOMES:
- Actionable knowledge against key performance measures
- Confident yet humble leaders, empowered teams
- Leadership, learning, and execution are integrated in the way work is done every day
- An agile organization that embraces change

WHEN TO USE:
- Where there are high stakes and/or complexity of interdependent actions and decision-making
- As a practical way to build or sustain a learning culture
- Built into existing operating cycles

WHEN NOT TO USE:
- As a one-time, backward-looking postmortem
- With a team or "panel" who will not be expected to take action—focusing After Action Reviews (AARs) on creating reports or recommendations for others not present undermines the ability to use it as a living practice

NUMBER OF PARTICIPANTS:
- 5–15 in a session (sessions can be cascaded to involve entire organization)

TYPES OF PARTICIPANTS:
- Teams and leaders with direct responsibility for an action or mission. Interdependent teams can do Before Action Reviews (BARs) and AARs together.

TYPICAL DURATION:
- Preparation: Collect performance data during action
- Depending on scope and skill: BAR: 15 minutes–2 hours; AAR: 15 minutes–3 hours
- Follow-up is continuous—this is a cycle

BRIEF EXAMPLE:
For Jeff Clanon of the Society of Organizational Learning, the ARC was a mechanism to get organizational members engaged in collectively taking responsibility for what happened in their quarterly meetings and acting on the implications of their discussions going forward. Using the BAR/AAR contributed to a step change in the way the groups coalesced in the last two years. Interactions became more grounded and disciplined, and embody what the organization preaches.

HISTORICAL CONTEXT:
Originated in 1981 at the U.S. Army's National Training Center, has evolved over 25 years. World's Best Practitioners: NTC Opposing Force (11th ACR).

Ancient Wisdom Council

Thumbnail
Adaptable Method
Chapter 13
Page 195

PURPOSE:
To awaken "whole" thinking using a holistic and collaborative process for deeper wisdom.

OUTCOMES:
- Enhances cohesion and energetic motivation
- Increases use of people resources
- Develops balanced and unbiased perspectives
- Clears blocked communication
- Builds trust and deepens relationships

WHEN TO USE:
- For complex issues that require innovation
- To slow down the cycle of act and react
- When dominant voices close out valuable contributions
- To make decisions that affect the collective's longevity
- To bring a more holistic view when many biases are present

WHEN NOT TO USE:
- Leadership is unwilling to cocreate
- Decisions have already been made
- The climate is one of mistrust and disrespect
- No trained facilitator is present

NUMBER OF PARTICIPANTS:
- 1–500
- 16 is ideal; one man and one woman in each of eight perspectives
- Can include a group in each perspective acting as a society or be used within oneself

TYPES OF PARTICIPANTS:
- Any team, community group, or board
- All those affected by decisions

TYPICAL DURATION:
- Preparation: 2–5 days
- Wisdom Council: 2–5 days
- Follow-up: 1–3 months
- Ongoing: 0.5 day monthly

BRIEF EXAMPLE:
World Business Academy called a meeting to bring together the diversity of issues among 80+ members. Over four days, using the Ancient Wisdom Council, the people worked through 60+ issues to become a cohesive group. The WBA adopted the Ancient Wisdom Council for their decision-making process, resulting in a sharp increase in morale, a deeper connection, and a renewed vision in the organization.

HISTORICAL CONTEXT:
Deeply rooted in Native American and pre-Mayan tribal cultures and made relevant to our current culture by WindEagle and RainbowHawk Kinney-Linton in 1987.

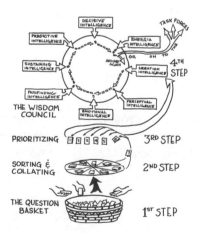

For More Information: Ehama Institute, www.ehama.org

Appreciative Inquiry

In-depth
Adaptable Method
Chapter 5
Page 73

PURPOSE:

To enable full-voice appreciative participation that taps the organization's positive change core and inspires collaborative action that serves the whole system.

OUTCOMES:

- Fundamental shift toward cooperation, equality of voice, and high participation
- A positive revolution, inquiry, and improvisational learning as daily practices
- Focus on life-giving forces—socially, financially, and ecologically

WHEN TO USE:

- To create a positive revolution
- To enhance strategic cooperation overcoming conflict, competition
- To catalyze whole system culture change
- To facilitate high-participation planning
- To mobilize global organization design and development
- To integrate multiple initiatives into a focused whole system effort
- To support large-scale mergers and acquisitions

WHEN NOT TO USE:

- If you are getting the results you desire
- When lacking commitment to a positive approach to change

NUMBER OF PARTICIPANTS:

- 20–2,000 involved in interviews, large-scale meetings, and collaborative actions

TYPES OF PARTICIPANTS:

- Internal and external stakeholders who hold images and tell stories about the organization

TYPICAL DURATION:

- Preparation: Work begins with the first question asked
- Process: 1 day–many months in nonconference format
- Appreciative Inquiry (AI) Summit: 4–6 days
- Total Transition: 3 months–1 year

BRIEF EXAMPLE:

Nutrimental Brazil closed the food processing plant for five days and invited 700 people to an AI Summit resulting in full-voice commitment to a renewed strategic plan and a 300 percent increase in sales within three months. The company chose to meet as a large group twice a year to ensure progress on the strategic plan.

HISTORICAL CONTEXT:

Created in 1987 by David Cooperrider and Suresh Srivastva, colleagues at Case Western Reserve University and the Taos Institute. Theory: Social Construction, Anticipatory Imagery Theory, and Narrative Theory.

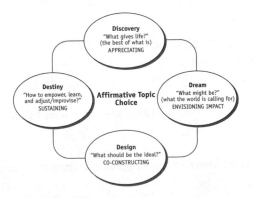

For More Information: Appreciative Inquiry Commons, http://ai.cwru.edu

Appreciative Inquiry Summit

Thumbnail
Adaptable Method
Chapter 14
Page 201

PURPOSE:

To accelerate positive change in organizations and communities by involving a broad range of internal and external stakeholders in the change process in real time.

OUTCOMES:

- Energizes the organization by putting the focus on strengths and potentials (rather than deficits and deficiencies)
- Generates innovation by connecting people in new configurations around promising ideas
- Builds leadership at all levels by involving everyone in envisioning, designing, and implementing change

WHEN TO USE:

- When you want to engage people, capitalize on their best thinking, and mobilize the entire organization quickly around a strategic change agenda

WHEN NOT TO USE:

- When leaders are not committed to full engagement, positive dialogue, and innovation throughout the organization

NUMBER OF PARTICIPANTS:

- 30–3,000 people, more using online technology

TYPES OF PARTICIPANTS:

- Ideally, every member of the system (e.g., internal or external stakeholders, multifunction, entire value chain)

TYPICAL DURATION:

- Planning: 2–6 months
- Conducting: 3–5 days
- Follow-up: 2 months–1 year; strategies and organization designs are altered for years to come

BRIEF EXAMPLE:

Since 2000, Roadway Express has held close to 40 summits across the organization to engage the workforce, improve margins, create service innovations, launch new strategies, and consolidate its merger with Yellow Corporation. The process has energized the workforce, produced millions of dollars of cost savings, and generated millions more in new revenues.

HISTORICAL CONTEXT:

Created in the early 1990s by Frank Barrett, John Carter, David Cooperrider, Ron Fry, Jim Ludema, Suresh Srivastva, Jane Watkins, Diana Whitney, and others at Case Western Reserve University; early roots in the work of Lewin, Homans, Bion, Von Bertalanffy, Emery and Trist, Berger and Luckmann, and Paulo Freire. More recent influences include Ken and Mary Gergen, Cooperrider and Srivastva, Weisbord, Owen, Dannemiller, and works from positive psychology and positive organizational scholarship.

For More Information: Appreciative Inquiry Commons, http://ai.cwru.edu

Balanced Scorecard

Thumbnail
Improving Method
Chapter 50
Page 490

PURPOSE:
To align everyone with financial and nonfinancial performance measures relevant to strategy implementation.

OUTCOMES:
- People think in terms of multiple types of organizational objectives that range from financial goals to people development goals
- Local behavior is driven by the overall strategy and relationships with other groups
- The strategic plan is shaped by feedback from all parts of the organization

WHEN TO USE:
- When you want people all working toward the same balanced objectives that include financial, customer, process, learning, and innovation perspectives.

WHEN NOT TO USE:
- When the organization's leadership desires a singular focus that is used to manage the organization, for example, managing only to financial goals.

NUMBER OF PARTICIPANTS:
- Up to 20 in the initial direction-setting session, followed by the entire organization as they (a) align local activities to the strategy and (b) contribute to the strategy based on customer and internal organizational feedback

TYPES OF PARTICIPANTS:
- All people in the organization participate in local goal setting, measurement, continuous improvement, and providing feedback for the next iteration of strategic planning

TYPICAL DURATION:
- Prework: 2–6 weeks
- Planning sessions: 1–3 days
- Local goal setting and feedback on the previous strategy and goals: 5 days–2 months, depending on the size of the organization
- Follow-up: 2–4 months

BRIEF EXAMPLE:
A biopharmaceutical company used the Balanced Scorecard to establish a portfolio of high-leverage goals to successfully move the company from a research and development mode to a commercial mode. Within 14 months, the company captured 63 percent of the market share.

HISTORICAL CONTEXT:
Created in the early 1990s by Robert Kaplan and David Norton.

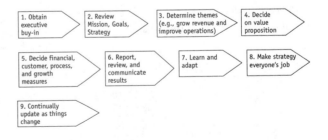

For More Information: The Balanced Scorecard Institute, www.balancedscorecard.org

Civic Engagement

Thumbnail
Improving Method
Chapter 51
Page 496

PURPOSE:

To shift the language of civic debate to questions that build accountability and commitment for a restored and reconciled community.

OUTCOMES:
- Shifts perspective to accountability and commitment belonging to the individuals in the community

WHEN TO USE:
- When a group wants to create an alternative and intentional future through accountability and commitment

WHEN NOT TO USE:
- When patriarchy is the dominant and preferred method for engagement
- When individuals can achieve the same outcomes as the group

NUMBER OF PARTICIPANTS:
- 15–200

TYPES OF PARTICIPANTS:
- Internal and external stakeholders (all levels of an organization)—volunteers for the cause!

TYPICAL DURATION:
- Preparation: 1 week
- Process: 2 weeks
- Follow-up: 1 week–6 months

BRIEF EXAMPLE:

Youth Dialogue: Adults (30+) and youth (under 25) were invited into conversations to establish an ongoing dialogue. Youth were required to attend (draftees). The questions, such as "What don't adults get about you?" made the most difference between the two groups. Breakthrough listening occurred. The result: The context shifted how adults see, hear, and respond to youth. The youth stopped posturing defensively and got "real." A diverse group made contact in a way they didn't think possible. The outcome: the group made a commitment to continue the conversation.

HISTORICAL CONTEXT:

Created in 1995, amended in 1999 and again in 2003 by Peter Block. This work is based on the works of Robert Putnam, John McKnight, and Peter Block.

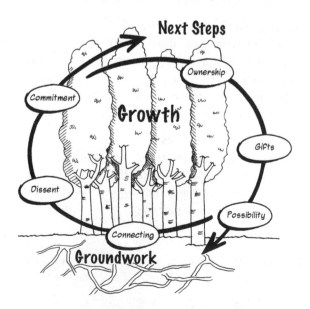

For More Information: A Small Group, www.asmallgroup.net

Collaborative Loops

In-depth
Adaptable Method
Chapter 6
Page 89

PURPOSE:
To teach people how to create their own change methodology.

OUTCOMES:
- Collaborative organizational and community change through a series of well-designed, strategically placed events
- People learn how to create their own change methodology
- People move from thinking they have to do everything themselves to working cooperatively with others

WHEN TO USE:
- The issues require employee engagement for success
- You have many different change projects going on in your organization
- To build organizational capacity for change
- To create partnerships throughout your organization
- If you want people to take responsibility for a change

WHEN NOT TO USE:
- If the results are predetermined
- If there isn't support for the people doing the work
- If you want complete control

NUMBER OF PARTICIPANTS:
- 6 teams of 10 people each is ideal, up to 20 teams possible
- 100–200 participants in events designed by teams

TYPES OF PARTICIPANTS:
- A broad range of internal and external stakeholders

TYPICAL DURATION:
- Workshop planning: 4–6 weeks
- Length: 2–3 days (workshop), 0.5 day–2 days (events designed during workshop)
- Follow-up: 3–12 months

BRIEF EXAMPLE:
Following the 1999 strike by Boeing engineers, Boeing Commercial Airplane engineering organization (20,000 people) and the Society of Professional Engineering Employees in Aerospace (SPEEA), the union that represents Boeing's engineers, addressed post-strike issues using engagement-based Collaborative Loops. Three years later, the same people who went on strike approved a new contract by 80 percent, and employee satisfaction in the engineering organization increased 40 percent.

HISTORICAL CONTEXT:
Created in 1995 by Dick and Emily Axelrod.
Influenced by Von Bertalanffy, Malcolm Knowles, Emery and Trist, Marvin Weisbord, and Sandra Janoff.

Gaining Insight - Getting Feedback

Achieving Results

For More Information: The Axelrod Group, www.AxelrodGroup.com

Collaborative Work Systems Design

*Thumbnail
Structuring Method
Chapter 44
Page 436*

PURPOSE:

To create a framework for successfully changing the organization to support collaboration and improve business results.

OUTCOMES:

- A holistic framework that incorporates the perspectives of a cross-section of the organization
- A plan of concrete actions to be accomplished
- Opportunity to bridge work across traditional boundaries

WHEN TO USE:

- Planning or renewing organizational change
- Building collaboration into the organization
- Integrating multiple change efforts

WHEN NOT TO USE:

- No commitment by decision makers to participate or act on the results
- Insufficient infrastructure and resources

NUMBER OF PARTICIPANTS:

- 5–30 per design event
- Multiple sessions may accommodate the whole organization

TYPES OF PARTICIPANTS:

- Change leaders
- Steering Committee members
- Design Team members
- Line managers
- Other internal stakeholders

TYPICAL DURATION:

- Assessment: 2–6 weeks
- Workshop: 1–5 days
- Change Process: Several months to many years, depending on scope of change

BRIEF EXAMPLE:

A glass plant recognized the need for broad organizational changes to achieve its desired business goals. The company used Collaborative Work Systems Design in conjunction with existing process, quality, and cultural initiatives. The result was a comprehensive, integrated design to take the organization to the next level.

HISTORICAL CONTEXT:

Created in 2000 by Michael Beyerlein, Cheryl Harris, and Sarah Bodner.

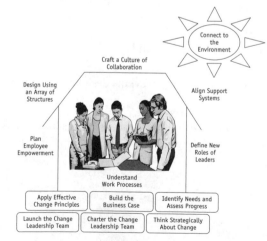

For More Information: Center for Collaborative Organizations, University of North Texas, www.workteams.unt.edu

Community Summits

Thumbnail
Planning Method
Chapter 36
Page 365

PURPOSE:
To help communities and large organizations invested in a complex issue quickly find the common ground necessary to support action.

OUTCOMES:
- Alignment of the broad community around a specific course of action
- The mobilization of energy for implementation
- The enlistment of individuals and organizations in follow-up

WHEN TO USE:
- When community alignment and participation around a course of action is required for the success of a change initiative

WHEN NOT TO USE:
- When all critical decisions have been made, and there is a desire to present the appearance of participation

NUMBER OF PARTICIPANTS:
- 64–2,048

TYPES OF PARTICIPANTS:
- All stakeholders, internal and external, necessary to achieve action around the central issue

TYPICAL DURATION:
- Plan: 2–4 weeks
- Solicit participants: 10–12 weeks
- Summit meeting: 2–3 days
- Follow-up: 6 months

BRIEF EXAMPLE:
United Way of Rhode Island used summits involving a microcosm of the state to build support for change from a dispersed funding model to a concentrated impact project model.

HISTORICAL CONTEXT:
Created in 2003 by Gil Steil and Mal Watlington. Emery's Open Systems Theory and Search Conference, Weisbord and Janoff's Future Search, Dannemiller's Whole Scale Change, and Harrison Owen's Open Space.

For More Information: Community Summits, www.gilsteil.com/communitysummits

Community Weaving

In-depth
Structuring Method
Chapter 42
Page 400

PURPOSE:

To weave the human and tangible resources of the grass roots with the knowledge and skills of formal systems using Web-based technology.

OUTCOMES:

- Builds and bridges social and human capital
- Maps and measures assets for community development
- Creates resilient, interdependent social networks
- Increases protective factors linked to community health and well-being
- Sparks initiative, innovation, ingenuity
- Creates microenterprises

WHEN TO USE:

- For establishing or strengthening social networks
- For collaborating among individuals, organizations, and systems
- For identifying assets and resources

WHEN NOT TO USE:

- There is no openness to outcomes
- There is no support for individual initiative

NUMBER OF PARTICIPANTS:

- Trainings: 25 maximum
- Events: Up to 2,500
- Formal Partners: Unlimited
- Participants: Infinite

TYPES OF PARTICIPANTS:

- Community members, community leaders, organization members, group members, students and parents, employees and managers, staff and clients

TYPICAL DURATION:

- Preparation:
  - Grassroots: None
  - Organizations: 2–4 weeks
  - Community-wide: 4–6 weeks
- Training: 1–4 days
- Summit: 1 day
- Total transition: Ongoing

BRIEF EXAMPLE:

One Community Weaver recruited, trained, and mobilized more than 150 Family Advocates and 800 Good Neighbors and established the Family Support Network, a nonprofit based in Bothell, Washington, with 15 agency partners.

HISTORICAL CONTEXT:

Created in 1993 by Cheryl Honey, C.P.P.

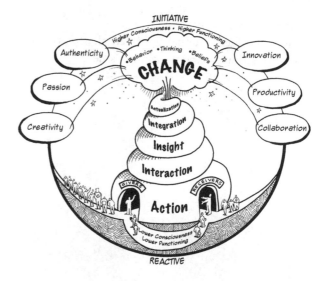

For More Information: Community Weaving, www.communityweaving.org

The Conference Model

PURPOSE:

To involve internal and external stakeholders in the redesign of processes and organizations.

OUTCOMES:
- People think systemically
- People think about whom to include when addressing issues
- Information and decision making are shared

WHEN TO USE:
- When you want to involve a critical mass of employees in the redesign of a process or organization

WHEN NOT TO USE:
- When the outcomes are known or you want the redesign done by a select few

NUMBER OF PARTICIPANTS:
- Up to 100 per conference
- Multiple conferences of 100 people can be run in parallel

TYPES OF PARTICIPANTS:
- Internal and external stakeholders, multilevel, multifunction

TYPICAL DURATION:
- Prework: 1–3 months
- Sessions: Three 2-day conferences, held 6 weeks apart
- Follow-up: 6 months–1 year

BRIEF EXAMPLE:

At Detroit Edison, a stalled supply-chain improvement process was revitalized using the Conference Model. Two 250-person conferences were held, resulting in 26 active supply-chain improvement process projects, with millions of dollars in savings.

HISTORICAL CONTEXT:

Created in 1991 by Dick and Emily Axelrod. Emery and Trist, Von Bertalanffy, Weisbord and Janoff.

For More Information: The Axelrod Group, www.AxelrodGroup.com

Consensus Decision Making

Thumbnail
Adaptable Method
Chapter 16
Page 212

PURPOSE:

To synthesize collective wisdom in order to generate decisions that best serve the needs of the whole.

OUTCOMES:

- High-quality decisions with strong support for follow-through and enhanced sense of connection among the participants.

WHEN TO USE:

- When the group participating has authority to make decisions
- When creative solutions are required to meet all the needs that are present
- When implementation will be ineffective unless everyone involved is really on board

WHEN NOT TO USE:

- When there is no common purpose or willingness to cooperate
- When there is strictly limited time combined with low trust within the group
- When the decision would more appropriately be delegated to an individual or committee

NUMBER OF PARTICIPANTS:

- 2–1,000+

TYPES OF PARTICIPANTS:

- All the members who are entrusted to make group decisions

TYPICAL DURATION:

- Preparation: Typically 1 hour outside meeting for every hour in the meeting
- Events: One or more meetings of <1 hour to several days
- Follow-up: Implementation of whatever decisions are reached

BRIEF EXAMPLE:

The Federation of Egalitarian Communities runs programs to support its affiliated groups in areas such as recruitment, labor exchange, and health care. In 2001, two of its groups were seeking to move the organization in a more politically active direction, drawing concerns from the largest community that such a change would alienate its membership base. The solution that emerged was to become more politically engaged in ways that also supported existing goals, for example, by doing recruitment at political events.

HISTORICAL CONTEXT:

Method of group decision making throughout human history. Contemporary secular tradition has roots in Quaker practices (1647), Free Speech Movement (1964), Movement for a New Society (1971).

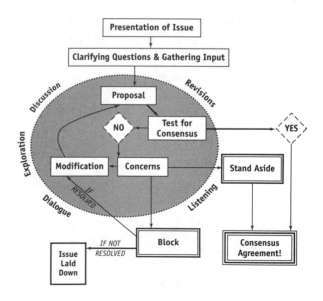

For More Information: Seeds for Change, http://seedsforchange.org.uk/free/consens

Conversation Café

Thumbnail
Adaptable Method
Chapter 17
Page 218

PURPOSE:
To build social trust and cohesion through safe, open, lively conversations in public places.

OUTCOMES:
- Conversation Café's impact is the culture itself—it is hard to measure its impact on social trust, greater citizen capacity for critical thinking, friendliness, and so on.

WHEN TO USE:
- To increase social glue
- To meet thoughtful neighbors
- To engage in meaningful conversation
- To shift, as we say, from small talk to BIG talk

WHEN NOT TO USE:
- Two traditions allow for the Conversation Café's safety and openness: "No committees will be formed" and "No marketing"
- Do not use Conversation Cafés to organize or motivate people toward a specific end, to convince others, or to form a club

NUMBER OF PARTICIPANTS:
- 3–8, plus a host per table with as many tables as the location can hold

TYPES OF PARTICIPANTS:
- Whoever comes; diverse members of the public

TYPICAL DURATION:
- Preparation: None
- Process: 60–90 minutes
- At conferences, "lite" Conversation Cafés of 30–60 minutes can be held
- Follow-up: None

BRIEF EXAMPLE:
The late Larry Gaffin hosted a Conversation Café for three years in several different cafés in Seattle, Washington. Participants ranged in age from their twenties to eighties, across the political spectrum, and while mostly white, had some cultural diversity. A core of a dozen people participated regularly, with newcomers at almost every meeting. A former minister, Larry easily generated topics each week ranging from ethical to philosophical to political to common personal issues and topics—people counted on this Conversation Café to make meaning of current events and said it felt a bit like church without the preaching. Ten to 20 other Conversation Cafés also met weekly, fostering civility—and community.

HISTORICAL CONTEXT:
Created in 2001 by Vicki Robin with Susan Partnow. Roots in a communication ritual called Heart Sharing, using similar agreements to dialogue circles and indigenous talking circles.

For More Information: Conversation Café, www.conversationcafe.org

The Cycle of Resolution

Quick Summaries

PURPOSE:

To generate a real, heartfelt, authentic dialogue that drives the creation of a joint vision and a detailed road map to desired results through conversational models and communication tools that get people unstuck.

OUTCOMES:

- Hierarchy flattened
- Individuals empowered to talk about anything; no fear sharing feelings and observations; feelings matter

WHEN TO USE:

- People not collaborating effectively
- Need for a clear unified vision

WHEN NOT TO USE:

- People won't engage or consider their own behavior

NUMBER OF PARTICIPANTS:

- 2–25 per group with up to 4 groups

TYPES OF PARTICIPANTS:

- All essential members of the system

TYPICAL DURATION:

- Preparation: Interview key players
- Process: 1–3 days
- Follow-up: 4–6 weeks with sustainability tool in the form of an eLearning program.

BRIEF EXAMPLE:

Total partnership breakdown between a private adoption agency and a county department of child welfare. The conflicts were resolved and an agreement was structured as the foundation for a healthy, productive working relationship with a new vision of collaborative partnership. In the following year, 109 "unadoptable" children destined for a life of foster care were placed in permanent families.

HISTORICAL CONTEXT:

Created in 1991 by Stewart Levine. Influenced by Dr. Stephen Covey and Dr. Fernando Flores.

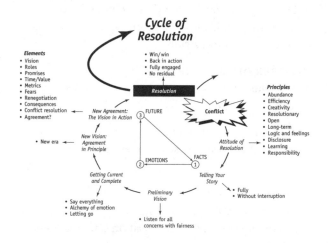

For More Information: Resolution Works, www.resolutionworks.org

Dialogue and Deliberation

PURPOSE:

To build and strengthen relationships, bridge gaps, resolve conflicts, generate innovative solutions to problems, inspire collaborative action, give people a voice in governance, and strengthen decision making.

OUTCOMES:

- Convinces those in power that ordinary people can understand complex issues, grapple with multiple perspectives and choices, and find common ground
- Convinces participants that a diverse group of people can make better decisions on tough issues than interest groups and power holders

WHEN TO USE:

- To create clarity/provide group with direction on an issue or situation
- To address contentious issues that attract only argument and debate
- To resolve long-standing conflicts and poor relations
- To inspire people to change, expand, or take time to reflect and heal
- To influence policy
- To empower people to solve complex problems

WHEN NOT TO USE:

- If there is not an adequately representative group participating
- When the organizing group is wedded to a specific outcome
- When buy-in and accountability cannot be obtained from those implementing the results
- If policy decision needs to be made before deliberative process is complete
- If the initiative is viewed as advocating for a particular group or interest

NUMBER OF PARTICIPANTS:

- 5–5,000

TYPES OF PARTICIPANTS:

- All major views/perspectives/roles on the issue at hand

TYPICAL DURATION:

- Preparation: 1–6 months
- Process: From a 90-minute forum to a multiyear sustained dialogue
- Follow-up: 1–3 months

BRIEF EXAMPLE:

The City of Waterloo Commission on Human Rights organized community-wide "study circles"—multiple small group dialogues held throughout the community culminating in collective action based on common ground.

HISTORICAL CONTEXT:

David Bohm's present-day revival—1985. Dialogue was created in indigenous cultures and used for centuries. Deliberation was born when people first developed the ability to consider options rationally. Created by numerous human societies over time.

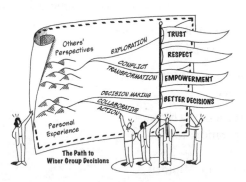

For More Information: National Coalition for Dialogue and Deliberation, www.thataway.org

The Drum Café

Thumbnail
Supportive Method
Chapter 62
Page 588

PURPOSE:

To break down barriers; promote unity and team building; leave the group stimulated, relaxed, and more receptive; challenge assumptions of what can be achieved as a group; spark creativity; have fun and transform colleagues into friends; and relieve stress.

OUTCOMES:

- The whole is greater than the sum of its parts—the individual must start to see him/herself as a function of the collective
- Preconceived notions of what is achievable should be challenged and can be surpassed
- Everyone can make music
- Cultural diversity can benefit the company if harnessed appropriately

WHEN TO USE:

- Conferences and road shows
- Year-end functions
- Incentive breakaways
- Mergers and product launches
- Celebrations

WHEN NOT TO USE:

- When people are not willing to participate
- When leadership is not willing to participate and model
- If there is trauma to the community or group that has happened too close to the event time and has not been properly processed or communicated

NUMBER OF PARTICIPANTS:

- 10–22,000 people

TYPES OF PARTICIPANTS:

- Anyone

TYPICAL DURATION:

- Preparation: 1 day
- Process: 1 day–2 weeks
- Follow-up: Minimal

BRIEF EXAMPLE:

A group of miners in South Africa came together in one room for the first time. They came in and tended to associate with others of the same color of skin. The drumming experience was part of the larger three-day planning event. By day three, blacks and whites together were drumming, laughing, and dancing together.

HISTORICAL CONTEXT:

Created by Warren Lieberman in 1995. Drumming is the most ancient form of music making, communication, and community building used in civilizations throughout the world.

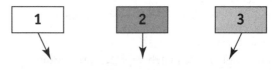

For More Information: Drum Café, www.drumcafe.com

Dynamic Facilitation

Thumbnail
Adaptable Method
Chapter 18
Page 223

PURPOSE:

To achieve breakthroughs on real, pressing, or "impossible" issues; arrive at better consensus decisions faster; and empower people to new levels of capability, trust, and mutual respect.

OUTCOMES:

- Sparks "shifts" and breakthroughs on difficult issues
- Creates a "we," where all work creatively together
- Awakens deeper understanding and a living-systems perspective

WHEN TO USE:

- To solve complex, difficult, conflicted, or impossible issues in small groups or with individuals
- To transform organizations through assuring creative, empowered teams
- To transform very large systems of unlimited size

WHEN NOT TO USE:

- When the problem is easy or has low interest
- When a group is expected to "buy-in" to a decision that has already been made

NUMBER OF PARTICIPANTS:

- 2–40
- One-on-one in therapeutic settings
- Within large work groups or teams of any size
- In systems of unlimited size, with the Center for Wise Democracy's Wisdom Council

TYPES OF PARTICIPANTS:

- People who care about the issue being solved
- People come as themselves, not representing their positions or organizations

TYPICAL DURATION:

- Preparation is less important, but it is valuable to know the situation through interviews and visits
- Process: Best in an ongoing series of meetings or, for instance, in 4 half-day meetings
- Follow-up: Written conclusion

BRIEF EXAMPLE:

Road crew workers met each week in dynamically facilitated meetings. They worked on what they considered to be an impossible-to-solve issue: getting full-time flaggers for directing traffic in construction zones. The county commissioners had already said "no" on this issue. The road crew became empowered to reassert themselves, getting the county commissioners to change their position. Not only did these workers get the policy changed, but they also ended the usual micromanaging from county commissioners that affected all departments.

HISTORICAL CONTEXT:

Created in the early 1980s by Jim Rough; public seminars held since 1990. Developed further through practitioners in different settings.

For More Information: Dynamic Faciliation, www.DynamicFacilitation.com

Dynamic Planning Charrettes

*In-depth
Planning Method
Chapter 32
Page 300*

PURPOSE:
To produce a feasible plan within an accelerated time frame that benefits from the support of all stakeholders throughout its implementation.

OUTCOMES:
- Master plan for reorganization, redevelopment, or new product design
- Multidisciplinary detailed studies (e.g., engineering, financial, market)
- Implementation mechanisms (e.g., policies, codes, standards)
- Action plans with roles, responsibilities, and timelines

WHEN TO USE:
- Company reorganization, product design, community planning, building design
- Projects that have multiple stakeholders with disparate agendas/needs
- Complex design and planning problems involving a number of different disciplines
- Projects with the potential to transform an organization (new policies)

WHEN NOT TO USE:
- When primary stakeholders will not participate in good faith
- Simple problems with little political and/or design complexity

NUMBER OF PARTICIPANTS:
- 10–100s

TYPES OF PARTICIPANTS:
- Primary—Company leadership, elected and appointed officials, agency staff, site property owners
- Secondary—Management, nongovernmental organizations, local nonprofits, businesses, and residences directly affected
- General—employees, community members

TYPICAL DURATION:
- Phase One—Research, Education, and Charrette Preparation: 6 weeks–4 months
- Phase Two—Charrette: 4–7 days.
- Phase Three—Implementation: 4–18 months

BRIEF EXAMPLE:
A dynamic planning process forged an agreement between Contra Costa County, California, and the Walden Improvement Association (neighborhood group) to develop the Pleasant Hill Bay Area Rapid Transit station area. After 25 years and several failed attempts, the transformative six-day Charrette created a plan with the input of all stakeholders.

HISTORICAL CONTEXT:
Created in 2001 by the National Charrette Institute. Historically rooted in collaborative design workshops by architectural and urban design firms.

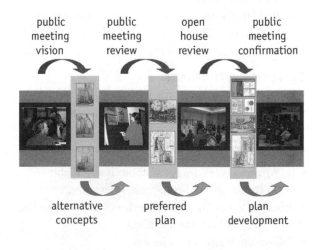

public meeting vision — public meeting review — open house review — public meeting confirmation

alternative concepts — preferred plan — plan development

For More Information: National Charrette Institute, www.charretteinstitute.org

Employee Engagement Process

PURPOSE:
To transform a "traditional" management culture into one that is more collaborative and team driven.

OUTCOMES:
- A more engaged workplace with increased cross-functional, cross-level communication and broad ownership of culture and results

WHEN TO USE:
- When morale or productivity is low or the culture is ready for a new level of results
- When there is a shift in the business, for example, new strategy or change in environment
- When quantitative data is needed to guide decisions about employee engagement or when there is fear about change efforts being too "soft"

WHEN NOT TO USE:
- When management is not ready for more employee engagement and involvement

NUMBER OF PARTICIPANTS:
- Any total number in groups up to about 100

TYPES OF PARTICIPANTS:
- Managers and frontline employees

TYPICAL DURATION:
- 1-year cycles; if possible, for the cycle, provide:
  - Preparation: 1–3 months
  - Process: 3–4 hours per session over 6–8 months
  - Follow-up: Varies with action teams, generally 1–3 months

BRIEF EXAMPLE:
Wyeth Distribution Centers began with survey process of broad and deep participation to identify the level of engagement across seven factors throughout the distribution centers. Resulted in employee-driven action plan to put systems and practices in place to increase meaningful employee engagement throughout the system. Communication across groups enriched learnings. More collaborative work groups ultimately drove change faster and had results that demonstrated improved productivity and morale.

HISTORICAL CONTEXT:
Created in 1999 by Marie McCormick, MBA, Ph.D. Roots in survey methodologies and large group methods such as Future Search and Open Space Technology.

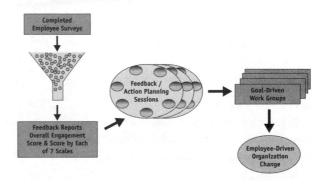

For More Information: InSyte Partners, www.insytepartners.com

Future Search

In-depth
Planning Method
Chapter 33
Page 316

PURPOSE:

To evolve a common ground future for an organization or community where stakeholders build high commitment to action and rapid implementation.

OUTCOMES:
- Discover and use common agendas and shared ideals
- The power of voluntary commitments made on common ground
- Experience shared leadership and self-management
- Experience the "whole elephant" before acting on any part of it
- Learn to accept polarities and differences

WHEN TO USE:
- A shared vision is desired and an action plan is needed
- Other efforts have stalled and time is growing short
- New leadership is taking over and a key transition is at hand
- Opposing parties need to meet and do not have a good forum

WHEN NOT TO USE:
- Leadership is reluctant and nobody but you wants it
- The agenda is preconceived and conditions for success not met

NUMBER OF PARTICIPANTS:
- 40–100 people
- Hundreds in parallel or sequential conferences

TYPES OF PARTICIPANTS:
- Broad cross-section of stakeholders
- Organizations: multilevel, multifunctional
- Communities: All sectors sponsors considered relevant

TYPICAL DURATION:
- Preparation: 3–6 months
- Process: 2.5 days
- Total Transition: Variable

BRIEF EXAMPLE:

Hopkinton, Massachusetts, a town of 9,000, more than doubled in size. A referendum left education level-funded. "Hopkinton 2002 AD" involved citizens; commissioners; police, fire, highway, and town department heads; business leaders; teachers; students; and school administrators. Their commitments included preserving the town's rural character and improving schools. Residents raised the school budget 12 percent. Within a year, a local firm donated $350,000 in computers and training, and pledged $300,000 more for the next two years.

HISTORICAL CONTEXT:

Created in 1982 by Marvin Weisbord and Sandra Janoff. Commitment to democratic ideals and whole system thinking—Lewin, Lippitt, Schindler-Rainman, Trist and Emery.

Gemeinsinn-Werkstatt

Thumbnail
Improving Method
Chapter 54
Page 513

PURPOSE:
To address complex issues within the framework of a large group project involving different people in a structured, motivated, and self-organized way.

OUTCOMES:
- Generates open-minded initiators and participants
- Enhanced voluntary engagement and responsibility for each other
- Better cooperation and synergy among institutions
- Optimizes use of human and material resources
- Supports sustainable networking processes and method-knowledge as a basis for further projects

WHEN TO USE:
- When there is an urgent issue and many are willing to act
- When many individuals and organizations volunteer
- When existing conflicts can be dealt with in a constructive manner

WHEN NOT TO USE:
- When dealing with a short-term issue, routine work, or well-defined projects
- When key participants are excluded
- When cooperation is impossible

NUMBER OF PARTICIPANTS:
- 27 to an open number

TYPES OF PARTICIPANTS:
- *Initiative circle:* Key figures from diverse interest groups, responsible for the project framework
- *Project circle:* The coordinators who work as volunteers, honorary, or full-time supporting the framework
- *Event circles:* Participants of at least two large group events
- *Action circles:* Participants who develop their various self-responsible action groups

TYPICAL DURATION:
- Activation phase: 6 weeks–6 months
- Realization phase: 3 months–2 years
- Integration phase: 6 weeks–6 months

BRIEF EXAMPLE:
A professor of the institute for educational sciences was interested in the new large-group procedure and saw a chance to improve cooperation within the university. With the support of the Gemeinsinn-Werkstatt, they not only succeeded in achieving midterm results, but also in developing an informal Gemeinsinn-Netzwerk (Community Spirit Network) that spans the university's functions, enhancing cooperation.

HISTORICAL CONTEXT:
Created in a project of the Bertelsmann Foundation with the Center for Applied Policy Research (2000–2004) by Wolfgang Faenderl in cooperation with the Support Network of consultants, researchers, and moderators.

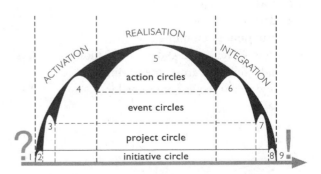

For More Information: Gemeinsinn-Werkstatt, www.gemeinsinn-werkstatt.de

The Genuine Contact Program

PURPOSE:
To sustain an organization at a higher, more holistic level of operating.

OUTCOMES:
- Understanding that the wisdom to do what needs to be done is in the organization
- Creates liberating structures and a participatory architecture and requires understanding and implementation of both

WHEN TO USE:
- To go from good to great
- In times of great challenge

WHEN NOT TO USE:
- If the senior leadership of the organization is not committed to leading and sustaining the change process and its results

NUMBER OF PARTICIPANTS:
- No limit
- Events: 500 people

TYPES OF PARTICIPANTS:
- All in the value chain

TYPICAL DURATION:
- 40 days over 9 months
- Preparation: 1–3 months
- Process: 4 events of 2–3 days over 8 months; 24 days of individual and group mentoring
- Follow-up: At request of leadership

BRIEF EXAMPLE:
A systemwide leadership development program was created in a 10,000-person global organization. Completed transformation of the corporate university that is leading the organization-wide change, including developing leadership and organizational capacity.

HISTORICAL CONTEXT:
Created in 1999 by Birgitt and Ward Williams. Rooted in the work of critical mass thinking and large group interventions, particularly in Harrison Owen's work with Open Space Technology and its historical context.

For More Information: Genuine Contact, http://genuinecontact.net

Human Systems Dynamics

Thumbnail
Adaptable Method
Chapter 20
Page 234

PURPOSE:

To see and influence self-organizing patterns for individuals, teams, organizations, and communities.

OUTCOMES:

- Improved understanding of shared or different cultural assumptions
- Opportunities emerge for new identity and shared assumptions

WHEN TO USE:

- Issues are complex with high interdependencies
- Situations are unpredictable
- Differences or concerns have persisted over time

WHEN NOT TO USE:

- Cause and effect are clear
- Systems are closed and predictable
- A single outcome is predicted or expected

NUMBER OF PARTICIPANTS:

- 10–200

TYPES OF PARTICIPANTS:

- Any

TYPICAL DURATION:

- 1–12 months
- Preparation: 4–12 hours
- Process: 2 hours–3 days
- Follow-up: 1 week–1 month

BRIEF EXAMPLE:

Collaboration of state and county government, university, and foundations to establish framework for well-being of children. Group of 25 met for six two-hour sessions and defined a framework of "well-being" for children—a model, objectives, measures, roles and responsibilities, and activities. The core theme selected, "How are the children?" is used by all governmental agencies when they interact with clients or the community.

HISTORICAL CONTEXT:

Human Systems Dynamics, as a field, was founded in 2002 by Glenda H. Eoyang, but the methods, tools, and techniques continue to be created by Associates of the Human Systems Dynamics Institute. Theoretical grounding of human systems dynamics is in complex adaptive systems theory and other areas of nonlinear dynamics. Some of the practical methods, tools, and techniques are based in complexity, while others are derived from a variety of social and organizational sciences including psychology, organization development management, and anthropology.

For More Information: Human Systems Dynamics Institute, www.hsdinstitute.org

Idealized Design

Thumbnail
Improving Method
Chapter 55
Page 519

PURPOSE:

To engage a large group of stakeholders in generating breakthrough solutions by first envisioning their ideal, then working backward to where they are.

OUTCOMES:

- Participants transform their assumptions about what is possible

WHEN TO USE:

- To design anything—for example, organization, product, service, system, process—whether there is a crisis or because an organization wants to become world-class

WHEN NOT TO USE:

- There is no chance to implement ideas

NUMBER OF PARTICIPANTS:

- 8–10 participants per facilitator
- Up to 50 participants per event. Wider involvement through asking others to improve the design

TYPES OF PARTICIPANTS:

- Participants can be any stakeholder type that is directly or indirectly affected by what is being designed

TYPICAL DURATION:

- Preparation: 2 days
- Process: 0.5–5 days
- Follow-up: 2 days

BRIEF EXAMPLE:

Idealized redesign of IKEA store. New Chicago store adopted designers' idea for an easy-to-navigate octagonal building with an open center—with no walls but instead pillars and railings—from which shoppers could see departments and quickly access them via escalators.

HISTORICAL CONTEXT:

Created in 1951 by Russell L. Ackoff at Bell Labs when its chief executive officer initiated a redesign of the telephone system from scratch. Ackoff recognized the potential and has applied it to many types of design over the past 50 years.

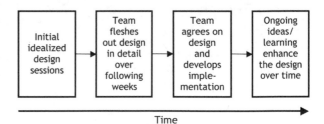

For More Information: Ackoff Center Web log, http://ackoffcenter.blogs.com/

Integrated Clarity

In-depth
Adaptable Method
Chapter 8
Page 118

PURPOSE:

To illuminate the authentic, collective Identity so people connect with it, operations become an extension of it, and a language model of empowerment supports it.

OUTCOMES:

- Fundamental shift from blame and finding fault to choice and personal responsibility
- Focus on core ideology *before* strategic action
- Capitalizing on the human element—namely, feelings and needs—rather than tolerating or "managing" it
- Values/principles-based vs. policy/procedure-based
- Aware of others and the whole system versus self-focus and isolated functions

WHEN TO USE:

- To invigorate or clarify a sense of collective identity and purpose
- To marshal resources into an organized and clear direction
- To shift communication from "blame" to personal responsibility
- To connect people to each other and the organization's needs
- To enhance the group's presence with stakeholders

WHEN NOT TO USE:

- When formal leaders are not engaged in the process

NUMBER OF PARTICIPANTS:

- 1–500

TYPES OF PARTICIPANTS:

- Executives, management/managers, team leaders, board of directors, midlevel to frontline workers
- Work teams or work groups
- Communities, associations, neighborhoods

TYPICAL DURATION:

- Preparation: 2 weeks–2 months
- Process: 1 day–many months
- Follow-up: Ongoing process and as needed

BRIEF EXAMPLE:

About 30 staff, faculty, and administration from all schools at the University of South Florida, College of Visual & Performing Arts, began conversations focused on the college's universal organizational needs. Eventually 30 percent of all college and faculty were engaged in the dialogue. Dean Ron Jones reported, "There's an exciting new energy in our College spreading like wildfire—a clarity about who we arc . . . and where we're going in the future."

HISTORICAL CONTEXT:

Earliest form developed in 2001 by Marie Miyashiro. Inspired by and based on the "needs-focused" Nonviolent Communication process developed by Marshall Rosenberg. Also incorporates work by William Bridges, Kimball Fisher, Jim Collins, Jerry I. Porras, Judith Orloff Faulk, and Marshall Thurber.

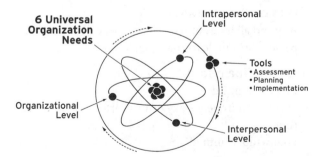

For More Information: Integrated Clarity, www.integratedclarity.com

JazzLab

Thumbnail
Supportive Method
Chapter 63
Page 593

PURPOSE:

To give participants a powerful and positive experience of deep listening, teamwork, diversity, synergy, creativity, and dynamic improvisation in a musical context.

OUTCOMES:

- Discovery that individuals have hidden talents and abilities
- Diversity is crucial to success; improvisation does not create chaos, but rather creates its own dynamic structure
- Everyone can discover and generate his or her own creativity and self-expression
- Listening is the key to an effective and progressive organization
- Leadership is not about control, but about trust, listening, engagement, and the encouragement of interaction and flow

WHEN TO USE:

- When an organization wants to provide a hands-on, musical experience of whole systems in action that is fun, engaging, and energetic

WHEN NOT TO USE:

- When participants are not attending voluntarily

NUMBER OF PARTICIPANTS:

- 20–2,000

TYPES OF PARTICIPANTS:

- Any and all levels of participants, as well as different personality and learning styles

TYPICAL DURATION:

- Preparation: 1 day
- Event: 60 minutes–1 day or in shorter modules over time
- Follow-up: Minimal

BRIEF EXAMPLE:

A group of participants had previously taken team-building and creativity programs and had understood these concepts in principle. With JazzLab, however, they actually experienced the synergy of diverse groups aligning together through active listening, the group creativity generated by jointly composing a piece of music, and the practice of working with ambiguity and chaos through musical improvisation to allow new structures to spontaneously arise. They were able to take skills they discovered through music and apply them back to their organization.

HISTORICAL CONTEXT:

Created by Brian Tate in 1996. Comes from earlier workshops on creativity and change, and from his career as a musician and facilitator. The effectiveness of group percussion comes from village culture in Africa, where it is recognized that making music together creates a healthy, interactive, and holistic community.

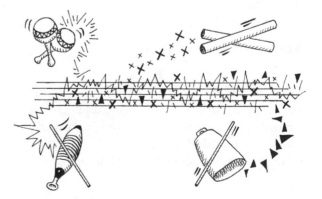

For More Information: Brian Tate, www.briantatemusic.com

Large Group Scenario Planning

Thumbnail Planning Method Chapter 37 Page 370

PURPOSE:
To enhance large group interventions involving a whole system by enabling participants to envision multiple ways the external environment may change in the future and how these environmental changes could affect the organization.

OUTCOMES:
- Future plans that have been clarified by questioning participant assumptions about the future, which is frequently not an extrapolation of the past

WHEN TO USE:
- To enhance strategic planning
- When multiple possibilities need to be considered
- When the imagination of the planners needs encouragement

WHEN NOT TO USE:
- When there are no critical uncertainties confronting the organization

NUMBER OF PARTICIPANTS:
- 32–512

TYPES OF PARTICIPANTS:
- All stakeholders

TYPICAL DURATION:
- Plan: 2–6 weeks
- Invite Participants: 2–10 weeks
- Meeting: 2–3 days
- Follow-up: 6 months

BRIEF EXAMPLE:
A dental school used Large Group Scenario Planning to plan for curricular change, admissions policy, and faculty development. The result was a restructured curriculum, some fresh approaches to admissions, and ideas for faculty development.

HISTORICAL CONTEXT:
Created in 2003 by Gil Steil and Michele Gibbons-Carr. Based on traditional scenario planning strategies of P. Schwartz, J. Ogillvy, G. Ringland, P. Schoemaker, and K. van der Heijden, and integrated into a whole system large group process.

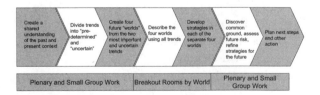

Activity Flow for Large Group Scenario Planning
(32 - 256 participants)

For More Information: Gil Steil Associates, www.gilsteil.com

Leadership Dojo

Thumbnail
Adaptable Method
Chapter 21
Page 239

PURPOSE:

To embody personal integrity, social dignity, and professional excellence in sustainable team and organizational change.

OUTCOMES:

- Transforms past behaviors into new actions
- Reveals importance of a leadership presence as a way to mobilize and motivate others
- Creates conversations for action
- Recognizes the importance of bringing the whole person to work

WHEN TO USE:

- To shift organizational culture connected to business results
- To build team alignment and cohesion
- To develop emerging leaders for succession planning

WHEN NOT TO USE:

- Client is not committed
- Conditions of success are vague
- When mediation is called for instead of learning
- Client cannot rearrange priorities so participants can be fully engaged

NUMBER OF PARTICIPANTS:

- 8–1,000

TYPES OF PARTICIPANTS:

- Broad cross-section, from senior executives to administrative assistants
- Multilevel, multifunctional

TYPICAL DURATION:

- Preparation: 2–3 days for client discovery
- Event: Two 4-day conferences over 6 months
- Follow-up: Coaching for individuals and teams
- Total Transition: Begins immediately through recurrent practices and covers a lifetime

BRIEF EXAMPLE:

The Board of Continuing Education Services of New York State (BOCES) contracted to work directly with their call centers. The call centers were consistently failing and drawing complaints from customers. During the discovery process, it was assessed that tech reps and support were quickly consumed by bad moods and lost effectiveness with customers. After a couple of 2-day conferences with follow-up coaching, BOCES reported that complaints fell 85 percent and that the improved cycle time with customers paid for their engagement and saved $250,000 over the year.

HISTORICAL CONTEXT:

Created in 1985 by Richard Strozzi-Heckler, influenced by his study and research of the Somatic Philosophy of Learning and his implementation of the Trojan Warrior Project on Leadership Development for the Army Special Forces. Additional contribution from Fernando Flores's Ontology of Language. Use of Aikido as a paradigm for conflict resolution and a leadership presence.

For More Information: Strozzi Institute, www.strozziinstitute.com

The Learning Map Approach

Thumbnail
Supportive Method
Chapter 64
Page 598

PURPOSE:
To create shared understanding, connection, and contribution to the future through dialogue and discovery.

OUTCOMES:
- Increased organizational alignment and employee engagement
- A line of sight from the marketplace to each individual
- Goals connected across the organization
- Skills and capabilities to deliver the strategy are developed
- Where cultural change has been measured, many employees offer statements such as "The company cares what I think," "Now I understand why we have to do it this way" or "I can see how I make a difference"

WHEN TO USE:
- To create a line of sight for everyone in the organization to understand the "why" of change, such as big-picture issues affecting the business—marketplace, customer, competitive, and technology issues
- To connect people to the organization and team goals—"what" is changing, including the specifics of the change, process information, and key metrics and measures
- To identify the "how" of change—how they can contribute to the success of the organization

WHEN NOT TO USE:
- In a "command and control" environment where leaders are uncomfortable and unwilling to share information and engage employees

NUMBER OF PARTICIPANTS:
- 8–10 people per table
- Organizations of 125–500,000+

TYPES OF PARTICIPANTS:
- Primarily internal stakeholders, multifunction and multilevel
- Has been used with external stakeholders

TYPICAL DURATION:
- Development: 3 weeks–6 months; average, 2 months
- Implementation timelines vary greatly and are determined by business needs

BRIEF EXAMPLE:
An innovative fashion retailer was focused on transforming its sales and customer service strategy, shifting from a task-focused culture to a customer-service culture. The company used the Root Learning Map process to help managers, associates, and other key stakeholders to become truly engaged in the brand, to live the new customer service approach, and to develop a sense of ownership in the business.

HISTORICAL CONTEXT:
Created in 1987 by James A. Haudan and Randall C. Root.

For More Information: Root Learning, www.rootlearning.com

Online Environments

PURPOSE:
To support and extend the impact of your change methodologies by using technology for both time-delimited and ongoing efforts.

OUTCOMES:
- Increases access by enabling distributed participation
- Creates a record of the interaction
- Increases transparency
- Changes the assumption that face-to-face is the only way to implement real change

WHEN TO USE:
- Networks and communities need to be nurtured over time/distance
- Events can be maximized through online support
- Cost or other factors prevent gathering face-to-face
- A process lasts a long time
- Records, ongoing conversation, and information sharing is useful
- Increased participation and more diverse voices are desired
- Complexity requires a variety of interaction and recording options
- To support greater transparency
- Special participant requirements lend themselves to online interactions

WHEN NOT TO USE:
- There is no leadership support
- There is no Internet access or participants are not skilled in the technology
- Insufficient motivation/attention to issues

NUMBER OF PARTICIPANTS:
- 2–10,000s

TYPES OF PARTICIPANTS:
- Everyone who needs or chooses to be present

TYPICAL DURATION:
- Preparation: Integrate into the change process
- Process: 1 hour–weeks or ongoing
- Follow-up: Integrate into the follow-up plan

BRIEF EXAMPLE:
In 2004, the Gender and Diversity Program of the Consultative Group on International Agricultural Research convened an online consultation to gather the needs and priorities of its member organizations. The program gathered input from more constituents than was possible face-to-face, resulting in knowing the priorities that might not have been heard otherwise. This input guided the program toward serving the actual needs of constituents rather than assumed needs.

HISTORICAL CONTEXT:
Created by people who have nurtured online interaction since the 1950s when computers were first networked. The history of online environments for change sits in the evolution of online communities (Rheingold, www.rheingold.com/vc/book), computer-supported communication, and distributed group work (teams).

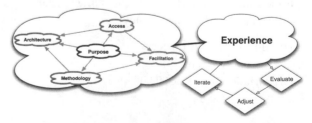

For More Information: Methods for Change, http://methodsforchange.com

Open Space Technology

In-depth
Adaptable Method
Chapter 9
Page 135

PURPOSE:

To enable groups to address complex, important issues as a high-performing system by inviting people to take responsibility for what they love for a few hours, a few days, or as an everyday practice.

OUTCOMES:

- Discover the capacity to operate as self-managed work teams with high levels of personal responsibility and leadership

WHEN TO USE:

- In critical situations requiring resolution characterized by high levels of complexity, diversity (of participants), and conflict (potential or actual), and with a decision time of yesterday

WHEN NOT TO USE:

- Specific predetermined outcomes are desired

NUMBER OF PARTICIPANTS:

- 5–2,000 people; no limit, theoretically, by using computer-connected, multisite, simultaneous events

TYPES OF PARTICIPANTS:

- Anybody who cares about the issue under consideration
- Diversity is a plus

TYPICAL DURATION:

- Preparation: The space opens with the first conversation
- Event: 1–3 days
- Total Transition: May last for the rest of the organization's life

BRIEF EXAMPLE:

In Bogotá, Colombia, 2,100 people—1,800 street kids, aged 15–22, and 300 of their teachers—convened for two days to consider the future of their jobs program. The core idea from the conference was responsibility.

The program was permanently altered, with the young people taking more responsibility for themselves and a much more responsible attitude toward their jobs. Lateness, laziness, and disrespect are almost gone. There were many structural changes in the schools. And finally, respect from the young peoples' bosses increased as their quality of work improved. The experience profoundly impacted the kids' approach to their lives.

HISTORICAL CONTEXT:

Created in 1985 by Harrison Owen with collegial assistance from a global cast of thousands. Open Space came initially from the wisdom and experience of indigenous people from around the world. Insights into the function of Open Space are from cultural anthropology, chaos and complexity theory, and non-Western (rational scientific) traditions.

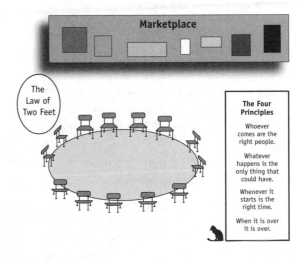

Marketplace

The Law of Two Feet

The Four Principles

Whoever comes are the right people.

Whatever happens is the only thing that could have.

Whenever it starts is the right time.

When it is over it is over.

For More Information: The Open Space Institutes, www.openspaceworld.org

Open Systems Theory

PURPOSE:
To address virtually any participative work, puzzle, or problem.

OUTCOMES:
- Greater cooperation, energy, and motivation for the task at hand
- A democratic team structure that supports sustainability and continuing motivation
- For unique designs, the selected application of Open Systems Theory principles and tools ensures productive participation and high levels of intrinsic motivation to perform the needed work

WHEN TO USE:
- When effective results are required in a complex environment of multiple perspectives, clashes of interests and values, and rapidly changing external and internal conditions

WHEN NOT TO USE:
- Insufficient educative preparation
- Top leadership is averse to distributing responsibilities downward

NUMBER OF PARTICIPANTS:
- 4–100s

TYPES OF PARTICIPANTS:
- May or may not be members of the system

TYPICAL DURATION:
- Preparation: 2 weeks–6 months
- Event: 1 hour to a series of meetings over months or longer
- Follow-up: Sustainable, if uses participative democratic structure and process

BRIEF EXAMPLE:
Since 2000, Roadway Express has held close to 40 summits across the organization to engage the workforce, improve margins, create service innovations, launch new strategies, and consolidate its merger with Yellow Corporation. The process has energized the workforce, produced millions of dollars of cost savings, and generated millions more in new revenues.

HISTORICAL CONTEXT:
Created in the early 1990s by Merrelyn Emery together with a cast of thousands. From a very good family—parents are Search Conference and Participative Design Workshop, grandmother was Social-Technical Systems. Lewin's work on democracy, autocracy, and laissez-faire. Asch's work on conditions for effective communication.

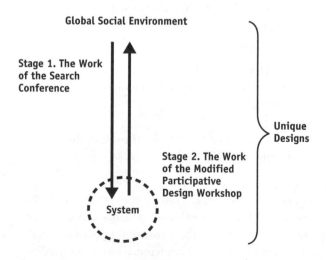

OpenSpace-Online Real-Time Methodology

Thumbnail
Adaptable Method
Chapter 23
Page 250

PURPOSE:

To enable a (r)evolutionary global "do-it-yourself" dimension of collaborative excellence and sustainable development in economy, society, politics and education across distance.

OUTCOMES:
- High level of co-creative excellence among many
- New ideas and agreements for next steps
- Results reported quickly on topics that really matter
- High commitment which sustains continued work
- Savings in travel costs, time, and natural resources
- Increased competencies to initiate and facilitate change
- Complementary synergies between different methods and activities (on-line and face-to-face)

WHEN TO USE:
- When groups or organizations are facing important questions or urgent issues and people are separated by distance
- When highly productive, liberated and joyful real-time collaboration is desired
- When immediately reported results and sustainable further work is important

WHEN NOT TO USE:
- Participants have no access to the Internet
- IT policies do not allow quick software installation
- The meeting agenda is already fixed and organizers want to play a dominant role during the event
- No trust that the right people will show up

NUMBER OF PARTICIPANTS:
- 5–125
- Parallel meetings are possible

TYPES OF PARTICIPANTS:
- Decentralized learning, interest, project, citizen, research, customer, stakeholder, network, and community groups

TYPICAL DURATION:
- Preparation: 1 hour–ongoing
- Real-time conference: 2–8 hours
- Follow-up: 1 hour—ongoing

BRIEF EXAMPLE:

An international marketing and sales company uses OpenSpace-Online with trainers, seminar groups, sales managers, and project leaders for diverse activities (e.g., ongoing project and team development, pre-meetings, and follow-ups of face-to-face activities).

HISTORICAL CONTEXT:

Created by Gabriela Ender (1999–2002) and supporting people after 30+ years of interdisciplinary work, the belief in the "do-it-yourself-power" of "passion and responsibility," grounded in the principles of Open Space Technology (Harrison Owen), and made possible through the invention of the Internet.

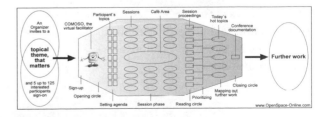

For More Information: OpenSpace-Online GmbH—The Power of People, www.OpenSpace-Online.com

Organization Workshop

Thumbnail
Adaptable Method
Chapter 24
Page 256

PURPOSE:
To create the knowledge and skills of system sight that enable us to create partnerships up, down, and across organizational lines.

OUTCOMES:
- Causes organization members to rethink their behaviors when they are in top, middle, bottom, and customer interactions
- Creates shared language and concrete strategies for partnership behavior in those relationships

WHEN TO USE:
- In any setting in which the client wants to redirect member energy from unproductive "sideshows" onto the business of the system
- Rapid change is desired to increase *individual power* and *overall organizational system power* to achieve previously unattainable stretch goals

WHEN NOT TO USE:
- It is being imposed on people
- Tops are using it on Bottoms to "straighten them out"
- People have not been adequately informed about the workshop's purposes and methods

NUMBER OF PARTICIPANTS:
- 24–50 people
- Variations for 50–100+ people

TYPES OF PARTICIPANTS:
- Can be internal and external stakeholders
- Cross-level, multifunction, or same function

TYPICAL DURATION:
- Preparation: 2–3 hours by telephone
- Event: 1-, 2-, or 3-day variations
- Total Transition: Variable

BRIEF EXAMPLE:
A Fortune 50 company has used the Organization Workshop on more than 25 separate occasions for various business leadership teams, multilevel cross-functional teams, top-to-bottom plants, and various functional groups (information systems, advertising, research and development, and several new product start-up ventures).

HISTORICAL CONTEXT:
Created in 1978 by Barry Oshry. Roots in experiential education with National Training Laboratories (now NTL Institute), experimental work at Boston University, but most directly from 30 years of work with the Power Lab.

For More Information: Power and Systems, www.powerandsystems.com

Participative Design Workshop

In-depth
Structuring Method
Chapter 43
Page 419

PURPOSE:
To produce a participative, democratic organizational system.

OUTCOMES:
- New behaviors evolve and assumptions change
- People cooperate rather than bicker and protect their turf
- Responsibility, motivation, care about overall business outcomes, and quality and productivity increase

WHEN TO USE:
- An organization wishes to increase productivity and innovation
- An agreement is in place

WHEN NOT TO USE:
- When above conditions are not in place

NUMBER OF PARTICIPANTS:
- 15–200 people per workshop; can run many Participative Design Workshops in parallel

TYPES OF PARTICIPANTS:
- Everyone who is part of the section of the structure being designed
- A deep-slice team covering these levels and as many functions and skills as possible

TYPICAL DURATION:
- Preparation: 2 weeks to many months
- Event: 1–3 days or session by session
- Ongoing: For the life of the agreement and usually longer

BRIEF EXAMPLE:
J. Robins & Sons Pty Ltd. increased output from 72 units per hour to 89 units per hour, up 25 percent; reduced shortages and thus stoppages in production; reduced absenteeism; reduced overall production time for a shoe from 6 to 8 weeks with 50 to 60 minutes actual processing time to less than 12 hours with 20 to 30 minutes processing; rejects have fallen from 4 percent to 0.5 percent.

HISTORICAL CONTEXT:
Created in 1971 by Fred Emery, based on nearly 60 years of intensive research.

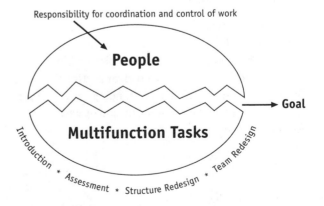

For More Information: Modern Times Workplace, www.moderntimesworkplace.com

PeerSpirit Circling

Thumbnail
Adaptable Method
Chapter 25
Page 261

PURPOSE:
To focus on the power of communication to release the full potential of working groups.

OUTCOMES:
- Wisdom is in the room
- Wise organizational decisions occur at all levels

WHEN TO USE:
- When you want to create a collaborative field

WHEN NOT TO USE:
- When thought leaders are invested in hierarchy and are not willing to change to a collaborative culture

NUMBER OF PARTICIPANTS:
- 5–20 people/per circle: numerous circles may function simultaneously

TYPES OF PARTICIPANTS:
- Anyone willing to work in a nonhierarchal, collaborative process

TYPICAL DURATION:
- Preparation: 3–4 hours
- Process: 1–2 hours to increase quality of communication, and 1–2 days to set the framework for initiating change
- Follow-up: As requested

BRIEF EXAMPLE:
A University Dean says: "We combined two departments and now everybody is playing lone ranger—protecting their own turf, or putting their friends forward for positions or funding. How do I get them to consider who's best for the job or what's best for the university?"

PeerSpirit response: "We worked with a combined faculty committee to reframe the situation from loss to gain. In a series of facilitated dialogues, the committee began to see the merging of departments as a chance to develop a new departmental culture with the potential to become a leading-edge model for the university. They included graduate students who documented and qualified their successful change."

HISTORICAL CONTEXT:
Created in 1994 by Christina Baldwin and Ann Linnea. Grounded in historical archetype of circle emerging from indigenous cultures throughout the world. Many indigenous scholars have helped circle emerge into modern consciousness: Willie Ermine, Eber Hampton, Fyre Jean Graveline, and Malidoma Patrice Somé represent a few of the many who have opened the way for circle.

For More Information: PeerSpirit, www.peerspirit.com

PlaybackTheatre

In-depth
Supportive Method
Chapter 60
Page 561

PURPOSE:
To promote dialogue, build empathy, surface critical issues, and mark transitions.

OUTCOMES:
- Makes corporate culture visible; gives voice to all levels of hierarchy

WHEN TO USE:
- To give a group a voice
- To build a sense of community
- To foster open discussion

WHEN NOT TO USE:
- When mistrust is too high
- When alcohol is being consumed

NUMBER OF PARTICIPANTS:
- 10–150+

TYPES OF PARTICIPANTS:
- Multifunction employees at all levels in an organization, grouped either heterogeneously or homogeneously. Could also include external clients and customers
- Audience format
- Workshop format

TYPICAL DURATION:
- Consultations: 0.5 day–2 days
- Process: 1- to 2-hour performance
- Follow-up: 0.5 day minimum

BRIEF EXAMPLE:
Line workers, support staff, and managers gather for a kickoff to visioning as part of strategic planning. A Playback Theatre team dramatizes in vivid fashion their stories of success and meaning in the workplace, along with systemwide frustrations they would like to see resolved. Understanding and empathy increases.

HISTORICAL CONTEXT:
Created in 1975 by Jonathan Fox, Jo Salas, and original Playback Theatre company. Influenced by Paolo Freire and J. L. Moreno.

For More Information: International Playback Theatre Network, www.playbacknet.org

Power of Imagination Studio

PURPOSE:

To build self-esteem and expertise on key themes; anchor individual strategies in organizations; and overcome hierarchical limitations and mental blocks.

OUTCOMES:
- Conviction that the future is alterable, that several possibilities ("futures") can be formed
- A stance of esteem and encouragement exists at all levels of the organization

WHEN TO USE:
- When participants are perceived to be the experts responsible for finding a solution and making changes
- In situations with negative changes
- When content is open

WHEN NOT TO USE:
- No chance of implementing/carrying out the conclusions
- No strength/financial resources/support
- Strategies/conclusions were decided long ago

NUMBER OF PARTICIPANTS:
- 12–120

TYPES OF PARTICIPANTS:
- All hierarchical levels
- Different backgrounds
- Less adroit in speech (lack of courage/spunk to speak freely)

TYPICAL DURATION:
- Preparation: 1–6 months
- Process: 1–5 days
- Follow-up: 1–3 months

BRIEF EXAMPLE:

Full-time and volunteer employees of the Red Cross from 20 different locations in northern Germany founded 13 statewide project teams after a three-day Imagination Studio. They published a handbook for members, devised a new concept for canvassing members, initiated an Internet information portal as a model project, organized an event to dissuade young people from drinking, inaugurated the annual meeting of all association members, issued guidelines for employees to improve their public image, and proposed teaching concepts in schools for strengthening volunteer involvement.

HISTORICAL CONTEXT:

Created in 2004 by Petra Eickhoff, Annegret Franz, Stephan G. Geffers, Fritz Letsch, Annette Schlemm, and Axel Weige. Builds on the Future Workshop created in 1965 by Professor Robert Jungk, Dr. Norbert R. Muellert, and Ruediger Lutz.

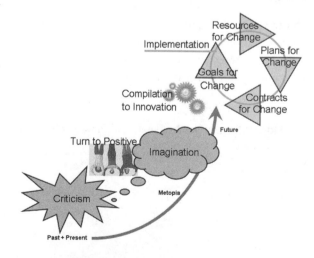

For More Information: Vernetzung von Zukunftswerkstätten, www.zwnetz.de

The Practice of Empowerment

PURPOSE:

To change behavior and develop talent in organizations. An alternative use is for community-based behavior change by public sector agencies and nonprofits.

OUTCOMES:
- An empowered organizational culture

WHEN TO USE:
- To change behavior and develop talent in organizations

WHEN NOT TO USE:
- When there is not a trained practitioner

NUMBER OF PARTICIPANTS:
- 15–40 per group

TYPES OF PARTICIPANTS:
- Any level

TYPICAL DURATION:
- Preparation: 30–90 days to plan and design with input of project champion and key leaders
- Process: 3-day training
- Follow-up: 12 months of coaching and master classes
- Project duration: 1–3 years

BRIEF EXAMPLE:

Senior industry leaders at Deloitte Consulting delivered a mentorship program to empower high-talent women and minorities to develop their full potential. The program was designed to retain and advance these people and build the capacity of senior leaders in talent development.

HISTORICAL CONTEXT:

Created in 1981 by David Gershon.

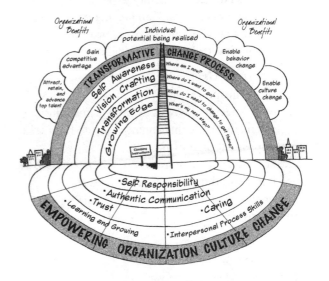

For More Information: Empowerment Institute, www.empowermentinstitute.net

Rapid Results

*In-depth
Improving Method
Chapter 46
Page 450*

PURPOSE:

To build capacity for large-scale change through the vehicle of short-term projects.

OUTCOMES:

- Change becomes an inherent part of the job
- Joint responsibility for shared objectives
- Parallel work flow
- Experimental, "let's try it" attitude
- Focused accountability
- "Better results with what we have"

WHEN TO USE:

- The most powerful driver of better performance is better performance itself. If you want to help an organization develop its ability to perform better, nothing is more effective than helping it to experience a tangible success on some of the dimensions it is trying to strengthen.

WHEN NOT TO USE:

- Guiding principles are not present
- Senior management wishes to hand teams solutions to implement versus challenging teams to both set and implement their own goals
- Senior management/sponsors are not prepared to be involved beyond the launch of the projects
- The organization does not exhibit "readiness" to move forward

NUMBER OF PARTICIPANTS:

- 7–10 people per team
- 100+ teams in successive waves

TYPES OF PARTICIPANTS:

- Any team composition where all members are committed to achieving results and learning
- Senior management sponsors prepared to be involved during the entire cycle

TYPICAL DURATION:

- Shape: 2 weeks
- Launch: 1 day
- Implement: 30–100 days
- Scale-up: 30+ days

BRIEF EXAMPLE:

In Nicaragua, farmers using Rapid Results witnessed measurable improvement in their productivity and income in 100–120 days. Daily milk production almost tripled among 60 producers; 30 farmers increased pig weight by 30 percent; and 30 chicken farmers' productivity increased by 20 percent.

HISTORICAL CONTEXT:

Created in the 1960s by Robert H. Schaffer and colleagues.

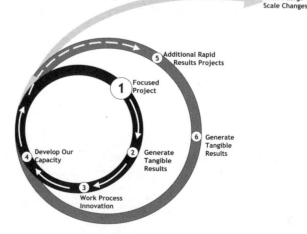

For More Information: Robert H. Schaffer & Associates, www.rhsa.com

RealTime Strategic Change

Thumbnail
Adaptable Method
Chapter 27
Page 273

PURPOSE:
To enable people to create their future—faster than they ever believed possible.

OUTCOMES:
- Better ways of doing business that lead to major improvements to key financial, quality, cost, timing, and other performance measures
- More flexible, resilient, and responsive organizations to meet emerging market demands
- Improved "changeability" that makes change a core competence
- Unleashing of organizational energy and commitment

WHEN TO USE:
- When you need to make big things happen—fast

WHEN NOT TO USE:
- When you don't have full commitment of leadership to support the development and implementation of better ways of doing business—for themselves and their organization

NUMBER OF PARTICIPANTS:
- 1–10,000 or more

TYPES OF PARTICIPANTS:
- Broad base of internal/external stakeholders who can help you create your future, faster

TYPICAL DURATION:
- With Real-Time Strategic Change (RTSC), "before, during, and after" don't exist. It's an approach to everyday work and major transformation efforts.

BRIEF EXAMPLE:
City of New York Out of School Time program involving several hundred providers, multiple funding streams, city agencies, and oversight bodies. Through applying RTSC, these diverse stakeholders with competing needs reached consensus on a common vision, goals, and operating principles. These agreements have ensured funding goes to programs that meet specifications and improved the overall care given to children before and after school and during holidays and weekends in New York City.

HISTORICAL CONTEXT:
Created in 1994 by Robert "Jake" Jacobs and Frank McKeown, RTSC is based on work by Kathleen Dannemiller, Chuck Tyson, Bruce Gibb, Al Davenport, and Nancy Badore. The method has undergone three generations of evolution.

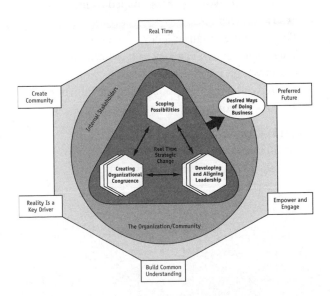

For More Information: Robert W. Jacobs Consulting, www.rwjacobs.com

Scenario Thinking

*In-depth
Planning Method
Chapter 34
Page 331*

PURPOSE:

To arrive at a deeper understanding of the world in which your organization operates, and use that understanding to inform your strategy and improve your ability to make better decisions today and in the future.

OUTCOMES:

- Set strategic direction
- Catalyze bold action
- Accelerate collaborative learning
- Alignment and visioning

WHEN TO USE:

- When the solution to a strategic issue is unclear
- You are working in a highly uncertain environment
- There is leadership support for scenario thinking
- Your organization is open to change and dialogue
- You have the resources for a successful initiative

WHEN NOT TO USE:

- The problem you are dealing with is not central to your organizational strategy and/or your problem and solution are clear
- The outcome will largely be shaped by internal or external forces
- There is not enough urgency for change
- There is too much urgency to step back for a reflective and creative conversation
- Desired outcomes are poorly aligned with your dedicated resources

NUMBER OF PARTICIPANTS:

- 10–20 interviewees
- 15–500 workshop participants

TYPES OF PARTICIPANTS:

- Decision makers
- Internal and external stakeholders representing a range of functions and perspectives
- Outsiders introducing provocative perspectives

TYPICAL DURATION:

- Orient phase: 1–2 months
- Explore, synthesize, and act phases: 2–4 months
- Monitor phase: Indefinite

BRIEF EXAMPLE:

A financial services company needs to better understand potential impact of emerging technologies and consumer behavior on the market for investment services during the dot-com bubble—and beyond. It engages in a scenario thinking process that involves the company's key decision makers. As a result, the company makes a decision that prevents overinvestment in growth during the peak of dot-com speculative bubble, and new product development is initiated.

HISTORICAL CONTEXT:

Scenario pioneers include Herman Kahn, Pierre Wack, Peter Schwartz, Kees van der Heijden, Ted Newland, and Napier Collyns. Roots in military planning and Wack's work at Shell in the 1970s.

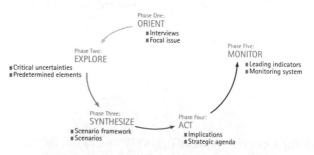

Search Conference

*In-depth
Planning Method
Chapter 35
Page 347*

PURPOSE:
To create a well-articulated, desirable, achievable future with action plans for implementation within a definite timetable by a community of people who want to and know how to do it.

OUTCOMES:
- A well-articulated set of goals.
- Coordinated action plans for achieving the goals.
- A community of people who have learned how to actively and adaptively plan.
- A shared commitment to, and energy for, implementing a plan to achieve the desired future.

WHEN TO USE:
- Strategic planning and the basis of policy making
- Creation of new systems to manage emergent or neglected issues
- Rationalization of major conflicts within a strategic context

WHEN NOT TO USE:
- When guarantees are not present to abide by the conditions governing the effective use of the method
- When the task is only about means to a preordained conclusion
- When there is not at least one trained and experienced Search Conference manager who knows their theory

NUMBER OF PARTICIPANTS:
- 20–35 people for a single Search Conference event. To involve more people, conduct a series and integrate the results.

TYPES OF PARTICIPANTS:
- Members of the system

TYPICAL DURATION:
- Preparation: 1–18 months recorded so far
- Event: 2 days and 2 nights consecutively
- Follow-up: Self-sustaining

BRIEF EXAMPLE:
Two national industrial relations Search Conferences held in 1972 and 1977 set the ground for the first national accord governing new directions for the democratization of work and revitalization of industry and business in Australia through "award restructuring" and other national processes.

HISTORICAL CONTEXT:
The method was conceptualized and designed by Fred Emery and Eric Trist in 1959. Fred and Merrelyn Emery and others have continued its development.

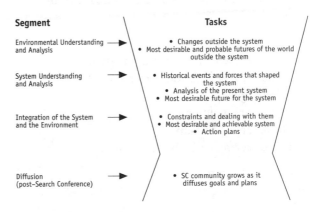

Segment	Tasks
Environmental Understanding and Analysis	• Changes outside the system • Most desirable and probable futures of the world outside the system
System Understanding and Analysis	• Historical events and forces that shaped the system • Analysis of the present system • Most desirable future for the system
Integration of the System and the Environment	• Constraints and dealing with them • Most desirable and achievable system • Action plans
Diffusion (post–Search Conference)	• SC community grows as it diffuses goals and plans

For More Information: www.moderntimesworkplace.com

SimuReal

PURPOSE:

To bring together key members of an organization or a community in a way that allows them to (a) experience/learn more about their interactions with one another, (b) work on real issues, (c) make decisions within a compressed time frame, and (d) gain skills and understandings they can use to deal more effectively with future challenges in their "back home" setting.

OUTCOMES:

- SimuReal holds a "mirror" to the organization about how it actually works (or does not work). It can be a powerful change agent, because everyone sees the impact of the system and can self-organize to improve it.

WHEN TO USE:

- To shorten the time it takes to make or implement decisions
- To "test drive" a restructuring plan before it is implemented
- To address a complex problem or decision
- To uncover the structural/procedural blocks to solving a problem effectively
- The organization is prepared to engage in self-examination

WHEN NOT TO USE:

- To focus on creating a common vision
- To align the organization around a given vision/strategy
- To do team building
- The organization is in crisis
- To redesign an entire business process

NUMBER OF PARTICIPANTS:

- 35–125

TYPES OF PARTICIPANTS:

- Flexible—can accommodate both internal and external stakeholders, as well as same-function or multifunction participants

TYPICAL DURATION:

- Preparation: 1-day design team meeting, 2 days in additional preparation
- Process: 1 day
- Follow-up: Typically ranges from immediate to a year, depending on initial contract with clients, SimuReal outcomes, and leadership needs in implementing those outcomes.

BRIEF EXAMPLE:

"Test drive" of a restructuring plan, involving all who would be affected. The "test drive" showed the design gaps and resulted in a 50 percent change in overall design in the days that followed the SimuReal, with support for implementation 3 months later.

HISTORICAL CONTEXT:

Created in the 1970s by Donald C. Klein.

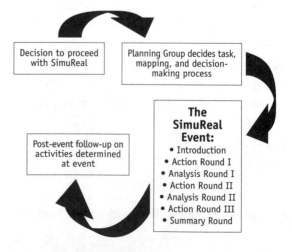

Decision to proceed with SimuReal

Planning Group decides task, mapping, and decision-making process

The SimuReal Event:
- Introduction
- Action Round I
- Analysis Round I
- Action Round II
- Analysis Round II
- Action Round III
- Summary Round

Post-event follow-up on activities determined at event

For More Information: Klein Consulting, www.kleinconsulting.com

The Six Sigma Approach

*In-depth
Improving Method
Chapter 47
Page 465*

Quick Summaries

PURPOSE:

To improve process performance and eliminate causes of mistakes in manufacturing and business processes by focusing on process outputs that are critically important to customers.

OUTCOMES:

- Process improvements resulting from completed improvement projects
- Human elements like leadership, teamwork, and customer focus integrated with the process aspects of improvement
- An infrastructure of management systems and permanent change agents is created to lead, deploy, and implement improvement projects
- Leaders are provided with the strategy, methods, and tools for changing their organizations
- Benefits produce culture change, rather than trying to change the culture to produce benefits

WHEN TO USE:

- To solve the problem by improving processes, whether they are manufacturing, financial, supply chain, or customer service

WHEN NOT TO USE:

- When the solution to a problem is already known— for example, installing a new piece of equipment, bringing information technology into line with new corporate guidelines, building a plant, most capital projects

NUMBER OF PARTICIPANTS:

- 4–6 team members per improvement project
- From 1 to more than 100 parallel teams

TYPES OF PARTICIPANTS:

- Leadership, Champions, Master Black Belts, Black Belts, Green Belts, functional support members

TYPICAL DURATION:

- Preparation: 2 days–1 months
- Process: 4–6 months per project
- Follow-up: Weekly management reviews; monthly for improvement projects, quarterly for the overall deployment, and annually to plan for the coming year

BRIEF EXAMPLE:

A major pharmaceutical manufacturer that anticipated being unable to meet demand for a blockbuster new product used Six Sigma's sequenced problem-solving methodology to improve the process and address underlying organizational issues.

HISTORICAL CONTEXT:

Early 1980s, stimulated by Japanese companies' use of statistical methods in manufacturing. Mid-1980s, created by Motorola and named Six Sigma. Mid-1990s, extended by G.E. to include all processes.

Major Deployment Phases

Major Transition Points

From Business as Usual to a Six Sigma Approach	From a New Launch to a Long Term Initiative	From THE Initiative to AN Initiative	From an Initiative to a Normal Part of the Job

Individual Project Methodology: DMAIC

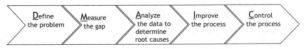

For More Information: American Society for Quality, www.asq.org

SOAR

*Thumbnail
Planning Method
Chapter 38
Page 375*

PURPOSE:

To accelerate the strategic planning process by allowing creativity and innovation while inspiring the organization's people to SOAR.

OUTCOMES:

- Develops a whole system perspective
- Uncovers the strengths and opportunities of the organization
- Cocreates the values, vision, and mission of stakeholders
- Develops a strategic and tactical plan
- Identifies the structures, systems, and processes
- Engenders continuous informed appreciative reflection and action

WHEN TO USE:

- For environmental scanning
- To accelerate existing strategic planning processes
- To create strategic and tactical plans
- To embrace a whole systems approach to strategic planning
- To heighten awareness of organizational relationships and how to best use these relationships

WHEN NOT TO USE:

- Leadership is not supportive (top-down approach)
- Participants are not empowered to act on their aspirations and plans

NUMBER OF PARTICIPANTS:

- 10–400

TYPES OF PARTICIPANTS:

- Internal and external organizational stakeholders

TYPICAL DURATION:

- Preparation: 0.5 day to 1.5 days
- Process: 0.5 day to 4 days (average is 2–3 days)
- Follow-up: Continuous

BRIEF EXAMPLE:

A health-care facility was in a shutdown state and needed a "last-ditch effort." The administrator gathered 76 stakeholders to discuss creating constructive accountability and strategic initiatives so corporate would not close the facility. The results were a 20 percent increase in census within six weeks, improved employee morale and resident satisfaction, and the facility broke even for the first time in three years.

HISTORICAL CONTEXT:

Created in 2000 by Jackie Stavros, David Cooperrider, and Lynn Kelley. Theory Base: Appreciative Inquiry, Dialogue, Whole Systems Approach to Change, Lippit's Preferred Futures, Strengths-Based Theory by Don Clifton, Social Construction, and Positive Organizational Scholarship.

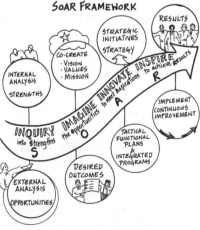

SOAR FRAMEWORK

STRENGTHS, OPPORTUNITIES, ASPIRATIONS, RESULTS
-Stavros, Cooperrider, Kelly, 2006

For More Information: Dynamic Relationships, www.dynamic-relationships.com

Strategic Forum

PURPOSE:
To help the organization and/or policy makers explore future scenarios when issues are complex, and multiple stakeholders see things differently.

OUTCOMES:
- Shared understanding of different futures
- Collective mental model for testing the efficacy of strategic choices
- Experiential (visceral) understanding of how a strategy should unfold
- Measure progress and/or to prepare for major shifts
- A dynamic and balanced scorecard

WHEN TO USE:
- There's a need to develop a balanced/holistic picture
- Groups are rushing down the solution path
- Discussion of a strategy has not resulted in a consensus
- There is a need to look at nonphysical variables
- It's important to see the impact of a strategy
- Wanting to understand potential unintended consequences

WHEN NOT TO USE:
- You can't find a competent modeler
- There is little time for exploration of assumptions
- It is considered a one-time event
- Organization is unwilling to embrace an ongoing systems thinking

NUMBER OF PARTICIPANTS:
- 2–50
- Ideally, 5 teams of 3–5 participants

TYPES OF PARTICIPANTS:
- At a minimum, should include participants from across multiple functions, silos, and levels
- Ideally, some participants will come from clients and suppliers to the organization

TYPICAL DURATION:
- Preparation: 1–6 months
- Process: 1–2 days
- Follow-up: 6 months

BRIEF EXAMPLE:
In the 1980s, a rapidly growing high-tech firm experienced "growing pains" and internal dissension as the service organization demanded a greater percentage of the organizaion's overall resource base. A Strategic Forum was developed to allow participants to understand the physics and to lay out several strategic choices they could pursue. As a result, the strategy team continued using the system dynamics approach to understanding issues, holding subsequent forums.

HISTORICAL CONTEXT:
Created in the 1980s by Barry Richmond.

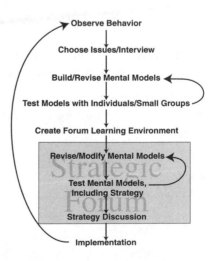

For More Information: Pontifex Consulting, www.pontifexconsulting.com

Strategic Visioning

PURPOSE:

To help leadership teams in organizations and communities combine historical hindsight with future-oriented foresight to support insight in present action.

OUTCOMES:

- Catalyzes real engagement
- Deepens relationships
- Shifts perspectives
- Develops appreciation of new factors and forces creation of a "perceptivity" to new ideas before they actually become viable in action

WHEN TO USE:

- Task force action planning, 2-day board retreats, 3–6 month Strategic Visioning processes, and special, large-scale change processes
- Planning processes needing involvement and breakthrough thinking
- Making leadership assumptions visible, shareable, and as a result, open to challenge and push-back

WHEN NOT TO USE:

- When leadership teams are locked into a top-down plan
- When leadership doesn't want to test their ideas and hear from people
- For situations in such crisis that no one has any room for reflection and big-picture thinking

NUMBER OF PARTICIPANTS:

- Leadership teams of 5–12 plus larger numbers of stakeholders

TYPES OF PARTICIPANTS:

- Leadership teams
- Other stakeholders

TYPICAL DURATION:

- Preparation: 6 weeks
- Process: 1–2 days
- Follow-up: 3–6 months

BRIEF EXAMPLE:

A national architectural firm engaged its 50 partners in appreciating systemwide opportunities and developed an aligned set of priorities. They reviewed their history, current environment, internal strengths and weaknesses, and then developed a vision, set of strategies, and fleshed out game plans over two 2-day meetings with some action teamwork in between.

HISTORICAL CONTEXT:

Created in 1995 by David Sibbet, Ed Claassen, and associate consultants who have contributed additional templates: Strategic Planning (Porter, Minzberg); Visioning (Fritz, Senge, Halprin); Large-Scale Change (Dannemiller Tyson, Weisbord), and Graphic Facilitation (Sibbet).

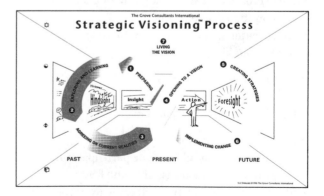

For More Information: Strategic Visioning, www.grove.com/learning_center/method_pm_svm.html

Study Circles

Thumbnail
Adaptable Method
Chapter 29
Page 283

PURPOSE:
To help communities develop their ability to solve problems by exploring ways for all kinds of people to think, talk, and create change together.

OUTCOMES:
- Helps communities develop a more democratic public culture
- Demonstrates the whole community is needed
- Embraces diversity
- Shares knowledge, resources, power, and decision making
- Combines dialogue and deliberation; builds understanding and explores a range of solutions
- Connects deliberative dialogue to social, political, and policy change

WHEN TO USE:
- An issue concerns the daily lives of many different types of people
- An issue captures widespread public attention
- An issue is best addressed through multiple forms of social, political, and policy change

WHEN NOT TO USE:
- On issues of personal transformation that do not include public and problem-solving dimensions

NUMBER OF PARTICIPANTS:
- 100 to 1,000s

TYPES OF PARTICIPANTS:
- Reflects the diversity of the community—in organizing, facilitation, and participation

TYPICAL DURATION:
- Preparation: 2–4 months
- Process: 4–6 weeks
- Follow-up: Ongoing

BRIEF EXAMPLE:
KCK Study Circles addressed neighborhood issues, as part of a public school reform initiative in Kansas City, Kansas. Since 1999, this United Way project has involved 1,800+ residents on neighborhood issues, education, and diversity. Study circles have led to: public housing residents starting a tenants' association, setting up a youth sports camp, and getting rid of about ten drug houses; 100+ young people conducting a downtown cleanup; Spanish-speaking parents forming a parents' association; young people doing minor home repairs and beautifying houses in their neighborhood to attract businesses where they can get jobs; a local church opening a food pantry.

HISTORICAL CONTEXT:
Created in 1989 by Paul J. Aicher, who founded the Study Circles Resource Center. Based in the deliberative traditions of town hall meetings, "study circles" were part of the Chautauqua movement in the U.S. Progressive Era (1870s–1920s). Swedish temperance and union movements brought them to Sweden where thousands are now government supported. They returned to the U.S. in the 1980s through National Issues Forums, unions, and the Study Circle Resource Center.

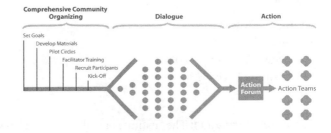

For More Information: Study Circles Resource Center, www.studycircles.org

Technology of Participation

PURPOSE:

To elicit participation of a group, organization, or community in creating a thoughtful discussion, consensus formation, or the collaborative creation of short-term or strategic plans.

OUTCOMES:

- Create solutions that represent a group's best thinking and which it will own
- Deeper understanding of and commitment to decisions and directions

WHEN TO USE:

- A group, organization, or community has a question or concern related to change and future action
- New strategies and focused directions are needed
- People need in-depth dialogue to allow them to operate with a common understanding and focus

WHEN NOT TO USE:

- Severe and unyielding group conflict is present
- The outcome is predetermined
- Key stakeholders will not be present
- No leadership support for decisions the group might make

NUMBER OF PARTICIPANTS:

- 5–1,000

TYPES OF PARTICIPANTS:

- Those directly involved in the issues or who will be affected by any solutions
- Those expected to support or implement any plans developed

TYPICAL DURATION:

- Preparation: 1–3 days
- Process: Typically 1–3 days
- Transition: Variable

BRIEF EXAMPLE:

A 40-person state government department used ToP methods to restore communications and trust and to develop a vision and new direction. Some outcomes: new in-house facilitators helped sections develop goals and mission statements; assessment of staff needs resulted in computer and quality training; and the office restructured, folding many functions into other departments.

HISTORICAL CONTEXT:

Developed by the Institute of Cultural Affairs in the 1960s and 1970s for change initiatives in different countries, especially community development and corporate strategic planning.

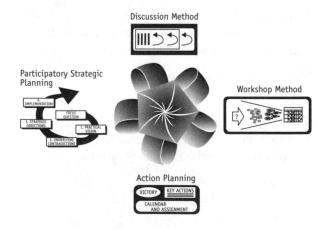

For More Information: The Institute of Cultural Affairs, www.ica-usa.org

Think Like a Genius

Quick Summaries

PURPOSE:

To express and represent people's ideas, feelings, knowledge, views, insights, experiences, and the like in new ways using multidimensional symbolic models that help improve human communication and foster understanding.

OUTCOMES:

- Uncovers "cultural assumptions" that are sinking an organization so that they can be changed, and the organization not only survives but flourishes
- Willingness to examine assumptions about using "unusual" methods to collaborate and to share personal knowledge and expertise while leveraging the organization's resources
- More openness to far-reaching, exploratory, and experimental approaches to innovation and "borderless thinking"

WHEN TO USE:

- To represent individual explicit and tacit knowledge or personal life experiences in memorable ways
- To collaboratively create new ideas
- To establish a sense of trust and true community
- To create and share new knowledge that can spark innovations

WHEN NOT TO USE:

- When you don't care what other people think about your ideas, your mission, your plans, your sense of success or purpose
- If you don't care to hear, see, or know what your coworkers have to say

NUMBER OF PARTICIPANTS:

- 12–1,200 or more

TYPES OF PARTICIPANTS:

- Internal and external stakeholders
- Experts in the field or profession
- Intact teams, cross-functional groups, consumers, clients, and the like

TYPICAL DURATION:

- Preparation: 3 hours–1 day
- Process: 3 hours–1 day
- Follow-up: Within 1 week

BRIEF EXAMPLE:

Immediately following a strategic planning and implementation workshop at NTT/Verio, the Verio CEO in America presented a detailed "Distillation Drawing" that translated the workshop's accomplishments to the NTT CEO in Japan. The drawing helped the NTT visionary quickly understand what needed to build on the recommendations offered by the senior executives of NTT who had participated in this hands-on workshop.

HISTORICAL CONTEXT:

Created by Todd Siler in 1978 with organizations and in 1993 with individuals. The Magdalenian cave painters of the Ice Age in Altimira, northern Spain, and Lascaux, France, were the first in recorded history to use symbolic objects as visual stories to express human experiences of the world.

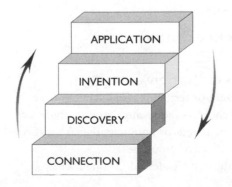

For More Information: Think Like a Genius, www.ThinkLikeAGenius.com

21st Century Town Meeting

PURPOSE:

To engage large numbers of citizens in government decision making on public policy issues by supporting deliberation that is well informed, synthesized, and directly connected to real opportunities for action.

OUTCOMES:
- Playing field leveled between citizens and special interests
- Decision makers incorporate citizen priorities in public policy development
- Increased expectations for transparent, accountable governance

WHEN TO USE:
- There is a direct link to the key decision makers and governance processes that can ensure results
- The nature of the issue requires people to deeply wrestle with strategies and choices
- Polling data indicate that citizens believe they can reach consensus even if partisan positioning means the politicians cannot

WHEN NOT TO USE:
- There is no commitment by decision makers to participate and/or act on the results
- The issue is in the early stages of development and action opportunities have not crystallized
- Insufficient availability of infrastructure and resources

NUMBER OF PARTICIPANTS:
- 100–5,000

TYPES OF PARTICIPANTS:
- Citizens or residents affected by the issue
- Stakeholders (advocates, community-based organizations, or representatives from affected businesses or industries)
- Community leaders, decision makers

TYPICAL DURATION:
- Development and Preparation: 6–12 months
- Meeting: 1 day (or partial day)
- Follow-up: Generally 3–12 months

BRIEF EXAMPLE:

In 2002, the Hamilton County, Ohio, Regional Planning Commission engaged the community in developing a comprehensive plan for issues including employment, housing, transportation, and education. In addition to a 1,300-person 21st Century Town Meeting, the effort included 11 community forums, one youth forum, and a weeklong online forum. Afterward, action teams produced 160 specific strategies for helping the county reach its goals. The county commissioners endorsed the citizens' vision statement, and in November 2004, the commission began implementing the citizen-driven priority initiatives.

HISTORICAL CONTEXT:

Created in 1995 by Carolyn J. Lukensmeyer and the America*Speaks* staff. Founding tenets of American Democracy: "government of the people, by the people and for the people," "consent of the governed."

For More Information: America*Speaks*, www.americaspeaks.org

Values Into Action

Thumbnail
Improving Method
Chapter 57
Page 530

PURPOSE:

To explore an issue through questions focused on its external (global and local) complexity and internal relationship to deeply held values, convictions, and perspectives, leading to individual commitments to act.

OUTCOMES:

- People of different views and values, stature and status understand and support each other
- People learn from the convictions of others without having to give up their own positions
- People make commitments and discover that individual acts unfolding over time can make a difference

WHEN TO USE:

- Positive change around an issue (e.g., AIDS, elimination of hunger, affordable housing, accessing clean water) is desired, and consensus vision and collaborative planning are not necessary or practical

WHEN NOT TO USE:

- A shared vision and collaborative planning and action are desired or there's not a compelling issue

NUMBER OF PARTICIPANTS:

- 30–1,000+

TYPES OF PARTICIPANTS:

- Within an organization: internal and external stakeholders
- Within a community: stakeholders from different segments of the community
- Across diverse geographies (regional or global gatherings): multisector teams from the same area

TYPICAL DURATION:

- Preparation: Up to 3 months
- Process: 1–3 days
- Follow-up: Optional tracking support

BRIEF EXAMPLE:

Carry the Vision: Building Cultures of Peace in Our Families, Our Communities and Our World was a one-day community-based conference with 400 participants from diverse segments of the regional community focused on how people can work for peace. Workshops and panels highlighted stories of what is working in the world. An afternoon reflecting on the Values Into Action questions moved from stories of connection to the issue, through reflection on values and convictions, culminating in commitment to individual simple and profound acts for peace. The conference collected 250 commitments.

HISTORICAL CONTEXT:

Created in 2003 by Susan Dupre, Ray Gordezky, Helen Spector, Billie Alban, Emily Axelrod, Jorge Estrada, Thava Govender, Sam Magill, Rita Schweitz, and Nan Voss in partnership with Dirk Ficca, executive director of the Council for a Parliament of the World's Religions. Principle-based processes including Future Search, Open Space, and Appreciative Inquiry.

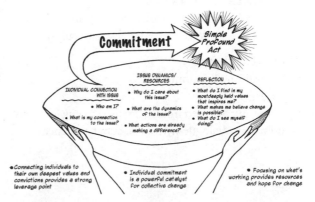

For More Information: Values into Action, www.valuesintoaction.net

Visual Explorer

Thumbnail
Supportive Method
Chapter 65
Page 603

PURPOSE:

To explore a complex issue using a visually mediated dialogue that fully engages each point of view in a fun, safe, relatively quick, and yet deep way.

OUTCOMES:

- Rapid depth of dialogue and shared understanding among differing perspectives
- Produces memorable metaphors and stories
- Produces a creative relationship to the ideas, emotions, and intuitions of self and others
- Produces a visual record of the dialogue for group memory and future reuse

WHEN TO USE:

- When a deep, creative, fun, and productive dialogue is in order among a variety of differing perspectives
- Best used at the front end of a creative, exploratory process as a group needs to make sense of a complex challenge

WHEN NOT TO USE:

- When a group is driving toward closure, or when analysis of data can produce a definitive answer to a group's issues

NUMBER OF PARTICIPANTS:

- 2–100s

TYPES OF PARTICIPANTS:

- Any; works well across vast differences in perspective, background, language, and culture.

TYPICAL DURATION:

- Preparation: 20 minutes
- Process: 1–4 hours
- Follow-up: Selected images are used to engage ideas and restart dialogue with subsequent audiences

BRIEF EXAMPLE:

A corporate e-commerce team opened their two-day planning retreat with a Visual Explorer (VE) session. Each member chose two images from the standard VE set of 224 images: One about "what its been like this year to work on the team," and another image about "what our work should look like in the next year." The resultant dialogue set a standard of candor and listening for the rest of the retreat. The team leader was pleased that this normally buttoned-down group was energized by the process of talking imaginatively about their recent history and their desired future.

HISTORICAL CONTEXT:

Created in 1997 by Charles J. Palus and David Magellan Horth with colleagues at the Center for Creative Leadership as a result of the work of Targeted Innovation, LeaderLab, and the Leading Creatively Project (see *The Leader's Edge*). VE has roots in the work of David Perkins at Harvard Project Zero (see *The Intelligent Eye*); in the field of dialogue; in the group dream-work process of Montague Ullman; and in the understanding of leadership as relational meaning making in the work of Bill Drath.

For More Information: Center for Creative Leadership Visual Explorer, www.ccl.org/visualexplorer

Visual Recording and Graphic Facilitation

*In-depth
Supportive Method
Chapter 61
Page 573*

PURPOSE:

To record ideas and facilitate conversation using images, symbols, words, and phrases, thereby supporting participants in a group process SEEing their ideas, noticing relationships and patterns, and reviewing and sharing the content of the event.

OUTCOMES:

- Open up individual and group creativity.
- Engage and connect people by supporting both linear and intuitive ways of working with information
- Challenge the notion that groups have to be clumsy, with unproductive means of getting things done

WHEN TO USE:

- At the inspiration and learning phases of process when imagery can be used in evocative ways to open up deeper understanding
- For planning and implementation, when clear thinking is critical

WHEN NOT TO USE:

- When a speaker has a slide or video presentation

NUMBER OF PARTICIPANTS:

- Groups of any size

TYPES OF PARTICIPANTS:

- Whatever mix is appropriate to the situation

TYPICAL DURATION:

- Preparation: Short process design meeting
- Process: The length of time of whatever process is being supported
- Follow-up: Digital and hardcopy reproductions available in 2–3 days

BRIEF EXAMPLE:

In 2005, 50 graphic recorders and facilitators gathered to assess the development of this field. The conference centered on 21st Century Literacy, opening with a session graphically facilitated on 16 running feet of paper. A former Apple multimedia leader posed key questions. Group dialogue was recorded, creating a huge map. Themes swirled and clustered in the visual space. Simple illustrations and diagrams complemented large headlines, building spontaneously. The mural became a springboard and backdrop for the rest of the conference.

HISTORICAL CONTEXT:

Visual recording and graphic facilitation adapted from architecture, design, and teaching in the early 1970s. David Sibbet and Nancy Margulies are among its modern pioneers. It's reflected in the design and visualization work of all creative people, and recently accelerated in acceptance with the integration of word and image in new digital tools.

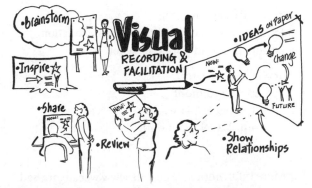

For More Information: The International Forum of Visual Practitioners, www.visualpractitioner.org

Web Lab's Small Group Dialogues

Thumbnail
Adaptable Method
Chapter 31
Page 294

PURPOSE:

To create an online "space" that fosters positive, transformative "dialogues across differences" on public, social, political, organizational development, and personal issues. Participants expressing divergent and sometimes conflicting perspectives work toward finding common ground and possible solutions.

OUTCOMES:
- Engages participants
- Fosters collaboration and builds trust
- Improves intergroup understanding
- Informs decision makers
- Transforms conflicts

WHEN TO USE:
- To enable a culture focused on information and constructive debate, allowing people with widely varied perspectives to learn from one another, and setting the stage for better decision making
- When disagreements are highly contentious

WHEN NOT TO USE:
- Where participants are compelled to join in or do not have a personal stake in the outcomes

NUMBER OF PARTICIPANTS:
- 200–10,000s
- Simultaneous small groups of 40–100 people

TYPES OF PARTICIPANTS:
- Internal or external stakeholders, same function, multifunction, and public stakeholders

TYPICAL DURATION:
- Preparation: 1–3 months
- Online Dialogue: 2–4 weeks
- Follow-up: 2 weeks–1 month

BRIEF EXAMPLE:

Fly into the Future Dialogues (FITF) was a two-week online dialogue addressing the San Diego region's long-term air transportation needs. FITF was organized with Viewpoint Learning, founded by public opinion researcher Daniel Yankelovich to foster "learning through dialogue." Participants' ideas, suggestions, and questions were reflected in subsequent official planning. See http://future.signonsandiego.com.

HISTORICAL CONTEXT:

Created in 1998 by Marc Weiss, Barry Joseph, and Brian Clark. Eric Trist: Social Technical Systems. Kurt Lewin: Experiential learning and action research. David Bohm: Theory of Dialogue. W. Barnett Pearce and Vernon Cronen: Coordinated Management of Meaning.

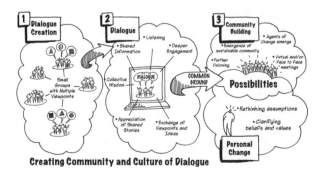

Creating Community and Culture of Dialogue

For More Information: Web Lab, www.weblab.org/sgd

Whole-Scale Change

PURPOSE:

To help organizations remain successful through fast, deep, and sustainable total system change.

OUTCOMES:

- Strategic alignment as one brain (all seeing the same things) and one heart (all committed to achieving the same preferred future)
- Intentionally designed and fully owned processes, skills, information, and guiding principles
- A new culture with the behaviors everyone desires to achieve common purpose

WHEN TO USE:

- With a particularly challenging, changing environment
- For quick, sustainable results

WHEN NOT TO USE:

- Sharing information, engaging and empowering people are not consistent with leaders' values

NUMBER OF PARTICIPANTS:

- 10–10,000 people (or more using Web-based tools)
- Critical mass (10 percent to 100 percent) to shift the paradigm

TYPES OF PARTICIPANTS:

- Microcosms of "the whole" system that's changing
- Cross-section of key stakeholders needed (physically and/or virtually) in order to achieve the purpose and outcomes

TYPICAL DURATION:

- Preparation: 2–4 days per event
- Events: Several 2- to 3-day events with 4–6 weeks of interim task team work
- Follow-up: 1 month–1 year

BRIEF EXAMPLE:

Best Friends Animal Society, a national humane organization, completely redesigned its organization structure and processes. It launched a new strategic vision, using four Whole-Scale events over 6 months, involving the entire 300 member staff. The results: an expanded mission; reorganized workgroups with people focused around the critical work to support the expanded mission; clarity of roles, work, and coordination across work groups; creation of a rapid response team that led the rescue of thousands of animals after hurricane Katrina; streamlined administration and board governance structures; and a succession strategy to free founders of day-to-day responsibilities and move them into public advocacy roles.

HISTORICAL CONTEXT:

Created in 1981, based on theory, principles and methods combined by Dannemiller, Tyson, Gibb, Davenport, and Badore for Ford Motor Company. In 1990, Paul Tolchinsky combined his sociotechnical systems expertise with Kathie Dannemiller's large-scale strategic change processes to develop Real-Time Work Design. The integrated approaches becameWhole-Scale in 1997.

For More Information: Dannemiller Tyson Associates, www.dannemillertyson.com

Whole Systems Approach

PURPOSE:

To effectively weave multiple organizational initiatives into a well-designed, highly effective organization-wide change effort that creates employee engagement, buy-in, and results.

OUTCOMES:

- Create a world of work where people and organizations thrive by streamlining work processes, creating shared meaning around work, and accelerating and substantially increasing results

WHEN TO USE:

- A need to fundamentally change or transform is evident
- A new organizational focus is required
- Existing efforts require integration into a comprehensive whole
- Large-scale engagement/commitment of stakeholders is desired

WHEN NOT TO USE:

- No top-level commitment, leadership, and full involvement

NUMBER OF PARTICIPANTS:

- All organizational members and stakeholder constituency representatives

TYPES OF PARTICIPANTS:

- Representatives from every stakeholder constituency and all employees

TYPICAL DURATION:

- Set the Stage: 3–12 months
- Change the Business: 12–18 months
- Transition: 6–12 months
- Run the Business: 6+ months
- Entire effort: 30–48 months

BRIEF EXAMPLE:

Carlson Companies, Inc., a privately-owned, family enterprise, has more than 190,000 employees in 50+ countries providing services in travel, hospitality (hotels and cruises), marketing, and the restaurant industry. For more than 50 years, Carlson operated as a holding company with six distinct business units managing more than 16 brands. In 2003, Carlson leaders strategically chose to move from a holding company to an integrated operating company focused on the customer. The changes have been massive, far-reaching, and impact every area and system of the organization. Carlson has realized substantial business results.

HISTORICAL CONTEXT:

Developed in 1985 by Bill Adams and Cindy Adams, encompassing years of research and "day in and day out" work partnering with leaders and organizations to successfully realize their change goals.

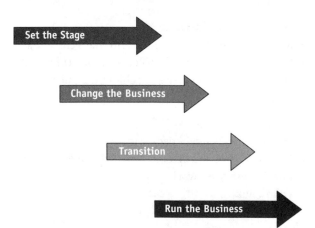

For More Information: Whole Systems, www.maxcomminc.com

WorkOut

PURPOSE:

To reduce bureaucracy, solve business problems, and streamline processes through fast and concentrated decision making and empowerment.

OUTCOMES:
- Drives business results through the resolution of complex business challenges across hierarchical, functional, and other boundaries
- Simultaneously facilitates cultural change—particularly speed, simplicity, empowered self-confidence, and rapid decision making

WHEN TO USE:
- Ambitious business challenge requires resolution of several issues
- Multiple functions, groups, and/or layers need to be involved in crafting an aligned solution
- Business processes need to be simplified—while improving quality and cycle time
- Fast, clear management decisions will stimulate action and focus people's energy and attention on an urgent issue

WHEN NOT TO USE:
- When the aim is to get buy-in for preconceived solutions
- When the obvious aim is to reduce head count

NUMBER OF PARTICIPANTS:
- 20–100

TYPES OF PARTICIPANTS:
- People across functions and levels who are able to contribute to the desired result
- Senior manager as a "sponsor" and decision maker
- Lead consultant and subgroup facilitators

TYPICAL DURATION:
- Design: 2–4 weeks
- Conduct Event: 1–3 days
- Implementation of Recommendations: 3–4 months

BRIEF EXAMPLE:
A UK insurance unit of Zurich Financial Services used WorkOut to transform its financial performance and corporate culture. In one year, more than 30 WorkOuts produced measurable savings in excess of $10 million.

HISTORICAL CONTEXT:
Conceived in 1988 by GE chairman Jack Welch with support from James Baughman, head of the company's Crotonville Leadership Center. Developed by an academic/consultant team led by Dave Ulrich, Len Schlesinger, and Todd Jick, and including Steve Kerr, Ron Ashkenas, and others.

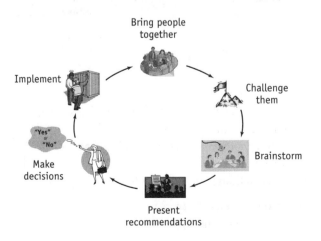

For More Information: Robert H. Schaffer & Associates, www.rhsa.com

The World Café

In-depth
Adaptable Method
Chapter 12
Page 179

PURPOSE:
To foster the conditions for the emergence of collective intelligence by engaging people in dynamic strategic conversations around questions that matter to their lives and work.

OUTCOMES:
- Surfaces unquestioned assumptions
- Redefines the relationship between talk and action and reveals conversation as core process for creating business/social value
- Clarifies the relationship of strategic questions, catalytic conversations, and networks of relationships in change efforts
- Fosters "coherence without control" among diverse stakeholders, even in very large groups

WHEN TO USE:
- Generate input, share knowledge, stimulate innovative thinking, and explore action possibilities around real-life issues and questions
- Engage people who are meeting for the first time in authentic conversation
- Conduct an in-depth exploration of key strategic challenges and opportunities
- Deepen relationships and mutual ownership of outcomes in an existing group
- Create meaningful interaction between a speaker and the audience
- Invite *all* voices into the conversation

WHEN NOT TO USE:
- Driving toward an already determined outcome, solution, or answer
- To convey only one-way information or to do implementation plans
- Have less than 90 minutes or fewer than 12 people

NUMBER OF PARTICIPANTS:
- 12–1,000s with no upper limit in theory

TYPES OF PARTICIPANTS:
- Diverse voices and perspectives on key issues

TYPICAL DURATION:
- Preparation: Less than 1 day to several months
- Process: 2 hours to several days. Regular ongoing Cafés may unfold over months or years
- Follow-up: As determined by designers, host, and participants

BRIEF EXAMPLE:
When faced with a budget shortfall, the Museum of Science and Industry used café dialogues to discover innovative revenue-producing programs enabling them to end fiscal year 2003 with a $267,000 surplus.

HISTORICAL CONTEXT:
Discovered in 1995 by Juanita Brown and David Isaacs with colleagues. Grounded in patterns of community organizing and the spread of social movements. Underpinnings include research by David Bohm, Humberto Maturana, Francisco Varela, Christopher Alexanderl, Fritjof Capra, Meg Wheatley, and other approaches to dialogue and collective consciousness. Deep commitment to democratic ideals.

For More Information: The World Café, www.theworldcafe.com

Part V: References Suggested by Multiple Contributing Authors

I'm astounded by people who want to know the universe, when it's hard enough to find your way around Chinatown.

—Woody Allen

Each chapter's contributors have identified source materials to help you develop a more in-depth understanding of their method. These references are located at the end of the chapter, under the heading "Where to Go for More Information." Some sources were cited more than once; when a work appeared multiple times we also included it in this section. (The method names associated with the authors who recommend the material appear in italics below the citation.)

Arrien, Angeles. *The Four-Fold Way: Walking the Paths of the Warrior, Teacher, Healer, and Visionary.* San Francisco: HarperSanFrancisco, 1993.
(Genuine Contact, Playback Theatre)

Atlee, Tom, with Rosa Zubizarreta. *The Tao of Democracy: Using Co-intelligence to Create a World That Works for All.* Cranston, RI: Writers' Collective, 2003.
(Dialogue and Deliberation, World Café)

Beer, Michael, Russell A. Eisenstat, and Bert A. Spector. "Why Change Programs Don't Produce Change." *Harvard Business Review* 68 (November/December 1990): 158–166.
(Collaborative Loops, Rapid Results)

Block, Peter. *Stewardship: Choosing Service over Self-Interest.* San Francisco: Berrett-Koehler, 1993.
(Civic Engagement, Collaborative Loops)

Cooperrider, David L., and Diana Whitney. *Appreciative Inquiry: Collaborating for Change* (booklet). Willston, VT: Berrett-Koehler Communications, 1999.
(Appreciative Inquiry, Values into Action)

Cooperrider, David L., Diana Whitney, and Jacqueline M. Stavros. *Appreciative Inquiry Handbook.* Bedford Heights, OH, and San Francisco: Lakeshore Communications and Berrett-Koehler Communications, 2003.
(Appreciative Inquiry, SOAR, World Café)

Dannemiller Tyson Associates. *Whole-Scale Change: Unleashing the Magic in Organizations.* San Francisco: Berrett-Koehler, 2000.
(Strategic Visioning, Whole-Scale Change)

Freire, Paulo. *Education for Critical Consciousness.* New York: Seabury Press, 1973.
(Playback Theatre, Technology of Participation)

Fry, Ronald, Frank Barrett, Jane Seiling, and Diana Whitney, eds. *Appreciative Inquiry and Organizational Transformation: Reports from the Field.* Westport, CT: Quorum Books, 2002.
(Appreciative Inquiry, Appreciative Inquiry Summit)

Kaner, Sam, with Lenny Lind, Catherine Toldi, Sarah Fisk, and Duane Berger. *Facilitator's Guide to Participatory Decision-Making.* Philadelphia: New Society Publishers, 1996.
(Charrettes, Visual Recording & Graphic Facilitation)

Kaplan, Robert S., and David P. Norton. *The Balanced Scorecard: Translating Strategy into Action.* Boston: Harvard Business School Press, 1996.
(Balanced Scorecard, Whole Systems Approach)

McKnight, John. *The Careless Society: Community and Its Counterfeits.* New York: BasicBooks, 1995.
(Civic Engagement, Community Weaving)

Oshry, Barry. *Seeing Systems: Unlocking the Mysteries of Organizational Life.* San Francisco: Berrett-Koehler, 1995.
(Employee Engagement, Organization Workshop)

Owen, Harrison. *Open Space Teachnology: A User's Guide,* 2d ed. San Francisco: Berrett-Koehler, 1997.
(Online Environments, Open Space Technology)

———. *The Power of Spirit: How Organizations Transform.* San Francisco: Berrett-Koehler, 2000.
(Genuine Contact, Open Space Technology)

Putnam, Robert D., with Robert Leonardi and Raffaella Y. Nanetti. *Making Democracy Work: Civic Traditions in Modern Italy.* Princeton, NJ: Princeton University Press, 1993.
(Civic Engagement, Community Weaving)

Schwartz, Peter. *Art of the Long View.* New York: Doubleday, 1991.
(Large Group Scenario Planning, Scenario Thinking)

Sheldrake, Rupert. *The Presence of the Past: Morphic Resonance and the Habits of Nature.* Rochester, VT: Park Street Press, 1988.
(Future Search, Online Environments)

Weisbord, Marvin R. *Productive Workplaces: Organizing and Managing for Dignity, Meaning, and Community.* San Francisco: Jossey-Bass, 1987.
(Future Search, Real Time Strategic Change)

Weisbord, Marvin R., and Sandra Janoff. *Future Search: An Action Guide to Finding Common Ground in Organizations and Communities.* San Francisco: Berrett-Koehler, 1995.
(Collaborative Loops, Future Search, Values into Action)

Welch, Jack, with John A. Byrne. *Jack: Straight from the Gut.* New York: Warner Books, 2001.
(Six Sigma, WorkOut)

Wheatley, Margaret J. *Leadership and the New Science: Learning about Organizations from an Orderly Universe.* San Francisco: Berrett-Koehler, 1992.
(Whole-Scale Change, Whole Systems Approach, World Café)

_____. *Turning to One Another: Simple Conversations to Restore Hope to the Future.* San Francisco: Berrett-Koehler, 2002.
(Community Weaving, PeerSpirit Circling)

Index

About the Lead Authors

Peggy Holman brings generative processes to organizations and communities, increasing their capacity for achieving what is important to them. Her work encourages people to take responsibility for what they love, resulting in stronger organizations, communities, and individuals. She believes in the promise of these processes to unleash the human spirit for individual and collective good. She has worked with a Swiss-based pharmaceutical company, a Colombian social service organization, the Israeli Ministry of Education, and U.S. journalists.

Tom Devane is an internationally known consultant and speaker specializing in transformation. He helps companies plan and implement transformations that utilize highly participative methods to achieve sustainable change. His clients include Microsoft, Hewlett-Packard, AT&T, Johnson & Johnson, and the Republic of South Africa.

Steven Cady is a scholar practitioner committed to using cutting-edge approaches that inspire system-wide change in organizations, and he is actively pursuing research and practice that unleash passion at the individual and organizational levels. Steven is a Graduate Faculty member at Bowling Green State University, where he is director of the Institute for Organizational Effectiveness and has served as the director of the Master of Organization Development Program. He has also served as the chief editor for the *Organization Development Journal*. Steven publishes, teaches, and consults on topics of organizational behavior and psychology, change management, and organization development. His clients include DaimlerChrysler, Dana Corporation, Diocese of NW Ohio (Toledo), and The Tavistock Group.

About Berrett-Koehler Publishers

Berrett-Koehler is an independent publisher dedicated to an ambitious mission: Creating a World that Works for All.

We believe that to truly create a better world, action is needed at all levels—individual, organizational, and societal. At the individual level, our publications help people align their lives with their values and with their aspirations for a better world. At the organizational level, our publications promote progressive leadership and management practices, socially responsible approaches to business, and humane and effective organizations. At the societal level, our publications advance social and economic justice, shared prosperity, sustainability, and new solutions to national and global issues.

A major theme of our publications is "Opening Up New Space." They challenge conventional thinking, introduce new ideas, and foster positive change. Their common quest is changing the underlying beliefs, mindsets, institutions, and structures that keep generating the same cycles of problems, no matter who our leaders are or what improvement programs we adopt.

We strive to practice what we preach—to operate our publishing company in line with the ideas in our books. At the core of our approach is *stewardship*, which we define as a deep sense of responsibility to administer the company for the benefit of all of our "stakeholder" groups: authors, customers, employees, investors, service providers, and the communities and environment around us.

We are grateful to the thousands of readers, authors, and other friends of the company who consider themselves to be part of the "BK Community." We hope that you, too, will join us in our mission.

Be Connected

Visit Our Website

Go to www.bkconnection.com to read exclusive previews and excerpts of new books, find detailed information on all Berrett-Koehler titles and authors, browse subject-area libraries of books, and get special discounts.

Subscribe to Our Free E-Newsletter

Be the first to hear about new publications, special discount offers, exclusive articles, news about bestsellers, and more! Get on the list for our free e-newsletter by going to www.bkconnection.com.

Participate in the Discussion

To see what others are saying about our books and post your own thoughts, check out our blogs at www.bkblogs.com.

Get Quantity Discounts

Berrett-Koehler books are available at quantity discounts for orders of ten or more copies. Please call us toll-free at (800) 929-2929 or email us at bkp.orders@aidcvt.com.

Host a Reading Group

For tips on how to form and carry on a book reading group in your workplace or community, see our website at www.bkconnection.com.

Join the BK Community

Thousands of readers of our books have become part of the "BK Community" by participating in events featuring our authors, reviewing draft manuscripts of forthcoming books, spreading the word about their favorite books, and supporting our publishing program in other ways. If you would like to join the BK Community, please contact us at bkcommunity@bkpub.com.